Texas Probate Code

2000 Edition
[Supersedes 1998 Edition]

WITH TABLE
AND INDEX

As Amended through the 1999 Regular Session of the 76th Legislature

WEST GROUP

ISBN 0–314–23926–X

PRINTED ON 10% POST CONSUMER RECYCLED PAPER

PREFACE

This Pamphlet contains the text of the Texas Probate Code, enacted by Acts 1955, 54th Leg., p. 88, ch. 55, as amended through the 1999 Regular Session of the 76th Legislature.

The Probate Code as enacted generally included the Chapter and Section headings which appear herein. The analyses of these headings in the Table of Contents and at the beginning of each chapter, coupled with an editorially prepared Index, provide a quick and easy means of finding particular provisions of the Code.

A Disposition Table is included preceding the Code, thus providing a means of tracing former Probate Articles of the Civil Statutes into the Code.

A Table of Sections Affected indicates sections of the Probate Code affected by the 1999 Regular Session of the 76th Legislature.

Comprehensive coverage of the judicial constructions and interpretations of the Code, together with cross references, references to law review commentaries discussing particular provisions, and other editorial features, is provided in the volumes of Vernon's Texas Statutes and Codes Annotated.

WEST GROUP

November, 1999

*

TABLE OF CONTENTS

*

EFFECTIVE DATES

The following table shows the date of adjournment and the effective date of ninety day bills enacted at sessions of the legislature beginning with the year 1945:

Year	Leg.	Session	Adjournment Date	Effective Date
1945	49	Regular	June 5, 1945	September 4, 1945
1947	50	Regular	June 6, 1947	September 5, 1947
1949	51	Regular	June 6, 1949	September 5, 1949
1951	52	Regular	June 8, 1951	September 7, 1951
1953	53	Regular	May 27, 1953	August 26, 1953
1954	53	1st C.S.	May 13, 1954	August 12, 1954
1955	54	Regular	June 7, 1955	September 6, 1955
1957	55	Regular	May 23, 1957	August 22, 1957
1957	55	1st C.S.	November 12, 1957	February 11, 1958
1957	55	2nd C.S.	December 3, 1957	March 4, 1958
1959	56	Regular	May 12, 1959	August 11, 1959
1959	56	1st C.S.	June 16, 1959	September 15, 1959
1959	56	2nd C.S.	July 16, 1959	October 15, 1959
1959	56	3rd C.S.	August 6, 1959	November 5, 1959
1961	57	Regular	May 29, 1961	August 28, 1961
1961	57	1st C.S.	August 8, 1961	November 7, 1961
1961	57	2nd C.S.	August 14, 1961	November 13, 1961
1962	57	3rd C.S.	February 1, 1962	May 3, 1962
1963	58	Regular	May 24, 1963	August 23, 1963
1965	59	Regular	May 31, 1965	August 30, 1965
1966	59	1st C.S.	February 23, 1966	*
1967	60	Regular	May 29, 1967	August 28, 1967
1968	60	1st C.S.	July 3, 1968	*
1969	61	Regular	June 2, 1969	September 1, 1969
1969	61	1st C.S.	August 26, 1969	*
1969	61	2nd C.S.	September 9, 1969	December 9, 1969
1971	62	Regular	May 31, 1971	August 30, 1971
1971	62	1st C.S.	June 4, 1971	September 3, 1971
1972	62	2nd C.S.	March 30, 1972	June 29, 1972
1972	62	3rd C.S.	July 7, 1972	*
1972	62	4th C.S.	October 17, 1972	January 16, 1973
1973	63	Regular	May 28, 1973	August 27, 1973
1973	63	1st C.S.	December 20, 1973	*
1975	64	Regular	June 2, 1975	September 1, 1975
1977	65	Regular	May 30, 1977	August 29, 1977
1977	65	1st C.S.	July 21, 1977	*
1978	65	2nd C.S.	August 8, 1978	November 7, 1978
1979	66	Regular	May 28, 1979	August 27, 1979
1981	67	Regular	June 1, 1981	August 31, 1981
1981	67	1st C.S.	August 11, 1981	November 10, 1981
1982	67	2nd C.S.	May 28, 1982	*
1982	67	3rd C.S.	September 9, 1982	*
1983	68	Regular	May 30, 1983	August 29, 1983

EFFECTIVE DATES

Year	Leg.	Session	Adjournment Date	Effective Date
1983	68	1st C.S.	June 25, 1983	September 23, 1983
1984	68	2nd C.S.	July 3, 1984	October 2, 1984
1985	69	Regular	May 27, 1985	August 26, 1985
1985	69	1st C.S.	May 30, 1985	August 29, 1985
1987	70	Regular	June 1, 1987	August 31, 1987
1987	70	1st C.S.	June 3, 1987	September 2, 1987
1987	70	2nd C.S.	July 21, 1987	October 20, 1987
1989	71	Regular	May 29, 1989	August 28, 1989
1989	71	1st C.S.	July 19, 1989	October 18, 1989
1989	71	2nd C.S.	December 12, 1989	*
1990	71	3rd C.S.	March 28, 1990	*
1990	71	4th C.S.	May 1, 1990	*
1990	71	5th C.S.	May 30, 1990	*
1990	71	6th C.S.	June 7, 1990	September 6, 1990
1991	72	Regular	May 27, 1991	August 26, 1991
1991	72	1st C.S.	August 13, 1991	November 12, 1991
1991	72	2nd C.S.	August 25, 1991	November 24, 1991
1992	72	3rd C.S.	January 8, 1992	April 8, 1992
1992	72	4th C.S.	December 3, 1992	*
1993	73	Regular	May 31, 1993	August 30, 1993
1995	74	Regular	May 29, 1995	August 28, 1995
1997	75	Regular	June 2, 1997	September 1, 1997
1999	76	Regular	May 31, 1999	August 30, 1999

* No legislation for which the ninety day effective date is applicable.

DISPOSITION TABLE

Showing where provisions of former Probate Articles of Vernon's Annotated Civil Statutes are covered in the Texas Probate Code as originally enacted.

Vernon's Ann.Civ.St. Article	Probate Code Section
932	Repealed
2570	38
2571	38
2572	39
2573 to 2575	41
2576	44
2577	43
2578	45
2579	45
2580	46
2581	42
2582	42
2583	41
2583a	47
3290	4
3291	5
3292	72
3293	6
3293–A	6
3294	8
3295	13
3296	15
3297	14
3298	16
3299	17
3300	18
3301	15
3302	23
3303	Repealed
3304	21
3305	11
3306	33
3307	24
3308	75
3309	25
3310	33
3310a	33
3310b	26, 33
3311	33
3312	32
3313	22
3314	37
3315	10
3316	19, 36
3317	3
3318	23
3319	26
3320	399, 404
3321	399
3322	189
3323	188
3324	27

Vernon's Ann.Civ.St. Article	Probate Code Section
3325	74
3326	73
3327	92
3328	11
3329 to 3331	81
3332	82
3333	128
3333a	129
3334	34, 128
3334a	129
3334b	129
3335 to 3338	128
3339	76
3340	80
3341	15, 80
3342	80
3343	80
3344	84
3345	85
3346	86
3347	86
3348	88
3349	85
3350	87
3351	89
3352	95
3353	78
3354 to 3356	178
3357	77
3358	77
3359	79
3360 to 3363	220
3364	83, 220
3365	105
3366	106
3367	223
3368	—
3369	88
3370	88
3371	181
3372	179
3373 to 3377	131
3378	132
3379	133
3380	134
3381	135
3382	190
3383 to 3385	190
3386	194
3387	196
3388	192
3389	149

DISPOSITION TABLE

Vernon's Ann.Civ.St. Article	Probate Code Section
3389	195
3390	199
3391	200
3392	203
3393	205
3393a	208
3394	204
3395	210
3396	33
3397	206
3398	207
3399	209
3400	218
3401	182
3402	183
3403	183, 186
3404	183
3405	187
3406	248
3407	249
3408	250
3409	250
3410	251
3410–a	251
3410–b	11
3411	252
3412	250
3413 to 3415	255
3416	256
3417, 3418	257
3419 to 3421	258
3422, 3423	259
3424	261
3425	260
3426	230
3427, 3428	238
3429	233
3430	234
3431	240
3432	240
3432a	234
3432b	239
3433	11
3434	33
3435	15
3436	145
3437	147
3438	149, 214
3439	149, 215
3440	216
3441	217
3442	150
3443 to 3447	148
3448	332
3449, 3450	——
3451	316
3452	224
3453	225
3454	224
3455	226
3456	227
3456A to 3456H	154
3456I	——
3457	262
3458	263
3459	264
3460	267
3461	266
3462, 3463	268
3464	269
3465	265
3466	213, 222
3467 to 3469	222
3470 to 3475	221
3476	286
3477	287
3478	288
3479	289
3480	291
3481	292
3482	293
3483	290
3484	291
3485	271
3486, 3487	273
3488	272
3489	274
3490	275
3491	276
3492	277
3493	278
3494	279
3495	280
3496	284
3497	285
3498	282
3499	270
3500	281
3501	283
3502 to 3504	294
3505, 3506	295
3507	296
3508	297
3509	298
3510	298
3511	300
3512	——
3513	323
3514	301
3515	303
3515a	306, 307
3516	309
3517	310
3518	311
3519 to 3521	312
3522	313
3523	313
3524	315
3525	312
3526 to 3528	317
3529	318
3530	314
3531	322
3532	321
3533	320
3534	319
3535	326
3536	325
3537	399
3538	400, 403

DISPOSITION TABLE

Vernon's Ann.Civ.St. Article	Probate Code Section
3539	399
3540	399
3541	327
3542	402
3543	328
3544	324
3545	359
3546	361
3547	360
3548	363
3549	365
3550	366
3551	362
3552	340
3553	331
3554	367
3554a	351
3555	367
3556	——
3557	331
3558	336
3559	337
3560	334
3561	334
3562	333
3563	334
3564	338
3565	341
3566	341, 342
3567, 3568	344
3569	15, 346
3570	349
3571	293, 332, 348, 349
3572	346, 348
3573 to 3575	349
3576	346, 348, 354
3577	347
3578	345
3579	352
3580	349
3581	349
3582	350
3582a	360
3583	353
3584	355
3585	339
3586	356
3587	357
3588	358
3589	357
3590	48
3591	49
3592	50, 51
3593	53
3594	54
3595	55
3596	56
3597	——
3597a	52
3598	373
3599, 3600	374
3601	375
3602	373
3603	377
3604	377
3605	376
3606	378
3607	379
3608 to 3613	380
3614	381
3615 to 3618	——
3619	381
3620	381
3621, 3622	382
3623	380
3624	380
3625	383
3626	384, 414
3627 to 3629	385
3630	235
3631	386
3632	387
3633	376
3634	404, 405
3635	405
3636	406
3637	407
3638	33
3639	407
3640 to 3643	408
3644	427
3645	427
3646, 3647	——
3648, 3649	428
3650	429
3651	430
3652 to 3656	433
3657	431
3658 to 3660	432
3661	156
3662	155
3663	157
3664	162
3665	163
3666	164
3667	165
3668	166
3669	167
3670	168
3671	170
3672	169
3673	171
3674	172, 173
3675, 3676	172
3677	174
3678	160
3679	——
3680	176
3681	175
3682	159
3683	158
3683a	Repealed
3684 to 3688	8
3689, 3690	241
3691	242
3692	244
3693	253
3694	380
3695	245
3696	——

DISPOSITION TABLE

Vernon's Ann.Civ.St. Article	Probate Code Section
3697	12
3698	28
3699	Repealed
3700	29
4102	4
4103	5
4104	3
4105	13, 14, 16, 17
4106	15
4107	23
4108	108
4109	10, 113
4110	19
4111	7
4112	33
4112a	144
4113	111
4114 to 4116	130
4117	112
4118	109
4119	117
4120	109
4121	109
4122	110
4123	21, 114, 115
4123a	114, 246
4123a–1	246
4124	116
4125	184
4126	118
4127	119
4128	120
4129 to 4131	136
4132	——
4133	185
4134 to 4137	131
4138	133, 135
4139	191
4140	193
4141	36, 194
4142	194
4143	194
4144	194, 214
4145	195
4146	199
4147	200
4148	203, 205, 208
4149	207
4150	209
4151	192
4152	209
4153	250
4154	251
4155	250, 252
4156	251
4157, 4158	256
4159	257
4160	258
4161	261
4162	229
4163	229
4164, 4165	230
4166	231
4167	232
4168, 4169	233

Vernon's Ann.Civ.St. Article	Probate Code Section
4170	236
4171	236
4172	235
4173	237
4174	238
4175	363
4176	359, 360
4177	361
4179	362
4180	389 to 391
4181	391, 394
4182 to 4186	393
4187	397
4188	397
4189	396
4190	392
4191	369, 395
4192	367
4192a	——
4192b	398
4193	333
4195	329, 341
4195a	341
4196	342
4197	347
4198	343
4199	340
4200	348
4201	346, 354
4201a	——
4202	350
4203	33, 349
4204	348
4205	352
4206	349
4207	349
4208	350
4209	338
4210	338
4211	234, 329
4212	329
4213 to 4215	353
4216	354, 355
4217	355
4218	339, 356, 357
4219	339, 356, 357
4220	358
4221	358
4222	357
4223	349
4223a	388
4224	399
4225	399, 401
4226	401
4227	400
4227a	330
4228	119, 220
4229 to 4232	221
4233	213, 222
4234, 4235	222
4236	——
4237	24, 220
4238	224
4239	301, 305
4240	301

DISPOSITION TABLE

Vernon's Ann.Civ.St. Article	Probate Code Section
4241	301, 304
4242	309
4243	310
4244	313
4245	313
4246	311
4247 to 4249	312
4250	14, 312
4251	303
4252	312
4253	317
4256	298
4257	299
4258	324
4259	313
4260	315
4261	14
4262	320, 321
4263	326
4264 to 4266	328
4267	416
4268, 4269	415
4270, 4271	417
4272	418
4273	419
4274	420
4275	421
4276	109
4277, 4278	422
4279	423
4280	424
4281	425
4282 to 4284	426
4285	124, 125
4286	126
4287	127
4288	126
4290 to 4294	121
4295	122
4296	404
4297	405

Vernon's Ann.Civ.St. Article	Probate Code Section
4298	406
4299 to 4301	407
4302, 4303	408
4304	—
4305	411
4306	412
4307	412, 413
4308	414
4309 to 4311	241
4312	242
4313	253
4314	245
4316	247
4317	12
4318	28
4328	31
4329	Repealed
6008b, § 3	369
8281	57
8282	58
8283	59
8284	60
8285	63
8286	64
8287	65, 86
8288	86
8289	86
8290	—
8291	Repealed
8292 to 8294	67
8295	68
8296	61
8297	62
8298	70
8299	90
8300	89
8301	96
8302	97
8303	98
8304	99
8305	107

PROBATE CODE
TABLE OF SECTIONS AFFECTED BY THE 76TH LEGISLATURE, REGULAR SESSION

Sec.	Effect	Acts 1999 Regular Session Ch.	Sec.
3(d)	Amended	344	6.001
3(p)	Amended	379	1
5(b)	Amended	1389	1
5A(b)	Amended	64	1
5A(e)	Amended	64	1
5B	Amended	1431	1
5B note	—	1431	3
5C	Added	1481	36
5C note	—	1481	52
10B	Amended	855	1
10B note	—	855	13
15	Amended	67	1
17	Amended	67	1
17A	Added	67	1
18	Amended	67	1
52	Amended	1538	1
52A	Added	1538	2
52A note	—	1538	3
95(c)	Amended	755	1
95 note	—	755	3
105A	Amended	344	6.002
128B	Added	855	2
149A(b)	Amended	855	3
149B(a)	Amended	855	4
149C(a)	Amended	855	5
149D	Added	855	6
149E	Added	855	6
149F	Added	855	6
149G	Added	855	6
194(5)	Amended	344	6.003
221A	Added	855	7
221A note	—	855	11
221B	Added	855	7
222(a)	Amended	855	8
222 note	—	855	12
270	Amended	487	1
		855	9
270 note	—	487	2
317(c)	Amended	1481	37
322	Amended	69	1
322 note	—	69	2
389	Repealed	828	1
389(b)	Amended	344	6.004
404	Amended	826	1
406	Amended	827	1
406 note	—	827	2
601	Amended	379	2
601(5)	Amended	344	6.005
601 note	—	379	11
606(b)	Amended	1389	2
607(b)	Amended	10	1

PROBATE CODE

Sec.	Effect	Acts 1999 Regular Session Ch.	Sec.
607(e)	Amended	10	2
608	Amended	1431	2
608 note	—	1431	3
610(d)	Repealed	379	10
625	Amended	67	2
627	Amended	67	2
627A	Added	67	2
628	Amended	67	2
633(b)	Amended	997	1
633(c)	Amended	379	3
		997	1
633 note	—	997	3
642(a)	Amended	829	2
642(b)	Amended	829	2
646	Amended	716	1
646(a)	Amended	379	4
647A	Added	716	2
647A note	—	716	3
648A(b)	Amended	829	3
665	Amended	905	1
665B(a)	Amended	905	2
665 note	—	905	6
677A(e)	Amended	1078	2
682	Amended	829	4
682A	Added	904	1
682A note	—	904	2
683	Amended	905	3
683A	Added	905	4
684(c)	Amended	379	5
685(a)	Amended	379	6
685(c)	Amended	379	6
686(a)	Amended	379	7
687(a)	Amended	379	8
694(b)	Amended	379	9
694(f)	Repealed	379	10
694I	Added	829	6
694A	Amended	829	5
694A note	—	829	7
694B	Added	829	6
694C	Added	829	6
694D	Added	829	6
694E	Added	829	6
694F	Added	829	6
694G	Added	829	6
694H	Added	829	6
694J	Added	829	6
694K	Added	829	6
695A	Added	906	1
697(a)	Amended	1116	2
697(e)	Added	1116	2
697 note	—	1116	4
698(a)	Amended	1116	3
702(c)	Amended	1078	1
702 note	—	1078	3
703(e)	Amended	344	6.006
703(g)	Amended	344	6.006
743(j)	Added	905	5
743 note	—	905	7
801	Amended	1481	38
855(b)	Amended	344	6.007
868(f)	Added	94	2

TABLE OF SECTIONS

Sec.	Effect	Acts 1999 Regular Session Ch.	Sec.
875(e)	Amended	997	2
875(f)	Amended	997	2
886	Repealed	1081	7
886A	Repealed	1081	7
886B	Repealed	1081	7
886C	Repealed	1081	7
886D	Repealed	1081	7
886E	Repealed	1081	7
886F	Repealed	1081	7

*

TEXAS PROBATE CODE

CHAPTER I. GENERAL PROVISIONS

§ 1. Short Title

This Act shall be known, and may be cited, as the "Texas Probate Code."

Acts 1955, 54th Leg., p. 88, ch. 55, eff. Jan. 1, 1956.

§ 2. Effective Date and Application

(a) Effective Date. This Code shall take effect and be in force on and after January 1, 1956. The procedure herein prescribed shall govern all probate proceedings in county and probate courts brought after the effective date of this Act, and also all further procedure in proceedings in probate then pending, except to the extent that in the opinion of the court, with respect to proceedings in probate then pending, its application in particular proceedings or parts thereof would not be feasible or would work injustice, in which event the former procedure shall apply.

(b) Rights Not Affected. No act done in any proceeding commenced before this Code takes effect, and no accrued right, shall be impaired by the provisions of this Code. When a right is acquired, extinguished, or barred upon the expiration of a prescribed period of time which has commenced to run by the provision of any statute in force before this Code takes effect, such provision shall remain in force and be deemed a part of this Code with respect to such right. All things properly done under any previously existing statute prior to the taking effect of this Code shall be treated as valid. Where citation or other process or notice is issued and served in compliance with existing statutes prior to the taking effect of this Code, the party upon whom such citation or other process has been served shall have the time provided for under such previously existing statutes in which to comply therewith.

(c) Subdivisions Have No Legal Effect. The division of this Code into Chapters, Parts, Sections, Subsections, and Paragraphs is solely for convenience and shall have no legal effect.

(d) Severability. If any provision of this Code, or the application thereof to any person or circumstance, is held invalid, such invalidity shall not affect other provisions or applications of the Code which can be given effect without the invalid provision or application, and to this end the provisions of this Code are declared to be severable, and the Legislature hereby states that it would have enacted such portions of the Code which can lawfully be given effect regardless of the possible invalidity of other provisions of the Code.

(e) Nature of Proceeding. The administration of the estate of a decedent, from the filing of the application for probate and administration, or for administration, until the decree of final distribution and the discharge of the last personal representative, shall be considered as one proceeding for purposes of jurisdiction. The entire proceeding is a proceeding in rem.

Acts 1955, 54th Leg., p. 88, ch. 55, eff. Jan. 1, 1956. Amended by Acts 1993, 73rd Leg., ch. 957, § 2, eff. Sept. 1, 1993.

§ 3. Definitions and Use of Terms

Except as otherwise provided by Chapter XIII of this Code, when used in this Code, unless otherwise apparent from the context:

(a) "Authorized corporate surety" means a domestic or foreign corporation authorized to do business in the State of Texas for the purpose of issuing surety, guaranty or indemnity bonds guaranteeing the fidelity of executors and administrators.

(b) "Child" includes an adopted child, whether adopted by any existing or former statutory procedure or by acts of estoppel, but, unless expressly so stated herein, does not include a child who has no presumed father.

(c) "Claims" include liabilities of a decedent which survive, including taxes, whether arising in contract or in tort or otherwise, funeral expenses, the expense of a tombstone, expenses of administration, estate and inheritance taxes, and debts due such estates.

(d) "Corporate fiduciary" means a financial institution as defined by Section 201.101, Finance Code, having trust powers, existing or doing business under the laws of this state, another state, or the United States, which is authorized by law to act under the order or appointment of any court of record, without giving bond, as receiver, trustee, executor, administrator, or, although without general depository powers, depository for any moneys paid into court, or to become sole guarantor or surety in or upon any bond required to be given under the laws of this state.

(e) "County Court" and "Probate Court" are synonymous terms and denote county courts in the exercise of their probate jurisdiction, courts created by statute and authorized to exercise original probate jurisdiction, and district courts exercising probate jurisdiction in contested matters.

(f) "County Judge," "Probate Judge," and "Judge" denote the presiding judge of any court having original jurisdiction over probate proceedings, whether it be a county court in the exercise of its probate jurisdiction, a court created by statute and authorized to exercise probate jurisdiction, or a district court exercising probate jurisdiction in contested matters.

(g) "Court" denotes and includes both a county court in the exercise of its probate jurisdiction, a court created by statute and authorized to exercise original probate jurisdiction, or a district court exercising original probate jurisdiction in contested matters.

(h) "Devise," when used as a noun, includes a testamentary disposition of real or personal property, or of both. When used as a verb, "devise" means to dispose of real or personal property, or of both, by will.

(i) "Devisee" includes legatee.

(j) "Distributee" denotes a person entitled to the estate of a decedent under a lawful will, or under the statutes of descent and distribution.

(k) "Docket" means the probate docket.

(*l*) "Estate" denotes the real and personal property of a decedent , both as such property originally existed and as from time to time changed in form by sale, reinvestment, or otherwise, and as augmented by any accretions and additions thereto (including any property to be distributed to the representative of the decedent by the trustee of a trust which terminates upon the decedent's death) and substitutions therefor, and as diminished by any decreases therein and distributions therefrom.

(m) "Exempt property" refers to that property of a decedent's estate which is exempt from execution or forced sale by the Constitution or laws of this State, and to the allowance in lieu thereof.

(n) Repealed by Acts 1995, 74th Leg., ch. 1039, § 73(1), eff. Sept. 1, 1995.

(*o*) "Heirs" denote those persons, including the surviving spouse, who are entitled under the statutes of descent and distribution to the estate of a decedent who dies intestate.

(p) "Incapacitated" or "Incapacitated person" means:

(1) a minor;

(2) an adult individual who, because of a physical or mental condition, is substantially unable to provide food, clothing, or shelter for himself or herself, to care for the individual's own physical health, or to manage the individual's own financial affairs; or

(3) a person who must have a guardian appointed to receive funds due the person from any governmental source.

(q) "Independent executor" means the personal representative of an estate under independent administration as provided in Section 145 of this Code. The term "independent executor" includes the term "independent administrator."

(r) "Interested persons" or "persons interested" means heirs, devisees, spouses, creditors, or any others having a property right in, or claim against, the estate being administered; and anyone interested in the welfare of a minor or incompetent ward.

(s) "Legacy" includes any gift or devise by will, whether of personalty or realty. "Legatee" includes any person entitled to a legacy under a will.

(t) "Minors" are all persons under eighteen years of age who have never been married or who have not had disabilities of minority removed for general purposes.

(u) "Minutes" means the probate minutes.

(v) "Mortgage" or "Lien" includes deed of trust, vendor's lien, chattel mortgage, mechanic's, materialman's or laborer's lien, judgment, attachment or garnishment lien, pledge by hypothecation, and Federal or State tax liens.

(w) "Net estate" means the real and personal property of a decedent, exclusive of homestead rights, exempt property, the family allowance and enforceable claims against the estate.

(x) "Person" includes natural persons and corporations.

(y) Repealed by Acts 1995, 74th Leg., ch. 1039, § 73(1), eff. Sept. 1, 1995.

(z) "Personal property" includes interests in goods, money, choses in action, evidence of debts, and chattels real.

(aa) "Personal representative" or "Representative" includes executor, independent executor, administrator, independent administrator, temporary administrator, together with their successors. The inclusion of independent executors herein shall not be held to subject such representatives to control of the courts in probate matters with respect to settlement of estates except as expressly provided by law.

(bb) "Probate matter," "Probate proceedings," "Proceeding in probate," and "Proceedings for probate" are synonymous and include a matter or proceeding relating to the estate of a decedent.

(cc) "Property" includes both real and personal property.

(dd) "Real property" includes estates and interests in lands, corporeal or incorporeal, legal or equitable, other than chattels real.

(ee) "Surety" includes both personal and corporate sureties.

(ff) "Will" includes codicil; it also includes a testamentary instrument which merely:

(1) appoints an executor or guardian;

(2) directs how property may not be disposed of; or

(3) revokes another will.

(gg) The singular number includes the plural; the plural number includes the singular.

(hh) The masculine gender includes the feminine and neuter.

(ii) "Statutory probate court" means a statutory court designated as a statutory probate court under Chapter 25, Government Code. A county court at law exercising probate jurisdiction is not a statutory probate court under this Code unless the court is designated a statutory probate court under Chapter 25, Government Code.

(jj) "Next of kin" includes an adopted child or his or her descendents and the adoptive parent of the adopted child.

(kk) "Charitable organization" means:

(1) a nonprofit corporation, trust, community chest, fund, foundation, or other entity that is exempt from federal income tax under Section 501(c)(3) of the Internal Revenue Code of 1986 [1] because the entity is organized and operated exclusively for religious, charitable, scientific, educational, or literary purposes, test-

ing for public safety, prevention of cruelty to children or animals, or promotion of amateur sports competition; or

(2) any other entity or organization that is organized and operated exclusively for the purposes listed in Section 501(c)(3) of the Internal Revenue Code of 1986.

(*ll*) "Governmental agency of the state" means:

(1) an incorporated city or town, a county, a public school district, a special-purpose district or authority, or a district, county, or justice of the peace court;

(2) a board, commission, department, office, or other agency in the executive branch of state government, including an institution of higher education as defined by Section 61.003, Education Code;

(3) the legislature or a legislative agency; and

(4) the supreme court, the court of criminal appeals, a court of appeals, or the State Bar of Texas or another judicial agency having statewide jurisdiction.

(mm) "Ward" is a person for whom a guardian has been appointed.

Acts 1955, 54th Leg., p. 88, ch. 55, eff. Jan. 1, 1956. Amended by Acts 1957, 55th Leg., p. 53, ch. 31, § 2(a), eff. Aug. 22, 1957; Acts 1961, 57th Leg., p. 44, ch. 30, § 2, eff. Aug. 28, 1961; Acts 1969, 61st Leg., p. 1703, ch. 556, § 1, eff. June 10, 1969; Acts 1969, 61st Leg., p. 1922, ch. 641, § 1, eff. June 12, 1969; Acts 1975, 64th Leg., p. 104, ch. 45, § 1, eff. Sept. 1, 1975; Acts 1975, 64th Leg., p. 2195, ch. 701, § 1, eff. June 21, 1975; Acts 1977, 65th Leg., p. 1061, ch. 390, §§ 1, 2, eff. Sept. 1, 1977; Acts 1979, 66th Leg., p. 1740, ch. 713, § 1, eff. Aug. 27, 1979; Acts 1985, 69th Leg., ch. 159, §§ 1, 2, eff. Sept. 1, 1985; Acts 1985, 69th Leg., ch. 591, § 1, eff. Sept. 1, 1985; Acts 1989, 71st Leg., ch. 375, § 33, eff. Sept. 1, 1989; Acts 1989, 71st Leg., ch. 1035, § 1, eff. Sept. 1, 1989; Acts 1991, 72nd Leg., ch. 14, § 284(96), eff. Sept. 1, 1991; Acts 1991, 72nd Leg., ch. 895, § 1, eff. Sept. 1, 1991; Acts 1993, 73rd Leg., ch. 957, § 3, eff. Sept. 1, 1993; Acts 1995, 74th Leg., ch. 1039, §§ 4, 73(1), eff. Sept. 1, 1995; Acts 1997, 75th Leg., ch. 52, § 1, eff. Sept. 1, 1997; Acts 1999, 76th Leg., ch. 344, § 6.001, eff. Sept. 1, 1999; Acts 1999, 76th Leg., ch. 379, § 1, eff. Sept. 1, 1999.

[1] 26 U.S.C.A. § 501(c)(3).

Section 78 of Acts 1985, 69th Leg., ch. 159, provides:

"(a) The intent of this Act is to remove certain derogatory terminology relating to mentally disabled persons. This Act is not intended to revive a law that was expressly or impliedly repealed by a law enacted by the 69th Legislature, Regular Session, 1985, or a previous legislature.

"(b) To the extent that a law enacted by the 69th Legislature, Regular Session, 1985, conflicts with this Act, the other law prevails, regardless of relative date of enactment or relative effective date."

Section 20 of Acts 1991, 72nd Leg., ch. 895, provides:

"(a) The changes in the law made by Sections 1, 3, 4, 6, 9, and 13 of this Act apply only to the estates of persons who die on or after the effective date of this Act. An estate of a person who dies before the effective date of this Act is covered by the law as it existed when the person died, and the former law is continued in effect for that purpose.

"(b) The change in the law made by Section 8 of this Act applies as to all persons who are living on or after the effective date of this Act, without regard to whether any relevant order, judgment, or decree was entered before or after the effective date of this Act.

"(c) The change in the law made by Section 14 of this Act applies only to sales made on or after the effective date of this Act. A sale of property made under Section 14 before the effective date of this Act is governed by the law in effect when the sale of property was made, and the former law is continued in effect for that purpose."

The amendment of this section by Acts 1993, 73rd Leg., ch. 905, § 6 failed to take effect under § 19(a), which provided that the amendment was not to take effect if both S.B. No. 236(ch. 905) and H.B. No. 2685(ch. 957) were enacted and became law.

Acts 1977, 65th Leg., p. 1067, ch. 390, which by §§ 1 to 8 amended subsecs. (q) and (aa) of this section, §§ 145, 147, 148, 149A(a), (b), and 150 and added § 154A, provided in §§ 9 and 10:

"Sec. 9. All other laws in conflict with this Act are hereby repealed to the extent they conflict.

"Sec. 10. This Act shall become effective September 1, 1977, and shall apply to estates of decedents who die intestate after September 1, 1977."

§ 4. Jurisdiction of County Court With Respect to Probate Proceedings

The county court shall have the general jurisdiction of a probate court. It shall probate wills, grant letters testamentary and of administration, settle accounts of personal representatives, and transact all business appertaining to estates subject to administration, including the settlement, partition, and distribution of such estates.

Acts 1955, 54th Leg., p. 88, ch. 55, eff. Jan. 1, 1956. Amended by Acts 1993, 73rd Leg., ch. 957, § 4, eff. Sept. 1, 1993.

§ 5. Jurisdiction of District Court and Other Courts of Record With Respect to Probate Proceedings and Appeals from Probate Orders

(a) The district court shall have original control and jurisdiction over executors and administrators under such regulations as may be prescribed by law.

(b) In those counties where there is no statutory probate court, county court at law or other statutory court exercising the jurisdiction of a probate court, all applications, petitions and motions regarding probate and administrations shall be filed and heard in the county court, except that in contested probate matters, the judge of the county court may on his own motion (or shall on the motion of any party to the proceeding, according to the motion) request as provided by Section 25.0022, Government Code, the assignment of a statutory probate court judge to hear the contested portion of the proceeding, or transfer the contested portion of the proceeding to the district court, which may then hear contested matter as if originally filed in district court. If the judge of the county court has not transferred a contested probate matter to the district court at the time a party files a motion for assignment of a statutory probate court judge, the county judge shall grant the motion and may not transfer the matter to district court unless the party withdraws the motion. A statutory probate court judge assigned to a contested probate matter as provided by this subsection has for that matter the jurisdiction and authority granted to a statutory probate court by Sections 5A and 5B of this code. The county court shall continue to exercise jurisdiction over the management of the estate with the exception of the contested matter until final disposition of the contested matter is made by the assigned judge or the district court. In contested matters transferred to the district court in those counties, the district court, concurrently with the county court, shall have the general jurisdiction of a probate court. Upon resolution of all pending contested matters, the contested portion of the probate proceeding shall be transferred by the district court to the county court for further proceedings not inconsistent with the orders of the district court. If a contested portion of the proceeding is transferred to a district court under this subsection, the clerk of the district court may perform in relation to the transferred portion of the proceeding any function a county clerk may perform in that type of contested proceeding.

(c) In those counties where there is a statutory probate court, county court at law, or other statutory court exercising the jurisdiction of a probate court, all applications, petitions and motions regarding probate and administrations shall be filed and heard in such courts and the constitutional county court, rather than in the district courts, unless otherwise provided by the legislature, and the judges of such courts may hear any of such matters sitting for the judge of any of such courts. In contested probate matters, the judge of the constitutional county court may on his own motion, and shall on the motion of any party to the proceeding, transfer the proceeding to the statutory probate court, county court at law, or other statutory court exercising the jurisdiction of a probate court, which may then hear the proceeding as if originally filed in such court.

(d) A statutory probate court has concurrent jurisdiction with the district court in all actions by or against a person in the person's capacity as a personal representative, in all actions involving an inter vivos trust, in all actions involving a charitable trust, and in all actions involving a testamentary trust.

(e) All courts exercising original probate jurisdiction shall have the power to hear all matters incident to an estate. When a surety is called on to perform in place of an administrator, all courts exercising original probate jurisdiction may award judgment against the personal representative in favor of his surety in the same suit.

(f) All final orders of any court exercising original probate jurisdiction shall be appealable to the courts of appeals.

(g) Notwithstanding any other law, a statutory county court created under Chapter 25, Government Code, that has the jurisdiction of a statutory probate court on August 31, 1997, retains that jurisdiction after that date. This subsection expires August 31, 1999.

Acts 1955, 54th Leg., p. 88, ch. 55, eff. Jan. 1, 1956. Amended by Acts 1973, 63rd Leg., p. 1684, ch. 610, § 1; Acts 1975, 64th Leg., p. 2195, ch. 701, § 2, eff. June 21, 1975; Acts 1977, 65th Leg., p. 1170, ch. 448, § 1, eff. Aug. 29, 1977; Acts 1979, 66th Leg., p. 1740, ch. 713, § 2, eff. Aug. 27, 1979; Acts 1983, 68th Leg., p. 4122, ch. 647, § 2, eff. Sept. 1, 1983; Acts 1983, 68th Leg., p. 5434, ch. 1015, § 1, eff. Aug. 29, 1983; Acts 1985, 69th Leg., ch. 159, § 3, eff. Sept. 1, 1985; Acts 1987, 70th Leg., ch. 459, § 4, eff. Sept. 1, 1987; Acts 1989, 71st Leg., ch. 1035, § 2, eff. Sept. 1, 1989; Acts 1993, 73rd Leg., ch. 957, § 5, eff. Sept. 1, 1993; Acts 1997, 75th Leg., ch. 1435, § 3, eff. Sept. 1, 1997; Acts 1999, 76th Leg., ch. 1389, § 1, eff. Aug. 30, 1999.

Section 2 of the 1973 Act amended § 21; § 3 of the Act provided:

"This Act takes effect only if a constitutional amendment [Acts 1973, 63rd Leg., p. 2471, S.J.R. No. 26, amending Const. Art. 5, § 8] deleting the constitutional requirement that district courts shall have only appellate jurisdiction and general control over probate matters is submitted by the 63rd Legislature and is adopted by the qualified electors of this state."

The constitutional amendment was so adopted on November 6, 1973.

Section 2 of Acts 1983, 68th Leg., p. 5435, ch. 1015, provides:

"This Act applies retroactively as an authorization for, and validation of, actions taken before the effective date of this Act by a district clerk if the clerk performed functions in a probate proceeding that would have been permissible for a county clerk to perform."

Section 5(b) of the 1987 amendatory act provides:

"Section 5(b), Texas Probate Code, as amended by this Act, applies to contested probate matters filed with the county court on or after September 1, 1987. A contested probate matter that was filed with the county court before the effective date of this Act is covered by the law as it existed on the date the matter was filed, and that law is continued in effect for that purpose."

Section 18(e) of the 1989 amendatory act provides:

"The change in the law made by Sections 2 and 3 of this Act applies only to a cause of action that accrues on or after the effective date of this Act. A cause of action that accrued before the effective date of this Act is governed by the law in effect at the time the cause of action accrued, and the former law is continued in effect for that purpose."

The amendment of this section by Acts 1993, 73rd Leg., ch. 905, § 8 failed to take effect under § 19(a), which provided that the amendment was not to take effect if both S.B. No. 236 (ch. 905) and H.B. No. 2685 (ch. 957) were enacted and became law.

§ 5A. Matters Appertaining and Incident to an Estate and Other Probate Court Jurisdiction

(a) In proceedings in the constitutional county courts and statutory county courts at law, the phrases "appertaining to estates" and "incident to an estate" in this Code include the probate of wills, the issuance of letters testamentary and of administration, the determination of heirship, and also include, but are not limited to, all claims by or against an estate, all actions for trial of title to land incident to an estate and for the enforcement of liens thereon incident to an estate, all actions for trial of the right of property incident to an estate, and actions to construe wills, and generally all matters relating to the settlement, partition, and distribution of estates of deceased persons.

(b) In proceedings in the statutory probate courts and district courts, the phrases "appertaining to estates" and "incident to an estate" in this Code include the probate of wills, the issuance of letters testamentary and of administration, and the determination of heirship, and also include, but are not limited to, all claims by or against an estate, all actions for trial of title to land and for the enforcement of liens thereon, all actions for trial of the right of property, all actions to construe wills, the interpretation and administration of testamentary trusts and the applying of constructive trusts, and generally all matters relating to the settlement, partition, and distribution of estates of deceased persons. All statutory probate courts may, in the exercise of their jurisdiction, notwithstanding any other provisions of this Code, hear all suits, actions, and applications filed against or on behalf of any heirship proceeding or decedent's estate, including estates administered by an independent executor; all such suits, actions, and applications are appertaining to and incident to an estate. This subsection shall be construed in conjunction with and in harmony with Section 145 and all other sections of this Code dealing with independent executors, but shall not be construed so as to increase permissible judicial control over independent executors. All statutory probate courts shall have the same powers over independent executors that are exercisable by the district courts. In situations where the jurisdiction of a statutory probate court is concurrent with that of a district court, any cause of action appertaining to estates or incident to an estate shall be brought in a statutory probate court rather than in the district court.

(c) A statutory probate court has concurrent jurisdiction with the district court in all actions:

(1) by or against a person in the person's capacity as a personal representative;

(2) involving an inter vivos trust;

(3) involving a charitable trust; and

(4) involving a testamentary trust.

(d) A statutory probate court may exercise the pendent and ancillary jurisdiction necessary to promote judicial efficiency and economy.

(e) Subsections (c)(2), (3), and (4) and Subsection (d) apply whether or not the matter is appertaining to or incident to an estate.

Added by Acts 1979, 66th Leg., p. 1741, ch. 713, § 3, eff. Aug. 27, 1979. Amended by Acts 1985, 69th Leg., ch. 875, § 1, eff. Aug. 26, 1985; Acts 1987, 70th Leg., ch. 459, § 1, eff. Sept. 1, 1987; Acts 1989, 71st Leg., ch. 1035, § 3, eff. Sept. 1, 1989; Acts 1993, 73rd Leg., ch. 957, § 6, eff. Sept. 1, 1993; Acts 1997, 75th Leg., ch. 1302, § 1, eff. Sept. 1, 1997; Acts 1999, 76th Leg., ch. 64, § 1, eff. Sept. 1, 1999.

Section 2 of the 1985 amendatory act provides:

"Because this Act is remedial, it applies to all cases filed under Section 5A(b), Texas Probate Code, on or after January 1, 1973."

Section 18(e) of the 1989 amendatory act provides:

"The change in the law made by Sections 2 and 3 of this Act applies only to a cause of action that accrues on or after the effective date of this Act. A cause of action that accrued before the effective date of this Act is governed by the law in effect at the time the cause of action accrued, and the former law is continued in effect for that purpose."

Section 16 of Acts 1997, 75th Leg., ch. 1302 provides:

"This Act takes effect September 1, 1997, and applies only to the estate of a person who dies on or after that date. An estate of a person who dies before the effective date of this Act is governed by the law in effect on the date of the person's death, and the former law is continued in effect for that purpose."

§ 5B. Transfer of Proceeding

A judge of a statutory probate court, on the motion of a party to the action or on the motion of a person interested in an estate, may transfer to his court from a district, county, or statutory court a cause of action appertaining to or incident to an estate pending in the statutory probate court or a cause of action in which a personal representative of an estate pending in the statutory probate court is a party and may consolidate the transferred cause of action with the other proceedings in the statutory probate court relating to that estate.

Added by Acts 1983, 68th Leg., p. 5228, ch. 958, § 1, eff. Sept. 1, 1983. Amended by Acts 1999, 76th Leg., ch. 1431, § 1, eff. Sept. 1, 1999.

Section 3 of Acts 1999, 76th Leg., ch. 1431 provides:

"This Act takes effect September 1, 1999, and applies only to a motion to transfer a cause of action filed on or after that date. A motion to transfer a cause of action filed before the effective date of this Act is governed by the law in effect on the date the motion was filed, and the former law is continued in effect for that purpose."

§ 5C. Actions to Collect Delinquent Property Taxes

(a) This section applies only to a decedent's estate that:

(1) is being administered in a pending probate proceeding;

(2) owns or claims an interest in property against which a taxing unit has imposed ad valorem taxes that are delinquent; and

(3) is not being administered as an independent administration under Section 145 of this code.

(b) Notwithstanding any provision of this code to the contrary, if the probate proceedings are pending in a foreign jurisdiction or in a county other than the county in which the taxes were imposed, a suit to foreclose the lien securing payment of the taxes or to enforce personal liability for the taxes must be brought under Section 33.41, Tax Code, in a court of competent jurisdiction in the county in which the taxes were imposed.

(c) If the probate proceedings have been pending for four years or less in the county in which the taxes were imposed, the taxing unit may present a claim for the delinquent taxes against the estate to the personal representative of the estate in the probate proceedings.

(d) If the taxing unit presents a claim against the estate under Subsection (c) of this section:

(1) the claim of the taxing unit is subject to each applicable provision in Parts 4 and 5, Chapter VIII,[1] of this code that relates to a claim or the enforcement of a claim in a probate proceeding; and

(2) the taxing unit may not bring a suit in any other court to foreclose the lien securing payment of the taxes or to enforce personal liability for the delinquent taxes before the first day after the fourth anniversary of the date the application for the probate proceeding was filed.

(e) To foreclose the lien securing payment of the delinquent taxes, the taxing unit must bring a suit under Section 33.41, Tax Code, in a court of competent jurisdiction for the county in which the taxes were imposed if:

(1) the probate proceedings have been pending in that county for more than four years; and

(2) the taxing unit did not present a delinquent tax claim under Subsection (c) of this section against the estate in the probate proceeding.

(f) In a suit brought under Subsection (e) of this section, the taxing unit:

(1) shall make the personal representative of the decedent's estate a party to the suit; and

(2) may not seek to enforce personal liability for the taxes against the estate of the decedent.

Added by Acts 1999, 76th Leg., ch. 1481, § 36, eff. Sept. 1, 1999.

[1] V.A.T.S. Probate Code, § 294 et seq. or § 331 et seq.

Section 52 of Acts 1999, 76th Leg., ch. 1481 provides:

"The changes in law made by Sections 36, 37, and 38 of this Act apply to the estates of all decedents, regardless of the date of death, and to the estates of all wards, regardless of the date the application for appointment of a guardian was filed, and to all causes of action pending on September 1, 1999, or brought after that date."

§ 6. Venue for Probate of Wills and Administration of Estates of Decedents

Wills shall be admitted to probate, and letters testamentary or of administration shall be granted:

(a) In the county where the deceased resided, if he had a domicile or fixed place of residence in this State.

(b) If the deceased had no domicile or fixed place of residence in this State but died in this State, then either in the county where his principal property was at the time of his death, or in the county where he died.

(c) If he had no domicile or fixed place of residence in this State, and died outside the limits of this State, then in any county in this State where his nearest of kin reside.

(d) But if he had no kindred in this State, then in the county where his principal estate was situated at the time of his death.

(e) In the county where the applicant resides, when administration is for the purpose only of receiving funds or money due to a deceased person or his estate from any governmental source or agency; provided, that unless the mother or father or spouse or adult child of the deceased is applicant, citation shall be served personally on the living parents and spouses and adult children, if any, of the deceased person, or upon those who are alive and whose addresses are known to the applicant. guardianship

Acts 1955, 54th Leg., p. 88, ch. 55, eff. Jan. 1, 1956.

§ 7. Repealed by Acts 1993, 73rd Leg., ch. 905, § 15, eff. Sept. 1, 1993; Acts 1993, 73rd Leg., ch. 957, § 75(1), eff. Sept. 1, 1993

Acts 1993, 73rd Leg., ch. 957, repealing this section, enacted Chapter XIII, Guardianship, of the Probate Code.

§ 8. Concurrent Venue and Transfer of Proceedings

(a) Concurrent Venue. When two or more courts have concurrent venue of an estate, the court in which application for probate proceedings thereon is first filed shall have and retain jurisdiction of the estate to the exclusion of the other court or courts. The proceedings shall be deemed commenced by the filing of an application averring facts sufficient to confer venue; and the proceeding first legally commenced shall extend to all of the property of the estate. Provided, however, that a bona fide purchaser of real property in reliance on any such subsequent proceeding, without knowledge of its invalidity, shall be protected in such purchase unless the decree admitting the will to probate or granting administration in the prior proceeding shall be recorded in the office of the county clerk of the county in which such property is located.

(b) Proceedings in More Than One County. If proceedings for probate are commenced in more than one county, they shall be stayed except in the county where first commenced until final determination of venue in the county where first commenced. If the proper venue is finally determined to be in another county, the clerk, after making and retaining a true copy of the entire file in the case, shall transmit the original file to the proper county, and proceedings shall thereupon be had in the proper county in the same manner as if the proceedings had originally been instituted therein.

(c) Transfer of Proceeding.

(1) Transfer for Want of Venue. If it appears to the court at any time before the final decree that the proceeding was commenced in a court which did not have priority of venue over such proceeding, the court shall, on the application of any interested person, transfer the proceeding to the proper county by transmitting to the proper court in such county the original file in such case, together with certified copies of all entries in the minutes theretofore made, and administration of the estate in such county shall be completed in the same manner as if the proceeding had originally been instituted therein; but, if the question as to priority of venue is not raised before final decree in the proceedings is announced, the finality of such decree shall not be affected by any error in venue.

(2) Transfer for Convenience of the Estate. If it appears to the court at any time before the estate is closed that it would be in the best interest of the estate, the court, in its discretion, may order the proceeding transferred to the proper court in any other county in this State. The clerk of the court from which the proceeding is transferred shall transmit to the court to which the proceeding is transferred the original file in the proceeding and a certified copy of the entries in the minutes that relate to the proceeding.

(d) Validation of Prior Proceedings. When a proceeding is transferred to another county under any provision of this Section of this Code, all orders entered in connection with the proceeding shall be valid and shall be recognized in the second court, provided such orders were made and entered in conformance with the procedure prescribed by this Code.

(e) Jurisdiction to Determine Venue. Any court in which there has been filed an application for proceedings in probate shall have full jurisdiction to determine the venue of such proceeding, and of any proceeding relating thereto, and its determination shall not be subject to collateral attack.

Acts 1955, 54th Leg., p. 88, ch. 55, eff. Jan. 1, 1956. Amended by Acts 1983, 68th Leg., p. 4754, ch. 833, § 1, eff. Sept. 1, 1983; Acts 1987, 70th Leg., ch. 786, § 1, eff. Aug. 31, 1987.

§ 9. Defects in Pleading

No defect of form or substance in any pleading in probate shall be held by any court to invalidate such pleading, or any order based upon such pleading, unless the defect has been timely objected to and called to the attention of the court in which such proceedings were or are pending.

Acts 1955, 54th Leg., p. 88, ch. 55, eff. Jan. 1, 1956.

§ 10. Persons Entitled to Contest Proceedings

Any person interested in an estate may, at any time before any issue in any proceeding is decided upon by the court, file opposition thereto in writing and shall be entitled to process for witnesses and evidence, and to be heard upon such opposition, as in other suits.

Acts 1955, 54th Leg., p. 88, ch. 55, eff. Jan. 1, 1956.

§ 10A. Necessary Party

(a) An institution of higher education as defined by Section 61.003, Education Code, a private institution of higher education, or a charitable organization is a necessary party to a will contest or will construction suit involving a will in which the institution or organization is a distributee.

(b) If an institution or organization is a necessary party under Subsection (a) of this section, the court shall serve the institution or organization in the manner provided for service on other parties by this code.

Added by Acts 1989, 71st Leg., ch. 1035, § 4, eff. Sept. 1, 1989. Amended by Acts 1991, 72nd Leg., ch. 675, § 1, eff. Sept. 1, 1991.

Section 18(d) of the 1989 Act provides:

"The change in the law made by Section 4 of this Act applies only to a will contest or will construction suit that is instituted on or after the effective date of this Act. A will contest or will construction suit that was instituted before the effective date of this Act is governed by the law in effect when the contest or suit was instituted, and the former law is continued in effect for that purpose."

Section 2 of the 1991 amendatory act provides:

"This Act takes effect September 1, 1991, and applies only to a will contest or will construction suit that is instituted on or after the effective date of this Act. A will contest or will construction suit that was instituted before the effective date of this Act is governed by the law in effect when the contest or suit was instituted, and the former law is continued in effect for that purpose."

§ 10B. Communications or Records Relating to Decedent's Condition Before Death

Notwithstanding the Medical Practice Act (Article 4495b, Vernon's Texas Civil Statutes), a person who is a party to a will contest or a proceeding in which a party relies on the mental or testamentary capacity of a decedent before the decedent's death as part of the party's claim or defense is entitled to production of all communications or records relevant to the decedent's condition before the decedent's death. On receipt of a subpoena of communications or records under this section and proof of filing of the will contest or proceeding, by file-stamped copy, the appropriate physician, hospital, medical facility, custodian of records, or other person in possession of the communications or records shall release the communications or records to the party requesting the records without further authorization.

Added by Acts 1997, 75th Leg., ch. 1302, § 2, eff. Sept. 1, 1997. Amended by Acts 1999, 76th Leg., ch. 855, § 1, eff. Sept. 1, 1999.

Section 13 of Acts 1999, 76th Leg., ch. 855 provides:

"Except as provided by Sections 11 and 12 of this Act, the changes in law made by this Act apply only to the estate of a person who dies on or after the effective date of this Act. An estate of a person who dies before the effective date of this Act is governed by the law in effect on the date of the person's death, and the former law is continued in effect for that purpose."

§ 11. Applications and Other Papers to be Filed With Clerk

All applications for probate proceedings, complaints, petitions and all other papers permitted or required by law to be filed in the court in probate matters, shall be filed with the county clerk of the proper county who shall file the same and endorse on each paper the date filed and the docket number, and his official signature.

Acts 1955, 54th Leg., p. 88, ch. 55, eff. Jan. 1, 1956.

§ 12. Costs and Security Therefor

(a) Applicability of Laws Regulating Costs. The provisions of law regulating costs in ordinary civil cases shall apply to all matters in probate when not expressly provided for in this Code.

(b) Security for Costs Required, When. When any person other than the personal representative of an estate files an application, complaint, or opposition in relation to the estate, he may be required by the clerk to give security for the probable cost of such proceeding before filing the same; or any one interested in the estate, or any officer of the court, may, at any time before the trial of such application, complaint, or opposition, obtain from the court, upon written motion, an order requiring such party to give security for the probable costs of such proceeding. The rules governing civil suits in the county court respecting this subject shall control in such cases.

(c) Suit for Fiduciary. No security for costs shall be required of an executor or administrator appointed by a court of this state in any suit brought by him in his fiduciary character.

Acts 1955, 54th Leg., p. 88, ch. 55, eff. Jan. 1, 1956. Amended by Acts 1985, 69th Leg., ch. 959, § 4, eff. Sept. 1, 1985; Acts 1993, 73rd Leg., ch. 957, § 7, eff. Sept. 1, 1993.

§ 13. Judge's Probate Docket

The county clerk shall keep a record book to be styled "Judge's Probate Docket," and shall enter therein:

(a) The name of each person upon whose person or estate proceedings are had or sought to be had.

(b) The name of the executor or administrator or of the applicant for letters.

(c) The date of the filing of the original application for probate proceedings.

(d) A minute of each order, judgment, decree, and proceeding had in each estate, with the date thereof.

(e) A number for each estate upon the docket in the order in which proceedings are commenced, and each paper filed in an estate shall be given the corresponding docket number of the estate.

Acts 1955, 54th Leg., p. 88, ch. 55, eff. Jan. 1, 1956. Amended by Acts 1993, 73rd Leg., ch. 957, § 8, eff. Sept. 1, 1993.

§ 14. Claim Docket

The county clerk shall also keep a record book to be styled "Claim Docket," and shall enter therein all claims presented against an estate for approval by the court. This docket shall be ruled in sixteen columns at proper intervals from top to bottom, with a short note of the contents at the top of each column. One or more pages shall be assigned to each estate. The following information shall be entered in the respective columns beginning with the first or marginal column: The names of claimants in the order in which their claims are filed; the amount of the claim; its date; the date of filing; when due; the date from which it bears interest; the rate of interest; when allowed by the executor or administrator; the amount allowed; the date of rejection; when approved; the amount approved; when disapproved; the class to which the claim belongs; when established by judgment of a court; the amount of such judgment.

Acts 1955, 54th Leg., p. 88, ch. 55, eff. Jan. 1, 1956. Amended by Acts 1993, 73rd Leg., ch. 957, § 9, eff. Sept. 1, 1993.

§ 15. Case Files

The county clerk shall maintain a case file for each decedent's estate in which a probate proceeding has been filed. The case file must contain all orders, judgments, and proceedings of the court and any other probate filing with the court, including all:

(1) applications for the probate of wills and for the granting of administration;

(2) citations and notices, whether published or posted, with the returns thereon;

(3) wills and the testimony upon which the same are admitted to probate, provided that the substance only of depositions shall be recorded;

(4) bonds and official oaths;

(5) inventories, appraisements, and lists of claims;

(6) exhibits and accounts;

(7) reports of hiring, renting, or sale;

(8) applications for sale or partition of real estate and reports of sale and of commissioners of partition;

(9) applications for authority to execute leases for mineral development, or for pooling or unitization of lands, royalty, or other interest in minerals, or to lend or invest money; and

(10) reports of lending or investing money.

Acts 1955, 54th Leg., p. 88, ch. 55, eff. Jan. 1, 1956. Amended by Acts 1993, 73rd Leg., ch. 957, § 10, eff. Sept. 1, 1993; Acts 1999, 76th Leg., ch. 67, § 1, eff. Sept. 1, 1999.

§ 16. Probate Fee Book

The county clerk shall keep a record book styled "Probate Fee Book," and shall enter therein each item of costs which accrues to the officers of the court, together with witness fees, if any, showing the party to whom the costs or fees are due, the date of the accrual of the same, the estate or party liable therefor, and the date on which any such costs or fees are paid.

Acts 1955, 54th Leg., p. 88, ch. 55, eff. Jan. 1, 1956.

§ 17. Maintaining Records in Lieu of Record Books

In lieu of keeping the record books described by Sections 13, 14, and 16 of this code, the county clerk may maintain the information relating to a person's or estate's probate proceedings maintained in those record books on a computer file, on microfilm, in the form of a digitized optical image, or in another similar form of data compilation.

Added by Acts 1999, 76th Leg., ch. 67, § 1, eff. Sept. 1, 1999.

§ 17A. Index

The county clerk shall properly index the records and keep the index open for public inspection, but may not release the index from the clerk's custody.

Acts 1955, 54th Leg., p. 88, ch. 55, eff. Jan. 1, 1956. Renumbered from V.A.T.S. Probate Code, § 17 and amended by Acts 1999, 76th Leg., ch. 67, § 1, eff. Sept. 1, 1999.

§ 18. Use of Records as Evidence

The record books or individual case files, including records on a computer file, on microfilm, in the form of a digitized optical image, or in another similar form of data compilation described in preceding sections of this code, or certified copies or reproductions of the records, shall be evidence in any court of this state.

Acts 1955, 54th Leg., p. 88, ch. 55, eff. Jan. 1, 1956. Amended by Acts 1999, 76th Leg., ch. 67, § 1, eff. Sept. 1, 1999.

§ 19. Call of the Dockets

The judge of the court in which probate proceedings are pending, at such times as he shall determine, shall call the estates of decedents in their regular order upon both the probate and claim dockets and make such orders as shall be necessary.

Acts 1955, 54th Leg., p. 88, ch. 55, eff. Jan. 1, 1956. Amended by Acts 1993, 73rd Leg., ch. 957, § 11, eff. Sept. 1, 1993.

§ 20. Clerk May Set Hearings

Whenever, on account of the county judge's absence from the county seat, or his being on vacation, disqualified, ill, or deceased, such judge is unable to designate the time and place for hearing a probate matter pending in his court, authority is hereby vested in the county clerk of the county in which such matter is pending to designate such time and place, entering such setting on the judge's docket and certifying thereupon why such judge is not acting by himself. If, after service of such notices and citations as required by law with reference to such time and place of hearing has been perfected, no qualified judge is present for the hearing, the same shall automatically be continued from day to day until a qualified judge is present to hear and determine the matter.

Acts 1955, 54th Leg., p. 88, ch. 55, eff. Jan. 1, 1956.

§ 21. Trial by Jury

In all contested probate and mental illness proceedings in the district court or in the county court or statutory probate court, county court at law or other statutory court exercising probate jurisdiction, the parties shall be entitled to trial by jury as in other civil actions.

Acts 1955, 54th Leg., p. 88, ch. 55, eff. Jan. 1, 1956. Amended by Acts 1973, 63rd Leg., p. 1685, ch. 610, § 2.

For effectiveness of 1973 amendatory act, see note under § 5.

§ 22. Evidence

In proceedings arising under the provisions of this Code, the rules relating to witnesses and evidence that govern in the District Court shall apply so far as practicable except that where a will is to be probated, and in other probate matters where there is no opposing party or attorney of record upon whom notice and copies of interrogatories may be served, service may be had by posting notice of intention to take depositions for a period of ten days as provided in this Code governing posting of notices. When such notice is filed with the clerk, a copy of the interrogatories shall also be filed, and at the expiration of ten days, commission may issue for taking the depositions, and the judge may file cross-interrogatories where no one appears, if he so desires.

Acts 1955, 54th Leg., p. 88, ch. 55, eff. Jan. 1, 1956.

§ 23. Decrees and Signing of Minutes

All decisions, orders, decrees, and judgments of the county court in probate matters shall be rendered in open court except in cases where it is otherwise specially provided. The probate minutes shall be approved and signed by the judge on the first day of each month, except, however, that if the first day of the month falls on a Sunday, such approval shall be entered on the preceding or succeeding day.

Acts 1955, 54th Leg., p. 88, ch. 55, eff. Jan. 1, 1956.

§ 24. Enforcement of Orders

The county or probate judge may enforce obedience to all his lawful orders against executors and administrators by attachment and imprisonment, but no such imprisonment shall exceed three days for any one offense, unless otherwise expressly so provided in this Code.

Acts 1955, 54th Leg., p. 88, ch. 55, eff. Jan. 1, 1956. Amended by Acts 1993, 73rd Leg., ch. 957, § 12, eff. Sept. 1, 1993.

§ 25. Executions

Executions in probate matters shall be directed "to any sheriff or any constable within the State of Texas," made returnable in sixty days, and shall be attested and signed by the clerk officially under the seal of the court. All proceedings under such executions shall be governed by the laws regulating proceedings under executions issued from the District Court so far as applicable. Provided, however, that no execution directed to the sheriff or any constable of a specific county within this State shall be held defective if such execution was properly executed within such county by such officer.

Acts 1955, 54th Leg., p. 88, ch. 55, eff. Jan. 1, 1956.

§ 26. Attachments for Property

Whenever complaint in writing, under oath, shall be made to the county or probate judge by any person interested in the estate of a decedent that the executor or administrator is about to remove said estate, or any part thereof, beyond the limits of the State, such judge may order a writ to issue, directed "to any sheriff or any constable within the State of Texas," commanding him to seize such estate, or any part thereof, and hold the same subject to such further orders as such judge shall make on such complaint. No such writ shall issue unless the complainant shall give bond, in such sum as the judge shall require, payable to the executor or administrator of such estate, conditioned for the payment of all damages and costs that shall be recovered for the wrongful suing out of such writ. Provided, however, that no writ of attachment directed to the sheriff or any constable of a specific county within this State shall be held defective if such writ was properly executed within such county by such officer.

Acts 1955, 54th Leg., p. 88, ch. 55, eff. Jan. 1, 1956. Amended by Acts 1993, 73rd Leg., ch. 957, § 13, eff. Sept. 1, 1993.

§ 27. Enforcement of Specific Performance

When any person shall sell property and enter into bond or other written agreement to make title thereto, and shall depart this life without having made such title, the owner of such bond or written agreement or his legal representatives, may file a complaint in writing in the court of the county where the letters testamentary or of administration on the estate of the deceased obligor were granted, and cause the personal representative of such estate to be cited to appear at a date stated in the citation and show cause why specific performance of such bond or written agreement should not be decreed. Such bond or other written agreement shall be filed with such complaint, or good cause shown under oath why the same cannot be filed; and if it cannot be so filed, the same or the substance thereof shall be set forth in the complaint. After the service of the citation, the court shall hear such complaint and the evidence thereon, and, if satisfied from the proof that such bond or written agreement was legally executed by the testator or intestate, and that the complainant has a right to demand specific performance thereof, a decree shall be made ordering the personal representative to make title to the property, according to the tenor of the obligation, fully describing the property in such decree. When a conveyance is made under the provisions of this Section, it shall refer to and identify the decree of the court authorizing it, and, when delivered, shall vest in the person to whom made all the right and title which the testator or intestate had to the property conveyed; and such conveyance shall be prima facie evidence that all requirements of the law have been complied with in obtaining the same.

Acts 1955, 54th Leg., p. 88, ch. 55, eff. Jan. 1, 1956.

§ 28. Personal Representative to Serve Pending Appeal of Appointment

Pending appeals from orders or judgments appointing administrators or temporary administrators, the appointees shall continue to act as such and shall continue the prosecution of any suits then pending in favor of the estate.

Acts 1955, 54th Leg., p. 88, ch. 55, eff. Jan. 1, 1956. Amended by Acts 1975, 64th Leg., p. 2196, ch. 701, § 3, eff. June 21, 1975; Acts 1993, 73rd Leg., ch. 957, § 14, eff. Sept. 1, 1993.

§ 29. Appeal Bonds of Personal Representatives

When an appeal is taken by an executor or administrator, no bond shall be required, unless such appeal personally concerns him, in which case he must give the bond.

Acts 1955, 54th Leg., p. 88, ch. 55, eff. Jan. 1, 1956. Amended by Acts 1993, 73rd Leg., ch. 957, § 15, eff. Sept. 1, 1993.

§ 30. Repealed by Acts 1975, 64th Leg., p. 2197, ch. 701, § 7, eff. June 21, 1975

§ 31. Bill of Review

Any person interested may, by a bill of review filed in the court in which the probate proceedings were had, have any decision, order, or judgment rendered by the court, or by the judge thereof, revised and corrected on showing error therein; but no process or action under such decision, order or judgment shall be stayed except by writ of injunction, and no bill of review shall be filed after two years have elapsed from the date of such decision, order, or judgment.

Acts 1955, 54th Leg., p. 88, ch. 55, eff. Jan. 1, 1956. Amended by Acts 1993, 73rd Leg., ch. 957, § 16, eff. Sept. 1, 1993.

§ 32. Common Law Applicable

The rights, powers and duties of executors and administrators shall be governed by the principles of the common law, when the same do not conflict with the provisions of the statutes of this State.

Acts 1955, 54th Leg., p. 88, ch. 55, eff. Jan. 1, 1956. Amended by Acts 1993, 73rd Leg., ch. 957, § 17, eff. Sept. 1, 1993.

§ 33. Issuance, Contents, Service, and Return of Citation, Notices, and Writs in Probate Matters

(a) When Citation or Notice Necessary. No person need be cited or otherwise given notice except in situations in which this Code expressly provides for citation or the giving of notice; provided, however, that even though this Code does not expressly provide for citation, or the issuance or return of notice in any probate matter, the court may, in its discretion, require that notice be given, and prescribe the form and manner of service and return thereof.

(b) Issuance by the Clerk or by Personal Representative. The county clerk shall issue necessary citations, writs, and process in probate matters, and all notices not required to be issued by personal representatives, without any order from the court, unless such order is required by a provision of this Code.

(c) Contents of Citation, Writ, and Notice. Citation and notices issued by the clerk shall be signed and sealed by him, and shall be styled "The State of Texas." Notices required to be given by a personal representative shall be in writing and shall be signed by the representative in his official capacity. All citations and notices shall be directed to the person or persons to be cited or notified, shall be dated, and shall state the style and number of the proceeding, the court in which it is pending, and shall describe generally the nature of the proceeding or matter to which the citation or notice relates. No precept directed to an officer is necessary. A citation or notice shall direct the person or persons cited or notified to appear by filing a written contest or answer, or to perform other acts required of him or them and shall state when and where such appearance or performance is required. No citation or notice shall be held to be defective because it contains a precept directed to an officer authorized to serve it. All writs and other process except citations and notices shall be directed "To any sheriff or constable within the State of Texas," but shall not be held defective because directed to the sheriff or any constable of a specific county if properly served within the named county by such officer.

(d) Where No Specific Form of Notice, Service, or Return is Prescribed, or When Provisions Are Insufficient or Inadequate. In all situations in which this Code requires that notice be given, or that a person be cited, and in which a specific method of giving such notice or of citing such person, or a specific method of service and return of such citation or notice is not given, or an insufficient or inadequate provision appears with respect to any of such matters, or when any interested person so requests, such notice or citation shall be issued, served, and returned in such manner as the court, by written order, shall direct in accordance with this Code and the Texas Rules of Civil Procedure, and shall have the same force and effect as if the manner of service and return had been specified in this Code.

(e) Service of Citation or Notice Upon Personal Representatives. Except in instances in which this Code expressly provides another method of service, any notice or citation required to be served upon any personal representative or receiver shall be served by the clerk issuing such citation or notice. The clerk shall serve the same by sending the original thereof by registered or certified mail to the attorney of record for the personal representative or receiver, but if there is no attorney of record, to the personal representative or receiver.

(f) Methods of Serving Citations and Notices.

(1) Personal Service. Where it is provided that personal service shall be had with respect to a citation or notice, any such citation or notice must be served upon the attorney of record for the person to be cited. Notwithstanding the requirement of personal service, service may be made upon such attorney by any of the methods hereinafter specified for service upon an attorney. If there is no attorney of record in the proceeding for such person, or if an attempt to make service upon the attorney was unsuccessful, a citation or notice directed to a person within this State must be served by the sheriff or constable upon the person to be cited or notified, in person, by delivering to him a true copy of such citation or notice at least ten (10) days before the return day thereof, exclusive of the date of service. Where the person to be cited or notified is absent from the State, or is a nonresident, such citation or notice may be served by any disinterested person competent to make oath of the fact. Said citation or notice shall be returnable at least ten (10) days after the date of service, exclusive of the date of service. The return of the person serving the citation or notice shall be endorsed on or attached to same; it shall show the time and place of service, certify that a true copy of the citation or notice was delivered to the person directed to be served, be subscribed and sworn to before some officer authorized by the laws of this State to take affidavits, under the hand and official seal of such officer, and returned to the county clerk who issued same. If in either case such citation or notice is returned with the notation that the person sought to be served, whether within or without this State, cannot be found, the clerk shall issue a new citation or notice directed to the person or persons sought to be served and service shall be by publication.

(2) Posting. When citation or notice is required to be posted, it shall be posted by the sheriff or constable at the courthouse door of the county in which the proceedings are pending, or at the place in or near the courthouse where public notices customarily are posted, for not less than ten (10) days before the return day thereof, exclusive of the date of posting. The clerk shall deliver the original and a copy of such citation or notice to the sheriff or any constable of the proper county, who shall post said copy as herein prescribed and return the original to the clerk, stating in a written return thereon the time when and the place where he posted such copy. The date of posting shall be the date of service. When posting of notice by a personal representative is authorized or required, the method herein prescribed shall be followed, such notices to be issued in the name of the representative, addressed and delivered to, posted and returned by, the proper officer, and filed with the clerk.

(3) Publication. When a person is to be cited or notified by publication, the citation or notice shall be published once in a newspaper of general circulation in the county in which the proceedings are pending, and said publication shall be not less than ten (10) days before the return day thereof, exclusive of the date of publication. The date of publication which said newspaper bears shall be the date of service. If no newspaper is published, printed, or of general circulation, in the county where citation or notice is to be had, service of such citation or notice shall be by posting.

(4) Mailing.

(A) When any citation or notice is required or permitted to be served by registered or certified mail, other than notices required to be given by personal representatives, the clerk shall issue such citation or notice and shall serve the same by sending the original thereof by registered or certified mail. Any notice required to be given by a personal representative by registered or certified mail shall be issued by him, and he shall serve the same by sending the original thereof by registered or certified mail. In either case the citation or notice shall be mailed with instructions to deliver to the addressee only, and with return receipt requested. The envelope containing such citation or notice shall be addressed to the attorney of record in the proceeding for the person to be cited or notified, but if there is none, or if returned undelivered, then to the person to be cited or notified. A copy of such citation or notice, together with the certificate of the clerk, or of the personal representative, as the case may be, showing the fact and date of mailing, shall be filed and recorded. If a receipt is returned, it shall be attached to the certificate.

(B) When any citation or notice is required or permitted to be served by ordinary mail, the clerk, or the personal representative when required by statute or by order of the court, shall serve the same by mailing the original to the person to be cited or notified. A copy of such citation or notice, together with a certificate of the person serving the same showing the fact and time of mailing, shall be filed and recorded.

(C) When service is made by mail, the date of mailing shall be the date of service. Service by mail shall be made not less than twenty (20) days before the return day thereof, exclusive of the date of service.

(D) If a citation or notice served by mailing is returned undelivered, a new citation or notice shall be issued, and such citation or notice shall be served by posting.

(g) Return of Citation or Notice. All citations and notices issued by the clerk and served by personal service, by mail, by posting, or by publication, shall be returnable to the court from which issued on the first Monday after the service is perfected.

(h) Sufficiency of Return in Cases of Posting. In any probate matter where citation or notice is required to be served by posting, and such citation or notice is issued in conformity with the applicable provision of this Code, the citation or notice and the service and return thereof shall be sufficient and valid if any sheriff or constable posts a copy or copies of such citation or notice at the place or places prescribed by this Code on a day which is sufficiently prior to the return day named in such citation or notice for the period of time for which such citation or notice is required to be posted to elapse before the return day of such citation or notice, and the fact that such sheriff or constable makes his return on such citation or notice and returns same into court before the period of time elapses for which such citation or notice is required to be posted, shall not affect the sufficiency or validity of such citation or notice or the service or return thereof, even though such return is made, and such citation or notice is returned into court, on the same day it is issued.

(i) Proof of Service. Proof of service in all cases requiring notice or citation, whether by publication, posting, mailing, or otherwise, shall be filed before the hearing. Proof of service made by a sheriff or constable shall be made by the return of service. Service made by a private person shall be proved by the affidavit of the person. Proof of service by publication shall be made by the affidavit of the publisher or that of an employee of the publisher, which affidavit shall show the date the issue of the newspaper bore, and have attached to or embodied in it a copy of the published notice or citation. In the case of service by mail, proof shall be made by the certificate of the clerk, or the affidavit of the personal representative or other person making such service, stating the fact and time of mailing. In the case of service by registered or certified mail, the return receipt shall be attached to the certificate, if a receipt has been returned.

(j) Request for Notice. At any time after an application is filed for the purpose of commencing any proceeding in probate, including, but not limited to, a proceeding for the probate of a will, grant of letters testamentary or of administration and determination of heirship, any person interested in the estate may file with the clerk a request in writing that he be notified of any and all, or of any specifically designated, motions, applications, or pleadings filed by any person, or by any particular persons specifically designated in the request. The fees and costs for such notices shall be borne by the person requesting them, and the clerk may require a deposit to cover the estimated costs of furnishing such person with the notice or notices requested. The clerk shall thereafter send to such person by ordinary mail copies of any of the documents specified in the request. Failure of the clerk to comply with the request shall not invalidate any proceeding.

Acts 1955, 54th Leg., p. 88, ch. 55, eff. Jan. 1, 1956. Amended by Acts 1957, 55th Leg., p. 53, ch. 31, § 1, eff. Aug. 22, 1957; Acts 1971, 62nd Leg., p. 967, ch. 173, § 1, eff. Jan. 1, 1972; Acts 1993, 73rd Leg., ch. 957, § 18, eff. Sept. 1, 1993.

§ 34. Service on Attorney

If any attorney shall have entered his appearance of record for any party in any proceeding in probate, all citations and notices required to be served on the party in such proceeding shall be served on the attorney, and such service shall be in lieu of service upon the party for whom the attorney appears. All notices served on attorneys in accordance with this section may be served by registered or certified mail or by delivery to the attorney in person. They may be served by a party to the proceeding or his attorney of record, or by the proper sheriff or constable, or by any other person competent to testify. A written statement by an attorney of record, or the return of the officer, or the affidavit of any other person showing service shall be prima facie evidence of the fact of service.

Acts 1955, 54th Leg., p. 88, ch. 55, eff. Jan. 1, 1956. Amended by Acts 1971, 62nd Leg., p. 970, ch. 173, § 2, eff. Jan. 1, 1972.

§ 34A. Attorneys Ad Litem

The judge of a probate court may appoint an attorney ad litem to represent the interests of a person having a legal disability, a nonresident, an unborn or unascertained person, or an unknown heir in any probate proceeding. Each attorney ad litem appointed under this section is entitled to reasonable compensation for services in the amount set by the court and to be taxed as costs in the proceeding.

Added by Acts 1983, 68th Leg., p. 747, ch. 178, § 1, eff. Aug. 29, 1983. Amended by Acts 1987, 70th Leg., ch. 467, § 1, eff. Sept. 1, 1987; Acts 1993, 73rd Leg., ch. 957, § 19, eff. Sept. 1, 1993.

Section 4 of the 1987 amendatory act provides:

"This Act takes effect September 1, 1987, and applies to interests of beneficiaries that arise on or after that date. An interest of a beneficiary that arises before the effective date of this Act is covered by the law as it existed when the interest arose, and that law is continued in effect for that purpose."

§ 35. Waiver of Notice

Any person legally competent who is interested in any hearing in a proceeding in probate may, in person or by attorney, waive in writing notice of such hearing. A trustee may make such a waiver on behalf of the beneficiary of his trust. A consul or other representative of a foreign government, whose appearance has been entered as provided by law on behalf of any person residing in a foreign country, may make such waiver of notice on behalf of such person. Any person who submits to the jurisdiction of the court in any hearing shall be deemed to have waived notice thereof.

Acts 1955, 54th Leg., p. 88, ch. 55, eff. Jan. 1, 1956. Amended by Acts 1993, 73rd Leg., ch. 957, § 20, eff. Sept. 1, 1993.

§ 36. Duty and Responsibility of Judge

(a) It shall be the duty of each county and probate court to use reasonable diligence to see that personal representatives of estates being administered under orders of the court and other officers of the court perform the duty enjoined upon them by law pertaining to such estates. The judge shall annually, if in his opinion the same be necessary, examine the condition of each of said estates and the solvency of the bonds of personal representatives of estates. He shall, at any time he finds that the personal representative's bond is not sufficient to protect such estate, require such personal representatives to execute a new bond in accordance with law. In each case, he shall notify the personal representative, and the sureties on the bond, as provided by law; and should damage or loss result to estates through the gross neglect of the judge to use reasonable diligence in the performance of his duty, he shall be liable on his bond to those damaged by such neglect.

(b) The court may request an applicant or court-appointed fiduciary to produce other information identifying an applicant, decedent, or personal representative, including social security numbers, in addition to identifying information the applicant or fiduciary is required to produce under this code. The court shall maintain the information required under this subsection, and the information may not be filed with the clerk.

Acts 1955, 54th Leg., p. 88, ch. 55, eff. Jan. 1, 1956. Amended by Acts 1975, 64th Leg., p. 979, ch. 375, § 1, eff. June 19, 1975; Acts 1993, 73rd Leg., ch. 957, § 21, eff. Sept. 1, 1993; Acts 1997, 75th Leg., ch. 1302, § 3, eff. Sept. 1, 1997.

§ 36A. Repealed by Acts 1993, 73rd Leg., ch. 49, § 2, eff. Sept. 1, 1993

Section 2 of the 1989 amendatory act provides:

"Section 36A(c), Texas Probate Code, as added by this Act, applies only to durable powers of attorney executed on or after the effective date of this Act. A durable power of attorney that was executed before the effective date of this Act is governed by the law in effect when the power of attorney was executed, and the former law is continued in effect for that purpose."

Section 2 of the 1993 repealing act provides:

Repealed

"Section 36A, Probate Code, is repealed. A power of attorney executed in compliance with that section before the effective date of this Act is valid according to the terms of that section as it existed at the time of the execution, and that section is continued in effect for that purpose."

See now, V.A.T.S. Probate Code, § 481 et seq.

§ 36B. Examination of Documents or Safe Deposit Box With Court Order

(a) A judge of a court having probate jurisdiction of a decedent's estate may order a person to permit a court representative named in the order to examine a decedent's documents or safe deposit box if it is shown to the judge that:

(1) the person may possess or control the documents or that the person leased the safe deposit box to the decedent; and

(2) the documents or safe deposit box may contain a will of the decedent, a deed to a burial plot in which the decedent is to be buried, or an insurance policy issued in the decedent's name and payable to a beneficiary named in the policy.

(b) The court representative shall examine the decedent's documents or safe deposit box in the presence of:

(1) the judge ordering the examination or an agent of the judge; and

(2) the person who has possession or control of the documents or who leased the safe deposit box or, if the person is a corporation, an officer of the corporation or an agent of an officer.

Added by Acts 1981, 67th Leg., 1st C.S., p. 193, ch. 17, art. 3, § 1, eff. Sept. 1, 1981.

§ 36C. Delivery of Document With Court Order

(a) A judge who orders an examination by a court representative of a decedent's documents or safe deposit box under Section 36B of this code may order the person who possesses or controls the documents or who leases the safe deposit box to permit the court representative to take possession of the following documents:

(1) a will of the decedent;

(2) a deed to a burial plot in which the decedent is to be buried; or

(3) an insurance policy issued in the decedent's name and payable to a beneficiary named in the policy.

(b) The court representative shall deliver:

(1) the will to the clerk of a court that has probate jurisdiction and that is located in the same county as the court of the judge who ordered the examination;

(2) the burial plot deed to the person designated by the judge in the order for the examination; or

(3) the insurance policy to a beneficiary named in the policy.

(c) A court clerk to whom a will is delivered under Subsection (b) of this section shall issue a receipt for the will to the court representative who delivers it.

Added by Acts 1981, 67th Leg., 1st C.S., p. 193, ch. 17, art. 3, § 1, eff. Sept. 1, 1981.

§ 36D. Examination of Document or Safe Deposit Box Without Court Order

(a) A person who possesses or controls a document delivered by a decedent for safekeeping or who leases a safe deposit box to a decedent may permit any of the following persons to examine the document or the contents of the safe deposit box:

(1) the spouse of the decedent;

(2) a parent of the decedent;

(3) a descendant of the decedent who is at least 18 years old; or

(4) a person named as executor of the decedent's estate in a copy of a document that the person has and that appears to be a will of the decedent.

(b) The examination shall be conducted in the presence of the person who possesses or controls the document or who leases the safe deposit box or, if the person is a corporation, an officer of the corporation.

Added by Acts 1981, 67th Leg., 1st C.S., p. 193, ch. 17, art. 3, § 1, eff. Sept. 1, 1981.

§ 36E. Delivery of Document Without Court Order

(a) A person who permits an examination of a decedent's document or safe deposit box under Section 36D of this code may deliver:

(1) a document appearing to be the decedent's will to the clerk of a court that has probate jurisdiction and that is located in the county in which the decedent resided or to the person named in the document as an executor of the decedent's estate;

(2) a document appearing to be a deed to a burial plot in which the decedent is to be buried or appearing to give burial instructions to the person making the examination; or

(3) a document appearing to be an insurance policy on the decedent's life to a beneficiary named in the policy.

(b) A person who has leased a safe deposit box to the decedent shall keep a copy of a document appearing to be a will that the person delivers under Subsection (a) of this section. The person shall keep the copy for four years after the day of delivery.

(c) A person may not deliver a document under Subsection (a) of this section unless requested to do so by the person examining the document and unless the person examining the document issues a receipt for the document to the person who is to deliver it.

Added by Acts 1981, 67th Leg., 1st C.S., p. 193, ch. 17, art. 3, § 1, eff. Sept. 1, 1981.

§ 36F. Restriction on Removal of Contents of Safe Deposit Box

A person may not remove the contents of a decedent's safe deposit box except as provided by Section 36C or 36E of this code or except as provided by another law.

Added by Acts 1981, 67th Leg., 1st C.S., p. 193, ch. 17, art. 3, § 1, eff. Sept. 1, 1981.

CHAPTER II. DESCENT AND DISTRIBUTION

§ 37. Passage of Title Upon Intestacy and Under a Will

When a person dies, leaving a lawful will, all of his estate devised or bequeathed by such will, and all powers of appointment granted in such will, shall vest immediately in the devisees or legatees of such estate and the donees of such powers; and all the estate of such person, not devised or bequeathed, shall vest immediately in his heirs at law; subject, however, to the payment of the debts of the testator or intestate, except such as is exempted by law, and subject to the payment of court-ordered child support payments that are delinquent on the date of the person's death; and whenever a person dies intestate, all of his estate shall vest immediately in his heirs at law, but with the exception aforesaid shall still be liable and subject in their hands to the payment of the debts of the intestate and the delinquent child support payments; but upon the issuance of letters testamentary or of administration upon any such estate, the executor or administrator shall have the right to possession of the estate as it existed at the death of the testator or intestate, with the exception aforesaid; and he shall recover possession of and hold such estate in trust to be disposed of in accordance with the law.

Acts 1955, 54th Leg., p. 88, ch. 55, eff. Jan. 1, 1956. Amended by Acts 1969, 61st Leg., p. 1703, ch. 556, § 2, eff. June 10, 1969; Acts 1981, 67th Leg., p. 2537, ch. 674, § 3, eff. Sept. 1, 1981.

Section 5 of the 1981 amendatory act provides:

"This Act takes effect September 1, 1981. Section 3 of this Act applies to the estates of persons who die on or after the effective date of this Act, and Section 37, Probate Code, as in effect before the effective date of this Act, applies to the estates of persons who die before the effective date of this Act."

§ 37A. Means of Evidencing Disclaimer or Renunciation of Property or Interest Receivable From a Decedent

Any person, or the guardian of an incapacitated person, the personal representative of a deceased person, or the guardian ad litem of an unborn or unascertained person, with prior court approval of the court having, or which would have, jurisdiction over such guardian, personal representative, or guardian ad litem, or any independent executor of a deceased person, without prior court approval, who may be entitled to receive any property as a beneficiary and who intends to effect disclaimer irrevocably on or after September 1, 1977, of the whole or any part of such property shall evidence same as herein provided. A disclaimer evidenced as provided herein shall be effective as of the death of decedent and shall relate back for all purposes to the death of the decedent and is not subject to the claims of any creditor of the disclaimant. Unless the decedent's will provides otherwise, the property subject to the disclaimer shall pass as if the person disclaiming or on whose behalf a disclaimer is made had predeceased the decedent and a future interest that would otherwise take effect in possession or enjoyment after the termination of the estate or interest that is disclaimed takes effect as if the disclaiming beneficiary had predeceased the decedent. Failure to comply with the provisions hereof shall render such disclaimer ineffective except as an assignment of such property to those who would have received same had the person attempting the disclaimer died prior to the decedent. The term "property" as used in this section shall include all legal and equitable interests, powers, and property, whether present or future, whether vested or contingent, and whether beneficial or burdensome, in whole or in part. The term "disclaimer" as used in this section shall include "renunciation." In this section "beneficiary" includes a person who would have been entitled, if the person had not made a disclaimer, to receive property as a result of the death of another person by inheritance, under a will, by an agreement between spouses for community property with a right of survivorship, by a joint tenancy with a right of survivorship, or by any other survivorship agreement, account, or interest in which the interest of the decedent passes to a surviving beneficiary, by an insurance, annuity, endowment, employment, deferred compensation, or other contract or arrangement, or under a pension, profit sharing, thrift, stock bonus, life insurance, survivor income, incentive, or other plan or program providing retirement, welfare, or fringe benefits with respect to an employee or a self-employed individual. Nothing in this section shall be construed to preclude a subsequent disclaimer by any person who shall be entitled to property as a result of a disclaimer. The following shall apply to such disclaimers:

(a) Written Memorandum of Disclaimer and Filing Thereof. In the case of property receivable by a beneficiary, the disclaimer shall be evidenced by a written memorandum, acknowledged before a notary public or other person authorized to take acknowledgements of conveyances of real estate. Unless the beneficiary is a charitable organization or governmental agency of the state, a written memorandum of disclaimer disclaiming a present interest shall be filed not later than nine months after the death of the decedent and a written memorandum of disclaimer disclaiming a future interest may be filed not later than nine months after the event determining that the taker of the property or interest is finally ascertained and his interest is indefeasibly vested. If the beneficiary is a charitable organization or a governmental agency of the state, a written memorandum of disclaimer disclaiming a present or future interest shall be filed not later than nine months after the beneficiary receives the notice required by Section 128A of this code. The written memorandum of disclaimer shall be filed in the probate court in which the decedent's will has been probated or in which proceedings have been commenced for the administration of the decedent's estate or which has before it an application for either of the same; provided, however, if the administration of the decedent's estate is closed, or after the expiration of one year following the date of the issuance of letters testamentary in an independent administration, or if there has been no will of the decedent probated or filed for probate, or if no administration of the decedent's estate has been commenced, or if no application for administration of the decedent's estate has been filed, the written memorandum of disclaimer shall be filed with the county clerk of the county of the decedent's residence, or, if the decedent is not a resident of this state but real property or an interest therein located in this state is disclaimed, a written memorandum of disclaimer shall be filed with the county clerk of the county in which such real property or interest therein is located, and recorded by such county clerk in the deed records of that county.

(b) Notice of Disclaimer. Unless the beneficiary is a charitable organization or governmental agency of the state, copies of any written memorandum of disclaimer shall be delivered in person to, or shall be mailed by registered or certified mail to and received by, the legal representative of the transferor of the interest or the holder of legal title to the property to which the disclaimer relates not later than nine months after the death of the decedent or, if the interest is a future interest, not later than nine months after the date the person who will receive the property or interest is finally ascertained and the person's interest is indefeasibly vested. If the beneficiary is a charitable organization or government agency of the state, the notices required by this section shall be filed not later than nine months after the beneficiary receives the notice required by Section 128A of this code.

(c) Power to Provide for Disclaimer. Nothing herein shall prevent a person from providing in a will, insurance policy, employee benefit agreement, or other instrument for the making of disclaimers by a beneficiary of an interest receivable under that instrument and for the disposition of disclaimed property in a manner different from the provisions hereof.

(d) Irrevocability of Disclaimer. Any disclaimer filed and served under this section shall be irrevocable.

(e) Partial Disclaimer. Any person who may be entitled to receive any property as a beneficiary may disclaim such property in whole or in part, including but not limited to specific powers of invasion, powers of appointment, and fee estate in favor of life estates; and a partial disclaimer or renunciation, in accordance with the provisions of this section, shall be effective whether the property so renounced or disclaimed constitutes a portion of a single, aggregate gift or constitutes part or all of a separate, independent gift; provided, however, that a partial disclaimer shall be effective only with respect to property expressly described or referred to by category in such disclaimer; and provided further, that a partial disclaimer of property which is subject to a burdensome interest created by the decedent's will shall not be effective unless such property constitutes a gift which is separate and distinct from undisclaimed gifts.

(f) Partial Disclaimer by Spouse. Without limiting Subsection (e) of this section, a disclaimer by the decedent's surviving spouse of a transfer by the decedent is not a disclaimer by the surviving spouse of all or any part of any other transfer from the decedent to or for the benefit of the surviving spouse, regardless of whether the property or interest that would have passed under the disclaimed transfer passes because of the disclaimer to or for the benefit of the surviving spouse by the other transfer.

(g) Disclaimer After Acceptance. No disclaimer shall be effective after the acceptance of the property by the beneficiary. For the purpose of this section, acceptance shall occur only if the person making such disclaimer has previously taken possession or exercised dominion and control of such property in the capacity of beneficiary.

(h) Interest in Trust Property. A beneficiary who accepts an interest in a trust is not considered to have a direct or indirect interest in trust property that relates to a licensed or permitted business and over which the beneficiary exercises no control. Direct or indirect beneficial ownership of not more than five percent of any class of equity securities that is registered under the Securities Exchange Act of 1934 shall not be deemed to be an ownership interest in the business of the issuer of such securities within the meaning of any statute, pursuant thereto.

Added by Acts 1971, 62nd Leg., p. 2954, ch. 979, § 1, eff. Aug. 30, 1971. Amended by Acts 1977, 65th Leg., p. 1918, ch. 769, § 1, eff. Aug. 29, 1977; Acts 1979, 66th Leg., p. 1741, ch. 713, § 4, eff. Aug. 27, 1979; Acts 1987, 70th Leg., ch. 467, § 2, eff. Sept. 1, 1987; Acts 1991, 72nd Leg., ch. 895, § 2, eff. Sept. 1, 1991; Acts 1993, 73rd Leg., ch. 846, § 1, eff. Sept. 1, 1993; Acts 1995, 74th Leg., ch. 1039, § 5, eff. Sept. 1, 1995.

Section 4 of the 1987 amendatory act provides:

"This Act takes effect September 1, 1987, and applies to interests of beneficiaries that arise on or after that date. An interest of a beneficiary that arises before the effective date of this Act is covered by the law as it existed when the interest arose, and that law is continued in effect for that purpose."

Section 35(a) of the 1993 amendatory act provides:

"The changes in law made by Sections 1, 2, and 3 of this Act apply only to a disclaimer made on or after the effective date of this Act. A disclaimer made before the effective date of this Act is covered by the law in effect when the disclaimer was made, and the former law is continued in effect for that purpose."

§ 37B. Assignment of Property Received from a Decedent

(a) A person entitled to receive property or an interest in property from a decedent under a will, by inheritance, or as a beneficiary under a life insurance contract, and who does not disclaim the property under Section 37A of this code, may assign the property or interest in property to any person.

(b) The assignment may, at the request of the assignor, be filed as provided for the filing of a disclaimer under Section 37A(a) of this code. The filing requires the service of notice under Section 37A(b) of this code.

(c) Failure to comply with the provisions of Section 37A of this code does not affect an assignment under this section.

(d) An assignment under this section is a gift to the assignee and is not a disclaimer or renunciation under Section 37A of this code.

(e) An assignment that would defeat a spendthrift provision imposed in a trust may not be made under this section.

Added by Acts 1985, 69th Leg., ch. 880, § 1, eff. Sept. 1, 1985.

§ 38. Persons Who Take Upon Intestacy

(a) Intestate Leaving No Husband or Wife. Where any person, having title to any estate, real, personal or mixed, shall die intestate, leaving no husband or wife, it shall descend and pass in parcenary to his kindred, male and female, in the following course:

1. To his children and their descendants.

2. If there be no children nor their descendants, then to his father and mother, in equal portions. But if only the father or mother survive the intestate, then his estate shall be divided into two equal portions, one of which shall pass to such survivor, and the other half shall pass to the brothers and sisters of the deceased, and to their descendants; but if there be none such, then the whole estate shall be inherited by the surviving father or mother.

3. If there be neither father nor mother, then the whole of such estate shall pass to the brothers and sisters of the intestate, and to their descendants.

4. If there be none of the kindred aforesaid, then the inheritance shall be divided into two moieties, one of which shall go to the paternal and the other to the maternal kindred, in the following course: To the

grandfather and grandmother in equal portions, but if only one of these be living, then the estate shall be divided into two equal parts, one of which shall go to such survivor, and the other shall go to the descendant or descendants of such deceased grandfather or grandmother. If there be no such descendants, then the whole estate shall be inherited by the surviving grandfather or grandmother. If there be no surviving grandfather or grandmother, then the whole of such estate shall go to their descendants, and so on without end, passing in like manner to the nearest lineal ancestors and their descendants.

(b) Intestate Leaving Husband or Wife. Where any person having title to any estate, real, personal or mixed, other than a community estate, shall die intestate as to such estate, and shall leave a surviving husband or wife, such estate of such intestate shall descend and pass as follows:

1. If the deceased have a child or children, or their descendants, the surviving husband or wife shall take one-third of the personal estate, and the balance of such personal estate shall go to the child or children of the deceased and their descendants. The surviving husband or wife shall also be entitled to an estate for life, in one-third of the land of the intestate, with remainder to the child or children of the intestate and their descendants.

2. If the deceased have no child or children, or their descendants, then the surviving husband or wife shall be entitled to all the personal estate, and to one-half of the lands of the intestate, without remainder to any person, and the other half shall pass and be inherited according to the rules of descent and distribution; provided, however, that if the deceased has neither surviving father nor mother nor surviving brothers or sisters, or their descendants, then the surviving husband or wife shall be entitled to the whole of the estate of such intestate.

Acts 1955, 54th Leg., p. 88, ch. 55, eff. Jan. 1, 1956.

§ 39. No Distinction Because of Property's Source

There shall be no distinction in regulating the descent and distribution of the estate of a person dying intestate between property which may have been derived by gift, devise or descent from the father, and that which may have been derived by gift, devise or descent from the mother; and all the estate to which such intestate may have had title at the time of death shall descend and vest in the heirs of such person in the same manner as if he had been the original purchaser thereof.

Acts 1955, 54th Leg., p. 88, ch. 55, eff. Jan. 1, 1956.

§ 40. Inheritance By and From an Adopted Child

For purposes of inheritance under the laws of descent and distribution, an adopted child shall be regarded as the child of the parent or parents by adoption, such adopted child and its descendants inheriting from and through the parent or parents by adoption and their kin the same as if such child were the natural child of such parent or parents by adoption, and such parent or parents by adoption and their kin inheriting from and through such adopted child the same as if such child were the natural child of such parent or parents by adoption. The natural parent or parents of such child and their kin shall not inherit from or through said child, but said child shall inherit from and through its natural parent or parents. Nothing herein shall prevent any parent by adoption from disposing of his property by will according to law. The presence of this Section specifically relating to the rights of adopted children shall in no way diminish the rights of such children, under the laws of descent and distribution or otherwise, which they acquire by virtue of their inclusion in the definition of "child" which is contained in this Code.

Acts 1955, 54th Leg., p. 88, ch. 55, eff. Jan. 1, 1956. Amended by Acts 1989, 71st Leg., ch. 375, § 34, eff. Sept. 1, 1989.

§ 41. Matters Affecting and Not Affecting the Right to Inherit

(a) Persons Not in Being. No right of inheritance shall accrue to any persons other than to children or lineal descendants of the intestate, unless they are in being and capable in law to take as heirs at the time of the death of the intestate.

(b) Heirs of Whole and Half Blood. In situations where the inheritance passes to the collateral kindred of the intestate, if part of such collateral be of the whole blood, and the other part be of the half blood only, of the intestate, each of those of half blood shall inherit only half so much as each of those of the whole blood; but if all be of the half blood, they shall have whole portions.

(c) Alienage. No person is disqualified to take as an heir because he or a person through whom he claims is or has been an alien.

(d) Convicted Persons and Suicides. No conviction shall work corruption of blood or forfeiture of estate, except in the case of a beneficiary in a life insurance policy or contract who is convicted and sentenced as a principal or accomplice in wilfully bringing about the death of the insured, in which case the proceeds of such insurance policy or contract shall be paid as provided in the Insurance Code of this

State, as same now exists or is hereafter amended; nor shall there be any forfeiture by reason of death by casualty; and the estates of those who destroy their own lives shall descend or vest as in the case of natural death.

Acts 1955, 54th Leg., p. 88, ch. 55, eff. Jan. 1, 1956. Amended by Acts 1969, 61st Leg., p. 1922, ch. 641, § 2, eff. June 12, 1969.

§ 42. Inheritance Rights of Children

(a) Maternal Inheritance. For the purpose of inheritance, a child is the child of his biological or adopted mother, so that he and his issue shall inherit from his mother and from his maternal kindred, both descendants, ascendants, and collaterals in all degrees, and they may inherit from him and his issue.

(b) Paternal Inheritance. (1) For the purpose of inheritance, a child is the child of his biological father if the child is born under circumstances described by Section 151.002, Family Code, is adjudicated to be the child of the father by court decree as provided by Chapter 160, Family Code, was adopted by his father, or if the father executed a statement of paternity as provided by Section 160.202, Family Code, or a like statement properly executed in another jurisdiction, so that he and his issue shall inherit from his father and from his paternal kindred, both descendants, ascendants, and collaterals in all degrees, and they may inherit from him and his issue. A person claiming to be a biological child of the decedent, who is not otherwise presumed to be a child of the decedent, or claiming inheritance through a biological child of the decedent, who is not otherwise presumed to be a child of the decedent, may petition the probate court for a determination of right of inheritance. If the court finds by clear and convincing evidence that the purported father was the biological father of the child, the child is treated as any other child of the decedent for the purpose of inheritance and he and his issue may inherit from his paternal kindred, both descendants, ascendants, and collaterals in all degrees, and they may inherit from him and his issue. This section does not permit inheritance by a purported father of a child, whether recognized or not, if the purported father's parental rights have been terminated.

(2) A person who purchases for valuable consideration any interest in real or personal property of the heirs of a decedent, who in good faith relies on the declarations in an affidavit of heirship that does not include a child who at the time of the sale or contract of sale of the property is not a presumed child of the decedent and has not under a final court decree or judgment been found to be entitled to treatment under this subsection as a child of the decedent, and who is without knowledge of the claim of that child, acquires good title to the interest that the person would have received, as purchaser, in the absence of any claim of the child not included in the affidavit. This subdivision does not affect the liability, if any, of the heirs for the proceeds of any sale described by this subdivision to the child who was not included in the affidavit of heirship.

(c) Homestead Rights, Exempt Property, and Family Allowances. A child as provided by Subsections (a) and (b) of this section is a child of his mother, and a child of his father, for the purpose of determining homestead rights, distribution of exempt property, and the making of family allowances.

(d) Marriages Void and Voidable. The issue of marriages declared void or voided by annulment shall be treated in the same manner as issue of a valid marriage.

Acts 1955, 54th Leg., p. 88, ch. 55, eff. Jan. 1, 1956. Amended by Acts 1977, 65th Leg., p. 762, ch. 290, § 1, eff. May 28, 1977; Acts 1979, 66th Leg., p. 40, ch. 24, § 25, eff. Aug. 27, 1979; Acts 1979, 66th Leg., p. 1743, ch. 713, § 5, eff. Aug. 27, 1979 ; Acts 1987, 70th Leg., ch. 464, § 1, eff. Sept. 1, 1987; Acts 1989, 71st Leg., ch. 375, § 35, eff. Sept. 1, 1989; Acts 1997, 75th Leg., ch. 165, § 7.54, eff. Sept. 1, 1997; Acts 1997, 75th Leg., ch. 1302, § 4, eff. Sept. 1, 1997.

§ 43. Determination of Per Capita and Per Stirpes Distribution

When the intestate's children, descendants, brothers, sisters, uncles, aunts, or any other relatives of the deceased standing in the first or same degree alone come into the distribution upon intestacy, they shall take per capita, namely: by persons; and, when a part of them being dead and a part living, the descendants of those dead shall have right to distribution upon intestacy, such descendants shall inherit only such portion of said property as the parent through whom they inherit would be entitled to if alive.

Acts 1955, 54th Leg., p. 88, ch. 55, eff. Jan. 1, 1956. Amended by Acts 1991, 72nd Leg., ch. 895, § 3, eff. Sept. 1, 1991.

For applicability provisions of the 1991 amendatory act, see note following § 3.

§ 44. Advancements

(a) If a decedent dies intestate as to all or a portion of the decedent's estate, property the decedent gave during the decedent's lifetime to a person who, on the date of the decedent's death, is the decedent's heir, or property received by a decedent's heir under a nontestamentary transfer under Chapter XI [1] of this code is an advancement against the heir's intestate share only if:

(1) the decedent declared in a contemporaneous writing or the heir acknowledged in writing that the gift or nontestamentary transfer is an advancement; or

(2) the decedent's contemporaneous writing or the heir's written acknowledgment otherwise indicates that the gift or nontestamentary transfer is to be taken into account in computing the division and distribution of the decedent's intestate estate.

(b) For purposes of Subsection (a) of this section, property that is advanced is valued at the time the heir came into possession or enjoyment of the property or at the time of the decedent's death, whichever occurs first.

(c) If the recipient of the property fails to survive the decedent, the property is not taken into account in computing the division and distribution of the decedent's intestate estate, unless the decedent's contemporaneous writing provides otherwise.

Acts 1955, 54th Leg., p. 88, ch. 55, eff. Jan. 1, 1956. Amended by Acts 1993, 73rd Leg., ch. 846, § 4, eff. Sept. 1, 1993.

[1] Section 436 et seq.

Section 35(b) of the 1993 Act provides:

"The changes in law made by Sections 4, 5, 6, 7, 8, 9, 10, 11, 12, and 24 of this Act apply only to the estates of persons who die on or after the effective date of this Act. The estate of a person who dies before the effective date of this Act is covered by the law in effect when the person died, and the former law is continued in effect for that purpose."

§ 45. Community Estate

(a) On the intestate death of one of the spouses to a marriage, the community property estate of the deceased spouse passes to the surviving spouse if:

(1) no child or other descendant of the deceased spouse survives the deceased spouse; or

(2) all surviving children and descendants of the deceased spouse are also children or descendants of the surviving spouse.

(b) On the intestate death of one of the spouses to a marriage, if a child or other descendant of the deceased spouse survives the deceased spouse and the child or descendant is not a child or descendant of the surviving spouse, one-half of the community estate is retained by the surviving spouse and the other one-half passes to the children or descendants of the deceased spouse. The descendants shall inherit only such portion of said property to which they would be entitled under Section 43 of this code. In every case, the community estate passes charged with the debts against it.

Acts 1955, 54th Leg., p. 88, ch. 55, eff. Jan. 1, 1956. Amended by Acts 1991, 72nd Leg., ch. 895, § 4, eff. Sept. 1, 1991; Acts 1993, 73rd Leg., ch. 846, § 33, eff. Sept. 1, 1993.

For applicability provisions of the 1991 amendatory act, see note following § 3.

§ 46. Joint Tenancies

(a) If two or more persons hold an interest in property jointly, and one joint owner dies before severance, the interest of the decedent in the joint estate shall not survive to the remaining joint owner or owners but shall pass by will or intestacy from the decedent as if the decedent's interest had been severed. The joint owners may agree in writing, however, that the interest of any joint owner who dies shall survive to the surviving joint owner or owners, but no such agreement shall be inferred from the mere fact that the property is held in joint ownership.

(b) Subsection (a) does not apply to agreements between spouses regarding their community property. Agreements between spouses regarding rights of survivorship in community property are governed by Part 3 of Chapter XI of this code.[1] § 451-462

Acts 1955, 54th Leg., p. 88, ch. 55, eff. Jan. 1, 1956. Amended by Acts 1961, 57th Leg., p. 233, ch. 120, § 1, eff. May 15, 1961; Acts 1969, 61st Leg., p. 1922, ch. 641, § 3, eff. June 12, 1969; Acts 1981, 67th Leg., p. 895, ch. 319, § 1, eff. Sept. 1, 1981; Acts 1987, 70th Leg., ch. 678, § 2; Acts 1989, 71st Leg., ch. 655, § 1, eff. Aug. 28, 1989.

[1] V.A.T.S. Probate Code § 451 et seq.

Section 3(b) of the 1987 amendatory act provides:

"Section 2 of this Act takes effect when the [1987] constitutional amendment proposed by the 70th Legislature, Regular Session, permitting spouses to make an agreement concerning the right of survivorship of certain community property is adopted [S.J.R.35]. If that amendment is not adopted, Section 2 of this Act has no effect."

Acts 1987, 70th Leg., S.J.R. 35, was adopted by the voters at the Nov. 3, 1987 election.

Section 3 of the 1989 amendatory act provides:

"(a) The amendments made by this Act apply:

"(1) to all agreements between spouses creating a right of survivorship in community property entered into on or after the effective date of the 1987 amendment to Article XVI, Section 15, of the Texas Constitution; and

"(2) to all such agreements entered into prior to that date if both spouses were living on that date, the agreement complies with the provisions of Part 3 of Chapter XI, Texas Probate Code, as added by Section 2 of this Act, and the property which was the subject of the agreement remained community property after the date of the agreement.

"(b) If an agreement between spouses which purported to create a right of survivorship in their community property was entered into prior to the effective date of the 1987 amendment to Article XVI, Section 15, of the Texas Constitution, and a spouse died prior to that date, the agreement is covered by the law as it existed prior to the constitutional amendment, and that law is continued in effect for that purpose."

survival statute

§ 47. **Requirement of Survival by 120 Hours**

(a) **Survival of Heirs.** A person who fails to survive the decedent by 120 hours is deemed to have predeceased the decedent for purposes of homestead allowance, exempt property, and intestate succession, and the decedent's heirs are determined accordingly, except as otherwise provided in this section. If the time of death of the decedent or of the person who would otherwise be an heir, or the times of death of both, cannot be determined, and it cannot be established that the person who would otherwise be an heir has survived the decedent by 120 hours, it is deemed that the person failed to survive for the required period. This subsection does not apply where its application would result in the escheat of an intestate estate.

(b) **Disposal of Community Property.** When a husband and wife have died, leaving community property, and neither the husband nor wife survived the other by 120 hours, one-half of all community property shall be distributed as if the husband had survived, and the other one-half thereof shall be distributed as if the wife had survived. The provisions of this subsection apply to proceeds of life or accident insurance which are community property and become payable to the estate of either the husband or the wife, as well as to other kinds of community property.

(c) **Survival of Devisees or Beneficiaries.** A devisee who does not survive the testator by 120 hours is treated as if he predeceased the testator, unless the will of the decedent contains some language dealing explicitly with simultaneous death or deaths in a common disaster, or requiring that the devisee survive the testator or survive the testator for a stated period in order to take under the will. If property is so disposed of that the right of a beneficiary to succeed to any interest therein is conditional upon his surviving another person, the beneficiary shall be deemed not to have survived unless he or she survives the person by 120 hours. However, if any interest in property is given alternatively to one of two or more beneficiaries, with the right of each to take being dependent upon his surviving the other or others, and all shall die within a period of less than 120 hours, the property shall be divided into as many equal portions as there are beneficiaries, and those portions shall be distributed respectively to those who would have taken in the event that each beneficiary had survived.

(d) **Joint Owners.** If any real or personal property, including community property with a right of survivorship, shall be so owned that one of two joint owners is entitled to the whole on the death of the other, and neither survives the other by 120 hours, these assets shall be distributed one-half as if one joint owner had survived and the other one-half as if the other joint owner had survived. If there are more than two joint owners and all have died within a period of less than 120 hours, these assets shall be divided into as many equal portions as there are joint owners and these portions shall be distributed respectively to those who would have taken in the event that each joint owner survived.

(e) **Insured and Beneficiary.** When the insured and a beneficiary in a policy of life or accident insurance have died within a period of less than 120 hours, the insured shall be deemed to have survived the beneficiary for the purpose of determining the rights under the policy of the beneficiary or beneficiaries as such. The provisions of this subsection shall not prevent the application of subsection (b) above to the proceeds of life or accident insurance which are community property.

(f) **Instruments Providing Different Disposition.** When provision has been made in the case of wills, living trusts, deeds, or contracts of insurance, or any other situation, for disposition of property different from the provisions of this Section, this Section shall not apply.

Acts 1955, 54th Leg., p. 88, ch. 55, eff. Jan. 1, 1956. Amended by Acts 1965, 59th Leg., p. 279, ch. 119, § 1, eff. Aug. 30, 1965; Acts 1979, 66th Leg., p. 1743, ch. 713, § 6, eff. Aug. 27, 1979; Acts 1993, 73rd Leg., ch. 846, § 5, eff. Sept. 1, 1993.

For application provisions of the 1993 amendatory act, see note under § 44.

CHAPTER III. DETERMINATION OF HEIRSHIP

Section

§ 48. **Proceedings to Declare Heirship. When and Where Instituted**

(a) When a person dies intestate owning or entitled to real or personal property in Texas, and there shall have been no administration in this State upon his estate; or when there has been a will probated in this State or elsewhere, or an administration in this State upon the estate of such decedent, and any real or personal property in this State has been omitted from such will or from such administration, or no final disposition thereof has been made in such administration, the court of the county in which such proceedings were last pending, or in the event no will of such decedent has been admitted to probate in this State, and no administration has been granted in this State upon the estate of such decedent, then the court of the county in which any of the real property belonging to such estate is situated, or if there is no such real estate, then of the county in which any personal property belonging to such estate is found, may determine and declare in the manner hereinafter provided who are the heirs and only heirs of such decedent, and their respective shares and interests, under the laws of this State, in the estate of such decedent, and proceedings therefor shall be known as proceedings to declare heirship.

(b) If an application for determination of heirship is filed within four (4) years from the date of the death of the decedent, the applicant may request that the court determine whether a necessity for administration exists. The court shall hear evidence upon the issue and make a determination thereof in its judgment.

(c) Notwithstanding any other provision of this section, a probate court in which the proceedings for the guardianship of the estate of a ward who dies intestate were pending at the time of the death of the ward may, if there is no administration pending in the estate, determine and declare who are the heirs and only heirs of the ward, and their respective shares and interests, under the laws of this State, in the estate of the ward.

Acts 1955, 54th Leg., p. 88, ch. 55, eff. Jan. 1, 1956. Amended by Acts 1971, 62nd Leg., p. 971, ch. 173, § 4, eff. Jan. 1, 1972; Acts 1977, 65th Leg., p. 1521, ch. 616, § 1, eff. Aug. 29, 1977.

§ 49. Who May Institute Proceedings to Declare Heirship

(a) Such proceedings may be instituted and maintained in any of the instances enumerated above by the qualified personal representative of the estate of such decedent, by any person or persons claiming to be a secured creditor or the owner of the whole or a part of the estate of such decedent, or by the guardian of the estate of a ward, if the proceedings are instituted and maintained in the probate court in which the proceedings for the guardianship of the estate were pending at the time of the death of the ward. In such a case an application shall be filed in a proper court stating the following information:

(1) the name of the decedent and the time and place of death;

(2) the names and residences of the decedent's heirs, the relationship of each heir to the decedent, and the true interest of the applicant and each of the heirs in the estate of the decedent;

(3) all the material facts and circumstances within the knowledge and information of the applicant that might reasonably tend to show the time or place of death or the names or residences of all heirs, if the time or place of death or the names or residences of all the heirs are not definitely known to the applicant;

(4) a statement that all children born to or adopted by the decedent have been listed;

(5) a statement that each marriage of the decedent has been listed with the date of the marriage, the name of the spouse, and if the marriage was terminated, the date and place of termination, and other facts to show whether a spouse has had an interest in the property of the decedent;

(6) whether the decedent died testate and if so, what disposition has been made of the will;

(7) a general description of all the real and personal property belonging to the estate of the decedent; and

(8) an explanation for the omission of any of the foregoing information that is omitted from the application.

(b) Such application shall be supported by the affidavit of each applicant to the effect that, insofar as is known to such applicant, all the allegations of such application are true in substance and in fact and that no such material fact or circumstance has, within the affiant's knowledge, been omitted from such application. The unknown heirs of such decedent, all persons who are named in the application as heirs of such decedent, and all persons who are, at the date of the filing of the application, shown by the deed records of the county in which any of the real property described in such application is situated to own any share or interest in any such real property, shall be made parties in such proceeding.

Acts 1955, 54th Leg., p. 88, ch. 55, eff. Jan. 1, 1956. Amended by Acts 1971, 62nd Leg., p. 971, ch. 173, § 4, eff. Jan. 1, 1972; Acts 1977, 65th Leg., p. 1522, ch. 616, § 2, eff. Aug. 29, 1977; Acts 1979, 66th Leg., p. 1744, ch. 713, § 7, eff. Aug. 27, 1979; Acts 1983, 68th Leg., p. 629, ch. 139, § 1, eff. Sept. 1, 1983; Acts 1985, 69th Leg., ch. 693, § 1, eff. Sept. 1, 1985.

§ 50. Notice

(a) Citation shall be served by registered or certified mail upon all distributees 12 years of age or older whose names and addresses are known, or whose names and addresses can be learned through the exercise of reasonable diligence, provided that the court may in its discretion require that service of citation shall be made by personal service upon some or all of those named as distributees in the application. Citation shall be served as provided by this subsection on the parent, managing conservator, or guardian of a distributee who is younger than 12 years of age, if the name and address of the parent, managing conservator, or guardian is known or can be reasonably ascertained.

(b) If the address of a person or entity on whom citation is required to be served cannot be ascertained, citation shall be served on the person or entity by publication in the county in which the proceedings are commenced, and if the decedent resided in another county, then a citation shall also be published in the county of his last residence. Unknown heirs shall also be served by publication in the manner provided by this subsection.

(c) Except in proceedings in which there is service of citation by publication as provided by Subsection (b) of this section, citation shall also be posted in the county in which the proceedings are commenced and in the county of the decedent's last residence.

(d) A party to the proceedings who has executed the application need not be served by any method.

Acts 1955, 54th Leg., p. 88, ch. 55, eff. Jan. 1, 1956. Amended by Acts 1971, 62nd Leg., p. 971, ch. 173, § 4, eff. Jan. 1, 1972; Acts 1979, 66th Leg., p. 1745, ch. 713, § 8, eff. Aug. 29, 1979; Acts 1997, 75th Leg., ch. 1130, § 1, eff. Sept. 1, 1997.

Section 2 of Acts 1997, 75th Leg., ch. 1130, provides:

"This Act takes effect September 1, 1997, and applies only to an application for determination of heirship filed on or after that date. An application for determination of heirship filed before the effective date of this Act is governed by the law in existence on the date on which the application was filed, and the former law is continued in effect for that purpose."

§ 51. Transfer of Proceeding When Will Probated or Administration Granted

If an administration upon the estate of any such decedent shall be granted in the State, or if the will of such decedent shall be admitted to probate in this State, after the institution of a proceeding to declare heirship, the court in which such proceeding is pending shall, by an order entered of record therein, transfer the cause to the court of the county in which such administration shall have been granted, or such will shall have been probated, and thereupon the clerk of the court in which such proceeding was originally filed shall send to the clerk of the court named in such order, a certified transcript of all pleadings, docket entries, and orders of the court in such cause. The clerk of the court to which such cause shall be transferred shall file the transcript and record the same in the minutes of the court and shall docket such cause, and the same shall thereafter proceed as though originally filed in that court. The court, in its discretion, may consolidate the cause so transferred with the pending proceeding.

Acts 1955, 54th Leg., p. 88, ch. 55, eff. Jan. 1, 1956. Amended by Acts 1971, 62nd Leg., p. 971, ch. 173, § 4, eff. Jan. 1, 1972.

§ 52. Recorded Instruments as Prima Facie Evidence

(a) A statement of facts concerning the family history, genealogy, marital status, or the identity of the heirs of a decedent shall be received in a proceeding to declare heirship, or in a suit involving title to real or personal property, as prima facie evidence of the facts therein stated, if the statement is contained in either an affidavit or any other instrument legally executed and acknowledged or sworn to before, and certified by, an officer authorized to take acknowledgments or oaths as applicable, or any judgment of a court of record, and if the affidavit or instrument has been of record for five years or more in the deed records of any county in this state in which such real or personal property is located at the time the suit is instituted, or in the deed records of any county of this state in which the decedent had his domicile or fixed place of residence at the time of his death. If there is any error in the statement of facts in such recorded affidavit or instrument, the true facts may be proved by anyone interested in the proceeding in which said affidavit or instrument is offered in evidence.

(b) An affidavit of facts concerning the identity of heirs of a decedent as to an interest in real property that is filed in a proceeding or suit described by Subsection (a) of this section may be in the form described by Section 52A of this code.

(c) An affidavit of facts concerning the identity of heirs of a decedent does not affect the rights of an omitted heir or a creditor of the decedent as otherwise provided by law. This statute shall be cumulative of all other statutes on the same subject, and shall not be construed as abrogating any right to present evidence or to rely on an affidavit of facts conferred by any other statute or rule of law.

Acts 1955, 54th Leg., p. 88, ch. 55, eff. Jan. 1, 1956. Amended by Acts 1969, 61st Leg., p. 1922, ch. 641, § 4, eff. June 12, 1969; Acts 1991, 72nd Leg., ch. 895, § 5, eff. Sept. 1, 1991; Acts 1999, 76th Leg., ch. 1538, § 1, eff. Sept. 1, 1999.

§ 52A. Form of Affidavit of Facts Concerning Identity of Heirs

An affidavit of facts concerning the identity of heirs of a decedent may be in substantially the following form:

AFFIDAVIT OF FACTS CONCERNING THE IDENTITY OF HEIRS

Before me, the undersigned authority, on this day personally appeared ________ ("Affiant") (insert name of affiant) who, being first duly sworn, upon his/her oath states:

1. My name is ________ (insert name of affiant), and I live at ________ (insert address of affiant's residence). I am personally familiar with the family and marital history of ________ ("Decedent") (insert name of decedent), and I have personal knowledge of the facts stated in this affidavit.

2. I knew decedent from ________ (insert date) until ________ (insert date). Decedent died on ________ (insert date of death). Decedent's place of death was ________ (insert place of death). At the time of decedent's death, decedent's residence was ________ (insert address of decedent's residence).

3. Decedent's marital history was as follows: ________ (insert marital history and, if decedent's spouse is deceased, insert date and place of spouse's death).

4. Decedent had the following children: ________ (insert name, birth date, name of other parent, and current address of child or date of death of child and descendants of deceased child, as applicable, for each child).

5. Decedent did not have or adopt any other children and did not take any other children into decedent's home or raise any other children, except: ________ (insert name of child or names of children, or state "none").

6. (Include if decedent was not survived by descendants.) Decedent's mother was: ________ (insert name, birth date, and current address or date of death of mother, as applicable).

7. (Include if decedent was not survived by descendants.) Decedent's father was: ________ (insert name, birth date, and current address or date of death of father, as applicable).

8. (Include if decedent was not survived by descendants or by both mother and father.) Decedent had the following siblings: ________ (insert name, birth date, and current address or date of death of each sibling and parents of each sibling and descendants of each deceased sibling, as applicable, or state "none").

9. (Optional.) The following persons have knowledge regarding the decedent, the identity of decedent's children, if any, parents, or siblings, if any: ________ (insert names of persons with knowledge, or state "none").

10. Decedent died without leaving a written will. (Modify statement if decedent left a written will.)

11. There has been no administration of decedent's estate. (Modify statement if there has been administration of decedent's estate.)

12. Decedent left no debts that are unpaid, except: ________ (insert list of debts, or state "none").

13. There are no unpaid estate or inheritance taxes, except: ________ (insert list of unpaid taxes, or state "none").

14. To the best of my knowledge, decedent owned an interest in the following real property: ________ (insert list of real property in which decedent owned an interest, or state "none").

15. (Optional.) The following were the heirs of decedent: ________ (insert names of heirs).

16. (Insert additional information as appropriate, such as size of the decedent's estate.)

Signed this ___ day of ________, ___.

____

(signature of affiant)

State of ________

County of ________

Sworn to and subscribed to before me on ________ (date) by ________ (insert name of affiant).

____

(signature of notarial officer)

(Seal, if any, of notary) ________

(printed name)

My commission expires: ________

Added by Acts 1999, 76th Leg., ch. 1538, § 2, eff. Sept. 1, 1999.

Section 3 of Acts 1999, 76th Leg., ch. 1538 provides:

"(a) This Act takes effect September 1, 1999, and applies only to an affidavit of facts concerning the identity of heirs of a decedent that is executed on or after the effective date of this Act.

"(b) An affidavit of facts concerning the identity of heirs of a decedent that is executed before the effective date of this Act is governed by the law in effect on the date the affidavit was executed, and the former law is continued in effect for that purpose."

§ 53. Evidence; Unknown Parties

(a) The court in its discretion may require all or any part of the evidence admitted in a proceeding to declare heirship to be reduced to writing, and subscribed and sworn to by the witnesses, respectively, and filed in the cause, and recorded in the minutes of the court.

(b) If it appears to the court that there are or may be living heirs whose names or whereabouts are unknown, or that any defendant is an incapacitated person, the court may, in its discretion, appoint an attorney ad litem or guardian ad litem to represent the interests of any such persons. The court may not appoint an attorney ad litem or guardian ad litem unless the court finds that the appointment is necessary to protect the interests of the living heir or incapacitated person.

Acts 1955, 54th Leg., p. 88, ch. 55, eff. Jan. 1, 1956. Amended by Acts 1971, 62nd Leg., p. 971, ch. 173, § 4, eff. Jan. 1, 1972; Acts 1995, 74th Leg., ch. 1039, § 6, eff. Sept. 1, 1995.

§ 54. Judgment

The judgment of the court in a proceeding to declare heirship shall declare the names and places of residence of the heirs of the decedent, and their respective shares and interests in the real and personal property of such decedent. If the proof is in any respect deficient, the judgment shall so state.

Acts 1955, 54th Leg., p. 88, ch. 55, eff. Jan. 1, 1956. Amended by Acts 1971, 62nd Leg., p. 971, ch. 173, § 4, eff. Jan. 1, 1972.

§ 55. Effect of Judgment

(a) Such judgment shall be a final judgment, and may be appealed or reviewed within the same time limits and in the same manner as may other judgments in probate matters at the instance of any interested person. If any person who is an heir of the decedent is not served with citation by registered or certified mail, or by personal service, he may at any time within four years from the date of such judgment have the same corrected by bill of review, or upon proof of actual fraud, after the passage of any length of time, and may recover from the heirs named in the judgment, and those claiming under them who are not bona fide purchasers for value, his just share of the property or its value.

(b) Although such judgment may later be modified, set aside, or nullified, it shall nevertheless be conclusive in any suit between any heir omitted from the judgment and a bona fide purchaser for value who has purchased real or personal property after entry of the judgment without actual notice of the claim of the omitted heir. Similarly, any person who has delivered funds or property of the decedent to the persons declared to be heirs in the judgment, or has engaged in any other transaction with them, in good faith, after entry of such judgment, shall not be liable therefor to any person.

(c) If the court states in its judgment that there is no necessity for administration on the estate, such recital shall constitute authorization to all persons owing any money to the estate of the decedent, or having custody of any property of such estate, or acting as registrar or transfer agent of any evidence of interest, indebtedness, property, or right belonging to the estate, and to persons purchasing from or otherwise dealing with the heirs as determined in the judgment, to pay, deliver, or transfer such property or evidence of property rights to such heirs, or to purchase property from such heirs, without liability to any creditor of the estate or other person. Such heirs shall be entitled to enforce their right to payment, delivery, or transfer by suit. Nothing in this chapter shall affect the rights or remedies of the creditors of the decedent except as provided in this subsection.

Acts 1955, 54th Leg., p. 88, ch. 55, eff. Jan. 1, 1956. Amended by Acts 1971, 62nd Leg., p. 971, ch. 173, § 4, eff. Jan. 1, 1972; Acts 1979, 66th Leg., p. 1746, ch. 713, § 9, eff. Aug. 29, 1979.

§ 56. Filing of Certified Copy of Judgment

A certified copy of such judgment may be filed for record in the office of the county clerk of the county in which any of the real property described in such judgment is situated, and recorded in the deed records of such county, and indexed in the name of such decedent as grantor and of the heirs named in such judgment as grantees; and, from and after such filing, such judgment shall constitute constructive notice of the facts set forth therein.

Acts 1955, 54th Leg., p. 88, ch. 55, eff. Jan. 1, 1956.

CHAPTER IV. EXECUTION AND REVOCATION OF WILLS

Section

§ 57. Who May Execute a Will

Every person who has attained the age of eighteen years, or who is or has been lawfully married, or who is a member of the armed forces of the United States or of the auxiliaries thereof or of the maritime service at the time the will is made, being of sound mind, shall have the right and power to make a last will and testament, under the rules and limitations prescribed by law.

Acts 1955, 54th Leg., p. 88, ch. 55, eff. Jan. 1, 1956. Amended by Acts 1967, 60th Leg., p. 801, ch. 334, § 1, eff. Aug. 28, 1967.

§ 58. Interests Which May Pass Under a Will

(a) Every person competent to make a last will and testament may thereby devise and bequeath all the estate, right, title, and interest in property the person has at the time of the person's death, subject to the limitations prescribed by law.

(b) A person who makes a last will and testament may:

(1) disinherit an heir; and

(2) direct the disposition of property or an interest passing under the will or by intestacy.

(c) A legacy of personal property does not include any contents of the property unless the will directs that the contents are included in the legacy. A devise of real property does not include any personal property located on or associated with the real property or any contents of personal property located on the real property unless the will directs that the personal property or contents are included in the devise.

(d) In this section:

(1) "Contents" means tangible personal property, other than titled personal property, found inside of or on a specifically bequeathed or devised item. The term includes clothing, pictures, furniture, coin collections, and other items of tangible personal property that do not require a formal transfer of title and that are located in another item of tangible personal property such as a cedar chest or other furniture.

(2) "Titled personal property" includes all tangible personal property represented by a certificate of title, certificate of ownership, written label, marking, or designation that signifies ownership by a person. The term includes a motor vehicle, motor home, motorboat, or other similar property that requires a formal transfer of title.

Acts 1955, 54th Leg., p. 88, ch. 55, eff. Jan. 1, 1956. Amended by Acts 1991, 72nd Leg., ch. 895, § 6, eff. Sept. 1, 1991; Acts 1993, 73rd Leg., ch. 846, § 6, eff. Sept. 1, 1993; Acts 1995, 74th Leg., ch. 642, § 1, eff. Sept. 1, 1995.

For applicability provisions of the 1991 amendatory act, see note following § 3.

For application provisions of the 1993 amendatory act, see note under § 44.

Section 17(a) of the 1995 amendatory act provides:

"The changes in law made by Sections 1–11 of this Act apply only to the estates of decedents who die on or after September 1, 1995. The estates of decedents who die before the effective date of this Act are governed by the law as it existed immediately before the effective date of this Act, and that law is continued in effect for that purpose."

§ 58a. Devises or Bequests to Trustees

(a) A testator may validly devise or bequeath property in a will to the trustee of a trust established or to be established:

(1) during the testator's lifetime by the testator, by the testator and another person, or by another person, including a funded or unfunded life insurance trust, in which the settlor has reserved any or all rights of ownership of the insurance contracts; or

(2) at the testator's death by the testator's devise or bequest to the trustee, if the trust is identified in the testator's will and its terms are in a written instrument, other than a will, that is executed before, with, or after the execution of the testator's will or in another person's will if that other person has predeceased the testator, regardless of the existence, size, or character of the corpus of the trust.

(b) A devise or bequest is not invalid because the trust is amendable or revocable or because the trust was amended after the execution of the will or the testator's death.

(c) Unless the testator's will provides otherwise, property devised or bequeathed to a trust described by Subsection (a) of this section is not held under a testamentary trust of the testator. The property becomes a part of the trust to which it is devised or bequeathed and must be administered and disposed of in accordance with the provisions of the instrument establishing the trust, including any amendments to the instrument made before or after the testator's death.

(d) Unless the testator's will provides otherwise, a revocation or termination of the trust before the testator's death causes the devise or bequest to lapse.

Added by Acts 1961, 57th Leg., p. 43, ch. 29, § 1. Amended by Acts 1993, 73rd Leg., ch. 846, § 7, eff. Sept. 1, 1993.

For application provisions of the 1993 amendatory act, see note under § 44.

§ 58b. Devises and Bequests That Are Void

(a) A devise or bequest of property in a will to an attorney who prepares or supervises the preparation of the will or a devise or bequest of property in a will to an heir or employee of the attorney who prepares or supervises the preparation of the will is void.

(b) This section does not apply to a bequest made to a person who is related within the second degree by consanguinity or affinity to the testator, nor to a bona fide purchaser for value from a devisee in a will.

Added by Acts 1997, 75th Leg., ch. 1054, § 1, eff. Sept. 1, 1997.

Section 2 of Acts 1997, 75th Leg., ch. 1054 provides:

"This Act takes effect September 1, 1997, and applies only to a will executed on or after that date. A will executed before the effective date of this Act is governed by the law in effect on the date the will was executed, and that law is continued in effect for that purpose."

§ 59. Requisites of a Will

(a) Every last will and testament, except where otherwise provided by law, shall be in writing and signed by the testator in person or by another person for him by his direction and in his presence, and shall, if not wholly in the handwriting of the testator, be attested by two or more credible witnesses above the age of fourteen years who shall subscribe their names thereto in their own handwriting in the presence of the testator. Such a will or testament may, at the time of its execution or at any subsequent date during the lifetime of the testator and the witnesses, be made self-proved, and the testimony of the witnesses in the probate thereof may be made unnecessary, by the affidavits of the testator and the attesting witnesses, made before an officer authorized to administer oaths under the laws of this State. Provided that nothing shall require an affidavit or certificate of any testator or testatrix as a prerequisite to self-proof of a will or testament other than the certificate set out below. The affidavits shall be evidenced by a certificate, with official seal affixed, of such officer attached or annexed to such will or testament in form and contents substantially as follows:

THE STATE OF TEXAS

COUNTY OF ______________

Before me, the undersigned authority, on this day personally appeared ______________, ______________, and ______________, known to me to be the testator and the witnesses, respectively, whose names are subscribed to the annexed or foregoing instrument in their respective capacities, and, all of said persons being by me duly sworn, the said ______________, testator, declared to me and to the said witnesses in my presence that said instrument is his last will and testament, and that he had willingly made and executed it as his free act and deed; and the said witnesses, each on his oath stated to me, in the presence and hearing of the said testator, that the said testator had declared to them that said instrument is his last will and testament, and that he executed same as such and wanted each of them to sign it as a witness; and upon their oaths each witness stated further that they did sign the same as witnesses in the presence of the said testator and at his request; that he was at that time eighteen years of age or over (or being under such age, was or had been lawfully married, or was then a member of the armed forces of the United States or of an auxiliary thereof or of the Maritime Service) and was of sound mind; and that each of said witnesses was then at least fourteen years of age.

____
Testator

____
Witness

____
Witness

Subscribed and sworn to before me by the said ______________, testator, and by the said ______________ and ______________, witnesses, this ______ day of ______________ A.D. ______________.

(SEAL)

(Signed) ______________
(Official Capacity of Officer)

(b) An affidavit in form and content substantially as provided by Subsection (a) of this section is a "self-proving affidavit." A will with a self-proving affidavit subscribed and sworn to by the testator and witnesses attached or annexed to the will is a "self-proved will." Substantial compliance with the form of such affidavit shall suffice to cause the will to be self-proved. For this purpose, an affidavit that is subscribed and acknowledged by the testator and subscribed and sworn to by the witnesses would suffice as being in substantial compliance. A signature on a self-proving affidavit is considered a signature to the will if necessary to prove that the will was signed by the testator or witnesses, or both, but in that case, the will may not be considered a self-proved will.

(c) A self-proved will may be admitted to probate without the testimony of any subscribing witness, but otherwise it shall be treated no differently than a will not self-proved. In particular and without limiting the generality of the foregoing, a self-proved will may be contested, or revoked or amended by a codicil in exactly the same fashion as a will not self-proved.

Acts 1955, 54th Leg., p. 88, ch. 55, eff. Jan. 1, 1956. Amended by Acts 1961, 57th Leg., p. 936, ch. 412, § 1, eff. June 17, 1961; Acts 1969, 61st Leg., p. 1922, ch. 641, § 5, eff. June 12, 1969; Acts 1971, 62nd Leg., p. 974, ch. 173, § 5, eff. Jan. 1, 1972; Acts 1991, 72nd Leg., ch. 895, § 7, eff. Sept. 1, 1991.

Section 2 of the 1961 amendatory act and § 6 of the 1971 amendatory act each provided:

"All wills self-proved prior to the passage of this Act which were executed in compliance with Section 59 of the Texas Probate Code are in all things relating to self-providing hereby ratified."

§ 59A. Contracts Concerning Succession

(a) A contract to make a will or devise, or not to revoke a will or devise, if executed or entered into on or after September 1, 1979, can be established only by provisions of a will stating that a contract does exist and stating the material provisions of the contract.

(b) The execution of a joint will or reciprocal wills does not by itself suffice as evidence of the existence of a contract.

Added by Acts 1979, 66th Leg., p. 1746, ch. 713, § 10, eff. Aug. 27, 1979.

§ 60. Exception Pertaining to Holographic Wills

Where the will is written wholly in the handwriting of the testator, the attestation of the subscribing witnesses may be dispensed with. Such a will may be made self-proved at any time during the testator's lifetime by the attachment or annexation thereto of an affidavit by the testator to the effect that the instrument is his last will; that he was at least eighteen years of age when he executed it (or, if under such age, was or had been lawfully married, or was then a member of the armed forces of the United States or of an auxiliary thereof or of the Maritime Service); that he was of sound mind; and that he has not revoked such instrument.

Acts 1955, 54th Leg., p. 88, ch. 55, eff. Jan. 1, 1956. Amended by Acts 1969, 61st Leg., p. 1922, ch. 641, § 6, eff. June 12, 1969.

§ 61. Bequest to Witness

Should any person be a subscribing witness to a will, and also be a legatee or devisee therein, if the will cannot be otherwise established, such bequest shall be void, and such witness shall be allowed and compelled to appear and give his testimony in like manner as if no such bequest had been made. But, if in such case the witness would have been entitled to a share of the estate of the testator had there been no will, he shall be entitled to as much of such share as shall not exceed the value of the bequest to him in the will.

Acts 1955, 54th Leg., p. 88, ch. 55, eff. Jan. 1, 1956.

§ 62. Corroboration of Testimony of Interested Witness

In the situation covered by the preceding Section, the bequest to the subscribing witness shall not be void if his testimony proving the will is corroborated by one or more disinterested and credible persons who testify that the testimony of the subscribing witness is true and correct, and such subscribing witness shall not be regarded as an incompetent or non-credible witness under Section 59 of this Code.

Acts 1955, 54th Leg., p. 88, ch. 55, eff. Jan. 1, 1956.

§ 63. Revocation of Wills

No will in writing, and no clause thereof or devise therein, shall be revoked, except by a subsequent will, codicil, or declaration in writing, executed with like formalities, or by the testator destroying or canceling the same, or causing it to be done in his presence.

Acts 1955, 54th Leg., p. 88, ch. 55, eff. Jan. 1, 1956.

§ 64. Capacity to Make a Nuncupative Will

Any person who is competent to make a last will and testament may dispose of his personal property by a nuncupative will made under the conditions and limitations prescribed in this Code.

Acts 1955, 54th Leg., p. 88, ch. 55, eff. Jan. 1, 1956.

§ 65. Requisites of a Nuncupative Will

No nuncupative will shall be established unless it be made in the time of the last sickness of the deceased, at his home or where he has resided for ten days or more next preceding the date of such will, except when the deceased is taken sick away from home and dies before he returns to such home; nor when the value exceeds Thirty Dollars, unless it be proved by three credible witnesses that the testator called on a person to take notice or bear testimony that such is his will, or words of like import.

Acts 1955, 54th Leg., p. 88, ch. 55, eff. Jan. 1, 1956.

§ 66. Repealed by Acts 1979, 66th Leg., p. 1746, ch. 713, § 11, eff. Aug. 27, 1979

§ 67. Pretermitted Child

(a) Whenever a pretermitted child is not mentioned in the testator's will, provided for in the testator's will, or otherwise provided for by the testator, the pretermitted child shall succeed to a portion of the testator's estate as provided by Subsection (a)(1) or (a)(2) of this section.

(1) If the testator has one or more children living when he executes his last will, and:

(A) No provision is made therein for any such child, a pretermitted child succeeds to the portion of the testator's separate and community estate to which the pretermitted child would have been entitled pursuant to Section 38(a) of this code had the testator died intestate without a surviving spouse owning only that portion of his estate not devised or bequeathed to the parent of the pretermitted child.

(B) Provision is made therein for one or more of such children, a pretermitted child is entitled to share in the testator's estate as follows:

(i) The portion of the testator's estate to which the pretermitted child is entitled is limited to the disposition made to children under the will.

(ii) The pretermitted child shall receive such share of the testator's estate, as limited in Subparagraph (i), as he would have received had the testator included all pretermitted children with the children upon whom benefits were conferred under the will, and given an equal share of such benefits to each such child.

(iii) To the extent that it is feasible, the interest of the pretermitted child in the testator's estate shall be of the same character, whether an equitable or legal life estate or in fee, as the interest that the testator conferred upon his children under the will.

(2) If the testator has no child living when he executes his last will, the pretermitted child succeeds to the portion of the testator's separate and community estate to which the pretermitted child would have been entitled pursuant to Section 38(a) of this code had the testator died intestate without a surviving spouse owning only that portion of his estate not devised or bequeathed to the parent of the pretermitted child.

(b) The pretermitted child may recover the share of the testator's estate to which he is entitled either from the other children under Subsection (a)(1)(B) or the testamentary beneficiaries under Subsections (a)(1)(A) and (a)(2) other than the parent of the pretermitted child, ratably, out of the portions of such estate passing to such persons under the will. In abating the interests of such beneficiaries, the character of the testamentary plan adopted by the testator shall be preserved to the maximum extent possible.

(c) A "pretermitted child," as used in this section, means a child of a testator who, during the lifetime of the testator, or after his death, is born or adopted after the execution of the will of the testator.

(d) For the purposes of this section, a child is provided for or a provision is made for a child if a disposition of property to or for the benefit of the pretermitted child, whether vested or contingent, is made:

(1) in the testator's will, including a devise or bequest to a trustee as authorized by Section 58(a) of this code; or

(2) outside the testator's will and is intended to take effect at the testator's death.

Acts 1955, 54th Leg., p. 88, ch. 55, eff. Jan. 1, 1956. Amended by Acts 1989, 71st Leg., ch. 1035, § 5, eff. Sept. 1, 1989; Acts 1991, 72nd Leg., ch. 895, § 8, eff. Sept. 1, 1991; Acts 1993, 73rd Leg., ch. 846, § 8, eff. Sept. 1, 1993.

Section 18(a) of the 1989 amendatory act provides:

"The change in the law made by Section 5 of this Act applies only to the estates of persons who die on or after the effective date of this Act. An estate of a person who dies before the effective date of this Act is covered by the law as it existed when the person died, and the former law is continued in effect for that purpose."

Section 20(b) of the 1991 amendatory act provides:

"The change in the law made by Section 8 of this Act applies as to all persons who are living on or after the effective date of this Act, without regard to whether any relevant order, judgment, or decree was entered before or after the effective date of this Act."

For application provisions of the 1993 amendatory act, see note under § 44.

§ 68. Prior Death of Legatee

(a) If a devisee who is a descendant of the testator or a descendant of a testator's parent is deceased at the time of the execution of the will, fails to survive the testator, or is treated as if the devisee predeceased the testator by Section 47 of this code or otherwise, the descendants of the devisee who survived the testator by 120 hours take the devised property in place of the devisee. The property shall be divided into as many shares as there are surviving descendants in the nearest degree of kinship to the devisee and deceased persons in the same degree whose descendants survived the testator. Each surviving descendant in the nearest degree receives one share, and the share of each deceased person in the same degree is divided among his descendants by representation. For purposes of this section, a person who would have been a devisee under a class gift if the person had survived the testator is treated as a devisee unless the person died before the date the will was executed.

(b) Except as provided by Subsection (a) of this section, if a devise or bequest, other than a residuary devise or bequest, fails for any reason, the devise or bequest becomes a part of the residuary estate.

(c) Except as provided by Subsection (a) of this section, if the residuary estate is devised to two or more persons and the share of one of the residuary devisees fails for any reason, the residuary devisee's share passes to the other residuary devisees, in proportion to the residuary devisee's interest in the residuary estate.

(d) Except as provided by Subsection (a) of this section, if all residuary devisees are dead at the time of the execution of the will, fail to survive the testator, or are treated as if they predeceased the testator, the residuary estate passes as if the testator had died intestate.

(e) This section applies unless the testator's last will and testament provides otherwise. For example, a devise or bequest in the testator's will such as "to my surviving children" or "to such of my children as shall survive me" prevents the application of Subsection (a) of this section.

Acts 1955, 54th Leg., p. 88, ch. 55, eff. Jan. 1, 1956. Amended by Acts 1991, 72nd Leg., ch. 895, § 9, eff. Sept. 1, 1991; Acts 1993, 73rd Leg., ch. 846, § 9, eff. Sept. 1, 1993.

For applicability provisions of the 1991 amendatory act, see note following § 3.

For applicability provisions of the 1993 amendatory act, see note under § 44.

§ 69. Voidness Arising From Divorce

(a) If, after making a will, the testator is divorced or the testator's marriage is annulled, all provisions in the will in favor of the testator's former spouse, or appointing such spouse to any fiduciary capacity under the will or with respect to the estate or person of the testator's children, must be read as if the former spouse failed to survive the testator, and shall be null and void and of no effect unless the will expressly provides otherwise.

(b) A person who is divorced from the decedent or whose marriage to the decedent has been annulled is not a surviving spouse unless, by virtue of a subsequent marriage, the person is married to the decedent at the time of death.

Acts 1955, 54th Leg., p. 88, ch. 55, eff. Jan. 1, 1956. Amended by Acts 1979, 66th Leg., p. 1746, ch. 713, § 12, eff. Aug. 27, 1979; Acts 1995, 74th Leg., ch. 642, § 2, eff. Sept. 1, 1995; Acts 1997, 75th Leg., ch. 1302, § 5, eff. Sept. 1, 1997.

For application provisions of the 1995 amendatory act, see notes following V.A.T.S. Probate Code, § 58.

§ 69A. Changing Wills

(a) A court may not prohibit a person from executing a new will or a codicil to an existing will.

(b) Notwithstanding Section 3(g) of this code, in this section, "court" means a constitutional county court, district court, or statutory county court, including a statutory probate court.

Added by Acts 1993, 73rd Leg., ch. 120, § 1, eff. Sept. 1, 1993.

§ 70. Provision in Will for Management of Separate Property

The husband or wife may, by last will and testament, give to the survivor of the marriage the power to keep testator's separate property together until each of the several distributees shall become of lawful age, and to manage and control the same under the provisions of law relating to community property, and subject to such other restrictions as are imposed by such will; provided, that any child or distributee entitled to any part of said property shall, at any time upon becoming of age, be entitled to receive his distributive portion of said estate.

Acts 1955, 54th Leg., p. 88, ch. 55, eff. Jan. 1, 1956.

§ 70A. Increase in Securities; Accessions

(a) Unless the will clearly provides otherwise, a devise of securities that are owned by the testator on the date of execution of the will includes the following additional securities subsequently acquired by the testator as a result of the testator's ownership of the devised securities:

(1) securities of the same organization acquired because of action initiated by the organization or any successor, related, or acquiring organization, including stock splits, stock dividends, and new issues of stock acquired in a reorganization, redemption, or exchange, other than securities acquired through the exercise of purchase options or through a plan of reinvestment; and

(2) securities of another organization acquired as a result of a merger, consolidation, reorganization, or other distribution by the organization or any successor, related, or acquiring organization, including stock

splits, stock dividends, and new issues of stock acquired in a reorganization, redemption, or exchange, other than securities acquired through the exercise of purchase options or through a plan of reinvestment.

(b) Unless the will clearly provides otherwise, a devise of securities does not include a cash distribution relating to the securities and accruing before death, whether or not the distribution is paid before death.

(c) In this section:

(1) "Securities" has the meaning assigned by Section 4, The Securities Act (Article 581–4, Vernon's Texas Civil Statutes), and its subsequent amendments.

(2) "Stock" means securities.

Added by Acts 1993, 73rd Leg., ch. 846, § 10, eff. Sept. 1, 1993.

For applicability provisions of the 1993 Act, see note under § 44.

§ 71. Deposit of Will With Court During Testator's Lifetime

(a) Deposit of Will. A will may be deposited by the person making it, or by another person for him, with the county clerk of the county of the testator's residence. Before accepting any will for deposit, the clerk may require such proof as shall be satisfactory to him concerning the testator's identity and residence. The clerk, on being paid a fee of Three Dollars therefor, shall receive and keep the will, and shall give a certificate of deposit for it.[1] All wills so filed shall be numbered by the clerk in consecutive order, and all certificates of deposit shall bear like numbers respectively.

(b) How Will Shall Be Enclosed. Every will intended to be deposited with a county clerk shall be enclosed in a sealed wrapper, which shall have indorsed thereon "Will of," followed by the name, address and signature of the testator. The wrapper must also be indorsed with the name and current address of each person who shall be notified of the deposit of the will after the death of the testator.

(c) Index To Be Kept of All Wills Deposited. Each county clerk shall keep an index of all wills so deposited with him.

(d) To Whom Will Shall Be Delivered. During the lifetime of the testator, a will so deposited shall be delivered only to the testator, or to another person authorized by him by a sworn written order. Upon delivery of the will to the testator or to a person so authorized by him, the certificate of deposit issued for the will shall be surrendered by the person to whom delivery of the will is made; provided, however, that in lieu of the surrender of such certificate, the clerk may, in his discretion, accept and file an affidavit by the testator to the effect that the certificate of deposit has been lost, stolen, or destroyed.

(e) Proceedings Upon Death of Testator. If there shall be submitted to the clerk an affidavit to the effect that the testator of any will deposited with the clerk has died, or if the clerk shall receive any other notice or proof of the death of such testator which shall suffice to convince him that the testator is deceased, the clerk shall notify by registered mail with return receipt requested the person or persons named on the indorsement of the wrapper of the will that the will is on deposit in his office, and, upon request, he shall deliver the will to such person or persons, taking a receipt therefor. If the notice by registered mail is returned undelivered, or if a clerk has accepted a will which does not specify on the wrapper the person or persons to whom it shall be delivered, the clerk shall open the wrapper and inspect the will. If an executor is named in the will, he shall be notified by registered mail, with return receipt requested, that the will is on deposit, and, upon request, the clerk shall deliver the will to the person so named as executor. If no executor is named in the will, or if the person so named is deceased, or fails to take the will within thirty days after the clerk's notice to him is mailed, or if notice to the person so named is returned undelivered, the clerk shall give notice by registered mail, with return receipt requested, to the devisees and legatees named in the will that the will is on deposit, and, upon request, the clerk shall deliver the will to any or all of such devisees and legatees.

(f) Depositing Has No Legal Significance. These provisions for the depositing of a will during the lifetime of a testator are solely for the purpose of providing a safe and convenient repository for such a will, and no will which has been so deposited shall be treated for purposes of probate any differently than any will which has not been so deposited. In particular, and without limiting the generality of the foregoing, a will which is not deposited shall be admitted to probate upon proof that it is the last will and testament of the testator, notwithstanding the fact that the same testator has on deposit with the court a prior will which has been deposited in accordance with the provisions of this Code.

(g) Depositing Does Not Constitute Notice. The fact that a will has been deposited as provided herein shall not constitute notice of any character, constructive or otherwise, to any person as to the existence of such will or as to the contents thereof.

Acts 1955, 54th Leg., p. 88, ch. 55, eff. Jan. 1, 1956.

[1] For provision requiring fee to be $5, see Civil Statutes, art. 3930(b), § 1, subsec. F.

CHAPTER V. PROBATE AND GRANT OF ADMINISTRATION

PART 1. ESTATES OF DECEDENTS

§ 72. Proceedings Before Death; Administration in Absence of Direct Evidence of Death; Distribution; Limitation of Liability; Restoration of Estate; Validation of Proceedings

(a) The probate of a will or administration of an estate of a living person shall be void; provided, however, that the court shall have jurisdiction to determine the fact, time and place of death, and where application is made for the grant of letters testamentary or of administration upon the estate of a person believed to be dead and there is no direct evidence that such person is dead but the death of such person shall be proved by circumstantial evidence to the satisfaction of the court, such letters shall be granted. Distribution of the estate to the persons entitled thereto shall not be made by the personal representative until after the expiration of three (3) years from the date such letters are granted. If in a subsequent action such person shall be proved by direct evidence to have been living at any time subsequent to the date of grant of such letters, neither the personal representative nor anyone who shall deliver said estate or any part thereof to another under orders of the court shall be liable therefor; and provided further, that such person shall be entitled to restoration of said estate or the residue thereof with the rents and profits therefrom, except real or personal property sold by the personal representative or any distributee, his successors or assigns, to bona fide purchasers for value, in which case the right of such person to the restoration shall be limited to the proceeds of such sale or the residue thereof with the increase thereof. In no event shall the bonds of such personal representative be void provided, however, that the surety shall have no liability for any acts of the personal representative which were done in compliance with or approved by an order of the court. Probate proceedings upon estates of persons believed to be dead brought prior to the effective date of this Act and all such probate proceedings then pending, except such probate proceedings contested in any litigation pending on the effective date of this Act, are hereby validated insofar as the court's finding of death of such person is concerned.

(b) In any case in which the fact of death must be proved by circumstantial evidence, the court, at the request of any interested person, may direct that citation be issued to the person supposed to be dead, and served upon him by publication and by posting, and by such additional means as the court may by its order direct. After letters testamentary or of administration have been issued, the court may also direct the personal representative to make a search for the person supposed to be dead by notifying law enforcement agencies and public welfare agencies in appropriate locations that such person has disappeared, and may further direct that the applicant engage the services of an investigative agency to make a search for such person. The expenses of search and notices shall be taxed as costs and shall be paid out of the property of the estate.

Acts 1955, 54th Leg., p. 88, ch. 55, eff. Jan. 1, 1956. Amended by Acts 1959, 56th Leg., p. 950, ch. 442, § 1, eff. May 30, 1959; Acts 1971, 62nd Leg., p. 975, ch. 173, § 7, eff. Jan. 1, 1972.

§ 73. Period for Probate

(a) No will shall be admitted to probate after the lapse of four years from the death of the testator unless it be shown by proof that the party applying for such probate was not in default in failing to present the same for probate within the four years aforesaid; and in no case shall letters testamentary be issued where a will is admitted to probate after the lapse of four years from the death of the testator.

(b) If any person shall purchase real or personal property from the heirs of a decedent more than four years from the date of the death of the decedent, for value, in good faith, and without knowledge of the existence of a will, such purchaser shall be held to have good title to the interest which such heir or heirs would have had in the absence of a will, as against the claims of any devisees or legatees under any will which may thereafter be offered for probate.

Acts 1955, 54th Leg., p. 88, ch. 55, eff. Jan. 1, 1956. Amended by Acts 1971, 62nd Leg., p. 976, ch. 173, § 8, eff. Jan. 1, 1972.

§ 74. Time to File Application for Letters Testamentary or Administration

All applications for the grant of letters testamentary or of administration upon an estate must be filed within four years after the death of the testator or intestate; provided, that this section shall not apply in any case where administration is necessary in order to receive or recover funds or other property due to the estate of the decedent.

Acts 1955, 54th Leg., p. 88, ch. 55, eff. Jan. 1, 1956. Amended by Acts 1971, 62nd Leg., p. 976, ch. 173, § 8, eff. Jan. 1, 1972.

§ 75. Duty and Liability of Custodian of Will

Upon receiving notice of the death of a testator, the person having custody of the testator's will shall deliver it to the clerk of the court which has jurisdiction of the estate. On sworn written complaint that any person has the last will of any testator, or any papers belonging to the estate of a testator or intestate, the county judge shall cause said person to be cited by personal service to appear before him and show cause why he should not deliver such will to the court for probate, or why he should not deliver such papers to the executor or administrator. Upon the return of such citation served, unless delivery is made or good cause shown, if satisfied that such person had such will or papers at the time of filing the complaint, such judge may cause him to be arrested and imprisoned until he shall so deliver them. Any person refusing to deliver such will or papers shall also be liable to any person aggrieved for all damages sustained as a result of such refusal, which damages may be recovered in any court of competent jurisdiction.

Acts 1955, 54th Leg., p. 88, ch. 55, eff. Jan. 1, 1956.

§ 76. Persons Who May Make Application

An executor named in a will or any interested person may make application to the court of a proper county:

(a) For an order admitting a will to probate, whether the same is written or unwritten, in his possession or not, is lost, is destroyed, or is out of the State.

(b) For the appointment of the executor named in the will.

(c) For the appointment of an administrator, if no executor is designated in the will, or if the person so named is disqualified, or refuses to serve, or is dead, or resigns, or if there is no will. An application for probate may be combined with an application for the appointment of an executor or administrator; and a person interested in either the probate of the will or the appointment of a personal representative may apply for both.

Acts 1955, 54th Leg., p. 88, ch. 55, eff. Jan. 1, 1956.

§ 77. Order of Persons Qualified to Serve

Letters testamentary or of administration shall be granted to persons who are qualified to act, in the following order:

(a) To the person named as executor in the will of the deceased.

(b) To the surviving husband or wife.

(c) To the principal devisee or legatee of the testator.

(d) To any devisee or legatee of the testator.

(e) To the next of kin of the deceased, the nearest in order of descent first, and so on, and next of kin includes a person and his descendants who legally adopted the deceased or who have been legally adopted by the deceased.

(f) To a creditor of the deceased.

(g) To any person of good character residing in the county who applies therefor.

(h) To any other person not disqualified under the following Section. When applicants are equally entitled, letters shall be granted to the applicant who, in the judgment of the court, is most likely to administer the estate advantageously, or they may be granted to any two or more of such applicants.

Acts 1955, 54th Leg., p. 88, ch. 55, eff. Jan. 1, 1956. Amended by Acts 1979, 66th Leg., p. 1763, ch. 713, § 34, eff. Aug. 27, 1979.

§ 78. Persons Disqualified to Serve as Executor or Administrator

No person is qualified to serve as an executor or administrator who is:

(a) An incapacitated person;

(b) A convicted felon, under the laws either of the United States or of any state or territory of the United States, or of the District of Columbia, unless such person has been duly pardoned, or his civil rights restored, in accordance with law;

(c) A non-resident (natural person or corporation) of this State who has not appointed a resident agent to accept service of process in all actions or proceedings with respect to the estate, and caused such appointment to be filed with the court;

(d) A corporation not authorized to act as a fiduciary in this State; or

(e) A person whom the court finds unsuitable.

Acts 1955, 54th Leg., p. 88, ch. 55, eff. Jan. 1, 1956. Amended by Acts 1957, 55th Leg., p. 53, ch. 31, § 2a, eff. Aug. 22, 1957; Acts 1969, 61st Leg., p. 1922, ch. 641, § 7, eff. June 12, 1969; Acts 1995, 74th Leg., ch. 1039, § 7, eff. Sept. 1, 1995.

§ 79. Waiver of Right to Serve

The surviving husband or wife, or, if there be none, the heirs or any one of the heirs of the deceased to the exclusion of any person not equally entitled, may, in open court, or by power of attorney duly authenticated and filed with the county clerk of the county where the application is filed, renounce his right to letters testamentary or of administration in favor of another qualified person, and thereupon the court may grant letters to such person.

Acts 1955, 54th Leg., p. 88, ch. 55, eff. Jan. 1, 1956.

§ 80. Prevention of Administration

(a) Method of Prevention. When application is made for letters of administration upon an estate by a creditor, and other interested persons do not desire an administration thereupon, they can defeat such application:

(1) By the payment of the claim of such creditor; or

(2) By proof to the satisfaction of the court that such claim is fictitious, fraudulent, illegal, or barred by limitation; or

(3) By executing a bond payable to, and to be approved by, the judge in double the amount of such creditor's debt, conditioned that the obligors will pay the debt of such applicant upon the establishment thereof by suit in any court in the county having jurisdiction of the amount.

(b) Filing of Bond. The bond provided for, when given and approved, shall be filed with the county clerk, and any creditor for whose protection it was executed may sue thereon in his own name for the recovery of his debt.

(c) **Bond Secured by Lien.** A lien shall exist on all of the estate in the hands of the distributees of such estate, and those claiming under them with notice of such lien, to secure the ultimate payment of the bond provided for herein.

Acts 1955, 54th Leg., p. 88, ch. 55, eff. Jan. 1, 1956.

§ 81. Contents of Application for Letters Testamentary

(a) **For Probate of a Written Will.** A written will shall, if within the control of the applicant, be filed with the application for its probate, and shall remain in the custody of the county clerk unless removed therefrom by order of a proper court. An application for probate of a written will shall state:

(1) The name and domicile of each applicant.

(2) The name, age if known, and domicile of the decedent, and the fact, time, and place of death.

(3) Facts showing that the court has venue.

(4) That the decedent owned real or personal property, or both, describing the same generally, and stating its probable value.

(5) The date of the will, the name and residence of the executor named therein, if any, and if none be named, then the name and residence of the person to whom it is desired that letters be issued, and also the names and residences of the subscribing witnesses, if any.

(6) Whether a child or children born or adopted after the making of such will survived the decedent, and the name of each such survivor, if any.

(7) That such executor or applicant, or other person to whom it is desired that letters be issued, is not disqualified by law from accepting letters.

(8) Whether the decedent was ever divorced, and if so, when and from whom.

(9) Whether the state, a governmental agency of the state, or a charitable organization is named by the will as a devisee.

The foregoing matters shall be stated and averred in the application to the extent that they are known to the applicant, or can with reasonable diligence be ascertained by him, and if any of such matters is not stated or averred in the application, the application shall set forth the reason why such matter is not so stated and averred.

(b) **For Probate of Written Will Not Produced.** When a written will cannot be produced in court, in addition to the requirements of Subsection (a) hereof, the application shall state:

(1) The reason why such will cannot be produced.

(2) The contents of such will, as far as known.

(3) The date of such will and the executor appointed therein, if any, as far as known.

(4) The name, age, marital status, and address, if known, and the relationship to the decedent, if any, of each devisee, and of each person who would inherit as an heir in the absence of a valid will, and, in cases of partial intestacy, of each heir.

(c) **Nuncupative Wills.** An application for probate of a nuncupative will shall contain all applicable statements required with respect to written wills in the foregoing subsections and also:

(1) The substance of testamentary words spoken.

(2) The names and residences of the witnesses thereto.

Acts 1955, 54th Leg., p. 88, ch. 55, eff. Jan. 1, 1956. Amended by Acts 1971, 62nd Leg., p. 976, ch. 173, § 9, eff. Jan. 1, 1972; Acts 1987, 70th Leg., ch. 463, § 1, eff. Sept. 1, 1987; Acts 1989, 71st Leg., ch. 1035, § 6, eff. Sept. 1, 1989; Acts 1997, 75th Leg., ch. 1302, § 6, eff. Sept. 1, 1997.

Section 4 of the 1987 amendatory act provides:

"This Act takes effect September 1, 1987, and applies to applications for the probate of written wills, letters of administration, and appointment of permanent guardians filed on or after that date. An application for the probate of written wills, letters of administration, or appointment of a permanent guardian filed before the effective date of this Act is covered by the law as it existed on the date that the application was filed, and that law is continued in effect for that purpose."

Section 18(b) of the 1989 amendatory act provides:

"The change in the law made by Sections 6 and 7 of this Act applies only to an application for probate of a written will, a written will not produced, or a nuncupative will filed on or after the effective date of this Act. An application filed before the effective date of this Act is covered by the law in effect when the application was filed, and the former law is continued in effect for that purpose."

Section 16 of Acts 1997, 75th Leg., ch. 1302 provides:

"This Act takes effect September 1, 1997, and applies only to the estate of a person who dies on or after that date. An estate of a person who dies before the effective date of this Act is governed by the law in effect on the date of the person's death, and the former law is continued in effect for that purpose."

§ 82. Contents of Application for Letters of Administration

An application for letters of administration when no will, written or oral, is alleged to exist shall state:

(a) The name and domicile of the applicant, relationship to the decedent, if any, and that the applicant is not disqualified by law to act as administrator;

(b) The name and intestacy of the decedent, and the fact, time and place of death;

(c) Facts necessary to show venue in the court to which the application is made;

(d) Whether the decedent owned real or personal property, with a statement of its probable value;

(e) The name, age, marital status and address, if known, and the relationship, if any, of each heir to the decedent;

(f) If known by the applicant at the time of the filing of the application, whether children were born to or adopted by the decedent, with the name and the date and place of birth of each;

(g) If known by the applicant at the time of the filing of the application, whether the decedent was ever divorced, and if so, when and from whom; and

(h) That a necessity exists for administration of the estate, alleging the facts which show such necessity.

Acts 1955, 54th Leg., p. 88, ch. 55, eff. Jan. 1, 1956. Amended by Acts 1979, 66th Leg., p. 1746, ch. 713, § 13, eff. Aug. 27, 1979; Acts 1987, 70th Leg., ch. 463, § 2, eff. Sept. 1, 1987; Acts 1997, 75th Leg., ch. 1302, § 7, eff. Sept. 1, 1997.

Section 4 of the 1987 amendatory act provides:

"This Act takes effect September 1, 1987, and applies to applications for the probate of written wills, letters of administration, and appointment of permanent guardians filed on or after that date. An application for the probate of written wills, letters of administration, or appointment of a permanent guardian filed before the effective date of this Act is covered by the law as it existed on the date that the application was filed, and that law is continued in effect for that purpose."

§ 83. Procedure Pertaining to a Second Application

(a) Where Original Application Has Not Been Heard. If, after an application for the probate of a will or for the appointment of a general personal representative has been filed, and before such application has been heard, an application for the probate of a will of the decedent, not theretofore presented for probate, is filed, the court shall hear both applications together and determine what instrument, if any, should be admitted to probate, or whether the decedent died intestate.

(b) Where First Will Has Been Admitted to Probate. If, after a will has been admitted to probate, an application for the probate of a will of the decedent, not theretofore presented for probate, is filed, the court shall determine whether the former probate should be set aside, and whether such other will should be admitted to probate, or whether the decedent died intestate.

(c) Where Letters of Administration Have Been Granted. Whenever letters of administration shall have been granted upon an estate, and it shall afterwards be discovered that the deceased left a lawful will, such will may be proved in the manner provided for the proof of wills; and, if an executor is named in such will, and he is not disqualified, he shall be allowed to qualify and accept as such executor, and the letters previously granted shall be revoked; but, if no such executor be named in the will, or if the executor named be disqualified, be dead, or shall renounce the executorship, or shall neglect or otherwise fail or be unable to accept and qualify within twenty days after the date of the probate of the will, or shall neglect for a period of thirty days after the discovery of such will to present it for probate, then administration with the will annexed of the estate of such testator shall be granted as in other cases. All acts done by the first administrator, prior to the qualification of the executor or of the administrator with the will annexed, shall be as valid as if no such will had been discovered.

Acts 1955, 54th Leg., p. 88, ch. 55, eff. Jan. 1, 1956.

§ 84. Proof of Written Will Produced in Court

(a) Self-Proved Will. If a will is self-proved as provided in this Code, no further proof of its execution with the formalities and solemnities and under the circumstances required to make it a valid will shall be necessary.

(b) Attested Written Will. If not self-proved as provided in this Code, an attested written will produced in court may be proved:

(1) By the sworn testimony or affidavit of one or more of the subscribing witnesses thereto, taken in open court.

(2) If all the witnesses are non-residents of the county, or those who are residents are unable to attend court, by the sworn testimony of any one or more of them by deposition, either written or oral, taken in the same manner and under the same rules as depositions taken in other civil actions; or, if no opposition in writing to such will is filed on or before the date set for hearing thereon, then by the sworn testimony or affidavit of two witnesses taken in open court, or by deposition in the manner provided herein, to the signature or the handwriting evidenced thereby of one or more of the attesting witnesses, or of the testator, if he signed the will; or, if it be shown under oath to the satisfaction of the court that, diligent search having been made, only one witness can be found who can make the required proof, then by the sworn testimony or affidavit of such one taken in open court, or by deposition in the manner provided herein, to such signatures or handwriting.

(3) If none of the witnesses is living, or if all of such witnesses are members of the armed forces of the United States of America or of any auxiliary thereof, or of the armed forces reserve of the United States of America or of any auxiliary thereof, or of the Maritime Service, and are beyond the jurisdiction of the court, by two witnesses to the handwriting of one or both of the subscribing witnesses thereto, or of the testator, if signed by him, and such proof may be either by sworn testimony or affidavit taken in open court, or by deposition, either written or oral, taken in the same manner and under the same rules as depositions taken in other civil actions; or, if it be shown under oath to the satisfaction of the court that, diligent search having been made, only one witness can be found who can make the required proof, then by the sworn testimony or affidavit of such one taken in open court, or by deposition in the manner provided herein, to such signatures or handwriting.

(b) Holographic Will. If not self-proved as provided in this Code, a will wholly in the handwriting of the testator may be proved by two witnesses to his handwriting, which evidence may be by sworn testimony or affidavit taken in open court, or, if such witnesses are non-residents of the county or are residents who are unable to attend court, by deposition, either written or oral, taken in the same manner and under the same rules as depositions taken in other civil actions.

(c) Depositions if No Contest Filed. If no contest has been filed, depositions for the purpose of establishing a will may be taken in the same manner as provided in this Code for the taking of depositions where there is no opposing party or attorney of record upon whom notice and copies of interrogatories may be served; and, in such event, this Subsection, rather than the preceding portions of this Section which provide for the taking of depositions under the same rules as depositions in other civil actions, shall be applicable.

Acts 1955, 54th Leg., p. 88, ch. 55, eff. Jan. 1, 1956.

§ 85. Proof of Written Will Not Produced in Court

A written will which cannot be produced in court shall be proved in the same manner as provided in the preceding Section for an attested written will or an holographic will, as the case may be, and the same amount and character of testimony shall be required to prove such will as is required to prove a written will produced in court; but, in addition thereto, the cause of its non-production must be proved, and such cause must be sufficient to satisfy the court that it cannot by any reasonable diligence be produced, and the contents of such will must be substantially proved by the testimony of a credible witness who has read it or heard it read.

Acts 1955, 54th Leg., p. 88, ch. 55, eff. Jan. 1, 1956.

§ 86. Proof of Nuncupative Will

(a) Notice and Proof of Nuncupative Will. No nuncupative will shall be proved within fourteen days after the death of the testator, or until those who would have been entitled by inheritance, had there been no will, have been summoned to contest the same, if they desire to do so.

(b) Testimony Pertaining to Nuncupative Wills. After six months have elapsed from the time of speaking the alleged testamentary words, no testimony shall be received to prove a nuncupative will, unless the testimony or the substance thereof shall have been committed to writing within six days after making the will.

(c) When Value of Estate Exceeds Thirty Dollars. When the value of the estate exceeds Thirty Dollars, a nuncupative will must be proved by three credible witnesses that the testator called on a person to take notice or bear testimony that such is his will, or words of like import.

Acts 1955, 54th Leg., p. 88, ch. 55, eff. Jan. 1, 1956.

§ 87. Testimony to Be Committed to Writing

All testimony taken in open court upon the hearing of an application to probate a will shall be committed to writing at the time it is taken, and subscribed, and sworn to in open court by the witness or witnesses, and filed by the clerk, provided, however, that in any contested case, the court may, upon agreement of the parties, and in the event of no agreement on its own motion, dismiss this requirement.

Acts 1955, 54th Leg., p. 88, ch. 55, eff. Jan. 1, 1956. Amended by Acts 1971, 62nd Leg., p. 976, ch. 173, § 9, eff. Jan. 1, 1972.

§ 88. Proof Required for Probate and Issuance of Letters Testamentary or of Administration

(a) General Proof. Whenever an applicant seeks to probate a will or to obtain issuance of letters testamentary or of administration, he must first prove to the satisfaction of the court:

(1) That the person is dead, and that four years have not elapsed since his decease and prior to the application; and

(2) That the court has jurisdiction and venue over the estate; and

(3) That citation has been served and returned in the manner and for the length of time required by this Code; and

(4) That the person for whom letters testamentary or of administration are sought is entitled thereto by law and is not disqualified.

(b) Additional Proof for Probate of Will. To obtain probate of a will, the applicant must also prove to the satisfaction of the court:

(1) If the will is not self-proved as provided by this Code, that the testator, at the time of executing the will, was at least eighteen years of age, or was or had been lawfully married, or was a member of the armed forces of the United States or of the auxiliaries thereof, or of the Maritime Service of the United States, and was of sound mind; and

(2) If the will is not self-proved as provided by this Code, that the testator executed the will with the formalities and solemnities and under the circumstances required by law to make it a valid will; and

(3) That such will was not revoked by the testator.

(c) Additional Proof for Issuance of Letters Testamentary. If letters testamentary are to be granted, it must appear to the court that proof required for the probate of the will has been made, and, in addition, that the person to whom the letters are to be granted is named as executor in the will.

(d) Additional Proof for Issuance of Letters of Administration. If letters of administration are to be granted, the applicant must also prove to the satisfaction of the court that there exists a necessity for an administration upon such estate.

(e) Proof Required Where Prior Letters Have Been Granted. If letters testamentary or of administration have previously been granted upon the estate, the applicant need show only that the person for whom letters are sought is entitled thereto by law and is not disqualified.

Acts 1955, 54th Leg., p. 88, ch. 55, eff. Jan. 1, 1956. Amended by Acts 1969, 61st Leg., p. 1922, ch. 641, § 8, eff. June 12, 1969.

§ 89. Action of Court on Probated Will

Upon the completion of hearing of an application for the probate of a will, if the Court be satisfied that such will should be admitted to probate, an order to that effect shall be entered. Certified copies of such will and the order , or of the record thereof, and the record of testimony, may be recorded in other counties, and may be used in evidence, as the original might be, on the trial of the same matter in any other court, when taken there by appeal or otherwise.

Acts 1955, 54th Leg., p. 88, ch. 55, eff. Jan. 1, 1956. Amended by Acts 1961, 57th Leg., p. 1072, ch. 480, § 1, eff. Aug. 28, 1961; Acts 1983, 68th Leg., p. 1155, ch. 260, § 1, eff. Sept. 1, 1983; Acts 1993, 73rd Leg., ch. 846, § 11, eff. Sept. 1, 1993.

Section 35(b) of the 1993 Act provides:

"The changes in law made by Sections 4, 5, 6, 7, 8, 9, 10, 11, 12, and 24 of this Act apply only to the estates of persons who die on or after the effective date of this Act. The estate of a person who dies before the effective date of this Act is covered by the law in effect when the person died, and the former law is continued in effect for that purpose."

§ 89A. Contents of Application for Probate of Will as Muniment of Title

(a) A written will shall, if within the control of the applicant, be filed with the application for probate as a muniment of title, and shall remain in the custody of the county clerk unless removed from the custody of the clerk by order of a proper court. An application for probate of a will as a muniment of title shall state:

(1) The name and domicile of each applicant.

(2) The name, age if known, and domicile of the decedent, and the fact, time, and place of death.

(3) Facts showing that the court has venue.

(4) That the decedent owned real or personal property, or both, describing the property generally, and stating its probable value.

(5) The date of the will, the name and residence of the executor named in the will, if any, and the names and residences of the subscribing witnesses, if any.

(6) Whether a child or children born or adopted after the making of such will survived the decedent, and the name of each such survivor, if any.

(7) That there are no unpaid debts owing by the estate of the testator, excluding debts secured by liens on real estate.

(8) Whether the decedent was ever divorced, and if so, when and from whom.

(9) The social security number of the applicant and of the decedent.

(10) Whether the state, a governmental agency of the state, or a charitable organization is named by the will as a devisee.

The foregoing matters shall be stated and averred in the application to the extent that they are known to the applicant, or can with reasonable diligence be ascertained by the applicant, and if any of such matters is not stated or averred in the application, the application shall set forth the reason why such matter is not so stated and averred.

(b) When a written will cannot be produced in court, in addition to the requirements of Subsection (a) of this section, the application shall state:

(1) The reason why such will cannot be produced.

(2) The contents of such will, to the extent known.

(3) The date of such will and the executor appointed in the will, if any, to the extent known.

(4) The name, age, marital status, and address, if known, and the relationship to the decedent, if any, of each devisee, and of each person who would inherit as an heir in the absence of a valid will, and, in cases of partial intestacy, of each heir.

(c) An application for probate of a nuncupative will as muniment of title shall contain all applicable statements required with respect to written wills in the foregoing subsections and also:

(1) The substance of testamentary words spoken.

(2) The names and residences of the witnesses thereto.

Added by Acts 1997, 75th Leg., ch. 540, § 1, eff. Sept. 1, 1997.

Section 6 of Acts 1997, 75th Leg., ch. 540 provides:

"This Act takes effect September 1, 1997, and applies only to the estate of a decedent who dies on or after that date. The estate of a decedent who dies before the effective date of this Act is governed by the law in effect at the time of the decedent's death, and the former law is continued in effect for that purpose."

§ 89B. Proof Required for Probate of a Will as a Muniment of Title

(a) General Proof. Whenever an applicant seeks to probate a will as a muniment of title, the applicant must first prove to the satisfaction of the court:

(1) That the person is dead, and that four years have not elapsed since the person's death and prior to the application; and

(2) That the court has jurisdiction and venue over the estate; and

(3) That citation has been served and returned in the manner and for the length of time required by this Code; and

(4) That there are no unpaid debts owing by the estate of the testator, excluding debts secured by liens on real estate.

(b) To obtain probate of a will as a muniment of title, the applicant must also prove to the satisfaction of the court:

(1) If the will is not self-proved as provided by this Code, that the testator, at the time of executing the will, was at least 18 years of age, or was or had been lawfully married, or was a member of the armed forces of the United States or of the auxiliaries of the armed forces of the United States, or of the Maritime Service of the United States, and was of sound mind; and

(2) If the will is not self-proved as provided by this Code, that the testator executed the will with the formalities and solemnities and under the circumstances required by law to make it a valid will; and

(3) That such will was not revoked by the testator.

Added by Acts 1997, 75th Leg., ch. 540, § 1 eff. Sept. 1, 1997.

§ 89C. Probate of Wills as Muniments of Title

(a) In each instance where the court is satisfied that a will should be admitted to probate, and where the court is further satisfied that there are no unpaid debts owing by the estate of the testator, excluding debts secured by liens on real estate, or for other reason finds that there is no necessity for administration upon such estate, the court may admit such will to probate as a muniment of title.

(b) If a person who is entitled to property under the provisions of the will cannot be ascertained solely by reference to the will or if a question of construction of the will exists, on proper application and notice as provided by Chapter 37, Civil Practice and Remedies Code, the court may hear evidence and include in the order probating the will as a muniment of title a declaratory judgment construing the will or determining those persons who are entitled to receive property under the will and the persons' shares or interests in the estate. The judgment is conclusive in any suit between any person omitted from the judgment and a bona fide purchaser for value who has purchased real or personal property after entry of the judgment without actual notice of the claim of the omitted person to an interest in the estate. Any person who has delivered property of the decedent to a person declared to be entitled to the property under the judgment or has engaged in any other transaction with the person in good faith after entry of the judgment is not liable to any person for actions taken in reliance on the judgment.

(c) The order admitting a will to probate as a muniment of title shall constitute sufficient legal authority to all persons owing any money to the estate of the decedent, having custody of any property, or acting as registrar or transfer agent of any evidence of interest, indebtedness, property, or right belonging to the estate, and to persons purchasing from or otherwise dealing with the estate, for payment or transfer, without liability, to the persons described in such will as entitled to receive the particular asset without administration. The person or persons entitled to property under the provisions of such wills shall be entitled to deal with and treat the properties to which they are so entitled in the same manner as if the record of title thereof were vested in their names.

(d) Unless waived by the court, before the 181st day, or such later day as may be extended by the court, after the date a will is admitted to probate as a muniment of title, the applicant for probate of the will shall file with the clerk of the court a sworn affidavit stating specifically the terms of the will that have been fulfilled and the terms of the will that have been unfulfilled. Failure of the applicant for probate of the will to file such affidavit shall not otherwise affect title to property passing under the terms of the will.

Added by Acts 1993, 73rd Leg., ch. 846, § 12, eff. Sept. 1, 1993. Renumbered from V.A.T.S. Probate Code, § 89A by Acts 1997, 75th Leg., ch. 540, § 1, eff. Sept. 1, 1997.

For applicability provisions of the 1993 Act, see note under § 89.

For application provisions of Acts 1997, 75th Leg., ch. 540, see note following V.A.T.S. Probate Code, § 89A.

§ 90. Custody of Probated Wills

All original wills, together with the probate thereof, shall be deposited in the office of the county clerk of the county wherein the same shall have been probated, and shall there remain, except during such time as they may be removed for inspection to another place upon order by the court where probated. If the court shall order an original will to be removed to another place for inspection, the person removing such original will shall give a receipt therefor, and the clerk of the court shall make and retain a copy of such original will.

Acts 1955, 54th Leg., p. 88, ch. 55, eff. Jan. 1, 1956.

§ 91. When Will Not in Custody of Court, or Oral

If for any reason a written will is not in the custody of the court, or if the will is oral, the court shall find the contents thereof by written order, and certified copies of same as so established by the court may be recorded in other counties, and may be used in evidence, as in the case of certified copies of written wills in the custody of the court.

Acts 1955, 54th Leg., p. 88, ch. 55, eff. Jan. 1, 1956.

§ 92. Period for Probate Does Not Affect Settlement

Where letters testamentary or of administration shall have once been granted, any person interested in the administration of the estate may proceed, after any lapse of time, to compel settlement of the estate when it does not appear from the record that the administration thereof has been closed.

Acts 1955, 54th Leg., p. 88, ch. 55, eff. Jan. 1, 1956.

§ 93. Period for Contesting Probate

After a will has been admitted to probate, any interested person may institute suit in the proper court to contest the validity thereof, within two years after such will shall have been admitted to probate, and not afterward, except that any interested person may institute suit in the proper court to cancel a will for forgery or other fraud within two years after the discovery of such forgery or fraud, and not afterward. Provided, however, that persons non compos mentis and minors shall have two years after the removal of their respective disabilities within which to institute such contest.

Acts 1955, 54th Leg., p. 88, ch. 55, eff. Jan. 1, 1956.

§ 94. No Will Effectual Until Probated

Except as hereinafter provided with respect to foreign wills, no will shall be effectual for the purpose of proving title to, or the right to the possession of, any real or personal property disposed of by the will, until such will has been admitted to probate.

Acts 1955, 54th Leg., p. 88, ch. 55, eff. Jan. 1, 1956.

PART 2. PROCEDURE PERTAINING TO FOREIGN WILLS

§ 95. Probate of Foreign Will Accomplished by Filing and Recording

(a) Foreign Will May Be Probated. The written will of a testator who was not domiciled in Texas at the time of his death which would affect any real or personal property in this State, may be admitted to probate upon proof that it stands probated or established in any of the United States, its territories, the District of Columbia, or any foreign nation.

(b) Application and Citation.

(1) Will probated in domiciliary jurisdiction. If a foreign will has been admitted to probate or established in the jurisdiction in which the testator was domiciled at the time of his death, the application need state only that probate is requested on the basis of the authenticated copy of the foreign proceedings in which the will was probated or established. No citation or notice is required.

(2) **Will probated in non-domiciliary jurisdiction.** If a foreign will has been admitted to probate or established in any jurisdiction other than the domicile of the testator at the time of his death, the application for its probate shall contain all of the information required in an application for the probate of a domestic will, and shall also set out the name and address of each devisee and each person who will be entitled to a portion of the estate as an heir in the absence of a will. Citations shall be issued and served on each such devisee and heir by registered or certified mail.

(c) **Copy of Will and Proceedings To Be Filed.** A copy of the will and of the judgment, order, or decree by which it was admitted to probate or otherwise established, attested by and with the original signature of the clerk of the court or of such other official as has custody of such will or is in charge of probate records, with the seal of the court affixed, if there is a seal, together with a certificate containing the original signature of the judge or presiding magistrate of such court that the said attestation is in due form, shall be filed with the application. Original signatures shall not be required for recordation in the deed records pursuant to Sections 96 through 99 or Section 107 of this code.

(d) **Probate Accomplished by Recording.**

(1) **Will admitted in domiciliary jurisdiction.** If the will has been probated or established in the jurisdiction in which the testator was domiciled at the time of his death, it shall be the ministerial duty of the clerk to record such will and the evidence of its probate or establishment in the minutes of the court. No order of the court is necessary. When so filed and recorded, the will shall be deemed to be admitted to probate, and shall have the same force and effect for all purposes as if the original will had been probated by order of the court, subject to contest in the manner and to the extent hereinafter provided.

(2) **Will admitted in non-domiciliary jurisdiction.** If the will has been probated or established in another jurisdiction not the domicile of the testator, its probate in this State may be contested in the same manner as if the testator had been domiciled in this State at the time of his death. If no contest is filed, the clerk shall record such will and the evidence of its probate or establishment in the minutes of the court, and no order of the court shall be necessary. When so filed and recorded, it shall be deemed to be admitted to probate, and shall have the same force and effect for all purposes as if the original will had been probated by order of the court, subject to contest in the manner and to the extent hereafter provided.

(e) **Effect of Foreign Will on Local Property.** If a foreign will has been admitted to probate or established in the jurisdiction in which the testator was domiciled at the time of his death, such will, when probated as herein provided, shall be effectual to dispose of both real and personal property in this State irrespective of whether such will was executed with the formalities required by this Code.

(f) **Protection of Purchasers.** When a foreign will has been probated in this State in accordance with the procedure prescribed in this section for a will that has been admitted to probate in the domicile of the testator, and it is later proved in a proceeding brought for that purpose that the foreign jurisdiction in which the will was admitted to probate was not in fact the domicile of the testator, the probate in this State shall be set aside. If any person has purchased property from the personal representative or any legatee or devisee, in good faith and for value, or otherwise dealt with any of them in good faith, prior to the commencement of the proceeding, his title or rights shall not be affected by the fact that the probate in this State is subsequently set aside.

Acts 1955, 54th Leg., p. 88, ch. 55, eff. Jan. 1, 1956. Amended by Acts 1971, 62nd Leg., p. 976, ch. 173, § 9, eff. Jan. 1, 1972; Acts 1999, 76th Leg., ch. 755, § 1, eff. Sept. 1, 1999.

Section 3 of Acts 1999, 76th Leg., ch. 755 provides:

"The change in law made by this Act applies only to an application for probate of a foreign will filed on or after the effective date of this Act. An application for probate of a foreign will that is filed before the effective date of this Act is governed by the law in effect on the date the application was filed, and the former law is continued in effect for that purpose."

§ 96. Filing and Recording Foreign Will in Deed Records

When any will or testamentary instrument conveying or in any manner disposing of land in this State has been duly probated according to the laws of any of the United States, or territories thereof, or the District of Columbia, or of any country out of the limits of the United States, a copy thereof and of its probate which bears the attestation, seal and certificate required by the preceding Section, may be filed and recorded in the deed records in any county of this State in which said real estate is situated, in the same manner as deeds and conveyances are required to be recorded under the laws of this State, and without further proof or authentication; provided that the validity of such a will or testamentary instrument filed under this Section may be contested in the manner and to the extent hereinafter provided.

Acts 1955, 54th Leg., p. 88, ch. 55, eff. Jan. 1, 1956.

§ 97. Proof Required for Recording in Deed Records

A copy of such foreign will or testamentary instrument, and of its probate attested as provided above, together with the certificate that said attestation is in due form, shall be prima facie evidence that said will or testamentary instrument has been duly admitted to probate, according to the laws of the state, territory, district, or country wherein it has allegedly been admitted to probate, and shall be sufficient to authorize the same to be recorded in the deed records in the proper county or counties in this State.

Acts 1955, 54th Leg., p. 88, ch. 55, eff. Jan. 1, 1956. Amended by Acts 1969, 61st Leg., p. 1925, ch. 641, § 9, eff. June 12, 1969.

§ 98. Effect of Recording Copy of Will in Deed Records

Every such foreign will, or testamentary instrument, and the record of its probate, which shall be attested and proved, as hereinabove provided, and delivered to the county clerk of the proper county in this State to be recorded in the deed records, shall take effect and be valid and effectual as a deed of conveyance of all property in this State covered by said foreign will or testamentary instrument; and the record thereof shall have the same force and effect as the record of deeds or other conveyances of land from the time when such instrument is delivered to the clerk to be recorded, and from that time only.

Acts 1955, 54th Leg., p. 88, ch. 55, eff. Jan. 1, 1956. Amended by Acts 1969, 61st Leg., p. 1925, ch. 641, § 9, eff. June 12, 1969.

§ 99. Recording in Deed Records Serves as Notice of Title

The record of any such foreign will, or testamentary instrument, and of its probate, duly attested and proved and filed for recording in the deed records of the proper county, shall be notice to all persons of the existence of such will or testamentary instrument, and of the title or titles conferred thereby.

Acts 1955, 54th Leg., p. 88, ch. 55, eff. Jan. 1, 1956. Amended by Acts 1969, 61st Leg., p. 1925, ch. 641, § 9, eff. June 12, 1969.

§ 100. Contest of Foreign Wills

(a) Will Admitted in Domiciliary Jurisdiction. A foreign will that has been admitted to probate or established in the jurisdiction in which the testator was domiciled at the time of his death, and either admitted to probate in this State or filed in the deed records of any county of this State, may be contested by any interested person but only upon the following grounds:

(1) That the foreign proceedings were not authenticated in the manner required for ancillary probate or recording in the deed records.

(2) That the will has been finally rejected for probate in this State in another proceeding.

(3) That the probate of the will has been set aside in the jurisdiction in which the testator died domiciled.

(b) Will Probated in Non-Domiciliary Jurisdiction. A foreign will that has been admitted to probate or established in any jurisdiction other than that of the testator's domicile at the time of his death may be contested on any grounds that are the basis for the contest of a domestic will. If a will has been probated in this State in accordance with the procedure applicable for the probate of a will that has been admitted in the state of domicile, without the service of citation required for a will admitted in another jurisdiction that is not the domicile of the testator, and it is proved that the foreign jurisdiction in which the will was probated was not in fact the domicile of the testator, the probate in this State shall be set aside. If otherwise entitled, the will may be reprobated in accordance with the procedure prescribed for the probate of a will admitted in a non-domiciliary jurisdiction, or it may be admitted to original probate in this State in the same or a subsequent proceeding.

(c) Time and Method. A foreign will that has been admitted to ancillary probate in this State or filed in the deed records in this State may be contested by the same procedures, and within the same time limits, as wills admitted to probate in this State in original proceedings.

Acts 1955, 54th Leg., p. 88, ch. 55, eff. Jan. 1, 1956. Amended by Acts 1971, 62nd Leg., p. 976, ch. 173, § 9, eff. Jan. 1, 1972.

§ 101. Notice of Contest of Foreign Will

Within the time permitted for the contest of a foreign will in this State, verified notice may be filed and recorded in the minutes of the court in this State in which the will was probated, or the deed records of any county in this State in which such will was recorded, that proceedings have been instituted to contest the will in the foreign jurisdiction where it was probated or established. Upon such filing and recording, the force and effect of the probate or recording of the will shall cease until verified proof is filed and recorded that the foreign proceedings have been terminated in favor of the will, or that such proceedings were never actually instituted.

Acts 1955, 54th Leg., p. 88, ch. 55, eff. Jan. 1, 1956. Amended by Acts 1969, 61st Leg., p. 1925, ch. 641, § 9, eff. June 12, 1969.

§ 102. Effect of Rejection of Will in Domiciliary Proceedings

Final rejection of a will or other testamentary instrument from probate or establishment in the jurisdiction in which the testator was domiciled shall be conclusive in this State, except where the will or other testamentary instrument has been rejected solely for a cause which is not ground for rejection of a will of a testator who died domiciled in this State, in which case the will or testamentary instrument may nevertheless be admitted to probate or continue to be effective in this State.

Acts 1955, 54th Leg., p. 88, ch. 55, eff. Jan. 1, 1956. Amended by Acts 1971, 62nd Leg., p. 976, ch. 173, § 9, eff. Jan. 1, 1972.

§ 103. Original Probate of Foreign Will in This State

Original probate of the will of a testator who died domiciled outside this State which, upon probate, may operate upon any property in this State, and which is valid under the laws of this State, may be granted in the same manner as the probate of other wills is granted under this Code, if the will does not stand rejected from probate or establishment in the jurisdiction where the testator died domiciled, or if it stands rejected from probate or establishment in the jurisdiction where the testator died domiciled solely for a cause which is not ground for rejection of a will of a testator who died domiciled in this State. The court may delay passing on the application for probate of a foreign will pending the result of probate or establishment, or of a contest thereof, at the domicile of the testator.

Acts 1955, 54th Leg., p. 88, ch. 55, eff. Jan. 1, 1956.

§ 104. Proof of Foreign Will in Original Probate Proceeding

If a testator dies domiciled outside this State, a copy of his will, authenticated in the manner required by this Code, shall be sufficient proof of the contents of the will to admit it to probate in an original proceeding in this State if no objection is made thereto. This Section does not authorize the probate of any will which would not otherwise be admissible to probate, or, in case objection is made to the will, relieve the proponent from offering proof of the contents and legal sufficiency of the will as otherwise required, except that the original will need not be produced unless the court so orders.

Acts 1955, 54th Leg., p. 88, ch. 55, eff. Jan. 1, 1956. Amended by Acts 1969, 61st Leg., p. 1925, ch. 641, § 9, eff. June 12, 1969.

§ 105. Executor of Will Probated in Another Jurisdiction

When a foreign will is admitted to ancillary probate in accordance with Section 95 of this Code, the executor named in such will shall be entitled to receive, upon application, letters testamentary upon proof that he has qualified as such in the jurisdiction in which the will was admitted to probate, and that he is not disqualified to serve as executor in this State. After such proof is made, the court shall enter an order directing that ancillary letters testamentary be issued to him. If letters of administration have previously been granted by such court in this State to any other person, such letters shall be revoked upon the application of the executor after personal service of citation upon the person to whom such letters were granted.

Acts 1955, 54th Leg., p. 88, ch. 55, eff. Jan. 1, 1956. Amended by Acts 1969, 61st Leg., p. 1925, ch. 641, § 9, eff. June 12, 1969.

§ 105A. Appointment and Service of Foreign Banks and Trust Companies in Fiduciary Capacity

(a) A corporate fiduciary that does not have its main office or a branch office in this state, hereinafter called "foreign corporate fiduciaries", having the corporate power to so act, may be appointed and may serve in the State of Texas as trustee (whether of a personal or corporate trust), executor, administrator, guardian of the estate, or in any other fiduciary capacity, whether the appointment be by will, deed, agreement, declaration, indenture, court order or decree, or otherwise, when and to the extent that the home state of the corporate fiduciary grants authority to serve in like fiduciary capacity to a corporate fiduciary whose home state is this state.

(b) Before qualifying or serving in the State of Texas in any fiduciary capacity, as aforesaid, such a foreign corporate fiduciary shall file in the office of the Secretary of the State of the State of Texas (1) a copy of its charter, articles of incorporation or of association, and all amendments thereto, certified by its secretary under its corporate seal; (2) a duly executed instrument in writing, by its terms of indefinite duration and irrevocable, appointing the Secretary of State and his successors its agent for service of process upon whom all notices and processes issued by any court of this state may be served in any action or proceeding relating to any trust, estate, fund or other matter within this state with respect to which such foreign corporate fiduciary is acting in any fiduciary capacity, including the acts or defaults of such foreign corporate fiduciary with respect to any such trust, estate or fund; and (3) a written certificate of designation, which may be changed from time to time thereafter by the filing of a new certificate of designation, specifying the name and address of the officer, agent or other person to whom such notice or process shall be forwarded by the Secretary of State. Upon receipt of such notice or process, it shall be the duty of the Secretary of State forthwith to forward same by registered or certified mail to the officer, agent or other person so designated. Service of notice or process upon the Secretary of State as agent for such a foreign corporate fiduciary shall in all ways and for all purposes have the same effect as if personal service had been had within this state upon such foreign corporate fiduciary.

(c) Any foreign corporate fiduciary acting in a fiduciary capacity in this state in strict accordance with the provisions of this Section shall not be deemed to be doing business in the State of Texas within the meaning of Article 8.01 of the Texas Business Corporation Act; and shall be deemed qualified to serve in such capacity under the provisions of Section 105 of this Code.

(d) The provisions hereof are in addition to, and not a limitation on, the provisions of Subtitle G, Finance Code, and the Texas Trust Company Act (Article 342a–1.001 et seq., Vernon's Texas Civil Statutes).

(e) Any foreign corporate fiduciary which shall violate any provision of this Section 105a shall be guilty of a misdemeanor and, upon conviction thereof, shall be subject to a fine of not exceeding Five Thousand Dollars ($5,000.00), and may, in the discretion of the court, be prohibited from thereafter serving in this state in any fiduciary capacity.

Added by Acts 1961, 57th Leg., p. 46, ch. 31, § 1, eff. Aug. 28, 1961. Amended by Acts 1995, 74th Leg., ch. 914, § 10, eff. Sept. 1, 1995; Acts 1997, 75th Leg., ch. 769, § 5, eff. Sept. 1, 1997; Acts 1999, 76th Leg., ch. 344, § 6.002, eff. Sept. 1, 1999.

§ 106. When Foreign Executor to Give Bond

A foreign executor shall not be required to give bond if the will appointing him so provides. If the will does not exempt him from giving bond, the provisions of this Code with respect to the bonds of domestic representatives shall be applicable.

Acts 1955, 54th Leg., p. 88, ch. 55, eff. Jan. 1, 1956. Amended by Acts 1971, 62nd Leg., p. 976, ch. 173, § 9, eff. Jan. 1, 1972.

§ 107. Power of Sale of Foreign Executor or Trustee

When by any foreign will recorded in the deed records of any county in this state in the manner provided herein, power is given an executor or trustee to sell any real or personal property situated in this state, no order of a court of this state shall be necessary to authorize such executor or trustee to make such sale and execute proper conveyance, and whenever any particular directions are given by a testator in any such will respecting the sale of any such property situated in this state, belonging to his estate, the same shall be followed unless such directions have been annulled or suspended by order of a court of competent jurisdiction.

Acts 1955, 54th Leg., p. 88, ch. 55, eff. Jan. 1, 1956. Amended by Acts 1969, 61st Leg., p. 1925, ch. 641, § 9, eff. June 12, 1969.

§ 107A. Suit for the Recovery of Debts by a Foreign Executor or Administrator

(a) On giving notice by registered or certified mail to all creditors of the decedent in this state who have filed a claim against the estate of the decedent for a debt due to the creditor, a foreign executor or administrator of a person who was a nonresident at the time of death may prosecute a suit in this state for the recovery of debts due to the decedent.

(b) The plaintiff's letters testamentary or letters of administration granted by a competent tribunal, properly authenticated, shall be filed with the suit.

(c) By filing suit in this state for the recovery of a debt due to the decedent, a foreign executor or administrator submits personally to the jurisdiction of the courts of this state in a proceeding relating to the recovery of a debt due by his decedent to a resident of this state. Jurisdiction under this subsection is limited to the money or value of personal property recovered in this state by the foreign executor or administrator.

(d) Suit may not be maintained in this state by a foreign executor or administrator if there is an executor or administrator of the decedent qualified by a court of this state or if there is pending in this state an application for appointment as an executor or administrator.

Added by Acts 1977, 65th Leg., p. 1190, ch. 457, § 1, eff. Aug. 29, 1977.

PART 3. EMERGENCY INTERVENTION PROCEEDINGS; FUNERAL AND BURIAL EXPENSES

Acts 1993, 73rd Leg., ch. 712, § 7 added Chapter XII, of which chapter Part 2 consisted of §§ 520 to 525. Acts 1997, 75th Leg., ch. 199, § 1 transfers and redesignates Chapter XII, Part 2, as Chapter V, Part 3.

Without reference to the transfer and redesignation of Chapter XII, Part 2, as Chapter V, Part 3, Acts 1997, 75th Leg., ch. 540, § 5 repeals Chapter XII effective September 1, 1997.

A former Part 3, Estates of Minors and Incompetents, added by Acts 1955, 54th Leg., p. 88, ch. 55, and consisting of §§ 108 to 127A, was repealed by Acts 1993, 73rd Leg., ch. 957, § 75(2), which Act also enacted Chapter XIII, Guardianship; see V.A.T.S. Probate Code, § 601 et seq.

§ 108. Time to File Emergency Application

An applicant may file an application requesting emergency intervention by a court exercising probate jurisdiction to provide for the payment of funeral and burial expenses or the protection and storage of personal property owned by the decedent that was located in rented accommodations on the date of the decedent's death with the clerk of the court in the county of domicile of the decedent or the county in which the rental accommodations that contain the decedent's personal property are located. The application must be filed not earlier than the third day after the date of the decedent's death and not later than the 90th day after the date of the decedent's death.

Added by Acts 1993, 73rd Leg., ch. 712, § 7, eff. Sept. 1, 1993. Amended by Acts 1995, 74th Leg., ch. 642, § 6, eff. Sept. 1, 1995. Renumbered from V.A.T.S. Probate Code, § 520 and amended by Acts 1997, 75th Leg., ch. 199, § 1, eff. Sept. 1, 1997.

Repeal

Without reference to the renumbering and amendment of this section by Acts 1997, 75th Leg., ch. 199, § 1, Acts 1997, 75th Leg., ch. 540, § 5 repeals Chapter XII, including the former designation of this section, effective September 1, 1997.

Section 8 of the 1993 law provides:

"The change in law made by this Act applies only to the estate of a person who dies on or after the effective date of this Act. An estate of a person who dies before the effective date of this Act is covered by the law in effect on the date of the person's death, and the former law continues in effect for that purpose."

Section 17(a) of the 1995 amendatory act provides:

"The changes in law made by Sections 1–11 of this Act apply only to the estates of decedents who die on or after September 1, 1995. The estates of decedents who die before the effective date of this Act are governed by the law as it existed immediately before the effective date of this Act, and that law is continued in effect for that purpose."

Section 2 of Acts 1997, 75th Leg., ch. 199 provides:

"This Act takes effect September 1, 1997. The changes in law made by this Act apply only to an application that is filed on or after the effective date of this Act. An application that is filed before the effective date of this Act is governed by the law in effect at the time the application was filed, and the former law is continued in effect for that purpose."

§ 109. Eligible Applicants for Emergency Intervention

A person qualified to serve as an administrator under Section 77 of this code may file an emergency intervention application.

Added by Acts 1993, 73rd Leg., ch. 712, § 7, eff. Sept. 1, 1993. Renumbered from V.A.T.S. Probate Code, § 521 and amended by Acts 1997, 75th Leg., ch. 199, § 1, eff. Sept. 1, 1997.

Repeal

Without reference to the renumbering and amendment of this section by Acts 1997, 75th Leg., ch. 199, § 1, Acts 1997, 75th Leg., ch. 540, § 5 repeals Chapter XII, including the former designation of this section, effective September 1, 1997.

For application provision of the 1993 Act, see note following V.A.T.S. Probate Code, § 108.

For application provision of Acts 1997, 75th Leg., ch. 199, see notes following V.A.T.S. Probate Code, § 108.

§ 110. Requirements for Emergency Intervention

An applicant may file an emergency application with the court under Section 108 of this code only if an application has not been filed and is not pending under Section 81, 82, 137, or 145 of this code and the applicant:

(1) needs to obtain funds for the funeral and burial of the decedent; or

(2) needs to gain access to rental accommodations in which the decedent's personal property is located and the applicant has been denied access to those accommodations.

Added by Acts 1995, 74th Leg., ch. 642, § 7, eff. Sept. 1, 1995. Renumbered from V.A.T.S. Probate Code, § 521A and amended by Acts 1997, 75th Leg., ch. 199, § 1, eff. Sept. 1, 1997.

Repeal

Without reference to the renumbering and amendment of this section by Acts 1997, 75th Leg., ch. 199, § 1, Acts 1997, 75th Leg., ch. 540, § 5 repeals Chapter XII, including the former designation of this section, effective September 1, 1997.

For application provisions of the 1995 Act, see notes following V.A.T.S. Probate Code, § 108.

For application provision of Acts 1997, 75th Leg., ch. 199, see notes following V.A.T.S. Probate Code, § 108.

§ 111. Contents of Emergency Intervention Application for Funeral and Burial Expenses

(a) An application for emergency intervention to obtain funds needed for a decedent's funeral and burial expenses must be sworn and must contain:

(1) the name, address, social security number, and interest of the applicant;

(2) the facts showing an immediate necessity for the issuance of an emergency intervention order under this section by the court;

(3) the date of the decedent's death, place of death, decedent's residential address, and the name and address of the funeral home holding the decedent's remains;

(4) any known or ascertainable heirs and devisees of the decedent and the reason:

(A) the heirs and devisees cannot be contacted; or

(B) the heirs and devisees have refused to assist in the decedent's burial;

(5) a description of funeral and burial procedures necessary and a statement from the funeral home that contains a detailed and itemized description of the cost of the funeral and burial procedures; and

(6) the name and address of an individual, entity, or financial institution, including an employer, that is in possession of any funds of or due to the decedent, and related account numbers and balances, if known by the applicant.

(b) The application shall also state whether there are any written instructions from the decedent relating to the type and manner of funeral or burial the decedent would like to have. The applicant shall attach the instructions, if available, to the application and shall fully comply with the instructions. If written instructions do not exist, the applicant may not permit the decedent's remains to be cremated unless the applicant obtains the court's permission to cremate the decedent's remains.

Added by Acts 1993, 73rd Leg., ch. 712, § 7, eff. Sept. 1, 1993. Amended by Acts 1995, 74th Leg., ch. 642, § 8, eff. Sept. 1, 1995. Renumbered from V.A.T.S. Probate Code, § 522 and amended by Acts 1997, 75th Leg., ch. 199, § 1, eff. Sept. 1, 1997.

Repeal

Without reference to the renumbering and amendment of this section by Acts 1997, 75th Leg., ch. 199, § 1, Acts 1997, 75th Leg., ch. 540, § 5 repeals Chapter XII, including the former designation of this section, effective September 1, 1997.

For application provision of the 1993 Act, see note following V.A.T.S. Probate Code, § 108.

For application provisions of the 1995 amendatory act, see notes following V.A.T.S. Probate Code, § 108.

For application provision of Acts 1997, 75th Leg., ch. 199, see notes following V.A.T.S. Probate Code, § 108.

§ 112. Contents for Emergency Intervention Application for Access to Personal Property

An application for emergency intervention to gain access to rental accommodations of a decedent at the time of the decedent's death that contain the decedent's personal property must be sworn and must contain:

(1) the name, address, social security number, and interest of the applicant;

(2) the facts showing an immediate necessity for the issuance of an emergency intervention order by the court;

(3) the date and place of the decedent's death, the decedent's residential address, and the name and address of the funeral home holding the decedent's remains;

(4) any known or ascertainable heirs and devisees of the decedent and the reason:

(A) the heirs and devisees cannot be contacted; or

(B) the heirs and devisees have refused to assist in the protection of the decedent's personal property;

(5) the type and location of the decedent's personal property and the name of the person in possession of the property; and

(6) the name and address of the owner or manager of the decedent's rental accommodations and whether access to the accommodations is necessary.

Added by Acts 1995, 74th Leg., ch. 642, § 9, eff. Sept. 1, 1995. Renumbered from V.A.T.S. Probate Code, § 522A and amended by Acts 1997, 75th Leg., ch. 199, § 1, eff. Sept. 1, 1997.

Repeal

Without reference to the renumbering and amendment of this section by Acts 1997, 75th Leg., ch. 199, § 1, Acts 1997, 75th Leg., ch. 540, § 5 repeals Chapter XII, including the former designation of this section, effective September 1, 1997.

For application provisions of the 1995 Act, see notes following V.A.T.S. Probate Code, § 108.

For application provision of Acts 1997, 75th Leg., ch. 199, see notes following V.A.T.S. Probate Code, § 108.

§ 112A. Repealed by Acts 1995, 74th Leg., ch. 1039, § 73(1), eff. Sept. 1, 1995

§ 113. Orders of Emergency Intervention

(a) If the court determines on review of an application filed under Section 108 of this code that emergency intervention is necessary to obtain funds needed for a decedent's funeral and burial expenses, the court may order funds of the decedent held by an employer, individual, or financial institution to be paid directly to a funeral home only for reasonable and necessary attorney's fees for the attorney who obtained the order granted under this section, for court costs for obtaining the order, and for funeral and burial expenses not to exceed $5,000 as ordered by the court to provide the decedent with a reasonable, dignified, and appropriate funeral and burial.

(b) If the court determines on review of an application filed under Section 108 of this code that emergency intervention is necessary to gain access to accommodations rented by the decedent at the time of the decedent's death that contain the decedent's personal property, the court may order one or more of the following:

(1) the owner or agent of the rental accommodations shall grant the applicant access to the accommodations at a reasonable time and in the presence of the owner or agent;

(2) the applicant and owner or agent of the rental accommodations shall jointly prepare and file with the court a list that generally describes the decedent's property found at the premises;

(3) the applicant or the owner or agent of the rental accommodations may remove and store the decedent's property at another location until claimed by the decedent's heirs;

(4) the applicant has only the powers that are specifically stated in the order and that are necessary to protect the decedent's property that is the subject of the application; or

(5) funds of the decedent held by an employer, individual, or financial institution to be paid to the applicant for reasonable and necessary attorney's fees and court costs for obtaining the order.

(c) The court clerk may issue certified copies of an emergency intervention order on request of the applicant only until the 90th day after the date the order was signed or the date a personal representative is qualified, whichever occurs first.

(d) A person who is furnished with a certified copy of an emergency intervention order within the period described by Subsection (c) of this section is not personally liable for the person's actions that are taken in accordance with and in reliance on the order.

Added by Acts 1993, 73rd Leg., ch. 712, § 7, eff. Sept. 1, 1993. Amended by Acts 1995, 74th Leg., ch. 642, § 10, eff. Sept. 1, 1995. Renumbered from V.A.T.S. Probate Code, § 523 and amended by Acts 1997, 75th Leg., ch. 199, § 1, eff. Sept. 1, 1997.

Repeal

Without reference to the renumbering and amendment of this section by Acts 1997, 75th Leg., ch. 199, § 1, Acts 1997, 75th Leg., ch. 540, § 5 repeals Chapter XII, including the former designation of this section, effective September 1, 1997.

For application provision of the 1993 Act, see note following V.A.T.S. Probate Code, § 108.

For application provisions of the 1995 amendatory act, see notes following V.A.T.S. Probate Code, § 108.

For application provision of Acts 1997, 75th Leg., ch. 199, see notes following V.A.T.S. Probate Code, § 108.

§ 113A. Repealed by Acts 1993, 73rd Leg., ch. 957, § 75(2), eff. Sept. 1, 1993

§ 114. Termination

(a) All power and authority of an applicant under an emergency intervention order cease to be effective or enforceable on the 90th day after the date the order was issued or on the date a personal representative is qualified, whichever occurs first.

(b) If a personal representative has not been appointed when an emergency intervention order issued under Section 113(b) of this code ceases to be effective, a person who is in possession of the decedent's personal property that is the subject of the order, without incurring civil liability, may:

(1) release the property to the decedent's heirs; or

(2) dispose of the property under Subchapter C, Chapter 54, Property Code,[1] or Section 7.209 or 7.210, Business & Commerce Code.

Added by Acts 1993, 73rd Leg., ch. 712, § 7, eff. Sept. 1, 1993. Amended by Acts 1995, 74th Leg., ch. 642, § 11, eff. Sept. 1, 1995. Renumbered from V.A.T.S. Probate Code, § 524 and amended by Acts 1997, 75th Leg., ch. 199, § 1, eff. Sept. 1, 1997.

[1] V.T.C.A., Property Code § 54.041 et seq.

Repeal

Without reference to the renumbering and amendment of this section by Acts 1997, 75th Leg., ch. 199, § 1, Acts 1997, 75th Leg., ch. 540, § 5 repeals Chapter XII, including the former designation of this section, effective September 1, 1997.

For application provision of the 1993 Act, see note following V.A.T.S. Probate Code, § 108.

For application provisions of the 1995 amendatory act, see notes following V.A.T.S. Probate Code, § 108.

For application provision of Acts 1997, 75th Leg., ch. 199, see notes following V.A.T.S. Probate Code, § 108.

§ 115. Limitation on Right of Surviving Spouse to Control Deceased's Burial or Cremation

(a) An application under this section may be filed by:

(1) the executor of the deceased's will; or

(2) the next of kin of the deceased, the nearest in order of descent first, and so on, and next of kin includes the deceased's descendants who legally adopted the deceased or who have been legally adopted by the deceased.

(b) An application under this section must be under oath and must establish:

(1) whether the deceased died intestate or testate;

(2) the surviving spouse is alleged to be a principal or accomplice in a wilful act which resulted in the death of the deceased; and

(3) good cause exists to limit the right of the surviving spouse to control the burial and interment or cremation of the deceased spouse.

(c) After notice and hearing, without regard to whether the deceased died intestate or testate, a court may limit the right of a surviving spouse, whether or not the spouse has been designated by the deceased's will as the executor of a deceased spouse's estate, to control the burial and interment or cremation of the deceased spouse if the court finds that there is good cause to believe that the surviving spouse is the principal or an accomplice in a wilful act which resulted in the death of the deceased spouse.

(d) If the court limits the surviving spouse's right of control, as provided by Subsection (c), the court shall designate and authorize a person to make burial or cremation arrangements.

Added by Acts 1995, 74th Leg., ch. 642, § 12, eff. Sept. 1, 1995. Renumbered from V.A.T.S. Probate Code, § 525 and amended by Acts 1997, 75th Leg., ch. 199, § 1, eff. Sept. 1, 1997.

Repeal

Without reference to the renumbering and amendment of this section by Acts 1997, 75th Leg., ch. 199, § 1, Acts 1997, 75th Leg., ch. 540, § 5 repeals Chapter XII, including the former designation of this section, effective September 1, 1997.

For application provision of Acts 1997, 75th Leg., ch. 199, see notes following V.A.T.S. Probate Code, § 108.

§§ 116, 117. Repealed by Acts 1993, 73rd Leg., ch. 957, § 75(2), eff. Sept. 1, 1993

Acts 1993, 73rd Leg., ch. 957, repealing former Part 3, Estates of Minors and Incompetents, enacted Chapter XIII, Guardianship, of the Probate Code.

The amendment of sections 116 and 117 by Acts 1993, 73rd Leg., ch. 905, § 7 failed to take effect under § 19(a), which provided that the amendment was not to take effect if both S.B. No. 236 (ch. 905) and H.B. No. 2685 (Acts 1993, 73rd Leg., ch. 957) were enacted and became law.

§ 118. Repealed by Acts 1993, 73rd Leg., ch. 957, § 75(2), eff. Sept. 1, 1993; Acts 1995, 74th Leg., ch. 1039, § 73(1), eff. Sept. 1, 1995

Acts 1993, 73rd Leg., ch. 957, repealing former Part 3, Estates of Minors and Incompetents, enacted Chapter XIII, Guardianship, of the Probate Code.

§§ 118A to 123. Repealed by Acts 1993, 73rd Leg., ch. 957, § 75(2), eff. Sept. 1, 1993

Acts 1993, 73rd Leg., ch. 957, repealing former Part 3, Estates of Minors and Incompetents, enacted Chapter XIII, Guardianship, of the Probate Code.

The amendment of sections 118A to 123 by Acts 1993, 73rd Leg., ch. 905, § 7 failed to take effect under § 19(a), which provided that the amendment was not to take effect if both S.B. No. 236 (ch. 905) and H.B. No. 2685 (ch. 957) were enacted and became law.

§ 123A. Repealed by Acts 1995, 74th Leg., ch. 1039, § 73(1), eff. Sept. 1, 1995

§§ 124 to 127. Repealed by Acts 1993, 73rd Leg., ch. 957, § 75(2), eff. Sept. 1, 1993

Acts 1993, 73rd Leg., ch. 957, repealing former Part 3, Estates of Minors and Incompetents, enacted Chapter XIII, Guardianship, of the Probate Code.

The amendment of sections 124 to 127 by Acts 1993, 73rd Leg., ch. 905, § 7 failed to take effect under § 19(a), which provided that the amendment was not to take effect if both S.B. No. 236 (ch. 905) and H.B. No. 2685 (Acts 1993, 73rd Leg., ch. 957) were enacted and became law.

§ 127A. Repealed by Acts 1993, 73rd Leg., ch. 957, § 75(2), eff. Sept. 1, 1993; Acts 1995, 74th Leg., ch. 1039, § 73(1), eff. Sept. 1, 1995

Acts 1993, 73rd Leg., ch. 957, repealing former Part 3, Estates of Minors and Incompetents, enacted Chapter XIII, Guardianship, of the Probate Code.

PART 4. CITATIONS AND NOTICES

§ 128. Citations With Respect to Applications for Probate or for Issuance of Letters

(a) Where Application Is for Probate of a Written Will Produced in Court or for Letters of Administration. When an application for the probate of a written will produced in court, or for letters of administration, is filed with the clerk, he shall issue a citation to all parties interested in such estate, which citation shall be served by posting and shall state:

(1) That such application has been filed, and the nature of it.

(2) The name of the deceased and of the applicant.

(3) The time when such application will be acted upon.

(4) That all persons interested in the estate should appear at the time named therein and contest said application, should they desire to do so.

(b) Where Application Is for Probate of a Written Will Not Produced or of a Nuncupative Will. When the application is for the probate of a nuncupative will, or of a written will which cannot be produced in court, the clerk shall issue a citation to all parties interested in such estate, which citation shall contain substantially the statements made in the application for probate, and the time when, place where, and the court before which such application will be acted upon. If the heirs of the testator be residents of this state, and their residence be known, the citation shall be served upon them by personal service. Service of such citation may be made by publication in the following cases:

(1) When the heirs are non-residents of this state; or

(2) When their names or their residences are unknown; or

(3) When they are transient persons.

(c) No Action Until Service Is Had. No application for the probate of a will or for the issuance of letters shall be acted upon until service of citation has been made in the manner provided herein.

Acts 1955, 54th Leg., p. 88, ch. 55, eff. Jan. 1, 1956.

§ 128A. Notice to Certain Entities After Probate

(a) If the address of the entity can be ascertained with reasonable diligence, an applicant under Section 81 of this code shall give the state, a governmental agency of the state, or a charitable organization notice that the entity is named as a devisee in a written will, a written will not produced, or a nuncupative will that has been admitted to probate.

(b) The notice required by Subsection (a) of this section must be given not later than the 30th day after the date of the probate of the will.

(c) The notice must be in writing and state the county in which the will was admitted to probate. A copy of the application and the order admitting the will to probate and, if the application is for probate of a written will, a copy of the will must be attached to the notice.

(d) An entity entitled to notice under Subsection (a) of this section must be notified by registered or certified mail, return receipt requested.

(e) The applicant must file a copy of the notice with the court in which the will was admitted to probate.

Added by Acts 1989, 71st Leg., ch. 1035, § 7, eff. Sept. 1, 1989.

Section 18(b) of the 1989 Act provides:

"The change in the law made by Sections 6 and 7 of this Act applies only to an application for probate of a written will, a written will not produced, or a nuncupative will filed on or after the effective date of this Act. An application filed before the effective date of this Act is covered by the law in effect when the application was filed, and the former law is continued in effect for that purpose."

§ 128B. Notice When Will Probated After Four Years

(a) Except as provided by Subsection (b) of this section, an applicant for the probate of a will under Section 73(a) of this code must give notice by service of process to each of the testator's heirs whose address can be ascertained by the applicant with reasonable diligence. The notice must be given before the probate of the testator's will.

(b) Notice under Subsection (a) of this section is not required to be provided to an heir who has delivered to the court an affidavit signed by the heir stating that the heir does not object to the offer of the testator's will for probate.

(c) The notice required by this section and an affidavit described by Subsection (b) of this section must also contain a statement that:

(1) the testator's property will pass to the testator's heirs if the will is not admitted to probate; and

(2) the person offering the testator's will for probate may not be in default for failing to present the will for probate during the four-year period immediately following the testator's death.

(d) If the address of any of the testator's heirs cannot be ascertained by the applicant with reasonable diligence, the court shall appoint an attorney ad litem to protect the interests of the unknown heirs after an application for the probate of a will is made under Section 73(a) of this code.

(e) In the case of an application for the probate of a will of a testator who has had another will admitted to probate, this section applies to a beneficiary of the testator's probated will instead of the testator's heirs.

Added by Acts 1999, 76th Leg., ch. 855, § 2, eff. Sept. 1, 1999.

For application provisions of Acts 1999, 76th Leg., ch. 855, see notes following V.A.T.S. Probate Code, § 10B.

§ 129. Validation of Prior Modes of Service of Citation

(a) In all cases where written wills produced in court have been probated prior to June 14, 1927, after publication of citation as provided by the then Article 28 of the Revised Civil Statutes of Texas (1925), without service of citation, the action of the courts in admitting said wills to probate is hereby validated in so far as service of citation is concerned.

(b) In all cases where written wills produced in court have been probated or letters of administration have been granted prior to May 18, 1939, after citation, as provided by the then Article 3334, Title 54, of the Revised Civil Statutes of Texas (1925), without service of citation as provided for in the then Article 3336, Title 54, of the Revised Civil Statutes of Texas (1925) as amended by Acts 1935, 44th Legislature, page 659, Chapter 273, Section 1, such service of citation and the action of the court in admitting said wills to probate and granting administration upon estates, are hereby validated in so far as service of citation is concerned.

(c) In all cases where written wills have been probated or letters of administration granted, prior to June 12, 1941, upon citation or notice duly issued by the clerk in conformance with the requirements of the then Article 3333 of Title 54 of the Revised Civil Statutes of Texas (1925), as amended, but not directed to the sheriff or any constable of the county wherein the proceeding was pending, and such citation or notice having been duly posted by the sheriff or any constable of said county and returned for or in the time, manner, and form required by law, such citation or notice and return thereof and the action of the court in admitting said wills to probate or granting letters of administration upon estates, are hereby validated in so far as said citation or notice, and the issuance, service and return thereof are concerned.

Acts 1955, 54th Leg., p. 88, ch. 55, eff. Jan. 1, 1956.

§ 129A. Service by Publication or Other Substituted Service

Notwithstanding any other provisions of this part of this chapter, if an attempt to make service under this part of this chapter is unsuccessful, service may be made in the manner provided by Rule 109 or 109a, Texas Rules of Civil Procedure, for the service of a citation on a party by publication or other substituted service.

Added by Acts 1993, 73rd Leg., ch. 712, § 2, eff. Sept. 1, 1993.

§ 130. Repealed by Acts 1993, 73rd Leg., ch. 905, § 15, eff. Sept. 1, 1993; Acts 1993, 73rd Leg., ch. 957, § 75(1), eff. Sept. 1, 1993

Acts 1993, 73rd Leg., ch. 957, repealing this section, enacted Chapter XIII, Guardianship, of the Probate Code.

PART 5. LIMITED GUARDIANSHIP PROCEEDINGS [REPEALED]

§§ 130A to 130*O*. Repealed by Acts 1993, 73rd Leg., ch. 905, § 15, eff. Sept. 1, 1993; Acts 1993, 73rd Leg., ch. 957, § 75(2), eff. Sept. 1, 1993

Acts 1993, 73rd Leg., ch. 957, repealing this part, enacted Chapter XIII, Guardianship, of the Probate Code.

CHAPTER VI. SPECIAL TYPES OF ADMINISTRATION

PART 1. TEMPORARY ADMINISTRATION IN THE INTEREST OF ESTATES OF DEPENDENTS

Section

PART 2. RECEIVERSHIP FOR MINORS AND INCOMPETENTS [REPEALED]

PART 1. TEMPORARY ADMINISTRATION IN THE INTEREST OF ESTATES OF DEPENDENTS

§ 131. Repealed by Acts 1993, 73rd Leg., ch. 957, § 75(1), eff. Sept. 1, 1993

Acts 1993, 73rd Leg., ch. 957, repealing this section, enacted Chapter XIII, Guardianship, of the Probate Code.

The amendment of this section by Acts 1993, 73rd Leg., ch. 905, § 9 failed to take effect under § 19(a), which provided that the amendment was not to take effect if both S.B. No. 236 (ch. 905) and H.B. No. 2685 (ch. 957) were enacted and became law.

§ 131A. Appointment of Temporary Administrators

(a) If a county judge determines that the interest of a decedent's estate requires the immediate appointment of a personal representative, he shall, by written order, appoint a temporary administrator with limited powers as the circumstances of the case require. The duration of the appointment must be specified in the court's order and may not exceed 180 days unless the appointment is made permanent as provided by Subsection (j) of this section.

(b) Any person may file with the clerk of the court a written application for the appointment of a temporary administrator of a decedent's estate under this section. The application must be verified and must include the information required by Section 81 of this code if the decedent died testate or Section 82 of this code if the decedent died intestate and an affidavit that sets out:

(1) the name, address, and interest of the applicant;

(2) the facts showing an immediate necessity for the appointment of a temporary administrator;

(3) the requested powers and duties of the temporary administrator;

(4) a statement that the applicant is entitled to letters of temporary administration and is not disqualified by law from serving as a temporary administrator; and

(5) a description of the real and personal property that the applicant believes to be in the decedent's estate.

(c) An order of appointment must:

(1) designate the appointee as "temporary administrator" of the decedent's estate for the specified period;

(2) define the powers conferred on the appointee; and

(3) set the amount of bond to be given by the appointee.

(d) On the date of the order, the appointee shall file with the county clerk a bond in the amount ordered by the court.

(e) Not later than the third day after the date on which an appointee qualifies, the county clerk shall issue to the appointee letters of appointment that set forth the powers to be exercised by the appointee as ordered by the court.

(f) On the date that the county clerk issues letters of appointment, the county clerk shall post a notice of the appointment to all interested persons on the courthouse door.

(g) On the date the county clerk issues letters of appointment, the appointee shall notify the known heirs of the decedent of his appointment by certified mail, return receipt requested.

(h) A notice required by Subsection (f) or (g) of this section must state that:

(1) an interested person or an heir may request a hearing to contest the appointment not later than the 15th day after the date that the letters of appointment are issued;

(2) if no contest is made within the period specified by the notice, the appointment will continue for the time specified in the order of appointment; and

(3) the court may make the appointment permanent.

(i) If an interested person or an heir requests a hearing to contest the appointment of a temporary administrator, a hearing shall be held and a determination made not later than the 10th day after the date the request was made. If a request is not made on or before the 15th day after the date that the letters of appointment are issued, the appointment of a temporary administrator continues for the period specified in the order, unless made permanent under Subsection (j) of this section. During the pendency of a contest of the appointment of a temporary administrator, the temporary appointee shall continue to act as administrator of the estate to the extent of the powers conferred by his appointment. If the court sets aside the appointment, the court may require the temporary administrator to prepare and file, under oath, a complete exhibit of the condition of the estate and detail the disposition the temporary administrator has made of the property of the estate.

(j) At the conclusion of the term of appointment of a temporary administrator, the court may, by written order, make the appointment permanent if the permanent appointment is in the interest of the estate.

Added by Acts 1987, 70th Leg., ch. 460, § 2, eff. Sept. 1, 1987. Amended by Acts 1989, 71st Leg., ch. 1035, § 8, eff. Sept. 1, 1989; Acts 1997, 75th Leg., ch. 540, § 2, eff. Sept. 1, 1997.

For application provisions of Acts 1997, 75th Leg., ch. 540, see note following V.A.T.S. Probate Code, § 89A.

§ 132. Temporary Administration Pending Contest of a Will or Administration

(a) **Appointment of Temporary Administrator.** Pending a contest relative to the probate of a will or the granting of letters of administration, the court may appoint a temporary administrator, with such limited powers as the circumstances of the case require; and such appointment may continue in force until the termination of the contest and the appointment of an executor or administrator with full powers. The power of appointment in this Subsection is in addition to the court's power of appointment under Section 131A of this Code.

(b) **Additional Powers Relative to Claims.** When temporary administration has been granted pending a will contest, or pending a contest on an application for letters of administration, the court may, at any time during the pendency of the contest, confer upon the temporary administrator all the power and authority of a permanent administrator with respect to claims against the estate, and in such case the court and the temporary administrator shall act in the same manner as in permanent administration in connection with such matters as the approval or disapproval of claims, the payment of claims, and the making of sales of real or personal property for the payment of claims; provided, however, that in the event such power and authority is conferred upon a temporary administrator, he shall be required to give bond in the full amount required of a permanent administrator. The provisions of this Subsection are cumulative and shall not be construed to exclude the right of the court to order a temporary administrator to do any and all of the things covered by this Subsection in other cases where the doing of such things shall be necessary or expedient to preserve the estate pending final determination of the contest.

Acts 1955, 54th Leg., p. 88, ch. 55, eff. Jan. 1, 1956. Amended by Acts 1987, 70th Leg., ch. 460, § 3, eff. Sept. 1, 1987.

§ 133. Powers of Temporary Administrators

Temporary administrators shall have and exercise only such rights and powers as are specifically expressed in the order of the court appointing them, and as may be expressed in subsequent orders of the court. Where a court, by a subsequent order, extends the rights and powers of a temporary administrator, it may require additional bond commensurate with such extension. Any acts performed by temporary administrators that are not so expressly authorized shall be void.

Acts 1955, 54th Leg., p. 88, ch. 55, eff. Jan. 1, 1956. Amended by Acts 1993, 73rd Leg., ch. 957, § 25, eff. Sept. 1, 1993.

§ 134. Accounting

At the expiration of a temporary appointment, the appointee shall file with the clerk of the court a sworn list of all property of the estate which has come into his hands, a return of all sales made by him, and a full exhibit and account of all his acts as such appointee.

Acts 1955, 54th Leg., p. 88, ch. 55, eff. Jan. 1, 1956.

§ 135. Closing Temporary Administration

The list, return, exhibit, and account so filed shall be acted upon by the court and, whenever temporary letters shall expire or cease to be of effect for any cause, the court shall immediately enter an order requiring such temporary appointee forthwith to deliver the estate remaining in his possession to the person or persons legally entitled to its possession. Upon proof of such delivery, the appointee shall be discharged and the sureties on his bond released as to any future liability.

Acts 1955, 54th Leg., p. 88, ch. 55, eff. Jan. 1, 1956. Amended by Acts 1993, 73rd Leg., ch. 957, § 26, eff. Sept. 1, 1993.

PART 2. RECEIVERSHIP FOR MINORS AND INCOMPETENTS [REPEALED]

§ 136. Repealed by Acts 1993, 73rd Leg., ch. 957, § 75(3), eff. Sept. 1, 1993

Acts 1993, 73rd Leg., ch. 957, repealing this part, enacted Chapter XIII, Guardianship, of the Probate Code.

PART 3. SMALL ESTATES

§ 137. Collection of Small Estates Upon Affidavit

(a) The distributees of the estate of a decedent who dies intestate shall be entitled thereto, to the extent that the assets, exclusive of homestead and exempt property, exceed the known liabilities of said estate, exclusive of liabilities secured by homestead and exempt property, without awaiting the appointment of a personal representative when:

(1) No petition for the appointment of a personal representative is pending or has been granted; and

(2) Thirty days have elapsed since the death of the decedent; and

(3) The value of the entire assets of the estate, not including homestead and exempt property, does not exceed $50,000; and

(4) There is filed with the clerk of the court having jurisdiction and venue an affidavit sworn to by two disinterested witnesses, by all such distributees that have legal capacity, and, if the facts warrant, by the natural guardian or next of kin of any minor or the guardian of any other incapacitated person who is also a distributee, which affidavit shall be examined by the judge of the court having jurisdiction and venue; and

(5) The affidavit shows the existence of the foregoing conditions and includes a list of all of the known assets and liabilities of the estate, the names and addresses of the distributees, and the relevant family history facts concerning heirship that show the distributees' rights to receive the money or property of the estate or to have such evidences of money, property, or other rights of the estate as are found to exist transferred to them as heirs or assignees; and

(6) The judge, in the judge's discretion, finds that the affidavit conforms to the terms of this section and approves the affidavit; and

(7) A copy of the affidavit, certified to by said clerk, is furnished by the distributees of the estate to the person or persons owing money to the estate, having custody or possession of property of the estate, or acting as registrar, fiduciary or transfer agent of or for evidences of interest, indebtedness, property, or other right belonging to the estate.

(b) This section does not affect the disposition of property under the terms of a will or other testamentary document nor, except as provided by Subsection (c) of this section, does it transfer title to real property.

(c) Title to a decedent's homestead that is the only real property in a decedent's estate may be transferred on an affidavit that meets the requirements of this section. An affidavit that is used to transfer title to a homestead under this section must be recorded in the deed records of a county in which the homestead is located. A bona fide purchaser for value may rely on a recorded affidavit under this section. A bona fide purchaser for value without actual or constructive notice of an heir who is not disclosed in a recorded affidavit under this section acquires title to a homestead free of the interests of the undisclosed heir, but the bona fide purchaser remains subject to any claim a creditor of the decedent has by law. A purchaser has constructive notice of an heir who is not disclosed in a recorded affidavit under this section if an affidavit, judgment of heirship, or title transaction in the chain of title in the deed records identifies the heir of the decedent who is not disclosed in the affidavit as an heir of the decedent. An heir who is not disclosed in a recorded affidavit under this section may recover from an heir who receives consideration from a purchaser in a transfer for value of title to a homestead passing under the affidavit.

(d) If the judge approves the affidavit under this section, the affidavit is to be recorded as an official public record under Chapter 194, Local Government Code. If the county has not adopted a microfilm or microphotographic process under Chapter 194, Local Government Code, the county clerk shall provide and keep in his office an appropriate book labeled "Small Estates," with an accurate index showing the name of the decedent and reference to land, if any, involved, in which he shall record every such affidavit so filed, upon being paid his legal recording fee.

Acts 1955, 54th Leg., p. 88, ch. 55, eff. Jan. 1, 1956. Amended by Acts 1957, 55th Leg., p. 53, ch. 31, § 4, eff. Aug. 22, 1957; Acts 1969, 61st Leg., p. 1978, ch. 670, § 1, eff. Sept. 1, 1969; Acts 1975, 64th Leg., p. 1402, ch. 543, § 1, eff. Sept. 1, 1975; Acts 1977, 65th Leg., p. 361, ch. 177, § 1, eff. May 20, 1977; Acts 1979, 66th Leg., p. 1747, ch. 713, § 14, eff. Aug. 27, 1979; Acts 1983, 68th Leg., p. 4560, ch. 757, § 1, eff. Sept. 1, 1983; Acts 1993, 73rd Leg., ch. 594, § 1, eff. Sept. 1, 1993; Acts 1995, 74th Leg., ch. 642, § 3, eff. Sept. 1, 1995; Acts 1995, 74th Leg., ch. 1039, § 8, eff. Sept. 1, 1995; Acts 1997, 75th Leg., ch. 540, § 3, eff. Sept. 1, 1997.

Repeal

Acts 1971, 62nd Leg., p. 2722, ch. 886, effective June 14, 1971, relating to the microfilming of records by counties, and classified as Vernon's Ann.Civ.St. art. 1941(a), provided in section 2 that all laws or parts of laws in conflict with the provisions of this Act are hereby repealed, to the extent of conflict only, including but not limited to subsections (d) and (e) of this section.

Section 2 of the 1993 amendatory act provides:

"This Act takes effect September 1, 1993, and applies only to the distribution of the estate of a decedent who dies on or after the effective date of this Act. The distribution of the estate of a decedent who dies before the effective date of this Act is covered by the law in effect when the decedent died, and the former law is continued in effect for that purpose."

Section 17(a) of Acts 1995, 74th Leg., ch. 642, provides:

"The changes in law made by Sections 1–11 of this Act apply only to the estates of decedents who die on or after September 1, 1995. The estates of decedents who die before the effective date of this Act are governed by the law as it existed immediately before the effective date of this Act, and that law is continued in effect for that purpose."

For application provisions of Acts 1997, 75th Leg., ch. 540, see note following V.A.T.S. Probate Code, § 89A.

§ 138. Effect of Affidavit

The person making payment, delivery, transfer or issuance pursuant to the affidavit described in the preceding Section shall be released to the same extent as if made to a personal representative of the decedent, and shall not be required to see to the application thereof or to inquire into the truth of any statement in the affidavit, but the distributees to whom payment, delivery, transfer, or issuance is made shall be answerable therefor to any person having a prior right and be accountable to any personal representative thereafter appointed. In addition, the person or persons who execute the affidavit shall be liable for any damage or loss to any person which arises from any payment, delivery, transfer, or issuance made in reliance on such affidavit. If the person to whom such affidavit is delivered refuses to pay, deliver, transfer, or issue the property as above provided, such property may be recovered in an action brought for such purpose by or on behalf of the distributees entitled thereto, upon proof of the facts required to be stated in the affidavit.

Acts 1955, 54th Leg., p. 88, ch. 55, eff. Jan. 1, 1956. Amended by Acts 1995, 74th Leg., ch. 642, § 4, eff. Sept. 1, 1995.

For application provisions of the 1995 amendatory act, see notes following V.A.T.S. Probate Code, § 137.

§ 139. Application for Order of No Administration

If the value of the entire assets of an estate, not including homestead and exempt property, does not exceed the amount to which the surviving spouse and minor children of the decedent are entitled as a family allowance, there may be filed by or on behalf of the surviving spouse or minor children an application in any court of proper venue for administration, or, if an application for the appointment of a personal representative has been filed but not yet granted, then in the court where such application has been filed, requesting the court to make a family allowance and to enter an order that no administration shall be necessary. The application shall state the names of the heirs or devisees, a list of creditors of the estate together with the amounts of the claims so far as the same are known, and a description of all real and personal property belonging to the estate, together with the estimated value thereof according to the best knowledge and information of the applicant, and the liens and encumbrances thereon, with a prayer that the court make a family allowance and that, if the entire assets of the estate, not including homestead and exempt property, are thereby exhausted, the same be set aside to the surviving spouse and minor children, as in the case of other family allowances provided for by this Code.

Acts 1955, 54th Leg., p. 88, ch. 55, eff. Jan. 1, 1956.

§ 140. Hearing and Order Upon the Application

Upon the filing of an application for no administration such as that provided for in the preceding Section, the court may hear the same forthwith without notice, or at such time and upon such notice as the court requires. Upon the hearing of the application, if the court finds that the facts contained therein are true and that the expenses of last illness, funeral charges, and expenses of the proceeding have been paid or secured, the court shall make a family allowance and, if the entire assets of the estate, not including homestead and exempt property, are thereby exhausted, shall order that no administration be had of the estate and shall assign to the surviving spouse and minor children the whole of the estate, in the same manner and with the same effect as provided in this Code for the making of family allowances to the surviving spouse and minor children.

Acts 1955, 54th Leg., p. 88, ch. 55, eff. Jan. 1, 1956.

§ 141. Effect of Order

The order that no administration be had on the estate shall constitute sufficient legal authority to all persons owing any money, having custody of any property, or acting as registrar or transfer agent of any evidence of interest, indebtedness, property, or right, belonging to the estate, and to persons purchasing from or otherwise dealing with the estate, for payment or transfer to the persons described in the order as entitled to receive the estate without administration, and the persons so described in the order shall be entitled to enforce their right to such payment or transfer by suit.

Acts 1955, 54th Leg., p. 88, ch. 55, eff. Jan. 1, 1956.

§ 142. Proceeding to Revoke Order

At any time within one year after the entry of an order of no administration, and not thereafter, any interested person may file an application to revoke the same, alleging that other property has been discovered, or that property belonging to the estate was not included in the application for no administration, or that the property described in the application was incorrectly valued, and that if said property were added, included, or correctly valued, as the case may be, the total value of the property would exceed that necessary to justify the court in ordering no administration. Upon proof of any of such grounds, the court shall revoke the order of no administration. In case of any contest as to the value of any property, the court may appoint two appraisers to appraise the same in accordance with the procedure hereinafter provided for inventories and appraisements, and the appraisement of such appraisers shall be received in evidence but shall not be conclusive.

Acts 1955, 54th Leg., p. 88, ch. 55, eff. Jan. 1, 1956.

§ 143. Summary Proceedings for Small Estates After Personal Representative Appointed

Whenever, after the inventory, appraisement, and list of claims has been filed by a personal representative, it is established that the estate of a decedent, exclusive of the homestead and exempt property and family allowance to the surviving spouse and minor children, does not exceed the amount sufficient to pay the claims of Classes One to Four, inclusive, as claims are hereinafter classified, the personal representative shall, upon order of the court, pay the claims in the order provided and to the extent permitted by the assets of the estate subject to the payment of such claims, and thereafter present his account with an application for the settlement and allowance thereof. Thereupon the court, with or without notice, may adjust, correct, settle, allow or disallow such account, and, if the account is settled and allowed, may decree final distribution, discharge the personal representative, and close the administration.

Acts 1955, 54th Leg., p. 88, ch. 55, eff. Jan. 1, 1956.

§ 144. Repealed by Acts 1993, 73rd Leg., ch. 957, § 75(1), eff. Sept. 1, 1993

Acts 1993, 73rd Leg., ch. 957, repealing this section, enacted Chapter XIII, Guardianship, of the Probate Code.

PART 4 INDEPENDENT ADMINISTRATION

§ 145. Independent Administration

(a) Independent administration of an estate may be created as provided in Subsections (b) through (e) of this section.

(b) Any person capable of making a will may provide in his will that no other action shall be had in the county court in relation to the settlement of his estate than the probating and recording of his will, and the return of an inventory, appraisement, and list of claims of his estate.

(c) In situations where an executor is named in a decedent's will, but the will does not provide for independent administration of the decedent's estate as provided in Subsection (b) of this section, all of the distributees of the decedent may agree on the advisability of having an independent administration and collectively designate in the application for probate of the decedent's will the executor named in the will to serve as independent executor and request in the application that no other action shall be had in the county court in relation to the settlement of the decedent's estate other than the probating and recording of the decedent's will, and the return of an inventory, appraisement, and list of claims of the decedent's estate. In such case the county court shall enter an order granting independent administration and appointing the person, firm, or corporation designated in the application as independent executor, unless the county court finds that it would not be in the best interest of the estate to do so.

(d) In situations where no executor is named in the decedent's will, or in situations where each executor named in the will is deceased or is disqualified to serve as executor or indicates by affidavit filed with the application for administration of the decedent's estate his inability or unwillingness to serve as executor, all of the distributees of the decedent may agree on the advisability of having an independent administration and collectively designate in the application for probate of the decedent's will a qualified person, firm, or corporation to serve as independent administrator and request in the application that no other action shall be had in the county court in relation to the settlement of the decedent's estate other than the probating and recording of the decedent's will, and the return of an inventory, appraisement, and list of claims of the decedent's estate. In such case the county court shall enter an order granting independent administration and appointing the person, firm, or corporation designated in the application as independent administrator, unless the county court finds that it would not be in the best interest of the estate to do so.

(e) All of the distributees of a decedent dying intestate may agree on the advisability of having an independent administration and collectively designate in the application for administration of the decedent's estate a qualified person, firm, or corporation to serve as independent administrator and request in the application that no other action shall be had in the county court in relation to the settlement of the decedent's estate other than the return of an inventory, appraisement, and list of claims of the decedent's estate. In such case the county court shall enter an order granting independent administration and appointing the person, firm, or corporation designated in the application as independent administrator, unless the county court finds that it would not be in the best interest of the estate to do so.

(f) In those cases where an independent administration is sought under the provisions of Subsections (c) through (e) above, all distributees shall be served with citation and notice of the application for independent administration unless the distributee waives the issuance or service of citation or enters an appearance in court.

(g) In no case shall any independent administrator be appointed by any court to serve in any intestate administration until those parties seeking the appointment of said independent administrator offer clear and convincing evidence to the court that they constitute all of the said decedent's heirs.

(h) When an independent administration has been created, and the order appointing an independent executor has been entered by the county court, and the inventory, appraisement, and list aforesaid has been filed by the executor and approved by the county court, as long as the estate is represented by an independent executor, further action of any nature shall not be had in the county court except where this Code specifically and explicitly provides for some action in the county court.

(i) If a distributee described in Subsections (c) through (e) of this section is an incapacitated person, the guardian of the person of the distributee may sign the application on behalf of the distributee. If the county court finds that either the granting of independent administration or the appointment of the person, firm, or corporation designated in the application as independent executor would not be in the best interests of the incapacitated person, then, notwithstanding anything to the contrary in Subsections (c) through (e) of this section, the county court shall not enter an order granting independent administration of the estate. If such distributee who is an incapacitated person has no guardian of the person, the county court may appoint a guardian ad litem to make application on behalf of the incapacitated person if the county court considers such an appointment necessary to protect the interest of the distributees.

(j) If a trust is created in the decedent's will, the person or class of persons first eligible to receive the income from the trust, when determined as if the trust were to be in existence on the date of the decedent's death, shall, for the purposes of Subsections (c) and (d) of this section, be deemed to be the distributee or distributees on behalf of such trust, and any other trust or trusts coming into existence upon the termination of such trust, and are authorized to apply for independent administration on behalf of the trusts without the consent or agreement of the trustee or any other beneficiary of the trust, or the trustee or any beneficiary of any other trust which may come into existence upon the termination of such trust.

(k) If a life estate is created either in the decedent's will or by law, the life tenant or life tenants, when determined as if the life estate were to commence on the date of the decedent's death, shall, for the purposes of Subsections (c) through (e) of this section, be deemed to be the distributee or distributees on behalf of the entire estate created, and are authorized to apply for independent administration on behalf of the estate without the consent or approval of any remainderman.

(*l*) If a decedent's will contains a provision that a distributee must survive the decedent by a prescribed period of time in order to take under the decedent's will, then, for the purposes of determining who shall be the distributee under Subsections (c), (d), (h), and (i) of this section, it shall be presumed that the distributees living at the time of the filing of the application for probate of the decedent's will survived the decedent by the prescribed period.

(m) In the case of all decedents, whether dying testate or intestate, for the purposes of determining who shall be the distributees under Subsections (c), (d), (e), (h), and (i) of this section, it shall be presumed that no distributee living at the time the application for independent administration is filed shall subsequently disclaim any portion of such distributee's interest in the decedent's estate.

(n) If a distributee of a decedent's estate should die and if by virtue of such distributee's death such distributee's share of the decedent's estate shall become payable to such distributee's estate, then the deceased distributee's personal representative may sign the application for independent administration of the decedent's estate under Subsections (c), (d), (e), (h), and (i) of this section.

(*o*) Notwithstanding anything to the contrary in this section, a person capable of making a will may provide in his will that no independent administration of his estate may be allowed. In such case, his estate, if administered, shall be administered and settled under the direction of the county court as other estates are required to be settled.

(p) If an independent administration of a decedent's estate is created pursuant to Subsections (c), (d), or (e) of this section, then, unless the county court shall waive bond on application for waiver, the independent executor shall be required to enter into bond payable to and to be approved by the judge and his or her successors in a sum that is found by the judge to be adequate under all circumstances, or a bond with one surety in a sum that is found by the judge to be adequate under all circumstances, if the surety is an authorized corporate surety. This subsection does not repeal any other section of this Code.

(q) Absent proof of fraud or collusion on the part of a judge, no judge may be held civilly liable for the commission of misdeeds or the omission of any required act of any person, firm, or corporation designated as an independent executor or independent administrator under Subsections (c), (d), and (e) of the section. Section 36 of this code does not apply to the appointment of an independent executor or administrator under Subsection (c), (d), or (e) of this section.

(r) A person who declines to serve or resigns as independent executor or administrator of a decedent's estate may be appointed an executor or administrator of the estate if the estate will be administered and settled under the direction of the court.

Acts 1955, 54th Leg., p. 88, ch. 55, eff. Jan. 1, 1956. Amended by Acts 1957, 55th Leg., p. 53, ch. 31, § 2(b); Acts 1977, 65th Leg., p. 1061, ch. 390, § 3, eff. Sept. 1, 1977; Acts 1979, 66th Leg., p. 1750, ch. 713, § 16, eff. Aug. 27, 1979; Acts 1991, 72nd Leg., ch. 895, § 10, eff. Sept. 1, 1991; Acts 1993, 73rd Leg., ch. 846, § 15, eff. Sept. 1, 1993; Acts 1995, 74th Leg., ch. 1039, § 9, eff. Sept. 1, 1995.

§ 146. Payment of Claims and Delivery of Exemptions and Allowances

(a) Duty of the Independent Executor. An independent executor, in the administration of an estate, independently of and without application to, or any action in or by the court:

(1) shall give the notices required under Sections 294 and 295,

(2) may give the notice permitted under Section 294(d) and bar a claim under that subsection;

(3) shall approve, classify, and pay, or reject, claims against the estate in the same order of priority, classification, and proration prescribed in this Code; and

(4) shall set aside and deliver to those entitled thereto exempt property and allowances for support, and allowances in lieu of exempt property, as prescribed in this Code, to the same extent and result as if the independent executor's actions had been accomplished in, and under orders of, the court.

(b) Secured Claims for Money. Within six months after the date letters are granted or within four months after the date notice is received under Section 295, whichever is later, a creditor with a claim for money secured by real or personal property of the estate must give notice to the independent executor of the creditor's election to have the creditor's claim approved as a matured secured claim to be paid in due course of administration. If the election is not made, the claim is a preferred debt and lien against the specific property securing the indebtedness and shall be paid according to the terms of the contract that secured the lien, and the claim may not be asserted against other assets of the estate. The independent executor may pay the claim before the claim matures if paying the claim before maturity is in the best interest of the estate.

(c) Liability of Independent Executor. An independent executor, in the administration of an estate, may pay at any time and without personal liability a claim for money against the estate to the extent approved and classified by the personal representative if:

(1) the claim is not barred by limitations; and

(2) at the time of payment, the independent executor reasonably believes the estate will have sufficient assets to pay all claims against the estate.

(d) Notice Required of Unsecured Creditor. An unsecured creditor who has a claim for money against an estate and receives a notice under Section 294(d) shall give notice to the independent executor of the nature and amount of the claim not later than the 120th day after the date on which the notice is received or the claim is barred.

(e) Placement of Notice. Notice required by Subsections (b) and (d) must be contained in:

(1) a written instrument that is hand-delivered with proof of receipt or mailed by certified mail, return receipt requested, to the independent executor or the executor's attorney;

(2) a pleading filed in a lawsuit with respect to the claim; or

(3) a written instrument or pleading filed in the court in which the administration of the estate is pending.

Acts 1955, 54th Leg., p. 88, ch. 55, eff. Jan. 1, 1956. Amended by Acts 1957, 55th Leg., p. 53, ch. 31, § 2(c), eff. Aug. 21, 1957; Acts 1995, 74th Leg., ch. 1054, § 1, eff. Jan. 1, 1996; Acts 1997, 75th Leg., ch. 1302, § 8, eff. Sept. 1, 1997.

Section 30 of the 1995 amendatory act provides:

"The change in law made by this Act applies only to the estates of persons who die on or after the effective date of this Act. An estate of a person who dies before the effective date of this Act is covered by the law in effect when the person died, and the former law continues in effect for that purpose."

§ 147. Enforcement of Claims by Suit

Any person having a debt or claim against the estate may enforce the payment of the same by suit against the independent executor; and, when judgment is recovered against the independent executor, the execution shall run against the estate of the decedent in the hands of the independent executor which is subject to such debt. The independent executor shall not be required to plead to any suit brought against him for money until after six months from the date that an independent administration was created and the order appointing an independent executor was entered by the county court.

Acts 1955, 54th Leg., p. 88, ch. 55, eff. Jan. 1, 1956. Amended by Acts 1975, 64th Leg., p. 980, ch. 376, § 1, eff. June 19, 1975; Acts 1977, 65th Leg., p. 1064, ch. 390, § 4, eff. Sept. 1, 1977.

§ 148. Requiring Heirs to Give Bond

When an independent administration is created and the order appointing an independent executor is entered by the county court, any person having a debt against such estate may, by written complaint filed in the county court where such order was entered, cause all distributees of the estate, heirs at law, and other persons entitled to any portion of such estate under the will, if any, to be cited by personal service to appear before such county court and execute a bond for an amount equal to the amount of the creditor's claim or the full value of such estate, as shown by the inventory and list of claims, whichever is the smaller, such bond to be payable to the judge, and his successors, and to be approved by said judge, and conditioned that all obligors shall pay all debts that shall be established against such estate in the manner provided by law. Upon the return of the citation served, unless such person so entitled to any portion of the estate, or some of them, or some other person for them, shall execute such bond to the satisfaction of the county court, such estate shall thereafter be administered and settled under the direction of the county court as other estates are required to be settled. If the bond is executed and approved, the independent administration shall proceed. Creditors of the estate may sue on such bond, and shall be entitled to judgment thereon for the amount of their debt, or they may have their action against those in possession of the estate.

Acts 1955, 54th Leg., p. 88, ch. 55, eff. Jan. 1, 1956. Amended by Acts 1977, 65th Leg., p. 1064, ch. 390, § 5, eff. Sept. 1, 1977; Acts 1979, 66th Leg., p. 1750, ch. 713, § 17, eff. Aug. 27, 1979.

§ 149. Requiring Independent Executor to Give Bond

When it has been provided by will, regularly probated, that an independent executor appointed by such will shall not be required to give bond for the management of the estate devised by such will, the direction shall be observed, unless it be made to appear at any time that such independent executor is mismanaging the property, or has betrayed or is about to betray his trust, or has in some other way become disqualified, in which case, upon proper proceedings had for that purpose, as in the case of executors or administrators acting under orders of the court, such executor may be required to give bond.

Acts 1955, 54th Leg., p. 88, ch. 55, eff. Jan. 1, 1956.

§ 149A. Accounting

(a) Interested Person May Demand Accounting. At any time after the expiration of fifteen months from the date that an independent administration was created and the order appointing an independent executor was entered by the county court, any person interested in the estate may demand an accounting from the independent executor. The independent executor shall thereupon furnish to the person or persons making the demand an exhibit in writing, sworn and subscribed by the independent executor, setting forth in detail:

1. The property belonging to the estate which has come into his hands as executor.
2. The disposition that has been made of such property.
3. The debts that have been paid.
4. The debts and expenses, if any, still owing by the estate.
5. The property of the estate, if any, still remaining in his hands.
6. Such other facts as may be necessary to a full and definite understanding of the exact condition of the estate.
7. Such facts, if any, that show why the administration should not be closed and the estate distributed.

Any other interested person shall, upon demand, be entitled to a copy of any exhibit or accounting that has been made by an independent executor in compliance with this section.

(b) Enforcement of Demand. Should the independent executor not comply with a demand for an accounting authorized by this section within sixty days after receipt of the demand, the person making the demand may compel compliance by an action in the county court, as that term is defined by Section 3 of this code. After a hearing, the court shall enter an order requiring the accounting to be made at such time as it deems proper under the circumstances.

(c) Subsequent Demands. After an initial accounting has been given by an independent executor, any person interested in an estate may demand subsequent periodic accountings at intervals of not less than twelve months, and such subsequent demands may be enforced in the same manner as an initial demand.

(d) Remedies Cumulative. The right to an accounting accorded by this section is cumulative of any other remedies which persons interested in an estate may have against the independent executor thereof.

Added by Acts 1971, 62nd Leg., p. 980, ch. 173, § 10, eff. Jan. 1, 1972. Amended by Acts 1973, 63rd Leg., p. 412, ch. 184, § 1, eff. May 25, 1973; Acts 1977, 65th Leg., p. 1065, ch. 390, § 6, eff. Sept. 1, 1977; Acts 1999, 76th Leg., ch. 855, § 3, eff. Sept. 1, 1999.

For application provisions of Acts 1999, 76th Leg., ch. 855, see notes following V.A.T.S. Probate Code, § 10B.

§ 149B. Accounting and Distribution

(a) In addition to or in lieu of the right to an accounting provided by Section 149A of this code, at any time after the expiration of two years from the date that an independent administration was created and the order appointing an independent executor was entered, a person interested in the estate may petition the county court, as that term is defined by Section 3 of this code, for an accounting and distribution. The court may order an accounting to be made with the court by the independent executor at such time as the court deems proper. The accounting shall include the information that the court deems necessary to determine whether any part of the estate should be distributed.

(b) On receipt of the accounting and, after notice to the independent executor and a hearing, unless the court finds a continued necessity for administration of the estate, the court shall order its distribution by the independent executor to the persons entitled to the property. If the court finds there is a continued necessity for administration of the estate, the court shall order the distribution of any portion of the estate that the court finds should not be subject to further administration by the independent executor. If any portion of the estate that is ordered to be distributed is incapable of distribution without prior partition or sale, the court shall order partition and distribution, or sale, in the manner provided for the partition and distribution of property incapable of division in estates administered under the direction of the county court.

(c) If all the property in the estate is ordered distributed by the executor and the estate is fully administered, the court also may order the independent executor to file a final account with the court and may enter an order closing the administration and terminating the power of the independent executor to act as executor.

Added by Acts 1979, 66th Leg., p. 1751, ch. 713, § 18, eff. Aug. 27, 1979. Amended by Acts 1985, 69th Leg., ch. 882, § 1, eff. Aug. 26, 1985; Acts 1987, 70th Leg., ch. 565, § 1, eff. June 18, 1987; Acts 1987, 70th Leg., ch. 760, § 1, eff. Aug. 31, 1987; Acts 1999, 76th Leg., ch. 855, § 4, eff. Sept. 1, 1999.

Section 2 of the 1985 amendatory act provides:

"The change in the law made by this Act applies only to a petition for an accounting and distribution filed under Section 149B, Texas Probate Code, on or after the effective date of this Act. A petition filed before the effective date of this Act is covered by the law in effect when the petition was filed, and that law is continued in effect for that purpose."

For application provisions of Acts 1999, 76th Leg., ch. 855, see notes following V.A.T.S. Probate Code, § 10B.

§ 149C. Removal of Independent Executor

(a) The county court, as that term is defined by Section 3 of this code, on its own motion or on motion of any interested person, after the independent executor has been cited by personal service to answer at a time and place fixed in the notice, may remove an independent executor when:

(1) the independent executor fails to return within ninety days after qualification, unless such time is extended by order of the court, an inventory of the property of the estate and list of claims that have come to his knowledge;

(2) sufficient grounds appear to support belief that he has misapplied or embezzled, or that he is about to misapply or embezzle, all or any part of the property committed to his care;

(3) he fails to make an accounting which is required by law to be made;

(4) he fails to timely file the notice required by Section 128A of this code;

(5) he is proved to have been guilty of gross misconduct or gross mismanagement in the performance of his duties; or

(6) he becomes an incapacitated person, or is sentenced to the penitentiary, or from any other cause becomes legally incapacitated from properly performing his fiduciary duties.

(b) The order of removal shall state the cause of removal and shall direct by order the disposition of the assets remaining in the name or under the control of the removed executor. The order of removal shall require that letters issued to the removed executor shall be surrendered and that all letters shall be canceled of record. If an independent executor is removed by the court under this section, the court may, on application, appoint a successor independent executor as provided by Section 154A of this code.

(c) An independent executor who defends an action for his removal in good faith, whether successful or not, shall be allowed out of the estate his necessary expenses and disbursements, including reasonable attorney's fees, in the removal proceedings.

(d) Costs and expenses incurred by the party seeking removal incident to removal of an independent executor appointed without bond, including reasonable attorney's fees and expenses, may be paid out of the estate.

Added by Acts 1979, 66th Leg., p. 1751, ch. 713, § 19, eff. Aug. 27, 1979. Amended by Acts 1987, 70th Leg., ch. 719, § 1, eff. Aug. 31, 1987; Acts 1989, 71st Leg., ch. 1035, § 10, eff. Sept. 1, 1989; Acts 1995, 74th Leg., ch. 1039, § 10, eff. Sept. 1, 1995; Acts 1999, 76th Leg., ch. 855, § 5, eff. Sept. 1, 1999.

For application provisions of Acts 1999, 76th Leg., ch. 855, see notes following V.A.T.S. Probate Code, § 10B.

§ 149D. Distribution of Remaining Estate Pending Judicial Discharge

(a) On or before filing an action under Section 149E of this code, the independent executor must distribute to the beneficiaries of the estate any of the remaining assets or property of the estate that remains in the hands of the independent executor after all of the estate's debts have been paid, except for a reasonable reserve of assets that the independent executor may retain in a fiduciary capacity pending court approval of the final account.

(b) The court may review the amount of assets on reserve and may order the independent executor to make further distributions under this section.

Added by Acts 1999, 76th Leg., ch. 855, § 6, eff. Sept. 1, 1999.

For application provisions of Acts 1999, 76th Leg., ch. 855, see notes following V.A.T.S. Probate Code, § 10B.

§ 149E. Judicial Discharge of Independent Executor

(a) After an estate has been administered and if there is no further need for an independent administration of the estate, the independent executor of the estate may file an action for declaratory judgment under Chapter 37, Civil Practice and Remedies Code, seeking to discharge the independent executor from any liability involving matters relating to the past administration of the estate that have been fully and fairly disclosed.

(b) On the filing of an action under this section, each beneficiary of the estate shall be personally served with citation, except for a beneficiary who has waived the issuance and service of citation.

(c) In a proceeding under this section, the court may require the independent executor to file a final account that includes any information the court considers necessary to adjudicate the independent executor's request for a discharge of liability. The court may audit, settle, or approve a final account filed under this subsection.

Added by Acts 1999, 76th Leg., ch. 855, § 6, eff. Sept. 1, 1999.

For application provisions of Acts 1999, 76th Leg., ch. 855, see notes following V.A.T.S. Probate Code, § 10B.

§ 149F. Court Costs and Other Charges Related to Final Account in Judicial Discharge

(a) Except as ordered by the court, the independent executor is entitled to pay from the estate legal fees, expenses, or other costs of a proceeding incurred in relation to a final account required under Section 149E of this code.

(b) The independent executor shall be personally liable to refund any amount not approved by the court as a proper charge against the estate.

Added by Acts 1999, 76th Leg., ch. 855, § 6, eff. Sept. 1, 1999.

For application provisions of Acts 1999, 76th Leg., ch. 855, see notes following V.A.T.S. Probate Code, § 10B.

§ 149G. Rights and Remedies Cumulative

The rights and remedies conferred by Sections 149D, 149E, and 149F of this code are cumulative of other rights and remedies to which a person interested in the estate may be entitled under law.

Added by Acts 1999, 76th Leg., ch. 855, § 6, eff. Sept. 1, 1999.

For application provisions of Acts 1999, 76th Leg., ch. 855, see notes following V.A.T.S. Probate Code, § 10B.

§ 150. Partition and Distribution or Sale of Property Incapable of Division

If the will does not distribute the entire estate of the testator, or provide a means for partition of said estate, or if no will was probated, the independent executor may file his final account in the county court in which the will was probated, or if no will was probated, in the county court in which the order appointing the independent executor was entered, and ask for either partition and distribution of the estate or an order of sale of any portion of the estate alleged by the independent executor and found by the court to be incapable of a fair and equal partition and distribution, or both; and the same either shall be partitioned and distributed or shall be sold, or both, in the manner provided for the partition and distribution of property and the sale of property incapable of division in estates administered under the direction of the county court.

Acts 1955, 54th Leg., p. 88, ch. 55, eff. Jan. 1, 1956. Amended by Acts 1977, 65th Leg., p. 1065, ch. 390, § 7, eff. Sept. 1, 1977; Acts 1979, 66th Leg., p. 1752, ch. 713, § 20, eff. Aug. 27, 1979.

§ 151. Closing Independent Administration by Affidavit

(a) Filing of Affidavit. When all of the debts known to exist against the estate have been paid, or when they have been paid so far as the assets in the hands of the independent executor will permit, when there is no pending litigation, and when the independent executor has distributed to the persons entitled thereto all assets of the estate, if any, remaining after payment of debts, the independent executor may file with the court:

(1) a closing report verified by affidavit that shows:

(i) The property of the estate which came into the hands of the independent executor;

(ii) The debts that have been paid;

(iii) The debts, if any, still owing by the estate;

(iv) The property of the estate, if any, remaining on hand after payment of debts; and

(v) The names and residences of the persons to whom the property of the estate, if any, remaining on hand after payment of debts has been distributed; and

(2) signed receipts or other proof of delivery of property to the distributees named in the closing report if the closing report reflects that there was property remaining on hand after payment of debts.

(b) Effect of Filing the Affidavit. (1) The filing of such an affidavit and proof of delivery, if required, shall terminate the independent administration and the power and authority of the independent executor, but shall not relieve the independent executor from liability for any mismanagement of the estate or from liability for any false statements contained in the affidavit. When such an affidavit has been filed, persons dealing with properties of the estate, or with claims against the estate, shall deal directly with the distributees of the estate; and the acts of such distributees with respect to such properties or claims shall in all ways be valid and binding as regards the persons with whom they deal, notwithstanding any false statements made by the independent executor in such affidavit.

(2) If the independent executor is required to give bond, the independent executor's filing of the affidavit and proof of delivery, if required, automatically releases the sureties on the bond from all liability for the future acts of the principal.

(c) Authority to Transfer Property of a Decedent After Filing the Affidavit. An independent executor's affidavit closing the independent administration shall constitute sufficient legal authority to all persons owing any money, having custody of any property, or acting as registrar or transfer agent or trustee of any evidence of interest, indebtedness, property, or right that belongs to the estate, for payment or transfer without additional administration to the persons described in the will as entitled to receive the particular asset or who as heirs at law are entitled to receive the asset. The persons described in the will as entitled to receive the particular asset or the heirs at law entitled to receive the asset may enforce their right to the payment or transfer by suit.

(d) Delivery Subject to Receipt or Proof of Delivery. An independent executor may not be required to deliver tangible or intangible personal property to a distributee unless the independent executor shall receive, at or before the time of delivery of the property, a signed receipt or other proof of delivery of the property to the distributee. An independent executor shall not require a waiver or release from the distributee as a condition of delivery of property to a distributee.

(e) Community Administration. A community administrator may use the procedures in this section to terminate community administration under Section 175 of this code. The independent executor's filing of the affidavit releases the sureties on the community administrator's bond from all liability for the future acts of the principal.

Acts 1955, 54th Leg., p. 88, ch. 55, eff. Jan. 1, 1956. Amended by Acts 1979, 66th Leg., p. 1752, ch. 713, § 21, eff. Aug. 27, 1979; Acts 1991, 72nd Leg., ch. 895, § 11, eff. Sept. 1, 1991; Acts 1995, 74th Leg., ch. 642, § 5, eff. Sept. 1, 1995.

For application provisions of the 1995 amendatory act, see notes following V.A.T.S. Probate Code, § 137.

§ 152. Closing Independent Administration Upon Application by Distributee

(a) At any time after an estate has been fully administered and there is no further need for an independent administration of such estate, any distributee may file an application to close the administration; and, after citation upon the independent executor, and upon hearing, the court may enter an order:

(1) requiring the independent executor to file a verified report meeting the requirements of Section 151(a) of this code;

(2) closing the administration;

(3) terminating the power of the independent executor to act as such; and

(4) releasing the sureties on any bond the independent executor was required to give from all liability for the future acts of the principal.

(b) The order of the court closing the independent administration shall constitute sufficient legal authority to all persons owing any money, having custody of any property, or acting as registrar or transfer agent or trustee of any evidence of interest, indebtedness, property, or right that belongs to the estate, for payment or transfer without additional administration to the persons described in the will as entitled to receive the particular asset or who as heirs at law are entitled to receive the asset. The persons described in the will as entitled to receive the particular asset or the heirs at law entitled to receive the asset may enforce their right to the payment or transfer by suit.

Acts 1955, 54th Leg., p. 88, ch. 55, eff. Jan. 1, 1956. Amended by Acts 1979, 66th Leg., p. 1752, ch. 713, § 22, eff. Aug. 27, 1979; Acts 1991, 72nd Leg., ch. 895, § 12, eff. Sept. 1, 1991.

§ 153. Issuance of Letters

At any time before the authority of an independent executor has been terminated in the manner set forth in the preceding Sections, the clerk shall issue such number of letters testamentary as the independent executor shall request.

Acts 1955, 54th Leg., p. 88, ch. 55, eff. Jan. 1, 1956.

§ 154. Powers of an Administrator Who Succeeds an Independent Executor

(a) Grant of Powers by Court. Whenever a person has died, or shall die, testate, owning property in Texas, and such person's will has been or shall be admitted to probate by the proper court, and such probated will names an independent executor or executors, or trustees acting in the capacity of independent executors, to execute the terms and provisions of said will, and such will grants to such independent executor, or executors, or trustees acting in the capacity of independent executors, the power to raise or borrow money and to mortgage, and such independent executor, or executors, or trustees, have died or shall die, resign, fail to qualify, or be removed from office, leaving unexecuted parts or portions of the will of the testator, and an administrator with the will annexed is appointed by the court having jurisdiction of the estate, and an administrator's bond is filed and approved by the court, then in all such cases, the court may, in addition to the powers conferred upon such administrator under other provisions of the laws of Texas, authorize, direct, and empower such administrator to do and perform the acts and deeds, clothed with the rights, powers, authorities, and privileges, and subject to the limitations, set forth in the subsequent portions of this Section.

(b) Power to Borrow Money and Mortgage or Pledge Property. The court, upon application, citation, and hearing, may, by its order, authorize, direct, and empower such administrator to raise or borrow such sums of money and incur such obligations and debts as the court shall, in its said order, direct, and to renew and extend same from time to time, as the court, upon application and order, shall provide; and, if authorized by the court's order, to secure such loans, obligations, and debts, by pledge or mortgage upon property or assets of the estate, real, personal, or mixed, upon such terms and conditions, and for such duration of time, as the court shall deem to be to the best interest of the estate, and by its order shall prescribe; and all such loans, obligations, debts, pledges, and mortgages shall be valid and enforceable against the estate and against such administrator in his official capacity.

(c) Powers Limited to Those Granted by the Will. The court may order and authorize such administrator to have and exercise the powers and privileges set forth in the preceding Subsections hereof only to the extent that same are granted to or possessed by the independent executor, or executors, or trustees acting in the capacity of independent executors, under the terms of the probated will of such deceased person, and then only in such cases as it appears, at the hearing of the application, that at the time of the appointment of such administrator, there are outstanding and unpaid obligations and debts of the estate, or of the independent executor, or executors, or trustees, chargeable against the estate, or unpaid expenses of administration, or when the court appointing such administrator orders the business of such estate to be carried on and it becomes necessary, from time to time, under orders of the court, for such administrator to borrow money and incur obligations and indebtedness in order to protect and preserve the estate.

(d) Powers Other Than Those Relating to Borrowing Money and Mortgaging or Pledging Property. The court, in addition, may, upon application, citation, and hearing, order, authorize and empower such administrator to assume, exercise, and discharge, under the orders and directions of said court, made from time to time, all or such part of the rights, powers, and authorities vested in and delegated to, or possessed by, the independent executor, or executors, or trustees acting in the capacity of independent executors, under the terms of the will of such deceased person, as the court finds to be to the best interest of the estate and shall, from time to time, order and direct.

(e) Application for Grant of Powers. The granting to such administrator by the court of some, or all, of the powers and authorities set forth in this Section shall be upon application filed by such administrator with the county clerk, setting forth such facts as, in the judgment of the administrator, require the granting of the power or authority requested.

(f) Citation. Upon the filing of such application, the clerk shall issue citation to all persons interested in the estate, stating the nature of the application, and requiring such persons to appear on the return day named in such citation and show cause why such application should not be granted, should they choose to do so. Such citation shall be served by posting.

(g) Hearing and Order. The court shall hear such application and evidence thereon, upon the return day named in the citation, or thereafter, and, if satisfied a necessity exists and that it would be to the best interest of the estate to grant said application in whole or in part, the court shall so order; otherwise, the court shall refuse said application.

Acts 1955, 54th Leg., p. 88, ch. 55, eff. Jan. 1, 1956.

§ 154A. Court-Appointed Successor Independent Executor

(a) If the will of a person who dies testate names an independent executor who, having qualified, fails for any reason to continue to serve, or is removed for cause by the court, and the will does not name a successor independent executor or if each successor executor named in the will fails for any reason to qualify as executor or indicates by affidavit filed with the application for an order continuing independent administration his inability or unwillingness to serve as successor independent executor, all of the distributees of the decedent as of the filing of the application for an order continuing independent administration may apply to the county court for the appointment of a qualified person, firm, or corporation to serve as successor independent executor. If the county court finds that continued administration of the estate is necessary, the county court shall enter an order continuing independent administration and appointing the person, firm, or corporation designated in the application as successor independent executor, unless the county court finds that it would not be in the best interest of the estate to do so. Such successor shall serve with all of the powers and privileges granted to his predecessor independent executor.

(b) If a distributee described in this section is an incapacitated person, the guardian of the person of the distributee may sign the application on behalf of the distributee. If the county court finds that either the continuing of independent administration or the appointment of the person, firm, or corporation designated in the application as successor independent executor would not be in the best interest of the incapacitated person, then, notwithstanding anything to the contrary in Subsection (a) of this section, the county court shall not enter an order continuing independent administration of the estate. If the distributee is an incapacitated person and has no guardian of the person, the court may appoint a guardian ad litem to make application on behalf of the incapacitated person if the county court considers such an appointment necessary to protect the interest of such distributee.

(c) If a trust is created in the decedent's will, the person or class of persons first eligible to receive the income from the trust, determined as if the trust were to be in existence on the date of the filing of the application for an order continuing independent administration, shall, for the purposes of this section, be deemed to be the distributee or distributees on behalf of such trust, and any other trust or trusts coming into existence upon the termination of such trust, and are authorized to apply for an order continuing independent administration on behalf of the trust without the consent or agreement of the trustee or any other beneficiary of the trust, or the trustee or any beneficiary of any other trust which may come into existence upon the termination of such trust.

(d) If a life estate is created either in the decedent's will or by law, and if a life tenant is living at the time of the filing of the application for an order continuing independent administration, then the life tenant or life tenants, determined as if the life estate were to commence on the date of the filing of the application for an order continuing independent administration, shall, for the purposes of this section, be deemed to the distributee or distributees on behalf of the entire estate created, and are authorized to apply for an order continuing independent administration on behalf of the estate without the consent or approval of any remainderman.

(e) If a decedent's will contains a provision that a distributee must survive the decedent by a prescribed period of time in order to take under the decedent's will, for the purposes of determining who shall be the distributee under this section, it shall be presumed that the distributees living at the time of the filing of the application for an order continuing independent administration of the decedent's estate survived the decedent for the prescribed period.

(f) In the case of all decedents, whether dying testate or intestate, for the purposes of determining who shall be the distributees under this section, it shall be presumed that no distributee living at the time the application for an order continuing independent administration of the decedent's estate is filed shall subsequently disclaim any portion of such distributee's interest in the decedent's estate.

(g) If a distributee of a decedent's estate should die, and if by virtue of such distributee's death such distributee's share of the decedent's estate shall become payable to such distributee's estate, then the deceased distributee's personal representative may sign the application for an order continuing independent administration of the decedent's estate under this section.

(h) If a successor independent executor is appointed pursuant to this section, then, unless the county court shall waive bond on application for waiver, the successor independent executor shall be required to enter into bond payable to and to be approved by the judge and his or her successors in a sum that is found by the judge to be adequate under all circumstances, or a bond with one surety in a sum that is found by the judge to be adequate under all circumstances, if the surety is an authorized corporate surety.

(i) Absent proof of fraud or collusion on the part of a judge, the judge may not be held civilly liable for the commission of misdeeds or the omission of any required act of any person, firm, or corporation designated as a successor independent executor under this section. Section 36 of this code does not apply to an appointment of a successor independent executor under this section.

Added by Acts 1977, 65th Leg., p. 1066, ch. 390, § 8, eff. Sept. 1, 1977. Amended by Acts 1979, 66th Leg., p. 1753, ch. 713, § 23, eff. Aug. 27, 1979; Acts 1993, 73rd Leg., ch. 846, § 16, eff. Sept. 1, 1993; Acts 1995, 74th Leg., ch. 1039, § 11, eff. Sept. 1, 1995.

PART 5. ADMINISTRATION OF COMMUNITY PROPERTY

§ 155. Administration of Community Property

When a husband or wife dies intestate and the community property passes to the survivor, no administration thereon, community or otherwise, shall be necessary.

Acts 1955, 54th Leg., p. 88, ch. 55, eff. Jan. 1, 1956. Amended by Acts 1971, 62nd Leg., p. 980, ch. 173, § 11, eff. Jan. 1, 1972.

§ 156. Liability of Community Property for Debts

The community property subject to the sole or joint management, control, and disposition of a spouse during marriage continues to be subject to the liabilities of that spouse upon death. In addition, the interest that the deceased spouse owned in any other nonexempt community property passes to his or her heirs or devisees charged with the debts which were enforceable against such deceased spouse prior to his or her death. In the administration of community estates, the survivor or personal representative shall keep a separate, distinct account of all community debts allowed or paid in the administration and settlement of such estate.

Acts 1955, 54th Leg., p. 88, ch. 55, eff. Jan. 1, 1956. Amended by Acts 1971, 62nd Leg., p. 980, ch. 173, § 11, eff. Jan. 1, 1972.

§ 157. Repealed by Acts 1993, 73rd Leg., ch. 957, § 75(1), eff. Sept. 1, 1993; Acts 1995, 74th Leg., ch. 1039, § 73(1), eff. Sept. 1, 1995

Acts 1993, 73rd Leg., ch. 957, repealing this section, enacted Chapter XIII, Guardianship, of the Probate Code.

§ 158. Repealed by Acts 1993, 73rd Leg., ch. 957, § 75(1), eff. Sept. 1, 1993

§ 159. Repealed by Acts 1995, 74th Leg., ch. 1039, § 73(1), eff. Sept. 1, 1995

§ 160. Powers of Surviving Spouse When No Administration is Pending

(a) When no one has qualified as executor or administrator of the estate of a deceased spouse, the surviving spouse, whether the husband or wife, as the surviving partner of the marital partnership, without qualifying as community administrator as hereinafter provided, has power to sue and be sued for the recovery of community property; to sell, mortgage, lease, and otherwise dispose of community property for the purpose of paying community debts; to collect claims due to the community estate; and has such other powers as shall be necessary to preserve the community property, discharge community obligations, and wind up community affairs.

(b) If an affidavit stating that the affiant is the surviving spouse and that no one has qualified as executor or administrator of the estate of the deceased spouse is furnished to a person owing money to the community estate for current wages at the time of the death of the deceased spouse, the person making payment or delivering to the affiant the deceased spouse's final paycheck for wages, including unpaid sick pay or vacation pay, if any, is released from liability to the same extent as if the payment or delivery was made to a personal representative of the deceased spouse. The person is not required to inquire into the truth of the affidavit. The affiant to whom the payment or delivery is made is answerable to any person having a prior right and is accountable to any personal representative who is appointed. The affiant is liable for any damage or loss to any person that arises from a payment or delivery made in reliance on the affidavit.

(c) This section does not affect the disposition of the property of the deceased spouse.

Acts 1955, 54th Leg., p. 88, ch. 55, eff. Jan. 1, 1956. Amended by Acts 1993, 73rd Leg., ch. 846, § 17, eff. Sept. 1, 1993.

§ 161. Community Administration

Whenever an interest in community property passes to someone other than the surviving spouse, the surviving spouse may qualify as community administrator in the manner hereinafter provided if

(a) The deceased spouse failed to name an executor in his will, or

(b) If the executor named in the will of the deceased spouse is for any reason unable or unwilling to qualify as such, or

(c) If the deceased spouse died intestate.

Acts 1955, 54th Leg., p. 88, ch. 55, eff. Jan. 1, 1956. Amended by Acts 1971, 62nd Leg., p. 980, ch. 173, § 11, eff. Jan. 1, 1972.

§ 162. Application for Community Administration

A surviving spouse who desires to qualify as a community administrator shall, within four years after the death of the other spouse, file a written application in the court having venue over the estate of the deceased spouse, stating:

(a) That the other spouse is dead, setting forth the time and place of such death; and

(b) The name and residence of each person to whom an interest in community property has passed by the will of the decedent or by intestacy; and

(c) That there is a community estate between the deceased spouse and the applicant, and the facts that authorize the applicant to be appointed as community administrator; and

(d) That, by virtue of facts set forth in the application, the court has venue over the estate of the deceased spouse; and

(e) If the applicant desires that appraisers be appointed, that not less than one nor more than three appraisers should be appointed to appraise such estate.

Acts 1955, 54th Leg., p. 88, ch. 55, eff. Jan. 1, 1956. Amended by Acts 1971, 62nd Leg., p. 980, ch. 173, § 11, eff. Jan. 1, 1972.

§ 163. Appointment of Appraisers

If the appointment of appraisers is requested by the applicant, or by any interested person, the judge shall, without notice or citation, enter an order appointing appraisers to appraise such estate as in other administrations.

Acts 1955, 54th Leg., p. 88, ch. 55, eff. Jan. 1, 1956. Amended by Acts 1971, 62nd Leg., p. 980, ch. 173, § 11, eff. Jan. 1, 1972.

§ 164. Inventory, Appraisement, and List of Claims

The surviving spouse, with the assistance of the appraisers, if any be appointed, shall make out a full, fair, and complete inventory, appraisement, and list of claims of the community estate as in other administrations, shall attach thereto a list of all indebtedness owing by said community estate to other parties, giving the amount of each debt and the name of the party or parties to whom it is owing, and his or their postoffice address, and shall return same to the court within ninety (90) days after the date of the order appointing appraisers, if any be appointed, unless a longer time shall be granted by the court. If no appraisers be appointed, such return shall be made within ninety (90) days after the date of the application for community administration, unless a longer time shall be granted by the court. In either event, the court may, for good cause shown, require the filing of the inventory and appraisement within a shorter period of time. Such inventory, list of claims, and list of indebtedness of such community estate shall be sworn to by said surviving spouse, and said inventory, appraisement, and list of claims owing said community estate shall be sworn to by said appraisers, if any appraisers have been appointed.

Acts 1955, 54th Leg., p. 88, ch. 55, eff. Jan. 1, 1956. Amended by Acts 1971, 62nd Leg., p. 980, ch. 173, § 11, eff. Jan. 1, 1972.

§ 165. Bond of Community Administrator

The community administrator shall at the time the inventory, appraisement, and list of claims are returned, present to the court a bond with two or more good and sufficient sureties, payable to and to be approved by the judge and his successors in a sum as is found by the judge to be adequate under all the circumstances, or a bond with one surety in a sum as is found by the judge to be adequate under all the circumstances, if the surety is an authorized corporate surety. The condition of the bond shall be that such surviving spouse will faithfully administer such community estate and will, after the payment of debts with which such property is properly chargeable, deliver to such person or persons as shall be entitled to receive the same the portion of the community estate devised or bequeathed to them under the terms of the will of the deceased spouse, or which passes to them under the laws of descent and distribution. Either spouse may by will apportion community indebtedness as between the devisees and legatees of such testator and the surviving spouse, but this shall not include the power to charge the community share of the surviving spouse with more than the portion of the community debts for which it would otherwise be liable.

Acts 1955, 54th Leg., p. 88, ch. 55, eff. Jan. 1, 1956. Amended by Acts 1965, 59th Leg., p. 717, ch. 339, § 1, eff. June 9, 1965; Acts 1971, 62nd Leg., p. 982, ch. 173, § 12, eff. Jan. 1, 1972.

§ 166. Order of the Court

When such inventory, appraisement, list of claims, and bond are returned to the judge, he shall examine the same and approve or disapprove them by an order to that effect and, when approved, the order approving them shall also authorize the survivor as community administrator to control, manage, and dispose of the community property in accordance with the provisions of this Code.

Acts 1955, 54th Leg., p. 88, ch. 55, eff. Jan. 1, 1956.

§ 167. Powers of Community Administrator

When the order mentioned in the preceding section has been entered, the survivor, without any further action in the court, shall have the power to control, manage, and dispose of the community property, as provided in this Code, as fully and completely as if he or she were the sole owner thereof, and to sue and be sued with regard to the same; and a certified copy of the order of the court shall be evidence of the qualification and right of such survivor. After paying community debts outstanding at the death of the deceased spouse, the qualified community administrator may carry on as statutory trustee for the owners of the community estate, investing and reinvesting the funds of the estate and continuing the operation of community enterprises until the termination of the trust as provided in this Code. The qualified community administrator is not entitled to mortgage community property to secure debts incurred for his individual benefit, or otherwise to appropriate the community estate to his individual benefit; but he may transfer or encumber his individual interest in the community estate.

Acts 1955, 54th Leg., p. 88, ch. 55, eff. Jan. 1, 1956. Amended by Acts 1971, 62nd Leg., p. 982, ch. 173, § 13, eff. Jan. 1, 1972.

§ 168. Accounting by Survivor

The survivor, whether qualified as community administrator or not, shall keep a fair and full account and statement of all community debts and expenses paid by him, and of the disposition made of the community property; and, upon final partition of such estate, shall deliver to the heirs, devisees or legatees of the deceased spouse their interest in such estate, and the increase and profits of the same, after deducting therefrom the proportion of the community debts chargeable thereto, unavoidable losses, necessary and reasonable expenses, and a reasonable commission for the management of the same. Neither the survivor nor his bondsmen shall be liable for losses sustained by the estate, except when the survivor has been guilty of gross negligence or bad faith.

Acts 1955, 54th Leg., p. 88, ch. 55, eff. Jan. 1, 1956. Amended by Acts 1971, 62nd Leg., p. 982, ch. 173, § 13, eff. Jan. 1, 1972.

§ 169. Payment of Debts

The community administrator shall pay all just and legal community debts within the time, and according to the classification, and in the order prescribed for the payment of debts in other administrations. Where there is a deficiency of assets to pay all claims of the same class, such claims shall be paid pro rata.

Acts 1955, 54th Leg., p. 88, ch. 55, eff. Jan. 1, 1956.

§ 170. New Appraisement or New Bond

Any person interested in a community estate may cause a new appraisement to be made of the same, or may cause a new bond to be required of the survivor, for the same causes and in like manner as provided in other administrations.

Acts 1955, 54th Leg., p. 88, ch. 55, eff. Jan. 1, 1956.

§ 171. Creditor May Require Exhibit

Any creditor of the community estate whose claim has not been paid in full, after the lapse of one year from the filing of the inventory, appraisement, list of claims, and bond by the survivor, may by written application to the court cause such survivor to be cited by personal service to appear and make an exhibit to the court in writing and under oath, showing fully and specifically:

(a) The debts that have been presented to him against such community estate and their class; and

(b) The debts that have been paid by him and those that remain unpaid, and the class of each; and

(c) The property that has been disposed of by him, and the amount received therefor; and

(d) The property remaining on hand; and

(e) An account of losses, expenses, and commissions.

Acts 1955, 54th Leg., p. 88, ch. 55, eff. Jan. 1, 1956.

§ 172. Action of Court Upon Exhibit

When such exhibit has been returned to the court and filed, the court shall examine the same and hear exceptions and objections thereto, and evidence in support of or against same. Should it appear to the court from such exhibit or from other evidence that such community estate has been improperly administered, or that there are still assets of said estate that are liable for the payment of the applicant's debt, or any part thereof, the court shall enter an order requiring the survivor to pay such debt, or a part thereof, as the evidence may show to be proper; and, should he neglect the same for thirty days after the date of such order, the following proceedings shall be had:

(a) If said debt be for the amount of One Thousand Dollars or less, exclusive of interest, the court shall order citation to issue for the sureties upon the bond of such survivor, citing them by personal service to appear before such court at a regular term thereof, and show cause why judgment should not be rendered against them for such debt and costs, which citation shall be returnable as in other civil suits; and the proceedings in such case shall be the same as in other civil suits in said court.

(b) If the amount due and payable to such creditor exceeds One Thousand Dollars, exclusive of interest, the creditor may have his action against such survivor and the sureties upon his bond in the District Court of the county where the survivor's bond is filed.

Acts 1955, 54th Leg., p. 88, ch. 55, eff. Jan. 1, 1956.

§ 173. Approval of Exhibit

If, after examining the exhibit and after receiving evidence in support of or against the same, the court is satisfied that the estate has been fairly administered in conformity to law, and that there remains no further property of such estate for the payment of debts, the court shall enter an order approving such exhibit and directing the same to be recorded, and shall also in such order declare the community administration closed.

Acts 1955, 54th Leg., p. 88, ch. 55, eff. Jan. 1, 1956.

§ 174. Failure to File Exhibit

Should the survivor, after being duly cited, fail to file an exhibit as required, the court shall proceed as if the creditor's right to the payment of his claim had been fully established.

Acts 1955, 54th Leg., p. 88, ch. 55, eff. Jan. 1, 1956.

§ 175. Termination of Community Administration

After the lapse of twelve months from the filing of the bond of the survivor, the community administration may be terminated whenever termination is desired by either the survivor or the persons entitled to the share of the deceased spouse, or to any portion thereof. Partition and distribution of the community estate may be had and the administration closed either by proceedings as in other independent administration or by proceedings in the appropriate District Court. When the community administration is closed, the community administrator shall be discharged and his bondsmen released from further liability.

Acts 1955, 54th Leg., p. 88, ch. 55, eff. Jan. 1, 1956.

§ 176. Remarriage of Surviving Spouse

The remarriage of a surviving spouse shall not terminate the surviving spouse's powers or liabilities as a qualified community administrator or administratrix; nor shall it terminate his or her powers as a surviving partner.

Acts 1955, 54th Leg., p. 88, ch. 55, eff. Jan. 1, 1956. Amended by Acts 1979, 66th Leg., p. 39, ch. 24, § 23, eff. Aug. 27, 1979.

§ 177. Distribution of Powers Among Personal Representatives and Surviving Spouse

(a) When Community Administrator Has Qualified. The qualified community administrator is entitled to administer the entire community estate, including the part which was by law under the management of the deceased spouse during the continuance of the marriage.

(b) When No Community Administrator Has Qualified. When an executor of the estate of a deceased spouse has duly qualified, such executor is authorized to administer, not only the separate property of the deceased spouse, but also the community property which was by law under the management of the deceased spouse during the continuance of the marriage and all of the community property that was by law under the joint control of the spouses during the continuance of the marriage. The surviving spouse, as surviving partner of the marital partnership, is entitled to retain possession and control of all community property which was legally under the sole management of the surviving spouse during the continuance of the marriage and to exercise over that property all the powers elsewhere in this part of this Code authorized to be exercised by the surviving spouse when there is no administration pending on the estate of the deceased spouse. The surviving spouse may by written instrument filed with the clerk waive any right to exercise powers as community survivor, and in such event the executor or administrator of the deceased spouse shall be authorized to administer upon the entire community estate.

Acts 1955, 54th Leg., p. 88, ch. 55, eff. Jan. 1, 1956. Amended by Acts 1971, 62nd Leg., p. 982, ch. 173, § 13, eff. Jan. 1, 1972.

CHAPTER VII. EXECUTORS AND ADMINISTRATORS

PART 1. APPOINTMENT AND ISSUANCE OF LETTERS

Section

PART 2. OATHS AND BONDS OF PERSONAL REPRESENTATIVES

PART 1. APPOINTMENT AND ISSUANCE OF LETTERS

§ 178. When Letters Testamentary or of Administration Shall Be Granted

(a) Letters Testamentary. When a will has been probated, the court shall, within twenty days thereafter, grant letters testamentary, if permitted by law, to the executor or executors appointed by such will, if any there be, or to such of them as are not disqualified, and are willing to accept the trust and qualify according to law.

(b) Letters of Administration. When a person shall die intestate, or where no executor is named in a will, or where the executor is dead or shall fail or neglect to accept and qualify within twenty days after the probate of the will, or shall neglect for a period of thirty days after the death of the testator to present the will for probate, then administration of the estate of such intestate, or administration with the will annexed of the estate of such testator, shall be granted, should administration appear to be necessary. No administration of any estate shall be granted unless there exists a necessity therefor, such necessity to be determined by the court hearing the application. Such necessity shall be deemed to exist if two or more debts exist against the estate, or if or when it is desired to have the county court partition the estate among the distributees, but mention of these two instances of necessity for administration shall not prevent the court from finding other instances of necessity upon proof before it.

(c) Failure to Issue Letters Within Prescribed Time. Failure of a court to issue letters testamentary within the twenty day period prescribed by this Section shall not affect the validity of any letters testamentary which are issued subsequent to such period, in accordance with law.

Acts 1955, 54th Leg., p. 88, ch. 55, eff. Jan. 1, 1956.

§ 179. Opposition to Grant of Letters of Administration

When application is made for letters of administration, any person may at any time before the application is granted, file his opposition thereto in writing, and may apply for the grant of letters to himself or to any other person; and, upon the trial, the court shall grant letters to the person that may seem best entitled to them, having regard to applicable provisions of this Code, without further notice than that of the original application.

Acts 1955, 54th Leg., p. 88, ch. 55, eff. Jan. 1, 1956.

§ 180. Effect of Finding That No Necessity for Administration Exists

When application is filed for letters of administration and the court finds that there exists no necessity for administration of the estate, the court shall recite in its order refusing the application that no necessity for administration exists. An order of the court containing such recital shall constitute sufficient legal authority to all persons owing any money, having custody of any property, or acting as registrar or transfer agent of any evidence of interest, indebtedness, property, or right belonging to the estate, and to persons purchasing or otherwise dealing with the estate, for payment or transfer to the distributees of the decedent, and such distributees shall be entitled to enforce their right to such payment or transfer by suit.

Acts 1955, 54th Leg., p. 88, ch. 55, eff. Jan. 1, 1956.

§ 181. Orders Granting Letters Testamentary or of Administration

When letters testamentary or of administration are granted, the court shall make an order to that effect, which shall specify:

(a) The name of the testator or intestate; and

(b) The name of the person to whom the grant of letters is made; and

(c) If bond is required, the amount thereof; and

(d) If any interested person shall apply to the court for the appointment of an appraiser or appraisers, or if the court deems an appraisal necessary, the name of not less than one nor more than three disinterested persons appointed to appraise the estate and return such appraisement to the court; and

(e) That the clerk shall issue letters in accordance with said order when the person to whom said letters are granted shall have qualified according to law.

Acts 1955, 54th Leg., p. 88, ch. 55, eff. Jan. 1, 1956. Amended by Acts 1967, 60th Leg., p. 1815, ch. 697, § 1, eff. Aug. 28, 1967; Acts 1969, 61st Leg., p. 1922, ch. 641, § 10, eff. June 12, 1969.

§ 182. When Clerk Shall Issue Letters

Whenever an executor or administrator has been qualified in the manner required by law, the clerk of the court granting the letters testamentary or of administration shall forthwith issue and deliver the letters to such executor or administrator. When two or more persons qualify as executors or administrators, letters shall be issued to each of them so qualifying.

Acts 1955, 54th Leg., p. 88, ch. 55, eff. Jan. 1, 1956.

§ 183. What Constitutes Letters

Letters testamentary or of administration shall be a certificate of the clerk of the court granting the same, attested by the seal of such court, and stating that the executor or administrator, as the case may be, has duly qualified as such as the law requires, the date of such qualification, and the name of the deceased.

Acts 1955, 54th Leg., p. 88, ch. 55, eff. Jan. 1, 1956.

§§ 184, 185. Repealed by Acts 1993, 73rd Leg., ch. 957, § 75(1), eff. Sept. 1, 1993

Acts 1993, 73rd Leg., ch. 957, repealing these sections, enacted Chapter XIII, Guardianship, of the Probate Code.

The amendment of § 185 by Acts 1993, 73rd Leg., ch. 905, § 10 failed to take effect under § 19(a), which provided that the amendment was not to take effect if both S.B. No. 236 (ch. 905) and H.B. No. 2685 (ch. 957) were enacted and became law.

§ 186. Letters or Certificate Made Evidence

Letters testamentary or of administration or a certificate of the clerk of the court which granted the same, under the seal of such court, that said letters have been issued, shall be sufficient evidence of the appointment and qualification of the personal representative of an estate and of the date of qualification.

Acts 1955, 54th Leg., p. 88, ch. 55, eff. Jan. 1, 1956. Amended by Acts 1993, 73rd Leg., ch. 957, § 28, eff. Sept. 1, 1993.

§ 187. Issuance of Other Letters

When letters have been destroyed or lost, the clerk shall issue other letters in their stead, which shall have the same force and effect as the original letters. The clerk shall also issue any number of letters as and when requested by the person or persons who hold such letters.

Acts 1955, 54th Leg., p. 88, ch. 55, eff. Jan. 1, 1956.

§ 188. Rights of Third Persons Dealing With Executors or Administrators

When an executor or administrator, legally qualified as such, has performed any acts as such executor or administrator in conformity with his authority and the law, such acts shall continue to be valid to all intents and purposes, so far as regards the rights of innocent purchasers of any of the property of the estate from such executor or administrator, for a valuable consideration, in good faith, and without notice of any illegality in the title to the same, notwithstanding such acts or the authority under which they were performed may afterward be set aside, annulled, and declared invalid.

Acts 1955, 54th Leg., p. 88, ch. 55, eff. Jan. 1, 1956.

PART 2. OATHS AND BONDS OF PERSONAL REPRESENTATIVES

§ 189. How Executors and Administrators Shall Qualify

A personal representative shall be deemed to have duly qualified when he shall have taken and filed his oath and made the required bond, had the same approved by the judge, and filed it with the clerk. In case of an executor who is not required to make bond, he shall be deemed to have duly qualified when he shall have taken and filed his oath required by law.

Acts 1955, 54th Leg., p. 88, ch. 55, eff. Jan. 1, 1956. Amended by Acts 1993, 73rd Leg., ch. 957, § 29, eff. Sept. 1, 1993.

§ 190. Oaths of Executors and Administrators

(a) Executor, or Administrator With Will Annexed. Before the issuance of letters testamentary or of administration with the will annexed, the person named as executor, or appointed administrator with the will annexed, shall take and subscribe an oath in form substantially as follows: "I do solemnly swear that the writing which has been offered for probate is the last will of ______, so far as I know or believe, and that I will well and truly perform all the duties of executor of said will (or of administrator with the will annexed, as the case may be) of the estate of said ______."

(b) Administrator. Before the issuance of letters of administration, the person appointed administrator shall take and subscribe an oath in form substantially as follows: "I do solemnly swear that ______, deceased, died without leaving any lawful will (or that the named executor in any such will is dead or has failed or neglected to offer the same for probate, or to accept and qualify as executor, within the time required, as the case may be), so far as I know or believe, and that I will well and truly perform all the duties of administrator of the estate of said deceased."

(c) Temporary Administrator. Before the issuance of temporary letters of administration, the person appointed temporary administrator shall take and subscribe an oath in form substantially as follows: "I do solemnly swear that I will well and truly perform the duties of temporary administrator of the estate of ______, deceased, in accordance with the law, and with the order of the court appointing me such administrator."

(d) Filing and Recording of Oaths. All such oaths may be taken before any officer authorized to administer oaths, and shall be filed with the clerk of the court granting the letters, and shall be recorded in the minutes of such court.

Acts 1955, 54th Leg., p. 88, ch. 55, eff. Jan. 1, 1956.

§ 191. Repealed by Acts 1993, 73rd Leg., ch. 957, § 75(1), eff. Sept. 1, 1993

Acts 1993, 73rd Leg., ch. 957, repealing this section, enacted Chapter XIII, Guardianship, of the Probate Code.

§ 192. Time for Taking Oath and Giving Bond

The oath of a personal representative may be taken and subscribed, or his bond may be given and approved, at any time before the expiration of twenty days after the date of the order granting letters testamentary or of administration, as the case may be, or before such letters shall have been revoked for a failure to qualify within the time allowed. All such oaths may be taken before any person authorized to administer oaths under the laws of this State.

Acts 1955, 54th Leg., p. 88, ch. 55, eff. Jan. 1, 1956. Amended by Acts 1993, 73rd Leg., ch. 957, § 30, eff. Sept. 1, 1993.

§ 193. Repealed by Acts 1993, 73rd Leg., ch. 957, § 75(1), eff. Sept. 1, 1993

Acts 1993, 73rd Leg., ch. 957, repealing this section, enacted Chapter XIII, Guardianship, of the Probate Code.

§ 194. Bonds of Personal Representatives of Estates

Except when bond is not required under the provisions of this Code, before the issuance of letters testamentary or of administration, the recipient of letters shall enter into bond conditioned as required by law, payable to the county judge or probate judge of the county in which the probate proceedings are pending and to his successors in office. Such bonds shall bear the written approval of either of such judges in his official capacity, and shall be executed and approved in accordance with the following rules:

1. **Court to Fix Penalty.** The penalty of the bond shall be fixed by the judge, in an amount deemed sufficient to protect the estate and its creditors, as hereinafter provided.

2. **Bond to Protect Creditors Only, When.** If the person to whom letters testamentary or of administration is granted is also entitled to all of the decedent's estate, after payment of debts, the bond shall be in an amount sufficient to protect creditors only, notwithstanding the rules applicable generally to bonds of personal representatives of estates.

3. **Before Fixing Penalty, Court to Hear Evidence.** In any case where a bond is, or shall be, required of a personal representative of an estate, the court shall, before fixing the penalty of the bond, hear evidence and determine:

(a) The amount of cash on hand and where deposited, and the amount of cash estimated to be needed for administrative purposes, including operation of a business, factory, farm or ranch owned by the estate, and expenses of administration for one (1) year; and

(b) The revenue anticipated to be received in the succeeding twelve (12) months from dividends, interest, rentals, or use of real or personal property belonging to the estate and the aggregate amount of any installments or periodical payments to be collected; and

(c) The estimated value of certificates of stock, bonds, notes, or securities of the estate or ward, the name of the depository, if any, in which said assets are held for safekeeping, the face value of life insurance or other policies payable to the person on whose estate administration is sought, or to such estate, and such other personal property as is owned by the estate, or by one under disability; and

(d) The estimated amount of debts due and owing by the estate or ward.

4. **Penalty of Bond.** The penalty of the bond shall be fixed by the judge in an amount equal to the estimated value of all personal property belonging to the estate, or to the person under disability, together with an additional amount to cover revenue anticipated to be derived during the succeeding twelve (12) months from interest, dividends, collectible claims, the aggregate amount of any installments or periodical payments exclusive of income derived or to be derived from federal social security payments, and rentals for use of real and personal property; provided, that the penalty of the original bond shall be reduced in proportion to the amount of cash or value of securities or other assets authorized or required to be deposited or placed in safekeeping by order of court, or voluntarily made by the representative or by his sureties as hereinafter provided in Subdivisions 6 and 7 hereof.

5. **Agreement as to Deposit of Assets.** It shall be lawful, and the court may require such action when deemed in the best interest of an estate, for a personal representative to agree with the surety or sureties, either corporate or personal, for the deposit of any or all cash, and safekeeping of other assets of the estate in a financial institution as defined by Section 201.101, Finance Code, with its main office or a branch office in this state and qualified to act as a depository in this State under the laws of this State or of the United States, if such deposit is otherwise proper, in such manner as to prevent the withdrawal of such moneys or other assets without the written consent of the surety, or an order of the court made on such notice to the surety as the court shall direct. No such agreement shall in any manner release from or change the liability of the principal or sureties as established by the terms of the bond.

6. **Deposits Authorized or Required, When.** Cash or securities or other personal assets of an estate or which an estate is entitled to receive may, and if deemed by the court in the best interest of such estate shall, be deposited or placed in safekeeping as the case may be, in one or more of the depositories hereinabove described upon such terms as shall be prescribed by the court. The court in which the proceedings are pending, upon its own motion, or upon written application of the representative or of any other person interested in the estate may authorize or require additional assets of the estate then on hand or as they accrue during the pendency of the probate proceedings to be deposited or held in safekeeping as provided above. The amount of the bond of the personal representative shall be reduced in proportion to the cash so deposited, or the value of the securities or other assets placed in safekeeping. Such cash so deposited, or securities or other assets held in safekeeping, or portions thereof, may be withdrawn from a depository only upon order of the court, and the bond of the personal representative shall be increased in proportion to the amount of cash or the value of securities or other assets so authorized to be withdrawn.

7. **Representative May Deposit Cash or Securities of His Own in Lieu of Bond.** It shall be lawful for the personal representative of an estate, in lieu of giving surety or sureties on any bond which shall be

required of him, or for the purpose of reducing the amount of such bond, to deposit out of his own assets cash or securities acceptable to the court, with a depository such as named above or with any other corporate depository approved by the court, if such deposit is otherwise proper, said deposit to be equal in amount or value to the amount of the bond required, or the bond reduced by the value of assets so deposited.

8. **Rules Applicable to Making and Handling Deposits in Lieu of Bond or to Reduce Penal Sum of Bond.** (a) A receipt for a deposit in lieu of surety or sureties shall be issued by the depository, showing the amount of cash or, if securities, the amount and description thereof, and agreeing not to disburse or deliver the same except upon receipt of a certified copy of an order of the court in which the proceedings are pending, and such receipt shall be attached to the representative's bond and be delivered to and filed by the county clerk after approval by the judge.

(b) The amount of cash or securities on deposit may be increased or decreased, by order of the court from time to time, as the interest of the estate shall require.

(c) Deposits in lieu of sureties on bonds, whether of cash or securities, may be withdrawn or released only on order of a court having jurisdiction.

(d) Creditors shall have the same rights against the representative and such deposits as are provided for recovery against sureties on a bond.

(e) The court may on its own motion, or upon written application by the representative or by any other person interested in the estate, require that adequate bond be given by the representative in lieu of such deposit, or authorize withdrawal of the deposit and substitution of a bond with sureties therefor. In either case, the representative shall file a sworn statement showing the condition of the estate, and unless the same be filed within twenty (20) days after being personally served with notice of the filing of an application by another, or entry of the court's motion, he shall be subject to removal as in other cases. The deposit may not be released or withdrawn until the court has been satisfied as to the condition of the estate, has determined the amount of bond, and has received and approved the bond.

9. **Withdrawal of Deposits When Estate Closed.** Upon the closing of an estate, any such deposit or portion thereof remaining on hand, whether of the assets of the representative, or of the assets of the estate, or of the surety, shall be released by order of court and paid over to the person or persons entitled thereto. No writ of attachment or garnishment shall lie against the deposit, except as to claims of creditors of the estate being administered, or persons interested therein, including distributees and wards, and then only in the event distribution has been ordered by the court, and to the extent only of such distribution as shall have been ordered.

10. **Who May Act as Sureties.** The surety or sureties on said bonds may be authorized corporate sureties, or personal sureties.

11. **Procedure When Bond Exceeds Fifty Thousand Dollars ($50,000).** When any such bond shall exceed Fifty Thousand Dollars ($50,000) in penal sum, the court may require that such bond be signed by two (2) or more authorized corporate sureties, or by one such surety and two (2) or more good and sufficient personal sureties. The estate shall pay the cost of a bond with corporate sureties.

12. **Qualifications of Personal Sureties.** If the sureties be natural persons, there shall not be less than two (2), each of whom shall make affidavit in the manner prescribed in this Code, and the judge shall be satisfied that he owns property within this State, over and above that exempt by law, sufficient to qualify as a surety as required by law. Except as provided by law, only one surety is required if the surety is an authorized corporate surety; provided, a personal surety, instead of making affidavit, or creating a lien on specific real estate when such is required, may, in the same manner as a personal representative, deposit his own cash or securities, in lieu of pledging real property as security, subject, so far as applicable, to the provisions covering such deposits when made by personal representatives.

13. **Bonds of Temporary Appointees.** In case of a temporary administrator, the bond shall be in such sum as the judge shall direct.

14. **Increased or Additional Bonds When Property Sold, Rented, Leased for Mineral Development, or Money Borrowed or Invested.** The provisions in this Section with respect to deposit of cash and safekeeping of securities shall cover, so far as they may be applicable, the orders to be entered by the court when real or personal property of an estate has been authorized to be sold or rented, or money borrowed thereon, or when real property, or an interest therein, has been authorized to be leased for mineral development or subjected to unitization, the general bond having been found insufficient.

Acts 1955, 54th Leg., p. 88, ch. 55, eff. Jan. 1, 1956. Amended by Acts 1957, 55th Leg., p. 53, ch. 31, § 6(b), eff. Aug. 22, 1957; Acts 1971, 62nd Leg., p. 983, ch. 173, § 14, eff. Jan. 1, 1972; Acts 1979, 66th Leg., p. 1754, ch. 713, § 25, eff. Aug. 27, 1979; Acts 1993, 73rd Leg., ch. 957, § 31, eff. Sept. 1, 1993; Acts 1999, 76th Leg., ch. 344, § 6.003, eff. Sept. 1, 1999.

§ 195. When No Bond Required

(a) By Will. Whenever any will probated in a Texas court directs that no bond or security be required of the person or persons named as executors, the court finding that such person or persons are qualified, letters testamentary shall be issued to the persons so named, without requirement of bond.

(b) Corporate Fiduciary Exempted From Bond. If a personal representative is a corporate fiduciary, as said term is defined in this Code, no bond shall be required.

Acts 1955, 54th Leg., p. 88, ch. 55, eff. Jan. 1, 1956. Amended by Acts 1995, 74th Leg., ch. 1039, § 12, eff. Sept. 1, 1995.

§ 196. Form of Bond

The following form, or the same in substance, may be used for the bonds of personal representatives:

"The State of Texas

"County of ______

"Know all men by these presents that we, A. B., as principal, and E. F., as sureties, are held and firmly bound unto the county (or probate) judge of the County of ______, and his successors in office, in the sum of ______ Dollars; conditioned that the above bound A. B., who has been appointed executor of the last will and testament of J. C., deceased (or has been appointed by the said judge of ______ County, administrator with the will annexed of the estate of J. C., deceased, or has been appointed by the said judge of ______ County, administrator of the estate of J. C., deceased, or has been appointed by the said judge of ______ County, temporary administrator of the estate of J. C., deceased, as the case may be), shall well and truly perform all of the duties required of him by law under said appointment."

Acts 1955, 54th Leg., p. 88, ch. 55, eff. Jan. 1, 1956. Amended by Acts 1993, 73rd Leg., ch. 957, § 32, eff. Sept. 1, 1993.

§ 197. Bonds to Be Filed

All bonds required by preceding provisions of this Code shall be subscribed by both principals and sureties, and, when approved by the court, be filed with the clerk.

Acts 1955, 54th Leg., p. 88, ch. 55, eff. Jan. 1, 1956.

§ 198. Bonds of Joint Representatives

When two or more persons are appointed representatives of the same estate or person and are required by the provisions of this Code or by the court to give a bond, the court may require either a separate bond from each or one joint bond from all of them.

Acts 1955, 54th Leg., p. 88, ch. 55, eff. Jan. 1, 1956.

§ 199. Bonds of Married Persons

When a married person is appointed personal representative, the person may, jointly with, or without, his or her spouse, execute such bond as the law requires; and such bond shall bind the person's separate estate, but shall bind his or her spouse only if signed by the spouse.

Acts 1955, 54th Leg., p. 88, ch. 55, eff. Jan. 1, 1956. Amended by Acts 1979, 66th Leg., p. 39, ch. 24, § 24, eff. Aug. 27, 1979.

§ 200. Bond of Married Person Under Eighteen Years of Age

When a person under eighteen years of age who is or has been married shall accept and qualify as executor or administrator, any bond required to be executed by him shall be as valid and binding for all purposes as if he were of lawful age.

Acts 1955, 54th Leg., p. 88, ch. 55, eff. Jan. 1, 1956. Amended by Acts 1975, 64th Leg., p. 105, ch. 45, § 3, eff. Sept. 1, 1975; Acts 1993, 73rd Leg., ch. 957, § 33, eff. Sept. 1, 1993.

§ 201. (a) Affidavit of Personal Surety; (b) Lien on Specific Property, When Required; (c) Subordination of Lien Authorized

(a) Affidavit of Personal Surety. Before the judge may consider a bond with personal sureties, each person offered as surety shall execute an affidavit stating the amount of his assets, reachable by creditors, of a value over and above his liabilities, the total of the worth of such sureties to be equal to at least double the amount of the bond, and such affidavit shall be presented to the judge for his consideration and, if approved, shall be attached to and form part of the bond.

(b) Lien on Specific Property, When Required. If the judge finds that the estimated value of personal property of the estate which cannot be deposited or held in safekeeping as hereinabove provided is such that personal sureties cannot be accepted without the creation of a specific lien on real property of such sureties, he shall enter an order requiring that each surety designate real property owned by him within this State subject to execution, of a value over and above all liens and unpaid taxes, equal at least to the amount of the bond, giving an adequate legal description of such property, all of which shall be incorporated in an affidavit by the surety, approved by the judge, and be attached to and form part of the bond.

If compliance with such order is not had, the judge may in his discretion require that the bond be signed by an authorized corporate surety, or by such corporate surety and two (2) or more personal sureties.

(c) Subordination of Lien Authorized. If a personal surety who has been required to create a lien on specific real estate desires to lease such property for mineral development, he may file his written application in the court in which the proceedings are pending, requesting subordination of such lien to the proposed lease, and the judge of such court may, in his discretion, enter an order granting such application. A certified copy of such order, filed and recorded in the deed records of the proper county, shall be sufficient to subordinate such lien to the rights of a lessee, in the proposed lease.

Acts 1955, 54th Leg., p. 88, ch. 55, eff. Jan. 1, 1956. Amended by Acts 1957, 55th Leg., p. 53, ch. 31, § 6(c).

§ 202. Bond as Lien on Real Property of Surety

When a personal surety has been required by the court to create a lien on specific real property as a condition of his acceptance as surety on a bond, a lien on the real property of the surety in this State which is described in the affidavit of the surety, and only upon such property, shall arise as security for the performance of the obligation of the bond. The clerk of the court shall, before letters are issued to the representative, cause to be mailed to the office of the county clerk of each county in which is located any real property as set forth in the affidavit of the surety, a statement signed by the clerk, giving a sufficient description of such real property, the name of the principal and sureties, the amount of the bond, and the name of the estate and the court in which the bond is given. The county clerk to whom such statement is sent shall record the same in the deed records of the county. All such recorded statements shall be duly indexed in such manner that the existence and character of the liens may conveniently be determined, and such recording and indexing of such statement shall constitute and be constructive notice to all persons of the existence of such lien on such real property situated in such county, effective as of date of such indexing.

Acts 1955, 54th Leg., p. 88, ch. 55, eff. Jan. 1, 1956. Amended by Acts 1957, 55th Leg., p. 53, ch. 31, § 6(d).

§ 203. When New Bond May Be Required

A personal representative may be required to give a new bond in the following cases:

(a) When the sureties upon the bond, or any one of them, shall die, remove beyond the limits of the state, or become insolvent; or

(b) When, in the opinion of the court, the sureties upon any such bond are insufficient; or

(c) When, in the opinion of the court, any such bond is defective; or

(d) When the amount of any such bond is insufficient; or

(e) When the sureties, or any one of them, petitions the court to be discharged from future liability upon such bond; or

(f) When the bond and the record thereof have been lost or destroyed.

Acts 1955, 54th Leg., p. 88, ch. 55, eff. Jan. 1, 1956.

§ 204. Demand for New Bond by Interested Person

Any person interested in an estate may, upon application in writing filed with the county clerk of the county where the probate proceedings are pending, alleging that the bond of the personal representative is insufficient or defective, or has been, together with the record thereof, lost or destroyed, cause such representative to be cited to appear and show cause why he should not give a new bond.

Acts 1955, 54th Leg., p. 88, ch. 55, eff. Jan. 1, 1956.

§ 205. Judge to Require New Bond

When it shall be known to him that any such bond is in any respect insufficient or that it has, together with the record thereof, been lost or destroyed, the judge shall without delay cause the representative to be cited to show cause why he should not give a new bond.

Acts 1955, 54th Leg., p. 88, ch. 55, eff. Jan. 1, 1956.

§ 206. Order Requiring New Bond

Upon the return of a citation ordering a personal representative to show cause why he should not give a new bond, the judge shall, on the day named therein for the hearing of the matter, proceed to inquire into the sufficiency of the reasons for requiring a new bond; and, if satisfied that a new bond should be required, he shall enter an order to that effect, stating in such order the amount of such new bond, and the time within which it shall be given, which shall not be later than twenty days from the date of such order.

Acts 1955, 54th Leg., p. 88, ch. 55, eff. Jan. 1, 1956.

§ 207. Order Suspends Powers of Personal Representative

When a personal representative is required to give a new bond, the order requiring such bond shall have the effect to suspend his powers, and he shall not thereafter pay out any money of said estate or do any other official act, except to preserve the property of the estate, until such new bond has been given and approved.

Acts 1955, 54th Leg., p. 88, ch. 55, eff. Jan. 1, 1956.

§ 208. Decrease in Amount of Bond

A personal representative required to give bond may at any time file with the clerk a written application to the court to have his bond reduced. Forthwith the clerk shall issue and cause to be posted notice to all persons interested and to the surety or sureties on the bond, apprising them of the fact and nature of the application and of the time when the judge will hear the application. The judge, in his discretion, upon the submission of proof that a smaller bond than the one in effect will be adequate to meet the requirements of the law and protect the estate, and upon the approval of an accounting filed at the time of the application, may permit the filing of a new bond in a reduced amount.

Acts 1955, 54th Leg., p. 88, ch. 55, eff. Jan. 1, 1956.

§ 209. Discharge of Sureties Upon Execution of New Bond

When a new bond has been given and approved, an order shall be entered discharging the sureties upon the former bond from all liability for the future acts of the principal.

Acts 1955, 54th Leg., p. 88, ch. 55, eff. Jan. 1, 1956.

§ 210. Release of Sureties Before Estate Fully Administered

The sureties upon the bond of a personal representative, or any one of them, may at any time file with the clerk a petition to the court in which the proceedings are pending, praying that such representative be required to give a new bond and that petitioners be discharged from all liability for the future acts of such representative; whereupon, such representative shall be cited to appear and give a new bond.

Acts 1955, 54th Leg., p. 88, ch. 55, eff. Jan. 1, 1956.

§ 211. Release of Lien Before Estate Fully Administered

If a personal surety who has given a lien on specific real property as security applies to the court to have the lien released, the court shall order the release requested, if the court is satisfied that the bond is sufficient without the lien on such property, or if sufficient other real or personal property of the surety is substituted on the same terms and conditions required for the lien which is to be released. If such personal surety who requests the release of the lien does not offer a lien on other real or personal property, and if the court is not satisfied of the sufficiency of the bond without the substitution of other property, the court shall order the personal representative to appear and give a new bond.

Acts 1955, 54th Leg., p. 88, ch. 55, eff. Jan. 1, 1956.

§ 212. Release of Recorded Lien on Surety's Property

A certified copy of the court's order describing the property, and releasing the lien, filed with the county clerk of the county where the property is located, and recorded in the deed records, shall have the effect of cancelling the lien on such property.

Acts 1955, 54th Leg., p. 88, ch. 55, eff. Jan. 1, 1956.

§ 213. Revocation of Letters for Failure to Give Bond

If at any time a personal representative fails to give bond as required by the court, within the time fixed by this Code, another person may be appointed in his stead.

Acts 1955, 54th Leg., p. 88, ch. 55, eff. Jan. 1, 1956.

§ 214. Executor Without Bond Required to Give Bond

Where no bond is required of an executor appointed by will, any person having a debt, claim, or demand against the estate, to the justice of which oath has been made by himself, his agent, or attorney, or any other person interested in such estate, whether in person or as the representative of another, may file a complaint in writing in the court where such will is probated, and the court shall thereupon cite such executor to appear and show cause why he should not be required to give bond.

Acts 1955, 54th Leg., p. 88, ch. 55, eff. Jan. 1, 1956. Amended by Acts 1993, 73rd Leg., ch. 957, § 34, eff. Sept. 1, 1993.

§ 215. Order Requiring Bond

Upon hearing such complaint, if it appears to the court that such executor is wasting, mismanaging, or misapplying such estate, and that thereby a creditor may probably lose his debt, or that thereby some person's interest in the estate may be diminished or lost, the court shall enter an order requiring such executor to give bond within ten days from the date of such order.

Acts 1955, 54th Leg., p. 88, ch. 55, eff. Jan. 1, 1956. Amended by Acts 1993, 73rd Leg., ch. 957, § 34, eff. Sept. 1, 1993.

§ 216. Bond in Such Case

Such bond shall be for an amount sufficient to protect the estate and its creditors, to be approved by, and payable to, the judge, conditioned that said executor will well and truly administer such estate, and that he will not waste, mismanage, or misapply the same.

Acts 1955, 54th Leg., p. 88, ch. 55, eff. Jan. 1, 1956. Amended by Acts 1993, 73rd Leg., ch. 957, § 34, eff. Sept. 1, 1993.

§ 217. Failure to Give Bond

Should the executor fail to give such bond within ten days after the order requiring him to do so, then if the judge does not extend the time, he shall, without citation, remove such executor and appoint some competent person in his stead who shall administer the estate according to the provisions of such will or the law, and who, before he enters upon the administration of said estate, shall take the oath required of an administrator with the will annexed, and shall give bond in the same manner and in the same amount provided in this Code for the issuance of original letters of administration.

Acts 1955, 54th Leg., p. 88, ch. 55, eff. Jan. 1, 1956. Amended by Acts 1993, 73rd Leg., ch. 957, § 34, eff. Sept. 1, 1993.

§ 218. Bonds Not Void Upon First Recovery

The bonds of personal representative shall not become void upon the first recovery, but may be put in suit and prosecuted from time to time until the whole amount thereof shall have been recovered.

Acts 1955, 54th Leg., p. 88, ch. 55, eff. Jan. 1, 1956.

§ 219. Repealed by Acts 1957, 55th Leg., p. 53, ch. 31, § 13, eff. Aug. 22, 1957

PART 3. REVOCATION OF LETTERS, DEATH, RESIGNATION, AND REMOVAL

§ 220. Appointment of Successor Representative

(a) Because of Death, Resignation or Removal. When a person duly appointed a personal representative fails to qualify, or, after qualifying, dies, resigns, or is removed, the court may, upon application appoint a successor if there be necessity therefor, and such appointment may be made prior to the filing of, or action upon, a final accounting. In case of death, the legal representatives of the deceased person shall account for, pay, and deliver to the person or persons legally entitled to receive the same, all the property of every kind belonging to the estate entrusted to his care, at such time and in such manner as the court shall order. Upon the finding that a necessity for the immediate appointment of a successor representative exists, the court may appoint such successor without citation or notice.

(b) Because of Existence of Prior Right. Where letters have been granted to one, and another whose right thereto is prior and who has not waived such right and is qualified, applies for letters, the letters previously granted shall be revoked and other letters shall be granted to the applicant.

(c) When Named Executor Becomes an Adult. If one named in a will as executor is not an adult when the will is probated and letters in any capacity have been granted to another, such nominated executor, upon proof that he has become an adult and is not otherwise disqualified, shall be entitled to have such former letters revoked and appropriate letters granted to him. And if the will names two or more persons as executor, any one or more of whom are minors when such will is probated, and letters have been issued to such only as are adults, said minor or minors, upon becoming adults, if not otherwise disqualified, shall be permitted to qualify and receive letters.

(d) Upon Return of Sick or Absent Executor. If one named in a will as executor was sick or absent from the State when the testator died, or when the will was proved, and therefore could not present the will for probate within thirty days after the testator's death, or accept and qualify as executor within twenty days after the probate of the will, he may accept and qualify as executor within sixty days after his return or recovery from sickness, upon proof to the court that he was absent or ill; and, if the letters have been issued to others, they shall be revoked.

(e) When Will Is Discovered After Administration Granted. If it is discovered after letters of administration have been issued that the deceased left a lawful will, the letters shall be revoked and proper letters issued to the person or persons entitled thereto.

(f) When Application and Service Necessary. Except when otherwise expressly provided in this Code, letters shall not be revoked and other letters granted except upon application, and after personal service of citation on the person, if living, whose letters are sought to be revoked, that he appear and show cause why such application should not be granted.

(g) Payment or Tender of Money Due During Vacancy. Money or other thing of value falling due to an estate while the office of the personal representative is vacant may be paid, delivered, or tendered to the clerk of the court for credit of the estate, and the debtor, obligor, or payor shall thereby be discharged of the obligation for all purposes to the extent and purpose of such payment or tender. If the clerk accepts such payment or tender, he shall issue a proper receipt therefor.

Acts 1955, 54th Leg., p. 88, ch. 55, eff. Jan. 1, 1956. Amended by Acts 1969, 61st Leg., p. 1922, ch. 641, § 11, eff. June 12, 1969; Acts 1993, 73rd Leg., ch. 957, § 35, eff. Sept. 1, 1993.

§ 221. Resignation

(a) Application to Resign. A personal representative who wishes to resign his trust shall file with the clerk his written application to the court to that effect, accompanied by a full and complete exhibit and final account, duly verified, showing the true condition of the estate entrusted to his care.

(b) Successor Representatives. If the necessity exists, the court may immediately accept a resignation and appoint a successor, but shall not discharge the person resigning, or release him or the sureties on his bond until final order or judgment shall have been rendered on his final account.

(c) Citation. Upon the filing of an application to resign, supported by exhibit and final account, the clerk shall call the application to the attention of the judge, who shall set a date for a hearing upon the matter. The clerk shall then issue a citation to all interested persons, showing that proper application has been filed, and the time and place set for hearing, at which time said persons may appear and contest the exhibit and account. The citation shall be posted, unless the court directs that it be published.

(d) Hearing. At the time set for hearing, unless it has been continued by the court, if the court finds that citation has been duly issued and served, he shall proceed to examine such exhibit and account, and hear all evidence for and against the same, and shall, if necessary, restate, and audit and settle the same. If the court is satisfied that the matters entrusted to the applicant have been handled and accounted for in accordance with law, he shall enter an order of approval, and require that the estate remaining in the possession of the applicant, if any, be delivered to the person or persons entitled by law to receive it.

(e) Requisites of Discharge. No resigning personal representative shall be discharged until the application has been heard, the exhibit and account examined, settled, and approved, and until he has satisfied the court that he has delivered the estate, if there be any remaining in his possession, or has complied with all lawful orders of the court with relation to his trust.

(f) Final Discharge. When the resigning applicant has complied in all respects with the orders of the court, an order shall be made accepting the resignation, discharging the applicant, and, if he is under bond, his sureties.

Acts 1955, 54th Leg., p. 88, ch. 55, eff. Jan. 1, 1956. Amended by Acts 1993, 73rd Leg., ch. 957, § 36, eff. Sept. 1, 1993.

§ 221A. Change of Resident Agent

(a) A personal representative may change its resident agent to accept service of process in a probate proceeding or other action relating to the estate by filing a statement of the change titled "Designation of Successor Resident Agent" with the court in which the probate proceeding is pending. The statement must contain the names and addresses of the:

(1) personal representative;

(2) resident agent; and

(3) successor resident agent.

(b) The designation of a successor resident agent made in a statement filed under this section takes effect on the date on which the statement is filed with the court.

Added by Acts 1999, 76th Leg., ch. 855, § 7, eff. Sept. 1, 1999.

Section 11 of Acts 1999, 76th Leg., ch. 855 provides:

"Sections 221A and 221B, Texas Probate Code, as added by this Act, apply only to a change in designation of or a resignation of a resident agent made on or after the effective date of this Act. The change in designation of or the resignation of a resident agent made before the effective date of this Act is governed by the law in effect when the change in designation of or the resignation of the resident agent occurred, and the former law is continued in effect for that purpose."

§ 221B. Resignation of Resident Agent

(a) A resident agent of a personal representative may resign as the resident agent by giving notice to the personal representative and filing with the court in which the probate proceeding is pending a statement titled "Resignation of Resident Agent" that:

(1) contains the name of the personal representative;

(2) contains the address of the personal representative most recently known by the resident agent;

(3) states that notice of the resignation has been given to the personal representative and that the

personal representative has not designated a successor resident agent; and

(4) contains the date on which the notice of the resignation was given to the personal representative.

(b) The resident agent shall send, by certified mail, return receipt requested, a copy of a resignation statement filed under Subsection (a) of this section to:

(1) the personal representative at the address most recently known by the agent; and

(2) each party in the case or the party's attorney or other designated representative of record.

(c) The resignation of a resident agent takes effect on the date on which the court enters an order accepting the agent's resignation. A court may not enter an order accepting the agent's resignation unless the agent complies with the requirements of this section.

Added by Acts 1999, 76th Leg., ch. 855, § 7, eff. Sept. 1, 1999.

Section 11 of Acts 1999, 76th Leg., ch. 855 provides:

"Sections 221A and 221B, Texas Probate Code, as added by this Act, apply only to a change in designation of or a resignation of a resident agent made on or after the effective date of this Act. The change in designation of or the resignation of a resident agent made before the effective date of this Act is governed by the law in effect when the change in designation of or the resignation of the resident agent occurred, and the former law is continued in effect for that purpose."

§ 222. Removal

(a) Without Notice. (1) The court, on its own motion or on motion of any interested person, and without notice, may remove any personal representative, appointed under provisions of this Code, who:

(A) Neglects to qualify in the manner and time required by law;

(B) Fails to return within ninety days after qualification, unless such time is extended by order of the court, an inventory of the property of the estate and list of claims that have come to his knowledge;

(C) Having been required to give a new bond, fails to do so within the time prescribed;

(D) Absents himself from the State for a period of three months at one time without permission of the court, or removes from the State;

(E) Cannot be served with notices or other processes because of the fact that the:

(i) personal representative's whereabouts are unknown;

(ii) personal representative is eluding service; or

(iii) personal representative is a nonresident of this state who does not have a resident agent to accept service of process in any probate proceeding or other action relating to the estate; or

(F) Has misapplied, embezzled, or removed from the State, or is about to misapply, embezzle, or remove from the State, all or any part of the property committed to the personal representative's care.

(2) The court may remove a personal representative under Paragraph (F), Subdivision (1), of this subsection only on the presentation of clear and convincing evidence given under oath.

(b) With Notice. The court may remove a personal representative on its own motion, or on the complaint of any interested person, after the personal representative has been cited by personal service to answer at a time and place fixed in the notice, when:

(1) Sufficient grounds appear to support belief that he has misapplied, embezzled, or removed from the state, or that he is about to misapply, embezzle, or remove from the state, all or any part of the property committed to his care;

(2) He fails to return any account which is required by law to be made;

(3) He fails to obey any proper order of the court having jurisdiction with respect to the performance of his duties;

(4) He is proved to have been guilty of gross misconduct, or mismanagement in the performance of his duties;

(5) He becomes an incapacitated person, or is sentenced to the penitentiary, or from any other cause becomes incapable of properly performing the duties of his trust;

(6) As executor or administrator, he fails to make a final settlement within three years after the grant of letters, unless the time be extended by the court upon a showing of sufficient cause supported by oath; or

(7) As executor or administrator, he fails to timely file the notice required by Section 128A of this code.

(c) Order of Removal. The order of removal shall state the cause thereof. It shall require that any letters issued to the one removed shall, if he has been personally served with citation, be surrendered, and that all such letters be cancelled of record, whether delivered or not. It shall further require, as to all the estate remaining in the hands of a removed person, delivery thereof to the person or persons entitled thereto, or to one who has been appointed and has qualified as successor representative.

Acts 1955, 54th Leg., p. 88, ch. 55, eff. Jan. 1, 1956. Amended by Acts 1969, 61st Leg., p. 1922, ch. 641, § 11, eff. June 12, 1969; Acts 1989, 71st Leg., ch. 1035, § 11, eff. Sept. 1, 1989; Acts 1993, 73rd Leg., ch. 905, § 11, eff. Sept. 1, 1993; Acts 1993, 73rd Leg., ch. 957, § 37, eff. Sept. 1, 1993; Acts 1995, 74th Leg., ch. 1039, § 13, eff. Sept. 1, 1995; Acts 1999, 76th Leg., ch. 855, § 8, eff. Sept. 1, 1999.

Section 18 of Acts 1993, 73rd Leg., ch. 905 provides:

"A court may modify any guardianship in effect on September 1, 1993, to conform with the requirements of the Texas Probate Code, as amended by this Act, on the court's own motion or on application by the ward, the guardian, or any other interested person or entity."

Section 12 of Acts 1999, 76th Leg., ch. 855 provides:

"The changes in law made by this Act to Section 222(a), Texas Probate Code, apply only to a motion for the removal of a personal representative made or filed on or after the effective date of this Act. A motion for the removal of a personal representative made or filed before the effective date of this Act is governed by the law in effect on the date the motion was made or filed, and the former law is continued in effect for that purpose."

§ 222A. Reinstatement After Removal

(a) Not later than the 10th day after the date the court signs the order of removal, a personal representative who is removed under Subsection (a)(1)(F) or (G), Section 222, of this code may file an application with the court for a hearing to determine whether the personal representative should be reinstated.

(b) On the filing of an application for a hearing under this section, the court clerk shall issue a notice stating that the application for reinstatement was filed, the name of the ward or decedent, and the name of the applicant. The clerk shall issue the notice to the applicant, the ward, a person interested in the welfare of the ward, the decedent's estate, or the ward's estate and, if applicable, to a person who has control of the care and custody of the ward. The notice must cite all persons interested in the estate or welfare of the ward to appear at the time and place stated in the notice if they wish to contest the application.

(c) If, at the conclusion of a hearing under this section, the court is satisfied by a preponderance of the evidence that the applicant did not engage in the conduct that directly led to the applicant's removal, the court shall set aside an order appointing a successor representative, if any, and shall enter an order reinstating the applicant as personal representative of the ward or estate.

(d) If the court sets aside the appointment of a successor representative under this section, the court may require the successor representative to prepare and file, under oath, an accounting of the estate and to detail the disposition the successor has made of the property of the estate.

Added by Acts 1993, 73rd Leg., ch. 905, § 12, eff. Sept. 1, 1993.

PART 4. SUBSEQUENT PERSONAL REPRESENTATIVES

§ 223. Further Administration With or Without Will Annexed

Whenever any estate is unrepresented by reason of the death, removal, or resignation of the personal representative of such estate, the court shall grant further administration of the estate when necessary, and with the will annexed where there is a will, upon application therefor by a qualified person interested in the estate. Such appointments shall be made on notice and after hearing, as in case of original appointments, except that when the court finds that there is a necessity for the immediate appointment of a successor representative, such successor may be appointed upon application but without citation or notice.

Acts 1955, 54th Leg., p. 88, ch. 55, eff. Jan. 1, 1956. Amended by Acts 1969, 61st Leg., p. 1922, ch. 641, § 11, eff. June 12, 1969.

§ 224. Successors Succeed to Prior Rights, Powers, and Duties

When a representative of the estate not administered succeeds another, he shall be clothed with all rights, powers, and duties of his predecessor, except such rights and powers conferred on the predecessor by will which are different from those conferred by this Code on personal representatives generally. Subject to this exception, the successor shall proceed to administer such estate in like manner as if his administration were a continuation of the former one. He shall be required to account for all the estate which came into the hands of his predecessor and shall be entitled to any order or remedy which the court has power to give in order to enforce the delivery of the estate and the liability of the sureties of his predecessor for so much as is not delivered. He shall be excused from accounting for such of the estate as he has failed to recover after due diligence.

Acts 1955, 54th Leg., p. 88, ch. 55, eff. Jan. 1, 1956.

§ 225. Additional Powers of Successor Appointee

In addition, such appointee may make himself, and may be made, a party to suits prosecuted by or against his predecessors. He may settle with the predecessor, and receive and receipt for all such portion of the estate as remains in his hands. He may bring suit on the bond or bonds of the predecessor in his own name and capacity, for all the estate that came into the hands of the predecessor and has not been accounted for by him.

Acts 1955, 54th Leg., p. 88, ch. 55, eff. Jan. 1, 1956.

§ 226. Subsequent Executors Also Succeed to Prior Rights and Duties

Whenever an executor shall accept and qualify after letters of administration shall have been granted upon the estate, such executor shall, in like manner, succeed to the previous administrator, and he shall administer the estate in like manner as if his administration were a continuation of the former one, subject, however, to any legal directions of the testator contained in the will in relation to the estate.

Acts 1955, 54th Leg., p. 88, ch. 55, eff. Jan. 1, 1956. Amended by Acts 1993, 73rd Leg., ch. 957, § 38, eff. Sept. 1, 1993.

§ 227. Successors Return of Inventory, Appraisement, and List of Claims

An appointee who has been qualified to succeed to a prior personal representative shall make and return to the court an inventory, appraisement, and list of claims of the estate, within ninety days after being qualified, in like manner as is required of original appointees; and he shall also in like manner return additional inventories, appraisements, and lists of claims. In all orders appointing successor representatives of estates, the court shall appoint appraisers as in original appointments upon the application of any person interested in the estate.

Acts 1955, 54th Leg., p. 88, ch. 55, eff. Jan. 1, 1956. Amended by Acts 1969, 61st Leg., p. 1922, ch. 641, § 11, eff. June 12, 1969.

PART 5. GENERAL POWERS OF PERSONAL REPRESENTATIVES

§§ 228, 229. Repealed by Acts 1993, 73rd Leg., ch. 957, § 75(1), eff. Sept. 1, 1993

Acts 1993, 73rd Leg., ch. 957, repealing these sections, enacted Chapter XIII, Guardianship, of the Probate Code.

§ 230. Care of Property of Estates

The executor or administrator shall take care of the property of the estate of his testator or intestate as a prudent man would take of his own property, and if there be any buildings belonging to the estate, he shall keep the same in good repair, extraordinary casualties excepted, unless directed not to do so by an order of the court.

Acts 1955, 54th Leg., p. 88, ch. 55, eff. Jan. 1, 1956. Amended by Acts 1975, 64th Leg., p. 268, ch. 114, § 1, eff. April 30, 1975; Acts 1993, 73rd Leg., ch. 957, § 39, eff. Sept. 1, 1993.

§ 231. Repealed by Acts 1993, 73rd Leg., ch. 957, § 75(1), eff. Sept. 1, 1993

Acts 1993, 73rd Leg., ch. 957, repealing this section, enacted Chapter XIII, Guardianship, of the Probate Code.

§ 232. Representative of Estate Shall Take Possession of Personal Property and Records

The personal representative of an estate, immediately after receiving letters, shall collect and take into possession the personal property, record books, title papers, and other business papers of the estate, and all such in his possession shall be delivered to the person or persons legally entitled thereto when the administration has been closed or a successor has received letters.

Acts 1955, 54th Leg., p. 88, ch. 55, eff. Jan. 1, 1956.

§ 233. Collection of Claims and Recovery of Property

(a) Every personal representative of an estate shall use ordinary diligence to collect all claims and debts due the estate and to recover possession of all property of the estate to which its owners have claim or title, provided there is a reasonable prospect of collecting such claims or of recovering such property. If he wilfully neglects to use such diligence, he and the sureties on his bond shall be liable, at the suit of any person interested in the estate, for the use of the estate, for the amount of such claims or the value of such property as has been lost by such neglect.

(b) Except as provided by Subsection (c) of this section, a personal representative may enter into a contract to convey, or may convey, a contingent interest in any property sought to be recovered, not exceeding one-third thereof, for services of attorneys, subject only to approval of the court in which the estate is being administered.

(c) A personal representative, including an independent executor or independent administrator, may convey or contract to convey for services of an attorney a contingent interest that exceeds one-third of the property sought to be recovered under this section only on the approval of the court in which the estate is being administered. The court must approve a contract entered into or conveyance made under this section before an attorney performs any legal services. A contract entered into or conveyance made in violation of this section is void, unless the court ratifies or reforms the contract or documents relating to the conveyance to the extent necessary to cause the contract or conveyance to meet the requirements of this section.

(d) In approving a contract or conveyance under Subsection (b) or (c) of this section for services of an attorney, the court shall consider:

(1) the time and labor that will be required, the novelty and difficulty of the questions to be involved, and the skill that will be required to perform the legal services properly;

(2) the fee customarily charged in the locality for similar legal services;

(3) the value of property recovered or sought to be recovered by the personal representative under this section;

(4) the benefits to the estate that the attorney will be responsible for securing; and

(5) the experience and ability of the attorney who will be performing the services.

(e) On satisfactory proof to the court, a personal representative of an estate is entitled to all necessary and reasonable expenses incurred by the personal representative in collecting or attempting to collect a claim or debt owed to the estate or in recovering or attempting to recover property to which the estate has a title or claim.

Acts 1955, 54th Leg., p. 88, ch. 55, eff. Jan. 1, 1956. Amended by Acts 1993, 73rd Leg., ch. 848, § 1, eff. Sept. 1, 1993.

Section 4 of the 1993 amendatory act provides:

"The change in law made by Section 1 of this Act applies only to a contract executed or a conveyance made by the personal representative of an estate on or after the effective date of this Act. A contract executed or a conveyance made by the personal representative of an estate before the effective date of this Act is governed by the law in effect on the date the contract was executed or the conveyance was made, and the former law is continued in effect for that purpose."

§ 233A. Suits by Executors or Administrators

Suits for the recovery of personal property, debts, or damages and suits for title or possession of lands or for any right attached to or growing out of the same or for injury or damage done thereto may be instituted by executors or administrators appointed in this state; and judgment in such cases shall be conclusive, but may be set aside by any person interested for fraud or collusion on the part of such executor or administrator.

Added by Acts 1985, 69th Leg., ch. 959, § 3, eff. Sept. 1, 1985. Amended by Acts 1993, 73rd Leg., ch. 957, § 40, eff. Sept. 1, 1993.

§ 234. Exercise of Powers With and Without Court Order

(a) Powers To Be Exercised Under Order of the Court. The personal representative of the estate of any person may, upon application and order authorizing same, renew or extend any obligation owing by or to such estate. When a personal representative deems it for the interest of the estate, he may, upon written application to the court, and by order granting authority:

(1) Purchase or exchange property;

(2) Take claims or property for the use and benefit of the estate in payment of any debt due or owing to the estate;

(3) Compound bad or doubtful debts due or owing to the estate;

(4) Make compromises or settlements in relation to property or claims in dispute or litigation;

(5) Compromise or pay in full any secured claim which has been allowed and approved as required by law against the estate by conveying to the holder of such claim the real estate or personalty securing the same, in full payment, liquidation, and satisfaction thereof, and in consideration of cancellation of notes, deeds of trust, mortgages, chattel mortgages, or other evidences of liens securing the payment of such claim;

(6) Abandon the administration of property of the estate that is burdensome or worthless. Abandoned real or personal property may be foreclosed by a secured party, trustee, or mortgagee without further order of the court.

(b) Powers To Be Exercised Without Court Order. The personal representative of the estate of any person may, without application to or order of the court, exercise the powers listed below, provided, however, that a personal representative under court control may apply and obtain an order if doubtful of the propriety of the exercise of any such powers:

(1) Release liens upon payment at maturity of the debt secured thereby;

(2) Vote stocks by limited or general proxy;

(3) Pay calls and assessments;

(4) Insure the estate against liability in appropriate cases;

(5) Insure property of the estate against fire, theft, and other hazards;

(6) Pay taxes, court costs, bond premiums.

Acts 1955, 54th Leg., p. 88, ch. 55, eff. Jan. 1, 1956. Amended by Acts 1971, 62nd Leg., p. 984, ch. 173, § 15, eff. Jan. 1, 1972; Acts 1997, 75th Leg., ch. 1302, § 9, eff. Sept. 1, 1997.

§ 235. Possession of Property Held in Common Ownership

If the estate holds or owns any property in common, or as part owner with another, the representative of the estate shall be entitled to possession thereof in common with the other part owner or owners in the same manner as other owners in common or joint owners would be entitled.

Acts 1955, 54th Leg., p. 88, ch. 55, eff. Jan. 1, 1956.

§ 236. Repealed by Acts 1993, 73rd Leg., ch. 957, § 75(1), eff. Sept. 1, 1993; Acts 1995, 74th Leg., ch. 1039, § 73(1), eff. Sept. 1, 1995

Acts 1993, 73rd Leg., ch. 957, repealing this section, enacted Chapter XIII, Guardianship, of the Probate Code.

§ 236A. Repealed by Acts 1995, 74th Leg., ch. 1039, § 73(1), eff. Sept. 1, 1995

§ 237. Repealed by Acts 1993, 73rd Leg., ch. 957, § 75(1), eff. Sept. 1, 1993

Acts 1993, 73rd Leg., ch. 957, repealing this section, enacted Chapter XIII, Guardianship, of the Probate Code.

§ 238. Operation of Farm, Ranch, Factory, or Other Business

If the estate owns a farm, ranch, factory, or other business, the disposition of which has not been specifically directed by will, and if the same be not required to be sold at once for the payment of debts or other lawful purposes, the representative, upon order of the court, shall carry on the operation of such farm, ranch, factory, or other business, or cause the same to be done, or rent the same, as shall appear to be for the best interest of the estate. In deciding, the court shall consider the condition of the estate, and the necessity that may exist for future sale of such property or business for the payment of debts, claims, or other lawful expenditures, and shall not extend the time of renting any of the property beyond what appears consistent with the speedy settlement of the estate of a deceased person or the settlement of his estate.

Acts 1955, 54th Leg., p. 88, ch. 55, eff. Jan. 1, 1956. Amended by Acts 1993, 73rd Leg., ch. 957, § 41, eff. Sept. 1, 1993.

§ 238A. Administration of Partnership Interest by Personal Representative

If the decedent was a partner in a general partnership and the articles of partnership provide that, on the death of a partner, his or her executor or other personal representative shall be entitled to the place of the deceased partner in the firm, the executor or other personal representative so contracting to come into the partnership shall, to the extent allowed by law, be liable to third persons only to the extent of the deceased partner's capital in the partnership and the estate's assets held by the executor or other personal representative. This section does not exonerate an executor or other personal representative from liability for his or her negligence.

Added by Acts 1979, 66th Leg., p. 71, ch. 46, § 1, eff. April 11, 1979.

§ 239. Payment or Credit of Income

In all cases where the estate of a deceased person is being administered under the direction, control, and orders of a court in the exercise of its probate jurisdiction, upon the application of the executor or administrator of said estate, or of any interested party, after notice thereof has been given by posting, if it appears from evidence introduced at the hearing upon said application, and the court finds, that the reasonable market value of the assets of the estate then on hand, exclusive of the annual income therefrom, is at least twice the aggregate amount of all unpaid debts, administration expenses, and legacies, and that no creditor or legatee of the estate has then appeared and objected, the court may order and direct the executor or administrator to pay to, or credit to the account of, those persons who the court finds will own the assets of the estate when the administration thereon is completed, and in the same proportions, such part of the annual net income received by or accruing to said estate, as the court believes and finds can conveniently be paid to such owners without prejudice to the rights of creditors, legatees, or other interested parties. Nothing herein contained shall authorize the court to order paid over to such owners of the estate any part of the corpus or principal of the estate, except as otherwise provided by sections of this Code; provided, however, in this connection, bonuses, rentals, and royalties received for, or from, an oil, gas, or other mineral lease shall be treated and regarded as income, and not as corpus or principal.

Acts 1955, 54th Leg., p. 88, ch. 55, eff. Jan. 1, 1956. Amended by Acts 1973, 63rd Leg., p. 407, ch. 182, § 1, eff. May 25, 1973.

§ 240. Joint Executors or Administrators

Should there be more than one executor or administrator of the same estate at the same time, the acts of one of them as such executor or administrator shall be as valid as if all had acted jointly; and, in case of the death, resignation or removal of an executor or administrator, if there be a co-executor or co-administrator of such estate, he shall proceed with the administration as if no such death, resignation or removal had occurred. Provided, however, that this Section shall not be construed to authorize one of several executors or administrators to convey real estate, but in such case all the executors or administrators who have qualified as such and are acting as such shall join in the conveyance, unless the court, after due hearing, authorizes less than all to act.

Acts 1955, 54th Leg., p. 88, ch. 55, eff. Jan. 1, 1956.

PART 6. COMPENSATION, EXPENSES, AND COURT COSTS

§ 241. Compensation of Personal Representatives

(a) Executors, administrators, and temporary administrators shall be entitled to receive a commission of five per cent (5%) on all sums they may actually receive in cash, and the same per cent on all sums they may actually pay out in cash, in the administration of the estate on a finding by the court that the executor or administrator has taken care of and managed the estate in compliance with the standards of this code; provided, no commission shall be allowed for receiving funds belonging to the testator or intestate which were on hand or were held for the testator or intestate at the time of his death in a financial institution or a brokerage firm, including cash or a cash equivalent held in a checking account, savings account, certificate of deposit, or money market account; nor for collecting the proceeds of any life insurance policy; nor for paying out cash to the heirs or legatees as such; provided, further, however, that in no event shall the executor or administrator be entitled in the aggregate to more than five per cent (5%) of the gross fair market value of the estate subject to administration. If the executor or administrator manages a farm, ranch, factory, or other business of the estate, or if the compensation as calculated above is unreasonably low, the court may allow him reasonable compensation for his services, including unusual effort to collect funds or life insurance. For this purpose, the county court shall have jurisdiction to receive, consider, and act on applications from independent executors. The court may, on application of an interested person or on its own motion, deny a commission allowed by this subsection in whole or in part if:

(1) the court finds that the executor or administrator has not taken care of and managed estate property prudently; or

(2) the executor or administrator has been removed under Section 149C or 222 of this code.

(b) Definition. In this section, "financial institution" means an organization authorized to do business under state or federal laws relating to financial institutions, including banks and trust companies, savings banks, building and loan associations, savings and loan companies or associations, and credit unions.

Acts 1955, 54th Leg., p. 88, ch. 55, eff. Jan. 1, 1956. Amended by Acts 1957, 55th Leg., p. 53, ch. 31, § 8; Acts 1987, 70th Leg., ch. 919, § 1, eff. Sept. 1, 1987; Acts 1991, 72nd Leg., ch. 468, §§ 1, 2, eff. Sept. 1, 1991; Acts 1993, 73rd Leg., ch. 957, § 42, eff. Sept. 1, 1993.

Section 3 of the 1991 amendatory act provides:

"This Act takes effect September 1, 1991, and applies only to commissions for funds paid or received by executors and administrators on or after that date. Commissions for funds paid or received by executors or administrators before the effective date of this Act are governed by the law in effect when the funds were paid or received, and the former law is continued in effect for that purpose."

The amendment of this section by Acts 1993, 73rd Leg., ch. 905, § 13 failed to take effect under § 19(a), which provided that the amendment was not to take effect if both S.B. No. 236 (ch. 905) and H.B. No. 2685 (ch. 957) were enacted and became law.

§ 242. Expenses Allowed

Personal representatives of estates shall also be entitled to all necessary and reasonable expenses incurred by them in the preservation, safekeeping, and management of the estate, and in collecting or attempting to collect claims or debts, and in recovering or attempting to recover property to which the estate has a title or claim, and all reasonable attorney's fees, necessarily incurred in connection with the proceedings and management of such estate, on satisfactory proof to the court.

Acts 1955, 54th Leg., p. 88, ch. 55, eff. Jan. 1, 1956.

§ 243. Allowance for Defending Will

When any person designated as executor in a will or an alleged will, or as administrator with the will or alleged will annexed, defends it or prosecutes any proceeding in good faith, and with just cause, for the purpose of having the will or alleged will admitted to probate, whether successful or not, he shall be allowed out of the estate his necessary expenses and disbursements, including reasonable attorney's fees, in such proceedings. When any person designated as a devisee, legatee, or beneficiary in a will or an alleged will, or as administrator with the will or alleged will annexed, defends it or prosecutes any proceeding in good faith, and with just cause, for the purpose of having the will or alleged will admitted to probate, whether successful or not, he may be allowed out of the estate his necessary expenses and disbursements, including reasonable attorney's fees, in such proceedings.

Acts 1955, 54th Leg., p. 88, ch. 55, eff. Jan. 1, 1956. Amended by Acts 1983, 68th Leg., p. 5227, ch. 957, § 1, eff. Sept. 1, 1983; Acts 1987, 70th Leg., ch. 462, § 1, eff. Sept. 1, 1987.

Section 2 of the 1987 amendatory act provides:

"This Act takes effect September 1, 1987, and applies only to actions instituted on or after that date."

§ 244. Expense Accounts

All expense charges shall be made in writing, showing specifically each item of expense and the date thereof, and shall be verified by affidavit of the representative, filed with the clerk and entered on the claim docket, and shall be acted on by the court in like manner as other claims against the estate.

Acts 1955, 54th Leg., p. 88, ch. 55, eff. Jan. 1, 1956.

§ 245. When Costs Are Adjudged Against Representative

When the personal representative of an estate or person neglects the performance of any duty required of him, and any costs are incurred thereby, or if he is removed for cause, he and the sureties on his bond shall be liable for costs of removal and other additional costs incurred that are not authorized expenditures, as defined by this code, and for reasonable attorney's fees incurred in removing him and in obtaining his compliance regarding any statutory duty he has neglected.

Acts 1955, 54th Leg., p. 88, ch. 55, eff. Jan. 1, 1956. Amended by Acts 1977, 65th Leg., p. 1171, ch. 448, § 3, eff. Aug. 29, 1977; Acts 1983, 68th Leg., p. 631, ch. 140, § 1, eff. Aug. 29, 1983.

§§ 246, 247. Repealed by Acts 1993, 73rd Leg., ch. 957, § 75(1), eff. Sept. 1, 1993

Acts 1993, 73rd Leg., ch. 957, repealing these sections, enacted Chapter XIII, Guardianship, of the Probate Code.

CHAPTER VIII. PROCEEDINGS DURING ADMINISTRATION

PART 1. INVENTORY, APPRAISEMENT, AND LIST OF CLAIMS

PART 2. WITHDRAWING ESTATES OF DECEASED PERSONS FROM ADMINISTRATION

PART 3. SETTING APART HOMESTEAD AND OTHER EXEMPT PROPERTY, AND FIXING THE FAMILY ALLOWANCE

PART 4. PRESENTMENT AND PAYMENT OF CLAIMS

PART 1. INVENTORY, APPRAISEMENT, AND LIST OF CLAIMS

§ 248. Appointment of Appraisers

At any time after the grant of letters testamentary or of administration, upon the application of any interested person or if the court shall deem necessary, the court shall appoint not less than one nor more than three disinterested persons, citizens of the county in which letters were granted, to appraise the property of the estate. In such event and when part of the estate is situated in a county other than the county in which letters were granted, if the court shall deem necessary it may appoint not less than one nor more than three disinterested persons, citizens of the county where such part of the estate is situated, to appraise the property of the estate situated therein.

Acts 1955, 54th Leg., p. 88, ch. 55, eff. Jan. 1, 1956. Amended by Acts 1967, 60th Leg., p. 1815, ch. 697, § 2, eff. Aug. 28, 1967; Acts 1993, 73rd Leg., ch. 957, § 44, eff. Sept. 1, 1993.

§ 249. Failure of Appraisers to Serve

If any appraiser so appointed shall fail or refuse to act, the court shall by a like order or orders remove such appraiser and appoint another appraiser or appraisers, as the case shall require.

Acts 1955, 54th Leg., p. 88, ch. 55, eff. Jan. 1, 1956. Amended by Acts 1967, 60th Leg., p. 1816, ch. 697, § 3, eff. Aug. 28, 1967.

§ 250. Inventory and Appraisement

Within ninety days after his qualification, unless a longer time shall be granted by the court, the representative shall file with the clerk of court a verified, full and detailed inventory, in one written instrument, of all the property of such estate which has come to his possession or knowledge, which inventory shall include:

(a) all real property of the estate situated in the State of Texas;

(b) all personal property of the estate wherever situated. The representative shall set out in the inventory his appraisement of the fair market value of each item thereof as of the date of death in the case of grant of letters testamentary or of administration, as the case may be; provided that if the court shall appoint an appraiser or appraisers of the estate, the representative shall determine the fair market value of each item of the inventory with the assistance of such appraiser or appraisers and shall set out in the inventory such appraisement. The inventory shall specify what portion of the property, if any, is separate property and what portion, if any, is community property. If any property is owned in common with others, the interest owned by the estate shall be shown, together with the names and relationship, if known, of co-owners. Such inventory, when approved by the court and duly filed with the clerk of court, shall constitute for all purposes the inventory and appraisement of the estate referred to in this Code. The court for good cause shown may require the filing of the inventory and appraisement at a time prior to ninety days after the qualification of the representative.

Acts 1955, 54th Leg., p. 88, ch. 55, eff. Jan. 1, 1956. Amended by Acts 1967, 60th Leg., p. 1816, ch. 697, § 4, eff. Aug. 28, 1967; Acts 1993, 73rd Leg., ch. 957, § 45, eff. Sept. 1, 1993.

§ 251. List of Claims

There shall also be made out and attached to said inventory a full and complete list of all claims due or owing to the estate, which shall state:

(a) The name of each person indebted to the estate and his address when known.

(b) The nature of such debt, whether by note, bill, bond, or other written obligation, or by account or verbal contract.

(c) The date of such indebtedness, and the date when the same was or will be due.

(d) The amount of each claim, the rate of interest thereon, and time for which the same bears interest.

(e) In the case of decedent's estate, which of such claims are separate property and which are of the community.

(f) What portion of the claims, if any, is held in common with others, giving the names and the relationships, if any, of other part owners, and the interest of the estate therein.

Acts 1955, 54th Leg., p. 88, ch. 55, eff. Jan. 1, 1956.

§ 252. Affidavit to be Attached

The representative of the estate shall also attach to such inventory and list of claims his affidavit subscribed and sworn to before an officer in the county authorized by law to administer oaths, that the said inventory and list of claims are a true and complete statement of the property and claims of the estate that have come to his knowledge.

Acts 1955, 54th Leg., p. 88, ch. 55, eff. Jan. 1, 1956.

§ 253. Fees of Appraisers

Each appraiser appointed by the court, as herein authorized, shall be entitled to receive a minimum compensation of Five Dollars ($5) per day, payable out of the estate, for each day that he actually serves in performance of his duties as such.

Acts 1955, 54th Leg., p. 88, ch. 55, eff. Jan. 1, 1956. Amended by Acts 1957, 55th Leg., p. 53, ch. 31, § 9.

§ 254. Repealed by Acts 1967, 60th Leg., p. 1816, ch. 697, § 6, eff. Aug. 28, 1967

Acts 1967, 60th Leg., p. 1815, ch. 697, §§ 1 to 5, amended §§ 181, 248 to 250 and 256 of the Probate Code; §§ 6 to 8 of the Act provided:

"Sec. 6. Section 254. Texas Probate Code, together with all laws or parts of laws in conflict with this Act, be and the same are hereby repealed. In the event that any of the provisions of this Act are in conflict with the provisions of any of the Sections of the Texas Probate Code or with any other law, the provisions hereof shall take precedence and shall prevail to the extent of such conflict.

"Sec. 7. The repeal of any law by this Act shall not affect or impair any act done, obligation or right accrued or existing under the authority of the Act repealed; and such law shall be treated as still remaining in force for the purposes of sustaining any proper action, obligation or right.

"Sec. 8. If the provisions of this Act or the application thereof to any person or circumstance is held invalid, such invalidity shall not affect other provisions or applications of the Act which can be given effect without the invalid provision or application, and to this end the provisions of this Act are declared to be severable."

§ 255. Action by the Court

Upon return of the inventory, appraisement, and list of claims, the judge shall examine and approve, or disapprove, them, as follows:

(a) Order of Approval. Should the judge approve the inventory, appraisement, and list of claims, he shall issue an order to that effect.

(b) Order of Disapproval. Should the judge not approve the inventory, appraisement, or list of claims, or any of them, an order to that effect shall be entered, and it shall further require the return of another inventory, appraisement, and list of claims, or whichever of them is disapproved, within a time specified in such order, not to exceed twenty days from the date of the order; and the judge may also, if deemed necessary, appoint new appraisers.

Acts 1955, 54th Leg., p. 88, ch. 55, eff. Jan. 1, 1956.

§ 256. Discovery of Additional Property

If, after the filing of the inventory and appraisement, property or claims not included in the inventory shall come to the possession or knowledge of the representative, he shall forthwith file with the clerk of court a verified, full and detailed supplemental inventory and appraisement.

Acts 1955, 54th Leg., p. 88, ch. 55, eff. Jan. 1, 1956. Amended by Acts 1967, 60th Leg., p. 1816, ch. 697, § 5, eff. Aug. 28, 1967.

§ 257. Additional Inventory or List of Claims Required by Court

Any representative of an estate, on the written complaint of any interested person that property or claims of the estate have not been included in the inventory and list of claims filed, shall be cited to appear before the court in which the cause is pending and show cause why he should not be required to make and return an additional inventory or list of claims, or both. After hearing such complaint, and being satisfied of the truth thereof, the court shall enter its order requiring such additional inventory or list of claims, or both, to be made and returned in like manner as original inventories, and within such time, not to exceed twenty days, from the date of said order, as may be fixed by the court, but to include only property or claims theretofore not inventoried or listed.

Acts 1955, 54th Leg., p. 88, ch. 55, eff. Jan. 1, 1956.

§ 258. Correction Required When Inventory, Appraisement, or List of Claims Erroneous or Unjust

Any person interested in an estate who deems an inventory, appraisement, or list of claims returned therein erroneous or unjust in any particular may file a complaint in writing setting forth and pointing out the alleged erroneous or unjust items, and cause the representative to be cited to appear before the court and show cause why such errors should not be corrected. If, upon the hearing of such complaint, the court be satisfied from the evidence that the inventory, appraisement, or list of claims is erroneous or unjust in any particular as alleged in the complaint, an order shall be entered specifying the erroneous or unjust items and the corrections to be made, and appointing appraisers to make a new appraisement correcting such erroneous or unjust items and requiring the return of said new appraisement within twenty days from the date of the order. The court may also, on its own motion or that of the personal representative of the estate, have a new appraisal made for the purposes above set out.

Acts 1955, 54th Leg., p. 88, ch. 55, eff. Jan. 1, 1956.

§ 259. Effect of Reappraisement

When any reappraisement is made, returned, and approved by the court, it shall stand in place of the original appraisement. Not more than one reappraisement shall be made, but any person interested in the estate may object to the reappraisement either before or after it is approved, and if the court finds that the reappraisement is erroneous or unjust, the court shall appraise the property upon the basis of the evidence before it.

Acts 1955, 54th Leg., p. 88, ch. 55, eff. Jan. 1, 1956.

§ 260. Failure of Joint Personal Representatives to Return an Inventory, Appraisement, and List of Claims

If there be more than one representative qualified as such, any one or more of them, on the neglect of the others, may make and return an inventory and appraisement and list of claims; and the representative so neglecting shall not thereafter interfere with the estate or have any power over same; but the representative so returning shall have the whole administration, unless, within sixty days after the return, the delinquent or delinquents shall assign to the court in writing and under oath a reasonable excuse which the court may deem satisfactory; and if no excuse is filed or if the excuse filed is not deemed sufficient, the court shall enter an order removing any and all such delinquents and revoking their letters.

Acts 1955, 54th Leg., p. 88, ch. 55, eff. Jan. 1, 1956.

§ 261. Use of Inventories, Appraisements, and Lists of Claims as Evidence

All inventories, appraisements, and lists of claims which have been taken, returned, and approved in accordance with law, or the record thereof, or copies of either the originals or the record thereof, duly certified under the seal of the county court affixed by the clerk, may be given in evidence in any of the courts of this State in any suit by or against the representative of the estate, but shall not be conclusive for or against him, if it be shown that any property or claims of the estate are not shown therein, or that the value of the property or claims of the estate actually was in excess of that shown in the appraisement and list of claims.

Acts 1955, 54th Leg., p. 88, ch. 55, eff. Jan. 1, 1956.

PART 2. WITHDRAWING ESTATES OF DECEASED PERSONS FROM ADMINISTRATION

§ 262. Executor or Administrator Required to Report on Condition of Estate

At any time after the return of inventory, appraisement, and list of claims of a deceased person, any one entitled to a portion of the estate may, by a written complaint filed in the court in which such case is pending, cause the executor or administrator of the estate to be cited to appear and render under oath an exhibit of the condition of the estate.

Acts 1955, 54th Leg., p. 88, ch. 55, eff. Jan. 1, 1956.

§ 263. Bond Required to Withdraw Estate From Administration

When the executor or administrator has rendered the required exhibit, the persons entitled to such estate, or any of them, or any persons for them, may execute and deliver to the court a bond payable to the judge, and his successors in office, to be approved by the court, for an amount equal to at least double the gross appraised value of the estate as shown by the appraisement and list of claims returned, conditioned that the persons who execute such bond shall pay all the debts against the estate not paid that have been or shall be allowed by the executor or administrator and approved by the court, or that have been or shall be established by suit against said estate, and will pay to the executor or administrator any balance that shall be found to be due him by the judgment of the court on his exhibit.

Acts 1955, 54th Leg., p. 88, ch. 55, eff. Jan. 1, 1956.

§ 264. Court's Order

When such bond has been given and approved, the court shall thereupon enter an order directing and requiring the executor or administrator to deliver forthwith to all persons entitled to any portion of the estate the portion or portions of such estate to which they are entitled.

Acts 1955, 54th Leg., p. 88, ch. 55, eff. Jan. 1, 1956.

§ 265. Order of Discharge

When an estate has been so withdrawn from further administration, an order shall be entered discharging the executor or administrator and declaring the administration closed.

Acts 1955, 54th Leg., p. 88, ch. 55, eff. Jan. 1, 1956.

§ 266. Lien on Property of Estate Withdrawn From Administration

A lien shall exist on all of the estate withdrawn from administration in the hands of the distributees, and those claiming under them with notice of such lien, to secure the ultimate payment of the aforesaid bond and of the debts and claims secured thereby.

Acts 1955, 54th Leg., p. 88, ch. 55, eff. Jan. 1, 1956.

§ 267. Partition of Estate Withdrawn From Administration

Any person entitled to any portion of the estate withdrawn from further administration may, on written application to the court, cause a partition and distribution to be made among the persons entitled thereto, in accordance with the provisions of this Code pertaining to the partition and distribution of estates.

Acts 1955, 54th Leg., p. 88, ch. 55, eff. Jan. 1, 1956.

§ 268. Creditors May Sue on Bond

Any creditor of an estate withdrawn from administration whose debt or claim is unpaid and is not barred by limitation shall have the right to sue on the bond in his own name, and shall be entitled to judgment thereon for such debt or claim as he shall establish against the estate.

Acts 1955, 54th Leg., p. 88, ch. 55, eff. Jan. 1, 1956.

§ 269. Creditors May Sue Distributees

Any creditor of an estate withdrawn from administration whose debt or claim is unpaid and is not barred by limitation may sue any distributee who has received any of the estate, or he may sue all the distributees together, but no one of such distributees shall be liable beyond his just proportion according to the amount of the estate he shall have received in the distribution.

Acts 1955, 54th Leg., p. 88, ch. 55, eff. Jan. 1, 1956.

PART 3. SETTING APART HOMESTEAD AND OTHER EXEMPT PROPERTY, AND FIXING THE FAMILY ALLOWANCE

§ 270. Liability of Homestead for Debts

The homestead shall not be liable for the payment of any of the debts of the estate, except for:

(1) the purchase money thereof;

(2) the taxes due thereon;

(3) work and material used in constructing improvements thereon if the requirements of Section 50(a)(5), Article XVI, Texas Constitution, are met;

(4) an owelty of partition imposed against the entirety of the property by court order or by a written agreement of the parties to the partition, including a debt of one spouse in favor of the other spouse resulting from a division or an award of a family homestead in a divorce proceeding;

(5) the refinance of a lien against a homestead, including a federal tax lien resulting from the tax debt of both spouses, if the homestead is a family homestead, or from the tax debt of the decedent;

(6) an extension of credit on the homestead if the requirements of Section 50(a)(6), Article XVI, Texas Constitution, are met; or

(7) a reverse mortgage.

Acts 1955, 54th Leg., p. 88, ch. 55, eff. Jan. 1, 1956. Amended by Acts 1979, 66th Leg., p. 35, ch. 24, § 1, eff. Aug. 27, 1979; Acts 1999, 76th Leg., ch. 487, § 1, eff. Sept. 1, 1999; Acts 1999, 76th Leg., ch. 855, § 9, eff. Sept. 1, 1999.

Section 2 of Acts 1999, 76th Leg., ch. 487 provides:

"The changes in law made by this Act apply only to the estate of a person who dies on or after the effective date of this Act. An estate of a person who dies before the effective date of this Act is governed by the law in effect on the date of the person's death, and the former law is continued in effect for that purpose."

Section 13 of Acts 1999, 76th Leg., ch. 855 provides:

"Except as provided by Sections 11 and 12 of this Act, the changes in law made by this Act apply only to the estate of a person who dies on or after the effective date of this Act. An estate of a person who dies before the effective date of this Act is governed by the law in effect on the date of the person's death, and the former law is continued in effect for that purpose."

§ 271. Exempt Property to Be Set Apart

(a) Unless an affidavit is filed under Subsection (b) of this section, immediately after the inventory, appraisement, and list of claims have been approved, the court shall, by order, set apart for the use and benefit of the surviving spouse and minor children and unmarried children remaining with the family of the deceased, all such property of the estate as is exempt from execution or forced sale by the constitution and laws of the state.

(b) Before the approval of the inventory, appraisement, and list of claims, a surviving spouse, any person who is authorized to act on behalf of minor children of the deceased, or any unmarried children remaining with the family of the deceased may apply to the court to have exempt property set aside by filing an application and a verified affidavit listing all of the property that the applicant claims is exempt. The applicant bears the burden of proof by a preponderance of the evidence at any hearing on the application. The court shall set aside property of the decedent's estate that the court finds is exempt.

Acts 1955, 54th Leg., p. 88, ch. 55, eff. Jan. 1, 1956. Amended by Acts 1979, 66th Leg., p. 35, ch. 24, § 2, eff. Aug. 27, 1979; Acts 1993, 73rd Leg., ch. 846, § 18, eff. Sept. 1, 1993.

§ 272. To Whom Delivered

The exempt property set apart to the surviving spouse and children shall be delivered by the executor or administrator without delay as follows: (a) If there be a surviving spouse and no children, or if the children be the children of the surviving spouse, the whole of such property shall be delivered to the surviving spouse. (b) If there be children and no surviving spouse, such property, except the homestead, shall be delivered to such children if they be of lawful age, or to their guardian if they be minors. (c) If there be children of the deceased of whom the surviving spouse is not the parent, the share of such children in such exempted property, except the homestead, shall be delivered to such children if they be of lawful age, or to their guardian, if they be minors. (d) In all cases, the homestead shall be delivered to the surviving spouse, if there be one, and if there be no surviving spouse, to the guardian of the minor children and unmarried children, if any, living with the family.

Acts 1955, 54th Leg., p. 88, ch. 55, eff. Jan. 1, 1956. Amended by Acts 1979, 66th Leg., p. 35, ch. 24, § 3, eff. Aug. 27, 1979.

§ 273. Allowance in Lieu of Exempt Property

In case there should not be among the effects of the deceased all or any of the specific articles exempted from execution or forced sale by the Constitution and laws of this state, the court shall make a reasonable allowance in lieu thereof, to be paid to such surviving spouse and children, or such of them as there are, as hereinafter provided. The allowance in lieu of a homestead shall in no case exceed $15,000 and the allowance for other exempted property shall in no case exceed $5,000, exclusive of the allowance for the support of the surviving spouse and minor children which is hereinafter provided for.

Acts 1955, 54th Leg., p. 88, ch. 55, eff. Jan. 1, 1956. Amended by Acts 1977, 65th Leg., p. 351, ch. 172, § 1, eff. Aug. 29, 1977; Acts 1979, 66th Leg., p. 35, ch. 24, § 4, eff. Aug. 27, 1979; Acts 1993, 73rd Leg., ch. 846, § 19, eff. Sept. 1, 1993.

§ 274. How Allowance Paid

The allowance made in lieu of any of the exempted property shall be paid either in money out of the funds of the estate that come to the hands of the executor or administrator, or in any property of the deceased that such surviving spouse or children, if they be of lawful age, or their guardian if they be minors, shall choose to take at the appraisement, or a part thereof, or both, as they shall select; provided, however, that property specifically bequeathed or devised to another may be so taken, or may be sold to raise funds for the allowance as hereinafter provided, only if the other available property shall be insufficient to provide the allowance.

Acts 1955, 54th Leg., p. 88, ch. 55, eff. Jan. 1, 1956. Amended by Acts 1979, 66th Leg., p. 36, ch. 24, § 5, eff. Aug. 27, 1979.

§ 275. To Whom Allowance Paid

The allowance in lieu of exempt property shall be paid by the executor or administrator, as follows: (a) If there be a surviving spouse and no children, or if all the children be the children of the surviving spouse, the whole shall be paid to such surviving spouse.

(b) If there be children and no surviving spouse, the whole shall be paid to and equally divided among them if they be of lawful age, but if any of such children are minors, their shares shall be paid to their guardian or guardians.

(c) If there be a surviving spouse, and children of the deceased, some of whom are not children of the surviving spouse, the surviving spouse shall receive one-half of the whole, plus the shares of the children of whom the survivor is the parent, and the remaining shares shall be paid to the children of whom the survivor is not the parent, or, if they are minors, to their guardian.

Acts 1955, 54th Leg., p. 88, ch. 55, eff. Jan. 1, 1956. Amended by Acts 1979, 66th Leg., p. 36, ch. 24, § 6, eff. Aug. 27, 1979.

§ 276. Sale to Raise Allowance

If there be no property of the deceased that such surviving spouse or children are willing to take for such allowance, or not a sufficiency, and there be no funds, or not sufficient funds, of the estate in the hands of such executor or administrator to pay such allowance, or any part thereof, the court, on the application in writing of such surviving spouse and children, shall order a sale of so much of the estate for cash as will be sufficient to raise the amount of such allowance, or a part thereof, as the case requires.

Acts 1955, 54th Leg., p. 88, ch. 55, eff. Jan. 1, 1956. Amended by Acts 1979, 66th Leg., p. 36, ch. 24, § 7, eff. Aug. 27, 1979.

§ 277. Preference of Liens

If property upon which there is a valid subsisting lien or encumbrance shall be set apart to the surviving spouse or children as exempt property, or appropriated to make up allowances made in lieu of exempt property or for the support of the surviving spouse or children, the debts secured by such lien shall, if necessity requires, be either paid or continued as against such property. This provision applies to all estates, whether solvent or insolvent.

Acts 1955, 54th Leg., p. 88, ch. 55, eff. Jan. 1, 1956. Amended by Acts 1979, 66th Leg., p. 36, ch. 24, § 8, eff. Aug. 27, 1979.

§ 278. When Estate Is Solvent

If, upon a final settlement of the estate, it shall appear that the same is solvent, the exempted property, except the homestead or any allowance in lieu thereof, shall be subject to partition and distribution among the heirs and distributees of such estate in like manner as the other property of the estate.

Acts 1955, 54th Leg., p. 88, ch. 55, eff. Jan. 1, 1956.

§ 279. When Estate is Insolvent

Should the estate, upon final settlement, prove to be insolvent, the title of the surviving spouse and children to all the property and allowances set apart or paid to them under the provisions of this Code shall be absolute, and shall not be taken for any of the debts of the estate except as hereinafter provided.

Acts 1955, 54th Leg., p. 88, ch. 55, eff. Jan. 1, 1956. Amended by Acts 1979, 66th Leg., p. 37, ch. 24, § 9, eff. Aug. 27, 1979.

§ 280. Exempt Property Not Considered in Determining Solvency

In ascertaining whether an estate is solvent or insolvent, the exempt property set apart to the surviving spouse or children, or the allowance in lieu thereof, and the family allowance hereinafter provided for, shall not be estimated or considered as assets of the estate.

Acts 1955, 54th Leg., p. 88, ch. 55, eff. Jan. 1, 1956. Amended by Acts 1979, 66th Leg., p. 37, ch. 24, § 10, eff. Aug. 27, 1979.

§ 281. Exempt Property Liable for Certain Debts

The exempt property, other than the homestead or any allowance made in lieu thereof, shall be liable for the payment of Class 1 claims, but such property shall not be liable for any other debts of the estate.

Acts 1955, 54th Leg., p. 88, ch. 55, eff. Jan. 1, 1956. Amended by Acts 1997, 75th Leg., ch. 1302, § 10, eff. Sept. 1, 1997.

Section 16 of Acts 1997, 75th Leg., ch. 1302 provides:

"This Act takes effect September 1, 1997, and applies only to the estate of a person who dies on or after that date. An estate of a person who dies before the effective date of this Act is governed by the law in effect on the date of the person's death, and the former law is continued in effect for that purpose."

§ 282. Nature of Homestead Property Immaterial

The homestead rights of the surviving spouse and children of the deceased are the same whether the homestead be the separate property of the deceased or community property between the surviving spouse and the deceased, and the respective interests of such surviving spouse and children shall be the same in one case as in the other.

Acts 1955, 54th Leg., p. 88, ch. 55, eff. Jan. 1, 1956. Amended by Acts 1979, 66th Leg., p. 37, ch. 24, § 11, eff. Aug. 27, 1979.

§ 283. Homestead Rights of Surviving Spouse

On the death of the husband or wife, leaving a spouse surviving, the homestead shall descend and vest in like manner as other real property of the deceased and shall be governed by the same laws of descent and distribution.

Acts 1955, 54th Leg., p. 88, ch. 55, eff. Jan. 1, 1956. Amended by Acts 1979, 66th Leg., p. 37, ch. 24, § 12, eff. Aug. 27, 1979.

§ 284. When Homestead Not Partitioned

The homestead shall not be partitioned among the heirs of the deceased during the lifetime of the surviving spouse, or so long as the survivor elects to use or occupy the same as a homestead, or so long as the guardian of the minor children of the deceased is permitted, under the order of the proper court having jurisdiction, to use and occupy the same.

Acts 1955, 54th Leg., p. 88, ch. 55, eff. Jan. 1, 1956. Amended by Acts 1979, 66th Leg., p. 37, ch. 24, § 13, eff. Aug. 27, 1979.

§ 285. When Homestead Can Be Partitioned

When the surviving spouse dies or sells his or her interest in the homestead, or elects no longer to use or occupy the same as a homestead, or when the proper court no longer permits the guardian of the minor children to use and occupy the same as a homestead, it may be partitioned among the respective owners thereof in like manner as other property held in common.

Acts 1955, 54th Leg., p. 88, ch. 55, eff. Jan. 1, 1956. Amended by Acts 1979, 66th Leg., p. 37, ch. 24, § 14, eff. Aug. 27, 1979.

§ 286. Family Allowance to Surviving Spouses and Minors

(a) Unless an affidavit is filed under Subsection (b) of this section, immediately after the inventory, appraisement, and list of claims have been approved, the court shall fix a family allowance for the support of the surviving spouse and minor children of the deceased.

(b) Before the approval of the inventory, appraisement, and list of claims, a surviving spouse or any person who is authorized to act on behalf of minor children of the deceased may apply to the court to have the court fix the family allowance by filing an application and a verified affidavit describing the amount necessary for the maintenance of the surviving spouse and minor children for one year after the date of the death of the decedent and describing the spouse's separate property and any property that minor children have in their own right. The applicant bears the burden of proof by a preponderance of the evidence at any hearing on the application. The court shall fix a family allowance for the support of the surviving spouse and minor children of the deceased.

Acts 1955, 54th Leg., p. 88, ch. 55, eff. Jan. 1, 1956. Amended by Acts 1979, 66th Leg., p. 38, ch. 24, § 15, eff. Aug. 27, 1979; Acts 1993, 73rd Leg., ch. 846, § 20, eff. Sept. 1, 1993.

§ 287. Amount of Family Allowance

Such allowance shall be of an amount sufficient for the maintenance of such surviving spouse and minor children for one year from the time of the death of the testator or intestate. The allowance shall be fixed with regard to the facts or circumstances then existing and those anticipated to exist during the first year after such death. The allowance may be paid either in a lump sum or in installments, as the court shall order.

Acts 1955, 54th Leg., p. 88, ch. 55, eff. Jan. 1, 1956. Amended by Acts 1979, 66th Leg., p. 38, ch. 24, § 16, eff. Aug. 27, 1979.

§ 288. When Family Allowance Not Made

No such allowance shall be made for the surviving spouse when the survivor has separate property adequate to the survivor's maintenance; nor shall such allowance be made for the minor children when they have property in their own right adequate to their maintenance.

Acts 1955, 54th Leg., p. 88, ch. 55, eff. Jan. 1, 1956. Amended by Acts 1979, 66th Leg., p. 38, ch. 24, § 17, eff. Aug. 27, 1979.

§ 289. Order Fixing Family Allowance

When an allowance has been fixed, an order shall be entered stating the amount thereof, providing how the same shall be payable, and directing the executor or administrator to pay the same in accordance with law.

Acts 1955, 54th Leg., p. 88, ch. 55, eff. Jan. 1, 1956.

§ 290. Family Allowance Preferred

The family allowance made for the support of the surviving spouse and minor children of the deceased shall be paid in preference to all other debts or charges against the estate, except Class 1 claims.

Acts 1955, 54th Leg., p. 88, ch. 55, eff. Jan. 1, 1956. Amended by Acts 1979, 66th Leg., p. 38, ch. 24, § 18, eff. Aug. 27, 1979; Acts 1997, 75th Leg., ch. 1302, § 11, eff. Sept. 1, 1997.

§ 291. To Whom Family Allowance Paid

The executor or administrator shall apportion and pay the family allowance:

(a) To the surviving spouse, if there be one, for the use of the survivor and the minor children, if such children be the survivor's.

(b) If the surviving spouse is not the parent of such minor children, or of some of them, the portion of such allowance necessary for the support of such minor child or children of which the survivor is not the parent shall be paid to the guardian or guardians of such child or children.

(c) If there be no surviving spouse, the allowance to the minor child or children shall be paid to the guardian or guardians of such minor child or children.

(d) If there be a surviving spouse and no minor child or children, the entire allowance shall be paid to the surviving spouse.

Acts 1955, 54th Leg., p. 88, ch. 55, eff. Jan. 1, 1956. Amended by Acts 1979, 66th Leg., p. 38, ch. 24, § 19, eff. Aug. 27, 1979.

§ 292. May Take Property for Family Allowance

The surviving spouse, or the guardian of the minor children, as the case may be, shall have the right to take in payment of such allowance, or any part thereof, any of the personal property of the estate at its appraised value as shown by the appraisement; provided, however, that property specifically devised or bequeathed to another may be so taken, or may be sold to raise funds for the allowance as hereinafter provided, only if the other available property shall be insufficient to provide the allowance.

Acts 1955, 54th Leg., p. 88, ch. 55, eff. Jan. 1, 1956. Amended by Acts 1979, 66th Leg., p. 39, ch. 24, § 20, eff. Aug. 27, 1979.

§ 293. Sale to Raise Funds for Family Allowance

If there be no personal property of the deceased that the surviving spouse or guardian is willing to take for such allowance, or not a sufficiency of them, and if there be no funds or not sufficient funds in the hands of such executor or administrator to pay such allowance, or any part thereof, then the court, as soon as the inventory, appraisement, and list of claims are returned and approved, shall order a sale of so much of the estate for cash as will be sufficient to raise the amount of such allowance, or a part thereof, as the case requires.

Acts 1955, 54th Leg., p. 88, ch. 55, eff. Jan. 1, 1956. Amended by Acts 1979, 66th Leg., p. 39, ch. 24, § 21, eff. Aug. 27, 1979.

PART 4. PRESENTMENT AND PAYMENT OF CLAIMS

§ 294. Notice by Representative of Appointment

(a) Giving of Notice Required. Within one month after receiving letters, personal representatives of estates shall send to the comptroller of public accounts by certified or registered mail if the decedent remitted or should have remitted taxes administered by the comptroller of public accounts and publish in some newspaper, printed in the county where the letters were issued, if there be one, a notice requiring all persons having claims against the estate being administered to present the same within the time prescribed by law. The notice shall include the date of issuance of letters held by the representative, the address to which claims may be presented, and an instruction of the representative's choice that claims be addressed in care of the representative, in care of the representative's attorney, or in care of "Representative, Estate of ________" (naming the estate).

(b) Proof of Publication. A copy of such printed notice, together with the affidavit of the publisher, duly sworn to and subscribed before a proper officer, to the effect that the notice was published as provided in this Code for the service of citation or notice by publication, shall be filed in the court where the cause is pending.

(c) When No Newspaper Printed in the County. When no newspaper is printed in the county, the notice shall be posted and the return made and filed as required by this Code.

(d) Permissive Notice to Unsecured Creditors. At any time before an estate administration is closed, the personal representative may give notice by certified or registered mail, with return receipt requested, to an unsecured creditor having a claim for money against the estate expressly stating that the creditor must present a claim within four months after the date of the receipt of the notice or the claim is barred, if the claim is not barred by the general statutes of limitation. The notice must include:

(1) the dates of issuance of letters held by the representative;

(2) the address to which claims may be presented; and

(3) an instruction of the representative's choice that the claim be addressed in care of:

(A) the representative;

(B) the representative's attorney; or

(C) "Representative, Estate of " (naming the estate).

Acts 1955, 54th Leg., p. 88, ch. 55, eff. Jan. 1, 1956. Amended by Acts 1981, 67th Leg., p. 243, ch. 102, § 9, eff. Aug. 31, 1981; Acts 1991, 72nd Leg., ch. 464, § 1, eff. Aug. 26, 1991; Acts 1995, 74th Leg., ch. 1054, § 2, eff. Jan. 1, 1996.

Section 30 of the 1995 amendatory act provides:

"The change in law made by this Act applies only to the estates of persons who die on or after the effective date of this Act. An estate of a person who dies before the effective date of this Act is covered by the law in effect when the person died, and the former law continues in effect for that purpose."

§ 295. Notice to Holders of Secured Claims

(a) When notice required for secured claimants. Within two months after receiving letters, the personal representative of an estate shall give notice of the issuance of such letters to each and every person known to the personal representative to have a claim for money against the estate of a decedent that is secured by real or personal property of the estate. Within a reasonable time after the personal representative obtains actual knowledge of the existence of a person having a secured claim for money and to whom notice was not previously given, the personal representative shall give notice to the person of the issuance of letters.

(b) How notice shall be given. The notice stating the original grant of letters shall be given by mailing same by certified or registered mail, with return receipt requested, addressed to the record holder of such indebtedness or claim at the record holder's last known post office address.

(c) Proof of service of notice. A copy of each notice required by Subsection (a) of this section and a copy of the return receipt and an affidavit of the representative, stating that said notice was mailed as required by law, giving the name of the person to whom the notice was mailed, if not shown on the notice or receipt, shall be filed with the clerk of the court from which letters were issued.

Acts 1955, 54th Leg., p. 88, ch. 55, eff. Jan. 1, 1956. Amended by Acts 1987, 70th Leg., ch. 461, § 1, eff. Sept. 1, 1987; Acts 1991, 72nd Leg., ch. 895, § 13, eff. Sept. 1, 1991; Acts 1993, 73rd Leg., ch. 957, § 46, eff. Sept. 1, 1993; Acts 1995, 74th Leg., ch. 1054, § 3, eff. Jan. 1, 1996.

For applicability provisions of the 1991 amendatory act, see note following § 3.

For application provisions of the 1995 amendatory act, see notes following V.A.T.S. Probate Code, § 294.

§ 296. One Notice Sufficient

If the notices required by the two preceding Sections have been given by a former representative, or by one where several are acting, that shall be sufficient, and need not be repeated by any successor or co-representative.

Acts 1955, 54th Leg., p. 88, ch. 55, eff. Jan. 1, 1956.

§ 297. Penalty for Failure to Give Notice

If the representative fails to give the notices required in preceding Sections, or to cause such notices to be given, the representative and the sureties on the representative's bond shall be liable for any damage which any person suffers by reason of such neglect, unless it appears that such person had notice otherwise.

Acts 1955, 54th Leg., p. 88, ch. 55, eff. Jan. 1, 1956. Amended by Acts 1995, 74th Leg., ch. 1054, § 4, eff. Jan. 1, 1996.

For application provisions of the 1995 amendatory act, see notes following V.A.T.S. Probate Code, § 294.

§ 298. Claims Against Estates of Decedents

(a) Time for Presentation of Claims. A claim may be presented to the personal representative at any time before the estate is closed if suit on the claim has not been barred by the general statutes of limitation. If a claim of an unsecured creditor for money is not presented within four months after the date of receipt of the notice permitted by Section 294(d), the claim is barred.

(b) Claims Barred by Limitation Not to Be Allowed or Approved. No claims for money against a decedent, or against the estate of the decedent, on which a suit is barred under Subsection (a) of this section, Section 313, or Section 317(a) or by a general statute of limitation applicable thereto shall be allowed by a personal representative. If allowed by the representative and the court is satisfied that the claim is barred or that limitation has run, the claim shall be disapproved.

Acts 1955, 54th Leg., p. 88, ch. 55, eff. Jan. 1, 1956. Amended by Acts 1971, 62nd Leg., p. 2992, ch. 988, § 1, eff. June 15, 1971; Acts 1993, 73rd Leg., ch. 957, § 47, eff. Sept. 1, 1993; Acts 1995, 74th Leg., ch. 1054, § 5, eff. Jan. 1, 1996.

For application provisions of the 1995 amendatory act, see notes following V.A.T.S. Probate Code, § 294.

§ 299. Tolling of General Statutes of Limitation

The general statutes of limitation are tolled on the date:

(1) a claim for money is filed or deposited with the clerk; or

(2) suit is brought against the personal representative of an estate with respect to a claim of the estate that is not required to be presented to the personal representative.

Acts 1955, 54th Leg., p. 88, ch. 55, eff. Jan. 1, 1956. Amended by Acts 1997, 75th Leg., ch. 1302, § 12, eff. Sept. 1, 1997.

§ 301. Claims for Money Must be Authenticated

No personal representative of a decedent's estate shall allow, and the court shall not approve, a claim for money against such estate, unless such claim be supported by an affidavit that the claim is just and that all legal offsets, payments, and credits known to the affiant have been allowed. If the claim is not founded on a written instrument or account, the affidavit shall also state the facts upon which the claim is founded. A photostatic copy of any exhibit or voucher necessary to prove a claim may be offered with and attached to the claim in lieu of the original.

Acts 1955, 54th Leg., p. 88, ch. 55, eff. Jan. 1, 1956. Amended by Acts 1993, 73rd Leg., ch. 957, § 48, eff. Sept. 1, 1993; Acts 1995, 74th Leg., ch. 1054, § 6, eff. Jan. 1, 1996.

For application provisions of the 1995 amendatory act, see notes following V.A.T.S. Probate Code, § 294.

§ 302. When Defects of Form Are Waived

Any defect of form, or claim of insufficiency of exhibits or vouchers presented, shall be deemed waived by the personal representative unless written objection thereto has been made within thirty days after presentment of the claim, and filed with the county clerk.

Acts 1955, 54th Leg., p. 88, ch. 55, eff. Jan. 1, 1956.

§ 303. Evidence Concerning Lost or Destroyed Claims

If evidence of a claim is lost or destroyed, the claimant or an authorized representative or agent of the claimant, may make affidavit to the fact of such loss or destruction, stating the amount, date, and nature of the claim and when due, and that the same is just, and that all legal offsets, payments and credits known to the affiant have been allowed, and that the claimant is still the owner of the claim; and the claim must be proved by disinterested testimony taken in open court, or by oral or written deposition, before the claim is approved. If such claim is allowed or approved without such affidavit, or if it is approved without satisfactory proof, such allowance or approval shall be void.

Acts 1955, 54th Leg., p. 88, ch. 55, eff. Jan. 1, 1956. Amended by Acts 1995, 74th Leg., ch. 1054, § 7, eff. Jan. 1, 1996.

For application provisions of the 1995 amendatory act, see notes following V.A.T.S. Probate Code, § 294.

§ 304. Authentication of Claim by Others Than Individual Owners

An authorized officer or representative of a corporation or other entity shall make the affidavit required to authenticate a claim of such corporation or entity. When an affidavit is made by an officer of a corporation, or by an executor, administrator, trustee, assignee, agent, representative, or attorney, it shall be sufficient to state in such affidavit that the person making it has made diligent inquiry and examination, and that he believes that the claim is just and that all legal offsets, payments, and credits made known to the affiant have been allowed.

Acts 1955, 54th Leg., p. 88, ch. 55, eff. Jan. 1, 1956. Amended by Acts 1993, 73rd Leg., ch. 957, § 49, eff. Sept. 1, 1993; Acts 1995, 74th Leg., ch. 1054, § 8, eff. Jan. 1, 1996.

For application provisions of the 1995 amendatory act, see notes following V.A.T.S. Probate Code, § 294.

§ 305. Repealed by Acts 1993, 73rd Leg., ch. 957, § 75(1), eff. Sept. 1, 1993

Acts 1993, 73rd Leg., ch. 957, repealing this section, enacted Chapter XIII, Guardianship, of the Probate Code.

§ 306. Method of Handling Secured Claims for Money

(a) Specifications of Claim. When a secured claim for money against an estate is presented, the claimant shall specify therein, in addition to all other matters required to be specified in claims:

(1) Whether it is desired to have the claim allowed and approved as a matured secured claim to be paid in due course of administration, in which event it shall be so paid if allowed and approved; or

(2) Whether it is desired to have the claim allowed, approved, and fixed as a preferred debt and lien against the specific property securing the indebtedness and paid according to the terms of the contract which secured the lien, in which event it shall be so allowed and approved if it is a valid lien; provided, however, that the personal representative may pay said claim prior to maturity if it is for the best interest of the estate to do so.

(b) Time for Specification of Secured Claim. Within six months after the date letters are granted, or within four months after the date notice is received under Section 295 of this code, whichever is later, the secured creditor may present the creditor's claim and shall specify whether the claim is to be allowed and approved under Paragraph (1) or (2) of Subsection (a) of this section. If a secured claim is not presented within the time prescribed by this subsection or if the claim is presented without specifying how the claim is to be paid, it shall be treated as a claim to be paid in accordance with Paragraph (2) of Subsection (a) hereof.

(c) Matured Secured Claims. If a claim has been allowed and approved as a matured secured claim under Paragraph (1) of Subsection (a) of this section, the claim shall be paid in due course of administration and the secured creditor is not entitled to exercise any other remedies in a manner that prevents the preferential payment of claims and allowances described by Paragraphs (1) through (3) of Section 320(a) of this code.

(d) Approved Claim as Preferred Lien Against Property. When an indebtedness has been allowed and approved under Paragraph (2) of Subsection (a) hereof, no further claim shall be made against other assets of the estate by reason thereof, but the same thereafter shall remain a preferred lien against the property securing same, and the property shall remain security for the debt in any distribution or sale thereof prior to final maturity and payment of the debt.

(e) Payment of Maturities on Preferred Debt and Lien Claims. If property securing a claim allowed, approved, and fixed under Paragraph (2) of Subsection (a) hereof is not sold or distributed within six months from the date letters are granted, the representative of the estate shall promptly pay all maturities which have accrued on the debt according to the terms thereof, and shall perform all the terms of any contract securing same. If the representative defaults in such payment or performance, on application of the claimholder, the court shall:

(1) require the sale of said property subject to the unmatured part of such debt and apply the proceeds of the sale to the liquidation of the maturities;

(2) require the sale of the property free of the lien and apply the proceeds to the payment of the whole debt; or

(3) authorize foreclosure by the claimholder as provided by Subsections (f) through (k) of this section.

(f) Foreclosure of Preferred Liens. An application by a claimholder under Subsection (e) of this section to foreclose the claimholder's lien or security interest on property securing a claim that has been allowed, approved, and fixed under Paragraph (2) of Subsection (a) of this section shall be supported by affidavit of the claimholder that:

(1) describes the property or part of the property to be sold by foreclosure;

(2) describes the amounts of the claimholder's outstanding debt;

(3) describes the maturities that have accrued on the debt according to the terms of the debt;

(4) describes any other debts secured by a mortgage, lien, or security interest against the property that are known by the claimholder;

(5) contains a statement that the claimholder has no knowledge of the existence of any debts secured by the property other than those described by the application; and

(6) requests permission for the claimholder to foreclose the claimholder's mortgage, lien, or security interest.

(g) Citation. On the filing of an application, the clerk shall issue citation by personal service to the personal representative and to any person described by the application as having other debts secured by a mortgage, lien, or security interest against the property and by posting to any other person interested in the estate. The citation must require the person to appear and show cause why foreclosure should or should not be permitted.

(h) Setting of Hearing on Application. When an application is filed, the clerk shall immediately notify the judge. The judge shall schedule in writing a date for a hearing on the application. The judge may, by entry on the docket or otherwise, continue the hearing for a reasonable time to allow an interested person to obtain an appraisal or other evidence concerning the fair market value of the property that is the subject of the application. If the interested person requests an unreasonable time for a continuance, the person must show good cause for the continuance.

(i) Hearing. (1) At the hearing, if the court finds that there is a default in payment or performance under the contract that secures the payment of the claim, the court shall:

(A) require the sale of the property subject to the unmatured part of the debt and apply the proceeds of the sale to the liquidation of the maturities;

(B) require the sale of the property free of the lien and apply the proceeds to the payment of the whole debt; or

(C) authorize foreclosure by the claimholder as provided by Subsection (f) of this section.

(2) When the court grants a claimholder the right of foreclosure, the court shall authorize the claimholder to foreclose the claimholder's mortgage, lien, or security interest in accordance with the provisions of the document creating the mortgage, lien, or security interest or in any other manner allowed by law. In the discretion of the court and based on the evidence presented at the hearing, the court may fix a minimum price for the property to be sold by foreclosure that does not exceed the fair market value of the property. If the court fixes a minimum price, the property may not be sold at the foreclosure sale for a lower price.

(j) Appeal. Any person interested in the estate may appeal an order issued under Subsection (i)(1)(C) of this section.

(k) Unsuccessful Foreclosure. If a foreclosure sale authorized under this section is conducted and the property is not sold because no bid at the sale met the minimum price set by the court, the claimholder may file another application under Subsection (f) of this section. The court may, in the court's discretion, eliminate or modify the minimum price requirement and grant permission for another foreclosure sale.

Acts 1955, 54th Leg., p. 88, ch. 55, eff. Jan. 1, 1956. Amended by Acts 1993, 73rd Leg., ch. 957, § 50, eff. Sept. 1, 1993; Acts 1995, 74th Leg., ch. 1054, § 9, eff. Jan. 1, 1996; Acts 1997, 75th Leg., ch. 1302, § 13, eff. Sept. 1, 1997.

For application provisions of the 1995 amendatory act, see notes following V.A.T.S. Probate Code, § 294.

§ 307. Claims Providing for Attorney's Fees

If the instrument evidencing or supporting a claim provides for attorney's fees, then the claimant may include as a part of the claim the portion of such fee that he has paid or contracted to pay to an attorney to prepare, present, and collect such claim.

Acts 1955, 54th Leg., p. 88, ch. 55, eff. Jan. 1, 1956.

§ 308. Depositing Claims With Clerk

Claims may also be presented by depositing same, with vouchers and necessary exhibits and affidavit attached, with the clerk, who, upon receiving same, shall advise the representative of the estate, or the representative's attorney, by letter mailed to the representative's last known address, of the deposit of same. Should the representative fail to act on said claim within thirty days after it is deposited, then it shall be presumed to be rejected. Failure of the clerk to give notice as required herein shall not affect the validity of the presentment or the presumption of rejection because not acted upon within said thirty day period. The clerk shall enter a deposited claim on the claim docket.

Acts 1955, 54th Leg., p. 88, ch. 55, eff. Jan. 1, 1956. Amended by Acts 1995, 74th Leg., ch. 1054, § 10, eff. Jan. 1, 1996.

For application provisions of the 1995 amendatory act, see notes following V.A.T.S. Probate Code, § 294.

§ 309. Memorandum of Allowance or Rejection of Claim

When a duly authenticated claim against an estate is presented to the representative, or deposited with the clerk as heretofore provided, the representative shall, within thirty days after the claim is presented or deposited, endorse thereon, annex thereto, or file with the clerk a memorandum signed by the representative, stating the date of presentation or depositing of the claim, and that the representative allows or rejects it, or what portion thereof the representative allows or rejects.

Acts 1955, 54th Leg., p. 88, ch. 55, eff. Jan. 1, 1956. Amended by Acts 1995, 74th Leg., ch. 1054, § 11, eff. Jan. 1, 1996.

For application provisions of the 1995 amendatory act, see notes following V.A.T.S. Probate Code, § 294.

§ 310. Failure to Endorse or Annex Memorandum

The failure of a representative of an estate to timely allow or reject a claim under Section 309 of this code shall constitute a rejection of the claim. If the claim is thereafter established by suit, the costs shall be taxed against the representative, individually, or the representative may be removed on the written complaint of any person interested in the claim, after personal service of citation, hearing, and proof, as in other cases of removal.

Acts 1955, 54th Leg., p. 88, ch. 55, eff. Jan. 1, 1956. Amended by Acts 1995, 74th Leg., ch. 1054, § 12, eff. Jan. 1, 1996.

For application provisions of the 1995 amendatory act, see notes following V.A.T.S. Probate Code, § 294.

§ 311. When Claims Entered in Docket

After a claim against an estate has been presented to and allowed or rejected by the personal representative, in whole or in part, the claim must be filed with the county clerk of the proper county. The clerk shall enter the claim on the claim docket.

Acts 1955, 54th Leg., p. 88, ch. 55, eff. Jan. 1, 1956. Amended by Acts 1971, 62nd Leg., p. 2992, ch. 988, § 2, eff. June 15, 1971; Acts 1993, 73rd Leg., ch. 957, § 51, eff. Sept. 1, 1993; Acts 1995, 74th Leg., ch. 1054, § 13, eff. Jan. 1, 1996.

For application provisions of the 1995 amendatory act, see notes following V.A.T.S. Probate Code, § 294.

§ 312. Contest of Claims, Action by Court, and Appeals

(a) Contest of Claims. Any person interested in an estate may, at any time before the court has acted upon a claim, appear and object in writing to the approval of the same, or any part thereof, and in such case the parties shall be entitled to process for witnesses, and the court shall hear proof and render judgment as in ordinary suits.

(b) Court's Action Upon Claims. All claims which have been allowed and entered upon the claim docket for a period of ten days shall be acted upon by the court and be either approved in whole or in part or rejected, and they shall also at the same time be classified by the court.

(c) Hearing on Claims. Although a claim may be properly authenticated and allowed, if the court is not satisfied that it is just, the court shall examine the claimant and the personal representative under oath, and hear other evidence necessary to determine the issue. If not then convinced that the claim is just, the court shall disapprove it.

(d) Order of the Court. When the court has acted upon a claim, the court shall also endorse thereon, or annex thereto, a written memorandum dated and signed officially, stating the exact action taken upon such claim, whether approved or disapproved, or approved in part or rejected in part, and stating the classification of the claim. Such orders shall have the force and effect of final judgments.

(e) Appeal. When a claimant or any person interested in an estate shall be dissatisfied with the action of the court upon a claim, the claimant or person may appeal therefrom to the courts of appeals, as from other judgments of the county court in probate matters.

Acts 1955, 54th Leg., p. 88, ch. 55, eff. Jan. 1, 1956. Amended by Acts 1975, 64th Leg., p. 2196, ch. 701, § 4, eff. June 21, 1975; Acts 1993, 73rd Leg., ch. 957, § 52, eff. Sept. 1, 1993; Acts 1995, 74th Leg., ch. 1054, § 14, eff. Jan. 1, 1996.

For application provisions of the 1995 amendatory act, see notes following V.A.T.S. Probate Code, § 294.

§ 313. Suit on Rejected Claim

When a claim or a part thereof has been rejected by the representative, the claimant shall institute suit thereon in the court of original probate jurisdiction in which the estate is pending or in any other court of proper jurisdiction within ninety days after such rejection, or the claim shall be barred. When a rejected claim is sued on, the endorsement made on or annexed thereto, or any memorandum of rejection filed with respect to the claim, shall be taken to be true without further proof, unless denied under oath. When a rejected claim or part thereof has been established by suit, no execution shall issue, but the judgment shall be certified within thirty days after rendition, if of any court other than the court of original probate jurisdiction, and filed in the court in which the cause is pending, entered upon the claim docket, classified by the court, and handled as if originally allowed and approved in due course of administration.

Acts 1955, 54th Leg., p. 88, ch. 55, eff. Jan. 1, 1956. Amended by Acts 1975, 64th Leg., p. 2196, ch. 701, § 5, eff. June 21, 1975; Acts 1995, 74th Leg., ch. 1054, § 15, eff. Jan. 1, 1996.

For application provisions of the 1995 amendatory act, see notes following V.A.T.S. Probate Code, § 294.

§ 314. Presentment of Claims a Prerequisite for Judgment

No judgment shall be rendered in favor of a claimant upon any claim for money which has not been legally presented to the representative of an estate, and rejected by the representative or by the court, in whole or in part.

Acts 1955, 54th Leg., p. 88, ch. 55, eff. Jan. 1, 1956. Amended by Acts 1993, 73rd Leg., ch. 957, § 53, eff. Sept. 1, 1993; Acts 1995, 74th Leg., ch. 1054, § 16, eff. Jan. 1, 1996.

For application provisions of the 1995 amendatory act, see notes following V.A.T.S. Probate Code, § 294.

§ 315. Costs of Suit With Respect to Claims

All costs incurred in the probate court with respect to claims shall be taxed as follows:

(a) If allowed and approved, the estate shall pay the costs.

(b) If allowed, but disapproved, the claimant shall pay the costs.

(c) If rejected, but established by suit, the estate shall pay the costs.

(d) If rejected, but not established by suit, the claimant shall pay the costs, except as provided by Section 310 of this code.

(e) In suits to establish a claim after rejection in part, if the claimant fails to recover judgment for a greater amount than was allowed or approved, the claimant shall pay all costs.

Acts 1955, 54th Leg., p. 88, ch. 55, eff. Jan. 1, 1956. Amended by Acts 1995, 74th Leg., ch. 1054, § 17, eff. Jan. 1, 1996.

For application provisions of the 1995 amendatory act, see notes following V.A.T.S. Probate Code, § 294.

§ 316. Claims Against Personal Representatives

The naming of an executor in a will shall not operate to extinguish any just claim which the deceased had against the person named as executor; and, in all cases where a personal representative is indebted to the testator or intestate, the representative shall account for the debt in the same manner as if it were cash in the representative's hands; provided, however, that if said debt was not due at the time of receiving letters, the representative shall be required to account for it only from the date when it becomes due.

Acts 1955, 54th Leg., p. 88, ch. 55, eff. Jan. 1, 1956. Amended by Acts 1995, 74th Leg., ch. 1054, § 18, eff. Jan. 1, 1996.

For application provisions of the 1995 amendatory act, see notes following V.A.T.S. Probate Code, § 294.

§ 317. Claims by Personal Representatives

(a) By Executors or Administrators. The foregoing provisions of this Code relative to the presentation of claims against an estate shall not be construed to apply to any claim of a personal representative against the testator or intestate; but a personal representative holding such claim shall file the same in the court granting the letters, verified by affidavit as required in other cases, within six months after the representative has qualified, or such claim shall be barred.

(b) Action on Such Claims. When a claim by a personal representative has been filed with the court within the required time, such claim shall be entered upon the claim docket and acted upon by the court in the same manner as in other cases, and, when the claim has been acted upon by the court, an appeal from the judgment of the court may be taken as in other cases.

(c) Provisions Not Applicable to Certain Claims. The foregoing provisions relative to the presentment of claims shall not be so construed as to apply to a claim:

(1) of any heir, devisee, or legatee who claims in such capacity;

(2) that accrues against the estate after the granting of letters for which the representative of the estate has contracted; or

(3) for delinquent ad valorem taxes against a decedent's estate that is being administered in probate in:

(A) a county other than the county in which the taxes were imposed; or

(B) the same county in which the taxes were imposed, if the probate proceedings have been pending for more than four years.

Acts 1955, 54th Leg., p. 88, ch. 55, eff. Jan. 1, 1956. Amended by Acts 1993, 73rd Leg., ch. 957, § 54, eff. Sept. 1, 1993; Acts 1995, 74th Leg., ch. 1054, § 19, eff. Jan. 1, 1996; Acts 1999, 76th Leg., ch. 1481, § 37, eff. Sept. 1, 1999.

For application provisions of the 1995 amendatory act, see notes following V.A.T.S. Probate Code, § 294.

Section 52 of Acts 1999, 76th Leg., ch. 1481 provides:

"The changes in law made by Sections 36, 37, and 38 of this Act apply to the estates of all decedents, regardless of the date of death, and to the estates of all wards, regardless of the date the application for appointment of a guardian was filed, and to all causes of action pending on September 1, 1999, or brought after that date."

§ 318. Claims Not Allowed After Order for Partition and Distribution

No claim for money against the estate of a decedent shall be allowed by a personal representative and no suit shall be instituted against the representative on any such claim, after an order for final partition and distribution has been made; but, after such an order has been made, the owner of any claim not barred by the laws of limitation shall have an action thereon against the heirs, devisees, legatees, or creditors of the estate, limited to the value of the property received by them in distributions from the estate.

Acts 1955, 54th Leg., p. 88, ch. 55, eff. Jan. 1, 1956. Amended by Acts 1995, 74th Leg., ch. 1054, § 20, eff. Jan. 1, 1996.

For application provisions of the 1995 amendatory act, see notes following V.A.T.S. Probate Code, § 294.

§ 319. Claims Not to be Paid Unless Approved

No claim for money against the estate of a decedent, or any part thereof, shall be paid until it has been approved by the court or established by the judgment of a court of competent jurisdiction.

Acts 1955, 54th Leg., p. 88, ch. 55, eff. Jan. 1, 1956. Amended by Acts 1993, 73rd Leg., ch. 957, § 55, eff. Sept. 1, 1993.

§ 320. Order of Payment of Claims and Allowances

(a) Priority of Payments. Personal representatives, when they have funds in their hands belonging to the estate, shall pay in the following order:

(1) Funeral expenses and expenses of last sickness, in an amount not to exceed Fifteen Thousand Dollars.

(2) Allowances made to the surviving spouse and children, or to either.

(3) Expenses of administration and the expenses incurred in the preservation, safekeeping, and management of the estate.

(4) Other claims against the estate in the order of their classification.

(b) Sale of Mortgaged Property. If a personal representative has the proceeds of a sale that has been made for the satisfaction of a mortgage, lien, or security interest, and the proceeds, or any part of the proceeds, are not required for the payment of any debts against the estate that have a preference over the mortgage, lien, or security interest, the personal representative shall pay the proceeds to any holder of a mortgage, lien, or security interest. If there is more than one mortgage, lien, or security interest against the property, the personal representative shall pay the holders in the order of the holders' priority. If the personal representative fails to pay proceeds under this subsection, a holder, on proof of the failure to pay, may obtain an order from the court directing the payment to be made.

(c) Claimant's Petition. A claimant whose claim has not been paid may petition the court for determination of his claim at any time before it is barred by the applicable statute of limitations and upon due proof procure an order for its allowance and payment from the estate.

(d) Permissive Order of Payment. After the sixth month after the date letters are granted and on application by the personal representative stating that the personal representative has no actual knowledge of any outstanding enforceable claims against the estate other than the claims already approved and classified by the court, the court may order the personal representative to pay any claim that is allowed and approved.

Acts 1955, 54th Leg., p. 88, ch. 55, eff. Jan. 1, 1956. Amended by Acts 1975, 64th Leg., p. 1818, ch. 554, § 1, eff. Sept. 1, 1975; Acts 1977, 65th Leg., p. 352, ch. 173, § 1, eff. Aug. 29, 1977; Acts 1979, 66th Leg., p. 1876, ch. 758, § 1, eff. Aug. 27, 1979; Acts 1987, 70th Leg., ch. 461, § 2, eff. Sept. 1, 1987; Acts 1993, 73rd Leg., ch. 957, § 56, eff. Sept. 1, 1993; Acts 1995, 74th Leg., ch. 1054, § 21, eff. Jan. 1, 1996; Acts 1997, 75th Leg., ch. 540, § 4, eff. Sept. 1, 1997; Acts 1997, 75th Leg., ch. 1361, § 1, eff. Sept. 1, 1997.

Section 3(b) of the 1987 amendatory act provides:

"Section 320, Texas Probate Code, as amended by this Act, applies to the estates of persons who die on or after September 1, 1987. An estate of a person who dies before that date is covered by the law as it existed when the person died, and that law is continued in effect for that purpose."

For application provisions of the 1995 amendatory act, see notes following V.A.T.S. Probate Code, § 294.

Section 3 of Acts 1997, 75th Leg., ch. 1361 provides:

"This Act takes effect September 1, 1997, and applies only to the estate of a person who dies on or after that date. The estate of a person who dies before the effective date of this Act is governed by the law in effect at the time of the person's death and that law is continued in effect for that purpose."

§ 320A. Funeral Expenses

When personal representatives pay claims for funeral expenses and for items incident thereto, such as tombstones, grave markers, crypts or burial plots, they shall charge the whole of such claims to the decedent's estate and shall charge no part thereof to the community share of a surviving spouse.

Added by Acts 1967, 60th Leg., p. 768, ch. 321, § 1, eff. May 27, 1967. Amended by Acts 1995, 74th Leg., ch. 1054, § 22, eff. Jan. 1, 1996.

For application provisions of the 1995 amendatory act, see notes following V.A.T.S. Probate Code, § 294.

§ 321. Deficiency of Assets

When there is a deficiency of assets to pay all claims of the same class, other than secured claims for money, the claims in such class shall be paid pro rata, as directed by the court, and in the order directed. No personal representative shall be allowed to pay the claims, whether the estate is solvent or insolvent, except with the pro rata amount of the funds of the estate that have come to hand.

Acts 1955, 54th Leg., p. 88, ch. 55, eff. Jan. 1, 1956. Amended by Acts 1993, 73rd Leg., ch. 957, § 57, eff. Sept. 1, 1993; Acts 1995, 74th Leg., ch. 1054, § 23, eff. Jan. 1, 1996.

For application provisions of the 1995 amendatory act, see notes following V.A.T.S. Probate Code, § 294.

§ 322. Classification of Claims Against Estates of Decedent

Claims against an estate of a decedent shall be classified and have priority of payment, as follows:

Class 1. Funeral expenses and expenses of last sickness for a reasonable amount to be approved by the court, not to exceed a total of Fifteen Thousand Dollars, with any excess to be classified and paid as other unsecured claims.

Class 2. Expenses of administration and expenses incurred in the preservation, safekeeping, and management of the estate.

Class 3. Secured claims for money under Section 306(a)(1), including tax liens, so far as the same can be paid out of the proceeds of the property subject to such mortgage or other lien, and when more than one mortgage, lien, or security interest shall exist upon the same property, they shall be paid in order of their priority.

Class 4. Claims for the principal amount of and accrued interest on delinquent child support and child support arrearages that have been confirmed and reduced to money judgment, as determined under Subchapter F, Chapter 157, Family Code.[1]

Class 5. Claims for taxes, penalties, and interest due under Title 2, Tax Code;[2] Chapter 8, Title 132, Revised Statutes;[3] Section 81.111, Natural Resources Code; the Municipal Sales and Use Tax Act (Chapter 321, Tax Code); Section 451.404, Transportation Code; or Subchapter I, Chapter 452, Transportation Code.[4]

Class 6. Claims for the cost of confinement established by the institutional division of the Texas Department of Criminal Justice under Section 501.017, Government Code.

Class 7. Claims for repayment of medical assistance payments made by the state under Chapter 32, Human Resources Code, to or for the benefit of the decedent.

Class 8. All other claims.

Acts 1955, 54th Leg., p. 88, ch. 55, eff. Jan. 1, 1956. Amended by Acts 1971, 62nd Leg., p. 2992, ch. 988, § 3, eff. June 15, 1971; Acts 1979, 66th Leg., p. 869, ch. 394, § 1, eff. Aug. 27, 1979; Acts 1981, 67th Leg., p. 242, ch. 102, § 8, eff. Aug. 31, 1981; Acts 1981, 67th Leg., p. 1785, ch. 389, §§ 38A, 39(*l*), eff. Jan. 1, 1982; Acts 1987, 70th Leg., ch. 1049, § 51, eff. Sept. 1, 1987; Acts 1987, 70th Leg., ch. 1052, § 2.07, eff. Sept. 1, 1987; Acts 1989, 71st Leg., ch. 2, § 14.27(a)(6), eff. Aug. 28, 1989; Acts 1989, 71st Leg., ch. 1035, § 13, eff. Sept. 1, 1989; Acts 1995, 74th Leg., ch. 1054, § 24, eff. Jan. 1, 1996; Acts 1997, 75th Leg., ch. 165, § 30.243, eff. Sept. 1, 1997; Acts 1997, 75th Leg., ch. 1361, § 2, eff. Sept. 1, 1997; Acts 1999, 76th Leg., ch. 69, § 1, eff. Sept. 1, 1999.

[1] V.T.C.A., Family Code § 157.261 et seq.

[2] V.T.C.A., Tax Code § 101.001 et seq.

[3] Vernon's Ann.Civ.St. art. 8801 et seq.

[4] V.T.C.A., Transportation Code § 452.401 et seq.

Section 1 of Acts 1981, 67th Leg., ch. 389, enacted Title 2 of the Tax Code.

Acts 1989, 71st Leg., ch. 2, § 1.02(b) provides:

"If any provision of this Act conflicts with a statute enacted by the 71st Legislature, Regular Session, 1989, the statute controls."

For application provisions of the 1995 amendatory act, see notes following V.A.T.S. Probate Code, § 294.

Section 3 of Acts 1997, 75th Leg., ch. 1361 provides:

"This Act takes effect September 1, 1997, and applies only to the estate of a person who dies on or after that date. The estate of a person who dies before the effective date of this Act is governed by the law in effect at the time of the person's death and that law is continued in effect for that purpose."

Section 2 of Acts 1999, 76th Leg., ch. 69 provides:

"(a) This Act takes effect September 1, 1999, and applies only to the estate of a decedent who dies on or after that date.

"(b) The estate of a decedent who dies before the effective date of this Act is governed by the law in effect on the date of the decedent's death, and the former law is continued in effect for that purpose."

§ 322A. Apportionment of Taxes

(a) In this section:

(1) "Estate" means the gross estate of a decedent as determined for the purpose of estate taxes.

(2) "Estate tax" means any estate, inheritance, or death tax levied or assessed on the property of a decedent's estate, because of the death of a person, imposed by federal, state, local, or foreign law, including the federal estate tax and the additional inheritance tax imposed by Chapter 211, Tax Code, and including interest and penalties imposed in addition to those taxes. Estate tax does not include a tax imposed under Section 2701(d)(1)(A), Internal Revenue Code of 1986 (26 U.S.C. Section 2701(d)).

(3) "Person" includes a trust, natural person, partnership, association, joint stock company, corporation, government, political subdivision, or governmental agency.

(4) "Person interested in the estate" means a person, or a fiduciary on behalf of that person, who is entitled to receive, or who has received, from a decedent or because of the death of the decedent, property included in the decedent's estate for purposes of the estate tax, but does not include a creditor of the decedent or of the decedent's estate.

(5) "Representative" means the representative, executor, or administrator of an estate, or any other person who is required to pay estate taxes assessed against the estate.

(b)(1) The representative shall charge each person interested in the estate a portion of the total estate tax assessed against the estate. The portion of each estate tax that is charged to each person interested in the estate must represent the same ratio as the taxable value of that person's interest in the estate included in determining the amount of the tax bears to the total taxable value of all the interests of all persons interested in the estate included in determining the amount of the tax. In apportioning an estate tax under this subdivision, the representative shall disregard a portion of the tax that is apportioned under the law imposing the tax, otherwise apportioned by federal law, or apportioned as otherwise provided by this section.

(2) Subdivision (1) of this subsection does not apply to the extent the decedent in a written inter vivos or testamentary instrument disposing of or creating an interest in property specifically directs the manner of apportionment of estate tax or grants a discretionary power of apportionment to another person. A direction for the apportionment or nonapportionment of estate tax is limited to the estate tax on the property passing under the instrument unless the instrument is a will that provides otherwise.

(3) If under Subdivision (2) of this subsection directions for the apportionment of an estate tax in two or more instruments executed by the same person conflict, the instrument disposing of or creating an interest in the property to be taxed controls. If directions for the apportionment of estate tax in two or more instruments executed by different persons conflict, the direction of the person in whose estate the property is included controls.

(4) Subdivisions (2) and (3) of this subsection do not grant or enlarge the power of a person to apportion estate tax to property passing under an instrument created by another person in excess of the estate tax attributable to the property. Subdivisions (2) and (3) of this subsection do not apply to the extent federal law directs a different manner of apportionment.

(c) Any deduction, exemption, or credit allowed by law in connection with the estate tax inures to a person interested in the estate as provided by Subsections (d)–(f) of this section.

(d) If the deduction, exemption, or credit is allowed because of the relationship of the person interested in the estate to the decedent, or because of the purpose of the gift, the deduction, exemption, or credit inures to the person having the relationship or receiving the gift, unless that person's interest in the estate is subject to a prior present interest that is not allowable as a deduction. The estate tax apportionable to the person having the present interest shall be paid from the corpus of the gift or the interest of the person having the relationship.

(e) A deduction for property of the estate that was previously taxed and a credit for gift taxes or death taxes of a foreign country that were paid by the decedent or his estate inures proportionally to all persons interested in the estate who are liable for a share of the estate tax.

(f) A credit for inheritance, succession, or estate taxes, or taxes of a similar nature applicable to property or interests includable in the estate, inures to the persons interested in the estate who are chargeable with payment of a portion of those taxes to the extent that the credit reduces proportionately those taxes.

(g) To the extent that property passing to or in trust for a surviving spouse or a charitable, public, or similar gift or devise is not an allowable deduction for purposes of the estate tax solely because of an inheritance tax or other death tax imposed on and deductible from the property, the property is not included in the computation provided for by Subsection (b) of this section, and to that extent no apportionment is made against the property. The exclusion provided by this subsection does not apply if the result would be to deprive the estate of a deduction otherwise allowable under Section 2053(d), Internal Revenue Code of 1986,[1] relating to deductions for state death taxes on transfers for public, charitable, or religious uses.

(h) Except as provided by Subsection (i)(3) of this section, an interest in income, an estate for years or for life, or another temporary interest in any property or fund is not subject to apportionment. The estate tax apportionable to the temporary interest and the remainder, if any, is chargeable against the corpus of the property or the funds that are subject to the temporary interest and remainder.

(i)(1) In this subsection, "qualified real property" has the meaning assigned by Section 2032A, Internal Revenue Code of 1986 (26 U.S.C. Section 2032A).

(2) If an election is made under Section 2032A, Internal Revenue Code of 1986 (26 U.S.C. Section 2032A), the representative shall apportion estate taxes according to the amount of federal estate tax that would be payable if the election were not made. The amount of the reduction of the estate tax resulting from the election shall be applied to reduce the amount of the estate tax allocated based on the value of the qualified real property that is the subject of the election. If the amount applied to reduce the taxes allocated based on the value of the qualified real property is greater than the amount of those taxes, the excess shall be applied to the portion of the taxes allocated for all other property. This amount is to be apportioned under Subsection (b)(1) of this section.

(3) If additional federal estate tax is imposed under Section 2032A(c), Internal Revenue Code of 1986 (26 U.S.C. Section 2032A) because of an early disposition or cessation of a qualified use, the additional tax shall be equitably apportioned among the persons who have an interest in the portion of the qualified real property to which the additional tax is attributable in proportion to their interests. The additional tax is a charge against such qualified real property. If the qualified real property is split between one or more life or term interests and remainder interests, the additional tax shall be apportioned to each person whose action or cessation of use caused the imposition of additional tax, unless all persons with an interest in the qualified real property agree in writing to dispose of the property, in which case the additional tax shall be apportioned among the remainder interests.

(j)(1) In this subsection, "excess retirement accumulation" has the meaning assigned by Section 4980A(d)(3), Internal Revenue Code of 1986 (26 U.S.C. Section 4980A).

(2) If the federal estate tax is increased under Section 4980A(d), Internal Revenue Code of 1986 (26 U.S.C. Section 4890A), the amount of the increase shall be charged against the persons who receive the excess retirement accumulation that gives rise to the increase and shall be apportioned among all persons who receive interests in qualified employer plans and individual retirement plans to which the excess retirement accumulation is attributable in accordance with Subsection (b)(1) of this section, as if those assets represented the only assets of the estate.

(k) If the date for the payment of any portion of an estate tax is extended, the amount of the extended tax shall be apportioned to the persons who receive the specific property that gives rise to the extension. Those persons are entitled to the benefits and shall bear the burdens of the extension.

(*l*) If federal law directs the apportionment of the federal estate tax, a similar state tax shall be apportioned in the same manner.

(m) Interest on an extension of estate tax and interest and penalties on a deficiency shall be apportioned equitably to reflect the benefits and burdens of the extension or deficiency and of any tax deduction associated with the interest and penalties, but if the assessment or penalty and interest is due to delay caused by the negligence of the representative, the representative shall be charged with the amount of assessed penalty and interest.

(n) If property includable in an estate does not come into possession of the representative obligated to pay the estate tax, the representative shall recover from each person interested in the estate the amount of the estate tax apportioned to the person under this section or assign to persons affected by the tax obligation the representative's right of recovery. The obligation to recover a tax under this subsection does not apply if:

(1) the duty is waived by the parties affected by the tax obligation or by the instrument under which the representative derives powers; or

(2) in the reasonable judgment of the representative, proceeding to recover the tax is not cost-effective.

(*o*) If a representative cannot collect from a person interested in the estate an unpaid amount of estate tax apportioned to the person, the amount not collected shall be apportioned among the other persons interested in the estate who are subject to apportionment in the same manner as provided by Subsection (b)(1) of this section. A person who is charged with or who pays an apportioned amount under this subsection because another person failed to pay an amount of estate tax apportioned to the person has a right of reimbursement for that amount from the person who failed to pay the tax. The representative may enforce the right of reimbursement, or the person who is charged with or who pays an apportioned amount under this subsection may enforce the right of reimbursement directly by an assignment from the representative. A person assigned the right under this subsection is subrogated to the rights of the representative. A representative who has a right of reimbursement may petition a court to determine the right of reimbursement.

(p) This section shall be applied after giving effect to any disclaimers made in accordance with Section 37A of this code.

(q) Interest and penalties assessed against the estate by a taxing authority shall be apportioned among and charged to the persons interested in the estate in the manner provided by Subsection (b) of this section, unless, on application by any person interested in the estate, the court determines that the proposed apportionment is not equitable or that the assessment of interest or penalties was caused by a breach of fiduciary duty of a representative. If the apportionment is not equitable, the court may apportion interest and penalties in an equitable manner. If the assessment of interest or penalties was caused by a breach of fiduciary duty of a representative, the court may charge the representative with the amount of the interest and penalties assessed attributable to his conduct.

(r) Expenses reasonably incurred by a representative in determination of the amount, apportionment, or collection of the estate tax shall be apportioned among and charged to persons interested in the estate in the manner provided by Subsection (b) of this section unless, on application by any person interested in the estate, the court determines that the proposed apportionment is not equitable. If the court determines that the assessment is not equitable, the court may apportion the expenses in an equitable manner.

(s) For the purposes of this section, "court" means a court in which proceedings for administration of the estate are pending or have been completed or, if no proceedings are pending or have been completed, a court in which venue lies for the administration of the estate of the decedent.

(t) A representative who has possession of any property of an estate that is distributable to a person interested in the estate may withhold from that property an amount equal to the person's apportioned share of the estate tax.

(u) A representative shall recover from any person interested in the estate the unpaid amount of the estate tax apportioned and charged to the person under this section, unless the representative determines in good faith that an attempt to recover this amount would be economically impractical.

(v) A representative required to recover unpaid amounts of estate tax apportioned to persons interested in the estate under this section may not be required to initiate the necessary actions until the expiration of 90 days after the date of the final determination of the amount of the estate tax by the Internal Revenue Service. A representative who initiates an action under this section within a reasonable time after the 90-day period is not subject to any liability or surcharge because any portion of the estate tax apportioned to any person interested in the estate was collectible at a time following the death of the decedent but thereafter became uncollectible.

(w) A representative acting in another state may initiate an action in a court of this state to recover a proportionate amount of the federal estate tax, of an estate tax payable to another state, or of a death duty due by a decedent's estate to another state, from a person interested in the estate who is domiciled in this state or owns property in this state subject to attachment or execution. In the action, a determination of apportionment by the court having jurisdiction of the administration of the decedent's estate in the other state is prima facie correct. This section applies only if the state in which the determination of apportionment was made affords a substantially similar remedy.

(x) A reference in this section to a section of the Internal Revenue Code of 1986 refers to the section as it exists at the time in question. The reference also includes a corresponding section of a subsequent Internal Revenue Code and the referenced section as renumbered if it is renumbered.

(y) The prevailing party in an action initiated by a person for the collection of estate taxes from a person interested in the estate to whom estate taxes were apportioned and charged under Subsection (b) of this section shall be awarded necessary expenses, including reasonable attorney's fees.

Added by Acts 1987, 70th Leg., ch. 742, § 1, eff. Sept. 1, 1987. Amended by Acts 1991, 72nd Leg., ch. 410, § 1, eff. Sept. 1, 1991.

[1] 26 U.S.C.A. § 2053(d).

Section 3 of the 1987 Act provides:

"This Act takes effect September 1, 1987, and applies to the estates of persons who die on or after that date. An estate of a person who dies before the effective date of this Act is covered by the law as it existed when the person died, and that law is continued in effect for that purpose."

Section 2 of the 1991 amendatory act provides:

"This Act takes effect September 1, 1991, and Section 322A, Texas Probate Code, as amended by this Act, applies only to the estates of persons who die on or after that date. An estate of a person who dies before that date is covered by the law as it existed when the person died, and that law is continued in effect for that purpose."

§ 322B. Abatement of Bequests

(a) Except as provided by Subsections (b)–(d) of this section, a decedent's property is liable for debts and expenses of administration other than estate taxes, and bequests abate in the following order:

(1) property not disposed of by will, but passing by intestacy;

(2) personal property of the residuary estate;

(3) real property of the residuary estate;

(4) general bequests of personal property;

(5) general devises of real property;

(6) specific bequests of personal property; and

(7) specific devises of real property.

(b) This section does not affect the requirements for payment of a claim of a secured creditor who elects to have the claim continued as a preferred debt and lien against specific property under Section 306 of this code.

(c) This section does not apply to the payment of estate taxes under Section 322A of this code.

(d) A decedent's intent, as expressed in a will, controls over the abatement of bequests provided by this section.

Added by Acts 1987, 70th Leg., ch. 742, § 2, eff. Sept. 1, 1987.

Section 3 of the 1987 Act provides:

"This Act takes effect September 1, 1987, and applies to the estates of persons who die on or after that date. An estate of a person who dies before the effective date of this Act is covered by the law as it existed when the person died, and that law is continued in effect for that purpose."

§ 323. Joint Obligation

When two or more persons are jointly bound for the payment of a debt, or for any other purpose, upon the death of any of the persons so bound, the decedent's estate shall be charged by virtue of such obligation in the same manner as if the obligors had been bound severally as well as jointly.

Acts 1955, 54th Leg., p. 88, ch. 55, eff. Jan. 1, 1956. Amended by Acts 1995, 74th Leg., ch. 1054, § 25, eff. Jan. 1, 1996.

For application provisions of the 1995 amendatory act, see notes following V.A.T.S. Probate Code, § 294.

§ 324. Representatives Not to Purchase Claims

It shall be unlawful, and cause for removal, for a personal representative whether acting under appointment by will or under orders of the court, to purchase for the personal representative's own use or for any purposes whatsoever, any claim against the estate the personal representative represents. Upon written complaint by any person interested in the estate, and satisfactory proof of violation of this provision, after citation and hearing, the court shall enter its order cancelling the claim, and no part thereof shall be paid out of the estate; and the court may, in the court's discretion, remove such representative.

Acts 1955, 54th Leg., p. 88, ch. 55, eff. Jan. 1, 1956. Amended by Acts 1993, 73rd Leg., ch. 957, § 58, eff. Sept. 1, 1993; Acts 1995, 74th Leg., ch. 1054, § 26, eff. Jan. 1, 1996.

For application provisions of the 1995 amendatory act, see notes following V.A.T.S. Probate Code, § 294.

§ 325. Repealed by Acts 1995, 74th Leg., ch. 1054, § 29, eff. Jan. 1, 1996

§ 326. Owner May Obtain Order for Payment

Any creditor of an estate of a decedent whose claim, or part thereof, has been approved by the court or established by suit, may, at any time after twelve months from the granting of letters testamentary, upon written application and proof showing that the estate has on hand sufficient available funds, obtain an order directing that payment be made; or, if there are no available funds, and if to await the receipt of funds from other sources would unreasonably delay payment, the court shall then order sale of property of the estate sufficient to pay the claim; provided, the representative of the estate shall have first been cited on such written complaint to appear and show cause why such order should not be made.

Acts 1955, 54th Leg., p. 88, ch. 55, eff. Jan. 1, 1956.

§ 327. Repealed by Acts 1995, 74th Leg., ch. 1054, § 29, eff. Jan. 1, 1996

§ 328. Liability for Nonpayment of Claims

(a) Procedure to Force Payment. If any representative of an estate shall fail to pay on demand any money ordered by the court to be paid to any person, except to the State Treasury, when there are funds of the estate available, the person or claimant entitled to such payment, upon affidavit of the demand and failure to pay, shall be authorized to have execution issued against the property of the estate for the amount due, with interest and costs; or

(b) Penalty Against Representative. Upon return of the execution not satisfied, or merely upon the affidavit of demand and failure to pay, the court may cite the representative and the sureties on the representative's bond to show cause why they should not be held liable for such debt, interest, costs, and damages. Upon return of citation duly served, if good cause to the contrary be not shown, the court shall render judgment against the representative and sureties so cited, in favor of the holder of such claim, for the amount theretofore ordered to be paid or established by suit, and remaining unpaid, together with interest and costs, and also for damages upon the amount neglected to be paid, at the rate of five per cent per month for each month, or fraction thereof, that the payment was neglected to be paid after demand made therefor, which damages may be collected in any court of competent jurisdiction.

Acts 1955, 54th Leg., p. 88, ch. 55, eff. Jan. 1, 1956. Amended by Acts 1995, 74th Leg., ch. 1054, § 27, eff. Jan. 1, 1996.

For application provisions of the 1995 amendatory act, see notes following V.A.T.S. Probate Code, § 294.

§ 329. Borrowing Money

(a) Circumstances Under Which Money May Be Borrowed. Any real or personal property of an estate may be mortgaged or pledged by deed of trust or otherwise as security for an indebtedness, under order of the court, when necessary for any of the following purposes:

(1) For the payment of any ad valorem, income, gift, estate, inheritance, or transfer taxes upon the transfer of an estate or due from a decedent or the estate, regardless of whether such taxes are assessed by a state, or any of its political subdivisions, or by the federal government or by a foreign country; or

(2) For payment of expenses of administration, including sums necessary for operation of a business, farm, or ranch owned by the estate; or

(3) For payment of claims allowed and approved, or established by suit, against the estate; or

(4) To renew and extend a valid, existing lien.

(b) Procedure for Borrowing Money. When it is necessary to borrow money for any of the aforementioned purposes, or to create or extend a lien upon property of the estate as security, a sworn application for such authority shall be filed with the court, stating fully and in detail the circumstances which the representative of the estate believes make necessary the granting of such authority. Thereupon, the clerk shall issue and cause to be posted a citation to all interested persons, stating the nature of the application and requiring such persons, if they choose so to do, to appear and show cause, if any, why such application should not be granted.

(c) Order Authorizing Such Borrowing, or Extension of Lien. The court, if satisfied by the evidence adduced at the hearing upon said application that it is to the interest of the estate to borrow money, or to extend and renew an existing lien, shall issue its order to that effect, setting out the terms and conditions of the authority granted; provided, however, the loan or renewal shall not be for a term longer than three years from the granting of original letters to the representative of such estate, but the court may authorize an extension of such lien for not more than one additional year without further citation or notice. If a new lien is created on property of an estate, the court may require that the representative's general bond be increased, or an additional bond given, for the protection of the estate and the creditors, as for the sale of real property belonging to the estate.

Acts 1955, 54th Leg., p. 88, ch. 55, eff. Jan. 1, 1956. Amended by Acts 1973, 63rd Leg., p. 408, ch. 182, § 3, eff. May 25, 1973; Acts 1987, 70th Leg., ch. 766, § 1, eff. Aug. 31, 1987; Acts 1993, 73rd Leg., ch. 957, § 59, eff. Sept. 1, 1993; Acts 1995, 74th Leg., ch. 1054, § 28, eff. Jan. 1, 1996.

For application provisions of the 1995 amendatory act, see notes following V.A.T.S. Probate Code, § 294.

§ 330. Repealed by Acts 1993, 73rd Leg., ch. 957, § 75(1), eff. Sept. 1, 1993

Acts 1993, 73rd Leg., ch. 957, repealing this section, enacted Chapter XIII, Guardianship, of the Probate Code.

PART 5. SALES

§ 331. Court Must Order Sales

Except as hereinafter provided, no sale of any property of an estate shall be made without an order of court authorizing the same. The court may order property sold for cash or on credit, at public auction or privately, as it may consider most to the advantage of the estate, except when otherwise specially provided herein.

Acts 1955, 54th Leg., p. 88, ch. 55, eff. Jan. 1, 1956.

§ 332. Sales Authorized by Will

Whenever by the terms of a will an executor is authorized to sell any property of the testator, no order of court shall be necessary to authorize the executor to make such sale, and the sale may be made at public auction or privately as the executor deems to be in the best interest of the estate and may be made for cash or upon such credit terms as the executor shall determine; provided, that when particular directions are given by a testator in his will respecting the sale of any property belonging to his estate, the same shall be followed, unless such directions have been annulled or suspended by order of the court.

Acts 1955, 54th Leg., p. 88, ch. 55, eff. Jan. 1, 1956.

§ 333. Certain Personal Property to Be Sold

(a) The representative of an estate, after approval of inventory and appraisement, shall promptly apply for an order of the court to sell at public auction or privately, for cash or on credit not exceeding six months, all of the estate that is liable to perish, waste, or deteriorate in value, or that will be an expense or disadvantage to the estate if kept. Property exempt from forced sale, specific legacies, and personal property necessary to carry on a farm, ranch, factory, or any other business which it is thought best to operate, shall not be included in such sales.

(b) In determining whether to order the sale of an asset under Subsection (a) of this section, the court shall consider:

(1) the representative's duty to take care of and manage the estate as a person of ordinary prudence, discretion, and intelligence would exercise in the management of the person's own affairs; and

(2) whether the asset constitutes an asset that a trustee is authorized to invest under Section 113.056 or Subchapter F, Chapter 113, Property Code.[1]

Acts 1955, 54th Leg., p. 88, ch. 55, eff. Jan. 1, 1956. Amended by Acts 1993, 73rd Leg., ch. 846, § 21, eff. Sept. 1, 1993.

[1] V.T.C.A. Property Code, § 113.171 et seq.

§ 334. Sales of Other Personal Property

Upon application by the personal representative of the estate or by any interested person, the court may order the sale of any personal property of the estate not required to be sold by the preceding Section, including growing or harvested crops or livestock, but not including exempt property or specific legacies, if the court finds that so to do would be in the best interest of the estate in order to pay expenses of administration, funeral expenses, expenses of last illness, allowances, or claims against the estate, from the proceeds of the sale of such property. In so far as possible, applications and orders for the sale of personal property shall conform to the requirements hereinafter set forth for applications and orders for the sale of real estate.

Acts 1955, 54th Leg., p. 88, ch. 55, eff. Jan. 1, 1956.

§ 335. Special Provisions Pertaining to Livestock

When the personal representative of an estate has in his possession any livestock which he deems necessary or to the advantage of the estate to sell, he may, in addition to any other method provided by law for the sale of personal property, obtain authority from the court in which the estate is pending to sell such livestock through a bonded livestock commission merchant, or a bonded livestock auction commission merchant. Such authority may be granted by the court upon written and sworn application by the personal representative, or by any person interested in the estate, describing the livestock sought to be sold, and setting out the reasons why it is deemed necessary or to the advantage of the estate that the application be granted. The court shall forthwith consider any such application, and may, in its discretion, hear evidence for or against the same, with or without notice, as the facts warrant. If the application be granted, the court shall enter its order to that effect, and shall authorize delivery of the livestock to any bonded livestock commission merchant or bonded livestock auction commission merchant for sale in the regular course of business. The commission merchant shall be paid his usual and customary charges, not to exceed three per cent of the sale price, for the sale of such livestock. A report of such sale, supported by a verified copy of the merchant's account of sale, shall be made promptly by the personal representative to the court, but no order of confirmation by the court is required to pass title to the purchaser of such livestock.

Acts 1955, 54th Leg., p. 88, ch. 55, eff. Jan. 1, 1956.

§ 336. Sales of Personal Property at Public Auction

All sales of personal property at public auction shall be made after notice has been issued by the representative of the estate and posted as in case of posting for original proceedings in probate, unless the court shall otherwise direct.

Acts 1955, 54th Leg., p. 88, ch. 55, eff. Jan. 1, 1956.

§ 337. Sales of Personal Property on Credit

No more than six months credit may be allowed when personal property is sold at public auction, based upon the date of such sale. The purchaser shall be required to give his note for the amount due, with good and solvent personal security, before delivery of such property can be made to him, but security may be waived if delivery is not to be made until the note, with interest, has been paid.

Acts 1955, 54th Leg., p. 88, ch. 55, eff. Jan. 1, 1956.

§ 338. Sale of Mortgaged Property

Any creditor holding a claim secured by a valid mortgage or other lien, which has been allowed and approved or established by suit, may obtain from the court in which the estate is pending an order that said property, or so much thereof as necessary to satisfy his claim, shall be sold, by filing his written application therefor. Upon the filing of such application, the clerk shall issue citation requiring the representative of the estate to appear and show cause why such application should not be granted. If it appears to the court that it would be advisable to discharge the lien out of the general assets of the estate or that it be refinanced, he may so order; otherwise, he shall grant the application and order that the property be sold at public or private sale, as deemed best, as in ordinary cases of sales of real estate.

Acts 1955, 54th Leg., p. 88, ch. 55, eff. Jan. 1, 1956.

§ 339. Sales of Personal Property to be Reported; Decree Vests Title

All sales of personal property shall be reported to the court, and the laws regulating sales of real estate as to confirmation or disapproval of sales shall apply, but no conveyance shall be necessary. The decree confirming the sale of personal property shall vest the right and title of the estate of the intestate in the purchaser who has complied with the terms of the sale, and shall be prima facie evidence that all requirements of the law in making the sale have been met. The representative of an estate may, upon request, issue a bill of sale without warranty to the purchaser as evidence of title, the expense thereof to be borne by the purchaser.

Acts 1955, 54th Leg., p. 88, ch. 55, eff. Jan. 1, 1956. Amended by Acts 1993, 73rd Leg., ch. 957, § 60, eff. Sept. 1, 1993.

§ 339A. Repealed by Acts 1993, 73rd Leg., ch. 957, § 75(1), eff. Sept. 1, 1993

Acts 1993, 73rd Leg., ch. 957, repealing this section, enacted Chapter XIII, Guardianship, of the Probate Code.

§ 340. Selection of Real Property to Be Sold for Payment of Debts

Real property of the estate which is selected to be sold for the payment of expenses or claims shall be that which the court deems most advantageous to the estate to be sold.

Acts 1955, 54th Leg., p. 88, ch. 55, eff. Jan. 1, 1956.

§ 341. Application for Sale of Real Estate

Application may be made to the court for an order to sell property of the estate when it appears necessary or advisable in order to:

(1) Pay expenses of administration, funeral expenses and expenses of last sickness of decedents, and allowances and claims against the estates of decedents.

(2) Dispose of any interest in real property of the estate of a decedent, when it is deemed to the best interest of the estate to sell such interest.

Acts 1955, 54th Leg., p. 88, ch. 55, eff. Jan. 1, 1956. Amended by Acts 1969, 61st Leg., p. 2030, ch. 695, § 1, eff. June 12, 1969; Acts 1973, 63rd Leg., p. 408, ch. 182, § 4, eff. May 25, 1973; Acts 1975, 64th Leg., p. 975, ch. 372, § 1, eff. June 19, 1975; Acts 1975, 64th Leg., p. 976, ch. 373, § 1, eff. June 19, 1975; Acts 1979, 66th Leg., p. 1755, ch. 713, § 27, eff. Aug. 27, 1979; Acts 1993, 73rd Leg., ch. 957, § 61, eff. Sept. 1, 1993.

§ 342. Contents of Application for Sale of Real Estate

An application for the sale of real estate shall be in writing, shall describe the real estate or interest in or part thereof sought to be sold, and shall be accompanied by an exhibit, verified by affidavit, showing fully and in detail the condition of the estate, the charges and claims that have been approved or established by suit, or that have been rejected and may yet be established, the amount of each such claim, the property of the estate remaining on hand liable for the payment of such claims, and any other facts tending to show the necessity or advisability of such sale.

Acts 1955, 54th Leg., p. 88, ch. 55, eff. Jan. 1, 1956.

§ 343. Setting of Hearing on Application

Whenever an application for the sale of real estate is filed, it shall immediately be called to the attention of the judge by the clerk, and the judge shall designate in writing a day for hearing said application, any opposition thereto, and any application for the sale of other land, together with the evidence pertaining thereto. The judge may, by entries on the docket, continue such hearing from time to time until he is satisfied concerning the application.

Acts 1955, 54th Leg., p. 88, ch. 55, eff. Jan. 1, 1956. Amended by Acts 1979, 66th Leg., p. 1755, ch. 713, § 28, eff. Aug. 27, 1979.

§ 344. Citation and Return on Application

Upon the filing of such application and exhibit, the clerk shall issue a citation to all persons interested in the estate, describing the land or interest or part thereof sought to be sold, requiring them to appear at the time set by the court as shown in the citation and show cause why the sale should not be made, if they so elect. Service of such citation shall be by posting.

Acts 1955, 54th Leg., p. 88, ch. 55, eff. Jan. 1, 1956.

§ 345. Opposition to Application

When an application for an order of sale is made, any person interested in the estate may, before an order is made thereon, file his opposition to the sale, in writing, or may make application for the sale of other property of the estate.

Acts 1955, 54th Leg., p. 88, ch. 55, eff. Jan. 1, 1956.

§ 346. Order of Sale

If satisfied upon hearing that the sale of the property of the estate described in the application is necessary or advisable, the court shall order the sale to be made; otherwise, the court may deny the application and may, if it deems best, order the sale of other property the sale of which would be more advantageous to the estate. An order for the sale of real estate shall specify:

(a) The property to be sold, giving such description as will identify it; and

(b) Whether the property is to be sold at public auction or at private sale, and, if at public auction, the time and place of such sale; and

(c) The necessity or advisability of the sale and its purpose; and

(d) Except in cases in which no general bond is required, that, having examined the general bond of the representative of the estate, the court finds it to be sufficient as required by law, or finds the same to be insufficient and specifies the necessary or increased bond, as the case may be; and

(e) That the sale shall be made and the report returned in accordance with law; and

(f) The terms of the sale.

Acts 1955, 54th Leg., p. 88, ch. 55, eff. Jan. 1, 1956.

§ 347. Procedure When Representative Neglects to Apply for Sale

When the representative of an estate neglects to apply for an order to sell sufficient property to pay the charges and claims against the estate that have been allowed and approved, or established by suit, any interested person may, upon written application, cause such representative to be cited to appear and make a full exhibit of the condition of such estate, and show cause why a sale of the property should not be ordered. Upon hearing such application, if the court is satisfied that a sale of the property is necessary or advisable in order to satisfy such claims, it shall enter an order of sale as provided in the preceding Section.

Acts 1955, 54th Leg., p. 88, ch. 55, eff. Jan. 1, 1956.

§ 348. Permissible Terms of Sale of Real Estate

(a) For Cash or Credit. The real estate may be sold for cash, or for part cash and part credit, or the equity in land securing an indebtedness may be sold subject to such indebtedness, or with an assumption of such indebtedness, at public or private sale, as appears to the court to be for the best interest of the estate. When real estate is sold partly on credit, the cash payment shall not be less than one-fifth of the purchase price, and the purchaser shall execute a note for the deferred payments payable in monthly, quarterly, semi-annual or annual installments, of such amounts as appears to the court to be for the best interest of the estate, to bear interest from date at a rate of not less than four percent (4%) per annum, payable as provided in such note. Default in the payment of principal or interest, or any part thereof when due, shall, at the election of the holder of such note, mature the whole debt. Such note shall be secured by vendor's lien retained in the deed and in the note upon the property sold, and be further secured by deed of trust upon the property sold, with the usual provisions for foreclosure and sale upon failure to make the payments provided in the deed and notes.

(b) Reconveyance Upon Redemption. When an estate owning real estate by virtue of foreclosure of vendor's lien or mortgage belonging to the estate, either by judicial sale or by a foreclosure suit or through sale under deed of trust or by acceptance of a deed in cancellation of a lien or mortgage owned by the estate, and it appears to the court that an application to redeem the property foreclosed upon has been made by the former owner of the real estate to any corporation or agency now created or hereafter to be created by any Act or Acts of the Congress of the United States or of the State of Texas in connection with legislation for the relief of owners of mortgaged or encumbered homes, farms, ranches, or other real estate, and it further appears to the court that it would be to the best interest of the estate to own bonds of one of the above named federal or state corporations or agencies instead of the real estate, then upon proper application and proof, the court may dispense with the provisions of credit sales as provided above, and may order reconveyance of the property to the former mortgage debtor, or former owner, reserving vendor's lien notes for the total amount of the indebtedness due or for the total amount of bonds which the corporation or agency above named is under its rules and regulations allowed to advance, and, upon obtaining such an order, it shall be proper for the representative to indorse and assign the notes so obtained over to any one of the corporations or agencies above named in exchange for bonds of that corporation or agency.

Acts 1955, 54th Leg., p. 88, ch. 55, eff. Jan. 1, 1956. Amended by Acts 1959, 56th Leg., p. 636, ch. 290, § 1, eff. May 30, 1959.

§ 349. Public Sales of Real Estate

(a) Notice of Sale. Except as hereinafter provided, all public sales of real estate shall be advertised by the representative of the estate by a notice published in the county in which the estate is pending, as provided in this Code for publication of notices or citations. Reference shall be made to the order of sale, the time, place, and the required terms of sale, and a brief description of the property to be sold shall be given. It need not contain field notes, but if rural property, the name of the original survey, the number of acres, its locality in the county, and the name by which the land is generally known, if any, shall be given.

(b) Method of Sale. All public sales of real estate shall be made at public auction to the highest bidder.

(c) Time and Place of Sale. All such sales shall be made in the county in which the proceedings are pending, at the courthouse door of said county, or other place in such county where sales of real estate are specifically authorized to be made, on the first Tuesday of the month after publication of notice shall have been completed, between the hours of ten o'clock A.M. and four o'clock P.M., provided, that if deemed advisable by the court, he may order such sale to be made in the county in which the land is situated, in which event notice shall be published both in such county and in the county where the proceedings are pending.

(d) Continuance of Sales. If sales are not completed on the day advertised, they may be continued from day to day by making public announcement verbally of such continuance at the conclusion of the sale each day, such continued sales to be within the same hours as hereinbefore prescribed. If sales are so continued, the fact shall be shown in the report of sale made to the court.

(e) Failure of Bidder to Comply. When any person shall bid off property of an estate offered for sale at public auction, and shall fail to comply with the terms of sale, such property shall be readvertised and sold without any further order; and the person so defaulting shall be liable to pay to the representative of the estate, for its benefit, ten per cent of the amount of his bid, and also any deficiency in price on the second sale, such amounts to be recovered by such representative by suit in any court having jurisdiction of the amount claimed, in the county in which the sale was made.

Acts 1955, 54th Leg., p. 88, ch. 55, eff. Jan. 1, 1956.

§ 350. Private Sales of Real Estate

All private sales of real estate shall be made in such manner as the court directs in its order of sale, and no further advertising, notice, or citation concerning such sale shall be required, unless the court shall direct otherwise.

Acts 1955, 54th Leg., p. 88, ch. 55, eff. Jan. 1, 1956. Amended by Acts 1979, 66th Leg., p. 1755, ch. 713, § 29, eff. Aug. 27, 1979.

§ 351. Sales of Easements and Right of Ways

It shall be lawful to sell and convey easements and rights of ways on, under, and over the lands of an estate being administered under orders of a court, regardless of whether the proceeds of such a sale are required for payment of charges or claims against the estate, or for other lawful purposes. The procedure for such sales shall be the same as now or hereafter provided by law for sales of real property of estates of decedents at private sale.

Acts 1955, 54th Leg., p. 88, ch. 55, eff. Jan. 1, 1956. Amended by Acts 1993, 73rd Leg., ch. 957, § 62, eff. Sept. 1, 1993.

§ 352. Representative Purchasing Property of the Estate

(a) Except as provided by Subsection (b), (c), or (d) of this section, the personal representative of an estate shall not become the purchaser, directly or indirectly, of any property of the estate sold by him, or by any co-representative if one be acting.

(b) A personal representative of an estate may purchase property from the estate if the will, duly admitted to probate, appointing the personal representative expressly authorizes the sale.

(c) A personal representative of a decedent may purchase property from the estate of the decedent in compliance with the terms of a written executory contract signed by the decedent, including a contract for deed, earnest money contract, buy/sell agreement, or stock purchase or redemption agreement.

(d) After issuing the notice required by this subsection, a personal representative of an estate, including an independent administrator, may purchase property from the estate on the court's determination that the sale is in the best interest of the estate. The personal representative shall give notice by certified mail, return receipt requested, unless the court requires another form of notice, to each distributee of a deceased person's estate and to each creditor whose claim remains unsettled after presenting a claim within six months of the original grant of letters. The court may require additional notice or it may allow for the waiver of the notice required for a sale made under this subsection.

(e) If a purchase is made in violation of this section, any person interested in the estate may file a written complaint with the court in which the proceedings are pending, and upon service of citation upon the representative, after hearing and proof, such sale shall be by the court declared void, and shall be set aside by the court and the property ordered to be reconveyed to the estate. All costs of the sale, protest, and suit, if found necessary, shall be adjudged against the representative.

Acts 1955, 54th Leg., p. 88, ch. 55, eff. Jan. 1, 1956. Amended by Acts 1985, 69th Leg., ch. 709, § 1, eff. Aug. 26, 1985; Acts 1989, 71st Leg., ch. 651, § 1, eff. June 14, 1989; Acts 1991, 72nd Leg., ch. 895, § 14, eff. Sept. 1, 1991; Acts 1993, 73rd Leg., ch. 957, § 63, eff. Sept. 1, 1993.

Section 2 of the 1985 amendatory act provides:

"The change in Section 352, Texas Probate Code, made by this Act applies only to the purchase of property from an estate that is the subject of a will filed for probate on or after the effective date of this Act. The purchase of property from an estate that is the subject of a will filed for probate before the effective date of this Act is covered by the law in effect when the will was filed, and the former law is continued in effect for that purpose."

Section 2 of the 1989 amendatory act provides:

"(a) The intent of the legislature is to clarify the law relating to the purchase of estate property from an estate of a decedent or ward by the personal representative of the estate.

"(b) Subsection (c), Section 352, Probate Code, as added by Section 1, Chapter 709, Acts of the 69th Legislature, Regular Session, 1985, applies only to the purchase of estate property from an estate of a decedent or ward by a personal representative of the estate whose application for appointment was filed on or after August 26, 1985. The purchase of estate property from an estate by a personal representative whose application for appointment was filed before August 26, 1985, is governed by the law in effect when the application for appointment was filed, and the former law is continued in effect for that purpose."

Section 20(c) of the 1991 amendatory act provides:

"The change in the law made by Section 14 of this Act applies only to sales made on or after the effective date of this Act. A sale of property made under Section 14 before the effective date of this Act is governed by the law in effect when the sale of property was made, and the former law is continued in effect for that purpose."

§ 353. Reports of Sale

All sales of real property of an estate shall be reported to the court ordering the same within thirty days after the sales are made. Reports shall be in writing, sworn to, and filed with the clerk, and noted on the probate docket. They shall show:

(a) The date of the order of sale.

(b) The property sold, describing it.

(c) The time and place of sale.

(d) The name of the purchaser.

(e) The amount for which each parcel of property or interest therein was sold.

(f) The terms of the sale, and whether made at public auction or privately.

(g) Whether the purchaser is ready to comply with the order of sale.

Acts 1955, 54th Leg., p. 88, ch. 55, eff. Jan. 1, 1956.

§ 354. Bond on Sale of Real Estate

If the personal representative of the estate is not required by this Code to furnish a general bond, the sale may be confirmed by the court if found to be satisfactory and in accordance with law. Otherwise, before any sale of real estate is confirmed, the court shall determine whether the general bond of said representative is sufficient to protect the estate after the proceeds of the sale are received. If the court so finds, the sale may be confirmed. If the general bond be found insufficient, the sale shall not be confirmed until and unless the general bond be increased to the amount required by the court, or an additional bond given, and approved by the court. The increase, or the additional bond, shall be equal to the amount for which such real estate is sold, plus, in either instance, such additional sum as the court shall find necessary and fix for the protection of the estate; provided, that where the real estate sold is encumbered by a lien to secure a claim against the estate and is sold to the owner or holder of such secured claim and is in full payment, liquidation, and satisfaction thereof, no increased general bond or additional bond shall be required except for the amount of cash, if any, actually paid to the representative of the estate in excess of the amount necessary to pay, liquidate, and satisfy such claim in full.

Acts 1955, 54th Leg., p. 88, ch. 55, eff. Jan. 1, 1956.

§ 355. Action of Court on Report of Sale

After the expiration of five days from the filing of a report of sale, the court shall inquire into the manner in which the sale was made, hear evidence in support of or against such report, and determine the sufficiency or insufficiency of the representative's general bond, if any has been required and given; and, if he is satisfied that the sale was for a fair price, was properly made and in conformity with law, and has approved any increased or additional bond which may have been found necessary to protect the estate, the court shall enter a decree confirming such sale, showing conformity with the foregoing provisions of the Code, and authorizing the conveyance of the property to be made by the representative of the estate upon compliance by the purchaser with the terms of the sale, detailing such terms. If the court is not satisfied that the sale was for a fair price, was properly made, and in conformity with law, an order shall be made setting the same aside and ordering a new sale to be made, if necessary. The action of the court in confirming or disapproving a report of sale shall have the force and effect of a final judgment; and any person interested in the estate or in the sale shall have the right to have such decrees reviewed as in other final judgments in probate proceedings.

Acts 1955, 54th Leg., p. 88, ch. 55, eff. Jan. 1, 1956. Amended by Acts 1975, 64th Leg., p. 2197, ch. 701, § 6, eff. June 21, 1975.

§ 356. Deed Conveys Title to Real Estate

When real estate is sold, the conveyance shall be by proper deed which shall refer to and identify the decree of the court confirming the sale. Such deed shall vest in the purchaser all right, title, and interest of the estate to such property, and shall be prima facie evidence that said sale has met all applicable requirements of the law.

Acts 1955, 54th Leg., p. 88, ch. 55, eff. Jan. 1, 1956.

§ 357. Delivery of Deed, Vendor's and Deed of Trust Lien

After a sale is confirmed by the court and the terms of sale have been complied with by the purchaser, the representative of the estate shall forthwith execute and deliver to the purchaser a proper deed conveying the property. If the sale is made partly on credit, the vendor's lien securing the purchase money note or notes shall be expressly retained in said deed, and in no event waived, and before actual delivery of said deed to purchaser, he shall execute and deliver to the representative of the estate a vendor's lien note or notes, with or without personal sureties as the court shall have ordered, and also a deed of trust or mortgage on the property as further security for the payment of said note or notes. Upon completion of the transaction, the personal representative shall promptly file or cause to be filed and recorded in the appropriate records in the county where the land is situated said deed of trust or mortgage.

Acts 1955, 54th Leg., p. 88, ch. 55, eff. Jan. 1, 1956.

§ 358. Penalty for Neglect

Should the representative of an estate neglect to comply with the preceding Section, or to file the deed of trust securing such lien in the proper county, he and the sureties on his bond shall, after complaint and citation, be held liable for the use of the estate, for all damages resulting from such neglect, which damages may be recovered in any court of competent jurisdiction, and he may be removed by the court.

Acts 1955, 54th Leg., p. 88, ch. 55, eff. Jan. 1, 1956.

PART 6. HIRING AND RENTING

§ 359. Hiring or Renting Without Order of Court

The personal representative of an estate may, without order of court, rent any of its real property or hire out any of its personal property, either at public auction or privately, as may be deemed in the best interest of the estate, for a period not to exceed one year.

Acts 1955, 54th Leg., p. 88, ch. 55, eff. Jan. 1, 1956.

§ 360. Liability of Personal Representative

If property of the estate is hired or rented without an order of court, the personal representative shall be required to account to the estate for the reasonable value of the hire or rent of such property, to be ascertained by the court upon satisfactory evidence, upon sworn complaint of any person interested in the estate.

Acts 1955, 54th Leg., p. 88, ch. 55, eff. Jan. 1, 1956.

§ 361. Order to Hire or Rent

Representatives of estates, if they prefer, may, and, if the proposed rental period exceeds one year, shall, file a written application with the court setting forth the property sought to be hired or rented. If the court finds that it would be to the interest of the estate, he shall grant the application and issue an order which shall describe the property to be hired or rented, state whether such hiring or renting shall be at public auction or privately, whether for cash or on credit, and, if on credit, the extent of same and the period for which the property may be rented. If to be hired or rented at public auction, the court shall also prescribe whether notice thereof shall be published or posted.

Acts 1955, 54th Leg., p. 88, ch. 55, eff. Jan. 1, 1956.

§ 362. Procedure in Case of Neglect to Rent Property

Any person interested in an estate may file his written and sworn complaint in a court where such estate is pending, and cause the personal representative of such estate to be cited to appear and show cause why he did not hire or rent any property of the estate, and the court, upon hearing such complaint, shall make such order as seems for the best interest of the estate.

Acts 1955, 54th Leg., p. 88, ch. 55, eff. Jan. 1, 1956.

§ 363. When Property is Hired or Rented on Credit

When property is hired or rented on credit, possession thereof shall not be delivered until the hirer or renter has executed and delivered to the representative of the estate a note with good personal security for the amount of such hire or rent; and, if any such property so hired or rented is delivered without receiving such security, the representative and the sureties on his bond shall be liable for the full amount of such hire or rent; provided, that when the hire or rental is payable in installments, in advance of the period of time to which they relate, this Section shall not apply.

Acts 1955, 54th Leg., p. 88, ch. 55, eff. Jan. 1, 1956.

§ 364. Property Hired or Rented to Be Returned in Good Condition

All property hired or rented, with or without an order of court, shall be returned to the possession of the estate in as good condition, reasonable wear and tear excepted, as when hired or rented, and it shall be the duty and responsibility of the representative of the estate to see that this is done, to report to the court any loss, damage or destruction of property hired or rented, and to ask for authority to take such action as is necessary; failing so to do, he and the sureties on his bond shall be liable to the estate for any loss or damage suffered through such fault.

Acts 1955, 54th Leg., p. 88, ch. 55, eff. Jan. 1, 1956.

§ 365. Report of Hiring or Renting

(a) When any property of the estate with an appraised value of Three Thousand Dollars or more has been hired or rented, the representative shall, within thirty days thereafter, file with the court a sworn and written report, stating:

(1) The property involved and its appraised value.

(2) The date of hiring or renting, and whether at public auction or privately.

(3) The name of the person or persons hiring or renting such property.

(4) The amount of such hiring or rental.

(5) Whether the hiring or rental was for cash or on credit, and, if on credit, the length of time, the terms, and the security taken therefor.

(b) When the value of the property involved is less than Three Thousand Dollars, the hiring or renting thereof may be reported upon in the next annual or final account which shall be filed as required by law.

Acts 1955, 54th Leg., p. 88, ch. 55, eff. Jan. 1, 1956.

§ 366. Action of Court on Report

At any time after five days from the time such report of hiring or renting is filed, it shall be examined by the court and approved and confirmed by order of the court if found just and reasonable; but, if disapproved, the estate shall not be bound and the court may order another offering of the property for hire or rent, in the same manner and subject to the same rules heretofore provided. If the report has been approved and it later appears that, by reason of any fault of the representative of the estate, the property has not been hired or rented for its reasonable value, the court shall cause the representative of the estate and his sureties to appear and show cause why the reasonable value of hire or rent of such property shall not be adjudged against him.

Acts 1955, 54th Leg., p. 88, ch. 55, eff. Jan. 1, 1956.

PART 7. MINERAL LEASES, POOLING OR UNITIZATION AGREEMENTS, AND OTHER MATTERS RELATING TO MINERAL PROPERTIES

§ 367. Mineral Leases After Public Notice

(a) Certain Words and Terms Defined. As used throughout in this Part of this Chapter, the words "land" or "interest in land" include minerals or any interest in any of such minerals in place. The word "property" includes land, minerals in place, whether solid, liquid or gaseous, as well as an interest of any kind in such property, including royalty, owned by the estate. "Mineral development" includes exploration, by geophysical or by any other means, drilling, mining, developing, and operating, and producing and saving oil, other liquid hydrocarbons, gas (including all liquid hydrocarbons in the gaseous phase in the reservoir), gaseous elements, sulphur, metals, and all other minerals, solid or otherwise.

(b) Mineral Leases, With or Without Pooling or Unitization. Personal representatives of the estates of decedents, appointed and qualified under the laws of this State, and acting solely under orders of court, may be authorized by the court in which the probate proceedings on such estates are pending to make, execute, and deliver leases, with or without unitization clauses or pooling provisions, providing for the exploration for, and development and production of, oil, other liquid hydrocarbons, gas (including all liquid hydrocarbons in the gaseous phase), metals, and other solid minerals, and other minerals, or any of such minerals in place, belonging to such estates.

(c) Rules Concerning Applications, Orders, Notices, and Other Essential Matters. All such leases, with or without pooling provisions or unitization clauses, shall be made and entered into pursuant to and in conformity with the following rules:

1. **Contents of Application.** The representative of the estate shall file with the county clerk of the county where the probate proceeding is pending his written application, addressed to the court or the judge of such court, asking for authority to lease property of the estate for mineral exploration and development, with or without pooling provisions or unitization clauses. The application shall (a) describe the property fully enough by reference to the amount of acreage, the survey name or number, or abstract number, or other description adequately identifying the property and its location in the county in which situated; (b) specify the interest thought to be owned by the estate, if less than the whole, but asking for authority to include all interest owned by the estate, if that be the intention; and (c) set out the reasons why such particular property of the estate should be leased. Neither the name of any proposed lessee, nor the terms, provisions, or form of any desired lease, need be set out or suggested in any such application for authority to lease for mineral development.

2. **Order Designating Time and Place for Hearing Application.**

(a) Duties of Clerk and Judge. When an application to lease, as above prescribed, is filed, the county clerk shall immediately call the filing of such application to the attention of the court, and the judge shall promptly make and enter a brief order designating the time and place for the hearing of such application.

(b) Continuance of Hearing. If the hearing is not had at the time originally designated by the court or by timely order or orders of continuance duly entered, then, in such event, the hearing shall be automatically continued, without further notice, to the same hour or time the following day (except Sundays and holidays on which the county courthouse is officially closed to business) and from day to day until the application is finally acted upon and disposed of by order of the court. No notice of such automatic continuance shall be required.

3. **Notice of Application to Lease, Service of Notice, and Proof of Service.**

(a) Notice and Its Contents. The personal representative, and not the county clerk, shall give notice in writing of the time designated by the judge for the hearing on the application to lease. The notice shall be directed to all persons interested in the estate. It shall state the date on which the application was filed, describe briefly the property sought to be leased, specifying the fractional interest sought to be leased if less than the entire interest in the tract or tracts identified, state the time and place designated by the judge for the hearing, and be dated.

(b) Service of Notice. The personal representative shall give at least ten days notice, exclusive of the date of notice and of the date set for hearing, by publication in one issue of a newspaper of general circulation in the county in which the proceeding is pending, or, if there be no such newspaper, then by posting by the personal representative or at his instance. The date of notice when published shall be the date the newspaper bears.

4. **Preceding Requirements Mandatory.** In the absence of: (a) a written order originally designating a time and place for hearing; (b) a notice issued by the personal representative of the estate in compliance with such order; and (c) proof of publication or posting of such notice as required, any order of the judge or court authorizing any acts to be performed pursuant to said application shall be null and void.

5. **Hearing on Application to Lease and Order Thereon.** At the time and place designated for the

hearing, or at any time to which it shall have been continued as hereinabove provided, the judge shall hear such application, requiring proof as to the necessity or advisability of leasing for mineral development the property described in the application and in the notice; and, if he is satisfied that the application is in due form, that notice has been duly given in the manner and for the time required by law, that the proof of necessity or advisability of leasing is sufficient, and that the application should be granted, then an order shall be entered so finding, and authorizing the making of one or more leases, with or without pooling provisions or unitization clauses (with or without cash consideration if deemed by the court to be in the best interest of the estate) affecting and covering the property, or portions thereof, described in the application. Said order authorizing leasing shall also set out the following mandatory contents:

(a) The name of the lessee.

(b) The actual cash consideration, if any, to be paid by the lessee.

(c) Finding that the personal representative is exempted by law from giving bond, if that be a fact and if not a fact, then a finding as to whether or not the representative's general bond on file is sufficient to protect the personal property on hand, inclusive of any cash bonus to be paid, if any. If the court finds the general bond insufficient to meet these requirements, the order shall show the amount of increased or additional bond required to cover the deficiency.

(d) A complete exhibit copy, either written or printed, of each lease thus authorized to be made, shall either be set out in the order or attached thereto and incorporated by reference in said order and made a part thereof. It shall show the name of the lessee, the date of the lease, an adequate description of the property being leased, the delay rental, if any, to be paid to defer commencement of operations, and all other terms and provisions authorized; provided, that if no date of the lease appears in such exhibit copy, or in the court's order, then the date of the court's order shall be considered for all purposes as the date of the authorized lease, and if the name and address of the depository bank, or either of them, for receiving rental is not shown in said exhibit copy, the same may be inserted or caused to be inserted in the lease by the estate's personal representative at the time of its execution, or at any other time agreeable to the lessee, his successors, or assigns.

6. Conditional Validity of Lease; Bond; Time of Execution; Confirmation Not Needed. If, upon the hearing of an application for authority to lease, the court shall grant the same as above provided, the personal representative of the estate shall then be fully authorized to make, within thirty days after date of the judge's order, but not afterwards unless an extension be granted by the court upon sworn application showing good cause, the lease or leases as evidenced by the aforesaid true exhibit copies, in accordance with said order; but, unless the personal representative is not required to give a general bond, no such lease, for which a cash consideration is required, though ordered, executed, and delivered, shall be valid unless the order authorizing same actually makes findings with respect to the general bond, and, in case such bond has been found insufficient, then unless and until the bond has been increased, or an additional bond given, as required by the court's order, with the sureties required by law, has been approved by the judge and filed with the clerk of the court in which the proceedings are pending. In the event two or more leases on different lands are authorized by the same order, the general bond shall be increased, or additional bonds given, to cover all. It shall not be necessary for the judge to make any order confirming such leases.

7. Term of Lease Binding. Every such lease, when executed and delivered in compliance with the rules hereinabove set out, shall be valid and binding upon the property or interest therein owned by the estate and covered by the lease for the full duration of the term as provided therein, subject only to its terms and conditions, even though the primary term shall extend beyond the date when the estate shall have been closed in accordance with law; provided the authorized primary term shall not exceed five (5) years, subject to terms and provisions of the lease extending it beyond the primary term by paying production, by bona fide drilling or reworking operations, whether in or on the same or additional well or wells, with no cessation of operations of more than sixty (60) consecutive days before production has been restored or obtained, or by the provisions of the lease relating to a shut-in gas well.

7(a). Validation of Certain Provisions of Leases Heretofore Executed by Personal Representatives. As to any valid mineral lease heretofore executed and delivered in compliance with the provisions of the Texas Probate Code and which lease is still in force, any provisions of any such lease continuing such lease in force after its five (5) year primary term by a shut-in gas well are hereby validated; provided, however, that this provision shall not be applicable to any such provision of any such lease which is involved in any lawsuit pending in this state on the effective date of this Act wherein the validity of such provision is an issue.

8. **Amendment of Leases.** Any oil, gas, and mineral lease heretofore or hereafter executed by a personal representative pursuant to the Texas Probate Code may be amended by an instrument which provides that a shut-in gas well on the land covered by the lease or on land pooled with all or some part thereof shall continue such lease in force after its five (5) year primary term. Such instrument shall be executed by the personal representative, with the approval of the court, and on such terms and conditions as may be prescribed therein.

Acts 1955, 54th Leg., p. 88, ch. 55, eff. Jan. 1, 1956. Amended by Acts 1957, 55th Leg., p. 53, ch. 31, § 10(a), eff. Aug. 22, 1957; Acts 1961, 57th Leg., p. 441, ch. 215, §§ 1 to 3, eff. May 25, 1961; Acts 1993, 73rd Leg., ch. 957, § 64, eff. Sept. 1, 1993.

§ 368. Mineral Leases at Private Sale

(a) Authorization Allowed. Notwithstanding the preceding mandatory requirements for setting a time and place for hearing of an application to lease and the issuance, service, and return of notice, the court may authorize the making of oil, gas, and mineral leases at private sale (without public notice or advertising) if, in the opinion of the court, sufficient facts are set out in the application required above to show that it would be more advantageous to the estate that a lease be made privately and without compliance with said mandatory requirements mentioned above. Leases so authorized may include pooling provisions or unitization clauses as in other cases.

(b) Action of the Court When Public Advertising Not Required. At any time after the expiration of five (5) days and prior to the expiration of ten (10) days from the date of filing and without an order setting time and place of hearing, the court shall hear the application to lease at private sale and shall inquire into the manner in which the proposed lease has been or will be made, and shall hear evidence for or against the same; and, if satisfied that the lease has been or will be made for a fair and sufficient consideration and on fair terms, and has been or will be properly made in conformity with law, the court shall enter an order authorizing the execution of such lease without the necessity of advertising, notice, or citation, said order complying in all other respects with the requirements essential to the validity of mineral leases as hereinabove set out, as if advertising or notice were required. No order confirming a lease or leases made at private sale need be issued, but no such lease shall be valid until the increased or additional bond required by the court, if any, has been approved by the court and filed with the clerk of the court.

Acts 1955, 54th Leg., p. 88, ch. 55, eff. Jan. 1, 1956. Amended by Acts 1957, 55th Leg., p. 53, ch. 31, § 10(b).

§ 369. Pooling or Unitization of Royalty or Minerals

(a) Authorization for Pooling or Unitization. When an existing lease or leases on property owned by the estate does not adequately provide for pooling or unitization, the court may authorize the commitment of royalty or mineral interests in oil, liquid hydrocarbons, gas (including all liquid hydrocarbons in the gaseous phase in the reservoir), gaseous elements, and other minerals, or any one or more of them, owned by the estate being administered, to agreements that provide for the operation of areas as a pool or unit for the exploration, development, and production of all such minerals, where the court finds that the pool or unit to which the agreement relates will be operated in such a manner as to protect correlative rights, or to prevent the physical or economic waste of oil, liquid hydrocarbons, gas (including all liquid hydrocarbons in the gaseous phase in the reservoir), gaseous elements, or other mineral subject thereto, and that it is to the best interest of the estate to execute the agreement. Any agreement so authorized to be executed may, among other things, provide:

(1) That operations incident to the drilling of or production from a well upon any portion of a pool or unit shall be deemed for all purposes to be the conduct of operations upon or production from each separately owned tract in the pool or unit.

(2) That any lease covering any part of the area committed to a pool or unit shall continue in force in its entirety as long as oil, gas, or other mineral subject to the agreement is produced in paying quantities from any part of the pooled or unitized area, or as long as operations are conducted as provided in the lease on any part of the pooled or unitized area, or as long as there is a shut-in gas well on any part of the pooled or unitized area, if the presence of such shut-in gas well is a ground for continuation of the lease by the terms of said lease.

(3) That the production allocated by the agreement to each tract included in a pool or unit shall, when produced, be deemed for all purposes to have been produced from such tract by a well drilled thereon.

(4) That the royalties provided for on production from any tract or portion thereof within the pool or unit shall be paid only on that portion of the produc-

tion allocated to the tract in accordance with the agreement.

(5) That the dry gas, before or after extraction of hydrocarbons, may be returned to a formation underlying any lands or leases committed to the agreement, and that no royalties are required to be paid on the gas so returned.

(6) That gas obtained from other sources or other lands may be injected into a formation underlying any lands or leases committed to the agreement, and that no royalties are required to be paid on the gas so injected when same is produced from the unit.

(b) Procedure for Authorizing Pooling or Unitization. Pooling or unitization, when not adequately provided for by an existing lease or leases on property owned by the estate, may be authorized by the court in which the proceedings are pending pursuant to and in conformity with the following rules:

(1) Contents of Application. The personal representative of the estate shall file with the county clerk of the county where the probate proceeding is pending his written application for authority (a) to enter into pooling or unitization agreements supplementing, amending, or otherwise relating to, any existing lease or leases covering property owned by the estate, or (b) to commit royalties or other interest in minerals, whether subject to lease or not, to a pooling or unitization agreement. The application shall also (c) describe the property sufficiently, as required in original application to lease, (d) describe briefly the lease or leases, if any, to which the interest of the estate is subject, and (e) set out the reasons why the proposed agreement concerning such property should be made. A true copy of the proposed agreement shall be attached to the application and by reference made a part thereof, but the agreement shall not be recorded in the minutes. The clerk shall immediately, after such application is filed, call it to the attention of the judge.

(2) Notice Not Necessary. No notice of the filing of such application by advertising, citation, or otherwise, is required.

(3) Hearing of Application. A hearing on such application may be held by the judge at any time agreeable to the parties to the proposed agreement, and the judge shall hear proof and satisfy himself as to whether or not it is to the best interest of the estate that the proposed agreement be authorized. The hearing may be continued from day to day and from time to time as the court finds to be necessary.

(4) Action of Court and Contents of Order. If the court finds that the pool or unit to which the agreement relates will be operated in such a manner as to protect correlative rights or to prevent the physical or economic waste of oil, liquid hydrocarbons, gas (including all liquid hydrocarbons in the gaseous phase in the reservoir), gaseous elements, or other mineral subject thereto; that it is to the best interest of the estate that the agreement be executed; and that the agreement conforms substantially with the permissible provisions of Subsection (a) hereof, he shall enter an order setting out the findings made by him, authorizing execution of the agreement (with or without payment of cash consideration according to the agreement). If cash consideration is to be paid for the agreement, findings as to the necessity of increased or additional bond, as in making of leases upon payment of the cash bonus therefor, shall also be made, and no such agreement shall be valid until the increased or additional bond required by the court, if any, has been approved by the judge and filed with the clerk. The date of the court's order shall be the effective date of the agreement, if not stipulated in such agreement.

Acts 1955, 54th Leg., p. 88, ch. 55, eff. Jan. 1, 1956. Amended by Acts 1961, 57th Leg., p. 441, ch. 215, § 4, eff. May 25, 1961.

§ 370. Special Ancillary Instruments Which May Be Executed Without Court Order

As to any valid mineral lease or pooling or unitization agreement, executed on behalf of the estate prior to the effective date of this Code, or pursuant to its provisions, or by a former owner of land, minerals, or royalty affected thereby, the personal representative of the estate which is being administered may, without further order of the court, and without consideration, execute division orders, transfer orders, instruments of correction, instruments designating depository banks for the reception of delay rentals or shut-in gas well royalty to accrue or become payable under the terms of any such lease or leases, and similar instruments pertaining to any such lease or agreement and the property covered thereby.

Acts 1955, 54th Leg., p. 88, ch. 55, eff. Jan. 1, 1956. Amended by Acts 1957, 55th Leg., p. 53, ch. 31, § 10(c).

§ 371. Procedure When Representative of Estate Neglects to Apply for Authority

When the personal representative of an estate shall neglect to apply for authority to subject property of the estate to a lease for mineral development, pooling or unitization, or to commit royalty or other interest in minerals to pooling or unitization, any person interested in the estate may, upon written application filed with the county clerk, cause such representative to be cited to show cause why it is not for the best interest of the estate for such a lease to be made, or such an agreement entered into. The clerk shall immediately call the filing of such application to the attention of the judge of the court in which the probate proceedings are pending, and the judge shall set a time and place for a hearing on the application, and the representative of the estate shall be cited to appear and show cause why the execution of such lease or agreement should not be ordered. Upon hearing, if satisfied from the proof that it would be in the best interest of the estate, the court shall enter an order requiring the personal representative forthwith to file his application to subject such property of the estate to a lease for mineral development, with or without pooling or unitization provisions, or to commit royalty or other minerals to unitization, as the case may be. The procedure prescribed with respect to original application to lease, or with respect to original application for authority to commit royalty or minerals to pooling or unitization, whichever is appropriate, shall then be followed.

Acts 1955, 54th Leg., p. 88, ch. 55, eff. Jan. 1, 1956.

§ 372. Validation of Certain Leases and Pooling or Unitization Agreements Based on Previous Statutes

All presently existing leases on the oil, gas, or other minerals, or one or more of them, belonging to the estates of decedents, and all agreements with respect to pooling, or unitization thereof, or one or more of them, or any interest therein, with like properties of others having been authorized by the court having venue, and executed and delivered by the executors, administrators, or other fiduciaries of their estates in substantial conformity to the rules set forth in statutes heretofore existing, providing for only seven days notice in some instances, and also for a brief order designating a time and place for hearing, are hereby validated in so far as said period of notice is concerned, and in so far as the absence of any order setting a time and place for hearing is concerned; provided, this shall not apply to any lease or pooling or unitization agreement involved in any suit pending on the effective date of this Code wherein either the length of time of said notice or the absence of such order is in issue.

Acts 1955, 54th Leg., p. 88, ch. 55, eff. Jan. 1, 1956. Amended by Acts 1993, 73rd Leg., ch. 957, § 65, eff. Sept. 1, 1993.

PART 8. PARTITION AND DISTRIBUTION OF ESTATES OF DECEDENTS

§ 373. Application for Partition and Distribution of Estates of Decedents

(a) Who May Apply. At any time after the expiration of twelve months after the original grant of letters testamentary or of administration, the executor or administrator, or the heirs, devisees, or legatees of the estate, or any of them, may, by written application filed in the court in which the estate is pending, request the partition and distribution of the estate.

(b) Contents of Application. The application shall state:

(1) The name of the person whose estate is sought to be partitioned and distributed; and

(2) The names and residences of all persons entitled to shares of such estate, and whether adults or minors; and, if these facts be unknown to the applicant, it shall be so stated in the application; and

(3) The reasons why partition and distribution should be had.

(c) Partial Distribution. At any time after the original grant of letters testamentary or of administration, and the filing and approval of the inventory, the executor or administrator, or the heirs, devisees, or legatees of the estate, or any of them, may, by written application filed in the court in which the estate is pending, request a distribution of any portion of the estate. All interested parties shall be personally cited, as in other distributions, including known creditors. The court may upon proper citation and hearing distribute any portion of the estate it deems advisable. In the event a distribution is to be made to one or more heirs or devisees, and not to all the heirs or devisees, the court shall require a refunding bond in an amount to be determined by the court to be filed with the court and, upon its approval, the court shall order the distribution of that portion of the estate, unless such requirement is waived in writing and the waiver is filed with the court by all interested parties. This section shall apply to corpus as well as income, notwithstanding any other provisions of this Code.

Acts 1955, 54th Leg., p. 88, ch. 55, eff. Jan. 1, 1956. Amended by Acts 1973, 63rd Leg., p. 408, ch. 182, § 2, eff. May 25, 1973.

§ 374. Citation of Interested Persons

Upon the filing of such application, the clerk shall issue a citation which shall state the name of the person whose estate is sought to be partitioned and distributed, and the date upon which the court will hear the application, and the citation shall require all persons interested in the estate to appear and show cause why such partition and distribution should not be made. Such citation shall be personally served upon each person residing in the state entitled to a share of the estate whose address is known; and, if there be any such persons whose identities or addresses are not known, or who are not residents of this state, or are residents of but absent from this state, such citation shall be served by publication.

Acts 1955, 54th Leg., p. 88, ch. 55, eff. Jan. 1, 1956.

§ 375. Citation of Executor or Administrator

When application for partition and distribution is made by any person other than the executor or administrator, such representative shall also be cited to appear and answer the application and to file in court a verified exhibit and account of the condition of the estate, as in the case of final settlements.

Acts 1955, 54th Leg., p. 88, ch. 55, eff. Jan. 1, 1956.

§ 376. Repealed by Acts 1993, 73rd Leg., ch. 957, § 75(1), eff. Sept. 1, 1993

Acts 1993, 73rd Leg., ch. 957, repealing this section, enacted Chapter XIII, Guardianship, of the Probate Code.

§ 377. Facts to Be Ascertained Upon Hearing

At the hearing upon the application for partition and distribution, the court shall ascertain:

(a) The residue of the estate subject to partition and distribution, which shall be ascertained by deducting from the entire assets of such estate remaining on hand the amount of all debts and expenses of every kind which have been approved or established by judgment, but not paid, or which may yet be established by judgment, and also the probable future expenses of administration.

(b) The persons who are by law entitled to partition and distribution, and their respective shares.

(c) Whether advancements have been made to any of the persons so entitled and their nature and value. If advancements have been made, the court shall require the same to be placed in hotchpotch as required by the law governing intestate succession.

Acts 1955, 54th Leg., p. 88, ch. 55, eff. Jan. 1, 1956.

§ 378. Decree of the Court

If the court is of the opinion that the estate should be partitioned and distributed, it shall enter a decree which shall state:

(a) The name and address, if known, of each person entitled to a share of the estate, specifying those who are known to be minors, and the names of their guardians, or the guardians ad litem, and the name of the attorney appointed to represent those who are unknown or who are not residents of the state.

(b) The proportional part of the estate to which each is entitled.

(c) A full description of all the estate to be distributed.

(d) That the executor or administrator retain in his hands for the payment of all debts, taxes, and expenses of administration a sufficient amount of money or property for that purpose, specifying the amount of money or the property to be so retained.

Acts 1955, 54th Leg., p. 88, ch. 55, eff. Jan. 1, 1956.

§ 378A. Satisfaction of Pecuniary Bequests

(a) Unless the governing instrument provides otherwise, if an executor, administrator, or trustee is authorized under the will or trust of a decedent to satisfy a pecuniary bequest, devise, or transfer in trust in kind with assets at their value for federal estate tax purposes, in satisfaction of a gift intended to qualify, or that otherwise would qualify, for a United States estate tax marital deduction, the executor, administrator, or trustee, in order to implement the bequest, devise, or transfer, shall distribute assets, including cash, fairly representative of appreciation or depreciation in the value of all property available for distribution in satisfaction of the pecuniary bequest, devise, or transfer.

(b) Unless the governing instrument provides otherwise, if a will or trust contains a pecuniary bequest, devise, or transfer that may be satisfied by distributing assets in kind and if the executor, administrator, or trustee determines to fund the bequest, devise, or transfer by distributing assets in kind, the property shall, for the purpose of funding the bequest, devise, or transfer, be valued at its value on the date or dates of distribution.

Added by Acts 1987, 70th Leg., ch. 1110, § 1, eff. Sept. 1, 1987. Amended by Acts 1991, 72nd Leg., ch. 895, § 15, eff. Sept. 1, 1991.

Section 2 of the 1987 Act provides:

"This Act takes effect September 1, 1987, and applies to the estates of persons who die on or after that date. An estate of a person who dies before the effective date of this Act is covered by the law as it existed when the person died, and that law is continued in effect for that purpose."

§ 378B. Allocation of Income and Expenses During Administration of Decedent's Estate

(a) Except as provided by Subsection (b) of this section and unless the will provides otherwise, all expenses incurred in connection with the settlement of a decedent's estate, including debts, funeral expenses, estate taxes, interest and penalties relating to estate taxes, and family allowances, shall be charged against the principal of the estate. Fees and expenses of an attorney, accountant, or other professional advisor, commissions and expenses of a personal representative, court costs, and all other similar fees or expenses relating to the administration of the estate shall be allocated between the income and principal of the estate as the executor determines in its discretion to be just and equitable.

(b) Unless the will provides otherwise, income from the assets of a decedent's estate that accrues after the death of the testator and before distribution, including income from property used to discharge liabilities, shall be determined according to the rules applicable to a trustee under the Texas Trust Code (Subtitle B, Title 9, Property Code)[1] and distributed as provided by Subsections (c), (d), and (e) of this section.

(c) The income from the property bequeathed or devised to a specific devisee shall be distributed to the devisee after reduction for property taxes, ordinary repairs, insurance premiums, interest accrued after the death of the testator, other expenses of management and operation of the property, and other taxes, including the taxes imposed on the income that accrues during the period of administration and that is payable to the devisee.

(d) Except as provided by Subsection (f) of this section, the balance of the net income shall be distributed to all other devisees after reduction for the balance of property taxes, ordinary repairs, insurance premiums, interest accrued, including interest accruing as provided by Subsection (f) of this section after the death of the testator, other expenses of management and operation of all property from which the estate is entitled to income, and taxes imposed on income that accrues during the period of administration and that is payable or allocable to the devisees, in proportion to the devisees' respective interests in the undistributed assets of the estate.

(e) If a charitable organization is entitled to receive income under Subsection (b) of this section, any amount allowed as a tax deduction to the estate for income payable to the charitable organization shall be paid, without reduction for taxes, to the charitable organization.

(f) A devisee of a pecuniary bequest, whether or not in trust, shall be paid interest on the bequest at the legal rate of interest as provided by Article 1.03, Revised Statutes (Article 5069–1.03, Vernon's Texas Civil Statutes), and its subsequent amendments, beginning one year after the date the court grants letters testamentary or letters of administration.

(g) Income received by a trustee under this section shall be treated as income of the trust as provided by Section 113.103, Property Code.

(h) In this section, "undistributed assets" includes funds used to pay debts, administration expenses, and federal and state estate, inheritance, succession, and generation-skipping transfer taxes until the date of payment of the debts, expenses, and taxes. Except as required by Sections 2055 and 2056 of the Internal Revenue Code of 1986 (26 U.S.C. Secs. 2055 and 2056), and its subsequent amendments, the frequency and method of determining the beneficiaries' respective interests in the undistributed assets of the estate shall be in the executor's sole and absolute discretion. The executor may consider all relevant factors, including administrative convenience and expense and the interests of the various beneficiaries of the estate in order to reach a fair and equitable result among beneficiaries.

Added by Acts 1993, 73rd Leg., ch. 846, § 24, eff. Sept. 1, 1993.

[1] V.T.C.A. Property Code, § 111.001 et seq.

§ 379. Partition When Estate Consists of Money or Debts Only

If the estate to be distributed shall consist only of money or debts due the estate, or both, the court shall fix the amount to which each distributee is entitled, and shall order the payment and delivery thereof by the executor or administrator.

Acts 1955, 54th Leg., p. 88, ch. 55, eff. Jan. 1, 1956.

§ 380. Partition and Distribution When Property Is Capable of Division

(a) Appointment of Commissioners. If the estate does not consist entirely of money or debts due the estate, or both, the court shall appoint three or more discreet and disinterested persons as commissioners, to make a partition and distribution of the estate, unless the court has already determined that the estate is incapable of partition.

(b) Writ of Partition and Service Thereof. When commissioners are appointed, the clerk shall issue a writ of partition directed to the commissioners appointed, commanding them to proceed forthwith to make partition and distribution in accordance with the decree of the court, a copy of which decree shall accompany the writ, and also command them to make due return of said writ, with their proceedings under it, on a date named in the writ. Such writ shall be served by delivering the same and the accompanying copy of the decree of partition to any one of the commissioners appointed, and by notifying the other commissioners, verbally or otherwise, of their appointment, and such service may be made by any person.

(c) Partition by Commissioners. The commissioners shall make a fair, just, and impartial partition and distribution of the estate in the following order:

(1) Of the land or other property, by allotting to each distributee a share in each parcel or shares in one or more parcels, or one or more parcels separately, either with or without the addition of a share or shares of other parcels, as shall be most for the interest of the distributees; provided, the real estate is capable of being divided without manifest injury to all or any of the distributees.

(2) If the real estate is not capable of a fair, just and equal division in kind, but may be made so by allotting to one or more of the distributees a proportion of the money or other personal property to supply the deficiency or deficiencies, the commissioners shall have power to make, as nearly as may be, an equal division of the real estate and supply the deficiency of any share or shares from the money or other property.

(3) The commissioners shall proceed to make a like division in kind, as nearly as may be, of the money and other personal property, and shall determine by lot, among equal shares, to whom each particular share shall belong.

(d) Report of Commissioners. The commissioners, having divided the whole or any part of the estate, shall make to the court a written sworn report containing a statement of the property divided by them, and also a particular description of the property allotted to each distributee, and its value. If it be real estate that has been divided, the report shall contain a general plat of said land with the division lines plainly set down and with the number of acres in each share. The report of a majority of the commissioners shall be sufficient.

(e) Action of the Court. Upon the return of such report, the court shall examine the same carefully and hear all exceptions and objections thereto, and evidence in favor of or against the same, and if it be informal, shall cause said informality to be corrected. If such division shall appear to have been fairly made according to law, and no valid exceptions are taken to it, the court shall approve it, and shall enter a decree vesting title in the distributees of their respective shares or portions of the property as set apart to them by the commissioners; otherwise, the court may set aside said report and division and order a new partition to be made.

(f) Delivery of Property. When the report of commissioners to make partition has been approved and ordered to be recorded, the court shall order the executor or administrator to deliver to the distributees their respective shares of the estate on demand, including all the title deeds and papers belonging to the same.

(g) Fees of Commissioners. Commissioners thus appointed who actually serve in partitioning and distributing an estate shall be entitled to receive Five Dollars each for every day that they are necessarily engaged in the performance of their duties as such commissioners, to be taxed and paid as other costs in cases of partition.

Acts 1955, 54th Leg., p. 88, ch. 55, eff. Jan. 1, 1956.

§ 381. Partition and Distribution When Property of an Estate Is Incapable of Division

(a) Finding by the Court. When, in the opinion of the court, the whole or any portion of an estate is not capable of a fair and equal partition and distribution, the court shall make a special finding in writing, specifying therein the property incapable of division.

(b) Order of Sale. When the court has found that the whole or any portion of the estate is not capable of fair and equal division, it shall order a sale of all property which it has found not to be capable of such division. Such sale shall be made by the executor or administrator in the same manner as when sales of real estate are made for the purpose of satisfying debts of the estate, and the proceeds of such sale, when collected, shall be distributed by the court among those entitled thereto.

(c) Purchase by Distributee. At such sale, if any distributee shall buy any of the property, he shall be required to pay or secure only such amount of his bid as exceeds the amount of his share of such property.

(d) Applicability of Provisions Relating to Sales of Real Estate. The provisions of this Code relative to reports of sales of real estate, the giving of an increased general or additional bond upon sales of real estate, and to the vesting of title to the property sold by decree or by deed, shall also apply to sales made under this Section.

Acts 1955, 54th Leg., p. 88, ch. 55, eff. Jan. 1, 1956.

§ 382. Property Located in Another County

(a) Court May Order Sale. When any portion of the estate to be partitioned lies in another county and cannot be fairly partitioned without prejudice to the interests of the distributees, the commissioners may report such facts to the court in writing; whereupon, if satisfied that the said property cannot be fairly divided, or that its sale would be more advantageous to the distributees, the court may order a sale thereof, which sale shall be conducted in the same manner as is provided in this Code for the sale of property which is not capable of fair and equal division.

(b) Court May Appoint Additional Commissioners. If the court is not satisfied that such property cannot be fairly and advantageously divided, or that its sale would be more advantageous to the distributees, three or more commissioners may be appointed in each county where any portion of the estate so reported is situated, and the same proceedings shall be had thereon as are provided in this Code for commissioners to make partition.

Acts 1955, 54th Leg., p. 88, ch. 55, eff. Jan. 1, 1956.

§ 383. Repealed by Acts 1993, 73rd Leg., ch. 957, § 75(1), eff. Sept. 1, 1993

Acts 1993, 73rd Leg., ch. 957, repealing this section, enacted Chapter XIII, Guardianship, of the Probate Code.

§ 384. Damages for Neglect to Deliver Property

If any executor or administrator shall neglect to deliver to the person entitled thereto, when demanded, any portion of an estate ordered to be delivered, such person may file with the clerk of the court his written complaint alleging the fact of such neglect, the date of his demand, and other relevant facts, whereupon the clerk shall issue a citation to be served personally on such representative, apprising him of the complaint and citing him to appear before the court and answer, if he so desires, at the time designated in the citation. If at the hearing the court finds that the citation was duly served and returned and that the representative is guilty of such neglect, the court shall enter an order to that effect, and the representative shall be liable to such complainant in damages at the rate of ten per cent of the amount or appraised value of the share so withheld, per month, for each and every month or fraction thereof that the share is and/or has been so withheld after date of demand, which damages may be recovered in any court of competent jurisdiction.

Acts 1955, 54th Leg., p. 88, ch. 55, eff. Jan. 1, 1956.

§ 385. Partition of Community Property

(a) Application for Partition. When a husband or wife shall die leaving any community property, the survivor may, at any time after letters testamentary or of administration have been granted, and an inventory, appraisement, and list of the claims of the estate have been returned, make application in writing to the court which granted such letters for a partition of such community property.

(b) Bond and Action of the Court. The survivor shall execute and deliver to the judge of said court a bond with a corporate surety or two or more good and sufficient personal sureties, payable to and approved by said judge, for an amount equal to the value of the survivor's interest in such community property, conditioned for the payment of one-half of all debts existing against such community property, and the court shall proceed to make a partition of said community property into two equal moieties, one to be delivered to the survivor and the other to the executor or administrator of the deceased. The provisions of this Code respecting the partition and distribution of estates shall apply to such partition so far as the same are applicable.

(c) Lien Upon Property Delivered. Whenever such partition is made, a lien shall exist upon the property delivered to the survivor to secure the payment of the aforementioned bond; and any creditor of said community estate may sue in his own name on such bond, and shall have judgment thereon for one-half of such debt as he shall establish, and for the other one-half he shall be entitled to be paid by the executor or administrator of the deceased.

Acts 1955, 54th Leg., p. 88, ch. 55, eff. Jan. 1, 1956.

§ 386. Partition of Property Jointly Owned

Any person having a joint interest with the estate of a decedent in any property, real or personal, may make application to the court from which letters testamentary or of administration have been granted thereon to have a partition thereof, whereupon the court shall make a partition of said property between the applicant and the estate of the deceased; and all the provisions of this Code in relation to the partition and distribution of estates shall govern partition hereunder, so far as the same are applicable.

Acts 1955, 54th Leg., p. 88, ch. 55, eff. Jan. 1, 1956.

§ 387. Expense of Partition

Expense of partition of the estate of a decedent shall be paid by the distributees pro rata. The portion of the estate allotted each distributee shall be liable for his portion of such expense, and, if not paid, the court may order execution therefor in the names of the persons entitled thereto.

Acts 1955, 54th Leg., p. 88, ch. 55, eff. Jan. 1, 1956.

PART 9. PARTITION OF WARD'S ESTATE IN REALTY [REPEALED]

§ 388. Repealed by Acts 1993, 73rd Leg., ch. 957, § 75(4), eff. Sept. 1, 1993

Acts 1993, 73rd Leg., ch. 957, repealing this part, enacted Chapter XIII, Guardianship, of the Probate Code.

PART 10. INVESTMENTS, LOANS, AND CONTRIBUTIONS OF ESTATES OF WARDS

§ 389. Investments Without Court Order

(a) Repealed by Acts 1999, 76th Leg., ch. 828, § 1, eff. June 18, 1999.

(b) If, at any time, the guardian of the estate shall have on hand money belonging to the ward beyond that which may be necessary for the education and maintenance of such ward or wards, he shall invest such money as follows:

(1) In bonds or other obligations of the United States;

(2) In tax-supported bonds of the State of Texas;

(3) In tax-supported bonds of any county, district, political subdivision, or incorporated city or town in the State of Texas; provided, that the bonds of counties, districts, subdivisions, cities, and towns may be purchased only subject to the following restrictions: the net funded debt of said issuing unit shall not exceed ten per cent of the assessed value of taxable property therein, "net funded debt" meaning the total funded debt less sinking funds on hand; and further, in the case of cities or towns, less that part of the debt incurred for acquisition or improvement of revenue-producing utilities, the revenues of which are not pledged to support other obligations; provided, however, that these restrictions shall not apply to bonds issued for road purposes in this state under authority of Section 52 of Article III of the Constitution of Texas, which bonds are supported by a tax unlimited as to rate or amount;

(4) In shares or share accounts of any state savings and loan association or savings bank with its main office or a branch office in this state, provided the payment of such shares or share accounts is insured by the Federal Deposit Insurance Corporation;

(5) In the shares or share accounts of any federal savings and loan association or savings bank with its main office or a branch office in this state, where the payment of such shares or share accounts is insured by the Federal Deposit Insurance Corporation;

(6) In collateral bonds of companies incorporated under the laws of the State of Texas, having a paid-in capital of One Million Dollars or more, when such bonds are a direct obligation of the company issuing them, and are specifically secured by first mortgage real estate notes or other securities pledged with a trustee; or

(7) In interest-bearing time deposits which may be withdrawn on or before one year after demand in any bank doing business in Texas where the payment of such time deposits is insured by the Federal Deposit Insurance Corporation.

Acts 1955, 54th Leg., p. 88, ch. 55, eff. Jan. 1, 1956. Amended by Acts 1961, 57th Leg., p. 42, ch. 28, § 1, eff. March 25, 1961; Acts 1993, 73rd Leg., ch. 846, § 22, eff. Sept. 1, 1993; Acts 1999, 76th Leg., ch. 344, § 6.004, eff. Sept. 1, 1999; Acts 1999, 76th Leg., ch. 828, § 1, eff. June 18, 1999.

Repeal

Without reference to the amendment of subsec. (b) by Acts 1999, 76th Leg., ch. 344, § 6.004, this section was repealed by Acts 1999, 76th Leg., ch. 828, § 1, eff. June 18, 1999.

§§ 389A to 398. Repealed by Acts 1993, 73rd Leg., ch. 957, § 75(4), eff. Sept. 1, 1993

Acts 1993, 73rd Leg., ch. 957, repealing this part, enacted Chapter XIII, Guardianship, of the Probate Code.

Without reference to the repeal of § 389A by Acts 1993, 73rd Leg., ch. 957, § 75(4), Acts 1993, 73rd Leg., ch. 846, § 23 amended the section heading to read, "Investments With Court Order".

PART 10A. STOCKS, BONDS AND OTHER PERSONAL PROPERTY

§ 398A. Holding of Stocks, Bonds and Other Personal Property by Personal Representatives in Name of Nominee

Unless otherwise provided by will, a personal representative may cause stocks, bonds, and other personal property of an estate to be registered and held in the name of a nominee without mention of the fiduciary relationship in any instrument or record constituting or evidencing title thereto. The personal representative is liable for the acts of the nominee with respect to any property so registered. The records of the personal representative shall at all times show the ownership of the property. Any property so registered shall be in the possession and control of the personal representative at all times and be kept separate from his individual property.

Added by Acts 1969, 61st Leg., p. 2106, ch. 719, § 1, eff. Sept. 1, 1969.

PART 11. ANNUAL ACCOUNTS AND OTHER EXHIBITS

§ 399. Annual Accounts Required

(a) Estates of Decedents Being Administered Under Order of Court. The personal representative of the estate of a decedent being administered under order of court shall, upon the expiration of twelve (12) months from the date of qualification and receipt of letters, return to the court an exhibit in writing under oath setting forth a list of all claims against the estate that were presented to him within the period covered by the account, specifying which have been allowed by him, which have been paid, which have been rejected and the date when rejected, which have been sued upon, and the condition of the suit, and show:

(1) All property that has come to his knowledge or into his possession not previously listed or inventoried as property of the estate.

(2) Any changes in the property of the estate which have not been previously reported.

(3) A complete account of receipts and disbursements for the period covered by the account, and the source and nature thereof, with receipts of principal and income to be shown separately.

(4) A complete, accurate and detailed description of the property being administered, the condition of the property and the use being made thereof, and, if rented, the terms upon and the price for which rented.

(5) The cash balance on hand and the name and location of the depository wherein such balance is kept; also, any other sums of cash in savings accounts or other form, deposited subject to court order, and the name and location of the depository thereof.

(6) A detailed description of personal property of the estate, which shall, with respect to bonds, notes, and other securities, include the names of obligor and obligee, or if payable to bearer, so state; the date of issue and maturity; the rate of interest; serial or other identifying numbers; in what manner the property is secured; and other data necessary to identify the same fully, and how and where held for safekeeping.

(7) A statement that, during the period covered by the account, all tax returns due have been filed and that all taxes due and owing have been paid and a complete account of the amount of the taxes, the date the taxes were paid, and the governmental entity to which the taxes were paid.

(8) If any tax return due to be filed or any taxes due to be paid are delinquent on the filing of the account, a description of the delinquency and the reasons for the delinquency.

(9) A statement that the personal representative has paid all the required bond premiums for the accounting period.

(b) Annual Reports Continue Until Estate Closed. Each personal representative of the estate of a decedent shall continue to file annual accounts conforming to the essential requirements of those in Subsection (a) hereof as to changes in the assets of the estate after rendition of the former account so that the true condition of the estate, with respect to money, securities, and other property, can be ascertained by the court or by any interested person, by adding to the balances forward the receipts, and then subtracting the disbursements. The description of property sufficiently described in an inventory or previous account may be by reference thereto.

(c) Supporting Vouchers, etc., Attached to Accounts. Annexed to all annual accounts of representatives of estates shall be:

(1) Proper vouchers for each item of credit claimed in the account, or, in the absence of such voucher, the item must be supported by evidence satisfactory to the court. Original vouchers may, upon application, be returned to the representative after approval of his account.

(2) An official letter from the bank or other depository in which the money on hand of the estate is deposited, showing the amounts in general or special deposits.

(3) Proof of the existence and possession of securities owned by the estate, or shown by the accounting, as well as other assets held by a depository subject to orders of the court, the proof to be by one of the following means:

a. By an official letter from the bank or other depository wherein said securities or other assets are held for safekeeping; provided, that if such depository is the representative, the official letter shall be signed by a representative of such depository other than the one verifying the account; or

b. By a certificate of an authorized representative of the corporation which is surety on the representative's bonds; or

c. By a certificate of the clerk or a deputy clerk of a court of record in this State; or

d. By an affidavit of any other reputable person designated by the court upon request of the representative or other interested party.

Such certificate or affidavit shall be to the effect that the affiant has examined the assets exhibited to him by the representative as assets of the estate in which the accounting is made, and shall describe the assets by reference to the account or otherwise sufficiently to identify those so exhibited, and shall state the time when and the place where exhibited. In lieu of using a certificate or an affidavit, the representative may exhibit the securities to the judge of the court who shall endorse on the account, or include in his order with respect thereto, a statement that the securities shown therein as on hand were in fact exhibited to him, and that those so exhibited were the same as those shown in the account, or note any variance. If the securities are exhibited at any place other than where deposited for safekeeping, it shall be at the expense and risk of the representative. The court may require additional evidence as to the existence and custody of such securities and other personal property as in his discretion he shall deem proper; and may require the representative to exhibit them to the court, or any person designated by him, at any time at the place where held for safekeeping.

(d) Verification of Account. The representative filing the account shall attach thereto his affidavit that it contains a correct and complete statement of the matters to which it relates.

Acts 1955, 54th Leg., p. 88, ch. 55, eff. Jan. 1, 1956. Amended by Acts 1957, 55th Leg., p. 53, ch. 31, § 11(a); Acts 1993, 73rd Leg., ch. 712, § 4, eff. Sept. 1, 1993, Acts 1993, 73rd Leg., ch. 957, § 66, eff. Sept. 1, 1993; Acts 1997, 75th Leg., ch. 1403, § 1, eff. Sept. 1, 1997.

Section 8 of Acts 1993, 73rd Leg., ch. 712 provides:

"The change in law made by this Act applies only to the estate of a person who dies on or after the effective date of this Act. An estate of a person who dies before the effective date of this Act is covered by the law in effect on the date of the person's death, and the former law continues in effect for that purpose."

The amendment of this section by Acts 1993, 73rd Leg., ch. 905, § 14 failed to take effect under § 19(a), which provided that the amendment was not to take effect if both S.B. No. 236 (ch. 905) and H.B. No. 2685 (ch. 957) were enacted and became law.

Sections 6 to 8 of Acts 1997, 75th Leg., ch. 1403 provide:

"Sec. 6. A court may modify any guardianship in effect on September 1, 1997, to conform with the requirements of Section 805, Texas Probate Code, as amended by this Act, on the court's own motion or on application by the ward, guardian, or any other interested person or entity.

"Sec. 7. The change in law made by Sections 1–4 of this Act to the Texas Probate Code apply only to an account or report filed on or after the effective date of this Act. An account or report filed before the effective date of this Act is governed by the law applicable on the date the account or report was filed, and that law is continued in effect for that purpose.

"Sec. 8. Except as provided by Section 6 of this Act:

"(1) the change in law made by this Act to Section 805, Texas Probate Code, applies only to proceedings for the appointment of a guardian instituted on or after the effective date of this Act; and

"(2) a proceeding for the appointment of a guardian that is instituted before the effective date of this Act is governed by the law in effect on the date the proceedings were instituted, and the former law is continued in effect for that purpose."

§ 400. Penalty for Failure to File Annual Account

Should any personal representative of an estate fail to return any annual account required by preceding sections of this Code, any person interested in said estate may, upon written complaint, or the court upon its own motion may, cause the personal representative to be cited to return such account, and show cause for such failure. If he fails to return said account after being so cited, or fails to show good cause for his failure so to do, the court, upon hearing, may revoke the letters of such representative, and may fine him in a sum not to exceed Five Hundred Dollars ($500). He and his sureties shall be liable for any fine imposed, and for all damages and costs sustained by reason of such failure, which may be recovered in any court of competent jurisdiction.

Acts 1955, 54th Leg., p. 88, ch. 55, eff. Jan. 1, 1956. Amended by Acts 1957, 55th Leg., p. 53, ch. 31, § 11(b); Acts 1993, 73rd Leg., ch. 957, § 67, eff. Sept. 1, 1993.

§ 401. Action Upon Annual Accounts

These rules shall govern the handling of annual accounts:

(a) They shall be filed with the county clerk, and the filing thereof shall be noted forthwith upon the judge's docket.

(b) Before being considered by the judge, the account shall remain on file ten (10) days.

(c) At any time after the expiration of ten (10) days after the filing of an annual account, the judge shall consider same, and may continue the hearing thereon until fully advised as to all items of said account.

(d) No accounting shall be approved unless possession of cash, listed securities, or other assets held in safekeeping or on deposit under order of court has been proved as required by law.

(e) If the account be found incorrect, it shall be corrected. When corrected to the satisfaction of the court, it shall be approved by an order of court, and the court shall then act with respect to unpaid claims, as follows:

(1) Order for Payment of Claims in Full. If it shall appear from the exhibit, or from other evidence, that

the estate is wholly solvent, and that the representative has in his hands sufficient funds for the payment of every character of claims against the estate, the court shall order immediate payment to be made of all claims allowed and approved or established by judgment.

(2) Order for Pro Rata Payment of Claims. If it shall appear from the account, or from other evidence, that the funds on hand are not sufficient for the payment of all the said claims, or if the estate is insolvent and the personal representative has any funds on hand, the court shall order such funds to be applied to the payment of all claims having a preference in the order of their priority if they, or any of them, be still unpaid, and then to the payment pro rata of the other claims allowed and approved or established by final judgment, taking into consideration also the claims that were presented within twelve (12) months after the granting of administration, and those which are in suit or on which suit may yet be instituted.

Acts 1955, 54th Leg., p. 88, ch. 55, eff. Jan. 1, 1956. Amended by Acts 1957, 55th Leg., p. 53, ch. 31, § 11(c).

§ 402. Additional Exhibits of Estates of Decedents

At any time after the expiration of fifteen months from the original grant of letters to an executor or administrator, any interested person may, by a complaint in writing filed in the court in which the estate is pending, cause the representative to be cited to appear and make an exhibit in writing under oath, setting forth fully, in connection with previous exhibits, the condition of the estate he represents; and, if it shall appear to the court by said exhibit, or by other evidence, that said representative has any funds of the estate in his hands subject to distribution among the creditors of the estate, the court shall order the same to be paid out to them according to the provisions of this Code; or any representative may voluntarily present such exhibit to the court; and, if he has any of the funds of the estate in his hands subject to distribution among the creditors of the estate, a like order shall be made.

Acts 1955, 54th Leg., p. 88, ch. 55, eff. Jan. 1, 1956.

§ 403. Penalty for Failure to File Exhibits or Reports

Should any personal representative fail to file any exhibit or report required by this Code, any person interested in the estate may, upon written complaint filed with the clerk of the court, cause him to be cited to appear and show cause why he should not file such exhibit or report; and, upon hearing, the court may order him to file such exhibit or report, and, unless good cause be shown for such failure, the court may revoke the letters of such personal representative and may fine him in an amount not to exceed One Thousand Dollars.

Acts 1955, 54th Leg., p. 88, ch. 55, eff. Jan. 1, 1956.

PART 12. FINAL SETTLEMENT, ACCOUNTING, AND DISCHARGE

§ 404. Closing Administration of Estates of Decedents

Administration of the estates of decedents shall be settled and closed when all the debts known to exist against the estate of a deceased person have been paid, or when they have been paid so far as the assets in the hands of an administrator or executor of such estate will permit, and when there is no further need for administration.

Acts 1955, 54th Leg., p. 88, ch. 55, eff. Jan. 1, 1956. Amended by Acts 1975, 64th Leg., p. 104, ch. 45, § 2, eff. Sept. 1, 1975; Acts 1985, 69th Leg., ch. 881, § 2, eff. Aug. 26, 1985; Acts 1989, 71st Leg., ch. 1035, § 15, eff. Sept. 1, 1989; Acts 1993, 73rd Leg., ch. 712, § 5, eff. Sept. 1, 1993; Acts 1993, 73rd Leg., ch. 957, § 68, eff. Sept. 1, 1993; Acts 1999, 76th Leg., ch. 826, § 1, eff. June 18, 1999.

Section 8 of Acts 1993, 73rd Leg., ch. 712 provides:

"The change in law made by this Act applies only to the estate of a person who dies on or after the effective date of this Act. An estate of a person who dies before the effective date of this Act is covered by the law in effect on the date of the person's death, and the former law continues in effect for that purpose."

§§ 404A, 404B. Repealed by Acts 1993, 73rd Leg., ch. 957, § 75(1), eff. Sept. 1, 1993

Acts 1993, 73rd Leg., ch. 957, repealing these sections, enacted Chapter XIII, Guardianship, of the Probate Code.

§ 405. Account for Final Settlement of Estates of Decedents

When administration of the estate of a decedent is to be settled and closed, the personal representative of such estate shall present to the court his verified account for final settlement. In such account it shall be sufficient to refer to the inventory without describing each item of property in detail, and to refer to and adopt any and all proceedings had in the administration concerning sales, renting or hiring, leasing for mineral development, or any other transactions on behalf of the estate including exhibits, accounts, and vouchers previously filed and approved, without restating the particular items thereof. Each final account, however, shall be accompanied by proper vouchers in support of each item thereof not already accounted for and shall show, either by reference to any proceedings authorized above or by statement of the facts:

1. The property belonging to the estate which has come into the hands of the executor or administrator.

2. The disposition that has been made of such property.

3. The debts that have been paid.

4. The debts and expenses, if any, still owing by the estate.

5. The property of the estate, if any, still remaining on hand.

6. The persons entitled to receive such estate, their relationship to the decedent, and their residence, if known, and whether adults or minors, and, if minors, the names of their guardians, if any.

7. All advancements or payments that have been made, if any, by the executor or administrator from such estate to any such person.

8. The tax returns due that have been filed and the taxes due and owing that have been paid and a complete account of the amount of taxes, the date the taxes were paid, and the governmental entity to which the taxes were paid.

9. If any tax return due to be filed or any taxes due to be paid are delinquent on the filing of the account, a description of the delinquency and the reasons for the delinquency.

10. The personal representative has paid all required bond premiums.

Acts 1955, 54th Leg., p. 88, ch. 55, eff. Jan. 1, 1956. Amended by Acts 1993, 73rd Leg., ch. 712, § 6, eff. Sept. 1, 1993; Acts 1993, 73rd Leg., ch. 957, § 69, eff. Sept. 1, 1993; Acts 1997, 75th Leg., ch. 1403, § 2, eff. Sept. 1, 1997.

Section 8 of Acts 1993, 73rd Leg., ch. 712 provides:

"The change in law made by this Act applies only to the estate of a person who dies on or after the effective date of this Act. An estate of a person who dies before the effective date of this Act is covered by the law in effect on the date of the person's death, and the former law continues in effect for that purpose."

Sections 6 to 8 of Acts 1997, 75th Leg., ch. 1403 provide:

"Sec. 6. A court may modify any guardianship in effect on September 1, 1997, to conform with the requirements of Section 805, Texas Probate Code, as amended by this Act, on the court's own motion or on application by the ward, guardian, or any other interested person or entity.

"Sec. 7. The change in law made by Sections 1–4 of this Act to the Texas Probate Code apply only to an account or report filed on or after the effective date of this Act. An account or report filed before the effective date of this Act is governed by the law applicable on the date the account or report was filed, and that law is continued in effect for that purpose.

"Sec. 8. Except as provided by Section 6 of this Act:

"(1) the change in law made by this Act to Section 805, Texas Probate Code, applies only to proceedings for the appointment of a guardian instituted on or after the effective date of this Act; and

"(2) a proceeding for the appointment of a guardian that is instituted before the effective date of this Act is governed by the law in effect on the date the proceedings were instituted, and the former law is continued in effect for that purpose."

§ 405A. Delivery of Property

The court may permit a resident executor or administrator who has any of the estate of a ward to deliver the estate to a duly qualified and acting guardian of the ward.

Added by Acts 1995, 74th Leg., ch. 1039, § 14, eff. Sept. 1, 1995.

§ 406. Procedure in Case of Neglect or Failure to File Final Account; Payments Due Meantime

(a) If a personal representative charged with the duty of filing a final account fails or neglects so to do at the proper time, the court shall, upon its own motion, or upon the written complaint of any one interested in the decedent's estate which has been administered, cause such representative to be cited to appear and present such account within the time specified in the citation.

(b) If the whereabouts of the personal representative and heirs of a decedent are unknown and a complaint has not been filed by anyone interested in the decedent's estate, the court may, on or after the fourth anniversary after the last date on which letters testamentary or of administration are issued by the court clerk, close the estate without a final accounting and without appointing a successor personal representative.

Acts 1955, 54th Leg., p. 88, ch. 55, eff. Jan. 1, 1956. Amended by Acts 1979, 66th Leg., p. 1876, ch. 758, § 3, eff. Aug. 27, 1979; Acts 1993, 73rd Leg., ch. 898, § 1, eff. June 19, 1993; Acts 1993, 73rd Leg., ch. 957, § 70, eff. Sept. 1, 1993; Acts 1999, 76th Leg., ch. 827, § 1, eff. Sept. 1, 1999.

Section 2 of Acts 1999, 76th Leg., ch. 827 provides:

"The change in law made by this Act applies only to the estates of persons who die on or after the effective date of this Act. The estate of a person who dies before the effective date of this Act is governed by the law in effect on the date of the person's death, and the former law is continued in effect for that purpose."

§ 407. Citation Upon Presentation of Account for Final Settlement

Upon the filing of an account for final settlement by temporary or permanent personal representatives of the estates of decedents, citation shall contain a statement that such final account has been filed, the time and place when it will be considered by the court, and a statement requiring the person or persons cited to appear and contest the same if they see proper. Such citation shall be issued by the county clerk to the persons and in the manner set out below.

1. In case of the estates of deceased persons, notice shall be given by the personal representative to each heir or beneficiary of the decedent by certified mail, return receipt requested, unless another type of notice is directed by the court by written order. The notice must include a copy of the account for final settlement.

2. If the court deems further additional notice necessary, it shall require the same by written order. In its discretion, the court may allow the waiver of notice of an account for final settlement in a proceeding concerning a decedent's estate.

Acts 1955, 54th Leg., p. 88, ch. 55, eff. Jan. 1, 1956. Amended by Acts 1959, 56th Leg., p. 641, ch. 294, § 1, eff. May 30, 1959; Acts 1979, 66th Leg., p. 1755, ch. 713, § 30, eff. Aug. 27, 1979; Acts 1983, 68th Leg., p. 4558, ch. 756, § 1, eff. Sept. 1, 1983; Acts 1993, 73rd Leg., ch. 957, § 71, eff. Sept. 1, 1993.

§ 408. Action of the Court

(a) Action Upon Account. Upon being satisfied that citation has been duly served upon all persons interested in the estate, the court shall examine the account for final settlement and the vouchers accompanying the same, and, after hearing all exceptions or objections thereto, and evidence in support of or against such account, shall audit and settle the same, and restate it if that be necessary.

(b) Distribution of Remaining Property. Upon final settlement of an estate, if there be any of such estate remaining in the hands of the personal representative, the court shall order that a partition and distribution be made among the persons entitled to receive such estate.

(c) Discharge of Representative When No Property Remains. If, upon such settlement, there be none of the estate remaining in the hands of the representative, he shall be discharged from his trust and the estate ordered closed.

(d) Discharge When Estate Fully Administered. Whenever the representative of an estate has fully administered the same in accordance with this Code and the orders of the court, and his final account has been approved, and he has delivered all of said estate remaining in his hands to the person or persons entitled to receive the same, it shall be the duty of the court to enter an order discharging such representative from his trust, and declaring the estate closed.

Acts 1955, 54th Leg., p. 88, ch. 55, eff. Jan. 1, 1956. Amended by Acts 1979, 66th Leg., p. 1877, ch. 758, § 4, eff. Aug. 27, 1979; Acts 1993, 73rd Leg., ch. 957, § 72, eff. Sept. 1, 1993.

§ 409. Money Becoming Due Pending Final Discharge

Until the order of final discharge of the personal representative is entered in the minutes of the court, money or other thing of value falling due to the estate while the account for final settlement is pending may be paid, delivered, or tendered to the personal representative, who shall issue receipt therefor, and the obligor and/or payor shall be thereby discharged of the obligation for all purposes.

Acts 1955, 54th Leg., p. 88, ch. 55, eff. Jan. 1, 1956. Amended by Acts 1993, 73rd Leg., ch. 957, § 73, eff. Sept. 1, 1993.

§ 410. Inheritance Taxes Must be Paid

No final account of an executor or administrator shall be approved, and no estate of a decedent shall be closed, unless the final account shows, and the court finds, that all inheritance taxes due and owing to the State of Texas with respect to all interests and properties passing through the hands of the representative have been paid.

Acts 1955, 54th Leg., p. 88, ch. 55, eff. Jan. 1, 1956. Amended by Acts 1989, 71st Leg., ch. 1035, § 16, eff. Sept. 1, 1989.

§ 411. Repealed by Acts 1993, 73rd Leg., ch. 957, § 75(1), eff. Sept. 1, 1993

Acts 1993, 73rd Leg., ch. 957, repealing this section, enacted Chapter XIII, Guardianship, of the Probate Code.

§ 412. Offsets, Credits, and Bad Debts

In the settlement of any of the accounts of the personal representative of an estate, all debts due the estate which the court is satisfied could not have been collected by due diligence, and which have not been collected, shall be excluded from the computation.

Acts 1955, 54th Leg., p. 88, ch. 55, eff. Jan. 1, 1956.

§ 413. Repealed by Acts 1993, 73rd Leg., ch. 957, § 75(1), eff. Sept. 1, 1993

Acts 1993, 73rd Leg., ch. 957, repealing this section, enacted Chapter XIII, Guardianship, of the Probate Code.

§ 414. Procedure if Representative Fails to Deliver Estate

If any personal representative of an estate, upon final settlement, shall neglect to deliver to the person entitled thereto when demanded any portion of an estate or any funds or money in his hands ordered to be delivered, such person may file with the clerk of the court his written complaint alleging the fact of such neglect, the date of his demand, and other relevant facts, whereupon the clerk shall issue a citation to be served personally upon such representative, apprising him of the complaint and citing him to appear before the court and answer, if he so desires, at the time designated in the citation. If at the hearing the court finds that the citation was duly served and returned and that the representative is guilty of the neglect charged, the court shall enter an order to that effect, and the representative shall be liable to such person in damages at the rate of ten per cent of the amount or appraised value of the money or estate so withheld, per month, for each and every month or fraction thereof that said estate or money or funds is and/or has been so withheld after date of demand, which damages may be recovered in any court of competent jurisdiction.

Acts 1955, 54th Leg., p. 88, ch. 55, eff. Jan. 1, 1956. Amended by Acts 1993, 73rd Leg., ch. 957, § 74, eff. Sept. 1, 1993.

CHAPTER IX. SPECIFIC PROVISIONS RELATING TO PERSONS OF UNSOUND MIND AND HABITUAL DRUNKARDS [REPEALED]

§§ 415 to 426. Repealed by Acts 1993, 73rd Leg., ch. 905, § 17, eff. Sept. 1, 1993; Acts 1993, 73rd Leg., ch. 957, § 75(5), eff. Sept. 1, 1993

Acts 1993, 73rd Leg., ch. 957, repealing this chapter, enacted Chapter XIII, Guardianship, of the Probate Code.

Section 28 of Acts 1993, 73rd Leg., ch. 905 provides:

"The change in law made by Section 17 of this Act applies only to the appointment of a guardian based on information that is filed under Section 415, Texas Probate Code, on or after the effective date of this Act. An appointment of a guardian based on information that is filed before the effective date of this Act is governed by the law in effect on the date the information was filed, and the former law is continued in effect for that purpose."

CHAPTER X. PAYMENT OF ESTATES INTO STATE TREASURY

Section

§ 427. When Estates to be Paid Into State Treasury

If any person entitled to a portion of an estate, except a resident minor without a guardian, shall not demand his portion from the executor or administrator within six months after an order of court approving the report of commissioners of partition, or within six months after the settlement of the final account of an executor or administrator, as the case may be, the court by written order shall require the executor or administrator to pay so much of said portion as is in money to the comptroller; and such portion as is in other property he shall order the executor or administrator to sell on such terms as the court thinks best, and, when the proceeds of such sale are collected, the court shall order the same to be paid to the comptroller, in all such cases allowing the executor or administrator reasonable compensation for his services. A suit to recover proceeds of the sale is governed by Section 433 of this Code.

Acts 1955, 54th Leg., p. 88, ch. 55, eff. Jan. 1, 1956. Amended by Acts 1991, 72nd Leg., ch. 153, § 27, eff. Sept. 1, 1991; Acts 1997, 75th Leg., ch. 1423, § 15.01, eff. Sept. 1, 1997.

§ 428. Indispensability of Comptroller as Party

The comptroller is an indispensable party to any judicial or administrative proceeding concerning the disposition and handling of any portion of an estate that is or may be payable to the comptroller under Section 427 of this Code. Whenever an order shall be made by the court for an executor or administrator to pay any funds to the comptroller under Section 427 of this Code, the clerk of the court in which such order is made shall serve on the comptroller by personal service of citation a certified copy of such order within five days after the same has been made.

Acts 1955, 54th Leg., p. 88, ch. 55, eff. Jan. 1, 1956. Amended by Acts 1991, 72nd Leg., ch. 153, § 27, eff. Sept. 1, 1991; Acts 1997, 75th Leg., ch. 1423, § 15.02, eff. Sept. 1, 1997.

§ 429. Penalty for Neglect to Notify Comptroller

Any clerk who shall neglect to have served on the comptroller by personal citation a certified copy of any such order within the time prescribed by Section 428 of this Code shall be liable in a penalty of One Hundred Dollars, to be recovered in an action in the name of the state, after personal service of citation, on the information of any citizen, one-half of which penalty shall be paid to the informer and the other one-half to the state.

Acts 1955, 54th Leg., p. 88, ch. 55, eff. Jan. 1, 1956. Amended by Acts 1991, 72nd Leg., ch. 153, § 27, eff. Sept. 1, 1991; Acts 1997, 75th Leg., ch. 1423, § 15.03, eff. Sept. 1, 1997.

§ 430. Receipt of Comptroller

Whenever an executor or administrator pays the comptroller any funds of the estate he represents, under the preceding provisions of this Code, he shall take from the comptroller a receipt for such payment, with official seal attached, and shall file the same with the clerk of the court ordering such payment; and such receipt shall be recorded in the minutes of the court.

Acts 1955, 54th Leg., p. 88, ch. 55, eff. Jan. 1, 1956. Amended by Acts 1997, 75th Leg., ch. 1423, § 15.04, eff. Sept. 1, 1997.

§ 431. Penalty for Failure to Make Payments to Comptroller

When an executor or administrator fails to pay to the comptroller any funds of an estate which he has been ordered by the court so to pay, within 30 days after such order has been made, such executor or administrator shall, after personal service of citation charging such failure and after proof thereof, be liable to pay out of his own estate to the comptroller damages thereon at the rate of five per cent per month for each month, or fraction thereof, that he fails to make such payment after 30 days from such order, which damages may be recovered in any court of competent jurisdiction.

Acts 1955, 54th Leg., p. 88, ch. 55, eff. Jan. 1, 1956. Amended by Acts 1991, 72nd Leg., ch. 153, § 28, eff. Sept. 1, 1991; Acts 1997, 75th Leg., ch. 1423, § 15.05, eff. Sept. 1, 1997.

§ 432. Comptroller May Enforce Payment and Collect Damages.

The Comptroller shall have the right in the name of the state to apply to the court in which the order for payment was made to enforce the payment of funds which the executor or administrator has failed to pay to him pursuant to order of court, together with the payment of any damages that shall have accrued under the provisions of the preceding section of this code, and the court shall enforce such payment in like manner as other orders of payment are required to be enforced. The comptroller shall also have the right to institute suit in the name of the state against such executor or administrator, and the sureties on his bond, for the recovery of the funds so ordered to be paid and such damages as have accrued. The county attorney or criminal district attorney of the county, the district attorney of the district, or the attorney general, at the election of the comptroller and with the approval of the attorney general, shall represent the comptroller in all such proceedings, and shall also represent the interests of the state in all other matters arising under any provisions of this Code.

Acts 1955, 54th Leg., p. 88, ch. 55, eff. Jan. 1, 1956. Amended by Acts 1991, 72nd Leg., ch. 153, § 28, eff. Sept. 1, 1991; Acts 1997, 75th Leg., ch. 1423, § 15.06, eff. Sept. 1, 1997.

§ 433. Suit for the Recovery of Funds Paid to the Comptroller

(a) Mode of Recovery. When funds of an estate have been paid to the comptroller, any heir, devisee, or legatee of the estate, or their assigns, or any of them, may recover the portion of such funds to which he, she, or they are entitled. The person claiming such funds shall institute suit on or before the fourth anniversary of the date of the order requiring payment to the comptroller, by petition filed in the district court of Travis County, against the comptroller, setting forth the plaintiff's right to such funds, and the amount claimed by him.

(b) Citation. Upon the filing of such petition, the clerk shall issue a citation for the comptroller, to be served by personal service, to appear and represent the interest of the state in such suit. As the comptroller elects and with the approval of the attorney general, the attorney general, the county attorney or criminal district attorney for the county, or the district attorney for the district shall represent the comptroller.

(c) Procedure. The proceedings in such suit shall be governed by the rules for other civil suits; and, should the plaintiff establish his right to the funds claimed, he shall have a judgment therefor, which shall specify the amount to which he is entitled; and a certified copy of such judgment shall be sufficient authority for the comptroller to pay the same.

(d) Costs. The costs of any such suit shall in all cases be adjudged against the plaintiff, and he may be required to secure the costs.

Acts 1955, 54th Leg., p. 88, ch. 55, eff. Jan. 1, 1956. Amended by Acts 1991, 72nd Leg., ch. 153, § 29, eff. Sept. 1, 1991; Acts 1997, 75th Leg., ch. 1423, § 15.07, eff. Sept. 1, 1997.

REPEAL OF LAWS—EMERGENCY CLAUSE

§ 434. Repeal of Laws Supplanted by This Code

The following statutes and laws of this State are supplanted by the provisions of this Code and are hereby repealed:

(a) Title 48 of the Revised Civil Statutes of Texas of 1925, as amended, and all Articles contained in said Title, as said Articles are amended; [1] Article 932 of the Revised Civil Statutes of Texas of 1925; [2] and Chapter 196, Acts of the 52nd Legislature (1951), page 322; [3] and

(b) Title 129 of the Revised Civil Statutes of Texas of 1925, as amended, and all Articles contained in said Title, as said Articles are amended; [4] and

(1) Sections 1 and 2 of Chapter 196, Acts of the 42nd Legislature (1931), page 329; [5] and

(2) Section 1 of Chapter 297, Acts of the 49th Legislature (1945), page 469; [6] and

(3) Sections 1 and 2 of Chapter 170, Acts of the 50th Legislature (1947), page 275; [7] and

(4) Section 1 of Chapter 120, Acts of the 51st Legislature (1949), page 218; [8] and

(c) Title 54 of the Revised Civil Statutes of Texas of 1925, as amended, and all Articles contained in said Title, as said Articles are amended; [9] and

(1) Acts of the 39th Legislature (1925), Section 1 of Chapter 82, page 253; [10] and

(2) Acts of the 40th Legislature (1927): Section 1 of Chapter 50, page 74; [11] Sections 1, 2 and 3 of Chapter 81, page 123; [12] Section 1 of Chapter 92, page 142; [13] Section 1 of Chapter 152, page 223; [14] and Section 1 of Chapter 244, page 362; [15] and

(3) Acts of the 41st Legislature (1929): Sections 1 and 2 of Chapter 29, page 63; [16] Section 1 of Chapter 63, page 130; [17] Section 2 of Chapter 100, page 235; [18] Section 1 of Chapter 132, page 288; [19] and Section 1 of Chapter 48, First Called Session, page 107; [20] and

(4) Acts of the 42nd Legislature (1931): Chapter 52, page 79; [21] Section 1 of Chapter 59, page 93; [22] Chapter 123, page 210; [20] Section 1 of Chapter 234, page 389; [23] Section 1 of Chapter 235, page 390; [24] Section 1 of Chapter 236, page 391; [25] and Section 1 of Chapter 35a, page 842; [26] and

(5) Acts of the 43rd Legislature, Third Called Session (1934): Section 1 of Chapter 25, page 48; [27] and

(6) Acts of the 44th Legislature (1935): Section 1 of Chapter 247, page 634; [28] Section 1 of Chapter 248, page 635; [18] Section 1 of Chapter 250, page 637; [29] Section 1 of Chapter 251, page 638; [30] Section 1 of Chapter 252, page 638; [31] Section 1 of Chapter 253, page 639; [32] Section 1 of Chapter 266, page 654; [33] Section 1 of Chapter 272, page 658; [34] Section 1 of Chapter 273, page 659; [35] Sections 1 and 2 of Chapter 277, page 662; [36] Section 1 of Chapter 278, page 664; [37] Section 1 of Chapter 280, page 665; [38] and Chapter 446, Second Called Session, page 1729; [39] and

(7) Acts of the 45th Legislature (1937): Section 1 of Chapter 193, page 391; [40] and Section 1 of Chapter 250, page 499; [41] and

(8) Acts of the 46th Legislature (1939): H.B.No.656, page 318; [42] H.B.No.158, page 319; [35] H.B.No.31, page 320; [43] and S.B.No.141, page 321; [44] and

(9) Acts of the 47th Legislature (1941): Section 1 of Chapter 382, page 633; [45] and Chapter 521, page 845; [46] and

(10) Acts of the 48th Legislature (1943): Section 1 of Chapter 234, page 356; [47] and

(11) Acts of the 49th Legislature (1945): Section 1 of Chapter 214, page 296; [48] Section 1 of Chapter 296, page 468; [49] Section 2 of Chapter 297, page 469; [50] and Sections 1 and 2 of Chapter 316, page 525; [16] and

(12) Acts of the 50th Legislature (1947): Section 1 of Chapter 401, page 942; [51] and

(13) Acts of the 52nd Legislature (1951): Chapter 37, page 62; [52] and

(d) Title 69 of the Revised Civil Statutes of Texas of 1925, as amended, and all Articles contained in said Title, as said Articles are amended; [53] and

(1) Acts of the 39th Legislature (1925): Section 1 of Chapter 156, page 367; [54] and Section 1 of Chapter 134, page 338; [55] and

(2) Acts of the 40th Legislature (1927): Section 1 of Chapter 16, page 22; [56] Section 2 of Chapter 31, page 43; [57] Section 1 of Chapter 164, page 237; [58] and Sections 1, 2 and 3 of Chapter 179, page 257; [59] and

(3) Acts of the 41st Legislature (1929): Section 1 of Chapter 31, page 65; [60] Chapter 126, page 281; [61] Sections 1 and 2 of Chapter 127, page 282; [62] Sections 1 and 2 of Chapter 128, page 283; [63] Sections 1 and 2 of Chapter 129, page 284; [64] Sections 1 and 2 of Chapter 130, page 285; [65] Sections 1, 2, 3, 4, 5 and 6 of Chapter 131, page 286; [66] Section 1 of Chapter 133, page 289; [67] and Chapter 305, page 684; [68] and

(4) Acts of the 42nd Legislature (1931): Section 1 of Chapter 237, page 392; [69] and

(5) Acts of the 43rd Legislature (1933): Chapter 47, page 93; [70] Chapter 239, page 838; [71] and Section 1 of Chapter 26, Third Called Session (1934), page 49; [57] and

(6) Acts of the 44th Legislature (1935): Section 1 of Chapter 13, page 5; [72] Section 1 of Chapter 79, page 196; [73] Section 1 of Chapter 84, page 206; [74] Section 1 of Chapter 254, page 640; [75] Section 1 of Chapter 279, page 664; [76] and

(7) Acts of the 45th Legislature (1937): Chapter 289, page 579;[77] Chapter 336, page 673; [68] Sections 1 and 2 of Chapter 27, First Called Session, page 1803; [78] and Section 1 of Chapter 54, Second Called Session, page 1964; [68] and

(8) Acts of the 46th Legislature (1939): S.B.No.189, page 340; [54] and

(9) Acts of the 47th Legislature (1941): Section 3 of Chapter 303, page 480; [79] and Sections 1, 2, 3, 4, 5, 6 and 7 of Chapter 541, page 867; [80] and

(10) Acts of the 48th Legislature (1943): Section 1 of Chapter 56, page 65; [68] Chapter 281, page 414; [81] and Section 1 of Chapter 378, page 684; [82] and

(11) Acts of the 49th Legislature (1945): Sections 3, 4 and 5 of Chapter 316, page 525; [83] and

(12) Acts of the 50th Legislature (1947): Section 1 of Chapter 39, page 51; [81] and Section 1 of Chapter 256, page 453; [84] and

(13) Acts of the 51st Legislature (1949): Section 1 of Chapter 499, page 923; [85] Section 1 of Chapter 556, page 1093; [86] Chapter 456, page 842; [87] and Section 3 of Chapter 259, page 447; [88] and

(14) Acts of the 52nd Legislature (1951): Section 1 of Chapter 34, page 56.[58]

(15) Acts of the 53rd Legislature (1953): Section 1 of Chapter 70, page 104.[89]

Acts 1955, 54th Leg., p. 88, ch. 55, eff. Jan. 1, 1956.

[1] Civil Statutes, arts. 2570 to 2583.
[2] Civil Statutes, art. 932.
[3] Civil Statutes, art. 2583a.
[4] Civil Statutes, arts. 8281 to 8305.
[5] Civil Statutes, arts. 8291, 8292.
[6] Civil Statutes, art. 8281.
[7] Civil Statutes, arts. 8283, 8284.
[8] Civil Statutes, art. 8293.
[9] Civil Statutes, arts. 3290 to 3703.
[10] Civil Statutes, art. 3678.
[11] Civil Statutes, art. 3654.
[12] Civil Statutes, arts. 3334, 3334a, 3336.
[13] Civil Statutes, art. 3351.
[14] Civil Statutes, art. 3386.
[15] Civil Statutes, art. 3597a.
[16] Civil Statutes, arts. 3386, 3576.
[17] Civil Statutes, art. 3393a.
[18] Civil Statutes, art. 3334.
[19] Civil Statutes, art. 3325.
[20] Civil Statutes, art. 3310a.
[21] Civil Statutes, art. 3515a.
[22] Civil Statutes, art. 3293–A.
[23] Civil Statutes, art. 3531.
[24] Civil Statutes, art. 3690.
[25] Civil Statutes, art. 3492.
[26] Probably should read: "and Section 1 of Chapter 352, page 842". Civil Statutes, art. 3432a.
[27] Civil Statutes, art. 3369.
[28] Civil Statutes, art. 3311.
[29] Civil Statutes, art. 3576.
[30] Civil Statutes, art. 3321.
[31] Civil Statutes, art. 3420.
[32] Civil Statutes, art. 3476.
[33] Civil Statutes, art. 3396.
[34] Civil Statutes, art. 3337.
[35] Civil Statutes, art. 3336.
[36] Civil Statutes, arts. 3430, 3576 note.
[37] Civil Statutes, art. 3417.
[38] Civil Statutes, art. 3317.
[39] Civil Statutes, arts. 3456A to 3456I.
[40] Civil Statutes, arts. 3410–a, 3410–b.
[41] Civil Statutes, art. 3605.
[42] Civil Statutes, art. 3334b.
[43] Civil Statutes, art. 3370.
[44] Civil Statutes, arts. 3393a, 3396.
[45] Civil Statutes, art. 3432b.
[46] Civil Statutes, arts. 3333a, 3333a note.
[47] Civil Statutes, art. 3554a.
[48] Civil Statutes, art. 3310b.
[49] Civil Statutes, art. 3344.
[50] Civil Statutes, art. 3348.
[51] Civil Statutes, art. 3683a.
[52] Civil Statutes, art. 3582a.
[53] Civil Statutes, arts. 4102 to 4329.
[54] Civil Statutes, art. 4225.
[55] Civil Statutes, arts. 4195, 4196.
[56] Civil Statutes, art. 4231.
[57] Civil Statutes, art. 4195a.
[58] Civil Statutes, art. 4192.
[59] Civil Statutes, arts. 4102, 4111, 4123.
[60] Civil Statutes, art. 4111.
[61] Civil Statutes, art. 4227a.
[62] Civil Statutes, art. 4233.
[63] Civil Statutes, art. 4143.
[64] Civil Statutes, art. 4234.
[65] Civil Statutes, art. 4148.
[66] Civil Statutes, arts. 4282 to 4284.
[67] Civil Statutes, art. 4142.
[68] Civil Statutes, art. 4180.
[69] Civil Statutes, art. 4200.
[70] Probably should read: "Chapter 47, page 96". Civil Statutes, art. 4295a.
[71] Civil Statutes, art. 4223a.
[72] Probably should read: "Section 1 of Chapter 13, page 35". Civil Statutes, art. 4204.
[73] Civil Statutes, art. 4216.
[74] Civil Statutes, art. 4201.
[75] Civil Statutes, art. 4115.
[76] Civil Statutes, art. 4291.
[77] Civil Statutes, art. 4112a.
[78] Civil Statutes, arts. 4285, 4286.
[79] Civil Statutes, art. 4203.
[80] Civil Statutes, arts. 4113, 4114, 4116, 4117, 4121 to 4123, 4128, 4228, 4229, 4272, 4123a, 4123a–1.
[81] Civil Statutes, art. 4296.
[82] Civil Statutes, arts. 4201, 4216.
[83] Civil Statutes, arts. 4141, 4201, 4216.
[84] Civil Statutes, art. 4141.
[85] Civil Statutes, art. 4123a–1.
[86] Civil Statutes, art. 4168.
[87] Probably should read "Chapter 458, page 842". Civil Statutes, art. 4192b.
[88] Probably should read "Section 3 of Chapter 259, page 477". Civil Statutes, art. 6008b, § 3.
[89] Civil Statutes, art. 4285.

§ 435. Emergency Clause

The need for revision of the probate statutes of this state creates an emergency and an imperative public necessity that the Constitutional Rule requiring bills to be read on three several days in each House be suspended, and said Rule is hereby suspended, and this Act shall take effect and be in force from and after its passage, and it is so enacted.

Acts 1955, 54th Leg., p. 88, ch. 55, eff. Jan. 1, 1956.

CHAPTER XI. NONTESTAMENTARY TRANSFERS

PART 1. MULTIPLE-PARTY ACCOUNTS

PART 2. PROVISIONS RELATING TO EFFECT OF DEATH

PART 3. COMMUNITY PROPERTY WITH RIGHT OF SURVIVORSHIP

PART 1. MULTIPLE-PARTY ACCOUNTS

§ 436. Definitions

In this part:

(1) "Account" means a contract of deposit of funds between a depositor and a financial institution, and includes a checking account, savings account, certificate of deposit, share account, and other like arrangement.

(2) "Beneficiary" means a person named in a trust account as one for whom a party to the account is named as trustee.

(3) "Financial institution" means an organization authorized to do business under state or federal laws relating to financial institutions, including, without limitation, banks and trust companies, savings banks, building and loan associations, savings and loan companies or associations, credit unions, and brokerage firms that deal in the sales and purchases of stocks, bonds, and other types of securities.

(4) "Joint account" means an account payable on request to one or more of two or more parties whether or not there is a right of survivorship.

(5) "Multiple-party account" means a joint account, a convenience account, a P.O.D. account, or a trust account. It does not include accounts established for deposit of funds of a partnership, joint venture, or other association for business purposes, or accounts controlled by one or more persons as the duly authorized agent or trustee for a corporation, unincorporated association, charitable or civic organization, or a regular fiduciary or trust account where the relationship is established other than by deposit agreement.

(6) "Net contribution" of a party to a joint account as of any given time is the sum of all deposits made to that account by or for him, less all withdrawals made by or for him which have not been paid to or applied to the use of any other party, plus a pro rata share of any interest or dividends included in the current balance. The term includes, in addition, any proceeds of deposit life insurance added to the account by reason of the death of the party whose net contribution is in question.

(7) "Party" means a person who, by the terms of the account, has a present right, subject to request, to payment from a multiple-party account. A P.O.D. payee or beneficiary of a trust account is a party only after the account becomes payable to him by reason of his surviving the original payee or trustee. Unless the context otherwise requires, it includes a guardian, personal representative, or assignee, including an attaching creditor, of a party. It also includes a person identified as a trustee of an account for another whether or not a beneficiary is named, but it does not include a named beneficiary unless the beneficiary has a present right of withdrawal.

(8) "Payment" of sums on deposit includes withdrawal, payment on check or other directive of a party, and any pledge of sums on deposit by a party and any set-off, or reduction or other disposition of all or part of an account pursuant to a pledge.

(9) "Proof of death" includes a certified copy of a death certificate or the judgment or order of a court

in a proceeding where the death of a person is proved by circumstantial evidence to the satisfaction of the court as provided by Section 72 of this code.

(10) "P.O.D. account" means an account payable on request to one person during lifetime and on his death to one or more P.O.D. payees, or to one or more persons during their lifetimes and on the death of all of them to one or more P.O.D. payees.

(11) "P.O.D. payee" means a person designated on a P.O.D. account as one to whom the account is payable on request after the death of one or more persons.

(12) "Request" means a proper request for withdrawal, or a check or order for payment, which complies with all conditions of the account, including special requirements concerning necessary signatures and regulations of the financial institution, but if the financial institution conditions withdrawal or payment on advance notice, for purposes of this part the request for withdrawal or payment is treated as immediately effective and a notice of intent to withdraw is treated as a request for withdrawal.

(13) "Sums on deposit" means the balance payable on a multiple-party account including interest, dividends, and in addition any deposit life insurance proceeds added to the account by reason of the death of a party.

(14) "Trust account" means an account in the name of one or more parties as trustee for one or more beneficiaries where the relationship is established by the form of the account and the deposit agreement with the financial institution and there is no subject of the trust other than the sums on deposit in the account. It is not essential that payment to the beneficiary be mentioned in the deposit agreement. A trust account does not include a regular trust account under a testamentary trust or a trust agreement which has significance apart from the account, or a fiduciary account arising from a fiduciary relation such as attorney-client.

(15) "Withdrawal" includes payment to a third person pursuant to check or other directive of a party.

Added by Acts 1979, 66th Leg., p. 1756, ch. 713, § 31, eff. Aug. 27, 1979. Amended by Acts 1993, 73rd Leg., ch. 846, § 25, eff. Sept. 1, 1993.

§ 437. Ownership as Between Parties and Others

The provisions of Sections 438 through 440 of this code that concern beneficial ownership as between parties, or as between parties and P.O.D. payees or beneficiaries of multiple-party accounts, are relevant only to controversies between these persons and their creditors and other successors, and have no bearing on the power of withdrawal of these persons as determined by the terms of account contracts.

Added by Acts 1979, 66th Leg., p. 1756, ch. 713, § 31, eff. Aug. 27, 1979. Amended by Acts 1981, 67th Leg., p. 895, ch. 319, § 2, eff. Sept. 1, 1981.

§ 438. Ownership During Lifetime

(a) A joint account belongs, during the lifetime of all parties, to the parties in proportion to the net contributions by each to the sums on deposit, unless there is clear and convincing evidence of a different intent.

(b) A P.O.D. account belongs to the original payee during his lifetime and not to the P.O.D. payee or payees. If two or more parties are named as original payees, during their lifetimes rights as between them are governed by Subsection (a) of this section.

(c) Unless a contrary intent is manifested by the terms of the account or the deposit agreement or there is other clear and convincing evidence of an irrevocable trust, a trust account belongs beneficially to the trustee during his lifetime, and if two or more parties are named as trustee on the account, during their lifetimes beneficial rights as between them are governed by Subsection (a) of this section. If there is an irrevocable trust, the account belongs beneficially to the beneficiary.

Added by Acts 1979, 66th Leg., p. 1756, ch. 713, § 31, eff. Aug. 27, 1979.

§ 438A. Convenience Account

(a) If an account is established at a financial institution by a party in the names of the party and a cosigner and the terms of the account provide that the sums on deposit are paid or delivered to the party or to the cosigner "for the convenience" of the party, the account is a convenience account.

(b) The making of a deposit in a convenience account does not affect the title to the deposit.

(c) The party to a convenience account is not considered to have made a gift of one-half of the deposit or of any additions or accruals to the deposit to the cosigner.

(d) On the death of the party, the cosigner shall have no right of survivorship in the account and ownership of the account remains in the party.

(e) If an addition is made to the account by anyone other than the party, the addition and accruals to the addition are considered to have been made by the party.

(f) All deposits to a convenience account and additions and accruals to the deposits may be paid to the party or to the cosigner. The financial institution is completely released from liability for a payment made from the account before the financial institution receives notice in writing signed by the party not to make the payment in accordance with the terms of the account. After receipt of the notice from the party, the financial institution may require the party to approve any further payments from the account.

(g) If the financial institution makes a payment of the sums on deposit in a convenience account to the cosigner after the death of the party and before the financial institution has received written notice of the party's death, the financial institution is completely released from liability for the payment. If a financial institution makes payment to the personal representative of the deceased party's estate after the death of the party and before service on the financial institution of a court order prohibiting payment, the financial institution is released to the extent of the payment from liability to any person claiming a right to the funds. The receipt by the representative to whom payment is made is a complete release and discharge of the financial institution.

Added by Acts 1993, 73rd Leg., ch. 795, § 1, eff. Aug. 30, 1993; Acts 1993, 73rd Leg., ch. 846, § 27, eff. Sept. 1, 1993.

§ 439. Right of Survivorship

(a) Sums remaining on deposit at the death of a party to a joint account belong to the surviving party or parties against the estate of the decedent if, by a written agreement signed by the party who dies, the interest of such deceased party is made to survive to the surviving party or parties. Notwithstanding any other law, an agreement is sufficient to confer an absolute right of survivorship on parties to a joint account under this subsection if the agreement states in substantially the following form: "On the death of one party to a joint account, all sums in the account on the date of the death vest in and belong to the surviving party as his or her separate property and estate." A survivorship agreement will not be inferred from the mere fact that the account is a joint account. If there are two or more surviving parties, their respective ownerships during lifetime shall be in proportion to their previous ownership interests under Section 438 of this code augmented by an equal share for each survivor of any interest the decedent may have owned in the account immediately before his death, and the right of survivorship continues between the surviving parties if a written agreement signed by a party who dies so provides.

(b) If the account is a P.O.D. account and there is a written agreement signed by the original payee or payees, on the death of the original payee or on the death of the survivor of two or more original payees, any sums remaining on deposit belong to the P.O.D. payee or payees if surviving, or to the survivor of them if one or more P.O.D. payees die before the original payee. If two or more P.O.D. payees survive, there is no right of survivorship in event of death of a P.O.D. payee thereafter unless the terms of the account or deposit agreement expressly provide for survivorship between them.

(c) If the account is a trust account and there is a written agreement signed by the trustee or trustees, on death of the trustee or the survivor of two or more trustees, any sums remaining on deposit belong to the person or persons named as beneficiaries, if surviving, or to the survivor of them if one or more beneficiaries die before the trustee dies. If two or more beneficiaries survive, there is no right of survivorship in event of death of any beneficiary thereafter unless the terms of the account or deposit agreement expressly provide for survivorship between them.

(d) In other cases, the death of any party to a multiple-party account has no effect on beneficial ownership of the account other than to transfer the rights of the decedent as part of his estate.

Added by Acts 1979, 66th Leg., p. 1756, ch. 713, § 31, eff. Aug. 27, 1979. Amended by Acts 1987, 70th Leg., ch. 297, § 1, eff. Aug. 31, 1987; Acts 1993, 73rd Leg., ch. 846, § 26, eff. Sept. 1, 1993.

Section 35(d) of the 1993 amendatory act provides:

The changes in law made by Section 26 of this Act apply only to an account created on or after the effective date of this Act. An account created before the effective date of this Act is covered by the law in effect when the account was created, and the former law is continued in effect for that purpose."

§ 439A. Uniform Single-Party or Multiple-Party Account Form

(a) A contract of deposit that contains provisions substantially the same as in the form provided by Subsection (b) of this section establishes the type of account selected by a party. The provisions of this part of Chapter XI of this code govern an account selected under the form, other than a single-party account without a P.O.D. designation. A contract of deposit that does not contain provisions substantially the same as in the form provided by Subsection (b) of this section is governed by the provisions of this chapter applicable to the account that most nearly conforms to the depositor's intent.

(b) A financial institution may use the following form to establish the type of account selected by a party:

UNIFORM SINGLE-PARTY OR MULTIPLE-PARTY ACCOUNT SELECTION FORM NOTICE: The type of account you select may determine how property passes on your death. Your will may not control the disposition of funds held in some of the following accounts.

Select one of the following accounts by placing your initials next to the account selected:

___ (1) SINGLE-PARTY ACCOUNT WITHOUT "P.O.D." (PAYABLE ON DEATH) DESIGNATION. The party to the account owns the account. On the death of the party, ownership of the account passes as a part of the party's estate under the party's will or by intestacy.

Enter the name of the party:

____

___ (2) SINGLE-PARTY ACCOUNT WITH "P.O.D." (PAYABLE ON DEATH) DESIGNATION. The party to the account owns the account. On the death of the party, ownership of the account passes to the P.O.D. beneficiaries of the account. The account is not a part of the party's estate.

Enter the name of the party:

____

Enter the name or names of the P.O.D. beneficiaries:

____

____

___ (3) MULTIPLE-PARTY ACCOUNT WITHOUT RIGHT OF SURVIVORSHIP. The parties to the account own the account in proportion to the parties' net contributions to the account. The financial institution may pay any sum in the account to a party at any time. On the death of a party, the party's ownership of the account passes as a part of the party's estate under the party's will or by intestacy.

Enter the names of the parties:

____

____

____

___ (4) MULTIPLE-PARTY ACCOUNT WITH RIGHT OF SURVIVORSHIP. The parties to the account own the account in proportion to the parties' net contributions to the account. The financial institution may pay any sum in the account to a party at any time. On the death of a party, the party's ownership of the account passes to the surviving parties.

Enter the names of the parties:

____

____

___ (5) MULTIPLE-PARTY ACCOUNT WITH RIGHT OF SURVIVORSHIP AND P.O.D. (PAYABLE ON DEATH) DESIGNATION. The parties to the account own the account in proportion to the parties' net contributions to the account. The financial institution may pay any sum in the account to a party at any time. On the death of the last surviving party, the ownership of the account passes to the P.O.D. beneficiaries.

Enter the names of the parties:

____

____

Enter the name or names of the P.O.D. beneficiaries:

____

____

___ (6) CONVENIENCE ACCOUNT. The party to the account owns the account. The cosigner to the account may make account transactions for the party. The cosigner does not own the account. On the death of the party, ownership of the account passes as a part of the party's estate under the party's will or by intestacy. The financial institution may pay funds in the account to the cosigner before the financial institution receives notice of the death of the party. The payment to the cosigner does not affect the party's ownership of the account.

Enter the name of the party:

____

Enter the name of the cosigner:

____

___ (7) TRUST ACCOUNT. The parties named as trustees to the account own the account in proportion to the parties' net contributions to the account. A trustee may withdraw funds from the account. A beneficiary may not withdraw funds from the account before all trustees are deceased. On the death of the last surviving trustee, the ownership of the account passes to the beneficiary. The trust account is not a part of a trustee's estate and does not pass under the trustee's will or by intestacy, unless the trustee survives all of the beneficiaries and all other trustees.

Enter the name or names of the trustees:

____

____

Enter the name or names of the beneficiaries:

____

____

(c) A financial institution shall be deemed to have adequately disclosed the information provided in this section if the financial institution uses the form set forth in Subsection (b) of this section. If a financial institution varies the format of the form set forth in Subsection (b) of this section, then such financial institution may make disclosures in the account agreement or in any other form which adequately discloses the information provided in this section.

(d) A financial institution may combine any of the provisions and vary the format of the selections form and notices described in Subsection (b) of this section provided that the customer receives adequate disclosure of the ownership rights and there is appropriate indication of the names of the parties. This may be accomplished in a universal account form with options listed for selection and additional disclosures provided in the account agreement, or in any other manner which adequately discloses the information provided in this section.

Added by Acts 1993, 73rd Leg., ch. 795, § 2, eff. Aug. 30, 1993.

§ 440. Effect of Written Notice to Financial Institution

The provisions of Section 439 of this code as to rights of survivorship are determined by the form of the account at the death of a party. Notwithstanding any other provision of the law, this form may be altered by written order given by a party to the financial institution to change the form of the account or to stop or vary payment under the terms of the account. The order or request must be signed by a party, received by the financial institution during the party's lifetime, and not countermanded by other written order of the same party during his lifetime.

Added by Acts 1979, 66th Leg., p. 1756, ch. 713, § 31, eff. Aug. 27, 1979.

§ 441. Accounts and Transfers Nontestamentary

Transfers resulting from the application of Section 439 of this code are effective by reason of the account contracts involved and this statute and are not to be considered as testamentary or subject to the testamentary provisions of this code.

Added by Acts 1979, 66th Leg., p. 1756, ch. 713, § 31, eff. Aug. 27, 1979.

§ 442. Rights of Creditors

No multiple-party account will be effective against an estate of a deceased party to transfer to a survivor sums needed to pay debts, taxes, and expenses of administration, including statutory allowances to the surviving spouse and minor children, if other assets of the estate are insufficient. A party, P.O.D. payee, or beneficiary who receives payment from a multiple-party account after the death of a deceased party shall be liable to account to the deceased party's personal representative for amounts the decedent owned beneficially immediately before his death to the extent necessary to discharge the claims and charges mentioned above remaining unpaid after application of the decedent's estate, but is not liable in an amount greater than the amount that the party, P.O.D. payee, or beneficiary received from the multiple-party account. No proceeding to assert this liability shall be commenced unless the personal representative has received a written demand by a surviving spouse, a creditor, or one acting for a minor child of the decedent, and no proceeding shall be commenced later than two years following the death of the decedent. Sums recovered by the personal representative shall be administered as part of the decedent's estate. This section shall not affect the right of a financial institution to make payment on multiple-party accounts according to the terms thereof, or make it liable to the estate of a deceased party unless before payment the institution received written notice from the personal representative stating the sums needed to pay debts, taxes, and expenses of administration.

Added by Acts 1979, 66th Leg., p. 1756, ch. 713, § 31, eff. Aug. 27, 1979.

§ 443. Protection of Financial Institutions

Sections 444 through 449 of this code govern the liability of financial institutions that make payments as provided in this chapter and the set-off rights of the institutions.

Added by Acts 1979, 66th Leg., p. 1756, ch. 713, § 31, eff. Aug. 27, 1979.

§ 444. Payment on Signature of One Party

Financial institutions may enter into multiple-party accounts to the same extent that they may enter into single-party accounts. A multiple-party account may be paid, on request, to any one or more of the parties.

A financial institution shall not be required to inquire as to the source of funds received for deposit to a multiple-party account, or to inquire as to the proposed application of any sum withdrawn from an account, for purposes of establishing net contributions.

Added by Acts 1979, 66th Leg., p. 1756, ch. 713, § 31, eff. Aug. 27, 1979.

§ 445. Payment of Joint Account After Death or Disability

Any sums in a joint account may be paid, on request, to any party without regard to whether any other party is incapacitated or deceased at the time the payment is demanded, but payment may not be made to the personal representative or heirs of a deceased party unless proofs of death are presented to the financial institution showing that the decedent was the last surviving party or unless there is no right of survivorship under Section 439 of this code. A financial institution that pays a sum from a joint account to a surviving party to that account pursuant to a written agreement under Section 439(a) of this code is not liable to an heir, devisee, or beneficiary of the decedent's estate.

Added by Acts 1979, 66th Leg., p. 1756, ch. 713, § 31, eff. Aug. 27, 1979. Amended by Acts 1987, 70th Leg., ch. 297, § 2, eff. Aug. 31, 1987.

§ 446. Payment of P.O.D. Account

A P.O.D. account may be paid, on request, to any original party to the account. Payment may be made, on request, to the P.O.D. payee or to the personal representative or heirs of a deceased P.O.D. payee upon presentation to the financial institution of proof of death showing that the P.O.D. payee survived all persons named as original payees. Payment may be made to the personal representative or heirs of a deceased original payee if proof of death is presented to the financial institution showing that his decedent was the survivor of all other persons named on the account either as an original payee or as P.O.D. payee.

Added by Acts 1979, 66th Leg., p. 1756, ch. 713, § 31, eff. Aug. 27, 1979.

§ 447. Payment of Trust Account

A trust account may be paid, on request, to any trustee. Unless the financial institution has received written notice that the beneficiary has a vested interest not dependent upon his surviving the trustee, payment may be made to the personal representative or heirs of a deceased trustee if proof of death is presented to the financial institution showing that his decedent was the survivor of all other persons named on the account either as trustee or beneficiary. Payment may be made, on request, to the beneficiary upon presentation to the financial institution of proof of death showing that the beneficiary or beneficiaries survived all persons named as trustees.

Added by Acts 1979, 66th Leg., p. 1756, ch. 713, § 31, eff. Aug. 27, 1979.

§ 448. Discharge from Claims

Payment made as provided by Section 444, 445, 446, or 447 of this code discharges the financial institution from all claims for amounts so paid whether or not the payment is consistent with the beneficial ownership of the account as between parties, P.O.D. payees, or beneficiaries, or their successors. The protection here given does not extend to payments made after a financial institution has received written notice from any party able to request present payment to the effect that withdrawals in accordance with the terms of the account should not be permitted. Unless the notice is withdrawn by the person giving it, the successor of any deceased party must concur in any demand for withdrawal if the financial institution is to be protected under this section. No other notice or any other information shown to have been available to a financial institution shall affect its right to the protection provided here. The protection here provided shall have no bearing on the rights of parties in disputes between themselves or their successors concerning the beneficial ownership of funds in, or withdrawn from, multiple-party accounts.

Added by Acts 1979, 66th Leg., p. 1756, ch. 713, § 31, eff. Aug. 27, 1979.

§ 449. Set-Off to Financial Institution

Without qualifying any other statutory right to set-off or lien and subject to any contractual provision, if a party to a multiple-party account is indebted to a financial institution, the financial institution has a right to set-off against the account in which the party has or had immediately before his death a present right of withdrawal. The amount of the account subject to set-off is that proportion to which the debtor is, or was immediately before his death, beneficially entitled, and in the absence of proof of net contributions, to an equal share with all parties having present rights of withdrawal.

Added by Acts 1979, 66th Leg., p. 1756, ch. 713, § 31, eff. Aug. 27, 1979.

PART 2. PROVISIONS RELATING TO EFFECT OF DEATH

§ 450. Provisions for Payment or Transfer at Death

(a) Any of the following provisions in an insurance policy, contract of employment, bond, mortgage, promissory note, deposit agreement, employees' trust, retirement account, deferred compensation arrangement, custodial agreement, pension plan, trust agreement, conveyance of real or personal property, securities, accounts with financial institutions as defined in Part 1 of this chapter, or any other written instrument effective as a contract, gift, conveyance, or trust is deemed to be nontestamentary, and this code does not invalidate the instrument or any provision:

(1) that money or other benefits theretofore due to, controlled, or owned by a decedent shall be paid after his death to a person designated by the decedent in either the instrument or a separate writing, including a will, executed at the same time as the instrument or subsequently;

(2) that any money due or to become due under the instrument shall cease to be payable in event of the death of the promisee or the promissor before payment or demand; or

(3) that any property which is the subject of the instrument shall pass to a person designated by the decedent in either the instrument or a separate writing, including a will, executed at the same time as the instrument or subsequently.

(b) Nothing in this section limits the rights of creditors under other laws of this state.

(c) In this section:

(1) "Employees' trust" means:

(A) a trust that forms a part of a stock-bonus, pension, or profit-sharing plan under Section 401, Internal Revenue Code of 1954 (26 U.S.C.A. Sec. 401 (1986));

(B) a pension trust under Chapter 111, Property Code; and

(C) an employer-sponsored benefit plan or program, or any other retirement savings arrangement, including a pension plan created under Section 3, Employee Retirement Income Security Act of 1974 (29 U.S.C.A. Sec. 1002 (1986)), regardless of whether the plan, program, or arrangement is funded through a trust.

(2) "Individual retirement account" means a trust, custodial arrangement, or annuity under Section 408(a) or (b), Internal Revenue Code of 1954 (26 U.S.C.A. Sec. 408 (1986)).

(3) "Retirement account" means a retirement-annuity contract, an individual retirement account, a simplified employee pension, or any other retirement savings arrangement.

(4) "Retirement-annuity contract" means an annuity contract under Section 403, Internal Revenue Code of 1954 (26 U.S.C.A. Sec. 403 (1986)).

(5) "Simplified employee pension" means a trust, custodial arrangement, or annuity under Section 408, Internal Revenue Code of 1954 (26 U.S.C.A. Sec. 408 (1986)).

Added by Acts 1979, 66th Leg., p. 1756, ch. 713, § 31, eff. Aug. 27, 1979. Amended by Acts 1987, 70th Leg., ch. 94, §§ 1, 2, eff. Aug. 31, 1987; Acts 1997, 75th Leg., ch. 1302, § 14, eff. Sept. 1, 1997.

PART 3. COMMUNITY PROPERTY WITH RIGHT OF SURVIVORSHIP

§ 451. Right of Survivorship

At any time, spouses may agree between themselves that all or part of their community property, then existing or to be acquired, becomes the property of the surviving spouse on the death of a spouse.

Added by Acts 1989, 71st Leg., ch. 655, § 2, eff. Aug. 28, 1989.

Section 3 of the 1989 Act provides:

"(a) The amendments made by this Act apply:

"(1) to all agreements between spouses creating a right of survivorship in community property entered into on or after the effective date of the 1987 amendment to Article XVI, Section 15, of the Texas Constitution; and

"(2) to all such agreements entered into prior to that date if both spouses were living on that date, the agreement complies with the provisions of Part 3 of Chapter XI, Texas Probate Code, as added by Section 2 of this Act, and the property which was the subject of the agreement remained community property after the date of the agreement.

"(b) If an agreement between spouses which purported to create a right of survivorship in their community property was entered into prior to the effective date of the 1987 amendment to Article XVI, Section 15, of the Texas Constitution, and a spouse died prior to that date, the agreement is covered by the law as it existed prior to the constitutional amendment, and that law is continued in effect for that purpose."

§ 452. Formalities

An agreement between spouses creating a right of survivorship in community property must be in writing and signed by both spouses. If an agreement in writing is signed by both spouses, the agreement shall be sufficient to create a right of survivorship in the community property described in the agreement if it includes any of the following phrases:

(1) "with right of survivorship";

(2) "will become the property of the survivor";

(3) "will vest in and belong to the surviving spouse"; or

(4) "shall pass to the surviving spouse."

An agreement that otherwise meets the requirements of this part, however, shall be effective without including any of those phrases.

Added by Acts 1989, 71st Leg., ch. 655, § 2, eff. Aug. 28, 1989.

For application of 1989 Act, see note under § 451.

§ 453. Ownership and Management During Marriage

Property subject to an agreement between spouses creating a right of survivorship in community property remains community property during the marriage of the spouses. Such an agreement does not affect the rights of the spouses concerning management, control, and disposition of the property subject to the agreement unless the agreement provides otherwise.

Added by Acts 1989, 71st Leg., ch. 655, § 2, eff. Aug. 28, 1989.

For application of 1989 Act, see note under § 451.

§ 454. Transfers Nontestamentary

Transfers at death resulting from agreements made in accordance with this part of this code are effective by reason of the agreement involved and are not testamentary transfers. Such transfers are not subject to the provisions of this code applicable to testamentary transfers except as expressly provided otherwise in this code.

Added by Acts 1989, 71st Leg., ch. 655, § 2, eff. Aug. 28, 1989.

For application of 1989 Act, see note under § 451.

§ 455. Revocation

An agreement between spouses made in accordance with this part of this code may be revoked in accordance with the terms of the agreement. If the agreement does not provide a method for revocation, the agreement may be revoked by a written instrument signed by both spouses or by a written instrument signed by one spouse and delivered to the other spouse. The agreement may be revoked with respect to specific property subject to the agreement by the disposition of such property by one or both of the spouses if such disposition is not inconsistent with specific terms of the agreement and applicable law.

Added by Acts 1989, 71st Leg., ch. 655, § 2, eff. Aug. 28, 1989.

For application of 1989 Act, see note under § 451.

§ 456. Proof of Agreement

(a) Application for Adjudication. An agreement between spouses creating a right of survivorship in community property that satisfies the requirements of this part is effective without an adjudication. After the death of a spouse, however, the surviving spouse or the personal representative of the surviving spouse may apply to the court for an order stating that the agreement satisfies the requirements of this code and is effective to create a right of survivorship in community property. The original agreement shall be filed with the application for an adjudication. An application for an adjudication under this section must include:

(1) the name and domicile of the surviving spouse;

(2) the name and former domicile of the decedent and the fact, time, and place of death;

(3) facts establishing venue in the court; and

(4) the social security number of the decedent, if known.

(b) Proof Required. An applicant for an adjudication under this section must prove to the satisfaction of the court:

(1) that the spouse whose community property interest is at issue is dead;

(2) that the court has jurisdiction and venue;

(3) that the agreement was executed with the formalities required by law;

(4) that the agreement was not revoked; and

(5) that citation has been served and returned in the manner and for the length of time required by this code.

(c) Method of Proof. The deceased spouse's signature to the agreement may be proved by the sworn testimony of one witness taken in open court, by the affidavit of one witness, or by the deposition of one witness, either written or oral, taken in the same manner and under the same rules as depositions in other civil actions. If the surviving spouse is competent to make an oath, the surviving spouse's signature to the agreement may be proved by the sworn testimony of the surviving spouse taken in open court, by the affidavit of the surviving spouse, or by the deposition of the surviving spouse either written or oral, taken in the same manner and under the same rules as depositions in other civil actions. If the surviving spouse is not competent to make an oath, the surviving spouse's signature to the agreement may be proved in the manner provided above for the proof of the deceased spouse's signature.

(d) Venue. An application for an adjudication under this section must be filed in the county of proper venue for administration of the deceased spouse's estate.

Added by Acts 1989, 71st Leg., ch. 655, § 2, eff. Aug. 28, 1989.

For application of 1989 Act, see note under § 451.

§ 457. Action of Court on Agreement

On completion of a hearing on an application under Section 456 of this code, if the court is satisfied that the requisite proof has been made, an order adjudging the agreement valid shall be entered. Certified copies of the agreement and order may be recorded in other counties and may be used in evidence, as the original might be, on the trial of the same matter in any other court, on appeal or otherwise.

Added by Acts 1989, 71st Leg., ch. 655, § 2, eff. Aug. 28, 1989.

For application of 1989 Act, see note under § 451.

§ 458. Effect of Order

An agreement between spouses creating a right of survivorship in community property that satisfies the requirements of this code is effective and enforceable without an adjudication. If an order adjudging such an agreement valid is obtained, however, the order shall constitute sufficient authority to all persons owing money, having custody of any property, or acting as registrar or transfer agent of any evidence of interest, indebtedness, property, or right, that is subject to the provisions of the agreement, and to persons purchasing from or otherwise dealing with the surviving spouse for payment or transfer to the surviving spouse, and the surviving spouse may enforce his or her right to such payment or transfer.

Added by Acts 1989, 71st Leg., ch. 655, § 2, eff. Aug. 28, 1989.

For application of 1989 Act, see note under § 451.

§ 459. Custody of Adjudicated Agreements

An original agreement creating a right of survivorship in community property that has been adjudicated together with the order adjudging it valid shall be deposited in the office of the county clerk of the county in which it was adjudicated and shall remain there, except during such time when it may be removed for inspection to another place on order of the court where adjudicated. If the court orders an original agreement to be removed to another place for inspection, the person removing the original agreement shall give a receipt therefor, and the clerk of the court shall make and retain a copy of the original agreement.

Added by Acts 1989, 71st Leg., ch. 655, § 2, eff. Aug. 28, 1989.

For application of 1989 Act, see note under § 451.

§ 460. Protection of Persons or Entities Acting Without Knowledge or Notice

(a) Personal Representatives. If the personal representative of a decedent's estate has no actual knowledge of the existence of an agreement creating a right of survivorship in community property in the decedent's surviving spouse, the personal representative shall not be liable to the surviving spouse or to any person claiming from the surviving spouse for selling, exchanging, distributing, or otherwise disposing of the property or an interest therein.

(b) Purchaser without Notice of Survivorship Agreement.

(1) If any person or entity purchases real or personal property from a person claiming from a decedent more than six months after the date of the decedent's death, for value, and without notice of the existence of an agreement creating a right of survivorship in the property in the decedent's surviving spouse, the purchaser shall have good title to the interest which the person claiming from the decedent would have had in the absence of the agreement, as against the claims of the surviving spouse or any person claiming from the surviving spouse.

(2) If any person or entity purchases real or personal property from the personal representative of a decedent's estate, for value, and without notice of the existence of an agreement creating a right of survivorship in the property in the decedent's surviving spouse, the purchaser shall have good title to the interest which the personal representative would have had the power to convey in the absence of the agreement, as against the claims of the surviving spouse or any person claiming from the surviving spouse.

(c) Purchaser without Notice of Revocation of Survivorship Agreement. If any person or entity purchases real or personal property from a decedent's surviving spouse more than six months after the date of the decedent's death, for value, and:

(1) with respect to real or personal property, the purchaser has received an original or certified copy of an agreement purporting to create a right of survivorship in such property in the decedent's surviving spouse, purportedly signed by the decedent and the surviving spouse; or

(2) with respect to real property, an agreement purporting to create a right of survivorship in such property in the decedent's surviving spouse, purportedly signed by the decedent and the surviving spouse, is properly recorded in a county in which a part of the property is located;

and the purchaser has no notice that the agreement was revoked, the purchaser shall have good title to the interest which the surviving spouse would have had in the absence of a revocation of the agreement, as against the claims of the personal representative of the decedent's estate and all persons claiming from the decedent or the personal representative of the decedent's estate.

(d) Debtors, Transfer Agents, and Other Persons Acting without Notice of Survivorship Agreement. If any person or entity owing money to a decedent or having custody of any property or acting as registrar or transfer agent of any evidence of interest, indebtedness, property, or right which was owned by a decedent prior to death has no actual knowledge of an agreement creating a right of survivorship in such property in the decedent's surviving spouse, that person or entity may pay or transfer such property to the personal representative of the decedent's estate or to the heirs, legatees, or devisees of the decedent's estate if no administration is pending on the estate, and the person or entity shall be discharged from all claims for amounts or property so paid or transferred.

(e) Debtors, Transfer Agents, and Persons Acting without Notice of Revocation of Survivorship Agreement. If any person or entity owing money to a decedent or having custody of any property or acting as registrar or transfer agent of any evidence of interest, indebtedness, property, or right which was owned by a decedent prior to death is presented with the original or a certified copy of an agreement creating a right of survivorship in such property in the decedent's surviving spouse, purportedly signed by the decedent and the decedent's surviving spouse and if such person or entity has no actual knowledge that the agreement was revoked, that person or entity may pay or transfer such property to the decedent's surviving spouse and shall be discharged from all claims for amounts or property so paid or transferred.

(f) Definitions. Under this section:

(1) a person or entity has "actual knowledge" of an agreement creating a right of survivorship in community property or of the revocation of such an agreement only if the person or entity has received written notice or has received the original or a certified copy of the agreement or revoking instrument;

(2) a person or entity has "notice" of an agreement creating a right of survivorship in community property or the revocation of such an agreement if the person or entity has actual knowledge of the agreement or revocation or, with respect to real property, if the agreement or revoking instrument is properly recorded in the county in which the real property is located; and

(3) a "certified copy" is a copy of an official record or of a document authorized by law to be recorded or filed and actually recorded or filed in a public office, certified as correct in accordance with the provisions of Rule 902 of the Texas Rules of Civil Evidence.

(g) Other Cases. Except as expressly provided in this section, the provisions of this section do not affect the rights of a surviving spouse or person claiming from the surviving spouse in disputes with persons claiming from a decedent or the successors of any of them concerning a beneficial interest in property or the proceeds therefrom, subject to a right of survivorship pursuant to an agreement that satisfies the requirements of this code.

Added by Acts 1989, 71st Leg., ch. 655, § 2, eff. Aug. 28, 1989.

For application of 1989 Act, see note under § 451.

§ 461. Rights of Creditors

The provisions of Part 1 of this chapter govern the rights of creditors in multiple-party accounts, as defined by Section 436 of Part 1. Except as expressly provided above in this section, the community property subject to the sole or joint management, control, and disposition of a spouse during marriage continues to be subject to the liabilities of that spouse upon death without regard to a right of survivorship in the decedent's surviving spouse under an agreement made in accordance with the provisions of this part. The surviving spouse shall be liable to account to the deceased spouse's personal representative for the property received by the surviving spouse pursuant to a right of survivorship to the extent necessary to discharge such liabilities. No proceeding to assert such a liability shall be commenced unless the personal representative has received a written demand by a creditor, and no proceeding shall be commenced later than two years following the death of the decedent. Property recovered by the personal representative shall be administered as part of the decedent's estate. This section does not affect the protection given to persons and entities under Section 460 of this code unless, before payment or transfer to the surviving spouse, the person or entity received a written notice from the decedent's personal representative stating the amount needed to satisfy the decedent's liabilities.

Added by Acts 1989, 71st Leg., ch. 655, § 2, eff. Aug. 28, 1989.

For application of 1989 Act, see note under § 451.

§ 462. Coordination With Part 1 of Chapter XI

The provisions of Part 1 of this chapter apply to multiple-party accounts held by spouses with a right of survivorship to the extent that such provisions are not inconsistent with the provisions of this part.

Added by Acts 1989, 71st Leg., ch. 655, § 2, eff. Aug. 28, 1989.

For application of 1989 Act, see note under § 451.

CHAPTER XII. DURABLE POWER OF ATTORNEY ACT

Chapter 12, Durable Power of Attorney Act, consisting of §§ 481 to 506, was added by Acts 1993, 73rd Leg., ch. 49, § 1.

Another Chapter 12, Informal Probate, added by Acts 1993, 73rd Leg., ch. 712, § 7, was repealed by Acts 1997, 75th Leg., ch. 540, § 5.

§ 481. Short Title

This chapter may be cited as the Durable Power of Attorney Act.

Added by Acts 1993, 73rd Leg., ch. 49, § 1, eff. Sept. 1, 1993.

§ 482. Definition

A "durable power of attorney" means a written instrument that:

(1) designates another person as attorney in fact or agent;

(2) is signed by an adult principal;

(3) contains the words "This power of attorney is not affected by subsequent disability or incapacity of the principal," or "This power of attorney becomes effective on the disability or incapacity of the principal," or similar words showing the principal's intent that the authority conferred on the attorney in fact or agent shall be exercised notwithstanding the principal's subsequent disability or incapacity; and

(4) is acknowledged by the principal before an officer authorized to take acknowledgments to deeds of conveyance and to administer oaths under the laws of this state or any other state.

Added by Acts 1993, 73rd Leg., ch. 49, § 1, eff. Sept. 1, 1993.

§ 483. Duration

A durable power of attorney does not lapse because of the passage of time unless the instrument creating the power of attorney specifically states a time limitation.

Added by Acts 1993, 73rd Leg., ch. 49, § 1, eff. Sept. 1, 1993.

§ 484. Effect of Acts by Attorney in Fact or Agent During Incapacity of Principal

All acts done by an attorney in fact or agent pursuant to a durable power of attorney during any period of disability or incapacity of the principal have the same effect and inure to the benefit of and bind the principal and the principal's successors in interest as if the principal were not disabled or incapacitated.

Added by Acts 1993, 73rd Leg., ch. 49, § 1, eff. Sept. 1, 1993.

§ 485. Relation of Attorney in Fact or Agent to Court-Appointed Guardian of Estate

If, after execution of a durable power of attorney, a court of the principal's domicile appoints a guardian of the estate of the principal, the powers of the attorney in fact or agent terminate on the qualification of the guardian of the estate, and the attorney in fact or agent shall deliver to the guardian of the estate all assets of the estate of the ward in the attorney's or agent's possession and shall account to the guardian of the estate as the attorney or agent would to the principal had the principal terminated his powers.

Added by Acts 1993, 73rd Leg., ch. 49, § 1, eff. Sept. 1, 1993.

§ 485A. Effect of Principal's Divorce or Marriage Annulment if Former Spouse is Attorney in Fact or Agent

If, after execution of a durable power of attorney, the principal is divorced from a person who has been appointed the principal's attorney in fact or agent or the principal's marriage to a person who has been appointed the principal's attorney in fact or agent is annulled, the powers of the attorney in fact or agent granted to the principal's former spouse shall terminate on the date on which the divorce or annulment of marriage is granted by a court, unless otherwise expressly provided by the durable power of attorney.

Added by Acts 1997, 75th Leg., ch. 455, § 1, eff. Sept. 1, 1997.

Section 8 of Acts 1997, 75th Leg., ch. 455 provides:

"This Act takes effect September 1, 1997, and applies only to a durable power of attorney or statutory durable power of attorney that is executed on or after that date. A durable power of attorney or statutory durable power of attorney that is executed before the effective date of this Act is governed by the law in effect on the date the power of attorney was executed, and the former law is continued in effect for that purpose."

§ 486. Knowledge of Death, Guardian of Estate, Revocation, Divorce, or Marriage Annulment; Good-Faith Acts

(a) The revocation by, the death of, or the qualification of a guardian of the estate of a principal who has executed a durable power of attorney does not revoke or terminate the agency as to the attorney in fact, agent, or other person who, without actual knowledge of the termination of the power by revocation, by the principal's death, or by the qualification of a guardian of the estate of the principal, acts in good faith under or in reliance on the power.

(b) The divorce of a principal from a person who has been appointed the principal's attorney in fact or agent before the date on which the divorce is granted or the annulment of the marriage of a principal and a person who has been appointed the principal's attorney in fact or agent before the date the annulment is granted does not revoke or terminate the agency as to a person other than the principal's former spouse if the person acts in good faith under or in reliance on the power.

(c) Any action taken under this section, unless otherwise invalid or unenforceable, binds successors in interest of the principal.

Added by Acts 1993, 73rd Leg., ch. 49, § 1, eff. Sept. 1, 1993. Amended by Acts 1997, 75th Leg., ch. 455, § 2, eff. Sept. 1, 1997.

For application provisions of Acts 1997, 75th Leg., ch. 455, see note following V.A.T.S., Probate Code § 485A.

§ 487. Affidavit of Lack of Knowledge or Termination of Power; Recording; Good-Faith Reliance

(a) As to acts undertaken in good-faith reliance on the durable power of attorney, an affidavit executed by the attorney in fact or agent under a durable power of attorney stating that the attorney in fact or agent did not have at the time of exercise of the power actual knowledge of the termination of the power by revocation, by the principal's death, by the principal's divorce or the annulment of the marriage of the principal if the attorney in fact or agent was the principal's spouse, or by the qualification of a guardian of the estate of the principal is conclusive proof as between the attorney in fact or agent and a person other than the principal or the principal's personal representative dealing with the attorney in fact or agent of the nonrevocation or nontermination of the power at that time.

(b) As to acts undertaken in good-faith reliance on the durable power of attorney, an affidavit executed by the attorney in fact or agent under a durable power of attorney stating that the principal is disabled or incapacitated, as defined by the power, is conclusive proof as between the attorney in fact or agent and a person other than the principal or the principal's personal representative dealing with the attorney in fact or agent of the disability or incapacity of the principal at that time.

(c) If the exercise of the power of attorney requires execution and delivery of any instrument that is to be recorded, an affidavit executed under Subsection (a) or (b) of this section, when authenticated for record, may also be recorded.

(d) This section does not affect any provision in a durable power of attorney for its termination by expiration of time or occurrence of an event other than express revocation.

(e) When a durable power of attorney is used, a third party who relies in good faith on the acts of an attorney in fact or agent within the scope of the power of attorney is not liable to the principal.

Added by Acts 1993, 73rd Leg., ch. 49, § 1, eff. Sept. 1, 1993. Amended by Acts 1997, 75th Leg., ch. 455, § 3, eff. Sept. 1, 1997.

For application provisions of Acts 1997, 75th Leg., ch. 455, see note following V.A.T.S., Probate Code § 485A.

§ 488. Revocation of Durable Power of Attorney

Unless otherwise provided by the durable power of attorney, a revocation of a durable power of attorney is not effective as to a third party relying on the power of attorney until the third party receives actual notice of the revocation.

Added by Acts 1993, 73rd Leg., ch. 49, § 1, eff. Sept. 1, 1993.

§ 489. Recording Durable Power of Attorney for Real Property Transactions

A durable power of attorney for a real property transaction requiring the execution and delivery of an instrument that is to be recorded, including a release, assignment, satisfaction, mortgage, security agreement, deed of trust, encumbrance, deed of conveyance, oil, gas, or other mineral lease, memorandum of a lease, lien, or other claim or right to real property, shall be recorded in the office of the county clerk of the county in which the property is located.

Added by Acts 1993, 73rd Leg., ch. 49, § 1, eff. Sept. 1, 1993.

§ 490. Statutory Durable Power of Attorney

(a) The following form is known as a "statutory durable power of attorney." A person may use a statutory durable power of attorney to grant an attorney in fact or agent powers with respect to a person's property and financial matters. A power of attorney in substantially the following form has the meaning and effect prescribed by this chapter. The validity of a power of attorney as meeting the requirements of a statutory durable power of attorney is not affected by the fact that one or more of the categories of optional powers listed in the form are struck or the form includes specific limitations on or additions to the attorney in fact's or agent's powers.

The following form is not exclusive, and other forms of power of attorney may be used.

STATUTORY DURABLE POWER OF ATTORNEY

NOTICE: THE POWERS GRANTED BY THIS DOCUMENT ARE BROAD AND SWEEPING. THEY ARE EXPLAINED IN THE DURABLE POWER OF ATTORNEY ACT, CHAPTER XII, TEXAS PROBATE CODE. IF YOU HAVE ANY QUESTIONS ABOUT THESE POWERS, OBTAIN COMPETENT LEGAL ADVICE. THIS DOCUMENT DOES NOT AUTHORIZE ANYONE TO MAKE MEDICAL AND OTHER HEALTH-CARE DECISIONS FOR YOU. YOU MAY REVOKE THIS POWER OF ATTORNEY IF YOU LATER WISH TO DO SO.

I, ________ (insert your name and address), appoint ________ (insert the name and address of the person appointed) as my agent (attorney-in-fact) to act for me in any lawful way with respect to all of the following powers except for a power that I have crossed out below.

TO WITHHOLD A POWER, YOU MUST CROSS OUT EACH POWER WITHHELD.

Real property transactions;

Tangible personal property transactions;

Stock and bond transactions;

Commodity and option transactions;

Banking and other financial institution transactions;

Business operating transactions;

Insurance and annuity transactions;

Estate, trust, and other beneficiary transactions;

Claims and litigation;

Personal and family maintenance;

Benefits from social security, Medicare, Medicaid, or other governmental programs or civil or military service;

Retirement plan transactions;

Tax matters.

IF NO POWER LISTED ABOVE IS CROSSED OUT, THIS DOCUMENT SHALL BE CONSTRUED AND INTERPRETED AS A GENERAL POWER OF ATTORNEY AND MY AGENT (ATTORNEY IN FACT) SHALL HAVE THE POWER AND AUTHORITY TO PERFORM OR UNDERTAKE ANY ACTION I COULD PERFORM OR UNDERTAKE IF I WERE PERSONALLY PRESENT.

SPECIAL INSTRUCTIONS:

Special instructions applicable to gifts (initial in front of the following sentence to have it apply):

I grant my agent (attorney in fact) the power to apply my property to make gifts, except that the amount of a gift to an individual may not exceed the amount of annual exclusions allowed from the federal gift tax for the calendar year of the gift.

ON THE FOLLOWING LINES YOU MAY GIVE SPECIAL INSTRUCTIONS LIMITING OR EXTENDING THE POWERS GRANTED TO YOUR AGENT.

____

____

____

____

____

____

____

____

____

____

UNLESS YOU DIRECT OTHERWISE ABOVE, THIS POWER OF ATTORNEY IS EFFECTIVE IMMEDIATELY AND WILL CONTINUE UNTIL IT IS REVOKED.

CHOOSE ONE OF THE FOLLOWING ALTERNATIVES BY CROSSING OUT THE ALTERNATIVE NOT CHOSEN:

(A) This power of attorney is not affected by my subsequent disability or incapacity.

(B) This power of attorney becomes effective upon my disability or incapacity.

YOU SHOULD CHOOSE ALTERNATIVE (A) IF THIS POWER OF ATTORNEY IS TO BECOME EFFECTIVE ON THE DATE IT IS EXECUTED.

IF NEITHER (A) NOR (B) IS CROSSED OUT, IT WILL BE ASSUMED THAT YOU CHOSE ALTERNATIVE (A).

If Alternative (B) is chosen and a definition of my disability or incapacity is not contained in this power of attorney, I shall be considered disabled or incapacitated for purposes of this power of attorney if a physician certifies in writing at a date later than the date this power of attorney is executed that, based on the physician's medical examination of me, I am mentally incapable of managing my financial affairs. I authorize the physician who examines me for this purpose to disclose my physical or mental condition to another person for purposes of this power of attorney. A third party who accepts this power of attorney is fully protected from any action taken under this power of attorney that is based on the determination made by a physician of my disability or incapacity.

I agree that any third party who receives a copy of this document may act under it. Revocation of the durable power of attorney is not effective as to a third party until the third party receives actual notice of the revocation. I agree to indemnify the third party for any claims that arise against the third party because of reliance on this power of attorney.

If any agent named by me dies, becomes legally disabled, resigns, or refuses to act, I name the following (each to act alone and successively, in the order named) as successor(s) to that agent: ________.

Signed this ______ day of __________, 19___

____

(your signature)

State of ______________________

County of _____________________

This document was acknowledged before me on

________________________(date) by ____________

(name of principal)

____

(signature of notarial officer)

(Seal, if any, of notary) ______________________________

(printed name)

My commission expires: __________

THE ATTORNEY IN FACT OR AGENT, BY ACCEPTING OR ACTING UNDER THE APPOINTMENT, ASSUMES THE FIDUCIARY AND OTHER LEGAL RESPONSIBILITIES OF AN AGENT.

(b) A statutory durable power of attorney is legally sufficient under this chapter if the wording of the form complies substantially with Subsection (a) of this section, the form is properly completed, and the signature of the principal is acknowledged.

(c) Repealed by Acts 1997, 75th Leg., ch. 455, § 7, eff. Sept. 1, 1997.

Added by Acts 1993, 73rd Leg., ch. 49, § 1, eff. Sept. 1, 1993. Amended by Acts 1997, 75th Leg., ch. 455, §§ 4, 7, eff. Sept. 1, 1997.

For application provisions of Acts 1997, 75th Leg., ch. 455, see note following V.A.T.S., Probate Code § 485A.

§ 491. Construction of Powers Generally

The principal, by executing a statutory durable power of attorney that confers authority with respect to any class of transactions, empowers the attorney in fact or agent for that class of transactions to:

(1) demand, receive, and obtain by litigation, action, or otherwise any money or other thing of value to which the principal is, may become, or may claim to be entitled;

(2) conserve, invest, disburse, or use any money or other thing of value received on behalf of the principal for the purposes intended;

(3) contract in any manner with any person, on terms agreeable to the attorney in fact or agent, to accomplish a purpose of a transaction and perform, rescind, reform, release, or modify the contract or another contract made by or on behalf of the principal;

(4) execute, acknowledge, seal, and deliver a deed, revocation, mortgage, lease, notice, check, release, or other instrument the agent considers desirable to accomplish a purpose of a transaction;

(5) prosecute, defend, submit to arbitration, settle, and propose or accept a compromise with respect to a claim existing in favor of or against the principal or intervene in an action or litigation relating to the claim;

(6) seek on the principal's behalf the assistance of a court to carry out an act authorized by the power of attorney;

(7) engage, compensate, and discharge an attorney, accountant, expert witness, or other assistant;

(8) keep appropriate records of each transaction, including an accounting of receipts and disbursements;

(9) prepare, execute, and file a record, report, or other document the attorney in fact or agent considers necessary or desirable to safeguard or promote the principal's interest under a statute or governmental regulation;

(10) reimburse the attorney in fact or agent for expenditures made in exercising the powers granted by the durable power of attorney; and

(11) in general, do any other lawful act that the principal may do with respect to a transaction.

Added by Acts 1993, 73rd Leg., ch. 49, § 1, eff. Sept. 1, 1993.

§ 492. Construction of Power Relating to Real Property Transactions

In a statutory durable power of attorney, the language conferring authority with respect to real property transactions empowers the attorney in fact or agent without further reference to a specific description of the real property to:

(1) accept as a gift or as security for a loan or reject, demand, buy, lease, receive, or otherwise acquire an interest in real property or a right incident to real property;

(2) sell, exchange, convey with or without covenants, quitclaim, release, surrender, mortgage, encumber, partition, consent to partitioning, subdivide, apply for zoning, rezoning, or other governmental permits, plat or consent to platting, develop, grant options concerning, lease or sublet, or otherwise dispose of an estate or interest in real property or a right incident to real property;

(3) release, assign, satisfy, and enforce by litigation, action, or otherwise a mortgage, deed of trust, encumbrance, lien, or other claim to real property that exists or is claimed to exist;

(4) do any act of management or of conservation with respect to an interest in real property, or a right incident to real property, owned or claimed to be owned by the principal, including power to:

(A) insure against a casualty, liability, or loss;

(B) obtain or regain possession or protect the interest or right by litigation, action, or otherwise;

(C) pay, compromise, or contest taxes or assessments or apply for and receive refunds in connection with them;

(D) purchase supplies, hire assistance or labor, or make repairs or alterations in the real property; and

(E) manage and supervise an interest in real property, including the mineral estate, by, for example, entering into a lease for oil, gas, and mineral purposes, making contracts for development of the mineral estate, or making pooling and unitization agreements;

(5) use, develop, alter, replace, remove, erect, or install structures or other improvements on real property in which the principal has or claims to have an estate, interest, or right;

(6) participate in a reorganization with respect to real property or a legal entity that owns an interest in or right incident to real property, receive and hold shares of stock or obligations received in a plan or

reorganization, and act with respect to the shares or obligations, including:

(A) selling or otherwise disposing of the shares or obligations;

(B) exercising or selling an option, conversion, or similar right with respect to the shares or obligations; and

(C) voting the shares or obligations in person or by proxy;

(7) change the form of title of an interest in or right incident to real property; and

(8) dedicate easements or other real property in which the principal has or claims to have an interest to public use, with or without consideration.

Added by Acts 1993, 73rd Leg., ch. 49, § 1, eff. Sept. 1, 1993. Amended by Acts 1997, 75th Leg., ch. 455, § 5, eff. Sept. 1, 1997.

For application provisions of Acts 1997, 75th Leg., ch. 455, see note following V.A.T.S., Probate Code § 485A.

§ 493. Construction of Power Relating to Tangible Personal Property Transactions

In a statutory durable power of attorney, the language conferring general authority with respect to tangible personal property transactions empowers the attorney in fact or agent to:

(1) accept as a gift or as security for a loan, reject, demand, buy, receive, or otherwise acquire ownership or possession of tangible personal property or an interest in tangible personal property;

(2) sell, exchange, convey with or without covenants, release, surrender, mortgage, encumber, pledge, hypothecate, create a security interest in, pawn, grant options concerning, lease or sublet to others, or otherwise dispose of tangible personal property or an interest in tangible personal property;

(3) release, assign, satisfy, or enforce by litigation, action, or otherwise a mortgage, security interest, encumbrance, lien, or other claim on behalf of the principal, with respect to tangible personal property or an interest in tangible personal property; and

(4) do an act of management or conservation with respect to tangible personal property or an interest in tangible personal property on behalf of the principal, including:

(A) insuring against casualty, liability, or loss;

(B) obtaining or regaining possession or protecting the property or interest by litigation, action, or otherwise;

(C) paying, compromising, or contesting taxes or assessments or applying for and receiving refunds in connection with taxes or assessments;

(D) moving from place to place;

(E) storing for hire or on a gratuitous bailment; and

(F) using, altering, and making repairs or alterations.

Added by Acts 1993, 73rd Leg., ch. 49, § 1, eff. Sept. 1, 1993.

§ 494. Construction of Power Relating to Stock and Bond Transactions

In a statutory durable power of attorney, the language conferring authority with respect to stock and bond transactions empowers the attorney in fact or agent to buy, sell, and exchange stocks, bonds, mutual funds, and all other types of securities and financial instruments other than commodity futures contracts and call and put options on stocks and stock indexes, receive certificates and other evidences of ownership with respect to securities, exercise voting rights with respect to securities in person or by proxy, enter into voting trusts, and consent to limitations on the right to vote.

Added by Acts 1993, 73rd Leg., ch. 49, § 1, eff. Sept. 1, 1993.

§ 495. Construction of Power Relating to Commodity and Option Transactions

In a statutory durable power of attorney, the language conferring authority with respect to commodity and option transactions empowers the attorney in fact or agent to buy, sell, exchange, assign, settle, and exercise commodity futures contracts and call and put options on stocks and stock indexes traded on a regulated options exchange and establish, continue, modify, or terminate option accounts with a broker.

Added by Acts 1993, 73rd Leg., ch. 49, § 1, eff. Sept. 1, 1993.

§ 496. Construction of Power Relating to Banking and Other Financial Institution Transactions

In a statutory durable power of attorney, the language conferring authority with respect to banking and other financial institution transactions empowers the attorney in fact or agent to:

(1) continue, modify, or terminate an account or other banking arrangement made by or on behalf of the principal;

(2) establish, modify, or terminate an account or other banking arrangement with a bank, trust company, savings and loan association, credit union, thrift

company, brokerage firm, or other financial institution selected by the attorney in fact or agent;

(3) hire a safe deposit box or space in a vault;

(4) contract to procure other services available from a financial institution as the attorney in fact or agent considers desirable;

(5) withdraw by check, order, or otherwise money or property of the principal deposited with or left in the custody of a financial institution;

(6) receive bank statements, vouchers, notices, or similar documents from a financial institution and act with respect to them;

(7) enter a safe deposit box or vault and withdraw or add to the contents;

(8) borrow money at an interest rate agreeable to the attorney in fact or agent and pledge as security real or personal property of the principal necessary to borrow, pay, renew, or extend the time of payment of a debt of the principal;

(9) make, assign, draw, endorse, discount, guarantee, and negotiate promissory notes, bills of exchange, checks, drafts, or other negotiable or nonnegotiable paper of the principal, or payable to the principal or the principal's order, to receive the cash or other proceeds of those transactions, to accept a draft drawn by a person on the principal, and to pay the principal when due;

(10) receive for the principal and act on a sight draft, warehouse receipt, or other negotiable or nonnegotiable instrument;

(11) apply for and receive letters of credit, credit cards, and traveler's checks from a financial institution and give an indemnity or other agreement in connection with letters of credit; and

(12) consent to an extension of the time of payment with respect to commercial paper or a financial transaction with a financial institution.

Added by Acts 1993, 73rd Leg., ch. 49, § 1, eff. Sept. 1, 1993.

§ 497. Construction of Power Relating to Business Operation Transactions

In a statutory durable power of attorney, the language conferring authority with respect to business operating transactions empowers the attorney in fact or agent to:

(1) operate, buy, sell, enlarge, reduce, or terminate a business interest;

(2) to the extent that an agent is permitted by law to act for a principal and subject to the terms of the partnership agreement:

(A) perform a duty or discharge a liability or exercise a right, power, privilege, or option that the principal has, may have, or claims to have under a partnership agreement, whether or not the principal is a general or limited partner;

(B) enforce the terms of a partnership agreement by litigation, action, or otherwise; and

(C) defend, submit to arbitration, settle, or compromise litigation or an action to which the principal is a party because of membership in the partnership;

(3) exercise in person or by proxy or enforce by litigation, action, or otherwise a right, power, privilege, or option the principal has or claims to have as the holder of a bond, share, or other instrument of similar character and defend, submit to arbitration, settle, or compromise a legal proceeding to which the principal is a party because of a bond, share, or similar instrument;

(4) with respect to a business owned solely by the principal:

(A) continue, modify, renegotiate, extend, and terminate a contract made with an individual or a legal entity, firm, association, or corporation by or on behalf of the principal with respect to the business before execution of the power of attorney;

(B) determine:

(i) the location of its operation;

(ii) the nature and extent of its business;

(iii) the methods of manufacturing, selling, merchandising, financing, accounting, and advertising employed in its operation;

(iv) the amount and types of insurance carried; and

(v) the mode of engaging, compensating, and dealing with its accountants, attorneys, and other agents and employees;

(C) change the name or form of organization under which the business is operated and enter into a partnership agreement with other persons or organize a corporation to take over all or part of the operation of the business; and

(D) demand and receive money due or claimed by the principal or on the principal's behalf in the operation of the business and control and disburse the money in the operation of the business;

(5) put additional capital into a business in which the principal has an interest;

(6) join in a plan of reorganization, consolidation, or merger of the business;

(7) sell or liquidate a business or part of it at the time and on the terms that the attorney in fact or agent considers desirable;

(8) establish the value of a business under a buy-out agreement to which the principal is a party;

(9) prepare, sign, file, and deliver reports, compilations of information, returns, or other papers with respect to a business that are required by a governmental agency, department, or instrumentality or that the attorney in fact or agent considers desirable and make related payments; and

(10) pay, compromise, or contest taxes or assessments and do any other act that the attorney in fact or agent considers desirable to protect the principal from illegal or unnecessary taxation, fines, penalties, or assessments with respect to a business, including attempts to recover, in any manner permitted by law, money paid before or after the execution of the power of attorney.

Added by Acts 1993, 73rd Leg., ch. 49, § 1, eff. Sept. 1, 1993.

§ 498. Construction of Power Relating to Insurance Transactions

In a statutory durable power of attorney, the language conferring authority with respect to insurance and annuity transactions empowers the attorney in fact or agent to:

(1) continue, pay the premium or assessment on, modify, rescind, release, or terminate a contract procured by or on behalf of the principal that insures or provides an annuity to either the principal or another person, whether or not the principal is a beneficiary under the contract;

(2) procure new, different, or additional contracts of insurance and annuities for the principal or the principal's spouse, children, and other dependents and select the amount, type of insurance or annuity, and mode of payment;

(3) pay the premium or assessment on or modify, rescind, release, or terminate a contract of insurance or annuity procured by the attorney in fact or agent;

(4) designate the beneficiary of the contract, except that an attorney in fact or agent may be named a beneficiary of the contract or an extension, renewal, or substitute for the contract only to the extent the attorney in fact or agent was named as a beneficiary under a contract procured by the principal before executing the power of attorney;

(5) apply for and receive a loan on the security of the contract of insurance or annuity;

(6) surrender and receive the cash surrender value;

(7) exercise an election;

(8) change the manner of paying premiums;

(9) change or convert the type of insurance contract or annuity with respect to which the principal has or claims to have a power described in this section;

(10) change the beneficiary of a contract of insurance or annuity, except that the attorney in fact or agent may be designated a beneficiary only to the extent authorized by Subdivision (4) of this section;

(11) apply for and procure government aid to guarantee or pay premiums of a contract of insurance on the life of the principal;

(12) collect, sell, assign, hypothecate, borrow on, or pledge the interest of the principal in a contract of insurance or annuity; and

(13) pay from proceeds or otherwise, compromise or contest, or apply for refunds in connection with a tax or assessment levied by a taxing authority with respect to a contract of insurance or annuity or its proceeds or liability accruing because of the tax or assessment.

Added by Acts 1993, 73rd Leg., ch. 49, § 1, eff. Sept. 1, 1993.

§ 499. Construction of Power Relating to Estate, Trust, and Other Beneficiary Transactions

In a statutory durable power of attorney, the language conferring authority with respect to estate, trust, and other beneficiary transactions empowers the attorney in fact or agent to act for the principal in all matters that affect a trust, probate estate, guardianship, conservatorship, escrow, custodianship, or other fund from which the principal is, may become, or claims to be entitled, as a beneficiary, to a share or payment, including to:

(1) accept, reject, disclaim, receive, receipt for, sell, assign, release, pledge, exchange, or consent to a reduction in or modification of a share in or payment from the fund;

(2) demand or obtain by litigation, action, or otherwise money or any other thing of value to which the principal is, may become, or claims to be entitled because of the fund;

(3) initiate, participate in, or oppose a legal or judicial proceeding to ascertain the meaning, validity, or effect of a deed, will, declaration of trust, or other instrument or transaction affecting the interest of the principal;

(4) initiate, participate in, or oppose a legal or judicial proceeding to remove, substitute, or surcharge a fiduciary;

(5) conserve, invest, disburse, or use anything received for an authorized purpose; and

(6) transfer all or part of an interest of the principal in real property, stocks, bonds, accounts with financial institutions, insurance, and other property to the trustee of a revocable trust created by the principal as settlor.

Added by Acts 1993, 73rd Leg., ch. 49, § 1, eff. Sept. 1, 1993.

§ 500. Construction of Power Relating to Claims and Litigation

In a statutory durable power of attorney, the language conferring general authority with respect to claims and litigation empowers the attorney in fact or agent to:

(1) assert and prosecute before a court or administrative agency a claim, a claim for relief, a counterclaim, or an offset or defend against an individual, a legal entity, or a government, including suits to recover property or other thing of value, to recover damages sustained by the principal, to eliminate or modify tax liability, or to seek an injunction, specific performance, or other relief;

(2) bring an action to determine adverse claims, intervene in an action or litigation, and act as amicus curiae;

(3) in connection with an action or litigation, procure an attachment, garnishment, libel, order of arrest, or other preliminary, provisional, or intermediate relief and use an available procedure to effect or satisfy a judgment, order, or decree;

(4) in connection with an action or litigation, perform any lawful act the principal could perform, including acceptance of tender, offer of judgment, admission of facts, submission of a controversy on an agreed statement of facts, consent to examination before trial, and binding of the principal in litigation;

(5) submit to arbitration, settle, and propose or accept a compromise with respect to a claim or litigation;

(6) waive the issuance and service of process on the principal, accept service of process, appear for the principal, designate persons on whom process directed to the principal may be served, execute and file or deliver stipulations on the principal's behalf, verify pleadings, seek appellate review, procure and give surety and indemnity bonds, contract and pay for the preparation and printing of records and briefs, or receive and execute and file or deliver a consent, waiver, release, confession of judgment, satisfaction of judgment, notice, agreement, or other instrument in connection with the prosecution, settlement, or defense of a claim or litigation;

(7) act for the principal with respect to bankruptcy or insolvency proceedings, whether voluntary or involuntary, concerning the principal or some other person, with respect to a reorganization proceeding or a receivership or application for the appointment of a receiver or trustee that affects an interest of the principal in real or personal property or other thing of value; and

(8) pay a judgment against the principal or a settlement made in connection with a claim or litigation and receive and conserve money or other thing of value paid in settlement of or as proceeds of a claim or litigation.

Added by Acts 1993, 73rd Leg., ch. 49, § 1, eff. Sept. 1, 1993.

§ 501. Construction of Power Relating to Personal and Family Maintenance

In a statutory durable power of attorney, the language conferring authority with respect to personal and family maintenance empowers the attorney in fact or agent to:

(1) perform the acts necessary to maintain the customary standard of living of the principal, the principal's spouse and children, and other individuals customarily or legally entitled to be supported by the principal, including providing living quarters by purchase, lease, or other contract, or paying the operating costs, including interest, amortization payments, repairs, and taxes on premises owned by the principal and occupied by those individuals;

(2) provide for the individuals described by Subdivision (1) of this section normal domestic help, usual vacations and travel expenses, and funds for shelter, clothing, food, appropriate education, and other current living costs;

(3) pay necessary medical, dental, and surgical care, hospitalization, and custodial care for the individuals described by Subdivision (1) of this section;

(4) continue any provision made by the principal, for the individuals described by Subdivision (1) of this

section, for automobiles or other means of transportation, including registering, licensing, insuring, and replacing the automobiles or other means of transportation;

(5) maintain or open charge accounts for the convenience of the individuals described by Subdivision (1) of this section and open new accounts the attorney in fact or agent considers desirable to accomplish a lawful purpose; and

(6) continue payments incidental to the membership or affiliation of the principal in a church, club, society, order, or other organization or to continue contributions to those organizations.

Added by Acts 1993, 73rd Leg., ch. 49, § 1, eff. Sept. 1, 1993.

§ 502. Construction of Power Relating to Benefits From Certain Governmental Programs or Civil or Military Service

In a statutory durable power of attorney, the language conferring authority with respect to benefits from social security, Medicare, Medicaid, or other governmental programs or civil or military service empowers the attorney in fact or agent to:

(1) execute vouchers in the name of the principal for allowances and reimbursements payable by the United States, a foreign government, or a state or subdivision of a state to the principal, including allowances and reimbursements for transportation of the individuals described by Section 501(1) of this code, and for shipment of their household effects;

(2) take possession and order the removal and shipment of property of the principal from a post, warehouse, depot, dock, or other place of storage or safekeeping, either governmental or private, and execute and deliver a release, voucher, receipt, bill of lading, shipping ticket, certificate, or other instrument for that purpose;

(3) prepare, file, and prosecute a claim of the principal to a benefit or assistance, financial or otherwise, to which the principal claims to be entitled under a statute or governmental regulation;

(4) prosecute, defend, submit to arbitration, settle, and propose or accept a compromise with respect to any benefits the principal may be entitled to receive; and

(5) receive the financial proceeds of a claim of the type described in this section and conserve, invest, disburse, or use anything received for a lawful purpose.

Added by Acts 1993, 73rd Leg., ch. 49, § 1, eff. Sept. 1, 1993.

§ 503. Construction of Power Relating to Retirement Plan Transactions

(a) In a statutory durable power of attorney, the language conferring authority with respect to retirement plan transactions empowers the attorney in fact or agent to do any lawful act the principal may do with respect to a transaction relating to a retirement plan, including to:

(1) apply for service or disability retirement benefits;

(2) select payment options under any retirement plan in which the principal participates, including plans for self-employed individuals;

(3) designate or change the designation of a beneficiary or benefits payable by a retirement plan, except that an attorney in fact or agent may be named a beneficiary only to the extent the attorney in fact or agent was a named beneficiary under the retirement plan before the durable power of attorney was executed;

(4) make voluntary contributions to retirement plans if authorized by the plan;

(5) exercise the investment powers available under any self-directed retirement plan;

(6) make "rollovers" of plan benefits into other retirement plans;

(7) borrow from, sell assets to, and purchase assets from retirement plans if authorized by the plan;

(8) waive the right of the principal to be a beneficiary of a joint or survivor annuity if the principal is a spouse who is not employed;

(9) receive, endorse, and cash payments from a retirement plan;

(10) waive the right of the principal to receive all or a portion of benefits payable by a retirement plan; and

(11) request and receive information relating to the principal from retirement plan records.

(b) In this section, "retirement plan" means:

(1) an employee pension benefit plan as defined by Section 1002, Employee Retirement Income Security Act of 1974 (ERISA) (29 U.S.C. Section 1002), without regard to the provisions of Section (2)(B) of that section;

(2) a plan that does not meet the definition of an employee benefit plan under ERISA because the plan does not cover common law employees;

(3) a plan that is similar to an employee benefit plan under ERISA, regardless of whether it is covered by Title I of ERISA, including a plan that provides death benefits to the beneficiary of employees; and

(4) an individual retirement account or annuity or a self-employed pension plan or similar plan or account.

Added by Acts 1993, 73rd Leg., ch. 49, § 1, eff. Sept. 1, 1993. Amended by Acts 1997, 75th Leg., ch. 455, § 6, eff. Sept. 1, 1997.

For application provisions of Acts 1997, 75th Leg., ch. 455, see note following V.A.T.S., Probate Code § 485A.

§ 504. Construction of Power Relating to Tax Matters

In a statutory durable power of attorney, the language conferring authority with respect to tax matters empowers the attorney in fact or agent to:

(1) prepare, sign, and file federal, state, local, and foreign income, gift, payroll, Federal Insurance Contributions Act, and other tax returns, claims for refunds, requests for extension of time, petitions regarding tax matters, and any other tax-related documents, including receipts, offers, waivers, consents, including consents and agreements under Section 2032A, Internal Revenue Code of 1986 (26 U.S.C. Section 2032A), closing agreements, and any power of attorney form required by the Internal Revenue Service or other taxing authority with respect to a tax year on which the statute of limitations has not run and 25 tax years following that tax year;

(2) pay taxes due, collect refunds, post bonds, receive confidential information, and contest deficiencies determined by the Internal Revenue Service or other taxing authority;

(3) exercise any election available to the principal under federal, state, local, or foreign tax law; and

(4) act for the principal in all tax matters for all periods before the Internal Revenue Service and any other taxing authority.

Added by Acts 1993, 73rd Leg., ch. 49, § 1, eff. Sept. 1, 1993.

§ 505. Existing Interest; Foreign Interests

The powers described in Sections 492 through 504 of this code may be exercised equally with respect to an interest the principal has at the time the durable power of attorney is executed or acquires later, whether or not the property is located in this state and whether or not the powers are exercised or the durable power of attorney is executed in this state.

Added by Acts 1993, 73rd Leg., ch. 49, § 1, eff. Sept. 1, 1993.

§ 506. Uniformity of Application and Construction

This chapter shall be applied and construed to effect its general purpose to make uniform the law with respect to the subject of this chapter among states enacting it.

Added by Acts 1993, 73rd Leg., ch. 49, § 1, eff. Sept. 1, 1993.

CHAPTER XII. INFORMAL PROBATE

For another Chapter 12, Durable Power of Attorney Act, added by Acts 1993, 73rd Leg., ch. 49, § 1, see § 481 et seq., ante.

PART 1. INFORMAL PROBATE WITH AND WITHOUT ISSUANCE OF LETTERS [REPEALED]

§§ 501 to 510. Repealed by Acts 1997, 75th Leg., ch. 540, § 5, eff. Sept. 1, 1997

PART 2. EMERGENCY INTERVENTION PROCEEDINGS; FUNERAL AND BURIAL EXPENSES [REDESIGNATED]

Acts 1997, 75th Leg., ch. 199, § 1 transfers and redesignates Chapter XII, Part 2, as Chapter V, Part 3, consisting of V.A.T.S. Probate Code, §§ 108 to 115.

Without reference to the transfer and redesignation of Chapter XII, Part 2, as Chapter V, Part 3, Acts 1997, 75th Leg., ch. 540, § 5 repeals Chapter XII effective September 1, 1997.

§§ 520 to 525. Renumbered as V.A.T.S. Probate Code §§ 108 to 115 by Acts 1997, 75th Leg., ch. 199, § 1, eff. Sept. 1, 1997

CHAPTER XIII. GUARDIANSHIP

PART 1. GENERAL PROVISIONS

SUBPART A. DEFINITIONS; PURPOSE; APPLICABILITY; PROCEEDINGS IN REM

Section

PART 2. GUARDIANSHIP PROCEEDINGS AND MATTERS

SUBPART A. JURISDICTION

GUARDIANSHIP

Section

694A. Complete Restoration of Ward's Capacity or Modification of Guardianship.
694B. Contents of Application.
694C. Appointment of Attorney ad Litem.
694D. Hearing.
694E. Findings Required.
694F. Examinations and Reports Relating to Complete Restoration of Ward's Capacity or Modification of Guardianship.
694G. Order of Complete Restoration of Ward's Capacity.
694H. Modification of Guardianship.
694I. Dismissal of Application.
694J. Contents of Order.
694K. Attorney Retained on Ward's Behalf.
695. Appointment of Successor Guardian.
695A. Successor Guardians for Wards of Guardianship Programs or Governmental Entities.
696. Appointment of Private Professional Guardians.
697. Registration of Private Professional Guardians.
698. Access to Criminal History Records.

SUBPART B. QUALIFICATION

699. How Guardians Qualify.
700. Oath of Guardian.
701. Time for Taking Oath and Giving Bond.
702. Bond Required of Guardian of the Person or Estate.
702A. Types of Bonds Acceptable for Guardian of the Person.
703. Bond of Guardian of the Estate.
704. Form of Bond.
705. Bond to be Filed.
706. Bond of Joint Guardians.
707. Bond of Married Persons.
708. Bond of Married Person Younger Than 18 Years of Age.
708A. Bond of Guardianship Program.
709. Affidavit of Personal Surety; Lien on Specific Property When Required; Subordination of Lien Authorized.
710. Bond as Lien on Real Property of Surety.
711. When New Bond May be Required.
712. Demand for New Bond by Interested Person.
713. Judge to Require New Bond.
714. Order Requiring New Bond.
715. Order Suspends Powers of Guardians.
716. Decrease in Amount of Bond.
717. Discharge of Sureties on Execution of New Bond.
718. Release of Sureties Before Guardianship Fully Administered.
719. Release of Lien Before Guardianship Fully Administered.
720. Release of Recorded Lien on Surety's Property.
721. Revocation of Letters for Failure to Give Bond.
722. Guardian Without Bond Required to Give Bond.
723. Order Requiring Bond.
724. Amount of Bond.
725. Failure to Give Bond.
726. Bonds Not Void on First Recovery.

PART 4. ADMINISTRATION OF GUARDIANSHIP

SUBPART A. INVENTORY, APPRAISEMENT, AND LIST OF CLAIMS

727. Appointment of Appraisers.

Section

728. Failure of Appraiser to Serve.
729. Inventory and Appraisement.
730. List of Claims.
731. Affidavit Attached.
732. Appraiser Fees.
733. Court Action.
734. Discovery of Additional Property.
735. Additional Inventory or List of Claims.
736. Correction When Inventory, Appraisement, or List of Claims Erroneous or Unjust.
737. Effect of Reappraisement.
738. Failure of Joint Guardians to Return an Inventory, Appraisement, and List of Claims.
739. Use of Inventories, Appraisements, and Lists of Claims as Evidence.

SUBPART B. ANNUAL ACCOUNTS, REPORTS, AND OTHER EXHIBITS

741. Annual Accounts Required.
742. Action on Annual Accounts.
743. Reports of Guardians of the Person.
744. Penalty for Failure to File Accountings, Exhibits, or Reports.

SUBPART C. FINAL SETTLEMENT, ACCOUNTING, AND DISCHARGE

745. Closing Guardianships of the Estate.
746. Payment of Funeral Expenses and Other Debts.
747. Termination of Guardianship of the Person.
748. Payment by Guardian of Taxes or Expenses.
749. Account for Final Settlement of Estates of Wards.
750. Procedure in Case of Neglect or Failure to File Final Account or Report.
751. Citation on Presentation of Account for Final Settlement.
752. Court Action.
753. Money Becoming Due Pending Final Discharge.
754. Inheritance Taxes Must be Paid.
755. Appointment of Attorney to Represent Ward.
756. Offsets, Credits, and Bad Debts.
757. Accounting for Labor or Services of a Ward.
758. Procedure if Representative Fails to Deliver Estate.

SUBPART D. REVOCATION OF LETTERS, DEATH, RESIGNATION, AND REMOVAL

759. Appointment of Successor Guardian.
760. Resignation.
761. Removal.
762. Reinstatement After Removal.
763. Additional Powers of Successor Guardian.
764. Subsequent Guardians Succeed to Prior Rights and Duties.
765. Successors' Return of Inventory, Appraisement, and List of Claims.

SUBPART E. GENERAL DUTIES AND POWERS OF GUARDIANS

767. Powers and Duties of Guardians of the Person.
768. General Powers and Duties of Guardian of the Estate.
769. Summary of Powers of Guardian of Person and Estate.
770. Care of Ward; Commitment.

Section

Section

TABLE

Showing generally the disposition into Chapter XIII, as enacted by Acts 1993, 73rd Leg., ch. 957, § 1, of the subject matter of specified sections repealed or repealed in part by Acts 1993, 73rd Leg., ch. 957, § 75.

Former Sections	New Sections
7	610
108	603
109	676
	677
110 (partially)	681
111	682
112	683
113	642
113A	646
114	684
115	643
116	690
117	676
118 (partially)	680
118A	679
119	695
120	694
121	612 to 616
122	617
123	618
124	881
	882
125	663
126	891
127	892
130	633
131	875
133(b)	877
136	885
144	887
157 (partially)	883
158	884
184	693
185	659
186	660
187	661
188	662
191	700
193	702
228	782
229	767
230(b)	768
	865
231	769
236 (partially)	776
237	778
247	669
305	792
330	636
339A	889
376	645

PART 1. GENERAL PROVISIONS

SUBPART A. DEFINITIONS; PURPOSE; APPLICABILITY; PROCEEDINGS IN REM

§ 601. Definitions

In this chapter:

(1) "Attorney ad litem" means an attorney who is appointed by a court to represent and advocate on behalf of a proposed ward, an incapacitated person, or an unborn person in a guardianship proceeding.

(2) "Authorized corporate surety" means a domestic or foreign corporation authorized to do business in this state to issue surety, guaranty, or indemnity bonds guaranteeing the fidelity of guardians.

(3) "Child" includes a biological or adopted child, whether adopted by a parent under a statutory procedure or by acts of estoppel.

(4) "Claims" includes a liability against the estate of a minor or an incapacitated person and debts due to the estate of a minor or an incapacitated person.

(5) "Corporate fiduciary" means a financial institution as defined by Section 201.101, Finance Code, having trust powers, existing or doing business under the laws of this state, another state, or the United States, that is authorized by law to act under the order or appointment of any court of record, without giving bond, as a guardian, receiver, trustee, executor, or administrator, or, although without general depository powers, as a depository for any money paid into court, or to become sole guarantor or surety in or on any bond required to be given under the laws of this state.

(6) "Court investigator" means a person appointed by a statutory probate court under Section 25.0025, Government Code.

(7) "Court" or "probate court" means a county court in the exercise of its probate jurisdiction, a court created by statute and authorized to exercise original probate jurisdiction, or a district court exercising original probate jurisdiction in contested matters.

(8) "Estate" or "guardianship estate" means the real and personal property of a ward or deceased ward, both as the property originally existed and as has from time to time changed in form by sale, reinvestment, or otherwise, and as augmented by any accretions and additions to (including any property to be distributed to the representative of the deceased ward by the trustee of a trust that terminates on the ward's death) or substitutions for the property, and as diminished by any decreases to or distributions from the property.

(9) "Exempt property" refers to that property of a deceased ward's estate that is exempt from execution or forced sale by the constitution or laws of this state, and to the allowance in lieu of the property.

(10) "Guardian" means a person who is appointed guardian under Section 693 of this code, or a temporary or successor guardian. Except as expressly provided otherwise, "guardian" includes the guardian of the estate and the guardian of the person of an incapacitated person.

(11) "Guardian ad litem" means a person who is appointed by a court to represent the best interests of an incapacitated person in a guardianship proceeding.

(12) "Guardianship program" means a local, county, or regional program that provides guardianship and related services to an incapacitated person or other person who needs assistance in making decisions concerning the person's own welfare or financial affairs.

(13) "Incapacitated person" means:

(A) a minor;

(B) an adult individual who, because of a physical or mental condition, is substantially unable to provide food, clothing, or shelter for himself or herself, to care for the individual's own physical health, or to manage the individual's own financial affairs; or

(C) a person who must have a guardian appointed to receive funds due the person from any governmental source.

(14) "Interested persons" or "persons interested" means an heir, devisee, spouse, creditor, or any other person having a property right in, or claim against,

the estate being administered or a person interested in the welfare of an incapacitated person, including a minor.

(15) "Minor" means a person who is younger than 18 years of age and who has never been married or who has not had the person's disabilities of minority removed for general purposes.

(16) "Minutes" means the guardianship minutes.

(17) "Mortgage" or "lien" includes a deed of trust; vendor's lien; chattel mortgage; mechanic's, materialman's, or laborer's lien; judgment, attachment, or garnishment lien; pledge by hypothecation; and a federal or state tax lien.

(18) "Next of kin" includes an adopted child, the descendants of an adopted child, and the adoptive parent of an adopted child.

(19) "Parent" means the mother of a child, a man presumed to be the biological father of a child, a man who has been adjudicated to be the biological father of a child by a court of competent jurisdiction, or an adoptive mother or father of a child, but does not include a parent as to whom the parent-child relationship has been terminated.

(20) "Person" includes natural persons, corporations, and guardianship programs.

(21) "Personal property" includes an interest in goods, money, choses in action, evidence of debts, and chattels real.

(22) "Personal representative" or "representative" includes a guardian, and a successor guardian.

(23) "Private professional guardian" means a person, other than an attorney or a corporate fiduciary, who is engaged in the business of providing guardianship services.

(24) "Proceedings in guardianship," "guardianship matter," "guardianship matters," "guardianship proceeding," and "proceedings for guardianship" are synonymous and include a matter or proceeding relating to a guardianship or any other matter addressed by this chapter.

(25) "Property" includes both real and personal property.

(26) "Proposed ward" means a person alleged to be incapacitated in a guardianship proceeding.

(27) "Real property" includes estates and interests in lands, corporeal or incorporeal, legal or equitable, other than chattels real.

(28) "Statutory probate court" means a statutory court designated as a statutory probate court under Chapter 25, Government Code. A county court at law exercising probate jurisdiction is not a statutory probate court under this chapter unless the court is designated a statutory probate court under Chapter 25, Government Code.

(29) "Surety" includes a personal and a corporate surety.

(30) "Ward" is a person for whom a guardian has been appointed.

(31) The singular number includes the plural; the plural number includes the singular.

(32) The masculine gender includes the feminine and neuter.

Added by Acts 1993, 73rd Leg., ch. 957, § 1, eff. Sept. 1, 1993. Amended by Acts 1995, 74th Leg., ch. 1039, § 15, eff. Sept. 1, 1995; Acts 1997, 75th Leg., ch. 52, § 2, eff. Sept. 1, 1997; Acts 1997, 75th Leg., ch. 1376, § 1, eff. Sept. 1, 1997; Acts 1999, 76th Leg., ch. 344, § 6.005, eff. Sept. 1, 1999; Acts 1999, 76th Leg., ch. 379, § 2, eff. Sept. 1, 1999.

Section 76 of the 1993 Act provides:

"(a) This Act applies to:

"(1) an application for the appointment of a guardian that is filed on or after September 1, 1993; and

"(2) an application for the appointment of a guardian that is filed before September 1, 1993, in which a guardianship has not been created.

"(b) An application described by Subsection (a)(2) of this section must be modified to conform to the changes in law made by this Act.

"(c) A guardianship existing on September 1, 1993, must be modified to conform to the changes in law made by this Act."

Section 6 of Acts 1997, 75th Leg., ch. 1376 provides:

"This Act takes effect September 1, 1997, and applies only to a proceeding for receivership of the estate of a missing person that is instituted on or after that date. A proceeding for receivership of the estate of a missing person that is instituted before the effective date of this Act is governed by the law in effect on the date on which the proceeding was instituted, and the former law is continued in effect for that purpose."

Section 11 of Acts 1999, 76th Leg., ch. 379 provides:

"(a) This Act takes effect September 1, 1999.

"(b) A guardianship for a missing person created under Chapter XIII, Texas Probate Code, before September 1, 1999, is abolished on the effective date of this Act.

"(c) On its own motion or on the motion of a person interested in the estate of the missing person, a court with jurisdiction to appoint a receiver for a missing person may convert a guardianship for a missing person abolished under this Act to a receivership:

"(1) under Section 79.017, Human Resources Code, as added by Chapter 1376, Acts of the 75th Legislature, Regular Session, 1997, and editorially redesignated as Article 62.023, Code of Criminal Procedure; or

"(2) under Section 886, Texas Probate Code."

§ 602. Policy; Purpose of Guardianship

A court may appoint a guardian with full authority over an incapacitated person or may grant a guardian limited authority over an incapacitated person as indicated by the incapacitated person's actual mental or physical limitations and only as necessary to promote and protect the well-being of the person. If the person is not a minor, the court may not use age as the sole factor in determining whether to appoint a guardian for the person. In creating a guardianship that gives a guardian limited power or authority over an incapacitated person, the court shall design the guardianship to encourage the development or maintenance of maximum self-reliance and independence in the incapacitated person.

Added by Acts 1993, 73rd Leg., ch. 957, § 1, eff. Sept. 1, 1993.

§ 603. Laws Applicable to Guardianships

(a) To the extent applicable and not inconsistent with other provisions of this code, the laws and rules governing estates of decedents apply to and govern guardianships.

(b) A reference in other sections of this code or in other law to a person who is mentally, physically, or legally incompetent, a person who is judicially declared incompetent, an incompetent or an incompetent person, a person of unsound mind, or a habitual drunkard means an incapacitated person.

Added by Acts 1993, 73rd Leg., ch. 957, § 1, eff. Sept. 1, 1993.

§ 604. Proceeding In Rem

From the filing of the application for the appointment of a guardian of the estate or person, or both, until the guardianship is settled and closed under this chapter, the administration of the estate of a minor or other incapacitated person is one proceeding for purposes of jurisdiction and is a proceeding in rem.

Added by Acts 1993, 73rd Leg., ch. 957, § 1, eff. Sept. 1, 1993.

PART 2. GUARDIANSHIP PROCEEDINGS AND MATTERS

SUBPART A. JURISDICTION

§ 605. County Court Jurisdiction

The county court has the general jurisdiction of a probate court. The county court shall appoint guardians of minors and other incapacitated persons, grant letters of guardianship, settle accounts of guardians, and transact all business appertaining to estates subject to guardianship, including the settlement, partition, and distribution of the estates. The county court may also enter other orders as may be authorized under this chapter.

Added by Acts 1993, 73rd Leg., ch. 957, § 1, eff. Sept. 1, 1993.

For applicability provisions of the 1993 Act, see notes following § 601.

§ 606. District Court and Other Court of Record Jurisdiction

(a) The district court has original control and jurisdiction over guardians and wards under regulations as may be prescribed by law.

(b) In those counties in which there is no statutory probate court, county court at law, or other statutory court exercising the jurisdiction of a probate court, all applications, petitions and motions regarding guardianships, mental health matters, and other matters covered by this chapter shall be filed and heard in the county court, except that in contested guardianship matters, the judge of the county court may on the judge's own motion, or shall on the motion of any party to the proceeding, according to the motion, request as provided by Section 25.0022, Government Code, the assignment of a statutory probate court judge to hear the contested portion of the proceeding, or transfer the contested portion of the proceeding to the district court, which may hear the transferred contested matters as if originally filed in the district court. If the judge of the county court has not transferred a contested guardianship matter to the district court at the time a party files a motion for assignment of a statutory probate court judge, the county judge shall grant the motion and may not transfer the matter to district court unless the party withdraws the motion. A statutory probate court judge assigned to a contested probate matter as provided by this subsection has for that matter the jurisdiction and authority granted to a statutory probate court by Sections 607 and 608 of this code. The county court continues to exercise jurisdiction over the management of the guardianship with the exception of the contested matter until final disposition of the contested matter is made by the assigned judge or the district court. In contested matters transferred to the district court as provided by this subsection, the district court, concurrently with the county court, has the general jurisdiction of a probate court. On resolution of all pending contested matters, the district court shall transfer the contested portion of the guardianship proceeding to the county court for further proceedings not inconsistent with the orders of the district court. If a contested portion of the proceeding is transferred to a district court under this subsection, the clerk of the district court may perform in relation to the transferred portion of the proceeding any function a county clerk may perform in that type of contested proceeding.

(c) In those counties in which there is a statutory probate court, county court at law, or other statutory court exercising the jurisdiction of a probate court, all applications, petitions and motions regarding guardianships, mental illness matters, or other matters addressed by this chapter shall be filed and heard in those courts and the constitutional county court, rather than in the district courts, unless otherwise provided by the legislature, and the judge of a county court may hear any of those matters sitting for the judge of any other county court. Except as provided by Section 608 of this code, in contested guardianship matters, the judge of the constitutional county court may on the judge's own motion, and shall on the motion of a party to the proceeding, transfer the proceeding to the statutory probate court, county court at law, or other statutory court exercising the jurisdiction of a probate court. The court to which the proceeding is transferred may hear the proceeding as if originally filed in the court.

(d) A statutory probate court has concurrent jurisdiction with the district court in all actions by or against a person in the person's capacity as guardian.

(e) A court that exercises original probate jurisdiction has the power to hear all matters incident to an estate. When a surety is called on to perform in place of a guardian or former guardian, a court exercising original probate jurisdiction may award judgment against the guardian or former guardian in favor of the surety of the guardian or former guardian in the same suit, even if the ward has died, regained capacity, or the ward's disabilities of minority have been removed.

(f) A final order of a court that exercises original probate jurisdiction is appealable to a court of appeals.

Added by Acts 1993, 73rd Leg., ch. 957, § 1, eff. Sept. 1, 1993. Amended by Acts 1995, 74th Leg., ch. 1039, §§ 16, 17, eff. Sept. 1, 1995; Acts 1999, 76th Leg., ch. 1389, § 2, eff. Aug. 30, 1999.

§ 607. Matters Appertaining and Incident to an Estate

(a) In a proceeding in a constitutional county court or a statutory county court at law, the phrases "appertaining to estates" and "incident to an estate" in this chapter include the appointment of guardians, the issuance of letters of guardianship, a claim by or against a guardianship estate, all actions for trial of title to land incident to a guardianship estate and for the enforcement of liens incident to a guardianship estate, all actions for trial of the right of property incident to a guardianship estate, and generally all matters relating to the settlement, partition, and distribution of a guardianship estate.

(b) In a proceeding in a statutory probate court or district court, the phrases "appertaining to estates" and "incident to an estate" in this chapter include the appointment of guardians, the issuance of letters of guardianship, all claims by or against a guardianship estate, all actions for trial of title to land and for the enforcement of liens on the land, all actions for trial of the right of property, and generally all matters relating to the settlement, partition, and distribution of a guardianship estate. A statutory probate court, in the exercise of its jurisdiction and notwithstanding any other provision of this chapter, may hear all suits, actions, and applications filed against or on behalf of any guardianship; all such suits, actions, and applications are appertaining to and incident to an estate. In a situation in which the jurisdiction of a statutory probate court is concurrent with that of a district court, a cause of action appertaining to or incident to a guardianship estate shall be brought in a statutory probate court rather than in the district court.

(c) In all actions by or against a person in the person's capacity as a guardian, a statutory probate court has concurrent jurisdiction with a district court.

(d) A statutory probate court may exercise the pendent and ancillary jurisdiction necessary to promote judicial efficiency and economy.

(e) Subsection (d) of this section applies whether or not the matter is appertaining to or incident to a guardianship estate.

Added by Acts 1993, 73rd Leg., ch. 957, § 1, eff. Sept. 1, 1993. Amended by Acts 1999, 76th Leg., ch. 10, §§ 1, 2, eff. Sept. 1, 1999.

§ 608. Transfer of Guardianship Proceeding

A judge of a statutory probate court, on the motion of a party to the action or of a person interested in a guardianship, may transfer to the judge's court from a district, county, or statutory court a cause of action appertaining to or incident to a guardianship estate that is pending in the statutory probate court or a cause of action in which a personal representative of an estate pending in the statutory probate court is a party and may consolidate the transferred cause of action with the other proceedings in the statutory probate court relating to the guardianship estate.

Added by Acts 1993, 73rd Leg., ch. 957, § 1, eff. Sept. 1, 1993. Amended by Acts 1999, 76th Leg., ch. 1431, § 2, eff. Sept. 1, 1999.

Section 3 of Acts 1999, 76th Leg., ch. 1431 provides:

"This Act takes effect September 1, 1999, and applies only to a motion to transfer a cause of action filed on or after that date. A motion to transfer a cause of action filed before the effective date of this Act is governed by the law in effect on the date the motion was filed, and the former law is continued in effect for that purpose."

§ 609. Contested Guardianship of the Person of a Minor

(a) If an interested person contests an application for the appointment of a guardian of the person of a minor or an interested person seeks the removal of a guardian of the person of a minor, the judge, on the judge's own motion, may transfer all matters relating to the guardianship of the person of the minor to a court of competent jurisdiction in which a suit affecting the parent-child relationship under the Family Code is pending.

(b) The probate court that transfers a proceeding under this section to a court with proper jurisdiction over suits affecting the parent-child relationship shall send to the court to which the transfer is made the complete files in all matters affecting the guardianship of the person of the minor and certified copies of all entries in the minutes. The transferring court shall keep a copy of the transferred files. If the transferring court retains jurisdiction of the guardianship of the estate of the minor or of another minor who was the subject of the suit, the court shall send a copy of the complete files to the court to which the transfer is made and shall keep the original files.

(c) The court to which a transfer is made under this section shall apply the procedural and substantive provisions of the Family Code, including Sections 155.005 and 155.205, in regard to enforcing an order rendered by the court from which the proceeding was transferred.

Added by Acts 1993, 73rd Leg., ch. 957, § 1, eff. Sept. 1, 1993. Amended by Acts 1997, 75th Leg., ch. 77, § 1, eff. Sept. 1, 1997; Acts 1997, 75th Leg., ch. 165, § 7.55, eff. Sept. 1, 1997.

SUBPART B. VENUE

§ 610. Venue for Appointment of Guardian

(a) Except as otherwise authorized by this section, a proceeding for the appointment of a guardian for the person or estate, or both, of an incapacitated person shall be brought in the county in which the proposed ward resides or is located on the date the application is filed or in the county in which the principal estate of the proposed ward is located.

(b) A proceeding for the appointment of a guardian for the person or estate, or both, of a minor may be brought:

(1) in the county in which both the minor's parents reside;

(2) if the parents do not reside in the same county, in the county in which the parent who is the sole managing conservator of the minor resides, or in the county in which the parent who is the joint managing conservator with the greater period of physical possession of and access to the minor resides;

(3) if only one parent is living and the parent has custody of the minor, in the county in which that parent resides;

(4) if both parents are dead but the minor was in the custody of a deceased parent, in the county in which the last surviving parent having custody resided; or

(5) if both parents of a minor child have died in a common disaster and there is no evidence that the parents died other than simultaneously, in the county in which both deceased parents resided at the time of their simultaneous deaths if they resided in the same county.

(c) A proceeding for the appointment of a guardian who was appointed by will may be brought in the county in which the will was admitted to probate or in the county of the appointee's residence if the appointee resides in this state.

(d) Repealed by Acts 1999, 76th Leg., ch. 379, § 10, eff. Sept. 1, 1999.

Added by Acts 1993, 73rd Leg., ch. 957, § 1, eff. Sept. 1, 1993. Amended by Acts 1999, 76th Leg., ch. 379, § 10, eff. Sept. 1, 1999.

For applicability provisions of the 1993 Act, see notes following § 601.

Section 11 of Acts 1999, 76th Leg., ch. 379 provides:

"(a) This Act takes effect September 1, 1999.

"(b) A guardianship for a missing person created under Chapter XIII, Texas Probate Code, before September 1, 1999, is abolished on the effective date of this Act.

"(c) On its own motion or on the motion of a person interested in the estate of the missing person, a court with jurisdiction to appoint a receiver for a missing person may convert a guardianship for a missing person abolished under this Act to a receivership:

"(1) under Section 79.017, Human Resources Code, as added by Chapter 1376, Acts of the 75th Legislature, Regular Session, 1997, and editorially redesignated as Article 62.023, Code of Criminal Procedure; or

"(2) under Section 886, Texas Probate Code."

§ 611. Concurrent Venue and Transfer for Want of Venue

(a) If two or more courts have concurrent venue of a guardianship matter, the court in which an application for a guardianship proceeding is initially filed has and retains jurisdiction of the guardianship matter. A proceeding is considered commenced by the filing of an application alleging facts sufficient to confer venue, and the proceeding initially legally commenced extends to all of the property of the guardianship estate.

(b) If a guardianship proceeding is commenced in more than one county, it shall be stayed except in the county in which it was initially commenced until final determination of proper venue is made by the court in the county in which it was initially commenced.

(c) If it appears to the court at any time before the guardianship is closed that the proceeding was commenced in a court that did not have venue over the proceeding, the court shall, on the application of any interested person, transfer the proceeding to the proper county.

(d) When a proceeding is transferred to another county under a provision of this chapter, all orders entered in connection with the proceeding shall be valid and shall be recognized in the court to which the guardianship was ordered transferred, if the orders were made and entered in conformance with the procedures prescribed by this code.

Added by Acts 1993, 73rd Leg., ch. 957, § 1, eff. Sept. 1, 1993.

§ 612. Application for Transfer of Guardianship to Another County

When a guardian or any other person desires to remove the transaction of the business of the guardianship from one county to another, the person shall file a written application in the court in which the guardianship is pending stating the reason for moving the transaction of business.

Added by Acts 1993, 73rd Leg., ch. 957, § 1, eff. Sept. 1, 1993.

§ 613. Notice

(a) On filing an application to remove a guardianship to another county, the sureties on the bond of the guardian shall be cited by personal service to appear and show cause why the application should not be granted.

(b) If an application is filed by a person other than the guardian, the guardian shall be cited by personal service to appear and show cause why the application should not be granted.

Added by Acts 1993, 73rd Leg., ch. 957, § 1, eff. Sept. 1, 1993.

§ 614. Court Action

On hearing an application under Section 612 of this code, if good cause is not shown to deny the application and it appears that removal of the guardianship is in the best interests of the ward, the court shall enter an order authorizing the removal on payment on behalf of the estate of all accrued costs.

Added by Acts 1993, 73rd Leg., ch. 957, § 1, eff. Sept. 1, 1993.

§ 615. Transcript of Record

When an order of removal is made under Section 614 of this code, the clerk shall record any unrecorded papers of the guardianship required to be recorded and make out a complete certified transcript of all the orders, decrees, judgments, and proceedings in the guardianship. On payment of the clerk's fees, the clerk shall transmit the transcript, with the original papers in the case, to the county clerk of the county to which the guardianship was ordered removed.

Added by Acts 1993, 73rd Leg., ch. 957, § 1, eff. Sept. 1, 1993.

§ 616. Removal Effective

The order removing a guardianship does not take effect until:

(1) the transcript required by Section 615 of this code is filed in the office of the county clerk of the county to which the guardianship was ordered removed; and

(2) a certificate under the clerk's official seal and reporting the filing of the transcript is filed in the court ordering the removal by the county clerk of the county to which the guardianship was ordered removed.

Added by Acts 1993, 73rd Leg., ch. 957, § 1, eff. Sept. 1, 1993.

§ 617. Continuation of Guardianship

When a guardianship is removed from one county to another in accordance with this subpart, the guardianship proceeds in the court to which it was removed as if it had been originally commenced in that court. It is not necessary to record in the receiving court any of the papers in the case that were recorded in the court from which the case was removed.

Added by Acts 1993, 73rd Leg., ch. 957, § 1, eff. Sept. 1, 1993.

§ 618. New Guardian Appointed on Removal

If it appears to the court that removal of the guardianship is in the best interests of the ward, but that because of the removal it will be unduly expensive or unduly inconvenient to the estate for the guardian of the estate to continue to serve in that capacity, the court may in its order of removal revoke the letters of guardianship and appoint a new guardian, and the former guardian shall account for and deliver the estate as provided by this chapter in a case in which a guardian resigns.

Added by Acts 1993, 73rd Leg., ch. 957, § 1, eff. Sept. 1, 1993.

SUBPART C. DUTIES AND RECORDS OF CLERK

§ 621. Application and Other Papers to be Filed With Clerk

(a) An application for a guardianship proceeding, a complaint, petition, or other paper permitted or required by law to be filed in the court in guardianship matters shall be filed with the county clerk of the proper county.

(b) The county clerk shall file the paper received under this section and endorse on each paper the date filed, the docket number, and the clerk's official signature.

Added by Acts 1993, 73rd Leg., ch. 957, § 1, eff. Sept. 1, 1993.

For applicability provisions of the 1993 Act, see notes following § 601.

§ 622. Costs and Security

(a) The laws regulating costs in ordinary civil cases apply to a guardianship matter unless otherwise expressly provided by this chapter.

(b) When a person other than the guardian, attorney ad litem, or guardian ad litem files an application, complaint, or opposition in relation to a guardianship matter, the clerk may require the person to give security for the probable costs of the guardianship proceeding before filing. A person interested in the guardianship or in the welfare of the ward, or an officer of the court, at any time before the trial of an application, complaint, or opposition in relation to a guardianship matter, may obtain from the court, on written motion, an order requiring the person who filed the application, complaint, or opposition to give security for the probable costs of the proceeding. The rules governing civil suits in the county court relating to this subject control in these cases.

(c) No security for costs shall be required of a guardian, attorney ad litem, or guardian ad litem appointed under this chapter by a court of this state in any suit brought by the guardian, attorney ad litem, or guardian ad litem in their respective fiduciary capacities.

Added by Acts 1993, 73rd Leg., ch. 957, § 1, eff. Sept. 1, 1993.

§ 623. Judge's Guardianship Docket

(a) The county clerk shall keep a record book to be styled "Judge's Guardianship Docket" and shall enter in the record book:

(1) the name of each person on whose person or estate a proceeding is had or is sought to be had;

(2) the name of the guardian of the estate or person or of the applicant for letters;

(3) the date the original application for a guardianship proceeding was filed;

(4) a minute, including the date, of each order, judgment, decree, and proceeding in each estate; and

(5) a number of each guardianship on the docket in the order in which a proceeding is commenced.

(b) Each paper filed in a guardianship proceeding shall be given the corresponding docket number of the estate.

Added by Acts 1993, 73rd Leg., ch. 957, § 1, eff. Sept. 1, 1993.

§ 624. Claim Docket

The county clerk shall keep a record book to be styled "Claim Docket" and shall enter in the claim docket all claims presented against a guardianship for court approval. The claim docket shall be ruled in 16 columns at proper intervals from top to bottom, with a short note of the contents at the top of each column. One or more pages shall be assigned to each guardianship. The following information shall be entered in the respective columns beginning with the first or marginal column: The names of claimants in the order in which their claims are filed; the amount of the claim; its date; the date of filing; when due; the date from which it bears interest; the rate of interest; when allowed by the guardian; the amount allowed; the date of rejection; when approved; the amount approved; when disapproved; the class to which the claim belongs; when established by judgment of a court; the amount of the judgment.

Added by Acts 1993, 73rd Leg., ch. 957, § 1, eff. Sept. 1, 1993.

§ 625. Case Files

The county clerk shall maintain a case file for each person's filed guardianship proceedings. The case file must contain all orders, judgments, and proceedings of the court and any other guardianship filing with the court, including all:

(1) applications for the granting of guardianship;

(2) citations and notices, whether published or posted, with the returns on the citations and notices;

(3) bonds and official oaths;

(4) inventories, appraisements, and lists of claims;

(5) exhibits and accounts;

(6) reports of hiring, renting, or sale;

(7) applications for sale or partition of real estate and reports of sale and of commissioners of partition;

(8) applications for authority to execute leases for mineral development, or for pooling or unitization of lands, royalty, or other interest in minerals, or to lend or invest money;

(9) reports of lending or investing money; and

(10) reports of guardians of the persons.

Added by Acts 1993, 73rd Leg., ch. 957, § 1, eff. Sept. 1, 1993. Amended by Acts 1999, 76th Leg., ch. 67, § 2, eff. Sept. 1, 1999.

§ 626. Guardianship Fee Book

The county clerk shall keep a record book styled "Guardianship Fee Book" and shall enter in the guardianship fee book each item of costs that accrue to the officers of the court, with witness fees, if any, showing the:

(1) party to whom the costs or fees are due;

(2) date of the accrual of the costs or fees;

(3) guardianship or party liable for the costs or fees; and

(4) date on which the costs or fees are paid.

Added by Acts 1993, 73rd Leg., ch. 957, § 1, eff. Sept. 1, 1993.

§ 627. Maintaining Records in Lieu of Record Books

In lieu of keeping the record books described by Sections 623, 624, and 626 of this code, the county clerk may maintain the information relating to a person's guardianship proceeding maintained in those record books on a computer file, on microfilm, in the form of a digitized optical image, or in another similar form of data compilation.

Added by Acts 1999, 76th Leg., ch. 67, § 2, eff. Sept. 1, 1999.

§ 627A. Index

The county clerk shall properly index the records and keep the index open for public inspection but may not release the index from the clerk's custody.

Added by Acts 1993, 73rd Leg., ch. 957, § 1, eff. Sept. 1, 1993. Renumbered from § 627 and amended by Acts 1999, 76th Leg., ch. 67, § 2, eff. Sept. 1, 1999.

§ 628. Use of Records as Evidence

The record books or individual case files, including records on a computer file, on microfilm, in the form of a digitized optical image, or in another similar form of data compilation described in other sections of this chapter, or certified copies or reproductions of the records, shall be evidence in any court of this state.

Added by Acts 1993, 73rd Leg., ch. 957, § 1, eff. Sept. 1, 1993. Amended by Acts 1999, 76th Leg., ch. 67, § 2, eff. Sept. 1, 1999.

§ 629. Call of the Dockets

The judge of the court in which a guardianship proceeding is pending, as the judge determines, shall call guardianship matters in their regular order on both the guardianship and claim dockets and shall make necessary orders.

Added by Acts 1993, 73rd Leg., ch. 957, § 1, eff. Sept. 1, 1993.

§ 630. Clerk May Set Hearings

If the county judge is absent from the county seat or is on vacation, disqualified, ill, or deceased and is unable to designate the time and place for hearing a guardianship matter pending in the judge's court, the county clerk of the county in which the matter is pending may designate the time and place for hearing, entering the setting on the judge's docket and certifying on the docket the reason that the judge is not acting to set the hearing. If a qualified judge is not present for the hearing, after service of the notices and citations required by law with reference to the time and place of hearing has been perfected, the hearing is automatically continued from day to day until a qualified judge is present to hear and determine the matter.

Added by Acts 1993, 73rd Leg., ch. 957, § 1, eff. Sept. 1, 1993.

§ 631. Clerk's Duties

(a) If the proper venue is finally determined to be in another county, the clerk, after making and retaining a true copy of the entire file in the case, shall transmit the original file to the proper county, and a proceeding shall be held in the proper county in the same manner as if the proceeding had originally been instituted in the proper county.

(b) By transmitting to the proper court in the proper county for venue purposes the original file in the case, with certified copies of all entries in the minutes made in the file, an administration of the guardianship in the proper county for venue purposes shall be completed in the same manner as if the proceeding had originally been instituted in that county.

(c) The clerk of the court from which the proceeding is transferred shall transmit to the court to which the proceeding is transferred the original file in the proceeding and a certified copy of the entries in the minutes that relate to the proceeding.

Added by Acts 1993, 73rd Leg., ch. 957, § 1, eff. Sept. 1, 1993.

SUBPART D. SERVICE AND NOTICE

§ 632. Issuance, Contents, Service, and Return of Citation, Notices, and Writs in Guardianship Matters

(a) A person does not need to be cited or otherwise given notice in a guardianship matter except in situations in which this chapter expressly provides for citation or the giving of notice. If this chapter does not expressly provide for citation or the issuance or return of notice in a guardianship matter, the court may require that notice be given. If the court requires that notice be given, the court shall prescribe the form and manner of service and return of service.

(b) Unless a court order is required by a provision of this chapter, the county clerk shall issue without a court order necessary citations, writs, and process in guardianship matters and all notices not required to be issued by guardians.

(c) A citation and notice issued by the clerk shall be signed and sealed by the clerk and shall be styled "The State of Texas." A notice required to be given by a guardian shall be in writing and signed by the guardian in the guardian's official capacity. A citation or notice shall be dated and directed to the person that is being cited or notified and must state the style and number of the proceeding and the court in which the proceeding is pending and must describe generally the nature of the proceeding or matter to which the citation or notice relates. A precept directed to an officer is not necessary. A citation or notice must direct the person cited or notified to appear by filing a written contest or answer or perform other required acts. A citation or notice must state when and where an appearance or performance by a person cited or notified is required. A citation or notice is not defective because it contains a precept directed to an officer authorized to serve it. A writ or other process other than a citation or notice shall be directed "To any sheriff or constable within the State of Texas" and may not be held defective because it is directed to the sheriff or any constable of a specific county if the writ or other process is properly served within the named county by an officer authorized to serve it.

(d) In all situations in which this chapter requires that notice be given or that a person be cited, and in which a specific method of giving the notice or citing the person, or a specific method of service and return of the citation or notice is not given, or an insufficient or inadequate provision appears with respect to any matter relating to citation or notice, or on request of an interested person, notice or citation shall be issued, served, and returned in the manner the court, by written order, directs in accordance with this chapter and the Texas Rules of Civil Procedure and has the same force and effect as if the manner of service and return had been specified in this chapter.

(e) Except in instances in which this chapter expressly provides for another method of service, a notice or citation required to be served on a guardian or receiver shall be served by the clerk that issues the citation or notice. The clerk shall serve the citation or notice by sending the original citation or notice by registered or certified mail to the attorney of record for the guardian or receiver or to the guardian or receiver, if the guardian or receiver does not have an attorney of record.

(f)(1) In cases in which it is provided that personal service shall be had with respect to a citation or notice, the citation or notice must be served on the attorney of record for the person who is being cited or notified. Notwithstanding the requirement of personal service, service may be made on the attorney by any method specified under this chapter for service on an attorney. If there is no attorney of record in the proceeding for the person who is being cited or notified, or if an attempt to make service on the attorney was unsuccessful, a citation or notice directed to a person within this state must be served in person by the sheriff or constable on the person who is being cited or notified by delivering to the person a true copy of the citation or notice at least 10 days before the return day on the citation or notice, exclusive of the date of service. If the person who is being cited or notified is absent from the state or is a nonresident, the citation or notice may be served by a disinterested person competent to make oath of the fact. The citation or notice served by a disinterested person shall be returnable at least 10 days after the date of service, exclusive of the date of service. The return of the person serving the citation or notice shall be endorsed on or attached to the citation or notice. The return must show the time and place of service, certify that a true copy of the citation or notice was delivered to the person directed to be served, be subscribed and sworn to before an officer authorized by the laws of this state to take affidavits, under the hand and official seal of the officer, and returned to the county clerk who issued the citation or notice. If the citation or notice is returned with the notation that the person sought to be served, whether or not within this state, cannot be found, the clerk shall issue a new citation or notice directed to the person sought to be served and service shall be by publication.

(2) When citation or notice is required to be posted, the sheriff or constable shall post the citation or notice at the courthouse door of the county in which the proceeding is pending, or at the place in or near the courthouse where public notices customarily are posted, for at least 10 days before the return day of the citation or notice, exclusive of the date of posting. The clerk shall deliver the original and a copy of the citation or notice to the sheriff or a constable of the proper county, who shall post the copy as prescribed by this section and return the original to the clerk, stating in a written return of the copy the time when and the place where the sheriff or constable posted the copy. The date of posting is the date of service. When posting of notice by a guardian is authorized or required, the method prescribed by this section shall be followed. The notice is to be issued in the name of the guardian, addressed and delivered to, posted and returned by, the proper officer, and filed with the clerk.

(3) When a person is to be cited or notified by publication, the citation or notice shall be published once in a newspaper of general circulation in the county in which the proceeding is pending, and the publication shall be not less than 10 days before the return date of the citation or notice, exclusive of the date of publication. The date of publication of the newspaper in which the citation or notice is published appears is the date of service. If there is no newspaper of general circulation published or printed in the county in which citation or notice is to be had, service of the citation or notice shall be by posting.

(4)(A) When a citation or notice is required or permitted to be served by registered or certified mail, other than a notice required to be given by a guardian, the clerk shall issue the citation or notice and shall serve the citation or notice by sending the original citation or notice by registered or certified mail. A guardian shall issue notice required to be given by the guardian by registered or certified mail, and the guardian shall serve the notice by sending the original notice by registered or certified mail. The citation or notice shall be mailed return receipt requested with instructions to deliver to the addressee only. The envelope containing the citation or notice shall be addressed to the attorney of record in the proceeding for the person who is being cited or notified, but if there is no attorney of record, or if the citation or notice is returned undelivered, the envelope containing the citation or notice shall be addressed to the person who is being cited or notified. A copy of the citation or notice and the certificate of the clerk or guardian showing the fact and date of mailing shall be filed and recorded. If a receipt is returned, it shall be attached to the certificate.

(B) When a citation or notice is required or permitted to be served by ordinary mail, the clerk or the guardian when required by statute or court order, shall serve the citation or notice by mailing the original to the person being cited or notified. A copy of the citation or notice and a certificate of the person serving the citation or notice that shows the fact and time of mailing shall be filed and recorded.

(C) When service is made by mail, the date of mailing is the date of service. Service by mail must be made not less than 20 days before the return day of the citation or notice, exclusive of the date of service.

(D) If a citation or notice served by mail is returned undelivered, a new citation or notice shall be issued, and the new citation or notice shall be served by posting.

(g) A citation or notice issued by the clerk and served by personal service, by mail, by posting, or by publication shall be returned to the court from which the citation or notice was issued on the first Monday after the service is perfected.

(h) In a guardianship matter in which citation or notice is required to be served by posting and issued in conformity with the applicable provision of this code, the citation or notice and the service of and return of the citation or notice is sufficient and valid if a sheriff or constable posts a copy of the citation or notice at the place or places prescribed by this chapter on a day that is sufficiently before the return day contained in the citation or notice for the period of time for which the citation or notice is required to be posted to elapse before the return day of the citation or notice. The sufficiency or validity of the citation or notice or the service of or return of the service of the citation or notice is not affected by the fact that the sheriff or constable makes his return on the citation or notice and returns the citation or notice to the court before the period elapses for which the citation or notice is required to be posted, even though the return is made, and the citation or notice is returned to the court, on the same day it is issued.

(i) Proof of service by publication, posting, mailing, or otherwise in all cases requiring notice or citation shall be filed before a hearing. Proof of service made by a sheriff or constable shall be made by the return of service. Service made by a private person shall be proved by the person's affidavit. Proof of service by publication shall be made by an affidavit of the publisher or of an employee of the publisher that shows the issue date of the newspaper that carried the notice or citation and that has attached to or embodied in the affidavit a copy of the notice or citation. Proof of service by mail shall be made by the certificate of the clerk, or the affidavit of the guardian or other person that makes the service that states the fact and time of mailing. The return receipt must be attached to the certificate, if a receipt has been returned if service is made by registered or certified mail.

(j) At any time after an application is filed for the purpose of commencing a guardianship proceeding, a person interested in the estate or welfare of a ward or an incapacitated person may file with the clerk a written request that the person be notified of any or all specifically designated motions, applications, or pleadings filed by any person, or by a person specifically designated in the request. The person who makes the request is responsible for the fees and costs associated with the documents specified in the request. The clerk may require a deposit to cover the estimated costs of furnishing the person with the requested notice. The clerk by ordinary mail shall send to the requesting person a copy of any document specified in the request. A proceeding is not invalid if the clerk fails to comply with the request under this subsection.

Added by Acts 1993, 73rd Leg., ch. 957, § 1, eff. Sept. 1, 1993.

For applicability provisions of the 1993 Act, see notes following § 601.

§ 633. Notice and Citation

(a) On the filing of an application for guardianship, notice shall be issued and served as provided by this section.

(b) The court clerk shall issue a citation stating that the application for guardianship was filed, the name of the proposed ward, the name of the applicant, and the name of the person to be appointed guardian as provided in the application, if that person is not the applicant. The citation must cite all persons interested in the welfare of the proposed ward to appear at the time and place stated in the notice if they wish to contest the application. The citation shall be posted.

(c) The sheriff or other officer shall personally serve citation to appear and answer the application for guardianship on:

(1) a proposed ward who is 12 years of age or older;

(2) the parents of a proposed ward if the whereabouts of the parents are known or can be reasonably ascertained;

(3) any court-appointed conservator or person having control of the care and welfare of the proposed ward;

(4) a proposed ward's spouse; [1]

(5) Deleted by Acts 1999, 76th Leg., ch. 379, § 3, eff. Sept. 1, 1999.

(6) the person named in the application to be appointed guardian, if that person is not the applicant.

(d) The court clerk, at the applicant's request, or the applicant shall mail a copy of the notice by registered or certified mail, return receipt requested, to the following persons if their whereabouts are known or can be reasonably ascertained:

(1) all adult siblings and all adult children of a proposed ward;

(2) the administrator of a nursing home facility or similar facility in which the proposed ward resides;

(3) the operator of a residential facility in which the proposed ward resides;

(4) a person whom the applicant knows to hold a power of attorney signed by the proposed ward;

(5) a person designated to serve as guardian of the proposed ward by a written declaration under Section 679 of this code, if the applicant knows of the existence of the declaration;

(6) a person designated to serve as guardian of the proposed ward in the probated will of the last surviving parent of the ward; and

(7) a person designated to serve as guardian of the proposed ward by a written declaration of the proposed ward's last surviving parent, if the declarant is deceased and the applicant knows of the existence of the declaration.

(e) A person other than the proposed ward who is entitled to receive notice or personal service of citation under Subsections (c) and (d) of this section may choose, in person or by attorney ad litem, by writing filed with the clerk, to waive the receipt of notice or the issuance and personal service of citation.

(f) The court may not act on an application for the creation of a guardianship until the Monday following the expiration of the 10-day period beginning the date service of notice and citation has been made as provided by Subsections (b), (c), and (d)(1) of this section. The validity of a guardianship created under this chapter is not affected by the failure of the clerk or applicant to comply with the requirements of Subsections (d)(2)–(7) of this section.

(g) It is not necessary for a person who files an application for the creation of a guardianship under this chapter to be served with citation or waive the issuance and personal service of citation under this section.

Added by Acts 1995, 74th Leg., ch. 1039, § 18, eff. Sept. 1, 1995. Amended by Acts 1997, 75th Leg., ch. 77, § 2, eff. Sept. 1, 1997; Acts 1999, 76th Leg., ch. 379, § 3, eff. Sept. 1, 1999; Acts 1999, 76th Leg., ch. 997, § 1, eff. Sept. 1, 1999.

[1] Due to the independent amendments by Acts 1999, 76th Leg., chs. 379 and 997 the word "; and" does not appear in the combined text.

The addition of a § 633 relating to notice and citation for application of guardianship, by Acts 1993, 73rd Leg., ch. 957, § 1, failed to take effect under Acts 1993, 73rd Leg., ch. 905, § 19(b), which provided that the addition of § 633 was not to take effect if both S.B. No. 236 (ch. 905) and H.B. No. 2685 (ch. 957) were enacted and became law. For related subject matter, see V.A.T.S. Probate Code, § 111 as amended by Acts 1993, 73rd Leg., ch. 905, § 7.

Section 3 of Acts 1999, 76th Leg., ch. 997 provides:

"(a) This Act takes effect September 1, 1999, and applies only to a proceeding for the appointment of a guardian instituted on or after the effective date of this Act.

"(b) A proceeding for the appointment of a guardian instituted before the effective date of this Act is governed by the law in effect on the date on which the proceeding was instituted, and the former law is continued in effect for that purpose."

§ 634. Service on Attorney

If an attorney has entered an appearance on record for a party in a guardianship proceeding, a citation or notice required to be served on the party shall be served on the attorney. Service on the attorney of record is in lieu of service on the party for whom the attorney appears. Except as provided by Section 633(f) of this code, an attorney ad litem may not waive personal service of citation. A notice served on an attorney under this section may be served by registered or certified mail or by delivery to the attorney in person. A party to the proceeding or the party's attorney of record, an appropriate sheriff or constable, or another person who is competent to testify may serve notice or citation to an attorney under this section. A written statement by an attorney of record, the return of the officer, or the affidavit of a person that shows service is prima facie evidence of the fact of service.

Added by Acts 1993, 73rd Leg., ch. 957, § 1, eff. Sept. 1, 1993.

§ 635. Waiver of Notice

A competent person who is interested in a hearing in a guardianship proceeding, in person or by attorney, may waive in writing notice of the hearing. A consul or other representative of a foreign government, whose appearance has been entered as provided by law on behalf of a person residing in a foreign country, may waive notice on behalf of the person. A person who submits to the jurisdiction of the court in a hearing is deemed to have waived notice of the hearing.

Added by Acts 1993, 73rd Leg., ch. 957, § 1, eff. Sept. 1, 1993.

§ 636. Notices to Department of Veterans Affairs by Guardians

.When an annual or other account of funds, or an application for the expenditure of or investment of funds is filed by a guardian whose ward is a beneficiary of the Department of Veterans Affairs, or when a claim against the estate of a ward who is a beneficiary of the Department of Veterans Affairs is filed, the court shall set a date for the hearing of the account, application, petition, or claim to be held not less than 20 days from the date of the filing of the account, application, petition, or claim. The person who files the account, application, petition, or claim shall give notice of the date of the filing to the office of the Department of Veterans Affairs in whose territory the court is located by mailing to the office a certified copy of the account, application, petition, or claim not later than five days after the date of the filing. An office of the Department of Veterans Affairs, through its attorney, may waive the service of notice and the time within which a hearing may be had in those cases.

Added by Acts 1993, 73rd Leg., ch. 957, § 1, eff. Sept. 1, 1993. Amended by Acts 1995, 74th Leg., ch. 1039, § 19, eff. Sept. 1, 1995.

Section 77 of the 1995 amendatory act provides:

"The changes in law made by this Act to Sections 636 and 665, Texas Probate Code, apply only to an application for the appointment of a guardian that is filed on or after the effective date of this Act. An application filed before the effective date of this Act is governed by the law in effect on the date the application was filed, and that law is continued in effect for that purpose."

SUBPART E. TRIAL AND HEARING MATTERS

§ 641. Defects in Pleading

A court may not invalidate a pleading in a guardianship matter or an order based on the pleading based on a defect of form or substance in the pleading, unless the defect has been timely objected to and called to the attention of the court in which the proceeding was or is pending.

Added by Acts 1993, 73rd Leg., ch. 957, § 1, eff. Sept. 1, 1993.

For applicability provisions of the 1993 Act, see notes following § 601.

§ 642. Standing to Commence or Contest Proceeding

(a) Except as provided by Subsection (b) of this section, any person has the right to commence any guardianship proceeding, including a proceeding for complete restoration of a ward's capacity or modification of a ward's guardianship, or to appear and contest any guardianship proceeding or the appointment of a particular person as guardian.

(b) A person who has an interest that is adverse to a proposed ward or incapacitated person may not:

(1) file an application to create a guardianship for the proposed ward or incapacitated person;

(2) contest the creation of a guardianship for the proposed ward or incapacitated person;

(3) contest the appointment of a person as a guardian of the person or estate, or both, of the proposed ward or incapacitated person; or

(4) contest an application for complete restoration of a ward's capacity or modification of a ward's guardianship.

(c) The court shall determine by motion in limine the standing of a person who has an interest that is adverse to a proposed ward or incapacitated person.

Added by Acts 1993, 73rd Leg., ch. 957, § 1, eff. Sept. 1, 1993. Amended by Acts 1995, 74th Leg., ch. 1039, § 20, eff. Sept. 1, 1995; Acts 1999, 76th Leg., ch. 829, § 2, eff. Sept. 1, 1999.

For application provisions of Acts 1999, 76th Leg., ch. 829, see notes following V.A.T.S. Probate Code, § 694A.

§ 643. Trial by Jury

A party in a contested guardianship proceeding is entitled, on request, to a jury trial.

Added by Acts 1993, 73rd Leg., ch. 957, § 1, eff. Sept. 1, 1993.

§ 644. Hearing by Submission

(a) A court may consider by submission a motion or application filed under this chapter unless the proceeding is:

(1) contested; or

(2) an application for the appointment of a guardian.

(b) The burden of proof at a hearing on a motion or application that is being considered by the court on submission is on the party who is seeking relief under the motion or application.

(c) The court may consider a person's failure to file a response to a motion or application that may be considered on submission as a representation that the person does not oppose the motion or application.

(d) A person's request for oral argument is not a response to a motion or application under this section.

(e) The court, on its own motion, may order oral argument on a motion or application that may be considered by submission.

Added by Acts 1993, 73rd Leg., ch. 957, § 1, eff. Sept. 1, 1993. Amended by Acts 1995, 74th Leg., ch. 1039, § 21, eff. Sept. 1, 1995.

§ 645. Guardians Ad Litem

(a) The judge may appoint a guardian ad litem to represent the interests of an incapacitated person in a guardianship proceeding.

(b) A guardian ad litem is entitled to reasonable compensation for services in the amount set by the court to be taxed as costs in the proceeding.

(c) A guardian ad litem is an officer of the court. The guardian ad litem shall protect the incapacitated person in a manner that will enable the court to determine what action will be in the best interests of the incapacitated person.

(d) If a guardian ad litem is appointed under Section 681(4) of this code, the fees and expenses of the guardian ad litem are costs of the litigation proceeding that made the appointment necessary.

(e) In the interest of judicial economy, the court may appoint as guardian ad litem under Section 681(4) of this code the person who has been appointed attorney ad litem under Section 646 of this code or the person who is serving as an ad litem for the benefit of the ward in any other proceeding.

Added by Acts 1993, 73rd Leg., ch. 957, § 1, eff. Sept. 1, 1993.

§ 646. Appointment of Attorney ad Litem and Interpreter

(a) In a proceeding under this chapter for the appointment of a guardian, the court shall appoint an attorney ad litem to represent the interests of the proposed ward. The attorney shall be supplied with copies of all of the current records in the case and may have access to all of the proposed ward's relevant medical, psychological, and intellectual testing records.

(b) To be eligible for appointment as an attorney ad litem, a person must have the certification required by Section 647A of this code.

(c) A person whose certificate has expired must obtain a new certificate to be eligible for appointment as an attorney ad litem.

(d) At the time of the appointment of the attorney ad litem, the court shall also appoint a language interpreter or a sign interpreter if necessary to ensure effective communication between the proposed ward and the attorney.

Added by Acts 1993, 73rd Leg., ch. 957, § 1, eff. Sept. 1, 1993. Amended by Acts 1995, 74th Leg., ch. 1039, §§ 22, 74, eff. Sept. 1, 1995; Acts 1999, 76th Leg., ch. 379, § 4, eff. Sept. 1, 1999; Acts 1999, 76th Leg., ch. 716, § 1, eff. Sept. 1, 1999.

For application provisions of Acts 1999, 76th Leg., ch. 716, see notes following V.A.T.S. Probate Code, § 647A.

§ 647. Duties of Attorney Ad Litem

(a) An attorney ad litem appointed under Section 646 of this code to represent a proposed ward shall, within a reasonable time before the hearing, interview the proposed ward. To the greatest extent possible, the attorney shall discuss with the proposed ward the law and facts of the case, the proposed ward's legal options regarding disposition of the case, and the grounds on which guardianship is sought.

(b) Before the hearing, the attorney shall review the application for guardianship, certificates of current physical, medical, and intellectual examinations, and all of the proposed ward's relevant medical, psychological, and intellectual testing records.

Added by Acts 1993, 73rd Leg., ch. 957, § 1, eff. Sept. 1, 1993.

§ 647A. Certification Requirement for Certain Court-Appointed Attorneys

(a) A court-appointed attorney in any guardianship proceeding must be certified by the State Bar of Texas or a person or other entity designated by the state bar as having successfully completed a course of study in guardianship law and procedure sponsored by the state bar or its designee.

(b) For certification under this section, the state bar shall require three hours of credit.

(c) Except as provided by Subsection (e) of this section, a certificate issued under this section expires on the second anniversary of the date the certificate is issued.

(d) To be eligible to be appointed by a court to represent a person at a guardianship proceeding, an attorney whose certificate has expired must obtain a new certificate.

(e) A new certificate obtained by a person who previously has been issued a certificate under this section expires on the fourth anniversary of the date the new certificate is issued if the person has been certified each of the four years immediately preceding the date the new certificate is issued.

Added by Acts 1999, 76th Leg., ch. 716, § 2, eff. Sept. 1, 1999.

Section 3 of Acts 1999, 76th Leg., ch. 716 provides:

"This Act applies only to guardianship proceedings for which a court has appointed an attorney to represent the interests of a ward or other person:

"(1) on or after the effective date of this Act; or

"(2) before the effective date of this Act if the proceeding is pending on the effective date of this Act."

§ 648. Court Visitor Program

(a) Each statutory probate court shall operate a court visitor program to assess the conditions of wards and proposed wards. Another court that has jurisdiction over a guardianship proceeding may operate a court visitor program in accordance with the population needs and financial abilities of the jurisdiction. A court that operates a court visitor program shall use persons willing to serve without compensation to the greatest extent possible.

(b) On request by any interested person, including a ward or proposed ward, or on its own motion, and at any time before the appointment of a guardian or during the pendency of a guardianship of the person or estate, a court may appoint a court visitor to evaluate the ward or proposed ward and provide a written report that substantially complies with Subsection (c) of this section.

(c) A court visitor's report must include:

(1) a description of the nature and degree of capacity and incapacity of the ward or proposed ward, including the medical history of the ward or proposed ward, if reasonably available and not waived by the court;

(2) a medical prognosis and a list of the treating physicians of the ward or proposed ward, when appropriate;

(3) a description of the living conditions and circumstances of the ward or proposed ward;

(4) a description of the social, intellectual, physical, and educational condition of the ward or proposed ward;

(5) a statement that the court visitor has personally visited or observed the ward or proposed ward;

(6) a statement of the date of the most recent visit by the guardian, if one has been appointed;

(7) a recommendation as to any modifications needed in the guardianship or proposed guardianship, including removal or denial of the guardianship; and

(8) any other information required by the court.

(d) The court visitor shall file the report not later than the 14th day after the date of the evaluation conducted by the court visitor, and the court visitor making the report must swear, under penalty of perjury, to its accuracy to the best of the court visitor's knowledge and belief.

(e) A court visitor who has not expressed a willingness to serve without compensation is entitled to reasonable compensation for services in an amount set by the court and to be taxed as costs in the proceeding.

(f) This section does not apply to a guardianship that is created only because it is necessary for a person to have a guardian appointed to receive funds from a governmental source.

Added by Acts 1993, 73rd Leg., ch. 957, § 1, eff. Sept. 1, 1993. Amended by Acts 1995, 74th Leg., ch. 1039, § 23, eff. Sept. 1, 1995.

§ 648A. Duties of Court Investigator

(a) On the filing of an application for guardianship under Section 682 of this code, a court investigator shall investigate the circumstances alleged in the application to determine whether a less restrictive alternative than guardianship is appropriate.

(b) A court investigator shall:

(1) supervise the court visitor program established under Section 648 of this code and in that capacity serve as the chief court visitor;

(2) investigate a complaint received from any person about a guardianship and report to the judge, if necessary; and

(3) perform other duties as assigned by the judge or required by this code.

(c) After making an investigation under Subsection (a) or (b) of this section, a court investigator shall file with the court a report of the court investigator's findings and conclusions. Disclosure to a jury of the contents of a court investigator's report is subject to the Texas Rules of Civil Evidence. In a contested case, the court investigator shall provide copies of the report to the attorneys for the parties before the earlier of:

(1) the seventh day after the day the report is completed; or

(2) the 10th day before the day the trial is scheduled to begin.

(d) Nothing in this section supersedes any duty or obligation of another to report or investigate abuse or neglect under any statute of this state.

Added by Acts 1995, 74th Leg., ch. 1039, § 24, eff. Sept. 1, 1995. Amended by Acts 1999, 76th Leg., ch. 829, § 3, eff. Sept. 1, 1999.

For application provisions of Acts 1999, 76th Leg., ch. 829, see notes following V.A.T.S. Probate Code, § 694A.

§ 649. Evidence

In a guardianship proceeding, the rules relating to witnesses and evidence that govern in the district court apply as far as practicable. If there is no opposing party or attorney of record on whom to serve notice and copies of interrogatories, service may be had by posting notice of the intention to take depositions for a period of 10 days as provided by this chapter in the provisions governing a posting of notice. When notice by posting under this section is filed with the clerk, a copy of the interrogatories shall also be filed. At the expiration of the 10-day period, commission may issue for taking the depositions and the judge may file cross-interrogatories if no person appears.

Added by Acts 1993, 73rd Leg., ch. 957, § 1, eff. Sept. 1, 1993.

§ 650. Decrees and Signing of Minutes

A decision, order, decree, or judgment of the court in a guardianship matter must be rendered in open court, except in a case in which it is otherwise expressly provided. The judge shall approve and sign the guardianship minutes on the first day of each month. If the first day of the month falls on a Saturday, Sunday, or legal holiday, the judge's approval shall be entered on the preceding or succeeding day.

Added by Acts 1993, 73rd Leg., ch. 957, § 1, eff. Sept. 1, 1993.

§ 651. Enforcement of Orders

The judge may enforce obedience to an order entered against a guardian by attachment and imprisonment. An imprisonment of a guardian may not exceed three days for any one offense, unless expressly provided otherwise in this chapter.

Added by Acts 1993, 73rd Leg., ch. 957, § 1, eff. Sept. 1, 1993.

SUBPART F. POST–TRIAL MATTERS

§ 653. Execution

An execution in a guardianship matter shall be directed "To any sheriff or any constable within the State of Texas," made returnable in 60 days, and attested and signed by the clerk officially under the seal of the court. A proceeding under an execution in a guardianship matter is governed so far as applicable by the laws regulating a proceeding under an execution issued from the district court. An execution directed to the sheriff or a constable of a specific county in this state may not be held defective if the execution was properly executed within the county by the officer to whom the direction for execution was given.

Added by Acts 1993, 73rd Leg., ch. 957, § 1, eff. Sept. 1, 1993.

For applicability provisions of the 1993 Act, see notes following § 601.

§ 654. Attachment for Property

When a complaint in writing and under oath that the guardian is about to remove the estate or any part of the estate beyond the limits of the state is made to the judge by a person interested in the estate of a minor or other incapacitated person, the judge may order a writ to issue, directed "To any sheriff or any constable within the State of Texas," commanding the sheriff or constable to seize the estate or any part of the estate and to hold the estate subject to further court order. The judge may not issue a writ unless the complainant gives a bond, in the sum the judge requires, payable to the guardian of the estate and conditioned on payment of all damages and costs that shall be recovered for a wrongful suit out of the writ. A writ of attachment directed to the sheriff or a constable of a specific county in this state is not defective if the writ was properly executed within the county by the officer to whom the direction to seize the estate was given.

Added by Acts 1993, 73rd Leg., ch. 957, § 1, eff. Sept. 1, 1993.

§ 655. Guardian to Serve Pending Appeal of Appointment

Pending an appeal from an order or judgment appointing a guardian, an appointee shall continue to act as guardian and shall continue the prosecution of a pending suit in favor of the guardianship.

Added by Acts 1993, 73rd Leg., ch. 957, § 1, eff. Sept. 1, 1993.

§ 656. Appeal Bond of Guardian

When a guardian appeals, a bond is not required, unless the appeal personally concerns the guardian, in which case the guardian must give the bond.

Added by Acts 1993, 73rd Leg., ch. 957, § 1, eff. Sept. 1, 1993.

§ 657. Bill of Review

A person interested, including a ward, by bill of review filed in the court in which a guardianship proceeding took place, may have a decision, order, or judgment rendered by the court, revised and corrected if an error is shown on the decision, order, or judgment. A process or action under the decision, order, or judgment is not stayed except by writ of injunction. A bill of review may not be filed after two years have elapsed from the date of the decision, order, or judgment. A person with a disability has two years after the removal of the person's respective disability to apply for a bill of review.

Added by Acts 1993, 73rd Leg., ch. 957, § 1, eff. Sept. 1, 1993.

SUBPART G. LETTERS OF GUARDIANSHIP

§ 659. Issuance of Letters of Guardianship

(a) When a person who is appointed guardian has qualified under Section 699 of this code, the clerk shall issue to the guardian a certificate under seal, stating the fact of the appointment, of the qualification, the date of the appointment and qualification, and the date the letters of guardianship expire. The certificate issued by the clerk constitutes letters of guardianship.

(b) All letters of guardianship expire one year and four months after the date of issuance unless renewed.

(c) The clerk may not renew letters of guardianship relating to the appointment of a guardian of the estate until the court receives and approves the guardian's annual accounting. The clerk may not renew letters of guardianship relating to the appointment of a guardian of the person until the court receives and approves the annual report. If the guardian's annual accounting or annual report is disapproved or not timely filed, the clerk may not issue further letters of guardianship to the delinquent guardian unless ordered by the court.

(d) Regardless of the date the court approves an annual accounting or annual report for purposes of this section, a renewal relates back to the date the original letters of guardianship are issued, unless the accounting period has been changed as provided by this chapter, in which case a renewal relates back to the first day of the accounting period.

Added by Acts 1993, 73rd Leg., ch. 957, § 1, eff. Sept. 1, 1993. Amended by Acts 1995, 74th Leg., ch. 1039, § 25, eff. Sept. 1, 1995.

For applicability provisions of the 1993 Act, see notes following § 601.

§ 660. Letters or Order Made Evidence

(a) Letters of guardianship or a certificate under seal of the clerk of the court that granted the letters issued under Section 659 of this code is sufficient evidence of the appointment and qualification of the guardian and of the date of qualification.

(b) The court order that appoints the guardian is evidence of the authority granted to the guardian and of the scope of the powers and duties that the guardian may exercise only after the date letters of guardianship or a certificate has been issued under Section 659 of this code.

Added by Acts 1993, 73rd Leg., ch. 957, § 1, eff. Sept. 1, 1993. Amended by Acts 1995, 74th Leg., ch. 1039, § 26, eff. Sept. 1, 1995.

§ 661. Issuance of New Letters

When letters of guardianship have been destroyed or lost, the clerk shall issue new letters that have the same force and effect as the original letters. The clerk shall also issue any number of letters on request of the person who holds the letters.

Added by Acts 1993, 73rd Leg., ch. 957, § 1, eff. Sept. 1, 1993.

§ 662. Rights of Third Persons Dealing With Guardian

When a guardian who has qualified performs any act as guardian that is in conformity with the guardian's authority and the law, the guardian's act continues to be valid for all intents and purposes in regard to the rights of an innocent purchaser of the property of the guardianship estate who purchased the property from the guardian for a valuable consideration, in good faith, and without notice of any illegality in the title to the property, even if the guardian's act or the authority under which the act was performed may later be set aside, annulled, or declared invalid.

Added by Acts 1993, 73rd Leg., ch. 957, § 1, eff. Sept. 1, 1993.

§ 663. Validation of Certain Letters of Guardianship

All presently existing letters of guardianship issued to a nonresident guardian, with or without the procedure provided in this subpart, in whole or in part, and with or without a notice or citation required of resident guardians, are validated as of each letter's date, insofar as the absence of the procedure, notice, or citations is concerned. An otherwise valid conveyance, mineral lease, or other act of a nonresident guardian qualified and acting in connection with the letters of guardianship under supporting orders of a county or probate court of this state are validated. This section does not apply to any letters, conveyance, lease, or other act of a nonresident guardian under this section if the absence of the procedure, notice, or citation involving the letters, conveyance, lease, or other act of the nonresident guardian is an issue in a lawsuit pending in this state on September 1, 1993.

Added by Acts 1993, 73rd Leg., ch. 957, § 1, eff. Sept. 1, 1993.

SUBPART H. COMPENSATION, EXPENSES, AND COURT COSTS

§ 665. Compensation of Guardians and Temporary Guardians

(a) The court may authorize compensation for a guardian or a temporary guardian serving as a guardian of the person alone from available funds of the ward's estate. The court shall set the compensation in an amount not exceeding five percent of the ward's gross income. In determining whether to authorize compensation for a guardian under this section, the court shall consider the ward's monthly income from all sources and whether the ward receives medical assistance under the state Medicaid program.

(b) The guardian or temporary guardian of an estate is entitled to a fee of five percent of the gross income of the ward's estate and five percent of all money paid out of the estate on a court finding that the guardian or temporary guardian has taken care of and managed the estate in compliance with the standards of this chapter. In this section, the term "money paid out" does not include any money loaned, invested, or paid over on the settlement of the guardianship or a tax-motivated gift made by the ward. If the fee is an unreasonably low amount, the court may authorize reasonable compensation to a guardian or temporary guardian for services as guardian or temporary guardian of the estate. The court, on application of an interested person or on its own motion, may deny a fee authorized under this section in whole, or in part, if:

(1) the court finds that the guardian or temporary guardian has not adequately performed the duties required of a guardian or temporary guardian under this chapter; or

(2) the guardian or temporary guardian has been removed for cause.

(c) Except as provided by Subsection (b) of this section for a fee that is determined by the court to be unreasonably low, the aggregate fee of the guardian of the person and guardian of the estate may not exceed an amount equal to five percent of the gross income of the ward's estate plus five percent of all money paid out of the estate.

(d) If the estate of a ward is insufficient to pay for the services of a private professional guardian or a licensed attorney serving as guardian of the ward's person, the court may authorize compensation for that guardian if funds in the county treasury are budgeted for that purpose.

(e) In this section "gross income" does not include Department of Veterans Affairs or Social Security benefits received by a ward.

Added by Acts 1993, 73rd Leg., ch. 957, § 1, eff. Sept. 1, 1993. Amended by Acts 1995, 74th Leg., ch. 1039, § 27, eff. Sept. 1, 1995; Acts 1999, 76th Leg., ch. 905, § 1, eff. Sept. 1, 1999.

For applicability provisions of the 1993 Act, see notes following § 601.

Section 77 of the 1995 amendatory act provides:

"The changes in law made by this Act to Sections 636 and 665, Texas Probate Code, apply only to an application for the appointment of a guardian that is filed on or after the effective date of this Act. An application filed before the effective date of this Act is governed by the law in effect on the date the application was filed, and that law is continued in effect for that purpose."

Section 6 of Acts 1999, 76th Leg., ch. 905 provides:

"(a) The changes in law made by this Act to Sections 665 and 665B(a), Texas Probate Code, apply only to compensation for a guardian of the person that is authorized by a court on or after the effective date of this Act.

"(b) Compensation for a guardian of the person that is authorized by a court before the effective date of this Act is governed by the law in effect on the date the compensation was authorized, and the former law is continued in effect for that purpose."

§ 665A. Payment for Professional Services

The court shall order the payment of a fee set by the court as compensation to the attorneys, mental health professionals, and interpreters appointed under Section 646 or 687 of this code, as applicable, to be taxed as costs in the case. If after examining the proposed ward's assets the court determines the proposed ward is unable to pay for services provided by an attorney, a mental health professional, or an interpreter appointed under Section 646 or 687 of this code, as applicable, the county is responsible for the cost of those services.

Added by Acts 1995, 74th Leg., ch. 1039, § 28, eff. Sept. 1, 1995.

§ 665B. Compensation of Certain Attorneys

(a) A court that creates a guardianship for a ward under this chapter, on request of a person who filed an application to be appointed guardian of the proposed ward, may authorize compensation of an attorney who represents the person at the application hearing, regardless of whether the person is appointed the ward's guardian, from:

(1) available funds of the ward's estate; or

(2) the county treasury if:

(A) the ward's estate is insufficient to pay for the services provided by the attorney; and

(B) funds in the county treasury are budgeted for that purpose.

(b) The court may not authorize compensation under this section unless the court finds that the applicant acted in good faith and for just cause in the filing and prosecution of the application.

Added by Acts 1995, 74th Leg., ch. 1039, § 28, eff. Sept. 1, 1995. Amended by Acts 1999, 76th Leg., ch. 905, § 2, eff. Sept. 1, 1999.

Section 6 of Acts 1999, 76th Leg., ch. 905 provides:

"(a) The changes in law made by this Act to Sections 665 and 665B(a), Texas Probate Code, apply only to compensation for a guardian of the person that is authorized by a court on or after the effective date of this Act.

"(b) Compensation for a guardian of the person that is authorized by a court before the effective date of this Act is governed by the law in effect on the date the compensation was authorized, and the former law is continued in effect for that purpose."

§ 665C. Compensation for Collection of Claims and Recovery of Property

(a) Except as provided by Subsection (b) of this section, a guardian of an estate may enter into a contract to convey, or may convey, a contingent interest in any property sought to be recovered, not exceeding one-third thereof for services of attorneys, subject only to the approval of the court in which the estate is being administered.

(b) A guardian of an estate may convey or contract to convey for services of attorneys a contingent interest that exceeds one-third of the property sought to be recovered under this section only on the approval of the court in which the estate is being administered. The court must approve a contract entered into or conveyance made under this section before an attorney performs any legal services. A contract entered into or conveyance made in violation of this section is void, unless the court ratifies or reforms the contract or documents relating to the conveyance to the extent necessary to cause the contract or conveyance to meet the requirements of this section.

(c) In approving a contract or conveyance under Subsection (a) or (b) of this section for services of an attorney, the court shall consider:

(1) the time and labor that will be required, the novelty and difficulty of the questions to be involved, and the skill that will be required to perform the legal services properly;

(2) the fee customarily charged in the locality for similar legal services;

(3) the value of property recovered or sought to be recovered by the personal representative under this section;

(4) the benefits to the estate that the attorney will be responsible for securing; and

(5) the experience and ability of the attorney who will be performing the services.

(d) On satisfactory proof to the court, a guardian of an estate is entitled to all necessary and reasonable expenses incurred by the guardian in collecting or attempting to collect a claim or debt owed to the estate or in recovering or attempting to recover property to which the estate has a title or claim.

Added by Acts 1995, 74th Leg., ch. 1039, § 28, eff. Sept. 1, 1995.

§ 666. Expenses Allowed

A guardian is entitled to be reimbursed from the guardianship estate for all necessary and reasonable expenses incurred in performing any duty as a guardian.

Added by Acts 1993, 73rd Leg., ch. 957, § 1, eff. Sept. 1, 1993.

§ 667. Expense Account

All expense charges shall be:

(1) in writing, showing specifically each item of expense and the date of the expense;

(2) verified by affidavit of the guardian;

(3) filed with the clerk and entered on the claim docket; and

(4) acted on by the court in the same manner as other claims against the guardianship estate.

Added by Acts 1993, 73rd Leg., ch. 957, § 1, eff. Sept. 1, 1993.

§ 668. Costs Adjudged Against Guardian

When costs are incurred because a guardian neglects to perform a required duty or if a guardian is removed for cause, the guardian and the sureties on the guardian's bond are liable for:

(1) costs of removal and other additional costs incurred that are not authorized expenditures under this chapter; and

(2) reasonable attorney's fees incurred in removing the guardian or in obtaining compliance regarding any statutory duty the guardian has neglected.

Added by Acts 1993, 73rd Leg., ch. 957, § 1, eff. Sept. 1, 1993.

§ 669. Costs Against Guardianship

(a) Except as provided by Subsection (b), in a guardianship matter, the cost of the proceeding, including the cost of the guardian ad litem or court visitor, shall be paid out of the guardianship estate, or, if the estate is insufficient to pay for the cost of the proceeding, the cost of the proceeding shall be paid out of the county treasury, and the judgment of the court shall be issued accordingly.

(b) If a court denies an application for the appointment of a guardian under this chapter based on the recommendation of a court investigator, the applicant shall pay the cost of the proceeding.

Added by Acts 1993, 73rd Leg., ch. 957, § 1, eff. Sept. 1, 1993. Amended by Acts 1995, 74th Leg., ch. 1039, § 29, eff. Sept. 1, 1995.

SUBPART I. DUTY AND RESPONSIBILITY OF COURT

§ 671. Judge's Duty

(a) The court shall use reasonable diligence to determine whether a guardian is performing all of the duties required of the guardian that pertain to the guardian's ward.

(b) The judge, at least annually, shall examine the well-being of each ward of the court and the solvency of the bonds of the guardians of the estates.

(c) If after examining the solvency of a guardian's bond under this section a judge determines that the guardian's bond is not sufficient to protect the ward or the ward's estate, the judge shall require the guardian to execute a new bond.

(d) The judge shall notify the guardian and the sureties on the bond as provided by law. If damage or loss results to a guardianship or ward because of gross neglect of the judge to use reasonable diligence in the performance of the judge's duty under this section, the judge shall be liable on the judge's bond to those damaged by the judge's neglect.

(e) The court may request an applicant or court-appointed fiduciary to produce other information identifying an applicant, ward, or guardian, including social security numbers, in addition to identifying information the applicant or fiduciary is required to produce under this code. The court shall maintain the information required under this subsection, and the information may not be filed with the clerk.

Added by Acts 1993, 73rd Leg., ch. 957, § 1, eff. Sept. 1, 1993. Amended by Acts 1997, 75th Leg., ch. 77, § 3, eff. Sept. 1, 1997.

For applicability provisions of the 1993 Act, see notes following § 601.

§ 672. Annual Determination Whether Guardianship Should be Continued, Modified, or Terminated

(a) A court in which a guardianship proceeding is pending shall review annually each guardianship in which the application to create the guardianship was filed after September 1, 1993, and may review annually any other guardianship to determine whether the guardianship should be continued, modified, or terminated.

(b) In reviewing a guardianship as provided by Subsection (a) of this section, a statutory probate court may:

(1) review any report prepared by a court investigator under Section 648A of this code;

(2) review any report prepared by a court visitor under Section 648 of this code;

(3) conduct a hearing; or

(4) review an annual account prepared under Section 741 of this code or a report prepared under Section 743 of this code.

(c) In reviewing a guardianship as provided by Subsection (a) of this section, a court that is not a statutory probate court may use any appropriate method determined by the court according to the court's caseload and the resources available to the court.

(d) A determination under this section must be in writing and filed with the clerk.

(e) This section does not apply to a guardianship that is created only because it is necessary for a person to have a guardian appointed to receive funds from a governmental source.

Added by Acts 1995, 74th Leg., ch. 1039, § 30, eff. Sept. 1, 1995.

SUBPART J. LIABILITY OF GUARDIAN FOR CONDUCT OF WARD

§ 673. Liability

A person is not liable to a third person solely because the person has been appointed guardian of a ward under this chapter.

Added by Acts 1993, 73rd Leg., ch. 957, § 1, eff. Sept. 1, 1993.

For applicability provisions of the 1993 Act, see notes following § 601.

PART 3. APPOINTMENT AND QUALIFICATION OF GUARDIANS

SUBPART A. APPOINTMENT

§ 675. Rights and Powers Retained by Ward

An incapacitated person for whom a guardian is appointed retains all legal and civil rights and powers except those designated by court order as legal disabilities by virtue of having been specifically granted to the guardian.

Added by Acts 1993, 73rd Leg., ch. 957, § 1, eff. Sept. 1, 1993.

For applicability provisions of the 1993 Act, see notes following § 601.

§ 676. Guardians of Minors

(a) Except as provided by Section 680 of this code, the selection of a guardian for a minor is governed by this section.

(b) If the parents live together, both parents are the natural guardians of the person of the minor children by the marriage, and one of the parents is entitled to be appointed guardian of the children's estates. If the parents disagree as to which parent should be appointed, the court shall make the appointment on the basis of which parent is better qualified to serve in that capacity. If one parent is dead, the survivor is the natural guardian of the person of the minor children and is entitled to be appointed guardian of their estates. The rights of parents who do not live together are equal, and the guardianship of their minor children shall be assigned to one or the other, considering only the best interests of the children.

(c) In appointing a guardian for a minor orphan:

(1) if the last surviving parent did not appoint a guardian, the nearest ascendant in the direct line of the minor is entitled to guardianship of both the person and the estate of the minor;

(2) if more than one ascendant exists in the same degree in the direct line, one ascendant shall be appointed, according to circumstances and considering the best interests of the minor;

(3) if the minor has no ascendant in the direct line, the nearest of kin shall be appointed, and if there are two or more persons in the same degree of kinship, one shall be appointed, according to circumstances and considering the best interests of the minor; and

(4) if no relative of the minor is eligible to be guardian, or if no eligible person applies to be guardian, the court shall appoint a qualified person as guardian.

(d) The surviving parent of a minor may by will or written declaration appoint any eligible person to be guardian of the person of the parent's minor children after the death of the parent. Unless the court finds that the person designated in the will or declaration to serve as guardian of the person of the parent's minor children is disqualified, is dead, refuses to serve, or would not serve the best interests of the minor children, the court shall appoint the person as guardian in preference to those otherwise entitled to serve as guardian under this chapter. On compliance with this code, an eligible person is also entitled to be appointed guardian of the children's estates after the death of the parent.

Added by Acts 1993, 73rd Leg., ch. 957, § 1, eff. Sept. 1, 1993. Amended by Acts 1995, 74th Leg., ch. 304, § 1, eff. Sept. 1, 1995.

Section 4 of the 1995 amendatory act provides:

"This Act takes effect September 1, 1995, and the change in law made by this Act applies only to a will or written declaration for the appointment of a guardian that is executed on or after the effective date of this Act. A will or written declaration for the appointment of a guardian that is executed before the effective date of this Act is governed by the law as it existed immediately before the effective date of this Act, and that law is continued in effect for that purpose."

§ 677. Guardians of Persons Other Than Minors

(a) The court shall appoint a guardian for a person other than a minor according to the circumstances and considering the best interests of the ward. If the court finds that two or more eligible persons are equally entitled to be appointed guardian:

(1) the ward's spouse is entitled to the guardianship in preference to any other person if the spouse is one of the eligible persons;

(2) the eligible person nearest of kin to the ward is entitled to the guardianship if the ward's spouse is not one of the eligible persons; or

(3) the court shall appoint the eligible person who is best qualified to serve as guardian if:

(A) the persons entitled to serve under Subdivisions (1) and (2) of this section refuse to serve;

(B) two or more persons entitled to serve under Subdivision (2) of this section are related in the same degree of kinship to the ward; or

(C) neither the ward's spouse or any person related to the ward is an eligible person.

(b) The surviving parent of an adult individual who, because of a physical or mental condition, is substantially unable to provide food, clothing, or shelter for himself or herself, to care for the individual's own physical health, or to manage the individual's own financial affairs, may by will or written declaration appoint an eligible person to be guardian of the person of the adult individual after the parent's death if the parent is the guardian of the person of the adult individual. Unless the court finds that the person designated in the will or declaration to serve as guardian is disqualified, is dead, refuses to serve, or would not serve the best interests of the adult individual, the court shall appoint the person as guardian in preference to those otherwise entitled to serve as guardian under this chapter. On compliance with this code, the eligible person appointed under this subsection is also entitled to be appointed guardian of the adult individual's estate after the death of the individual's parent if the individual's parent is the guardian of the individual's estate.

Added by Acts 1993, 73rd Leg., ch. 957, § 1, eff. Sept. 1, 1993. Amended by Acts 1995, 74th Leg., ch. 304, § 2, eff. Sept. 1, 1995.

Section 4 of the 1995 amendatory act provides:

"This Act takes effect September 1, 1995, and the change in law made by this Act applies only to a will or written declaration for the appointment of a guardian that is executed on or after the effective date of this Act. A will or written declaration for the appointment of a guardian that is executed before the effective date of this Act is governed by the law as it existed immediately before the effective date of this Act, and that law is continued in effect for that purpose."

§ 677A. Written Declarations by Certain Parents to Appoint Guardians for Their Children

(a) A written declaration appointing an eligible person to be guardian of the person of the parent's child under Section 677(b) of this code must be attested to by at least two credible witnesses 14 years of age or older who are not named as guardian or alternate guardian in the declaration.

(b) The declaration must have attached a self-proving affidavit signed by the declarant and the witnesses attesting to the competence of the declarant and the execution of the declaration. A properly executed and witnessed declaration and affidavit are prima facie evidence that the declarant was competent at the time the declarant executed the declaration and that the guardian named in the declaration would serve the best interests of the ward.

(c) The declaration and affidavit may be filed with the court at any time after the application for appointment of a guardian is filed and before a guardian is appointed. If the designated guardian does not qualify, is dead, refuses to serve, resigns, or dies after being appointed guardian, or is otherwise unavailable to serve as guardian, the court shall appoint the next eligible designated alternate guardian named in the declaration. If the guardian and all alternate guardians do not qualify, are dead, refuse to serve, or later die or resign, the court shall appoint another person to serve as otherwise provided by this code.

(d) The declarant may revoke a declaration in any manner provided for the revocation of a will under Section 63 of this code, including the subsequent reexecution of the declaration in the manner required for the original declaration.

(e) A declaration and affidavit may be in any form adequate to clearly indicate the declarant's intention to designate a guardian for the declarant's child. The following form may, but need not, be used:

I, __________, make this Declaration to appoint as guardian for my child or children, listed as follows, in the event of my death:

DECLARATION OF APPOINTMENT OF GUARDIAN FOR MY CHILDREN IN THE EVENT OF MY DEATH

__________ __________

__________ __________

__________ __________

(add blanks as appropriate)

I designate __________ to serve as guardian of the person of my (child or children), __________ as first alternate guardian of the person of my (child or children), __________ as second alternate guardian of the person of my (child or children), and __________ as third alternate guardian of the person of my (child or children).

I direct that the guardian of the person of my (child or children) serve (with or without) bond.

(If applicable) I designate __________ to serve as guardian of the estate of my (child or children), __________ as first alternate guardian of the estate of my (child or children), __________ as second alternate guardian of the estate of my (child or children), and __________ as third alternate guardian of the estate of my (child or children).

If any guardian or alternate guardian dies, does not qualify, or resigns, the next named alternate guardian becomes guardian of my (child or children).

Signed this __________ day of __________, 19___.

____

Declarant

__________ __________

Witness Witness

SELF-PROVING AFFIDAVIT

Before me, the undersigned authority, on this date personally appeared the declarant, and __________ and __________ as witnesses, and all being duly sworn, the declarant said that the above instrument was his or her Declaration of Appointment of Guardian for the Declarant's Children in the Event of Declarant's Death and that the declarant had made and executed it for the purposes expressed in the declaration. The witnesses declared to me that they are each 14 years of age or older, that they saw the declarant sign the declaration, that they signed the declaration as witnesses, and that the declarant appeared to them to be of sound mind.

____

Declarant

__________ __________

Affiant Affiant

Subscribed and sworn to before me by the above named declarant and affiants on this ___ day of __________, 19___.

____

Notary Public in and for the State of Texas
My Commission expires:

____

Added by Acts 1995, 74th Leg., ch. 304, § 3, eff. Sept. 1, 1995. Amended by Acts 1997, 75th Leg., ch. 77, § 4, eff. Sept. 1, 1997; Acts 1999, 76th Leg., ch. 1078, § 2, eff. Sept. 1, 1999.

Section 4 of the 1995 Act provides:

"This Act takes effect September 1, 1995, and the change in law made by this Act applies only to a will or written declaration for the appointment of a guardian that is executed on or after the effective date of this Act. A will or written declaration for the appointment of a guardian that is executed before the effective date of this Act is governed by the law as it existed immediately before the effective date of this Act, and that law is continued in effect for that purpose."

Section 3 of Acts 1999, 76th Leg., ch. 1078 provides:

"This Act takes effect September 1, 1999, and the change in law made by this Act applies only to a written declaration for the appointment of a guardian that is executed on or after the effective date of this Act. A written declaration for the appointment of a guardian that is executed before the effective date of this Act is governed by the law as it existed immediately before the effective date of this Act, and that law is continued in effect for that purpose."

§ 678. Presumption Concerning Best Interest

It is presumed not to be in the best interests of a ward to appoint a person as guardian of the ward if the person has been finally convicted of any sexual offense, sexual assault, aggravated assault, aggravated sexual assault, injury to a child, to an elderly individual, or to a disabled individual, abandoning or endangering a child, or incest.

Added by Acts 1993, 73rd Leg., ch. 957, § 1, eff. Sept. 1, 1993. Amended by Acts 1995, 74th Leg., ch. 612, § 1, eff. Aug. 28, 1995.

§ 679. Designation of Guardian Before Need Arises

(a) A person other than an incapacitated person may designate by a written declaration persons to serve as guardian of the person of the declarant or the estate of the declarant if the declarant becomes incapacitated. The declaration must be attested to by at least two credible witnesses 14 years of age or older who are not named as guardian or alternate guardian in the declaration.

(b) A declarant may, in the declaration, disqualify named persons from serving as guardian of the declarant's person or estate, and the persons named may not be appointed guardian under any circumstances.

(c) The declaration must have attached a self-proving affidavit signed by the declarant and the witnesses attesting to the competence of the declarant and the execution of the declaration. A properly executed and witnessed declaration and affidavit are prima facie evidence that the declarant was competent at the time the declarant executed the declaration and that the guardian named in the declaration would serve the best interests of the ward.

(d) The declaration and affidavit may be filed with the court at any time after the application for appointment of a guardian is filed and before a guardian is appointed. Unless the court finds that the person designated in the declaration to serve as guardian is disqualified or would not serve the best interests of the ward, the court shall appoint the person as guardian in preference to those otherwise entitled to serve as guardian under this code. If the designated guardian does not qualify, is dead, refuses to serve, resigns, or dies after being appointed guardian, or is otherwise unavailable to serve as guardian, the court shall appoint the next eligible designated alternate guardian named in the declaration. If the guardian and all alternate guardians do not qualify, are dead, refuse to serve, or later die or resign, the court shall appoint another person to serve as otherwise provided by this code.

(e) The declarant may revoke a declaration in any manner provided for the revocation of a will under Section 63 of this code, including the subsequent reexecution of the declaration in the manner required for the original declaration.

(f) If a declarant designates the declarant's spouse to serve as guardian under this section, and the declarant is subsequently divorced from that spouse before a guardian is appointed, the provision of the declaration designating the spouse has no effect.

(g) A declaration and affidavit may be in any form adequate to clearly indicate the declarant's intention to designate a guardian. The following forms may, but need not, be used:

DECLARATION OF GUARDIAN IN THE EVENT OF LATER INCAPACITY OR NEED OF GUARDIAN

I, ________, make this Declaration of Guardian, to operate if the need for a guardian for me later arises.

1. I designate ________ to serve as guardian of my person, ________ as first alternate guardian of my person, ________ as second alternate guardian of my person, and ________ as third alternate guardian of my person.

2. I designate ________ to serve as guardian of my estate, ________ as first alternate guardian of my estate, ________ as second alternate guardian of my estate, and ________ as third alternate guardian of my estate.

3. If any guardian or alternate guardian dies, does not qualify, or resigns, the next named alternate guardian becomes my guardian.

4. I expressly disqualify the following persons from serving as guardian of my person: ________, ________, and ________.

5. I expressly disqualify the following persons from serving as guardian of my estate: ________, ________, and ________.

Signed this ___ day of ________, 19___.

____
Declarant

______________ ______________
Witness Witness

SELF-PROVING AFFIDAVIT

Before me, the undersigned authority, on this date personally appeared the declarant, and __________ and __________ as witnesses, and all being duly sworn, the declarant said that the above instrument was his or her Declaration of Guardian and that the declarant had made and executed it for the purposes expressed in the declaration. The witnesses declared to me that they are each 14 years of age or older, that they saw the declarant sign the declaration, that they signed the declaration as witnesses, and that the declarant appeared to them to be of sound mind.

____
Declarant

______________ ______________
Affiant Affiant

Subscribed and sworn to before me by the above named declarant and affiants on this ____ day of __________, 19__.

____
Notary Public in and for
the State of Texas
My Commission expires:
____

Added by Acts 1993, 73rd Leg., ch. 957, § 1, eff. Sept. 1, 1993.

§ 680. Selection of Guardian by Minor

(a) When an application is filed for the guardianship of the person or estate, or both, of a minor at least 12 years of age, the minor, by writing filed with the clerk, may choose the guardian if the court approves the choice and finds that the choice is in the best interest of the minor.

(b) A minor at least 12 years of age may select another guardian of either the minor's person or estate, or both, if the minor has a guardian appointed by the court or the minor has a guardian appointed by will or written declaration of the parent of the minor and that guardian dies, resigns, or is removed from guardianship. If the court is satisfied that the person selected is suitable and competent and that the appointment of the person is in the best interest of the minor, it shall make the appointment and revoke the letters of guardianship of the former guardian. The minor shall make the selection by filing an application in open court in person or by attorney.

Added by Acts 1993, 73rd Leg., ch. 957, § 1, eff. Sept. 1, 1993. Amended by Acts 1995, 74th Leg., ch. 1039, § 31, eff. Sept. 1, 1995.

§ 681. Persons Disqualified to Serve as Guardians

A person may not be appointed guardian if the person is:

(1) a minor;

(2) a person whose conduct is notoriously bad;

(3) an incapacitated person;

(4) a person who is a party or whose parent is a party to a lawsuit concerning or affecting the welfare of the proposed ward, unless the court:

(A) determines that the lawsuit claim of the person who has applied to be appointed guardian is not in conflict with the lawsuit claim of the proposed ward; or

(B) appoints a guardian ad litem to represent the interests of the proposed ward throughout the litigation of the ward's lawsuit claim;

(5) a person indebted to the proposed ward unless the person pays the debt before appointment;

(6) a person asserting a claim adverse to the proposed ward or the proposed ward's property, real or personal;

(7) a person who, because of inexperience, lack of education, or other good reason, is incapable of properly and prudently managing and controlling the ward or the ward's estate;

(8) a person, institution, or corporation found unsuitable by the court;

(9) a person disqualified in a declaration made under Section 679 of this code; or

(10) a nonresident person who has not filed with the court the name of a resident agent to accept service of process in all actions or proceedings relating to the guardianship.

Added by Acts 1993, 73rd Leg., ch. 957, § 1, eff. Sept. 1, 1993. Amended by Acts 1995, 74th Leg., ch. 1039, § 32, eff. Sept. 1, 1995.

§ 682. Application; Contents

Any person may commence a proceeding for the appointment of a guardian by filing a written application in a court having jurisdiction and venue. The application must be sworn to by the applicant and state:

(1) the name, sex, date of birth, and address of the proposed ward;

(2) the name, relationship, and address of the person the applicant desires to have appointed as guardian;

(3) whether guardianship of the person or estate, or both, is sought;

(4) the nature and degree of the alleged incapacity, the specific areas of protection and assistance requested, and the limitation of rights requested to be included in the court's order of appointment;

(5) the facts requiring that a guardian be appointed and the interest of the applicant in the appointment;

(6) the nature and description of any guardianship of any kind existing for the proposed ward in any other state;

(7) the name and address of any person or institution having the care and custody of the proposed ward;

(8) the approximate value and description of the proposed ward's property, including any compensation, pension, insurance, or allowance to which the proposed ward may be entitled;

(9) the name and address of any person whom the applicant knows to hold a power of attorney signed by the proposed ward and a description of the type of power of attorney;

(10) if the proposed ward is a minor, the names of the parents and next of kin of the proposed ward and whether either or both of the parents are deceased;

(11) if the proposed ward is a minor, whether the minor was the subject of a legal or conservatorship proceeding within the preceding two-year period and, if so, the court involved, the nature of the proceeding, and the final disposition, if any, of the proceeding;

(12) if the proposed ward is 60 years of age or older, the names and addresses, to the best of the applicant's knowledge, of the proposed ward's spouse, siblings, and children, or, if there is no spouse, sibling, or child, the names and addresses of the proposed ward's next of kin;

(13) facts showing that the court has venue over the proceeding; and

(14) if applicable, that the person whom the applicant desires to have appointed as a guardian is a private professional guardian who has complied with the requirements of Section 697 of this code.

Added by Acts 1993, 73rd Leg., ch. 957, § 1, eff. Sept. 1, 1993. Amended by Acts 1997, 75th Leg., ch. 77, § 5, eff. Sept. 1, 1997; Acts 1997, 75th Leg., ch. 1376, § 2, eff. Sept. 1, 1997; Acts 1999, 76th Leg., ch. 829, § 4, eff. Sept. 1, 1999.

For application provisions of Acts 1999, 76th Leg., ch. 829, see notes following V.A.T.S. Probate Code, § 694A.

§ 682A. Application for Appointment of Guardian for Certain Persons

(a) If a minor is a person who, because of incapacity, will require a guardianship after the ward is no longer a minor, a person may file an application under Section 682 of this code for the appointment of a guardian of the person and/or the estate of the proposed ward not earlier than the 60th day before the proposed ward's 18th birthday.

(b) Notwithstanding Section 694(b) of this code, the guardianship of the person of a minor who is the subject of an application for the appointment of a guardian of the person filed under Subsection (a) of this section is settled and closed when:

(1) the court, after a hearing on the application, determines that the appointment of a guardian of the person for the proposed ward is not necessary; or

(2) the guardian appointed by the court after a hearing on the application has qualified under Section 699 of this code.

Added by Acts 1999, 76th Leg., ch. 904, § 1, eff. Sept. 1, 1999.

Section 2 of Acts 1999, 76th Leg., ch. 904 provides:

"(a) This Act takes effect September 1, 1999, and applies only to an application for the appointment of a guardian filed on or after the effective date of this Act.

"(b) An application for the appointment of a guardian filed before the effective date of this Act is governed by the law in effect on the date the application was filed, and the former law is continued in effect for that purpose."

§ 683. Court's Initiation of Guardianship Proceedings

(a) If a court has probable cause to believe that a person domiciled or found in the county in which the court is located is an incapacitated person, and the person does not have a guardian in this state, the court shall appoint a guardian ad litem or court investigator to investigate and file an application for the appointment of a guardian of the person or estate, or both, of the person believed to be incapacitated.

(b) To establish probable cause under this section, the court may require:

(1) an information letter about the person believed to be incapacitated that is submitted by an interested

person and satisfies the requirements of Section 683A of this code; or

(2) a written letter or certificate from a physician who has examined the person believed to be incapacitated that satisfies the requirements of Section 687(a) of this code, except that the letter must be dated not earlier than the 120th day before the date of the filing of an application under Subsection (a) of this section and be based on an examination the physician performed not earlier than the 120th day before that date.

(c) A court that creates a guardianship for a ward under this chapter may authorize compensation of a guardian ad litem who files an application under Subsection (a) of this section from available funds of the ward's estate. If after examining the ward's assets the court determines the ward is unable to pay for services provided by the guardian ad litem, the court may authorize compensation from the county treasury.

Added by Acts 1993, 73rd Leg., ch. 957, § 1, eff. Sept. 1, 1993. Amended by Acts 1999, 76th Leg., ch. 905, § 3, eff. Sept. 1, 1999.

§ 683A. Information Letter

An information letter under Section 683(b)(1) of this code about a person believed to be incapacitated may:

(1) include the name, address, telephone number, county of residence, and date of birth of the person;

(2) state whether the residence of the person is a private residence, health care facility, or other type of residence;

(3) describe the relationship between the interested person and the person;

(4) contain the names and telephone numbers of any known friends and relatives of the person;

(5) state whether a guardian of the person or estate of the person has been appointed in this state;

(6) state whether the person has executed a power of attorney and, if so, the designee's name, address, and telephone number;

(7) describe any property of the person, including the estimated value of that property;

(8) list any amount and source of monthly income of the person; and

(9) describe the nature and degree of the person's alleged incapacity and include a statement of whether the person is in imminent danger of serious impairment to the person's physical health, safety, or estate.

Added by Acts 1999, 76th Leg., ch. 905, § 4, eff. Sept. 1, 1999.

§ 684. Findings Required

(a) Before appointing a guardian, the court must find by clear and convincing evidence that:

(1) the proposed ward is an incapacitated person;

(2) it is in the best interest of the proposed ward to have the court appoint a person as guardian of the proposed ward; and

(3) the rights of the proposed ward or the proposed ward's property will be protected by the appointment of a guardian.

(b) Before appointing a guardian, the court must find by a preponderance of the evidence that:

(1) the court has venue of the case;

(2) the person to be appointed guardian is eligible to act as guardian and is entitled to appointment, or, if no eligible person entitled to appointment applies, the person appointed is a proper person to act as guardian;

(3) if a guardian is appointed for a minor, the guardianship is not created for the primary purpose of enabling the minor to establish residency for enrollment in a school or school district for which the minor is not otherwise eligible for enrollment; and

(4) the proposed ward is totally without capacity as provided by this code to care for himself or herself and to manage the individual's property, or the proposed ward lacks the capacity to do some, but not all, of the tasks necessary to care for himself or herself or to manage the individual's property.

(c) The court may not grant an application to create a guardianship unless the applicant proves each element required by this code. A determination of incapacity of an adult proposed ward, other than a person who must have a guardian appointed to receive funds due the person from any governmental source, must be evidenced by recurring acts or occurrences within the preceding six-month period and not by isolated instances of negligence or bad judgment.

(d) A court may not appoint a guardian of the estate of a minor when a payment of claims is made under Section 887 of this code.

(e) A certificate of the executive head or a representative of the bureau, department, or agency of the government, to the effect that the appointment of a guardian is a condition precedent to the payment of any funds due the proposed ward from that governmental entity, is prima facie evidence of the necessity for the appointment of a guardian.

Added by Acts 1993, 73rd Leg., ch. 957, § 1, eff. Sept. 1, 1993. Amended by Acts 1995, 74th Leg., ch. 1039, § 33, eff. Sept. 1, 1995; Acts 1997, 75th Leg., ch. 1376, § 3, eff. Sept. 1, 1997; Acts 1999, 76th Leg., ch. 379, § 5, eff. Sept. 1, 1999.

§ 685. Hearing for Appointment of Guardian; Right to Jury Trial

(a) A proposed ward must be present at a hearing to appoint a guardian unless the court, on the record or in the order, determines that a personal appearance is not necessary. The court may close the hearing if the proposed ward or the proposed ward's counsel requests a closed hearing.

(b) The proposed ward is entitled, on request, to a jury trial.

(c) At the hearing, the court shall:

(1) inquire into the ability of any allegedly incapacitated adult person to feed, clothe, and shelter himself or herself, to care for the individual's own physical health, and to manage the individual's property or financial affairs;

(2) ascertain the age of any proposed ward who is a minor;

(3) inquire into the governmental reports for any person who must have a guardian appointed to receive funds due the person from any governmental source; and

(4) inquire into the qualifications, abilities, and capabilities of the person seeking to be appointed guardian.

Added by Acts 1993, 73rd Leg., ch. 957, § 1, eff. Sept. 1, 1993. Amended by Acts 1995, 74th Leg., ch. 1039, § 34, eff. Sept. 1, 1995; Acts 1999, 76th Leg., ch. 379, § 6, eff. Sept. 1, 1999.

§ 686. Use of Records in Hearing to Appoint Guardian

(a) Before a hearing may be held for the appointment of a guardian, current and relevant medical, psychological, and intellectual testing records of the proposed ward must be provided to the attorney ad litem appointed to represent the proposed ward unless:

(1) the proposed ward is a minor or a person who must have a guardian appointed to receive funds due the person from any governmental source; or

(2) the court makes a finding on the record that no current or relevant records exist and examining the proposed ward for the purpose of creating the records is impractical.

(b) Current medical, psychological, and intellectual testing records are a sufficient basis for a determination of guardianship.

(c) The findings and recommendations contained in the medical, psychological, and intellectual testing records are not binding on the court.

Added by Acts 1993, 73rd Leg., ch. 957, § 1, eff. Sept. 1, 1993. Amended by Acts 1999, 76th Leg., ch. 379, § 7, eff. Sept. 1, 1999.

§ 687. Examinations and Reports

(a) The court may not grant an application to create a guardianship for an incapacitated person, other than a minor, person whose alleged incapacity is mental retardation, or person for whom it is necessary to have a guardian appointed only to receive funds from a governmental source, unless the applicant presents to the court a written letter or certificate from a physician licensed in this state that is dated not earlier than the 120th day before the date of the filing of the application and based on an examination the physician performed not earlier than the 120th day before the date of the filing of the application. The letter or certificate must:

(1) describe the nature and degree of incapacity, including the medical history if reasonably available;

(2) provide a medical prognosis specifying the estimated severity of the incapacity;

(3) state how or in what manner the proposed ward's ability to make or communicate responsible decisions concerning himself or herself is affected by the person's physical or mental health;

(4) state whether any current medication affects the demeanor of the proposed ward or the proposed ward's ability to participate fully in a court proceeding;

(5) describe the precise physical and mental conditions underlying a diagnosis of senility, if applicable; and

(6) include any other information required by the court.

(b) Except as provided by Subsection (c) of this section, if the court determines it is necessary, the court may appoint the necessary physicians to examine the proposed ward. A physician who examines the proposed ward, other than a physician or psychologist who examines the proposed ward under Subsection (c) of this section, shall make available to an attorney ad litem appointed to represent the proposed ward, for inspection, a written letter or certificate from the physician that complies with the requirements of Subsection (a) of this section.

(c) If the basis of the proposed ward's alleged incapacity is mental retardation, the proposed ward shall be examined by a physician or psychologist licensed in this state or certified by the Texas Department of Mental Health and Mental Retardation to perform the examination, unless there is written documentation filed with the court that shows that the proposed ward has been examined according to the rules adopted by the Texas Department of Mental Health and Mental Retardation not earlier than six months before the date of a hearing to appoint a guardian for the proposed ward. The physician or psychologist shall conduct the examination according to the rules adopted by the Texas Department of Mental Health and Mental Retardation and shall submit written findings and recommendations to the court.

Added by Acts 1995, 74th Leg., ch. 1039, § 35, eff. Sept. 1, 1995. Amended by Acts 1999, 76th Leg., ch. 379, § 8, eff. Sept. 1, 1999.

§§ 688, 688A. Repealed by Acts 1995, 74th Leg., ch. 1039, § 73(1), eff. Sept. 1, 1995

§ 689. Preference of Ward

Before appointing a guardian, the court shall make a reasonable effort to consider the incapacitated person's preference of the person to be appointed guardian and, to the extent not inconsistent with other provisions of this chapter, shall give due consideration to the preference indicated by the incapacitated person.

Added by Acts 1993, 73rd Leg., ch. 957, § 1, eff. Sept. 1, 1993.

§ 690. Persons Appointed Guardian

Only one person may be appointed as guardian of the person or estate, but one person may be appointed guardian of the person and another of the estate, if it is in the best interest of the ward. Nothing in this section prohibits the joint appointment of a husband and wife, of joint managing conservators, or of co-guardians appointed under the laws of a jurisdiction other than this state.

Added by Acts 1993, 73rd Leg., ch. 957, § 1, eff. Sept. 1, 1993. Amended by Acts 1995, 74th Leg., ch. 1039, § 36, eff. Sept. 1, 1995.

§ 691. Repealed by Acts 1997, 75th Leg., ch. 809, § 2, eff. Sept. 1, 1997

Section 3 of Acts 1997, 75th Leg., ch. 809 provides:

"This Act takes effect September 1, 1997, and applies only to an application for mental retardation services made on or after that date."

§ 692. Dismissal of Application

If it is found that an adult person possesses the capacity to care for himself or herself and to manage the individual's property as would a reasonably prudent person, the court shall dismiss the application for guardianship.

Added by Acts 1993, 73rd Leg., ch. 957, § 1, eff. Sept. 1, 1993. Amended by Acts 1995, 74th Leg., ch. 1039, § 38, eff. Sept. 1, 1995.

§ 693. Order of Court

(a) If it is found that the proposed ward is totally without capacity as provided by this code to care for himself or herself and to manage the individual's property, the court may appoint a guardian of the individual's person or estate, or both, with full authority over the incapacitated person except as provided by law. An order appointing a guardian under this subsection must contain findings of fact and specify:

(1) the information required by Subsection (c) of this section;

(2) that the guardian has full authority over the incapacitated person; and

(3) if necessary, the amount of funds from the corpus of the person's estate the court will allow the guardian to expend for the education and maintenance of the person under Section 776 of this code.

(b) If it is found that the person lacks the capacity to do some, but not all, of the tasks necessary to care for himself or herself or to manage the individual's property, the court may appoint a guardian with limited powers and permit the individual to care for himself or herself or to manage the individual's property commensurate with the individual's ability.

An order appointing a guardian under this subsection must contain findings of fact and specify:

(1) the information required by Subsection (c) of this section;

(2) the specific powers, limitations, or duties of the guardian with respect to the care of the person or the management of the person's property by the guardian; and

(3) if necessary, the amount of funds from the corpus of the person's estate the court will allow the guardian to expend for the education and maintenance of the person under Section 776 of this code.

(c) The order of the court appointing a guardian must specify:

(1) the name of the person appointed;

(2) the name of the ward;

(3) whether the guardian is of the person or the estate, or of both, of the ward;

(4) the amount of any bond required;

(5) if it is a guardianship of the estate and the court deems an appraisal is necessary, one or more but not more than three disinterested persons to appraise the estate and to return the appraisement to the court; and

(6) that the clerk will issue letters of guardianship to the person appointed when the person has qualified according to law.

(d) An order appointing a guardian may not duplicate or conflict with the powers and duties of any other guardian.

(e) An order appointing a guardian or a successor guardian may specify a period of not more than one year during which a petition for adjudication that the incapacitated person no longer requires the guardianship may not be filed without special leave.

Added by Acts 1993, 73rd Leg., ch. 957, § 1, eff. Sept. 1, 1993. Amended by Acts 1995, 74th Leg., ch. 1039, § 39, eff. Sept. 1, 1995.

§ 694. Term of Appointment of Guardian

(a) Unless otherwise discharged as provided by law, a guardian remains in office until the estate is closed.

(b) The guardianship shall be settled and closed when the incapacitated person:

(1) dies and, if the person was married, the person's spouse qualifies as survivor in community;

(2) is found by the court to have full capacity to care for himself or herself and to manage the person's property;

(3) is no longer a minor; or

(4) no longer must have a guardian appointed to receive funds due the person from any governmental source.

(c) An order appointing a guardian or a successor guardian may specify a period of not more than one year during which a petition for adjudication that the incapacitated person no longer requires the guardianship may not be filed without special leave.

(d) A request for an order under this section may be made by informal letter to the court. A person who knowingly interferes with the transmission of the request to the court may be adjudged guilty of contempt of court.

(e) If a nonresident guardian of a nonresident ward qualifies as guardian under this chapter, the guardianship of any resident guardian may be terminated.

(f) Repealed by Acts 1999, 76th Leg., ch. 379, § 10, eff. Sept. 1, 1999.

Added by Acts 1993, 73rd Leg., ch. 957, § 1, eff. Sept. 1, 1993. Amended by Acts 1995, 74th Leg., ch. 1039, § 40, eff. Sept. 1, 1995; Acts 1999, 76th Leg., ch. 379, §§ 9, 10, eff. Sept. 1, 1999.

Section 11 of Acts 1999, 76th Leg., ch. 379 provides:

"(a) This Act takes effect September 1, 1999.

"(b) A guardianship for a missing person created under Chapter XIII, Texas Probate Code, before September 1, 1999, is abolished on the effective date of this Act.

"(c) On its own motion or on the motion of a person interested in the estate of the missing person, a court with jurisdiction to appoint a receiver for a missing person may convert a guardianship for a missing person abolished under this Act to a receivership:

"(1) under Section 79.017, Human Resources Code, as added by Chapter 1376, Acts of the 75th Legislature, Regular Session, 1997, and editorially redesignated as Article 62.023, Code of Criminal Procedure; or

"(2) under Section 886, Texas Probate Code."

§ 694A. Complete Restoration of Ward's Capacity or Modification of Guardianship

(a) A ward or any person interested in the ward's welfare may file a written application with the court for an order:

(1) finding that the ward is no longer an incapacitated person and ordering the settlement and closing of the guardianship;

(2) finding that the ward lacks the capacity to do some or all of the tasks necessary to provide food, clothing, or shelter for himself or herself, to care for the ward's own physical health, or to manage the ward's own financial affairs and granting additional powers or duties to the guardian; or

(3) finding that the ward has the capacity to do some, but not all, of the tasks necessary to provide food, clothing, or shelter for himself or herself, to care for the ward's own physical health, or to manage the ward's own financial affairs and:

(A) limiting the powers or duties of the guardian; and

(B) permitting the ward to care for himself or herself or to manage the ward's own financial affairs commensurate with the ward's ability.

(b) A ward may make a request for an order under this section by informal letter to the court. A person who knowingly interferes with the transmission of the request to the court may be adjudged guilty of contempt of court.

(c) On receipt of an informal letter under Subsection (b) of this section, the court shall appoint the court investigator or a guardian ad litem to file an application under Subsection (a) of this section on the ward's behalf. A guardian ad litem appointed under this subsection may also be appointed by the court to serve as attorney ad litem under Section 694C of this code.

(d) When an application is filed under this section, citation shall be served on the ward's guardian and on the ward if the ward is not the applicant.

(e) Except as otherwise provided by the court, on good cause shown by the applicant, a person may not reapply for complete restoration of a ward's capacity or modification of a ward's guardianship before the first anniversary of the date of the hearing on the last preceding application.

Added by Acts 1995, 74th Leg., ch. 1039, § 41, eff. Sept. 1, 1995. Amended by Acts 1999, 76th Leg., ch. 829, § 5, eff. Sept. 1, 1999.

Section 7 of Acts 1999, 76th Leg., ch. 829 provides:

"(a) The changes in law made by this Act apply to:

"(1) an application for the appointment of a guardian, restoration of a ward's capacity, or modification of a guardianship that is filed on or after the effective date of this Act; or

"(2) an application for the appointment of a guardian, restoration of a ward's capacity, or modification of a guardianship that is filed before the effective date of this Act in which a final determination on the application has not been made by the court.

"(b) An application described by Subsection (a)(2) of this section must be modified to conform to the changes in law made by this Act."

§ 694B. Contents of Application

An application filed under Section 694A of this code must be sworn to by the applicant and must:

(1) contain the name, sex, date of birth, and address of the ward;

(2) contain the name and address of any person serving as guardian of the person of the ward on the date the application is filed;

(3) contain the name and address of any person serving as guardian of the estate of the ward on the date the application is filed;

(4) state the nature and description of the ward's guardianship;

(5) state the specific areas of protection and assistance and any limitation of rights that exist;

(6) state whether the relief being sought is:

(A) a restoration of the ward's capacity because the ward is no longer an incapacitated person;

(B) the granting of additional powers or duties to the guardian; or

(C) the limitation of powers granted to or duties performed by the guardian;

(7) if the relief being sought under the application is described by Subdivision (6)(B) or (C) of this section, state:

(A) the nature and degree of the ward's incapacity;

(B) the specific areas of protection and assistance to be provided to the ward and requested to be included in the court's order; and

(C) any limitation of the ward's rights requested to be included in the court's order;

(8) state the approximate value and description of the ward's property, including any compensation, pension, insurance, or allowance to which the ward is or may be entitled; and

(9) if the ward is 60 years of age or older, contain the names and addresses, to the best of the applicant's knowledge, of the ward's spouse, siblings, and children or, if there is no known spouse, sibling, or child, the names and addresses of the ward's next of kin.

Added by Acts 1999, 76th Leg., ch. 829, § 6, eff. Sept. 1, 1999.

For application provisions of Acts 1999, 76th Leg., ch. 829, see notes following V.A.T.S. Probate Code, § 694A.

§ 694C. Appointment of Attorney ad Litem

(a) The court shall appoint an attorney ad litem to represent a ward in a proceeding for the complete restoration of the ward's capacity or for the modification of the ward's guardianship.

(b) Unless otherwise provided by the court, an attorney ad litem appointed under this section shall represent the ward only for purposes of the restoration or modification proceeding.

Added by Acts 1999, 76th Leg., ch. 829, § 6, eff. Sept. 1, 1999.

For application provisions of Acts 1999, 76th Leg., ch. 829, see notes following V.A.T.S. Probate Code, § 694A.

§ 694D. Hearing

(a) At a hearing on an application for complete restoration of a ward's capacity or modification of a ward's guardianship, the court shall consider only evidence regarding the ward's mental or physical capacity at the time of the hearing that is relevant to the restoration of capacity or modification of the guardianship, as appropriate.

(b) The party who filed the application has the burden of proof at the hearing.

Added by Acts 1999, 76th Leg., ch. 829, § 6, eff. Sept. 1, 1999.

For application provisions of Acts 1999, 76th Leg., ch. 829, see notes following V.A.T.S. Probate Code, § 694A.

§ 694E. Findings Required

(a) Before ordering the settlement and closing of the guardianship under an application filed under Section 694A of this code, the court must find by a preponderance of the evidence that the ward is no longer partially or fully incapacitated.

(b) Before granting additional powers to the guardian or requiring the guardian to perform additional duties under an application filed under Section 694A of this code, the court must find by a preponderance of the evidence that the current nature and degree of the ward's incapacity warrants a modification of the guardianship and that some or all of the ward's rights need to be further restricted.

(c) Before limiting the powers granted to or duties required to be performed by the guardian under an application filed under Section 694A of this code, the court must find by a preponderance of the evidence that the current nature and degree of the ward's incapacity warrants a modification of the guardianship and that some of the ward's rights need to be restored.

Added by Acts 1999, 76th Leg., ch. 829, § 6, eff. Sept. 1, 1999.

For application provisions of Acts 1999, 76th Leg., ch. 829, see notes following V.A.T.S. Probate Code, § 694A.

§ 694F. Examinations and Reports Relating to Complete Restoration of Ward's Capacity or Modification of Guardianship

(a) The court may not grant an order completely restoring a ward's capacity or modifying a ward's guardianship under an application filed under Section 694A of this code unless, in addition to other requirements prescribed by this code, the applicant presents to the court a written letter or certificate from a physician licensed in this state that is dated not earlier than the 120th day before the date of the filing of the application or dated after the date on which the application was filed but before the date of the hearing. The letter or certificate must:

(1) describe the nature and degree of incapacity, including the medical history if reasonably available, or state that, in the physician's opinion, the ward has the capacity to provide food, clothing, and shelter for himself or herself, to care for the ward's own physical health, and to manage the financial affairs of the ward;

(2) provide a medical prognosis specifying the estimated severity of any incapacity;

(3) state how or in what manner the ward's ability to make or communicate responsible decisions concerning himself or herself is affected by the person's physical or mental health;

(4) state whether any current medication affects the demeanor of the ward or the ward's ability to participate fully in a court proceeding;

(5) describe the precise physical and mental conditions underlying a diagnosis of senility, if applicable; and

(6) include any other information required by the court.

(b) If the court determines it is necessary, the court may appoint the necessary physicians to examine the ward in the same manner and to the same extent as a ward is examined by a physician under Section 687 of this code.

Added by Acts 1999, 76th Leg., ch. 829, § 6, eff. Sept. 1, 1999.

For application provisions of Acts 1999, 76th Leg., ch. 829, see notes following V.A.T.S. Probate Code, § 694A.

§ 694G. Order of Complete Restoration of Ward's Capacity

If the court finds that a ward is no longer an incapacitated person, the order completely restoring the ward's capacity must contain findings of fact and specify:

(1) the information required by Section 694J of this code;

(2) that the ward is no longer an incapacitated person;

(3) that there is no further need for a guardianship of the person or estate of the ward;

(4) that the guardian is required to:

(A) immediately settle and close the guardianship in accordance with Section 745 of this code; and

(B) deliver all of the remaining guardianship estate to the ward; and

(5) that the clerk shall revoke letters of guardianship when the guardianship is finally settled and closed.

Added by Acts 1999, 76th Leg., ch. 829, § 6, eff. Sept. 1, 1999.

For application provisions of Acts 1999, 76th Leg., ch. 829, see notes following V.A.T.S. Probate Code, § 694A.

§ 694H. Modification of Guardianship

If the court finds that a guardian's powers or duties should be expanded or limited, the order modifying the guardianship must contain findings of fact and specify:

(1) the information required by Section 694J of this code;

(2) the specific powers, limitations, or duties of the guardian with respect to the care of the ward or the management of the property of the ward, as appropriate;

(3) the specific areas of protection and assistance to be provided to the ward;

(4) any limitation of the ward's rights; and

(5) that the clerk shall modify the letters of guardianship to the extent applicable to conform to the order.

Added by Acts 1999, 76th Leg., ch. 829, § 6, eff. Sept. 1, 1999.

For application provisions of Acts 1999, 76th Leg., ch. 829, see notes following V.A.T.S. Probate Code, § 694A.

§ 694I. Dismissal of Application

If the court finds that a modification of the ward's guardianship is not necessary, including that the ward's capacity has not been restored, the court shall dismiss the application and enter an order that contains findings of fact and specifies:

(1) the information required by Section 694J of this code; and

(2) that the powers, limitations, or duties of the guardian with respect to the care of the ward or the management of the ward's property will remain unchanged.

Added by Acts 1999, 76th Leg., ch. 829, § 6, eff. Sept. 1, 1999.

For application provisions of Acts 1999, 76th Leg., ch. 829, see notes following V.A.T.S. Probate Code, § 694A.

§ 694J. Contents of Order

(a) A court order entered with respect to a request made under Section 694A of this code to completely restore a ward's capacity or modify a ward's guardianship must:

(1) contain the name of the guardian;

(2) contain the name of the ward; and

(3) state whether the type of guardianship being addressed at the proceeding is a:

(A) guardianship of the person;

(B) guardianship of the estate; or

(C) guardianship of both the person and the estate.

(b) In an order described by this section, the court may not grant a power to a guardian or require the guardian to perform a duty that is a power granted to or a duty required to be performed by another guardian.

Added by Acts 1999, 76th Leg., ch. 829, § 6, eff. Sept. 1, 1999.

For application provisions of Acts 1999, 76th Leg., ch. 829, see notes following V.A.T.S. Probate Code, § 694A.

§ 694K. Attorney Retained on Ward's Behalf

(a) A ward may retain an attorney for a proceeding involving the complete restoration of the ward's capacity or modification of the ward's guardianship.

(b) The court may order that compensation for services provided by an attorney retained under this section be paid from funds in the ward's estate only if the court finds that the attorney had a good-faith belief that the ward had the capacity necessary to retain the attorney's services.

Added by Acts 1999, 76th Leg., ch. 829, § 6, eff. Sept. 1, 1999.

For application provisions of Acts 1999, 76th Leg., ch. 829, see notes following V.A.T.S. Probate Code, § 694A.

§ 695. Appointment of Successor Guardian

(a) If a guardian dies, resigns, or is removed, the court may, on application and on service of notice as directed by the court, appoint a successor guardian.

(b) A successor guardian has the powers and rights and is subject to all of the duties of the preceding guardian.

Added by Acts 1993, 73rd Leg., ch. 957, § 1, eff. Sept. 1, 1993.

§ 695A. Successor Guardians for Wards of Guardianship Programs or Governmental Entities

(a) If a guardianship program or governmental entity serving as a guardian for a ward under this chapter becomes aware of a family member or friend of the ward or any other interested person who is willing and able to serve as the ward's successor guardian, the program or entity shall notify the court in which the guardianship is pending of the individual's willingness and ability.

(b) When the court is notified of the existence of a proposed successor guardian under Subsection (a) of this section or the court otherwise becomes aware of a family member, friend, or any other interested person who is willing and able to serve as a successor guardian for a ward of a guardianship program or governmental entity, the court shall determine whether the proposed successor guardian is qualified to serve under this chapter as the ward's successor guardian.

(c) If the court finds under Subsection (b) of this section that the proposed successor guardian for a ward is not disqualified from being appointed as the ward's successor guardian under Section 681 of this code and that the appointment is in the ward's best interests, the guardianship program or governmental entity serving as the ward's guardian or the court, on the court's own motion, may file an application to appoint the individual as the ward's successor guardian. Service of notice on an application filed under this subsection shall be made as directed by the court.

Added by Acts 1999, 76th Leg., ch. 906, § 1, eff. Sept. 1, 1999.

§ 696. Appointment of Private Professional Guardians

A court may not appoint a private professional guardian to serve as a guardian or permit a private professional guardian to continue to serve as a guardian under this code if the private professional guardian has not complied with the requirements of Section 697 of this code.

Added by Acts 1993, 73rd Leg., ch. 957, § 1, eff. Sept. 1, 1993.

§ 697. Registration of Private Professional Guardians

(a) A private professional guardian must apply annually to the clerk of the county having venue over the proceeding for the appointment of a guardian for certification. The application must include a sworn statement containing the following information concerning a private professional guardian or each person who represents or plans to represent the interests of a ward as a guardian on behalf of the private professional guardian:

(1) educational background and professional experience;

(2) three or more professional references;

(3) the names of all of the wards the private professional guardian or person is or will be serving as a guardian;

(4) the aggregate fair market value of the property of all wards that is being or will be managed by the private professional guardian or person;

(5) place of residence, business address, and business telephone number; and

(6) whether the private professional guardian or person has ever been removed as a guardian by the court or resigned as a guardian in a particular case, and, if so, a description of the circumstances causing the removal or resignation, and the style of the suit, the docket number, and the court having jurisdiction over the proceeding.

(b) The application must be accompanied by a nonrefundable fee set by the clerk in an amount necessary to cover the cost of administering this section.

(c) The term of the certification begins on the date that the requirements are met and extends through December 31 of the initial year. After the initial year of certification, the term of the certification begins on January 1 and ends on December 31 of each year. A renewal application must be completed during December of the year preceding the year for which the renewal is requested.

(d) The clerk shall bring the information received under this section to the judge's attention for review. The judge shall use the information only in determining whether to appoint, remove, or continue the appointment of a private professional guardian.

(e) Not later than February 1 of each year, the clerk shall submit to the Health and Human Services Commission the names and business addresses of private professional guardians who have satisfied the certification requirements under this section during the preceding year.

Added by Acts 1993, 73rd Leg., ch. 957, § 1, eff. Sept. 1, 1993. Amended by Acts 1999, 76th Leg., ch. 1116, § 2, eff. Sept. 1, 1999.

Section 4 of Acts 1999, 76th Leg., ch. 1116 provides:

"The changes in law made by this Act to Sections 697(a) and 698(a), Texas Probate Code, apply only to an application for certification that is filed on or after the effective date of this Act. An application for certification that is filed before the effective date of this Act is governed by the law in effect when the application was filed, and the former law is continued in effect for that purpose."

§ 698. Access to Criminal History Records

(a) The clerk of the county having venue over the proceeding for the appointment of a guardian shall obtain criminal history record information that is maintained by the Department of Public Safety or the Federal Bureau of Investigation identification division relating to:

(1) a private professional guardian;

(2) each person who represents or plans to represent the interests of a ward as a guardian on behalf of the private professional guardian; or

(3) each person employed by a private professional guardian who will:

(A) have personal contact with a ward or proposed ward;

(B) exercise control over and manage a ward's estate; or

(C) perform any duties with respect to the management of a ward's estate.

(b) The criminal history record information obtained under this section is for the exclusive use of the court and is privileged and confidential. The criminal history record information may not be released or otherwise disclosed to any person or agency except on court order or consent of the person being investigated. The clerk may destroy the criminal history information records after the records are used for the purposes authorized by this section.

(c) The court shall use the information obtained under this section only in determining whether to appoint, remove, or continue the appointment of a private professional guardian.

(d) A person commits an offense if the person releases or discloses any information received under this section without the authorization prescribed by Subsection (b) of this section. An offense under this subsection is a Class A misdemeanor.

(e) The clerk may charge a reasonable fee sufficient to recover the costs of obtaining criminal history information records authorized by Subsection (a) of this section.

Added by Acts 1993, 73rd Leg., ch. 957, § 1, eff. Sept. 1, 1993. Amended by Acts 1999, 76th Leg., ch. 1116, § 3, eff. Sept. 1, 1999.

Section 4 of Acts 1999, 76th Leg., ch. 1116 provides:

"The changes in law made by this Act to Sections 697(a) and 698(a), Texas Probate Code, apply only to an application for certification that is filed on or after the effective date of this Act. An application for certification that is filed before the effective date of this Act is governed by the law in effect when the application was filed, and the former law is continued in effect for that purpose."

SUBPART B. QUALIFICATION

§ 699. How Guardians Qualify

A guardian is deemed to have duly qualified when the guardian has taken and filed the oath required under Section 700 of this code, has made the required bond, and has filed it with the clerk, and has the bond approved by the judge. A guardian who is not required to make bond, is deemed to have duly qualified when the guardian has taken and filed the required oath.

Added by Acts 1993, 73rd Leg., ch. 957, § 1, eff. Sept. 1, 1993.

For applicability provisions of the 1993 Act, see notes following § 601.

§ 700. Oath of Guardian

(a) The guardian shall take an oath to discharge faithfully the duties of guardian for the person or estate, or both, of a ward.

(b) A representative of the Department of Protective and Regulatory Services shall take the oath required by Subsection (a) of this section if the department is appointed guardian.

Added by Acts 1993, 73rd Leg., ch. 957, § 1, eff. Sept. 1, 1993. Amended by Acts 1997, 75th Leg., ch. 1022, § 101, eff. Sept. 1, 1997.

§ 701. Time for Taking Oath and Giving Bond

The oath of a guardian may be taken and subscribed, or the bond of a guardian may be given and approved, at any time before the expiration of the 20th day after the date of the order granting letters of guardianship, or before the letters have been revoked for a failure to qualify within the time allowed. An oath may be taken before any person authorized to administer oaths under the laws of this state.

Added by Acts 1993, 73rd Leg., ch. 957, § 1, eff. Sept. 1, 1993.

§ 702. Bond Required of Guardian of the Person or Estate

(a) Except as provided by Subsections (b) and (c) of this section, a guardian of the person or of the estate of a ward is required to give bond.

(b) A bond is not required to be given by a guardian that is:

(1) a corporate fiduciary, as defined by Section 601(5) of this code; or

(2) a guardianship program operated by a county.

(c) When a will that is made by a surviving parent and is probated in a court in this state or a written declaration that is made by a surviving parent directs that the guardian appointed in the will or declaration serve without bond, the court finding that the person is qualified shall issue letters of guardianship of the person to the person named to be appointed guardian in the will or declaration without requirement of bond. The court may not waive the requirement of a bond for the guardian of the estate of a ward, regardless of whether a surviving parent's will or declaration directs the court to waive the bond.

Added by Acts 1993, 73rd Leg., ch. 957, § 1, eff. Sept. 1, 1993. Amended by Acts 1995, 74th Leg., ch. 642, § 13, eff. Sept. 1, 1995; Acts 1995, 74th Leg., ch. 1039, § 42, eff. Sept. 1, 1995; Acts 1997, 75th Leg., ch. 924, § 1, eff. Sept. 1, 1997; Acts 1999, 76th Leg., ch. 1078, § 1, eff. Sept. 1, 1999.

Section 78 of Acts 1995, 74th Leg., ch. 1039 provides:

"The change in law made by this Act to Section 702, Texas Probate Code, applies only to a person appointed by a court to serve as guardian on or after the effective date of this Act. A person who is appointed by a court to serve as guardian before the effective date of this Act is governed by the law in effect immediately before the effective date of this Act, and that law is continued in effect for that purpose."

Section 5 of Acts 1997, 75th Leg., ch. 924 provides:

"This Act takes effect September 1, 1997, and applies only to a proceeding for the appointment of a guardian that is instituted on or after that date. A proceeding for the appointment of a guardian that is instituted before the effective date of this Act is governed by the law in effect on the date on which the proceeding was instituted, and the former law is continued in effect for that purpose."

Section 3 of Acts 1999, 76th Leg., ch. 1078 provides:

"This Act takes effect September 1, 1999, and the change in law made by this Act applies only to a written declaration for the appointment of a guardian that is executed on or after the effective date of this Act. A written declaration for the appointment of a guardian that is executed before the effective date of this Act is governed by the law as it existed immediately before the effective date of this Act, and that law is continued in effect for that purpose."

§ 702A. Types of Bonds Acceptable for Guardian of the Person

(a) This section applies only to a bond required to be posted by a guardian of the person of a ward when there is no guardian of the ward's estate.

(b) To ensure the performance of the guardian's duties, the court may accept only:

(1) a corporate surety bond;

(2) a personal surety bond;

(3) a deposit of money instead of a surety bond; or

(4) a personal bond.

(c) In determining the appropriate type and amount of bond to set for the guardian, the court shall consider:

(1) the familial relationship of the guardian to the ward;

(2) the guardian's ties to the community;

(3) the guardian's financial condition;

(4) the guardian's past history of compliance with the court; and

(5) the reason the guardian may have previously been denied a corporate surety bond.

Added by Acts 1997, 75th Leg., ch. 924, § 2, eff. Sept. 1, 1997.

For application provision of Acts 1997, 75th Leg., ch. 924, see notes following V.A.T.S. Probate Code § 702.

§ 703. Bond of Guardian of the Estate

(a) Except when bond is not required under this chapter, before being issued letters of guardianship of estates, the recipient of letters shall give a bond that is conditioned as required by law and that is payable to the judge of the county in which the guardianship proceedings are pending or to the judge's successors in office. A bond of the guardian of the estate must have the written approval of either of the judges in the judge's official capacity and shall be executed and approved in accordance with Subsections (b)–(q) of this section.

(b) The judge shall set the penalty of the bond in an amount that is sufficient to protect the guardianship and its creditors, as provided by this chapter.

(c) If a bond is or will be required of a guardian of an estate, the court, before setting the penalty of the bond, shall hear evidence and determine:

(1) the amount of cash on hand and where deposited, and the amount of cash estimated to be needed for administrative purposes, including the operation of a business, factory, farm, or ranch owned by the guardianship estate, and administrative expenses for one year;

(2) the revenue anticipated to be received in the succeeding 12 months from dividends, interest, rentals, or use of real or personal property belonging to the guardianship estate and the aggregate amount of any installments or periodic payments to be collected;

(3) the estimated value of certificates of stock, bonds, notes, or securities of the ward, the name of the depository in which the stocks, bonds, notes, or securities of the ward are held for safekeeping, the face value of life insurance or other policies payable to the person on whose guardianship administration is sought or to the person's estate, and other personal property that is owned by the guardianship, or by a person with a disability; and

(4) the estimated amount of debts due and owing by the ward.

(d) The judge shall set the penalty of the bond in an amount equal to the estimated value of all personal property belonging to the ward, with an additional amount to cover revenue anticipated to be derived during the succeeding 12 months from interest, dividends, collectible claims, the aggregate amount of any installments or periodic payments exclusive of income derived or to be derived from federal social security payments, and rentals for use of real and personal property, provided that the penalty of the original bond shall be reduced in proportion to the amount of cash or value of securities or other assets authorized or required to be deposited or placed in safekeeping by court order, or voluntarily made by the guardian or by the sureties on the bond of the guardian as provided in Subsections (f) and (g) of this section.

(e) If the court considers it to be in the best interests of the ward, the court may require that the guardian and the corporate or personal sureties on the bond of the guardian of the ward agree to deposit any or all cash and safekeeping of other assets of the guardianship estate in a financial institution as defined by Section 201.101, Finance Code, with its main office or a branch office in this state and qualified to act as a depository in this state under the laws of this state or of the United States, and, if the depository is otherwise proper, the court may require the deposit to be made in a manner so as to prevent the withdrawal of the money or other assets in the guardianship estate without the written consent of the surety or on court order made on the notice to the surety. An agreement made by a guardian and the sureties on the bond of the guardian under this section does not release from liability or change the liability of the principal or sureties as established by the terms of the bond.

(f) Cash, securities, or other personal assets of a ward that a ward is entitled to receive may, and if it is deemed by the court in the best interests of the ward shall, be deposited or placed in safekeeping in one or more of the depositories described in this section on the terms prescribed by the court. The court in which the guardianship proceeding is pending, on its own motion or on written application of the guardian or of any other person interested in the ward, may authorize or require additional assets of the guardianship estate then on hand or as they accrue during the pendency of the guardianship proceeding to be deposited or held in safekeeping as provided by this section. The amount of the guardian's bond shall be reduced in proportion to the cash deposited or the value of the securities or other assets placed in safekeeping. Cash that is deposited, securities or other assets held in safekeeping, or portions of the cash, securities, or other assets held in safekeeping may be withdrawn from a depository only on court order. The bond of the guardian shall be increased in proportion to the amount of cash or the value of securities or other assets that are authorized to be withdrawn.

(g) In lieu of giving a surety or sureties on a bond that is required of the guardian, or for purposes of reducing the amount of the bond, the guardian of an estate may deposit out of the guardian's own assets cash or securities that are acceptable to the court with a financial institution as defined by Section 201.101, Finance Code, with its main office or a branch office in this state. If the deposit is otherwise proper, the deposit must be equal in amount or value to the amount of the bond required or the bond shall be reduced by the value of assets that are deposited.

(h) The depository shall issue a receipt for a deposit in lieu of a surety showing the amount of cash or, if securities, the amount and description of the securities and agreeing not to disburse or deliver the cash or securities except on receipt of a certified copy of an order of the court in which the proceeding is pending. The receipt must be attached to the guardian's bond and be delivered to and filed by the county clerk after the receipt is approved by the judge.

(i) The amount of cash or securities on deposit may be increased or decreased by court order from time to time as the interests of the guardianship shall require.

(j) A cash or security deposit in lieu of a surety on the bond may be withdrawn or released only on order of a court that has jurisdiction.

(k) A creditor has the same rights against the guardian and the deposits as are provided for recovery against sureties on a bond.

(*l*) The court on its own motion or on written application by the guardian or any other person interested in the guardianship may require that the guardian give adequate bond in lieu of the deposit or may authorize withdrawal of the deposit and substitution of a bond with sureties on the bond. In either case, the guardian shall file a sworn statement showing the condition of the guardianship. The guardian is subject to removal as in other cases if the guardian does not file the sworn statement before the 21st day after the guardian is personally served with notice of the filing of the application or before the 21st day after the date the court enters its motion. The deposit may not be released or withdrawn until the court is satisfied as to the condition of the guardianship estate, determines the amount of bond, and receives and approves the bond.

(m) On the closing of a guardianship, a deposit or a portion of a deposit that remains on hand, whether of the assets of the guardian, the guardianship, or surety, shall be released by court order and paid to the person entitled to the assets. A writ of attachment or garnishment does not lie against the deposit except as to claims of creditors of the guardianship being administered or of persons interested in the guardianship, including distributees and wards, and only if the court has ordered distribution, and only to the extent of the ordered distribution.

(n) The surety on the bond may be an authorized corporate or personal surety.

(*o*) When the bond is more than $50,000, the court may require that the bond be signed by two or more authorized corporate sureties or by one corporate surety and two or more good and sufficient personal sureties. The guardianship shall pay the cost of a bond with corporate sureties.

(p) If the sureties are natural persons, there may not be less than two sureties, each of whom shall make affidavit in the manner prescribed by this chapter. The judge must be satisfied that each surety owns property in this state, over and above that exempt by law, sufficient to qualify as a surety as required by law. Except as otherwise provided by law, only one surety is required if the surety is an authorized corporate surety. A personal surety, instead of making an affidavit or creating a lien on specific real estate when an affidavit or lien is required, may deposit the personal surety's own cash or securities in the same manner as a guardian in lieu of pledging real property as security, subject to the provisions covering the deposits when made by guardians.

(q) If the guardian is a temporary guardian, the judge shall set the amount of the bond.

(r) The provisions of this section relating to the deposit of cash and safekeeping of securities cover, as far as they may apply, the orders entered by the court when:

(1) real or personal property of a guardianship has been authorized to be sold or rented;

(2) money is borrowed from the guardianship;

(3) real property, or an interest in real property, has been authorized to be leased for mineral development or made subject to unitization;

(4) the general bond has been found insufficient; or

(5) money is borrowed or invested on behalf of a ward.

(s) In determining the amount of the bond, the court may not take into account the assets of the estate that are placed in a management trust under Subpart N, Part 4,[1] of this code.

Added by Acts 1993, 73rd Leg., ch. 957, § 1, eff. Sept. 1, 1993. Amended by Acts 1999, 76th Leg., ch. 344, § 6.006, eff. Sept. 1, 1999.

[1] Section 867 et seq.

§ 704. Form of Bond

The following form, or the same in substance, may be used for the bonds of guardians:

"The State of Texas

"County of ________

"Know all men by these presents that we, A. B., as principal, and E. F., as sureties, are held and firmly bound to the county judge of the County of ____ and his successors in office, in the sum of $______; conditioned that the above bound A. B., who has been appointed by the judge of the county as guardian or temporary guardian of the person or of the estate, or both, ________, stating in each case whether or not the person is a minor or an incapacitated person other than a minor, shall well and truly perform all of the duties required of the guardian or temporary guardian of the estate by law under appointment."

Added by Acts 1993, 73rd Leg., ch. 957, § 1, eff. Sept. 1, 1993.

§ 705. Bond to be Filed

A bond required under this chapter shall be subscribed by the principals and sureties, and shall be filed with the clerk when approved by the court.

Added by Acts 1993, 73rd Leg., ch. 957, § 1, eff. Sept. 1, 1993.

§ 706. Bond of Joint Guardians

When two or more persons are appointed guardians and are required to give a bond by the court or under this chapter, the court may require either a separate bond from each person or one joint bond from all of the persons.

Added by Acts 1993, 73rd Leg., ch. 957, § 1, eff. Sept. 1, 1993.

§ 707. Bond of Married Persons

When a married person is appointed guardian, the person may jointly execute, with or without, the person's spouse, the bond required by law. The bond shall bind the person's separate estate and may bind the person's spouse only if the bond is signed by the spouse.

Added by Acts 1993, 73rd Leg., ch. 957, § 1, eff. Sept. 1, 1993.

§ 708. Bond of Married Person Younger Than 18 Years of Age

When a person who is younger than 18 years of age and is or has been married accepts and qualifies as guardian, a bond required to be executed by the person shall be as valid and binding for all purposes as if the person were of lawful age.

Added by Acts 1993, 73rd Leg., ch. 957, § 1, eff. Sept. 1, 1993.

§ 708A. Bond of Guardianship Program

The judge may require a guardianship program that is appointed guardian under this chapter to file one bond that:

(1) meets all the conditions required under this chapter; and

(2) is in an amount that is sufficient to protect the guardianship and the creditors of the guardianship of all of the wards of the guardianship program.

Added by Acts 1993, 73rd Leg., ch. 957, § 1, eff. Sept. 1, 1993.

§ 709. Affidavit of Personal Surety; Lien on Specific Property When Required; Subordination of Lien Authorized

(a) Before a judge considers a bond with a personal surety, each personal surety shall execute an affidavit stating the amount of the surety's assets, reachable by creditors, of a value over and above the surety's liabilities. The total of the surety's worth must be equal to at least double the amount of the bond. The affidavit shall be presented to the judge for the judge's consideration and, if approved, shall be attached to and form part of the bond.

(b) If the judge finds that the estimated value of personal property of the guardianship that cannot be deposited or held in safekeeping as provided by this section is such that personal sureties cannot be accepted without the creation of a specific lien on the real property of the sureties, the judge shall enter an order requiring that each surety designate real property owned by the surety in this state subject to execution. The designated property must be of a value over and above all liens and unpaid taxes, equal at least to the amount of the bond, giving an adequate legal description of the property, all of which shall be incorporated in an affidavit by the surety, approved by the judge, and attached to and form part of the bond. If the surety does not comply with the order, the judge may require that the bond be signed by an authorized corporate surety or by an authorized corporate surety and two or more personal sureties.

(c) If a personal surety who has been required to create a lien on specific real estate desires to lease the real property for mineral development, the personal surety may file the surety's written application in the court in which the proceeding is pending to request subordination of the lien to the proposed lease. The judge of the court in which the proceeding is pending may enter an order granting the application. A certified copy of an order entered under this subsection that is filed and recorded in the deed records of the proper county is sufficient to subordinate the lien to the rights of a lessee in the proposed lease.

Added by Acts 1993, 73rd Leg., ch. 957, § 1, eff. Sept. 1, 1993.

§ 710. Bond as Lien on Real Property of Surety

When a personal surety is required by the court to create a lien on specific real property as a condition of the personal surety's acceptance as surety on a bond, a lien on the surety's real property in this state that is described in the affidavit of the surety, and only on the property, shall arise as security for the performance of the obligation of the bond. Before letters are issued to the guardian, the clerk of the court shall mail to the office of the county clerk of each county in which any real property set forth in the surety's affidavit is located a statement signed by the clerk that gives a sufficient description of the real property, the name of the principal and sureties, the amount of the bond, the name of the guardianship, and the court in which the bond is given. The county clerk to whom such statement is sent shall record the statement in the deed records of the county. The recorded statement shall be duly indexed in such a manner that the existence and character of a lien may conveniently be determined, and the recording and indexing of the statement is constructive notice to a person of the existence of the lien on the real property located in the county, effective as of the date of the indexing.

Added by Acts 1993, 73rd Leg., ch. 957, § 1, eff. Sept. 1, 1993.

§ 711. When New Bond May be Required

A guardian may be required to give a new bond when:

(1) one of the sureties on the bond dies, removes beyond the limits of the state, or becomes insolvent;

(2) in the opinion of the court, the sureties on the bond are insufficient;

(3) in the opinion of the court, the bond is defective;

(4) the amount of the bond is insufficient;

(5) one of the sureties petitions the court to be discharged from future liability on the bond; or

(6) the bond and the record of the bond has been lost or destroyed.

Added by Acts 1993, 73rd Leg., ch. 957, § 1, eff. Sept. 1, 1993.

§ 712. Demand for New Bond by Interested Person

A person interested in a guardianship may allege, on application in writing that is filed with the county clerk of the county in which the guardianship proceeding is pending, that the guardian's bond is insufficient or defective or has been, with the record of the bond, lost or destroyed, and may cause the guardian to be cited to appear and show cause why the guardian should not give a new bond.

Added by Acts 1993, 73rd Leg., ch. 957, § 1, eff. Sept. 1, 1993.

§ 713. Judge to Require New Bond

When it is made known to a judge that a bond is insufficient or that the bond has, with the record of the bond, been lost or destroyed, the judge without delay shall cause the guardian to be cited to show cause why the guardian should not give a new bond.

Added by Acts 1993, 73rd Leg., ch. 957, § 1, eff. Sept. 1, 1993.

§ 714. Order Requiring New Bond

On the return of a citation ordering a guardian to show cause why the guardian should not give a new bond, the judge on the day contained in the return of citation as the day for the hearing of the matter, shall proceed to inquire into the sufficiency of the reasons for requiring a new bond. If the judge is satisfied that a new bond should be required, the judge shall enter an order to that effect that states the amount of the new bond and the time within which the new bond shall be given, which may not be later than 20 days from the date of the order issued by the judge under this section.

Added by Acts 1993, 73rd Leg., ch. 957, § 1, eff. Sept. 1, 1993.

§ 715. Order Suspends Powers of Guardians

When a guardian is required to give a new bond, the order requiring the bond has the effect of suspending the guardian's powers, and the guardian may not pay out any money of the guardianship or do any other official act, except to preserve the property of the guardianship, until a new bond has been given and approved.

Added by Acts 1993, 73rd Leg., ch. 957, § 1, eff. Sept. 1, 1993.

§ 716. Decrease in Amount of Bond

A guardian required to give bond at any time may file with the clerk a written application to the court to have the bond reduced. After an application has been filed by the guardian under this section, the clerk shall issue and cause to be posted notice to all persons interested in the estate and to a surety on the bond, apprising the persons and surety of the fact and nature of the application and of the time at which the judge will hear the application. The judge may permit the filing of a new bond in a reduced amount on the submission of proof that a smaller bond than the one in effect will be adequate to meet the requirements of the law and protect the guardianship and on the approval of an accounting filed at the time of the application.

Added by Acts 1993, 73rd Leg., ch. 957, § 1, eff. Sept. 1, 1993.

§ 717. Discharge of Sureties on Execution of New Bond

When a new bond has been given and approved, the judge shall enter an order discharging the sureties on the former bond from all liability for the future acts of the principal.

Added by Acts 1993, 73rd Leg., ch. 957, § 1, eff. Sept. 1, 1993.

§ 718. Release of Sureties Before Guardianship Fully Administered

A surety on the guardian's bond at any time may file with the clerk a petition with the court in which the proceeding is pending, praying that the guardian be required to give a new bond and that the petitioner be discharged from all liability for the future acts of the guardian. If a petition is filed, the guardian shall be cited to appear and give a new bond.

Added by Acts 1993, 73rd Leg., ch. 957, § 1, eff. Sept. 1, 1993.

§ 719. Release of Lien Before Guardianship Fully Administered

If a personal surety who has given a lien on specific real property as security applies to the court to have the lien released, the court shall order the release requested if the court is satisfied that the bond is sufficient without the lien on the property or if sufficient other real or personal property of the surety is substituted on the same terms and conditions required for the lien that is to be released. If the personal surety who requests the release of the lien does not offer a lien on other real or personal property and if the court is not satisfied that the bond is sufficient without the substitution of other property, the court shall order the guardian to appear and give a new bond.

Added by Acts 1993, 73rd Leg., ch. 957, § 1, eff. Sept. 1, 1993.

§ 720. Release of Recorded Lien on Surety's Property

A certified copy of the court order that describes the property, releases the lien, and is filed with the county clerk and recorded in the deed records of the county in which the property is located has the effect of cancelling the lien on the property.

Added by Acts 1993, 73rd Leg., ch. 957, § 1, eff. Sept. 1, 1993.

§ 721. Revocation of Letters for Failure to Give Bond

If a guardian of a ward fails to give the bond required by the court within the time required under this chapter, another person may be appointed guardian of the ward.

Added by Acts 1993, 73rd Leg., ch. 957, § 1, eff. Sept. 1, 1993.

§ 722. Guardian Without Bond Required to Give Bond

If a bond is not required of an individual guardian of the estate, a person who has a debt, claim, or demand against the guardianship, to the justice of which oath has been made by the person, the person's agent or attorney, or any other person interested in the guardianship, in person or as the representative of another person, may file a complaint under oath in writing in the court in which the guardian was appointed, and the court, after a complaint is filed under this section, shall cite the guardian to appear and show cause why the guardian should not be required to give bond.

Added by Acts 1993, 73rd Leg., ch. 957, § 1, eff. Sept. 1, 1993.

§ 723. Order Requiring Bond

On hearing a complaint under Section 722 of this code, if it appears to the court that a guardian is wasting, mismanaging, or misapplying the guardianship estate and that a creditor may probably lose his debt, or that a person's interest in the guardianship may be diminished or lost, the court shall enter an order requiring the guardian to give a bond not later than the 10th day after the date of the order.

Added by Acts 1993, 73rd Leg., ch. 957, § 1, eff. Sept. 1, 1993.

§ 724. Amount of Bond

A bond that is required under Section 723 of this code shall be in an amount that is sufficient to protect the guardianship and its creditors. The bond shall be approved by and payable to the judge and shall be conditioned that the guardian will well and truly administer the guardianship and that the guardian will not waste, mismanage, or misapply the guardianship estate.

Added by Acts 1993, 73rd Leg., ch. 957, § 1, eff. Sept. 1, 1993.

§ 725. Failure to Give Bond

If the guardian fails to give the bond required under Section 723 of this code, and the judge does not extend the time, the judge, without citation, shall remove the guardian and appoint a competent person as guardian of the ward who:

(1) shall administer the guardianship according to the provisions of a will or law;

(2) shall take the oath required of a guardian as the case may be before the person enters on the administration of the guardianship; and

(3) shall give bond in the same manner and in the same amount provided in this chapter for the issuance of original letters of guardianship.

Added by Acts 1993, 73rd Leg., ch. 957, § 1, eff. Sept. 1, 1993.

§ 726. Bonds Not Void on First Recovery

The bond of a guardian is not void on the first recovery, but the bond may be sued on and prosecuted from time to time until the whole amount of the bond is recovered.

Added by Acts 1993, 73rd Leg., ch. 957, § 1, eff. Sept. 1, 1993.

PART 4. ADMINISTRATION OF GUARDIANSHIP

SUBPART A. INVENTORY, APPRAISEMENT, AND LIST OF CLAIMS

§ 727. Appointment of Appraisers

After letters of guardianship of the estate have been granted and on the application of any interested person, or if the court deems it necessary, the court shall appoint at least one but not more than three disinterested persons who are citizens of the county in which letters were granted to appraise the property of the ward. If the court appoints an appraiser under this section and part of the estate is located in a county other than the county in which letters were granted, the court may appoint at least one but not more than three disinterested persons who are citizens of the county in which the part of the estate is located to appraise the property of the estate located in the county if the court considers it necessary to appoint an appraiser.

Added by Acts 1993, 73rd Leg., ch. 957, § 1, eff. Sept. 1, 1993.

For applicability provisions of the 1993 Act, see notes following § 601.

§ 728. Failure of Appraiser to Serve

If an appraiser appointed under Section 727 of this code fails or refuses to act, the court shall remove the appraiser and appoint one or more appraisers.

Added by Acts 1993, 73rd Leg., ch. 957, § 1, eff. Sept. 1, 1993.

§ 729. Inventory and Appraisement

(a) Not later than the 90th day after the date the guardian of the estate qualifies as guardian, unless a longer time is granted by the court, the guardian of the estate shall file with the clerk of court a verified, full and detailed inventory, in one written instrument, of all the property of the ward that has come into the guardian's possession or knowledge. The inventory filed by the guardian under this section must include:

(1) all real property of the ward that is located in this state; and

(2) all personal property of the ward wherever located.

(b) The guardian shall set out in the inventory the guardian's appraisement of the fair market value of each item of the property on the date of the grant of letters of guardianship. If the court appoints an appraiser of the estate, the guardian shall determine the fair market value of each item of the inventory with the assistance of the appraiser and shall set out in the inventory the appraisement made by the appraiser.

(c) An inventory made under this section must specify what portion of the property is separate property and what portion is community property. If any property is owned in common with other persons, the interest owned by the ward shall be shown in the inventory, together with the names and relationship, if known, of co-owners.

(d) The inventory, when approved by the court and duly filed with the clerk of court, is for purposes of this chapter the inventory and appraisement of the estate referred to in this chapter.

(e) The court for good cause shown may require the filing of the inventory and appraisement at a time not later than the 90th day after the date of qualification of the guardian.

Added by Acts 1993, 73rd Leg., ch. 957, § 1, eff. Sept. 1, 1993.

§ 730. List of Claims

The guardian shall make and attach to an inventory under Section 729 of this code a full and complete list of all claims due or owing to the ward that must state:

(1) the name of each person indebted to the ward and the address of the person if known;

(2) the nature of the debt, whether it is a note, bill, bond, or other written obligation or whether it is an account or verbal contract;

(3) the date of the indebtedness and the date when the debt is or was due;

(4) the amount of each claim, the rate of interest on each claim, and time for which the claim bears interest; and

(5) what portion of the claim is held in common with others, including the names and the relationships of other part owners and the interest of the estate in the claim.

Added by Acts 1993, 73rd Leg., ch. 957, § 1, eff. Sept. 1, 1993.

§ 731. Affidavit Attached

The guardian of the estate shall attach to the inventory and list of claims the guardian's affidavit subscribed and sworn to before an officer in the county authorized by law to administer oaths that the inventory and list of claims are a true and complete statement of the property and claims of the estate that have come to the guardian's knowledge.

Added by Acts 1993, 73rd Leg., ch. 957, § 1, eff. Sept. 1, 1993.

§ 732. Appraiser Fees

An appraiser appointed by the court is entitled to receive a reasonable fee for the performance of the appraiser's duties as an appraiser that are to be paid out of the estate.

Added by Acts 1993, 73rd Leg., ch. 957, § 1, eff. Sept. 1, 1993.

§ 733. Court Action

(a) On return of the inventory, appraisement, and list of claims, the judge shall examine and approve or disapprove the inventory, appraisement, or list of claims as follows:

(1) if the judge approves the inventory, appraisement, and list of claims, the judge shall issue an order to that effect; and

(2) if the judge does not approve the inventory, appraisement, or list of claims, the judge shall enter an order to that effect.

(b) The court order shall require the return of another inventory, appraisement, and list of claims, or whichever of them is disapproved, within a time specified in the order but not later than 20 days after the date of the order. The judge may appoint new appraisers if the judge deems it necessary.

Added by Acts 1993, 73rd Leg., ch. 957, § 1, eff. Sept. 1, 1993.

§ 734. Discovery of Additional Property

The guardian of the estate shall promptly file with the clerk of court a verified, full, and detailed supplemental inventory and appraisement if property or claims that are not included in the inventory come to the guardian's possession or knowledge after the guardian files the inventory and appraisement required under Section 729 of this code.

Added by Acts 1993, 73rd Leg., ch. 957, § 1, eff. Sept. 1, 1993.

§ 735. Additional Inventory or List of Claims

(a) On the written complaint of an interested person that property or claims of the estate have not been included in the inventory and list of claims filed by the guardian, the guardian of an estate shall be cited to appear before the court in which the cause is pending and show cause why the guardian should not be required to make and return an additional inventory or list of claims, or both.

(b) After hearing a complaint filed under this section and being satisfied of the truth of the complaint, the court shall enter an order requiring the additional inventory or list of claims, or both, to be made and returned in like manner as the original inventory, not later than 20 days after the date of the order, as may be set by the court. The additional inventory or list of claims must include only property or claims that were not inventoried or listed by the guardian.

Added by Acts 1993, 73rd Leg., ch. 957, § 1, eff. Sept. 1, 1993.

§ 736. Correction When Inventory, Appraisement, or List of Claims Erroneous or Unjust

A person interested in an estate who deems an inventory, appraisement, or list of claims returned by the guardian erroneous or unjust in any particular form may file a written complaint that sets forth and points out the alleged erroneous or unjust items and cause the guardian to be cited to appear before the court and show cause why the errors should not be corrected. On the hearing of a complaint filed under this section, if the court is satisfied from the evidence that the inventory, appraisement, or list of claims is erroneous or unjust in any particular form as alleged in the complaint, the court shall enter an order that specifies the erroneous or unjust items and the corrections to be made and that appoints an appraiser to make a new appraisement correcting the erroneous or unjust items and requires the return of the new appraisement not later than the 20th day after the date of the order. The court may also, on its own motion or on motion of the guardian of the estate, have a new appraisal made for the purposes described by this section.

Added by Acts 1993, 73rd Leg., ch. 957, § 1, eff. Sept. 1, 1993.

§ 737. Effect of Reappraisement

When a reappraisement is made, returned, and approved by the court, the reappraisement stands in place of the original appraisement. Not more than one reappraisement shall be made, but any person interested in the estate may object to the reappraisement before or after the reappraisement is approved. If the court finds that the reappraisement is erroneous or unjust, the court shall appraise the property on the basis of the evidence before the court.

Added by Acts 1993, 73rd Leg., ch. 957, § 1, eff. Sept. 1, 1993.

§ 738. Failure of Joint Guardians to Return an Inventory, Appraisement, and List of Claims

If there is more than one qualified guardian of the estate, one or more of the guardians, on the neglect of the other guardians, may make and return an inventory and appraisement and list of claims. The guardian so neglecting may not thereafter interfere with the estate or have any power over the estate. The guardian that returns an inventory, appraisement, and list of claims has the whole administration, unless, not later than the 60th day after the date of return, each of the delinquent guardians assigns to the court in writing and under oath a reasonable excuse that the court may deem satisfactory. If no excuse is filed or if the excuse filed by a delinquent guardian is insufficient, the court shall enter an order removing the delinquent guardian and revoking the guardian's letters.

Added by Acts 1993, 73rd Leg., ch. 957, § 1, eff. Sept. 1, 1993.

§ 739. Use of Inventories, Appraisements, and Lists of Claims as Evidence

All inventories, appraisements, and lists of claims that have been taken, returned, and approved in accordance with the law, or the record of an inventory, appraisement, or list of claims, or copies of either the originals or the record, duly certified under the seal of the county court affixed by the clerk, may be given in evidence in any of the courts of this state in any suit by or against the guardian of the estate, but may not be conclusive for or against the guardian of the estate if it is shown that any property or claims of the estate are not shown in the inventory, appraisement, or list of claims or that the value of the property or claims of the estate actually was in excess of the value shown in the appraisement and list of claims.

Added by Acts 1993, 73rd Leg., ch. 957, § 1, eff. Sept. 1, 1993.

SUBPART B. ANNUAL ACCOUNTS, REPORTS, AND OTHER EXHIBITS

§ 741. Annual Accounts Required

(a) Not later than the 60th day after the expiration of 12 months from the date of qualification, unless the court extends that time period, the guardian of the estate of a ward shall return to the court an exhibit in writing under oath setting forth a list of all claims against the estate that were presented to the guardian within the period covered by the account and specifying which claims have been allowed, paid, or rejected by the guardian and the date when any claim was rejected and which claims have been the subject of a lawsuit and the status of the lawsuit, and showing:

(1) all property that has come to the guardian's knowledge or into the guardian's possession that has not been previously listed or inventoried as property of the ward;

(2) any changes in the property of the ward that have not been previously reported;

(3) a complete account of receipts and disbursements for the period covered by the account, and the source and nature of the receipts and disbursements, with receipts of principal and income shown separately;

(4) a complete, accurate, and detailed description of the property being administered, the condition of the property, and the use being made of the property and, if rented, the terms of the rental and the price for which the property is being rented;

(5) the cash balance on hand and the name and location of the depository where the cash balance is kept and any other sums of cash in savings accounts or other form, deposited subject to court order, and the name and location of the depository of the cash; and

(6) a detailed description of personal property of the estate, that, with respect to bonds, notes, and other securities, includes the names of obligor and obligee, or if payable to bearer, so state; the date of issue and maturity; the rate of interest; serial or other identifying numbers; in what manner the property is secured; and other data necessary to identify the same fully, and how and where held for safekeeping.

(b) A guardian of the estate shall file annual accounts conforming to the essential requirements of those in Subsection (a) of this section as to changes in the assets of the estate after rendition of the former account so that the true condition of the estate, with respect to money or securities or other property, can be ascertained by the court or by any interested person, by adding to the balances forward the receipts, and then subtracting the disbursements. The description of property sufficiently described in an inventory or previous account may be by reference to the property.

(c) The following shall be annexed to all annual accounts of guardians of estates:

(1) proper vouchers for each item of credit claimed in the account, or, in the absence of a voucher, the item must be supported by evidence satisfactory to the court, and original vouchers may, on application, be returned to the guardian after approval of the guardian's account;

(2) an official letter from the bank or other depository in which the money on hand of the estate or ward is deposited that shows the amounts in general or special deposits; and

(3) proof of the existence and possession of securities owned by the estate, or shown by the accounting, and other assets held by a depository subject to court order, the proof by one of the following means:

(A) an official letter from the bank or other depository that holds the securities or other assets for safekeeping; provided, that if the depository is the representative, the official letter shall be signed by a representative of the depository other than the depository that verifies the account;

(B) a certificate of an authorized representative of the corporation that is the surety on the representative's bonds;

(C) a certificate of the clerk or a deputy clerk of a court of record in this state; or

(D) an affidavit of any other reputable person designated by the court on request of the guardian or other interested party.

(d) A certificate or affidavit under this section shall be to the effect that the affiant has examined the assets exhibited to the affiant by the guardian as assets of the estate in which the accounting is made, shall describe the assets by reference to the account or otherwise sufficiently to identify those assets exhibited, and shall state the time when and the place where the assets were exhibited. Instead of using a certificate or an affidavit, the representative may exhibit the securities to the judge of the court who shall endorse on the account, or include in the judge's order with respect to the account, a statement that the securities shown to the judge as on hand were in fact exhibited to the judge and that those securities exhibited to the judge were the same as those shown in the account, or note any variance. If the securities are exhibited at any place other than where deposited for safekeeping, it shall be at the expense and risk of the representative. The judge may require additional evidence as to the existence and custody of the securities and other personal property as in the judge's discretion the judge considers proper, and the judge may require the representative to exhibit the securities to the judge, or any person designated by the judge, at any time at the place where the securities are held for safekeeping.

(e) The guardian of the estate filing the account shall attach to the account the guardian's affidavit that:

(1) the account contains a correct and complete statement of the matters to which the account relates;

(2) the guardian has paid the bond premium for the next accounting period;

(3) the guardian has filed all tax returns of the ward due during the accounting period; and

(4) the guardian has paid all taxes the ward owed during the accounting period, showing:

(A) the amount of the taxes;

(B) the date the guardian paid the taxes; and

(C) the name of the governmental entity to which the guardian paid the taxes.

(f) If the guardian, on the ward's behalf, has not filed a tax return or paid taxes that are due on the filing of the account under this section, the guardian of the estate filing the account shall attach to the account a description of the taxes and the reasons for the guardian's failure to file the return or pay the taxes.

(g) If the estate produces negligible or fixed income, the court has the power to waive the filing of annual accounts, and the court may permit the guardian to receive all income and apply it to the support, maintenance, and education of the ward and account to the court for income and corpus of the estate when the estate must be closed.

Added by Acts 1993, 73rd Leg., ch. 957, § 1, eff. Sept. 1, 1993.

For applicability provisions of the 1993 Act, see notes following § 601.

§ 742. Action on Annual Accounts

(a) The rules in this section govern the handling of annual accounts.

(b) Annual accounts shall be filed with the county clerk, and the filing of the accounts shall be noted on the judge's docket.

(c) Before being considered by the judge, the account must remain on file for 10 days.

(d) After the expiration of 10 days after the filing of an annual account, the judge shall consider the annual account, and may continue the hearing on the account until the judge is fully advised as to all items of the account.

(e) An accounting may not be approved unless possession of cash, listed securities, or other assets held in safekeeping or on deposit under court order has been proved as required by law.

(f) If an account is found to be incorrect, it shall be corrected. When corrected to the satisfaction of the court, the account shall be approved by a court order, and the court shall act with respect to unpaid claims, as follows:

(1) if it appears from the exhibit, or from other evidence, that the estate is wholly solvent, and that the guardian has sufficient funds for the payment of

every claim against the estate, the court shall order immediate payment made of all claims allowed and approved or established by judgment; and

(2) if it appears from the account, or from other evidence, that the funds on hand are not sufficient for the payment of all the claims, or if the estate is insolvent and the guardian has any funds on hand, the court shall order the funds to be applied to the payment of all claims having a preference in the order of their priority if any claim is still unpaid, and then to the payment pro rata of the other claims allowed and approved or established by final judgment, taking into consideration also the claims that were presented not later than 12 months after the date of the granting of letters of guardianship and those claims that are in suit or on which suit may yet be instituted.

Added by Acts 1993, 73rd Leg., ch. 957, § 1, eff. Sept. 1, 1993. Amended by Acts 1995, 74th Leg., ch. 1039, § 43, eff. Sept. 1, 1995.

§ 743. Reports of Guardians of the Person

(a) The guardian of the person of a ward shall return to the court a sworn, written report showing each item of receipts and disbursements for the support and maintenance of the ward, the education of the ward when necessary, and support and maintenance of the ward's dependents, when authorized by order of court.

(b) The guardian of the person, whether or not there is a separate guardian of the estate, shall submit to the court an annual report by sworn affidavit that contains the following information:

(1) the guardian's current name, address, and phone number;

(2) the ward's current:

(A) name, address, and phone number; and

(B) age and date of birth;

(3) the type of home in which the ward resides, described as the ward's own; a nursing, guardian's, foster, or boarding home; a relative's home, and the ward's relationship to the relative; a hospital or medical facility; or other type of residence;

(4) the length of time the ward has resided in the present home and, if there has been a change in the ward's residence in the past year, the reason for the change;

(5) the date the guardian most recently saw the ward, and how frequently the guardian has seen the ward in the past year;

(6) a statement indicating whether or not the guardian has possession or control of the ward's estate;

(7) the following statements concerning the ward's health during the past year:

(A) whether the ward's mental health has improved, deteriorated, or remained unchanged, and a description if there has been a change; and

(B) whether the ward's physical health has improved, deteriorated, or remained unchanged, and a description if there has been a change;

(8) a statement concerning whether or not the ward has regular medical care, and the ward's treatment or evaluation by any of the following persons during the last year, including the name of that person, and the treatment involved:

(A) a physician;

(B) a psychiatrist, psychologist, or other mental health care provider;

(C) a dentist;

(D) a social or other caseworker; or

(E) another individual who provided treatment;

(9) a description of the ward's activities during the past year, including recreational, educational, social, and occupational activities, or if no activities are available or if the ward is unable or has refused to participate in them, a statement to that effect;

(10) the guardian's evaluation of the ward's living arrangements as excellent, average, or below average, including an explanation if the conditions are below average;

(11) the guardian's evaluation of whether the ward is content or unhappy with the ward's living arrangements;

(12) the guardian's evaluation of unmet needs of the ward;

(13) a statement of whether or not the guardian's power should be increased, decreased, or unaltered, including an explanation if a change is recommended;

(14) a statement that the guardian has paid the bond premium for the next reporting period; and

(15) any additional information the guardian desires to share with the court regarding the ward.

(c) If the ward is deceased, the guardian shall provide the court with the date and place of death, if known, in lieu of the information about the ward otherwise required to be provided in the annual report.

(d) Unless the judge is satisfied that the facts stated are true, he shall issue orders as are necessary for the best interests of the ward.

(e) If the judge is satisfied that the facts stated in the report are true, the court shall approve the report.

(f) The court on the court's own motion may waive the costs and fees related to the filing of a report approved under Subsection (e) of this section.

(g) Once each year for the duration of the guardianship, a guardian of the person shall file the report that contains the information required by Subsections (a) and (b) of this section. Except as provided by Subsection (h) of this section, the report must cover a 12-month reporting period that begins on the date the guardian qualifies to serve.

(h) The court may change a reporting period for purposes of this section but may not extend a reporting period so that it covers more than 12 months.

(i) Each report is due not later than the 60th day after the date on which the reporting period ends.

(j) A guardian of the person may complete and file the report required under this section without the assistance of an attorney.

Added by Acts 1993, 73rd Leg., ch. 957, § 1, eff. Sept. 1, 1993. Amended by Acts 1995, 74th Leg., ch. 1039, §§ 44, 45, eff. Sept. 1, 1995; Acts 1997, 75th Leg., ch. 1403, § 3, eff. Sept. 1, 1997; Acts 1999, 76th Leg., ch. 905, § 5, eff. Sept. 1, 1999.

Sections 6 to 8 of Acts 1997, 75th Leg., ch. 1403 provide:

"Sec. 6. A court may modify any guardianship in effect on September 1, 1997, to conform with the requirements of Section 805, Texas Probate Code, as amended by this Act, on the court's own motion or on application by the ward, guardian, or any other interested person or entity.

"Sec. 7. The change in law made by Sections 1–4 of this Act to the Texas Probate Code apply only to an account or report filed on or after the effective date of this Act. An account or report filed before the effective date of this Act is governed by the law applicable on the date the account or report was filed, and that law is continued in effect for that purpose.

"Sec. 8. Except as provided by Section 6 of this Act:

"(1) the change in law made by this Act to Section 805, Texas Probate Code, applies only to proceedings for the appointment of a guardian instituted on or after the effective date of this Act; and

"(2) a proceeding for the appointment of a guardian that is instituted before the effective date of this Act is governed by the law in effect on the date the proceedings were instituted, and the former law is continued in effect for that purpose."

Section 7 of Acts 1999, 76th Leg., ch. 905 provides:

"(a) Section 743(j), Texas Probate Code, as added by this Act, applies only to an account or report filed on or after the effective date of this Act.

"(b) An account or report filed before the effective date of this Act is governed by the law in effect on the date the account or report was filed, and the former law is continued in effect for that purpose."

§ 744. Penalty for Failure to File Accountings, Exhibits, or Reports

If a guardian fails to file any accounting, exhibit, report of the guardian of the person, or other report required by this chapter, any person interested in the estate may, on written complaint filed with the clerk of the court, or the court on its own motion, may cause the guardian to be cited to appear and show cause why the guardian should not file the account, exhibit, or report; and, on hearing, the court may order the guardian to file the account, exhibit, or report, and, unless good cause is shown for the failure to file the account, exhibit, or report, the court may fine the guardian an amount not to exceed $1,000, revoke the letters of the guardian, or fine the guardian an amount not to exceed $1,000 and revoke the letters of the guardian.

Added by Acts 1993, 73rd Leg., ch. 957, § 1, eff. Sept. 1, 1993. Amended by Acts 1995, 74th Leg., ch. 1039, § 46, eff. Sept. 1, 1995.

SUBPART C. FINAL SETTLEMENT, ACCOUNTING, AND DISCHARGE

§ 745. Closing Guardianships of the Estate

(a) A guardianship of the estate of a ward is settled and closed when:

(1) a minor ward dies or becomes an adult by becoming 18 years of age, or by removal of disabilities of minority according to the law of this state, or by marriage;

(2) an incapacitated ward dies, or is decreed as provided by law to have been restored to full legal capacity;

(3) the spouse of a married ward has qualified as survivor in community and the ward owns no separate property;

(4) the estate of a ward becomes exhausted;

(5) the foreseeable income accruing to a ward or to his estate is so negligible that maintaining the guardianship in force would be burdensome;

(6) all of the assets of the estate have been placed in a management trust under Subpart N, Part 4, of this code and the court determines that a guardianship for the ward is no longer necessary; or

(7) the court determines for any other reason that a guardianship for the ward is no longer necessary.

(b) In a case arising under Subsection (a)(5) of this section, the court may authorize the income to be paid to a parent, or other person who has acted as guardian of the ward, to assist in the maintenance of the ward and without liability to account to the court for the income.

(c) When the estate of a minor ward consists only of cash or cash equivalents in an amount of $25,000 or less, the guardianship of the estate may be terminated and the assets paid to the county clerk of the county in which the guardianship proceeding is pending, and the clerk shall manage the funds as provided by Section 887 of this code.

(d) In the settlement and closing of a guardianship, the court may appoint an attorney ad litem to represent the interests of the ward, and may allow the attorney reasonable compensation for services provided by the attorney out of the ward's estate.

Added by Acts 1993, 73rd Leg., ch. 957, § 1, eff. Sept. 1, 1993. Amended by Acts 1995, 74th Leg., ch. 1039, § 47, eff. Sept. 1, 1995.

For applicability provisions of the 1993 Act, see notes following § 601.

§ 746. Payment of Funeral Expenses and Other Debts

Notwithstanding Section 745 of this code, before the guardianship of a person or estate of a ward is closed on the death of a ward, the guardian, subject to the approval of the court, may make all funeral arrangements, pay for the funeral expenses out of the estate of the deceased ward, and pay all other debts out of the estate. If a personal representative of the estate of a deceased ward is appointed, the court shall on the written complaint of the personal representative cause the guardian to be cited to appear and present a final account as provided in Section 749 of this code.

Added by Acts 1993, 73rd Leg., ch. 957, § 1, eff. Sept. 1, 1993.

§ 747. Termination of Guardianship of the Person

(a) When the guardianship of an incapacitated person is settled and closed as provided by Section 745 of this code, the guardian of the person shall deliver all property of the ward in the possession or control of the guardian to the emancipated ward or other person entitled to the property. If the ward is deceased, the guardian shall deliver the property to the personal representative of the deceased ward's estate or other person entitled to the property.

(b) If there is no property of the ward in the possession or control of the guardian of the person, the guardian shall file with the court a sworn affidavit that states the reason the guardianship was terminated and to whom the property of the ward in the guardian's possession was delivered. The judge may issue orders as necessary for the best interests of the ward or of the estate of a deceased ward. This section does not discharge a guardian of the person from liability for breach of the guardian's fiduciary duties.

Added by Acts 1993, 73rd Leg., ch. 957, § 1, eff. Sept. 1, 1993.

§ 748. Payment by Guardian of Taxes or Expenses

Notwithstanding any other provision of this chapter, a probate court in which proceedings to declare heirship are maintained may order the payment by the guardian of any and all taxes or expenses of administering the estate and may order the sale of properties in the ward's estate, when necessary, for the purpose of paying the taxes or expenses of administering the estate or for the purpose of distributing the estate among the heirs.

Added by Acts 1993, 73rd Leg., ch. 957, § 1, eff. Sept. 1, 1993.

§ 749. Account for Final Settlement of Estates of Wards

When a guardianship of the estate is settled and closed, the guardian shall present to the court the guardian's verified account for final settlement. In the account it shall be sufficient to refer to the inventory without describing each item of property in detail and to refer to and adopt any and all guardianship proceedings that concern sales, renting or hiring, leasing for mineral development, or any other transaction on behalf of the guardianship estate, including an exhibit, account, or voucher previously filed and approved, without restating the particular items. Each final account shall be accompanied by proper vouchers in support of each item not already accounted for and shall show, either by reference to any proceedings authorized above or by statement of the facts:

(1) the property, rents, revenues, and profits received by the guardian, and belonging to the ward, during the term of the guardianship;

(2) the disposition made of the property, rents, revenues, and profits;

(3) the expenses and debts against the estate that remain unpaid, if any;

(4) the property of the estate that remains in the hands of the guardian, if any;

(5) that the guardian has paid all required bond premiums;

(6) the tax returns the guardian has filed during the guardianship;

(7) the amount of taxes the ward owed during the guardianship that the guardian has paid;

(8) a complete account of the taxes the guardian has paid during the guardianship, including the amount of the taxes, the date the guardian paid the taxes, and the name of the governmental entity to which the guardian paid the taxes;

(9) a description of all current delinquencies in the filing of tax returns and the payment of taxes and a reason for each delinquency; and

(10) other facts as appear necessary to a full and definite understanding of the exact condition of the guardianship.

Added by Acts 1993, 73rd Leg., ch. 957, § 1, eff. Sept. 1, 1993. Amended by Acts 1997, 75th Leg., ch. 1403, § 4, eff. Sept. 1, 1997.

Sections 6 to 8 of Acts 1997, 75th Leg., ch. 1403 provide:

"Sec. 6. A court may modify any guardianship in effect on September 1, 1997, to conform with the requirements of Section 805, Texas Probate Code, as amended by this Act, on the court's own motion or on application by the ward, guardian, or any other interested person or entity.

"Sec. 7. The change in law made by Sections 1–4 of this Act to the Texas Probate Code apply only to an account or report filed on or after the effective date of this Act. An account or report filed before the effective date of this Act is governed by the law applicable on the date the account or report was filed, and that law is continued in effect for that purpose.

"Sec. 8. Except as provided by Section 6 of this Act:

"(1) the change in law made by this Act to Section 805, Texas Probate Code, applies only to proceedings for the appointment of a guardian instituted on or after the effective date of this Act; and

"(2) a proceeding for the appointment of a guardian that is instituted before the effective date of this Act is governed by the law in effect on the date the proceedings were instituted, and the former law is continued in effect for that purpose."

§ 750. Procedure in Case of Neglect or Failure to File Final Account or Report

(a) If a guardian charged with the duty of filing a final account or report fails or neglects so to do at the proper time, the court may, on the court's own motion, or on the written complaint of the emancipated ward or anyone interested in the ward or the ward's estate, shall cause the guardian to be cited to appear and present the account or report within the time specified in the citation.

(b) If a written complaint has not been filed by anyone interested in the guardianship of a person or estate of a minor or deceased ward, the court may, on or after the third anniversary after the date of the death of the ward or after the date the minor reaches the age of majority, remove the estate from the court's active docket without a final accounting and without appointing a successor personal representative.

(c) If a complaint has not been filed by anyone interested in the estate of a ward whose whereabouts are unknown to the court, the court may, on or after the fourth anniversary after the ward's whereabouts became unknown to the court, remove the estate from the court's active docket without a final accounting and without appointing a successor personal representative.

Added by Acts 1993, 73rd Leg., ch. 957, § 1, eff. Sept. 1, 1993.

§ 751. Citation on Presentation of Account for Final Settlement

(a) On the filing of an account for final settlement by a guardian of the estate of a ward, citation must contain a statement that the final account has been filed, the time and place when it will be considered by the court, and a statement requiring the person cited to appear and contest the final account if the person determines it is proper. The county clerk shall issue the citation to the following persons and in the manner provided by this section.

(b) If a ward is a living resident of this state who is 14 years of age or older, and the ward's residence is known, the ward shall be cited by personal service, unless the ward, in person or by attorney, by writing filed with the clerk, waives the issuance and personal service of citation.

(c) If one who has been a ward is deceased, the ward's executor or administrator, if one has been appointed, shall be personally served, but no service is required if the executor or administrator is the same person as the guardian.

(d) If a ward's residence is unknown, or if the ward is a nonresident of this state, or if the ward is deceased and no representative of the ward's estate has been appointed and qualified in this state, the citation to the ward or to the ward's estate shall be by publication, unless the court by written order directs citation by posting.

(e) If the court deems further additional notice necessary, it shall require the additional notice by written order. In its discretion, the court may allow the waiver of notice of an account for final settlement in a guardianship proceeding.

Added by Acts 1993, 73rd Leg., ch. 957, § 1, eff. Sept. 1, 1993.

§ 752. Court Action

(a) On being satisfied that citation has been duly served on all persons interested in the estate, the court shall examine the account for final settlement and the vouchers accompanying the account. After hearing all exceptions or objections to the account and evidence in support of or against the account, the court shall audit and settle the same, and restate it if that is necessary.

(b) On final settlement of an estate, if there is any part of the estate remaining in the hands of the guardian, the court shall order that it be delivered, in case of a ward, to the ward, or in the case of a deceased ward, to the personal representative of the deceased ward's estate if one has been appointed, or to any other person legally entitled to the estate.

(c) If on final settlement of an estate there is no part of the estate remaining in the hands of the guardian, the court shall discharge the guardian from the guardian's trust and order the estate closed.

(d) When the guardian of an estate has fully administered the estate in accordance with this chapter and the orders of the court and the guardian's final account has been approved, and the guardian has delivered all of the estate remaining in the guardian's hands to any person entitled to receive the estate, the court shall enter an order discharging the guardian from the guardian's trust, and declaring the estate closed.

Added by Acts 1993, 73rd Leg., ch. 957, § 1, eff. Sept. 1, 1993.

§ 753. Money Becoming Due Pending Final Discharge

Money or any other thing of value falling due to the estate or ward while the account for final settlement is pending, other than money or any other thing of value held under Section 703(c) of this code, until the order of final discharge of the guardian is entered in the minutes of the court, may be paid, delivered, or tendered to the emancipated ward, the guardian, or the personal representative of the deceased ward's estate, who shall issue a receipt for the money or other thing of value, and the obligor or payor shall be discharged of the obligation for all purposes.

Added by Acts 1993, 73rd Leg., ch. 957, § 1, eff. Sept. 1, 1993.

§ 754. Inheritance Taxes Must be Paid

If the guardian has been ordered to make payment of inheritance taxes under this code, an estate of a deceased ward may not be closed unless the final account shows and the court finds that all inheritance taxes due and owing to this state with respect to all interests and properties passing through the hands of the guardian have been paid.

Added by Acts 1993, 73rd Leg., ch. 957, § 1, eff. Sept. 1, 1993.

§ 755. Appointment of Attorney to Represent Ward

When the ward is dead and there is no executor or administrator of the ward's estate, or when the ward is a nonresident, or the ward's residence is unknown, the court may appoint an attorney ad litem to represent the interest of the ward in the final settlement with the guardian, and shall allow the attorney reasonable compensation out of the ward's estate for any services provided by the attorney.

Added by Acts 1993, 73rd Leg., ch. 957, § 1, eff. Sept. 1, 1993.

§ 756. Offsets, Credits, and Bad Debts

In the settlement of any of the accounts of the guardian of an estate, all debts due the estate that the court is satisfied could not have been collected by due diligence, and that have not been collected, shall be excluded from the computation.

Added by Acts 1993, 73rd Leg., ch. 957, § 1, eff. Sept. 1, 1993.

§ 757. Accounting for Labor or Services of a Ward

The guardian of a ward shall account for the reasonable value of the labor or services of the ward of the guardian, or the proceeds of the labor or services, if the labor or services have been rendered by the ward, but the guardian is entitled to reasonable credits for the board, clothing, and maintenance of the ward.

Added by Acts 1993, 73rd Leg., ch. 957, § 1, eff. Sept. 1, 1993.

§ 758. Procedure if Representative Fails to Deliver Estate

If a guardian, on final settlement or termination of the guardianship of the estate, neglects to deliver to the person entitled when legally demanded any portion of the estate or any funds or money in the hands of the guardian ordered to be delivered, a person entitled to the estate, funds, or money may file with the clerk of the court a written complaint alleging the fact of the guardian's neglect, the date of the person's demand, and other relevant facts. After the person files a complaint under this section, the clerk shall issue a citation to be served personally on the guardian, appraising the guardian of the complaint and citing the guardian to appear before the court and answer, if the guardian desires, at the time designated in the citation. If at the hearing the court finds that the citation was duly served and returned and that the guardian is guilty of the neglect charged, the court shall enter an order to that effect, and the guardian shall be liable to the person who filed the complaint in damages at the rate of 10 percent of the amount or appraised value of the money or estate withheld, per month, for each month or fraction of a month that the estate or money of a guardianship of the estate, or on termination of guardianship of the person, or funds is or has been withheld by the guardian after the date of demand, which damages may be recovered in any court of competent jurisdiction.

Added by Acts 1993, 73rd Leg., ch. 957, § 1, eff. Sept. 1, 1993.

SUBPART D. REVOCATION OF LETTERS, DEATH, RESIGNATION, AND REMOVAL

§ 759. Appointment of Successor Guardian

(a) In case of the death of the guardian of the person or of the estate of a ward, a personal representative of the deceased guardian shall account for, pay, and deliver to a person legally entitled to receive the property, all the property belonging to the guardianship that is entrusted to the care of the representative, at the time and in the manner as the court orders. On a finding that a necessity for the immediate appointment of a successor guardian exists, the court may appoint a successor guardian without citation or notice.

(b) If letters have been granted to a person, and another person whose right to be appointed successor guardian is prior and who has not waived the right and is qualified, applies for letters, the letters previously granted shall be revoked and other letters shall be granted to the applicant.

(c) If a person named in a will as guardian is not an adult when the will is probated and letters in any capacity have been granted to another person, the nominated guardian, on proof that the nominated guardian has become an adult and is not otherwise disqualified from serving as a guardian, is entitled to have the former letters revoked and appropriate letters granted to the nominated guardian. If the will names two or more persons as guardian, any one or more of whom are minors when the will is probated and letters have been issued to the persons who are adults, a minor, on becoming an adult, if not otherwise disqualified, is permitted to qualify and receive letters.

(d) If a person named in a will as guardian was ill or absent from the state when the testator died, or when the will was proved, and for that reason could not present the will for probate not later than the 30th day after the testator's death, or accept and qualify as guardian not later than the 20th day after the date the will was probated, the person may accept and qualify as guardian not later than the 60th day after the person's return or recovery from illness, on proof to the court that the person was absent or ill. If the letters have been issued to another person, the letters shall be revoked.

(e) If it is discovered after letters of guardianship have been issued that the deceased person left a lawful will, the letters shall be revoked and proper letters of guardianship issued to a person entitled to receive the letters.

(f) Except when otherwise expressly provided in this chapter, letters may not be revoked and other letters granted except on application, and after personal service of citation on the person, if living, whose letters are sought to be revoked, that the person appear and show cause why the application should not be granted.

(g) Money or any other thing of value falling due to a ward while the office of the guardian is vacant may be paid, delivered, or tendered to the clerk of the court for credit of the ward, and the debtor, obligor, or payor shall be discharged of the obligation for all purposes to the extent and purpose of the payment or tender. If the clerk accepts the payment or tender, the clerk shall issue a proper receipt for the payment or tender.

(h) The court may appoint as successor guardian a spouse, parent, or child of a proposed ward who has been disqualified from serving as guardian because of a litigation conflict under Section 681(4) of this code on removal of the conflict that caused the initial disqualification if the spouse, parent, or child is otherwise qualified to serve as a guardian.

Added by Acts 1993, 73rd Leg., ch. 957, § 1, eff. Sept. 1, 1993. Amended by Acts 1995, 74th Leg., ch. 1039, § 48, eff. Sept. 1, 1995.

For applicability provisions of the 1993 Act, see notes following § 601.

§ 760. Resignation

(a) A guardian of the estate who wishes to resign the guardian's trust shall file with the clerk a written application to the court to that effect, accompanied by a full and complete exhibit and final account, duly verified, showing the true condition of the guardianship estate entrusted to the guardian's care. A guardian of the person who wishes to resign the guardian's trust shall file with the clerk a written application to the court to that effect, accompanied by a report setting forth the information required in the annual report required under this chapter, duly verified, showing the condition of the ward entrusted to the guardian's care.

(b) If the necessity exists, the court may immediately accept a resignation and appoint a successor but may not discharge the person resigning as guardian of the estate or release the person or the sureties on the person's bond until final order or judgment is rendered on the final account of the guardian.

(c) On the filing of an application to resign, supported by an exhibit and final account, the clerk shall call the application to the attention of the judge, who shall set a date for a hearing on the matter. The clerk shall then issue a citation to all interested persons, showing that proper application has been filed and the time and place set for hearing, at which time the interested persons may appear and contest the exhibit and account or report. The citation shall be posted, unless the court directs that it be published.

(d) At the time set for hearing, unless it has been continued by the court, if the court finds that citation has been duly issued and served, the court shall proceed to examine the exhibit and account or report and hear all evidence for and against the exhibit, account, or report and shall, if necessary, restate, and audit and settle the exhibit, account, or report. If the court is satisfied that the matters entrusted to the applicant have been handled and accounted for in accordance with the law, the court shall enter an order of approval and require that the estate remaining in the possession of the applicant, if any, be delivered to the person entitled by law to receive it. A guardian of the person is required to comply with all orders of the court concerning the ward of the guardian.

(e) A resigning guardian may not be discharged until the application has been heard, the exhibit and account or report examined, settled, and approved, and the guardian has satisfied the court that the guardian has delivered the estate, if there is any part of the estate remaining in the possession of the guardian, or has complied with all orders of the court with relation to the guardian's trust.

(f) When the resigning guardian has complied in all respects with the orders of the court, an order shall be made accepting the resignation, discharging the applicant, and, if the applicant is under bond, the sureties of the guardian.

(g) The court at any time may order a resigning guardian who has all or part of the estate of a ward to deliver all or part of the ward's estate to a person who has been appointed and has qualified as successor guardian.

Added by Acts 1993, 73rd Leg., ch. 957, § 1, eff. Sept. 1, 1993. Amended by Acts 1995, 74th Leg., ch. 1039, § 49, eff. Sept. 1, 1995.

§ 761. Removal

(a) The court, on its own motion or on motion of any interested person, including the ward, and without notice, may remove any guardian, appointed under this chapter, who:

(1) neglects to qualify in the manner and time required by law;

(2) fails to return within 90 days after qualification, unless the time is extended by order of the court, an inventory of the property of the guardianship estate and list of claims that have come to the guardian's knowledge;

(3) having been required to give a new bond, fails to do so within the time prescribed;

(4) absents himself from the state for a period of three months at one time without permission of the court, or removes from the state;

(5) cannot be served with notices or other processes because the guardian's whereabouts are unknown, or because the guardian is eluding service;

(6) has misapplied, embezzled, or removed from the state, or is about to misapply, embezzle, or remove from the state, all or any part of the property committed to the guardian's care; or

(7) has cruelly treated a ward, or has neglected to educate or maintain the ward as liberally as the means of the ward and the condition of the ward's estate permit.

(b) The court may remove a personal representative under Subsection (a)(6) or (7) of this section only on the presentation of clear and convincing evidence given under oath.

(c) The court may remove a guardian on its own motion, or on the complaint of an interested person, after the guardian has been cited by personal service to answer at a time and place set in the notice, when:

(1) sufficient grounds appear to support belief that the guardian has misapplied, embezzled, or removed from the state, or that the guardian is about to

misapply, embezzle, or remove from the state, all or any part of the property committed to the care of the guardian;

(2) the guardian fails to return any account or report that is required by law to be made;

(3) the guardian fails to obey any proper order of the court having jurisdiction with respect to the performance of the guardian's duties;

(4) the guardian is proved to have been guilty of gross misconduct or mismanagement in the performance of the duties of the guardian;

(5) the guardian becomes incapacitated, or is sentenced to the penitentiary, or from any other cause becomes incapable of properly performing the duties of the guardian's trust;

(6) as guardian of the person, the guardian cruelly treats the ward, or neglects to educate or maintain the ward as liberally as the means of the ward's estate and the ward's ability or condition permit;

(7) the guardian interferes with the ward's progress or participation in programs in the community; or

(8) the guardian fails to comply with the requirements of Section 697 of this code.

(d) The order of removal shall state the cause of the removal. It must require that any letters issued to the person who is removed shall, if the removed person has been personally served with citation, be surrendered and that all those letters be cancelled of record, whether or not delivered. It must further require, as to all the estate remaining in the hands of a removed person, delivery of the estate to the person or persons entitled to the estate, or to one who has been appointed and has qualified as successor guardian, and as to the person of a ward, that control be relinquished as required in the order.

(e) If the necessity exists, the court may immediately appoint a successor but may not discharge the person removed as guardian of the estate or release the person or the sureties on the person's bond until final order or judgment is rendered on the final account of the guardian.

(f) The court at any time may order a person removed as guardian under this section who has all or part of the estate of a ward to deliver all or part of the ward's estate to a person who has been appointed and has qualified as successor guardian.

Added by Acts 1993, 73rd Leg., ch. 957, § 1, eff. Sept. 1, 1993. Amended by Acts 1995, 74th Leg., ch. 1039, § 50, eff. Sept. 1, 1995.

§ 762. Reinstatement After Removal

(a) Not later than the 10th day after the date the court signs the order of removal, a personal representative who is removed under Subsection (a)(6) or (7), Section 761, of this code may file an application with the court for a hearing to determine whether the personal representative should be reinstated.

(b) On the filing of an application for a hearing under this section, the court clerk shall issue a notice stating that the application for reinstatement was filed, the name of the ward or decedent, and the name of the applicant. The clerk shall issue the notice to the applicant, the ward, a person interested in the welfare of the ward, the decedent's estate, or the ward's estate, and, if applicable, to a person who has control of the care and custody of the ward. The notice must cite all persons interested in the estate or welfare of the ward to appear at the time and place stated in the notice if they wish to contest the application.

(c) If, at the conclusion of a hearing under this section, the court is satisfied by a preponderance of the evidence that the applicant did not engage in the conduct that directly led to the applicant's removal, the court shall set aside an order appointing a successor representative, if any, and shall enter an order reinstating the applicant as personal representative of the ward or estate.

(d) If the court sets aside the appointment of a successor representative under this section, the court may require the successor representative to prepare and file, under oath, an accounting of the estate and to detail the disposition the successor has made of the property of the estate.

Added by Acts 1993, 73rd Leg., ch. 957, § 1, eff. Sept. 1, 1993.

§ 763. Additional Powers of Successor Guardian

In addition, a successor guardian may make himself, and may be made, a party to a suit prosecuted by or against the predecessor of the successor guardian. The successor guardian may settle with the predecessor and receive and receipt for all the portion of the estate as remains in the hands of the successor guardian. The successor guardian may bring suit on the bond or bonds of the predecessor in the guardian's own name and capacity for all the estate that came into the hands of the predecessor and has not been accounted for by the predecessor.

Added by Acts 1993, 73rd Leg., ch. 957, § 1, eff. Sept. 1, 1993.

§ 764. Subsequent Guardians Succeed to Prior Rights and Duties

Whenever a guardian shall accept and qualify after letters of guardianship are granted on the estate, the guardian shall, in like manner, succeed to the previous guardian, and the guardian shall administer the estate in like manner as if the administration by the guardian were a continuation of the former one.

Added by Acts 1993, 73rd Leg., ch. 957, § 1, eff. Sept. 1, 1993.

§ 765. Successors' Return of Inventory, Appraisement, and List of Claims

A successor guardian who has qualified to succeed a prior guardian shall make and return to the court an inventory, appraisement, and list of claims of the estate, not later than 90 days after the date of qualification, in the same manner as is required of an original appointee. The successor guardian shall in like manner as is required of an original appointee return additional inventories, appraisements, and lists of claims. In all orders appointing a successor guardian, the court shall appoint an appraiser as in original appointments on the application of any person interested in the estate.

Added by Acts 1993, 73rd Leg., ch. 957, § 1, eff. Sept. 1, 1993.

SUBPART E. GENERAL DUTIES AND POWERS OF GUARDIANS

§ 767. Powers and Duties of Guardians of the Person

The guardian of the person is entitled to the charge and control of the person of the ward, and the duties of the guardian correspond with the rights of the guardian. A guardian of the person has:

(1) the right to have physical possession of the ward and to establish the ward's legal domicile;

(2) the duty of care, control, and protection of the ward;

(3) the duty to provide the ward with clothing, food, medical care, and shelter; and

(4) the power to consent to medical, psychiatric, and surgical treatment other than the in-patient psychiatric commitment of the ward.

Added by Acts 1993, 73rd Leg., ch. 957, § 1, eff. Sept. 1, 1993.

For applicability provisions of the 1993 Act, see notes following V.A.T.S. Probate Code, § 601.

§ 768. General Powers and Duties of Guardian of the Estate

The guardian of the estate of a ward is entitled to the possession and management of all property belonging to the ward, to collect all debts, rentals, or claims that are due to the ward, to enforce all obligations in favor of the ward, and to bring and defend suits by or against the ward; but, in the management of the estate, the guardian is governed by the provisions of this chapter. It is the duty of the guardian of the estate to take care of and manage the estate as a prudent person would manage the person's own property. The guardian of the estate shall account for all rents, profits, and revenues that the estate would have produced by such prudent management.

Added by Acts 1993, 73rd Leg., ch. 957, § 1, eff. Sept. 1, 1993.

§ 769. Summary of Powers of Guardian of Person and Estate

The guardian of both the person of and estate of a ward has all the rights and powers and shall perform all the duties of the guardian of the person and of the guardian of the estate.

Added by Acts 1993, 73rd Leg., ch. 957, § 1, eff. Sept. 1, 1993.

§ 770. Care of Ward; Commitment

(a) The guardian of an adult may expend funds of the guardianship as provided by court order to care for and maintain the incapacitated person. The guardian may apply for residential care and services provided by a public or private facility on behalf of an incapacitated person who has decision-making ability if the person agrees to be placed in the facility. The guardian shall report the condition of the person to the court at regular intervals at least annually, unless the court orders more frequent reports. If the person is receiving residential care in a public or private residential care facility, the guardian shall include in any report to the court a statement as to the necessity for continued care in the facility.

(b) Except as provided by Subsection (c) or (d) of this section, a guardian may not voluntarily admit an incapacitated person to a public or private in-patient psychiatric facility or to a residential facility operated by the Texas Department of Mental Health and Mental Retardation for care and treatment. If care and treatment in a psychiatric or a residential facility are necessary, the person or the person's guardian may apply for services under Section 593.027 or 593.028, Health and Safety Code, or apply to a court to commit the person under Subtitle D, Title 7, Health and

Safety Code (Persons with Mental Retardation Act),[1] Subtitle C, Title 7, Health and Safety Code (Texas Mental Health Code),[2] or Chapter 462, Health and Safety Code.

(c) A guardian of a person younger than 16 years of age may voluntarily admit an incapacitated person to a public or private inpatient psychiatric facility for care and treatment.

(d) A guardian of a person may voluntarily admit an incapacitated person to a residential care facility for emergency care or respite care under Section 593.027 or 593.028, Health and Safety Code.

Added by Acts 1993, 73rd Leg., ch. 957, § 1, eff. Sept. 1, 1993.

[1] V.T.C.A., Health & Safety Code § 591.001 et seq.

[2] V.T.C.A., Health & Safety Code § 571.001 et seq.

SUBPART F. SPECIFIC DUTIES AND POWERS OF GUARDIANS

§ 771. Guardian of Estate: Possession of Personal Property and Records

The guardian of an estate, immediately after receiving letters of guardianship, shall collect and take into possession the personal property, record books, title papers, and other business papers of the ward and shall deliver the personal property, books, or papers, of the ward to a person who is legally entitled to that property when the guardianship has been closed or a successor guardian has received letters.

Added by Acts 1993, 73rd Leg., ch. 957, § 1, eff. Sept. 1, 1993.

For applicability provisions of the 1993 Act, see notes following § 601.

§ 772. Collection of Claims and Recovery of Property

Every guardian of an estate shall use ordinary diligence to collect all claims and debts due the ward and to recover possession of all property of the ward to which the ward has claim or title, if there is a reasonable prospect of collecting the claims or of recovering the property. If the guardian wilfully neglects to use ordinary diligence, the guardian and the sureties on the guardian's bond shall be liable, at the suit of any person interested in the estate, for the use of the estate, for the amount of the claims or for the value of the property that has been lost due to the guardian's neglect.

Added by Acts 1993, 73rd Leg., ch. 957, § 1, eff. Sept. 1, 1993. Amended by Acts 1995, 74th Leg., ch. 1039, § 51, eff. Sept. 1, 1995.

§ 773. Suit by Guardian of Estate

A guardian of a ward's estate appointed in this state may institute suits for the recovery of personal property, debts, or damages and suits for title to or possession of land or for any right attached to or growing out of the same or for injury or damage done. Judgment in those cases shall be conclusive but may be set aside by any person interested for fraud or collusion on the part of the guardian.

Added by Acts 1993, 73rd Leg., ch. 957, § 1, eff. Sept. 1, 1993. Amended by Acts 1995, 74th Leg., ch. 1039, § 52, eff. Sept. 1, 1995.

§ 774. Exercise of Power With or Without Court Order

(a) On application, and if authorized by an order, the guardian of the estate may renew or extend any obligation owed by or to the ward. On written application to the court and when a guardian of the estate deems it is in the best interest of the estate, the guardian may, if authorized by an order of the court:

(1) purchase or exchange property;

(2) take a claim or property for the use and benefit of the estate in payment of a debt due or owing to the estate;

(3) compound a bad or doubtful debt due or owing to the estate;

(4) make a compromise or a settlement in relation to property or a claim in dispute or litigation;

(5) compromise or pay in full any secured claim that has been allowed and approved as required by law against the estate by conveying to the holder of the secured claim the real estate or personalty securing the claim, in full payment, liquidation, and satisfaction of the claim, and in consideration of cancellation of a note, deed of trust, mortgage, chattel mortgage, or other evidence of a lien that secures the payment of the claim; and

(6) abandon worthless or burdensome property and the administration of that property. Abandoned real or personal property may be foreclosed on by a secured party, trustee, or mortgagee without further order of the court.

(b) The guardian of the estate of a person, without application to or order of the court, may exercise the following powers provided, however, that a guardian may apply and obtain an order if doubtful of the propriety of the exercise of any such power:

(1) release a lien on payment at maturity of the debt secured by the lien;

(2) vote stocks by limited or general proxy;

(3) pay calls and assessments;

(4) insure the estate against liability in appropriate cases;

(5) insure property of the estate against fire, theft, and other hazards; and

(6) pay taxes, court costs, and bond premiums.

Added by Acts 1993, 73rd Leg., ch. 957, § 1, eff. Sept. 1, 1993. Amended by Acts 1997, 75th Leg., ch. 77, § 6, eff. Sept. 1, 1997.

§ 775. Possession of Property Held in Common Ownership

If the ward holds or owns any property in common, or as part owner with another person, the guardian of the estate is entitled to possession of the property of the ward held or owned in common with a part owner in the same manner as another owner in common or joint owner would be entitled.

Added by Acts 1993, 73rd Leg., ch. 957, § 1, eff. Sept. 1, 1993.

§ 776. Sums Allowable for Education and Maintenance of Ward

(a) Subject to Section 777 of this code, the court may direct the guardian of the person to expend, for the education and maintenance of the guardian's ward, a sum in excess of the income of the ward's estate. Otherwise, the guardian may not be allowed, for the education and maintenance of the ward, more than the net income of the estate. When different persons have the guardianship of the person and estate of a ward, the guardian of the estate shall pay to the guardian of the person a sum that is set by the court, at a time specified by the court, for the education and maintenance of the ward. If the guardian of the estate fails to pay to the guardian of the person the sum set by the court, the guardian of the estate shall be compelled to make the payment by court order after the guardian is duly cited to appear.

(b) When a guardian has in good faith expended funds from the corpus of the estate of the ward of the guardian for support and maintenance for the ward under this section or Section 777 of this code, and when it is not convenient or possible for the guardian to first secure court approval, if the proof is clear and convincing that the expenditures were reasonable and proper, and are expenditures that the court would have granted authority to make the expenditures out of the corpus, and the ward received the benefits of the expenditures, the court may approve the expenditures in the same manner as if the expenditures were made by the guardian out of the income from the ward's estate. An expenditure under this subsection may not exceed $5,000 per ward during an annual accounting period, unless the expenditure is made to a nursing home in which case the court may ratify any amount.

Added by Acts 1993, 73rd Leg., ch. 957, § 1, eff. Sept. 1, 1993. Amended by Acts 1995, 74th Leg., ch. 1039, § 53, eff. Sept. 1, 1995.

§ 776A. Sums Allowable for Education and Maintenance of Ward's Spouse or Dependent

(a) Subject to Section 777 of this code and on application to the court, the court may order the guardian of the estate of a ward to expend funds from the ward's estate for the education and maintenance of the ward's spouse or dependent.

(b) In determining whether to order the expenditure of funds from a ward's estate for the ward's spouse or dependent, as appropriate, in accordance with this section, the court shall consider:

(1) the circumstances of the ward, the ward's spouse, and the ward's dependents;

(2) the ability and duty of the ward's spouse to support himself or herself and the ward's dependent;

(3) the size of the ward's estate;

(4) a beneficial interest the ward or the ward's spouse or dependent has in a trust; and

(5) an existing estate plan, including a trust or will, that provides a benefit to the ward's spouse or dependent.

(c) A person who makes an application to the court under this section shall mail notice of the application by certified mail to all interested persons.

Added by Acts 1997, 75th Leg., ch. 77, § 7, eff. Sept. 1, 1997.

§ 777. Sums Allowed Parents for Education and Maintenance of Minor Ward

(a) Except as provided by Subsection (b) of this section, a parent who is the guardian of the person of a ward who is 17 years of age or younger may not use the income or the corpus from the ward's estate for the ward's support, education, or maintenance.

(b) A court with proper jurisdiction may authorize the guardian of the person to spend the income or the corpus from the ward's estate to support, educate, or maintain the ward if the guardian presents clear and convincing evidence to the court that the ward's parents are unable without unreasonable hardship to pay for all of the expenses related to the ward's support.

Added by Acts 1993, 73rd Leg., ch. 957, § 1, eff. Sept. 1, 1993.

§ 778. Title of Wards Not to be Disputed

A guardian or the heirs, executors, administrators, or assigns of a guardian may not dispute the right of the ward to any property that came into the possession of the guardian as guardian of the ward, except property that is recovered from the guardian or property on which there is a personal action pending.

Added by Acts 1993, 73rd Leg., ch. 957, § 1, eff. Sept. 1, 1993.

§ 779. Operation of Farm, Ranch, Factory, or Other Business

If the ward owns a farm, ranch, factory, or other business and if the farm, ranch, factory, or other business is not required to be sold at once for the payment of debts or other lawful purposes, the guardian of the estate on order of the court shall carry on the operation of the farm, ranch, factory, or other business, or cause the same to be done, or rent the same, as shall appear to be for the best interests of the estate. In deciding, the court shall consider the condition of the estate and the necessity that may exist for the future sale of the property or business for the payment of a debt, claim, or other lawful expenditure and may not extend the time of renting any of the property beyond what appears consistent with the maintenance and education of a ward or the settlement of the estate of the ward.

Added by Acts 1993, 73rd Leg., ch. 957, § 1, eff. Sept. 1, 1993.

§ 780. Administration of Partnership Interest by Guardian

If the ward was a partner in a general partnership and the articles of partnership provide that, on the incapacity of a partner, the guardian of the estate of the partner is entitled to the place of the incapacitated partner in the firm, the guardian who contracts to come into the partnership shall, to the extent allowed by law, be liable to a third person only to the extent of the incapacitated partner's capital in the partnership and the assets of the estate of the partner that are held by the guardian. This section does not exonerate a guardian from liability for the negligence of the guardian.

Added by Acts 1993, 73rd Leg., ch. 957, § 1, eff. Sept. 1, 1993.

§ 781. Borrowing Money

(a) The guardian may mortgage or pledge any real or personal property of a guardianship estate by deed of trust or otherwise as security for an indebtedness, under court order, when necessary for any of the following purposes:

(1) for the payment of any ad valorem, income, gift, or transfer taxes due from a ward, regardless of whether the taxes are assessed by a state, a political subdivision of the state, the federal government, or a foreign country;

(2) for the payment of any expenses of administration, including sums necessary for the operation of a business, farm, or ranch owned by the estate;

(3) for the payment of any claims allowed and approved, or established by suit, against the ward or the estate of the ward;

(4) to renew and extend a valid, existing lien;

(5) to make improvements or repairs to the real estate of the ward if:

(A) the real estate of the ward is not revenue producing but could be made revenue producing by certain improvements and repairs; or

(B) the revenue from the real estate could be increased by making improvements or repairs to the real estate;

(6) court-authorized borrowing of money that the court finds to be in the best interests of the ward for the purchase of a residence for the ward or a dependent of the ward; and

(7) if the guardianship is kept open after the death of the ward, funeral expenses of the ward and expenses of the ward's last illness.

(b) When it is necessary to borrow money for any of the purposes authorized under Subsection (a) of this section, or to create or extend a lien on property of the estate as security, a sworn application for the authority to borrow money shall be filed with the court, stating fully and in detail the circumstances that the guardian of the estate believes make necessary the granting of the authority. On the filing of an application under this subsection, the clerk shall issue and cause to be posted a citation to all interested persons, stating the nature of the application and requiring the interested persons to appear and show cause why the application should not be granted.

(c) If the court is satisfied by the evidence adduced at the hearing on the application that it is in the interest of the ward or the ward's estate to borrow money under Subsection (b) of this section, or to extend and renew an existing lien, the court shall issue an order to that effect, setting out the terms and conditions of the authority granted. The term of the loan or renewal shall be for the length of time that the court determines to be for the best interests of the ward or the ward's estate. If a new lien is created on the property of a guardianship estate, the court may require that the guardian's general bond be increased, or that an additional bond be given, for the protection of the guardianship estate and its creditors, as for the sale of real property belonging to the estate.

Added by Acts 1993, 73rd Leg., ch. 957, § 1, eff. Sept. 1, 1993.

§ 782. Powers, Duties, and Obligations of Guardian of Person Entitled to Government Funds

(a) A guardian of the person for whom it is necessary to have a guardian appointed to receive funds from a governmental source has the power to administer only the funds received from the governmental source, all earnings, interest, or profits derived from the funds, and all property acquired with the funds. The guardian has the power to receive the funds and pay out the expenses of administering the guardianship and the expenses for the support, maintenance, or education of the ward or the ward's dependents. Expenditures for the support, maintenance, or education of the ward or the ward's dependents may not exceed $12,000 during any 12-month period without the court's approval.

(b) All acts performed before September 1, 1993, by guardians of the estate of a person for whom it is necessary to have a guardian appointed to receive and disburse funds that are due the person from a governmental source are validated if the acts are performed in conformance with orders of a court that has venue with respect to the support, maintenance, and education of the ward or the ward's dependents and the investment of surplus funds of the ward under this chapter and if the validity of the act is not an issue in a probate proceeding or civil lawsuit that is pending on September 1, 1993.

Added by Acts 1993, 73rd Leg., ch. 957, § 1, eff. Sept. 1, 1993. Amended by Acts 1995, 74th Leg., ch. 1039, § 54, eff. Sept. 1, 1995.

SUBPART G. CLAIMS PROCEDURES

§ 783. Notice by Guardian of Appointment

(a) Within one month after receiving letters, personal representatives of estates shall send to the comptroller of public accounts by certified or registered mail if the ward remitted or should have remitted taxes administered by the comptroller of public accounts and publish in some newspaper, printed in the county where the letters were issued, if there be one, a notice requiring all persons having a claim against the estate being administered to present the claim within the time prescribed by law. The notice must include the time of issuance of letters held by the representative, the address to which a claim may be presented, and an instruction of the representative's choice that a claim be addressed in care of the representative, in care of the representative's attorney, or in care of "Representative, Estate of __________" (naming the estate).

(b) A copy of the printed notice, with the affidavit of the publisher, duly sworn to and subscribed before a proper officer, to the effect that the notice was published as provided in this chapter for the service of citation or notice by publication, shall be filed in the court in which the cause is pending.

(c) When no newspaper is printed in the county, the notice shall be posted and the return made and filed as required by this chapter.

Added by Acts 1993, 73rd Leg., ch. 957, § 1, eff. Sept. 1, 1993. Amended by Acts 1997, 75th Leg., ch. 77, § 8, eff. Sept. 1, 1997.

For applicability provisions of the 1993 Act, see notes following § 601.

§ 784. Notice to Holders of Recorded Claims

(a) Within four months after receiving letters, the guardian of an estate shall give notice of the issuance of the letters to each and every person having a claim for money against the estate of a ward if the claim is secured by a deed of trust, mortgage, or vendor's, mechanic's or other contractor's lien on real estate belonging to the estate.

(b) Within four months after receiving letters, the guardian of an estate shall give notice of the issuance of the letters to each person having an outstanding claim for money against the estate of a ward if the guardian has actual knowledge of the claim.

(c) The notice stating the original grant of letter shall be given by mailing the notice by certified mail or registered letter, with return receipt requested, addressed to the record holder of the indebtedness or claim at the last known post office address of the record holder.

(d) A copy of each notice required by Subsection (a) of this section, with the return receipt and an affidavit of the representative, stating that the notice was mailed as required by law, giving the name of the person to whom the notice was mailed, if not shown on the notice or receipt, shall be filed in the court from which letters were issued.

Added by Acts 1993, 73rd Leg., ch. 957, § 1, eff. Sept. 1, 1993.

§ 785. One Notice Sufficient; Penalty for Failure to Give Notice

(a) If the notice required by Section 784 of this code has been given by a former representative, or by one when several representatives are acting, the notice given by the former representative or co-representative is sufficient and need not be repeated by any successor or co-representative.

(b) If the guardian fails to give the notice required in other sections of this chapter or to cause the notices to be given, the guardian and the sureties on the bond of the guardian shall be liable for any damage that any person suffers because of the neglect, unless it appears that the person had notice otherwise.

Added by Acts 1993, 73rd Leg., ch. 957, § 1, eff. Sept. 1, 1993.

§ 786. Claims Against Wards

(a) A claim may be presented to the guardian of the estate at any time when the estate is not closed and when suit on the claim has not been barred by the general statutes of limitation.

(b) A claim against a ward on which a suit is barred by a general statute of limitation applicable to the claim may not be allowed by a guardian. If allowed by the guardian and the court is satisfied that limitation has run, the claim shall be disapproved.

Added by Acts 1993, 73rd Leg., ch. 957, § 1, eff. Sept. 1, 1993.

§ 787. Tolling of General Statutes of Limitation

The general statutes of limitation are tolled:

(1) by filing a claim that is legally allowed and approved; or

(2) by bringing a suit on a rejected and disapproved claim not later than the 90th day after the date of rejection or disapproval.

Added by Acts 1993, 73rd Leg., ch. 957, § 1, eff. Sept. 1, 1993.

§ 788. Claims Must be Authenticated

Except as provided by this section, with respect to the payment of an unauthenticated claim by a guardian, a guardian of the estate may not allow and the court may not approve a claim for money against the estate, unless the claim is supported by an affidavit that the claim is just and that all legal offsets, payments, and credits known to the affiant have been allowed. If the claim is not founded on a written instrument or account, the affidavit must also state the facts on which the claim is founded. A photostatic copy of an exhibit or voucher necessary to prove a claim under this section may be offered with and attached to the claim instead of the original.

Added by Acts 1993, 73rd Leg., ch. 957, § 1, eff. Sept. 1, 1993.

§ 789. When Defects of Form are Waived

Any defect of form or claim of insufficiency of exhibits or vouchers presented is deemed waived by the guardian unless written objection to the form, exhibit, or voucher is made not later than the 30th day after the date of presentment of the claim and is filed with the county clerk.

Added by Acts 1993, 73rd Leg., ch. 957, § 1, eff. Sept. 1, 1993.

§ 790. Evidence Concerning Lost or Destroyed Claims

If evidence of a claim is lost or destroyed, the claimant or a representative of the claimant may make affidavit to the fact of the loss or destruction, stating the amount, date, and nature of the claim and when due, that the claim is just, that all legal offsets, payments, and credits known to the affiant have been allowed, and that the claimant is still the owner of the claim. The claim must be proved by disinterested testimony taken in open court, or by oral or written deposition, before the claim is approved. If the claim is allowed or approved without the affidavit or if the claim is approved without satisfactory proof, the allowance or approval is void.

Added by Acts 1993, 73rd Leg., ch. 957, § 1, eff. Sept. 1, 1993.

§ 791. Authentication of Claim by Others Than Individual Owners

The cashier, treasurer, or managing official of a corporation shall make the affidavit required to authenticate a claim of the corporation. When an affidavit is made by an officer of a corporation, or by an executor, administrator, guardian, trustee, assignee, agent, or attorney, it is sufficient to state in the affidavit that the person making the affidavit has made diligent inquiry and examination and that the person believes that the claim is just and that all legal offsets, payments, and credits made known to the person making the affidavit have been allowed.

Added by Acts 1993, 73rd Leg., ch. 957, § 1, eff. Sept. 1, 1993.

§ 792. Guardian's Payment of Unauthenticated Claims

A guardian may pay an unauthenticated claim against the estate of the guardian's ward that the guardian believes to be just, but the guardian and the sureties on the bond of the guardian shall be liable for the amount of any payment of the claim if the court finds that the claim is not just.

Added by Acts 1993, 73rd Leg., ch. 957, § 1, eff. Sept. 1, 1993.

§ 793. Method of Handling Secured Claims

(a) When a secured claim against a ward is presented, the claimant shall specify in the claim, in addition to all other matters required to be specified in claims:

(1) whether the claim shall be allowed and approved as a matured secured claim to be paid in due course of administration, in which event it shall be so paid if allowed and approved; or

(2) whether the claim shall be allowed, approved, and fixed as a preferred debt and lien against the specific property securing the indebtedness and paid according to the terms of the contract that secured the lien, in which event it shall be so allowed and approved if it is a valid lien; provided, however, the guardian may pay the claim prior to maturity if it is in the best interests of the estate to do so.

(b) If a secured claim is not presented within the time provided by law, it shall be treated as a claim to be paid in accordance with Subsection (a)(2) of this section.

(c) When an indebtedness has been allowed and approved under Subsection (a)(2) of this section, no further claim shall be made against other assets of the estate because of the indebtedness, but the claim remains a preferred lien against the property securing the claim, and the property remains security for the debt in any distribution or sale of the property before final maturity and payment of the debt.

(d) If property that secures a claim allowed, approved, and fixed under Subsection (a)(2) of this section is not sold or distributed not later than the 12th month after the date letters of guardianship are granted, the guardian of the estate shall promptly pay all maturities that have accrued on the debt according to the terms of the maturities and shall perform all the terms of any contract securing the maturities. If the guardian defaults in the payment or performance, the court, on motion of the claim holder, shall require the sale of the property subject to the unmatured part of the debt and apply the proceeds of the sale to the liquidation of the maturities or, at the option of the claim holder, a motion may be made in a like manner to require the sale of the property free of the lien and to apply the proceeds to the payment of the whole debt.

Added by Acts 1993, 73rd Leg., ch. 957, § 1, eff. Sept. 1, 1993.

§ 794. Claims Providing for Attorney's Fees

If the instrument that evidences or supports a claim provides for attorney's fees, the claimant may include as a part of the claim the portion of the fee that the claimant has paid or contracted to pay to an attorney to prepare, present, and collect the claim.

Added by Acts 1993, 73rd Leg., ch. 957, § 1, eff. Sept. 1, 1993.

§ 795. Depositing Claims With Clerk

A claim may also be presented by depositing the claim, with vouchers and necessary exhibits and affidavit attached to the claim, with the clerk. The clerk, on receiving the claim, shall advise the guardian of the estate or the guardian's attorney by letter mailed to the last known address of the guardian of the deposit of the claim. If the guardian fails to act on the claim within 30 days after it is filed, the claim is presumed to be rejected. Failure of the clerk to give notice as required under this section does not affect the validity of the presentment or the presumption of rejection of the claim because not acted on within the 30-day period.

Added by Acts 1993, 73rd Leg., ch. 957, § 1, eff. Sept. 1, 1993.

§ 796. Memorandum of Allowance or Rejection of Claim

When a duly authenticated claim against a guardianship estate is presented to the guardian or filed with the clerk as provided by this subpart, the guardian shall, not later than the 30th day after the date the claim is presented or filed, endorse or annex to the claim a memorandum signed by the guardian stating the time of presentation or filing of the claim and that the guardian allows or rejects the claim, or what portion of the claim the guardian allows or rejects.

Added by Acts 1993, 73rd Leg., ch. 957, § 1, eff. Sept. 1, 1993.

§ 797. Failure to Endorse or Annex Memorandum

The failure of a guardian of an estate to endorse on or annex to a claim presented to the guardian, or the failure of a guardian to allow or reject the claim or portion of the claim within 30 days after the claim was presented constitutes a rejection of the claim. If the claim is later established by suit, the costs shall be taxed against the guardian, individually, or the guardian may be removed as in other cases of removal on the written complaint of any person interested in the claim, after personal service of citation, hearing, and proof.

Added by Acts 1993, 73rd Leg., ch. 957, § 1, eff. Sept. 1, 1993.

§ 798. Claims Entered in Docket

After a claim against a ward's estate has been presented to and allowed by the guardian, either in whole or in part, the claim shall be filed with the county clerk of the proper county who shall enter it on the claim docket.

Added by Acts 1993, 73rd Leg., ch. 957, § 1, eff. Sept. 1, 1993.

§ 799. Contest of Claims, Action by Court, and Appeals

(a) Any person interested in a ward, at any time before the court has acted on a claim, may appear and object in writing to the approval of the claim, or any part of the claim. The parties are entitled to process for witnesses, and the court shall hear proof and render judgment as in ordinary suits.

(b) The court shall either approve in whole or in part or reject a claim that has been allowed and entered on the claim docket for a period of 10 days and shall at the same time classify the claim.

(c) Although a claim may be properly authenticated and allowed, if the court is not satisfied that it is just, the court shall examine the claimant and the guardian under oath and hear other evidence necessary to determine the issue. If after the examination and hearing the court is not convinced that the claim is just, the court shall disapprove the claim.

(d) When the court has acted on a claim, the court shall endorse on or annex to the claim a written memorandum dated and signed officially that states the exact action taken by the court on the claim, whether the court approved or disapproved the claim or approved in part or rejected in part the claim, and that states the classification of the claim. An order under this subsection has the force and effect of a final judgment.

(e) When a claimant or any person interested in a ward is dissatisfied with the action of the court on a claim, the claimant or person interested may appeal the action to the courts of appeals, as from other judgments of the county court in probate matters.

Added by Acts 1993, 73rd Leg., ch. 957, § 1, eff. Sept. 1, 1993.

§ 800. Suit on Rejected Claim

When a claim or a part of a claim has been rejected by the guardian, the claimant shall institute suit on the claim in the court of original probate jurisdiction in which the guardianship is pending or in any other court of proper jurisdiction not later than the 90th day after the date of the rejection of the claim or the claim is barred. When a rejected claim is sued on, the endorsement made on or annexed to the claim is taken to be true without further proof, unless denied under oath. When a rejected claim or part of a claim has been established by suit, no execution shall issue but the judgment shall be certified not later than the 30th day after the date of rendition if the judgment is from a court other than the court of original probate jurisdiction, filed in the court in which the cause is pending entered on the claim docket, classified by the court, and handled as if originally allowed and approved in due course of administration.

Added by Acts 1993, 73rd Leg., ch. 957, § 1, eff. Sept. 1, 1993.

§ 801. Presentment of Claims a Prerequisite for Judgment

(a) A judgment may not be rendered in favor of a claimant on any claim for money that has not been legally presented to the guardian of the estate of the ward and rejected by the guardian or by the court, in whole or in part.

(b) Subsection (a) does not apply to a claim for delinquent ad valorem taxes against the estate of a ward that is being administered in probate in a county other than the county in which the taxes were imposed.

Added by Acts 1993, 73rd Leg., ch. 957, § 1, eff. Sept. 1, 1993. Amended by Acts 1999, 76th Leg., ch. 1481, § 38, eff. Sept. 1, 1999.

Section 52 of Acts 1999, 76th Leg., ch. 1481 provides:

"The changes in law made by Sections 36, 37, and 38 of this Act apply to the estates of all decedents, regardless of the date of death, and to the estates of all wards, regardless of the date the application for appointment of a guardian was filed, and to all causes of action pending on September 1, 1999, or brought after that date."

§ 802. Costs of Suit With Respect to Claims

All costs incurred in the probate court with respect to claims are taxed as follows:

(1) if allowed and approved, the guardianship estate shall pay the costs;

(2) if allowed, but disapproved, the claimant shall pay the costs;

(3) if rejected, but established by suit, the guardianship estate shall pay the costs;

(4) if rejected, but not established by suit, the claimant shall pay the costs; or

(5) in suits to establish a claim after rejection in part, if the claimant fails to recover judgment for a greater amount than was allowed or approved, the claimant shall pay all costs.

Added by Acts 1993, 73rd Leg., ch. 957, § 1, eff. Sept. 1, 1993.

§ 803. Claims by Guardians

(a) A claim that a guardian of the person or estate held against the ward at the time of the appointment of the guardian, or that has since accrued, shall be verified by affidavit as required in other cases and presented to the clerk of the court in which the guardianship is pending. The clerk shall enter the claim on the claim docket, after which it shall take the same course as other claims.

(b) When a claim by a guardian has been filed with the court within the required time, the claim shall be entered on the claim docket and acted on by the court in the same manner as in other cases. When the claim has been acted on by the court, an appeal from the judgment of the court may be taken as in other cases.

Added by Acts 1993, 73rd Leg., ch. 957, § 1, eff. Sept. 1, 1993.

§ 804. Claims Not to be Paid Unless Approved

Except as provided for payment at the risk of a guardian of an unauthenticated claim, a claim for money against the estate of a ward or any part of a claim may not be paid until it has been approved by the court or established by the judgment of a court of competent jurisdiction.

Added by Acts 1993, 73rd Leg., ch. 957, § 1, eff. Sept. 1, 1993.

§ 805. Order of Payment of Claims

(a) The guardian shall pay a claim against the estate of the guardian's ward that has been allowed and approved or established by suit, as soon as practicable, in the following order, except as provided by Subsection (b) of this section:

(1) expenses for the care, maintenance, and education of the ward or the ward's dependents;

(2) funeral expenses of the ward and expenses of the ward's last illness, if the guardianship is kept open after the death of the ward as provided under this chapter, except that any claim against the estate of a ward that has been allowed and approved or established by suit before the death of the ward shall be paid before the funeral expenses and expenses of the last illness;

(3) expenses of administration; and

(4) other claims against the ward or the ward's estate.

(b) If the estate is insolvent, the guardian shall give first priority to the payment of a claim relating to the administration of the guardianship. The guardian shall pay other claims against the ward's estate in the order prescribed by Subsection (a) of this section.

(c) A claimant whose claim has not been paid may petition the court for determination of the claim at any time before it is barred by the applicable statute of limitations and on due proof procure an order for its allowance and payment from the estate.

Added by Acts 1993, 73rd Leg., ch. 957, § 1, eff. Sept. 1, 1993. Amended by Acts 1997, 75th Leg., ch. 1403, § 5, eff. Sept. 1, 1997.

Sections 6 to 8 of Acts 1997, 75th Leg., ch. 1403 provide:

"Sec. 6. A court may modify any guardianship in effect on September 1, 1997, to conform with the requirements of Section 805, Texas Probate Code, as amended by this Act, on the court's own motion or on application by the ward, guardian, or any other interested person or entity.

"Sec. 7. The change in law made by Sections 1–4 of this Act to the Texas Probate Code apply only to an account or report filed on or after the effective date of this Act. An account or report filed before the effective date of this Act is governed by the law applicable on the date the account or report was filed, and that law is continued in effect for that purpose.

"Sec. 8. Except as provided by Section 6 of this Act:

"(1) the change in law made by this Act to Section 805, Texas Probate Code, applies only to proceedings for the appointment of a guardian instituted on or after the effective date of this Act; and

"(2) a proceeding for the appointment of a guardian that is instituted before the effective date of this Act is governed by the law in effect on the date the proceedings were instituted, and the former law is continued in effect for that purpose."

§ 806. Deficiency of Assets

When there is a deficiency of assets to pay all claims of the same class, the claims in the same class shall be paid pro rata, as directed by the court, and in the order directed. A guardian may not be allowed to pay any claims, whether the estate is solvent or insolvent, except with the pro rata amount of the funds of the guardianship estate that have come to hand.

Added by Acts 1993, 73rd Leg., ch. 957, § 1, eff. Sept. 1, 1993.

§ 807. Guardian Not to Purchase Claims

A guardian may not purchase for the guardian's own use or for any purposes whatsoever a claim against the guardianship the guardian represents. On written complaint by a person interested in the guardianship estate and satisfactory proof of violation of this provision, the court after citation and hearing shall enter its order cancelling the claim and no part of the claim shall be paid out of the guardianship. The judge may remove the guardian for a violation of this section.

Added by Acts 1993, 73rd Leg., ch. 957, § 1, eff. Sept. 1, 1993.

§ 808. Proceeds of Sale of Mortgaged Property

When a guardian has on hand the proceeds of a sale that has been made for the satisfaction of a mortgage or other lien and the proceeds, or any part of the proceeds, are not required for the payment of any debts against the estate that have a preference over the mortgage or other lien, the guardian shall pay the proceeds to a holder of the mortgage or other lien. If the guardian fails to pay the proceeds as required by this section, the holder, on proof of the mortgage or other lien, may obtain an order from the court directing the payment to be made.

Added by Acts 1993, 73rd Leg., ch. 957, § 1, eff. Sept. 1, 1993.

§ 809. Liability for Nonpayment of Claims

(a) If a guardian of an estate fails to pay on demand any money ordered by the court to be paid to any person, except to the state treasury, when there are funds of the guardianship estate available, the person or claimant entitled to the payment, on affidavit of the demand and failure to pay, is authorized to have execution issued against the property of the guardianship for the amount due, with interest and costs.

(b) On return of the execution not satisfied, or merely on the affidavit of demand and failure to pay, the court may cite the guardian and the sureties on the bond of the guardian to show cause why the guardian or the sureties should not be held liable for the debt, interest, costs, or damages. On return of citation duly served, if good cause to the contrary is not shown, the court shall render judgment against the guardian and sureties that are cited under this subsection in favor of the holder of the claim for the unpaid amount ordered to be paid or established by suit, with interest and costs, and for damages on the amount neglected to be paid, at the rate of five percent per month for each month or fraction of a month that the payment was neglected to be paid after demand was made for payment. The damages may be collected in any court of competent jurisdiction.

Added by Acts 1993, 73rd Leg., ch. 957, § 1, eff. Sept. 1, 1993.

SUBPART H. SALES

§ 811. Court Must Order Sales

Except as provided by this subpart, the sale of any property of the ward may not be made without an order of court authorizing the sale. The court may order property sold for cash or on credit, at public auction or privately, as it may consider most to the advantage of the estate, except when otherwise specifically provided in this chapter.

Added by Acts 1993, 73rd Leg., ch. 957, § 1, eff. Sept. 1, 1993.

For applicability provisions of the 1993 Act, see notes following § 601.

§ 812. Certain Personal Property to be Sold

(a) The guardian of an estate, after approval of inventory and appraisement, shall promptly apply for an order of the court to sell at public auction or privately, for cash or on credit not exceeding six months, all of the estate that is liable to perish, waste, or deteriorate in value or that will be an expense or disadvantage to the estate if kept. Property exempt from forced sale, a specific legacy, or personal property necessary to carry on a farm, ranch, factory, or any other business that it is thought best to operate, may not be included in a sale under this section.

(b) In determining whether to order the sale of an asset under Subsection (a) of this section, the court shall consider:

(1) the guardian's duty to take care of and manage the estate as a person of ordinary prudence, discretion, and intelligence would exercise in the management of the person's own affairs; and

(2) whether the asset constitutes an asset that a trustee is authorized to invest under Section 113.056 or Subchapter F, Chapter 113, Property Code.[1]

Added by Acts 1993, 73rd Leg., ch. 957, § 1, eff. Sept. 1, 1993.

[1] V.T.C.A., Property Code § 113.171 et seq.

§ 813. Sales of Other Personal Property

On application by the guardian of the estate or by any interested person, the court may order the sale of any personal property of the estate not required to be sold by Section 812 of this code, including growing or harvested crops or livestock but not including exempt property, if the court finds that the sale of the property would be in the best interests of the ward or the ward's estate in order to pay expenses of the care, maintenance, and education of the ward or the ward's dependents, expenses of administration, allowances, or claims against the ward or the ward's estate, and funeral expenses of the ward and expenses of the ward's last illness, if the guardianship is kept open after the death of the ward, from the proceeds of the sale of the property. Insofar as possible, applications and orders for the sale of personal property must conform to the requirements set forth under this chapter for applications and orders for the sale of real estate.

Added by Acts 1993, 73rd Leg., ch. 957, § 1, eff. Sept. 1, 1993.

§ 814. Special Provisions Pertaining to Livestock

When the guardian of an estate has in the guardian's possession any livestock that the guardian deems necessary or to the advantage of the estate to sell, the guardian may, in addition to any other method provided by law for the sale of personal property, obtain authority from the court in which the estate is pending to sell the livestock through a bonded livestock commission merchant or a bonded livestock auction commission merchant. On written and sworn application by the guardian or by any person interested in the estate that describes the livestock sought to be sold and that sets out the reasons why it is deemed necessary or to the advantage of the estate that the application be granted, the court may authorize the sale. The court shall consider the application and may hear evidence for or against the application, with or without notice, as the facts warrant. If the application is granted, the court shall enter its order to that effect and shall authorize delivery of the livestock to any bonded livestock commission merchant or bonded livestock auction commission merchant for sale in the regular course of business. The commission merchant shall be paid his usual and customary charges, not to exceed three percent of the sale price, for the sale of the livestock. A report of the sale, supported by a verified copy of the merchant's account of sale, shall be made promptly by the guardian to the court, but no order of confirmation by the court is required to pass title to the purchaser of the livestock.

Added by Acts 1993, 73rd Leg., ch. 957, § 1, eff. Sept. 1, 1993.

§ 815. Sales of Personal Property at Public Auction

All sales of personal property at public auction shall be made after notice has been issued by the guardian of the estate and posted as in case of posting for original proceedings in probate, unless the court shall otherwise direct.

Added by Acts 1993, 73rd Leg., ch. 957, § 1, eff. Sept. 1, 1993.

§ 816. Sales of Personal Property on Credit

No more than six months' credit may be allowed when personal property is sold at public auction, based on the date of the sale. The purchaser shall be required to give his note for the amount due, with good and solvent personal security, before delivery of the property can be made to the purchaser, but security may be waived if delivery is not to be made until the note, with interest, has been paid.

Added by Acts 1993, 73rd Leg., ch. 957, § 1, eff. Sept. 1, 1993.

§ 817. Sale of Mortgaged Property

On the filing of a written application, a creditor who holds a claim that is secured by a valid mortgage or other lien and that has been allowed and approved or established by suit may obtain from the court in which the guardianship is pending an order that the property, or so much of the property as necessary to satisfy the creditor's claim, shall be sold. On the filing of the application, the clerk shall issue citation requiring the guardian of the estate to appear and show cause why an application filed under this section should not be granted. If it appears to the court that it would be advisable to discharge the lien out of the general assets of the estate or that it be refinanced, the court may so order. Otherwise, the court shall grant the application and order that the property be sold at public or private sale, as the court considers best, as in ordinary cases of sales of real estate.

Added by Acts 1993, 73rd Leg., ch. 957, § 1, eff. Sept. 1, 1993.

§ 818. Sales of Personal Property Reported; Decree Vests Title

All sales of personal property shall be reported to the court. The laws regulating the confirmation or disapproval of sales of real estate apply to sales of personal property, but no conveyance shall be necessary. The decree confirming the sale of personal property shall vest the right and title of the estate of the ward in the purchaser who has complied with the terms of the sale and shall be prima facie evidence that all requirements of the law in making the sale have been met. The guardian of an estate may, on request, issue a bill of sale without warranty to the purchaser as evidence of title. The expense of the bill of sale if requested is to be borne by the purchaser.

Added by Acts 1993, 73rd Leg., ch. 957, § 1, eff. Sept. 1, 1993.

§ 819. Selection of Real Property Sold for Payment of Debts

Real property of the ward that is selected to be sold for the payment of expenses or claims shall be that property that the court deems most advantageous to the guardianship to be sold.

Added by Acts 1993, 73rd Leg., ch. 957, § 1, eff. Sept. 1, 1993.

§ 820. Application For Sale of Real Estate

An application may be made to the court for an order to sell real property of the estate when it appears necessary or advisable in order to:

(1) pay expenses of administration, allowances, and claims against the ward or the ward's estate, and to pay funeral expenses of the ward and expenses of the ward's last illness, if the guardianship is kept open after the death of the ward;

(2) make up the deficiency when the income of a ward's estate, the personal property of the ward's estate, and the proceeds of previous sales, are insufficient to pay for the education and maintenance of the ward or to pay debts against the estate;

(3) dispose of property of the ward's estate that consists in whole or in part of an undivided interest in real estate when it is deemed in the best interests of the estate to sell the interest;

(4) dispose of real estate of a ward, any part of which is nonproductive or does not produce sufficient revenue to make a fair return on the value of the real estate, when the improvement of the real estate with a view to making it productive is not deemed advantageous or advisable and it appears that the sale of the real estate and the investment of the money derived from the sale of the real estate would be in the best interests of the estate; or

(5) conserve the estate of a ward by selling mineral interest or royalties on minerals in place owned by a ward.

Added by Acts 1993, 73rd Leg., ch. 957, § 1, eff. Sept. 1, 1993.

§ 821. Contents of Application For Sale of Real Estate

An application for the sale of real estate shall be in writing, must describe the real estate or an interest in or part of the real estate sought to be sold, and shall be accompanied by an exhibit, verified by affidavit that shows fully and in detail:

(1) the condition of the estate;

(2) the charges and claims that have been approved or established by suit, or that have been rejected and may be established later;

(3) the amount of each claim that has been approved or established by suit, or that has been rejected but may be established later;

(4) the property of the estate remaining on hand liable for the payment of those claims; and

(5) any other facts that show the necessity or advisability of the sale.

Added by Acts 1993, 73rd Leg., ch. 957, § 1, eff. Sept. 1, 1993.

§ 822. Setting of Hearing on Application

When an application for the sale of real estate is filed, it shall immediately be called to the attention of the judge by the clerk. The judge shall designate in writing a day for hearing the application, any opposition to the application, and any application for the sale of other land, with the evidence pertaining to the application. The judge may, by entries on the docket, continue the hearing from time to time until the judge is satisfied concerning the application.

Added by Acts 1993, 73rd Leg., ch. 957, § 1, eff. Sept. 1, 1993.

§ 823. Citation and Return on Application

On the filing of an application for the sale of real estate under Section 820 of this code and exhibit, the clerk shall issue a citation to all persons interested in the guardianship that describes the land or interest or part of the land or interest sought to be sold and that requires the persons to appear at the time set by the court as shown in the citation and show cause why the sale should not be made, if they so elect. Service of citation shall be by posting.

Added by Acts 1993, 73rd Leg., ch. 957, § 1, eff. Sept. 1, 1993.

§ 824. Opposition to Application

When an application for an order of sale is made, a person interested in the guardianship, before an order of sale is made by the court, may file the person's opposition to the sale, in writing, or may make application for the sale of other property of the estate.

Added by Acts 1993, 73rd Leg., ch. 957, § 1, eff. Sept. 1, 1993.

§ 825. Order of Sale

If satisfied on hearing that the sale of the property of the guardianship described in the application made under Section 820 of this code is necessary or advisable, the court shall order the sale to be made. Otherwise, the court may deny the application and, if the court deems best, may order the sale of other property the sale of which would be more advantageous to the estate. An order for the sale of real estate must specify:

(1) the property to be sold, giving a description that will identify the property;

(2) whether the property is to be sold at public auction or at private sale, and, if at public auction, the time and place of the sale;

(3) the necessity or advisability of the sale and its purpose;

(4) except in cases in which no general bond is required, that, having examined the general bond of the representative of the estate, the court finds it to be sufficient as required by law, or finds the bond to be insufficient and specifies the necessary or increased bond;

(5) that the sale shall be made and the report returned in accordance with law; and

(6) the terms of the sale.

Added by Acts 1993, 73rd Leg., ch. 957, § 1, eff. Sept. 1, 1993.

§ 826. Procedure When Guardian Neglects to Apply For Sale

When the guardian of an estate neglects to apply for an order to sell sufficient property to pay the charges and claims against the estate that have been allowed and approved or established by suit, an interested person, on written application, may cause the guardian to be cited to appear and make a full exhibit of the condition of the estate, and show cause why a sale of the property should not be ordered. On hearing an application made under this section, if the court is satisfied that a sale of the property is necessary or advisable in order to satisfy the claims, it shall enter an order of sale as provided by Section 825 of this code.

Added by Acts 1993, 73rd Leg., ch. 957, § 1, eff. Sept. 1, 1993.

§ 827. Permissible Terms of Sale of Real Estate

(a) The real estate may be sold for cash, or for part cash and part credit, or the equity in land securing an indebtedness may be sold subject to the indebtedness, or with an assumption of the indebtedness, at public or private sale, as appears to the court to be in the best interests of the estate. When real estate is sold partly on credit, the cash payment may not be less than one-fifth of the purchase price, and the purchaser shall execute a note for the deferred payments payable in monthly, quarterly, semiannual or annual installments, of the amounts as appear to the court to be for the best interests of the guardianship, to bear interest from date at a rate of not less than four percent per annum, payable as provided in the note. Default in the payment of principal or interest, or any part of the payment when due, at the election of the holder of the note, matures the whole debt. The note shall be secured by vendor's lien retained in the deed and in the note on the property sold and shall be further secured by deed of trust on the property sold, with the usual provisions for foreclosure and sale on failure to make the payments provided in the deed and the note.

(b) When an estate owning real estate by virtue of foreclosure of a vendor's lien or mortgage belonging to the estate either by judicial sale or by a foreclosure suit, by sale under deed of trust, or by acceptance of a deed in cancellation of a lien or mortgage owned by the estate, and it appears to the court that an application to redeem the property foreclosed on has been made by the former owner of the real estate to any corporation or agency created by any act of the Congress of the United States or of this state in connection with legislation for the relief of owners of mortgaged or encumbered homes, farms, ranches, or other real estate and that it would be in the best interests of the estate to own bonds of one of the above named federal or state corporations or agencies instead of the real estate, then on proper application and proof, the court may dispense with the provisions of credit sales as provided by Subsection (a) of this section, and may order reconveyance of the property to the former mortgage debtor, or former owner, reserving vendor's lien notes for the total amount of the indebtedness due or for the total amount of bonds that the corporation or agency above named is under its rules and regulations allowed to advance. On obtaining the order, it shall be proper for the guardian to endorse and assign the notes so obtained over to any one of the corporations or agencies above named in exchange for bonds of that corporation or agency.

Added by Acts 1993, 73rd Leg., ch. 957, § 1, eff. Sept. 1, 1993.

§ 828. Public Sale of Real Estate

(a) Except as otherwise provided by this chapter, all public sales of real estate shall be advertised by the guardian of the estate by a notice published in the county in which the estate is pending, as provided by this chapter for publication of notices or citations. A reference in the notice shall be made to the order of sale, the time, place, and the required terms of sale, and a brief description of the property to be sold. A reference made under this section does not have to contain field notes, but if the real estate consists of rural property, the name of the original survey, the number of acres, its locality in the county, and the name by which the land is generally known must be contained in the reference.

(b) All public sales of real estate shall be made at public auction to the highest bidder.

(c) All public sales of real estate shall be made in the county in which the guardianship proceedings are pending, at the courthouse door of the county, or at another place in the county where sales of real estate are specifically authorized to be made, on the first Tuesday of the month after publication of notice has been completed, between the hours of 10 a.m. and 4 p.m. If deemed advisable by the court, the court may order the sale to be made in the county in which the land is located, in which event notice shall be published both in that county and in the county in which the proceedings are pending.

(d) If a sale is not completed on the day advertised, the sale may be continued from day to day by making an oral public announcement of the continuance at the conclusion of the sale each day. The continued sale is to be made within the same hours as prescribed by Subsection (c) of this section. If sales are so continued, the fact shall be shown in the report of sale made to the court.

(e) When a person who bids on property of a guardianship estate offered for sale at public auction fails to comply with the terms of sale, the property shall be readvertised and sold without any further order. The person who defaults shall be liable to pay to the guardian of the estate, for the benefit of the estate, 10 percent of the amount of the person's bid and any deficiency in price on the second sale. The guardian shall recover the amounts by suit in any court in the county in which the sale was made that has jurisdiction over the amount claimed.

Added by Acts 1993, 73rd Leg., ch. 957, § 1, eff. Sept. 1, 1993.

§ 829. Private Sale of Real Estate

All private sales of real estate shall be made in the manner the court directs in its order of sale, and no further advertising, notice, or citation concerning the sale shall be required unless the court shall direct otherwise.

Added by Acts 1993, 73rd Leg., ch. 957, § 1, eff. Sept. 1, 1993.

§ 830. Sales of Easements and Rights of Way

The guardian may sell and convey easements and rights of way on, under, and over the land of a guardianship estate that is being administered under orders of a court, regardless of whether the proceeds of the sale are required for payment of charges or claims against the estate, or for other lawful purposes. The procedure for the sale is the same as provided by law for a sale of real property of wards at private sale.

Added by Acts 1993, 73rd Leg., ch. 957, § 1, eff. Sept. 1, 1993.

§ 831. Guardian Purchasing Property of the Estate

(a) Except as provided by Subsection (b) or (c) of this section, the guardian of an estate may not purchase, directly or indirectly, any property of the estate sold by the guardian, or by any co-representative of a guardian.

(b) A guardian may purchase property from the estate in compliance with the terms of a written executory contract signed by the ward before the ward became incapacitated, including a contract for deed, earnest money contract, buy/sell agreement, or stock purchase or redemption agreement.

(c) After issuing the notice required by this subsection, a guardian of an estate may purchase property from the estate on the court's determination that the sale is in the best interest of the estate. The guardian shall give notice by certified mail, return receipt requested, unless the court requires another form of notice, to each distributee of a deceased person's estate and to each creditor whose claim remains unsettled after presenting a claim within six months of the original grant of letters. In the case of an application filed by the guardian of the estate of a ward, the court shall appoint an attorney ad litem to represent the ward with respect to the sale. The court may require additional notice or it may allow for the waiver of the notice required for a sale made under this subsection.

(d) If a purchase is made in violation of this section, a person interested in the estate may file a written complaint with the court in which the guardianship proceedings are pending. On service of citation on the guardian and after hearing and proof, the court shall declare the sale void, set aside the sale, and order that the property be reconveyed to the estate. All costs of the sale, protest, and suit, if found necessary, shall be adjudged against the guardian.

Added by Acts 1993, 73rd Leg., ch. 957, § 1, eff. Sept. 1, 1993.

§ 832. Report of Sale

A sale of real property of an estate shall be reported to the court that orders the sale not later than the 30th day after the date the sale is made. A report must be in writing, sworn to, filed with the clerk, and noted on the probate docket. A report made under this section must contain:

(1) the date of the order of sale;

(2) a description of the property sold;

(3) the time and place of sale;

(4) the name of the purchaser;

(5) the amount for which each parcel of property or interest in the parcel of property was sold;

(6) the terms of the sale, and whether the sale was private or made at a public auction; and

(7) whether the purchaser is ready to comply with the order of sale.

Added by Acts 1993, 73rd Leg., ch. 957, § 1, eff. Sept. 1, 1993.

§ 833. Bond on Sale of Real Estate

If the guardian of the estate is not required by this chapter to furnish a general bond, the court may confirm the sale if the court finds the sale is satisfactory and in accordance with law. Otherwise, before a sale of real estate is confirmed, the court shall determine whether the general bond of the guardian is sufficient to protect the estate after the proceeds of the sale are received. If the court finds the bond is sufficient, the court may confirm the sale. If the general bond is found by the court to be insufficient, the court may not confirm the sale until the general bond is increased to the amount required by the court, or an additional bond is given and approved by the court. The increase in the amount of the bond, or the additional bond, shall be equal to the amount for which the real estate is sold in addition to any additional sum the court finds necessary and sets for the protection of the estate. If the real estate sold is encumbered by a lien to secure a claim against the estate, is sold to the owner or holder of the secured claim, and is in full payment, liquidation, and satisfaction of the claim, an increased general bond or additional bond may not be required except for the amount of cash actually paid to the guardian of the estate in excess of the amount necessary to pay, liquidate, and satisfy the claim in full.

Added by Acts 1993, 73rd Leg., ch. 957, § 1, eff. Sept. 1, 1993.

§ 834. Action of Court on Report of Sale

After the expiration of five days from the date a report of sale is filed under Section 832 of this code, the court shall inquire into the manner in which the sale was made, hear evidence in support of or against the report, and determine the sufficiency or insufficiency of the guardian's general bond, if any has been required and given. If the court is satisfied that the sale was for a fair price, was properly made, and conforms with the law and the court has approved any increased or additional bond that may have been found necessary to protect the estate, the court shall enter a decree confirming the sale showing conformity with other provisions of this chapter relating to the sale and authorizing the conveyance of the property to be made by the guardian of the estate on compliance by the purchaser with the terms of the sale, detailing those terms. If the court is not satisfied that the sale was for a fair price, was properly made, and conforms with the law, the court shall issue an order that sets the sale aside and order a new sale to be made, if necessary. The action of the court in confirming or disapproving a report of sale has the force and effect of a final judgment. Any person interested in the guardianship estate or in the sale has the right to have the decrees reviewed as in other final judgments in probate proceedings.

Added by Acts 1993, 73rd Leg., ch. 957, § 1, eff. Sept. 1, 1993.

§ 835. Deed Conveys Title to Real Estate

When real estate is sold, the conveyance of real estate shall be by proper deed that refers to and identifies the decree of the court that confirmed the sale. The deed shall vest in the purchaser all right, title, and interest of the estate to the property and shall be prima facie evidence that the sale has met all applicable requirements of the law.

Added by Acts 1993, 73rd Leg., ch. 957, § 1, eff. Sept. 1, 1993.

§ 836. Delivery of Deed, Vendor's Lien, and Deed of Trust Lien

After a sale is confirmed by the court and one purchaser has complied with the terms of sale, the guardian of the estate shall execute and deliver to the purchaser a proper deed conveying the property. If the sale is made partly on credit, the vendor's lien securing a purchase money note shall be expressly retained in the deed and may not be waived. Before actual delivery of the deed to the purchaser, the purchaser shall execute and deliver to the guardian of the estate a vendor's lien note, with or without personal sureties as the court has ordered and a deed of trust or mortgage on the property as further security for the payment of the note. On completion of the transaction, the guardian shall promptly file and record in the appropriate records in the county where the land is located the deed of trust or mortgage.

Added by Acts 1993, 73rd Leg., ch. 957, § 1, eff. Sept. 1, 1993.

§ 837. Penalty for Neglect

If the guardian of an estate neglects to comply with Section 836 of this code or fails to file the deed of trust securing the lien in the proper county, the guardian, after complaint and citation, may be removed. The guardian and the sureties on the bond of the guardian shall be held liable for the use of the estate and for all damages resulting from the neglect of the guardian. Damages under this section may be recovered in a court of competent jurisdiction.

Added by Acts 1993, 73rd Leg., ch. 957, § 1, eff. Sept. 1, 1993.

SUBPART I. HIRING AND RENTING

§ 839. Hiring or Renting Without Order of Court

The guardian of an estate, without court order, may rent any real property of the estate or hire out any personal property of the estate for one year or less, either at public auction or privately, as may be deemed in the best interests of the estate.

Added by Acts 1993, 73rd Leg., ch. 957, § 1, eff. Sept. 1, 1993.

§ 840. Liability of Guardian

If property of the guardianship estate is hired or rented without court order, on the sworn complaint of any person interested in the estate, the guardian of the estate shall be required to account to the estate for the reasonable value of the hire or rent of the property to be ascertained by the court on satisfactory evidence.

Added by Acts 1993, 73rd Leg., ch. 957, § 1, eff. Sept. 1, 1993.

§ 841. Order to Hire or Rent

A guardian of an estate may file a written application with the court setting forth the property sought to be hired or rented. If the proposed rental period is one year or more, the guardian of the estate shall file a written application with the court setting forth the property sought to be hired or rented. If the court finds that it would be in the interests of the estate, the court shall grant the application and issue an order that describes the property to be hired or rented and states whether the hiring or renting shall be at public auction or privately, whether for cash or on credit, and, if on credit, the extent of the credit and the period for which the property may be rented. If the property is to be hired or rented at public auction, the court shall prescribe whether notice shall be published or posted.

Added by Acts 1993, 73rd Leg., ch. 957, § 1, eff. Sept. 1, 1993.

§ 842. Procedure in Case of Neglect to Rent Property

A person interested in a guardianship may file a written and sworn complaint in a court in which the estate is pending and cause the guardian of the estate to be cited to appear and show cause why the guardian did not hire or rent any property of the estate. The court, on hearing the complaint, shall make an order that is in the best interests of the estate.

Added by Acts 1993, 73rd Leg., ch. 957, § 1, eff. Sept. 1, 1993.

§ 843. Property Hired or Rented on Credit

When property is hired or rented on credit, possession of the property may not be delivered until the hirer or renter has executed and delivered to the guardian of the estate a note with good personal security for the amount of the hire or rental. If the property that is hired or rented is delivered without the receipt of the security required under this section, the guardian and the sureties on the bond of the guardian shall be liable for the full amount of the hire or rental. This section does not apply to a hire or rental that is paid in installments in advance of the period of time to which they relate.

Added by Acts 1993, 73rd Leg., ch. 957, § 1, eff. Sept. 1, 1993.

§ 844. Property Hired or Rented Returned in Good Condition

All property that is hired or rented, with or without a court order, shall be returned to the possession of the guardianship in as good a condition, reasonable wear and tear excepted, as when the property was hired or rented. It shall be the duty and responsibility of the guardian of the estate to see that the property is returned as provided by this section, to report to the court any loss, damage, or destruction of property that is hired or rented under this chapter, and to ask for authority to take action as is necessary. If the guardian fails to act as required by this section, the guardian and the sureties on the bond of the guardian shall be liable to the guardianship for any loss or damage suffered through the fault of the guardian to act as required under this section.

Added by Acts 1993, 73rd Leg., ch. 957, § 1, eff. Sept. 1, 1993.

§ 845. Report of Hiring or Renting

(a) When any property of the guardianship estate with an appraised value of $3,000 or more has been hired or rented, the guardian of the estate, not later than the 30th day after the date of the hire or rental, shall file with the court a sworn and written report that states:

(1) the property involved and its appraised value;

(2) the date of hiring or renting, and whether at public auction or privately;

(3) the name of the person who hired or rented the property;

(4) the amount of the hiring or rental; and

(5) whether the hiring or rental was for cash or on credit, and, if on credit, the length of time, the terms, and the security taken for the hiring or rental.

(b) When the value of the property involved is less than $3,000, the hiring or renting of the property may be reported in the next annual or final account that is to be filed as required by law.

Added by Acts 1993, 73rd Leg., ch. 957, § 1, eff. Sept. 1, 1993.

§ 846. Court Action on Report

After five days from the time the report of the hiring or rental is filed, the court shall examine the report and shall approve and confirm the hiring or rental by court order if the court finds the hire or rental just and reasonable. If the court disapproves the hiring or rental, the guardianship may not be bound and the court may order another offering of the property for hire or rent in the same manner and subject to the same rules provided in this chapter for property for hire or rent. If the report has been approved by the court and it later appears that, due to the fault of the guardian of the estate, the property has not been hired or rented for its reasonable value, the court shall cause the guardian of the estate and the sureties on the bond of the guardian to appear and show cause why the reasonable value of the hire or rental of the property should not be adjudged against the guardian or sureties.

Added by Acts 1993, 73rd Leg., ch. 957, § 1, eff. Sept. 1, 1993.

SUBPART J. MINERAL LEASES, POOLING OR UNITIZATION AGREEMENTS, AND OTHER MATTERS RELATING TO MINERAL PROPERTIES

§ 847. Mineral Leases After Public Notice

(a) In this subpart:

(1) "Land" or "interest in land" includes minerals or any interest in any of the minerals in place.

(2) "Mineral development" includes exploration, by geophysical or by any other means, drilling, mining, developing, and operating, and producing and saving oil, other liquid hydrocarbons, gas (including all liquid hydrocarbons in the gaseous phase in the reservoir), gaseous elements, sulphur, metals, and all other minerals, solid or otherwise.

(3) "Property" includes land, minerals in place, whether solid, liquid, or gaseous, as well as an interest of any kind in the property, including royalty, owned by the estate.

(b) A guardian acting solely under an order of a court, may be authorized by the court in which the guardianship proceeding is pending to make, execute, and deliver leases, with or without unitization clauses or pooling provisions, that provide for the exploration for, and development and production of, oil, other liquid hydrocarbons, gas (including all liquid hydrocarbons in the gaseous phase), metals, and other solid minerals, and other minerals, or any of those minerals in place, belonging to the estate.

(c) All leases authorized by Subsection (b) of this section, with or without pooling provisions or unitization clauses, shall be made and entered into pursuant to and in conformity with Subsections (d)–(m) of this section.

(d) The guardian of the estate shall file a written application with the court seeking authority to lease property of the estate for mineral exploration and development, with or without pooling provisions or unitization clauses. The name of any proposed lessee or the terms, provisions, or form of any desired lease do not need to be set out or suggested in the application. The application shall:

(1) describe the property fully enough by reference to the amount of acreage, the survey name or number, abstract number, or other description that adequately identifies the property and its location in the county in which the property is located;

(2) specify the interest thought to be owned by the estate if less than the whole, but asking for authority to include all interest owned by the estate if that is the intention; and

(3) set out the reasons why the particular property of the estate should be leased.

(e) When an application to lease is filed, under this section, the county clerk shall immediately call the filing of the application to the attention of the court. The judge shall promptly make and enter a brief order designating the time and place for the hearing of the application. If the hearing does not take place at the time originally designated by the court or by timely order of continuance duly entered, the hearing shall be automatically continued without further notice to the same hour or time the following day, except Sundays and holidays on which the county courthouse is officially closed to business, and from day to day until the application is finally acted on and disposed of by order of the court. No notice of the automatic continuance shall be required.

(f) The guardian shall give written notice directed to all persons interested in the estate of the time designated by the judge for the hearing on the application to lease. The notice must be dated, state the date on which the application was filed, describe briefly the property sought to be leased, specify the fractional interest sought to be leased if less than the entire interest in the tract identified, and state the time and place designated by the judge for the hearing. Exclusive of the date of notice and of the date set for hearing, the guardian shall give at least 10 days' notice by publishing in one issue of a newspaper of general circulation in the county in which the proceeding is pending or by posting if there is no newspaper in the county. Posting under this section may be done at the guardian's instance. The date of notice when published shall be the date the newspaper bears.

(g) A court order authorizing any acts to be performed pursuant to the application is null and void in the absence of:

(1) a written order originally designating a time and place for hearing;

(2) a notice issued by the guardian of the estate in compliance with the order; and

(3) proof of publication or posting of the notice as required.

(h) At the time and place designated for the hearing, or at any time to which the hearing has been continued as provided by this section, the judge shall hear the application and require proof as to the necessity or advisability of leasing for mineral development the property described in the application and in the notice. If the judge is satisfied that the application is in due form, that notice has been duly given in the manner and for the time required by law, that the proof of necessity or advisability of leasing is sufficient, and that the application should be granted, the judge shall enter an order so finding and authorizing the making of one or more leases, with or without pooling provisions or unitization clauses (with or without cash consideration if deemed by the court to be in the best interest of the estate) that affects and covers the property or portions of the property described in the application. The order that authorizes the leasing must also set out the following mandatory contents:

(1) the name of the lessee;

(2) the actual cash consideration, if any, to be paid by the lessee;

(3) a finding that the guardian is exempt by law from giving bond if that is a fact, and if the guardian is required to give a bond, then a finding as to whether or not the guardian's general bond on file is sufficient to protect the personal property on hand, inclusive of any cash bonus to be paid; but if the court finds the general bond is insufficient to meet these requirements, the order shall show the amount of increased or additional bond required to cover the deficiency;

(4) a complete exhibit copy, either written or printed, of each lease authorized to be made, either set out

in, attached to, incorporated by reference in, or made a part of the order.

(i) An exhibit copy must show the name of the lessee, the date of the lease, an adequate description of the property being leased, the delay rental, if any, to be paid to defer commencement of operations, and all other terms and provisions authorized. If no date of the lease appears in the exhibit copy or in the court's order, then the date of the court's order is considered for all purposes as the date of the authorized lease. If the name and address of a depository bank for receiving rental is not shown in the exhibit copy, the name or address of the depository bank may be inserted or caused to be inserted in the lease by the estate's guardian at the time of its execution or at any other time agreeable to the lessee, his successors, or assigns.

(j) On the hearing of an application for authority to lease, if the court grants the authority to lease, the guardian of the estate is fully authorized to make, not later than the 30th day after the date of the judge's order, unless an extension is granted by the court on a sworn application showing good cause, the lease as evidenced by the true exhibit copies in accordance with the order. Unless the guardian is not required to give a general bond, a lease for which a cash consideration is required, though ordered, executed, and delivered, is not valid unless the order authorizing the lease actually makes a finding with respect to the general bond. If the general bond has been found insufficient, the lease is not valid until the bond has been increased or an additional bond given with the sureties required by law as required by the court order, has been approved by the judge, and has been filed with the clerk of the court in which the proceeding is pending. If two or more leases on different lands are authorized by the same order, the general bond shall be increased or additional bonds given to cover all. It is not necessary for the judge to make any order confirming the leases.

(k) Every lease when executed and delivered in compliance with the rules set out in this section shall be valid and binding on the property or interest owned by the estate and covered by the lease for the full duration of the term as provided in the lease and is subject only to its terms and conditions even though the primary term extends beyond the date when the estate is closed in accordance with law. In order for a lease to be valid and binding on the property or interest owned by the estate under this section, the authorized primary term in the lease may not exceed five years, subject to terms and provisions of the lease extending it beyond the primary term by paying production, by bona fide drilling or reworking operations, whether in or on the same or additional well or wells with no cessation of operations of more than 60 consecutive days before production has been restored or obtained, or by the provisions of the lease relating to a shut-in gas well.

(*l*) As to any existing valid mineral lease executed and delivered in compliance with this chapter before September 1, 1993, a provision of the lease continuing the lease in force after its five-year primary term by a shut-in gas well is validated, unless the validity of the provision is an issue in a lawsuit pending in this state on September 1, 1993.

(m) Any oil, gas, and mineral lease executed by a guardian under this chapter may be amended by an instrument that provides that a shut-in gas well on the land covered by the lease or on land pooled with all or some part of the land covered by the lease shall continue the lease in force after its five-year primary term. The instrument shall be executed by the guardian, with court approval, and on the terms and conditions as may be prescribed in the instrument.

Added by Acts 1993, 73rd Leg., ch. 957, § 1, eff. Sept. 1, 1993.

For applicability provisions of the 1993 Act, see note following § 601.

§ 848. Mineral Leases at Private Sale

(a) Notwithstanding the mandatory requirements for setting a time and place for hearing of an application to lease under Section 847 of this code and the issuance, service, and return of notice, the court may authorize the making of oil, gas, and mineral leases at private sale without public notice or advertising if, in the opinion of the court, sufficient facts are set out in the application to show that it would be more advantageous to the estate that a lease be made privately and without compliance with the mandatory requirements under Section 847 of this code. Leases authorized under this section may include pooling provisions or unitization clauses as in other cases.

(b) At any time after the expiration of five days and before the expiration of the 10th day after the date of filing and without an order setting the time and place of hearing, the court shall hear the application to lease at a private sale. The court shall inquire into the manner in which the proposed lease has been or will be made and shall hear evidence for or against the application. If the court is satisfied that the lease has been or will be made for a fair and sufficient consideration and on fair terms and has been or will be properly made in conformity with the law, the court shall enter an order authorizing the execution of the lease without the necessity of advertising, notice, or citation. An order entered under this subsection must comply in all other respects with the requirements essential to the validity of mineral leases set out in this chapter as if advertising or notice were required. An order that confirms a lease made at a private sale does not need to be issued. A lease made at a private sale is not valid until the increased or additional bond required by the court, if any, has been approved by the court and filed with the clerk of the court.

Added by Acts 1993, 73rd Leg., ch. 957, § 1, eff. Sept. 1, 1993.

§ 849. Pooling or Unitization of Royalty or Minerals

(a) When an existing lease on property owned by the estate does not adequately provide for pooling or unitization, the court may authorize the commitment of royalty or mineral interests in oil, liquid hydrocarbons, gas (including all liquid hydrocarbons in the gaseous phase in the reservoir), gaseous elements, and other minerals or any one or more of them owned by the estate being administered to agreements that provide for the operation of areas as a pool or unit for the exploration, development, and production of all those minerals, if the court finds that the pool or unit to which the agreement relates will be operated in such a manner as to protect correlative rights, or to prevent the physical or economic waste of oil, liquid hydrocarbons, gas (including all liquid hydrocarbons in the gaseous phase in the reservoir), gaseous elements, or other mineral subject thereto, and that it is in the best interests of the estate to execute the agreement. Any agreement so authorized to be executed may provide that:

(1) operations incident to the drilling of or production from a well on any portion of a pool or unit are deemed for all purposes to be the conduct of operations on or production from each separately owned tract in the pool or unit;

(2) any lease covering any part of the area committed to a pool or unit shall continue in force in its entirety as long as oil, gas, or other mineral subject to the agreement is produced in paying quantities from any part of the pooled or unitized area, as long as operations are conducted as provided in the lease on any part of the pooled or unitized area, or as long as there is a shut-in gas well on any part of the pooled or unitized area if the presence of the shut-in gas well is a ground for continuation of the lease on the terms of the lease;

(3) the production allocated by the agreement to each tract included in a pool or unit shall, when produced, be deemed for all purposes to have been produced from the tract by a well drilled on the tract;

(4) the royalties provided for on production from any tract or portion of a tract within the pool or unit shall be paid only on that portion of the production allocated to the tract in accordance with the agreement;

(5) the dry gas, before or after extraction of hydrocarbons, may be returned to a formation underlying any lands or leases committed to the agreement, and that no royalties are required to be paid on the gas so returned; and

(6) gas obtained from other sources or another tract of land may be injected into a formation underlying any land or lease committed to the agreement, and that no royalties are required to be paid on the gas so injected when same is produced from the unit.

(b) Pooling or unitization, when not adequately provided for by an existing lease on property owned by the estate, may be authorized by the court in which the proceeding is pending pursuant to and in conformity with Subsections (c)–(g) of this section.

(c) The guardian of the estate shall file with the county clerk of the county in which the guardianship proceeding is pending the guardian's written application for authority to enter into a pooling or unitization agreement supplementing, amending, or otherwise relating to, any existing lease covering property owned by the estate, or to commit royalties or other interest in minerals, whether subject to lease or not, to a pooling or unitization agreement. The application must also describe the property sufficiently as required in the original application to lease, describe briefly the lease to which the interest of the estate is subject, and set out the reasons the proposed agreement concerning the property should be made. A true copy of the proposed agreement shall be attached to the application and by reference made a part of the application, but the agreement may not be recorded in the minutes. The clerk shall immediately, after the application is filed, call it to the attention of the judge.

(d) Notice of the filing of the application by advertising, citation, or otherwise is not required.

(e) The judge may hold a hearing on the application at a time that is agreeable to the parties to the proposed agreement. The judge shall hear proof and be satisfied as to whether it is in the best interests of the estate that the proposed agreement be authorized.

The hearing may be continued from day to day and from time to time as the court finds to be necessary.

(f) If the court finds that the pool or unit to which the agreement relates will be operated in such a manner as to protect correlative rights or to prevent the physical or economic waste of oil, liquid hydrocarbons, gas (including all liquid hydrocarbons in the gaseous phase in the reservoir), gaseous elements, or other mineral subject to the pool or unit, that it is in the best interests of the estate that the agreement be executed, and that the agreement conforms substantially with the permissible provisions of Subsection (a) of this section, the court shall enter an order setting out the findings made by the court and authorizing execution of the agreement, with or without payment of cash consideration according to the agreement. If cash consideration is to be paid for the agreement, the court shall make a finding as to the necessity of increased or additional bond as a finding is made in the making of leases on payment of the cash bonus for the lease. The agreement is not valid until the increased or additional bond required by the court, if any, has been approved by the judge and filed with the clerk. If the date is not stipulated in the agreement, the date of the court's order shall be the effective date of the agreement.

Added by Acts 1993, 73rd Leg., ch. 957, § 1, eff. Sept. 1, 1993.

§ 850. Special Ancillary Instruments Executed Without Court Order

As to any valid mineral lease or pooling or unitization agreement, executed on behalf of the estate before September 1, 1993, pursuant to provisions, or by a former owner of land, minerals, or royalty affected by the lease, pooling, or unitization agreement, the guardian of the estate that is being administered, without further order of the court and without consideration, may execute division orders, transfer orders, instruments of correction, instruments designating depository banks for the reception of delay rentals or shut-in gas well royalty to accrue or become payable under the terms of the lease, or similar instruments pertaining to the lease or agreement and the property covered by the lease or agreement.

Added by Acts 1993, 73rd Leg., ch. 957, § 1, eff. Sept. 1, 1933.

§ 851. Procedure When Guardian of Estate Neglects to Apply for Authority

When the guardian of an estate neglects to apply for authority to subject property of the estate to a lease for mineral development, pooling, or unitization, or authority to commit royalty or other interest in minerals to pooling or unitization, any person interested in the estate, on written application filed with the county clerk, may cause the guardian to be cited to show cause why it is not in the best interests of the estate for the lease to be made or an agreement to be entered into. The clerk shall immediately call the filing of the application under this section to the attention of the judge of the court in which the guardianship proceeding is pending. The judge shall set a time and place for a hearing on the application. The guardian of the estate shall be cited to appear and show cause why the execution of the lease or agreement should not be ordered. On hearing and if satisfied from the proof that it would be in the best interests of the estate, the court shall enter an order requiring the guardian to file the guardian's application to subject the property of the estate to a lease for mineral development, with or without pooling or unitization provisions, or to commit royalty or other minerals to unitization, as the case may be. The procedures prescribed with respect to original application to lease or with respect to original application for authority to commit royalty or minerals to pooling or unitization shall be followed.

Added by Acts 1993, 73rd Leg., ch. 957, § 1, eff. Sept. 1, 1993.

§ 852. Validation of Certain Leases and Pooling or Unitization Agreements Based on Previous Statutes

All leases on the oil, gas, or other minerals existing on September 1, 1993, belonging to the estates of minors or other incapacitated persons and all agreements with respect to the pooling or unitization of oil, gas, or other minerals or any interest in oil, gas, or other minerals with like properties of others that have been authorized by the court having venue, executed, and delivered by a guardian or other fiduciary of the estate of a minor or incapacitated person in substantial conformity to the rules set forth in statutes on execution or delivery providing for only seven days' notice in some instances and for a brief order designating a time and place for hearing, are validated insofar as the period of notice or absence of an order setting a time and place for hearing is concerned, unless the length of time of the notice or the absence of the order is an issue in a lease or pooling or unitization agreement that is involved in a lawsuit pending on September 1, 1993.

Added by Acts 1993, 73rd Leg., ch. 957, § 1, eff. Sept. 1, 1993.

SUBPART K. PARTITION OF WARD'S ESTATE IN REALTY

§ 853. Partition of Ward's Interest in Realty

(a) If a ward owns an interest in real estate in common with another part owner or one or more part owners, and if, in the opinion of the guardian of the estate, it is in the best interests of the ward's estate to partition the real estate, the guardian may agree on a partition with the other part owners subject to the approval of the court in which the guardianship proceeding is pending.

(b) When a guardian has reached an agreement with the other part owners on how to partition the real estate, the guardian shall file with the court an application to have the agreement approved. The application filed by the guardian under this subsection shall describe the land that is to be divided and shall state why it is in the best interests of the ward's estate to partition the real estate and shall show that the proposed partition agreement is fair and just to the ward's estate.

(c) When the application required by Subsection (b) of this section is filed, the county clerk shall immediately call the filing of the application to the attention of the judge of the court in which the guardianship proceeding is pending. The judge shall designate a day to hear the application. The application must remain on file at least 10 days before any orders are made, and the judge may continue the hearing from time to time until the judge is satisfied concerning the application.

(d) If the judge is satisfied that the proposed partition of the real estate is in the best interests of the ward's estate, the court shall enter an order approving the partition and directing the guardian to execute the necessary agreement for the purpose of carrying the order and partition into effect.

(e) When a guardian has executed an agreement or will execute an agreement to partition any land in which the ward has an interest without court approval as provided by this section, the guardian shall file with the court in which the guardianship proceedings are pending an application for the approval and ratification of the partition agreement. The application must refer to the agreement in such a manner that the court can fully understand the nature of the partition and the land being divided. The application must state that, in the opinion of the guardian, the agreement is fair and just to the ward's estate and is in the best interests of the estate. When the application is filed, a hearing shall be held on the application as provided by Subsection (c) of this section. If the court is of the opinion that the partition is fairly made and that the partition is in the best interests of the ward's estate, the court shall enter an order ratifying and approving the partition agreement. When the partition is ratified and approved, the partition shall be effective and binding as if originally executed after a court order.

(f) If the guardian of the estate of a ward is of the opinion that it is in the best interests of the ward's estate that any real estate that the ward owns in common with others should be partitioned, the guardian may bring a suit in the court in which the guardianship proceeding is pending against the other part owner or part owners for the partition of the real estate. The court, if after hearing the suit is satisfied that the necessity for the partition of the real estate exists, may enter an order partitioning the real estate to the owner of the real estate.

Added by Acts 1993, 73rd Leg., ch. 957, § 1, eff. Sept. 1, 1993.

For applicability provisions of the 1993 Act, see notes following V.A.T.S. Probate Code, § 601.

SUBPART L. INVESTMENTS AND LOANS OF ESTATES OF WARDS

§ 855. Investments Without Court Order

(a) The guardian of the estate may retain, without regard to diversification of investments and without liability for any depreciation or loss resulting from the retention, any property received into a guardianship estate at its inception or added to the estate by gift, devise, or inheritance or by mutation or increase. A guardian of the estate is not relieved from the duty to take care of and manage the estate as a person of ordinary prudence, discretion, and intelligence would exercise in the management of the person's own affairs.

(b) If the guardian of the estate has on hand money that belongs to the ward that exceeds that amount of money that may be necessary for the education and maintenance of the ward, the guardian shall invest the money as follows:

(1) in bonds or other obligations of the United States;

(2) in tax-supported bonds of this state;

(3) except as limited by Subsections (c) and (d) of this section, in tax-supported bonds of a county, district, political subdivision, or incorporated city or town in this state;

(4) in shares or share accounts of a state savings and loan association or savings bank with its main office or a branch office in this state if the payment of the shares or share accounts is insured by the Federal Deposit Insurance Corporation;

(5) in the shares or share accounts of a federal savings and loan association or savings bank with its main office or a branch office in this state if the payment of the shares or share accounts is insured by the Federal Deposit Insurance Corporation;

(6) in collateral bonds of companies incorporated under the laws of this state, having a paid-in capital of $1,000,000 or more, when the bonds are a direct obligation of the company that issues the bonds and are specifically secured by first mortgage real estate notes or other securities pledged with a trustee; or

(7) in interest-bearing time deposits that may be withdrawn on or before one year after demand in a bank that does business in this state where the payment of the time deposits is insured by the Federal Deposit Insurance Corporation.

(c) The bonds of a county, district, or subdivision may be purchased only if the net funded debt of the county, district, or subdivision that issues the bonds does not exceed 10 percent of the assessed value of taxable property in the county, district, or subdivision.

(d) The bonds of a city or town may be purchased only if the net funded debt of the city or town does not exceed 10 percent of the assessed value of taxable property in the city or town less that part of the debt incurred for acquisition or improvement of revenue-producing utilities, the revenues of which are not pledged to support other obligations of the city or town.

(e) The limitations in Subsections (c) and (d) of this section do not apply to bonds issued for road purposes in this state under Section 52, Article III, of the Texas Constitution that are supported by a tax unlimited as to rate or amount.

(f) In this section, "net funded debt" means the total funded debt less sinking funds on hand.

Added by Acts 1993, 73rd Leg., ch. 957, § 1, eff. Sept. 1, 1993. Amended by Acts 1999, 76th Leg., ch. 344, § 6.007, eff. Sept. 1, 1999.

For applicability provisions of the 1993 Act, see notes following V.A.T.S. Probate Code, § 601.

§ 856. Other Investments

(a) If a guardian of an estate deems it is in the best interests of the ward the guardian is appointed to represent to invest on behalf of the ward in the Texas Tomorrow Fund established by Subchapter F, Chapter 54, Education Code,[1] or to invest in or sell any property or security in which a trustee is authorized to invest by either Section 113.056 or Subchapter F, Chapter 113, of the Texas Trust Code (Subtitle B, Title 9, Property Code),[2] and the investment or sale is not expressly permitted by other sections of this chapter, the guardian may file a written application in the court in which the guardianship is pending that asks for an order authorizing the guardian to make the desired investment or sale and states the reason why the guardian is of the opinion that the investment or sale would be beneficial to the ward. A citation or notice is not necessary under this subsection unless ordered by the court.

(b) On the hearing of the application filed under this section, the court shall enter an order authorizing the investment or sale if the court is satisfied that the investment or sale will be beneficial to the ward. The court order must specify the investment or sale to be made and contain other directions as the court finds advisable.

(c) The procedure specified in this section does not need to be followed in making an investment or sale specifically authorized by other statutes and does not apply if a different procedure is prescribed for an investment or sale by a guardian.

Added by Acts 1993, 73rd Leg., ch. 957, § 1, eff. Sept. 1, 1993. Amended by Acts 1997, 75th Leg., ch. 434, § 1, eff. Sept. 1, 1997.

[1] V.T.C.A., Education Code § 54.6001 et seq.

[2] V.T.C.A., Property Code § 111.001 et seq.

Sections 2 and 3 of Acts 1997, 75th Leg., ch. 434 provide:

"Sec. 2. A court may modify any guardianship in effect on September 1, 1997, to conform to the requirements of the Texas Probate Code, as amended by this Act, on the court's own motion or on application by the guardian or any other interested person or entity.

"Sec. 3. This Act takes effect September 1, 1997. Except as provided by Section 2 of this Act, the change in law made by this Act applies only to a person appointed by a court to serve as guardian on or after the effective date of this Act. A person appointed by a court to serve as guardian before the effective date of this Act is governed by the law in effect on the date of the person's appointment, and that law continues in effect for that purpose."

§ 857. Investment in Life Insurance or Annuities

(a) In this section, "life insurance company" means a stock or mutual legal reserve life insurance company that maintains the full legal reserves required under the laws of this state and that is licensed by the State Board of Insurance to transact the business of life insurance in this state.

(b) The guardian of the estate may invest in life, term, or endowment insurance policies, or in annuity contracts, or both, issued by a life insurance company or administered by the Veterans Administration, subject to conditions and limitations in this section.

(c) The guardian shall first apply to the court for an order that authorizes the guardian to make the investment. The application filed under this subsection must include a report that shows:

(1) in detail the financial condition of the estate at the time the application is made;

(2) the name and address of the life insurance company from which the policy or annuity contract is to be purchased and that the company is licensed by the State Board of Insurance to transact that business in this state on the date the application is filed, or that the policy or contract is administered by the Veterans Administration;

(3) a statement of the face amount and plan of the policy of insurance sought to be purchased and of the amount, frequency, and duration of the annuity payments to be provided by the annuity contract sought to be purchased;

(4) a statement of the amount, frequency, and duration of the premiums required by the policy or annuity contract; and

(5) a statement of the cash value of the policy or annuity contract at its anniversary nearest the 21st birthday of the ward, assuming that all premiums to the anniversary are paid and that there is no indebtedness against the policy or contract incurred in accordance with its terms.

(d) An insurance policy must be issued on the life of the ward, or the father, mother, spouse, child, brother, sister, grandfather, or grandmother of the ward or a person in whose life the ward may have an insurable interest.

(e) Only the ward, the ward's estate, or the father, mother, spouse, child, brother, sister, grandfather, or grandmother of the ward may be a beneficiary of the insurance policy and of the death benefit of the annuity contract, and the ward must be the annuitant in the annuity contract.

(f) The control of the policy or the annuity contract and of the incidents of ownership in the policy or annuity contract is vested in the guardian during the life and disability of the ward.

(g) The policy or annuity contract may not be amended or changed during the life and disability of the ward except on application to and order of the court.

(h) If a life, term, or endowment insurance policy or a contract of annuity is owned by the ward when a proceeding for the appointment of a guardian is begun, and it is made to appear that the company issuing the policy or contract of annuity is a life insurance company as defined by this section or the policy or contract is administered by the Veterans Administration, the policy or contract may be continued in full force and effect. All future premiums may be paid out of surplus funds of the ward's estate. The guardian shall apply to the court for an order to continue the policy or contract, or both, according to the existing terms of the policy or contract or to modify the policy or contract to fit any new developments affecting the welfare of the ward. Before any application filed under this subsection is granted, the guardian shall file a report in the court that shows in detail the financial condition of the ward's estate at the time the application is filed.

(i) The court, if satisfied by the application and the evidence adduced at the hearing that it is in the interests of the ward to grant the application, shall enter an order granting the application.

(j) A right, benefit, or interest that accrues under an insurance or annuity contract that comes under the provisions of this section shall become the exclusive property of the ward when the ward's disability is terminated.

Added by Acts 1993, 73rd Leg., ch. 957, § 1, eff. Sept. 1, 1993.

§ 858. Loans and Security for Loans

If, at any time, the guardian of the estate has on hand money belonging to the ward in an amount that is beyond what may be necessary for the education and maintenance of the ward, the guardian may lend the money for the highest rate of interest that can be obtained for the money. The guardian shall take the note of the borrower for the money that is loaned, secured by a mortgage with a power of sale on unencumbered real estate located in this state worth at least twice the amount of the note, or by collateral notes secured by vendor's lien notes, as collateral, or the guardian may purchase vendor's lien notes if at least one-half has been paid in cash or its equivalent on the land for which the notes were given.

Added by Acts 1993, 73rd Leg., ch. 957, § 1, eff. Sept. 1, 1993.

§ 859. Guardian's Liability for Loans

When the borrower of money lent by the guardian of the estate under the court's direction and on security approved by the court is unable to repay the money or the security fails, the guardian of the estate is not personally responsible for the money unless the guardian has been guilty of fraud or negligence with respect to the loan or the collection of the loan, in which case the guardian and the sureties on the bond of the guardian shall be liable for whatever loss the ward sustains because of the guardian's fraud or negligence.

Added by Acts 1993, 73rd Leg., ch. 957, § 1, eff. Sept. 1, 1993.

§ 860. Guardian's Investments in Real Estate

(a) When the guardian of the estate of a ward thinks it is best for the ward who has a surplus of money on hand to invest the money in real estate, the guardian shall file a written application in the court in which the guardianship is pending requesting a court order authorizing the guardian to make the desired investment and stating the reasons why the guardian is of the opinion that the investment would be for the benefit of the ward.

(b) When an application is filed by the guardian under this section, the judge's attention shall be called to the application, and the judge shall make investigation as necessary to obtain all the facts concerning the investment. The judge may not render an opinion or make an order on the application until 10 days from the date of the filing of the application have expired. On the hearing of the application, if the court is satisfied that the investment benefits the ward, the court shall issue an order that authorizes the guardian to make the investment. The order shall specify the investment to be made and contain other directions the court thinks are advisable.

(c) When a contract is made for the investment of money in real estate under court order, the guardian shall report the contract in writing to the courts. The court shall inquire fully into the contract. If satisfied that the investment will benefit the estate of the ward and that the title of the real estate is valid and unencumbered, the court may approve the contract and authorize the guardian to pay over the money in performance of the contract. The guardian may not pay any money on the contract until the contract is approved by court order to that effect.

(d) When the money of the ward has been invested in real estate, the title to the real estate shall be made to the ward. The guardian shall inventory, appraise, manage, and account for the real estate as other real estate of the ward.

Added by Acts 1993, 73rd Leg., ch. 957, § 1, eff. Sept. 1, 1993.

§ 861. Opinion of Attorney With Respect to Loans

When the guardian of the estate of a ward lends the money of the ward, the guardian may not pay over or transfer any money in consummation of the loan until the guardian has submitted to a reputable attorney for examination all bonds, notes, mortgages, documents, abstracts, and other papers pertaining to the loan and the guardian has received a written opinion from the attorney that all papers pertaining to the loan are regular and that the title to the bonds, notes, or real estate is good. The attorney's fee shall be paid by the borrower. The guardian may obtain a mortgagee's title insurance policy on any real estate loan instead of an abstract and attorney's opinion.

Added by Acts 1993, 73rd Leg., ch. 957, § 1, eff. Sept. 1, 1993. Amended by Acts 1995, 74th Leg., ch. 1039, § 55, eff. Sept. 1, 1995.

§ 862. Report of Loans

Not later than the 30th day after the date money belonging to a ward's estate is lent, the guardian of the ward's estate shall report to the court in writing, verified by affidavit, stating fully the facts of the loan, unless the loan was made pursuant to a court order.

Added by Acts 1993, 73rd Leg., ch. 957, § 1, eff. Sept. 1, 1993. Amended by Acts 1995, 74th Leg., ch. 1039, § 56, eff. Sept. 1, 1995.

§ 863. Liability of Guardian for Failure to Lend or Invest Funds

If the guardian of the estate neglects to invest or lend surplus money on hand at interest when the guardian can do so by using reasonable diligence, the guardian shall be liable for the principal and for the highest legal rate of interest on the principal for the time the guardian neglects to invest or lend the surplus money. The amount of principal and interest on the principal may be recovered in a court of competent jurisdiction.

Added by Acts 1993, 73rd Leg., ch. 957, § 1, eff. Sept. 1, 1993.

§ 864. Requiring Guardian to Invest or Lend Surplus Funds

If there is any surplus money of the estate in the hands of the guardian of the estate, the court, on its own motion or on written complaint filed by any person, may cause the guardian to be cited to appear and show cause why the surplus money should not be invested or lent at interest. On the hearing of a complaint filed under this section, the court shall enter an order as the law and the facts require.

Added by Acts 1993, 73rd Leg., ch. 957, § 1, eff. Sept. 1, 1993.

SUBPART M. TAX MOTIVATED AND CHARITABLE GIFTS

§ 865. Power to Make Tax-Motivated Gifts

(a) On application of the guardian of the estate or any interested party and after the posting of notice, the court, after hearing, may enter an order that authorizes the guardian to apply the principal or income of the ward's estate that is not required for the support of the ward or the ward's family during the ward's lifetime toward the establishment of an estate plan for the purpose of minimizing income, estate, inheritance, or other taxes payable out of the ward's estate on a showing that the ward will probably remain incapacitated during the ward's lifetime. On the ward's behalf, the court may authorize the guardian to make gifts, outright or in trust, of the ward's personal property or real estate to or for the benefit of:

(1) an organization to which charitable contributions may be made under the Internal Revenue Code and in which it is shown the ward would reasonably have an interest;

(2) the ward's spouse, descendant, or other person related to the ward by blood or marriage who are identifiable at the time of the order;

(3) a devisee under the ward's last validly executed will, trust, or other beneficial instrument if the instrument exists; and

(4) a person serving as guardian of the ward if the person is eligible under either Subdivision (2) or (3) of this subsection.

(b) The person making an application to the court under this section shall outline the proposed estate plan and set forth all the benefits that are to be derived from the estate plan. The application must indicate that the planned disposition is consistent with the ward's intentions if the ward's intentions can be ascertained. If the ward's intentions cannot be ascertained, the ward will be presumed to favor reduction in the incidence of the various forms of taxation and the partial distribution of the ward's estate as provided by this section.

(c) The court may appoint a guardian ad litem for the ward or any interested party at any stage of the proceedings if it is deemed advisable for the protection of the ward or the interested party.

(d) A subsequent modification of an approved plan may be made by similar application to the court.

(e) A person who makes an application to the court under this section shall mail notice of the application by certified mail to:

(1) all devisees under a will, trust, or other beneficial instrument relating to the ward's estate;

(2) the ward's spouse;

(3) the ward's dependents; and

(4) any other person as directed by the court.

Added by Acts 1993, 73rd Leg., ch. 957, § 1, eff. Sept. 1, 1993. Amended by Acts 1997, 75th Leg., ch. 77, § 9, eff. Sept. 1, 1997.

For applicability provisions of the 1993 Act, see notes following V.A.T.S. Probate Code, § 601.

§ 866. Contributions

(a) The guardian of the estate may at any time file the guardian's sworn application in writing with the county clerk requesting an order from the court in which the guardianship is pending authorizing the guardian to contribute from the income of the ward's estate a specific amount of money as stated in the application, to one or more:

(1) designated corporations, trusts, or community chests, funds, or foundations, organized and operated exclusively for religious, charitable, scientific, literary, or educational purposes; or

(2) designated nonprofit federal, state, county, or municipal projects operated exclusively for public health or welfare.

(b) When an application is filed under this section, the county clerk shall immediately call the filing of the application to the attention of the judge of the court. The judge, by written order filed with the clerk, shall designate a day to hear the application. The application shall remain on file at least 10 days before the hearing is held. The judge may postpone or continue the hearing from time to time until the judge is satisfied concerning the application.

(c) On the conclusion of a hearing under this section, the court may enter an order authorizing the guardian to make a contribution from the income of the ward's estate to a particular donee designated in the application and order if the court is satisfied and finds from the evidence that:

(1) the amount of the proposed contribution stated in the application will probably not exceed 20 percent

of the net income of the ward's estate for the current calendar year;

(2) the net income of the ward's estate for the current calendar year exceeds, or probably will exceed, $25,000;

(3) the full amount of the contribution, if made, will probably be deductible from the ward's gross income in determining the net income of the ward under applicable federal income tax laws and rules;

(4) the condition of the ward's estate justifies a contribution in the proposed amount; and

(5) the proposed contribution is reasonable in amount and is for a worthy cause.

Added by Acts 1993, 73rd Leg., ch. 957, § 1, eff. Sept. 1, 1993.

SUBPART N. MANAGEMENT TRUSTS

§ 867. Creation of Management Trust

On application by the guardian of a ward or by a ward's attorney ad litem at any time after the date of the attorney's appointment under Section 646 of this code, the court in which the guardianship proceeding is pending may enter an order that creates for the ward's benefit a trust for the management of guardianship funds if the court finds that the creation of the trust is in the ward's best interests. The order shall direct the guardian or another person to deliver all or part of the assets of the guardianship to a trust company or a state or national bank that has trust powers in this state. The order shall include terms, conditions, and limitations placed on the trust. The court shall maintain the trust under the same cause number as the guardianship proceeding.

Added by Acts 1993, 73rd Leg., ch. 957, § 1, eff. Sept. 1, 1993. Amended by Acts 1995, 74th Leg., ch. 1039, § 57, eff. Sept. 1, 1995; Acts 1997, 75th Leg., ch. 1375, § 1, eff. Sept. 1, 1997.

For applicability provisions of the 1993 Act, see notes following § 601.

Sections 7 and 8 of Acts 1997, 75th Leg., ch. 1375 provide:

"Sec. 7. (a) A trust may be created under Section 867, Texas Probate Code, as amended by this Act, regardless of the date on which the guardianship was created.

"(b) A trust otherwise valid under Section 867, Texas Probate Code, is not invalid solely because it was created for a guardianship that was in existence before September 1, 1993, and those trusts are validated as of the date of the creation of the trust.

"Sec. 8. This Act takes effect September 1, 1997, and applies to all trusts created under Section 867, Texas Probate Code, as amended by this Act, regardless of the date on which the trusts were created."

§ 868. Terms of Management Trust

(a) Except as provided by Subsection (d) of this section, a trust created under Section 867 of this code must provide that:

(1) the ward is the sole beneficiary of the trust;

(2) the trustee may disburse an amount of the trust's principal or income as the trustee determines is necessary to expend for the health, education, support, or maintenance of the ward;

(3) the income of the trust that the trustee does not disburse under Subdivision (2) of this subsection must be added to the principal of the trust;

(4) the trustee serves without giving a bond; and

(5) the trustee, on annual application to the court and subject to the court's approval, is entitled to receive reasonable compensation for services that the trustee provided to the ward as the ward's trustee that is:

(A) to be paid from the trust's income, principal, or both; and

(B) determined in the same manner as compensation of a guardian of an estate under Section 665 of this code.

(b) The trust may provide that a trustee make a distribution, payment, use, or application of trust funds for the health, education, support, or maintenance of the ward or of another person whom the ward is legally obligated to support, as necessary and without the intervention of a guardian or other representative of the ward, to:

(1) the ward's guardian;

(2) a person who has physical custody of the ward or another person whom the ward is legally obligated to support; or

(3) a person providing a good or service to the ward or another person whom the ward is legally obligated to support.

(c) Repealed by Acts 1997, 75th Leg., ch. 1375, § 6, eff. Sept. 1, 1997.

(d) When creating or modifying a trust, the court may omit or modify terms required by Subsection (a)(1) or (2) of this section only if the court determines that the omission or modification:

(1) is necessary and appropriate for the ward to be eligible to receive public benefits or assistance under a state or federal program that is not otherwise available to the ward; and

(2) is in the ward's best interests.

(e) The court may include additional provisions in a trust created or modified under this section if the court determines an addition does not conflict with Subsection (a) and, if appropriate, Subsection (d) of this section.

(f) If the trustee determines that it is in the best interest of the ward, the trustee may invest funds of the trust in the Texas tomorrow fund established by Subchapter F, Chapter 54, Education Code.

Added by Acts 1993, 73rd Leg., ch. 957, § 1, eff. Sept. 1, 1993. Amended by Acts 1995, 74th Leg., ch. 1039, §§ 58, 59, eff. Sept. 1, 1995; Acts 1997, 75th Leg., ch. 1375, §§ 2, 6, eff. Sept. 1, 1997; Acts 1999, 76th Leg., ch. 94, § 2, eff. May 17, 1999.

§ 868A. Discharge of Guardian of Estate and Continuation of Trust

On or at any time after the creation of a trust under this subpart, the court may discharge the guardian of the ward's estate only if a guardian of the ward's person remains and the court determines that the discharge is in the ward's best interests.

Added by Acts 1997, 75th Leg., ch. 1375, § 3, eff. Sept. 1, 1997.

§ 869. Trust Amendment, Modification, or Revocation

(a) The court may amend, modify, or revoke the trust at any time before the date of the trust's termination.

(b) The ward or guardian of the ward's estate may not revoke the trust.

Added by Acts 1993, 73rd Leg., ch. 957, § 1, eff. Sept. 1, 1993.

§ 869A. Successor Trustee

The court may appoint a corporate fiduciary as successor trustee if the trustee resigns, becomes ineligible, or is removed.

Added by Acts 1995, 74th Leg., ch. 1039, § 60, eff. Sept. 1, 1995.

§ 869B. Applicability of Texas Trust Code

(a) A trust created under Section 867 of this code is subject to Subtitle B, Title 9, Property Code.

(b) To the extent of a conflict between Subtitle B, Title 9, Property Code, and a provision of this subpart or of the trust, the provision of the subpart or trust controls.

Added by Acts 1997, 75th Leg., ch. 1375, § 3, eff. Sept. 1, 1997.

§ 869C. Jurisdiction Over Trust Matters

A court that creates a trust under Section 867 of this code has the same jurisdiction to hear matters relating to the trust as the court has with respect to the guardianship and other matters covered by this chapter.

Added by Acts 1997, 75th Leg., ch. 1375, § 3, eff. Sept. 1, 1997.

§ 870. Termination of Trust

(a) If the ward is a minor, the trust terminates:

(1) on the death of the ward or the ward's 18th birthday, whichever is earlier; or

(2) on the date provided by court order which may not be later than the ward's 25th birthday.

(b) If the ward is an incapacitated person other than a minor, the trust terminates on the date the court determines that continuing the trust is no longer in the ward's best interests or on the death of the ward.

Added by Acts 1993, 73rd Leg., ch. 957, § 1, eff. Sept. 1, 1993. Amended by Acts 1995, 74th Leg., ch. 1039, § 61, eff. Sept. 1, 1995; Acts 1997, 75th Leg., ch. 1375, § 4, eff. Sept. 1, 1997.

§ 871. Annual Accounting

(a) The trustee shall prepare and file with the court an annual accounting of transactions in the trust in the same manner and form that is required of a guardian under this chapter.

(b) The trustee shall provide a copy of the annual account to the guardian of the ward's estate or person.

(c) The annual account is subject to court review and approval in the same manner that is required of an annual account prepared by a guardian under this chapter.

Added by Acts 1993, 73rd Leg., ch. 957, § 1, eff. Sept. 1, 1993.

§ 872. Liability

The guardian of the person or of the estate of the ward or the surety on the bond of the guardian is not liable for an act or omission of the trustee.

Added by Acts 1993, 73rd Leg., ch. 957, § 1, eff. Sept. 1, 1993. Amended by Acts 1995, 74th Leg., ch. 1039, § 62, eff. Sept. 1, 1995.

§ 873. Distribution of Trust Property

Unless otherwise provided by the court, the trustee shall:

(1) prepare a final account in the same form and manner that is required of a guardian under Section 749 of this code; and

(2) on court approval, distribute the principal or any undistributed income of the trust:

(A) to the ward when the trust terminates on its own terms;

(B) to the successor trustee on appointment of a successor trustee; or

(C) to the representative of the deceased ward's estate on the ward's death.

Added by Acts 1993, 73rd Leg., ch. 957, § 1, eff. Sept. 1, 1993. Amended by Acts 1995, 74th Leg., ch. 1039, § 63, eff. Sept. 1, 1995.

PART 5. SPECIAL PROCEEDINGS AND ORDERS

SUBPART A. TEMPORARY GUARDIANSHIPS

§ 875. Temporary Guardian—Procedure

(a) If a court is presented with substantial evidence that a person may be a minor or other incapacitated person, and the court has probable cause to believe that the person or person's estate, or both, requires the immediate appointment of a guardian, the court shall appoint a temporary guardian with limited powers as the circumstances of the case require.

(b) A person for whom a temporary guardian has been appointed may not be presumed to be incapacitated. The person retains all rights and powers that are not specifically granted to the person's temporary guardian by court order.

(c) A sworn, written application for the appointment of a temporary guardian may be filed before the court appoints a temporary guardian. The application must be filed not later than the end of the next business day of the court after the date of appointment of the temporary guardian. The application must state:

(1) the name and address of the person who is the subject of the guardianship proceeding;

(2) the danger to the person or property alleged to be imminent;

(3) the type of appointment and the particular protection and assistance being requested;

(4) the facts and reasons supporting the allegations and requests;

(5) the name, address, and qualification of the proposed temporary guardian;

(6) the name, address, and interest of the applicant;

(7) the social security numbers of the applicant and proposed ward; and

(8) if applicable, that the proposed temporary guardian is a private professional guardian who has complied with the requirements of Section 697 of this code.

(d) At the earliest of the filing of an application for temporary guardianship or the appointment of a temporary guardian, the court shall appoint an attorney to represent the proposed ward in all guardianship proceedings in which independent counsel has not been retained by or on behalf of the proposed ward.

(e) On the filing of an application for temporary guardianship, the clerk shall issue notice that shall be served on the respondent, the respondent's appointed attorney, and the proposed temporary guardian named in the application, if that person is not the applicant. The notice must describe the rights of the parties and the date, time, place, purpose, and possible consequences of a hearing on the application. A copy of the application and, if applicable, a copy of the order appointing the temporary guardian must be attached to the notice.

(f)(1) A hearing shall be held not later than the 10th day after the date of the filing of the application for temporary guardianship unless the hearing date is extended as provided by Subdivision (2) of this subsection. At a hearing under this section, the respondent has the right to:

(A) receive prior notice;

(B) have representation by counsel;

(C) be present;

(D) present evidence and confront and cross-examine witnesses; and

(E) a closed hearing if requested by the respondent or the respondent's attorney.

(2) Every temporary guardianship granted before a hearing on the application required by Subdivision (1) of this subsection expires on its own terms at the conclusion of the hearing unless the respondent or the respondent's attorney consents that the order appointing the temporary guardian may be extended for a longer period not to exceed 60 days after the date of the filing of the application for temporary guardianship.

(3) Every temporary guardianship granted before a hearing on the application required by Subdivision (1) of this subsection shall be set for hearing at the earliest possible date and takes precedence over all matters except older matters of the same character.

(4) Every temporary guardianship granted before a hearing on the application required by Subdivision (1) of this subsection must include an order that sets a certain date for hearing on the application for temporary guardianship.

(5) On one day's notice to the party who obtained a temporary guardianship before a hearing on the application required by Subdivision (1) of this subsection, the respondent or the respondent's attorney may appear and move for the dissolution or modification of the temporary guardianship. If a motion is made for dissolution or modification of the temporary guardianship, the court shall hear and determine the motion as expeditiously as the ends of justice require.

(6) If the applicant is not the proposed temporary guardian, a temporary guardianship may not be granted before a hearing on the application required by Subdivision (1) of this subsection unless the proposed temporary guardian appears in court.

(g) If at the conclusion of the hearing required by Subsection (f)(1) of this section the court determines that the applicant has established that there is substantial evidence that the person is a minor or other incapacitated person, that there is imminent danger that the physical health or safety of the respondent will be seriously impaired, or that the respondent's estate will be seriously damaged or dissipated unless immediate action is taken, the court shall appoint a temporary guardian by written order. The court shall assign to the temporary guardian only those powers and duties that are necessary to protect the respondent against the imminent danger shown. The powers and duties must be described in the order of appointment.

(h) Except as provided by Subsection (k) of this section, a temporary guardianship may not remain in effect for more than 60 days.

(i) If the court appoints a temporary guardian after the hearing required by Subsection (f)(1) of this section, all court costs, including attorney's fees, may be assessed as provided in Section 665A, 665B, or 669 of this code.

(j) The court may not customarily or ordinarily appoint the Department of Protective and Regulatory Services as a temporary guardian under this section. The appointment of the department as a temporary guardian under this section should be made only as a last resort.

(k) If an application for a temporary guardianship, for the conversion of a temporary guardianship to a permanent guardianship, or for a permanent guardianship is challenged or contested, the court, on the court's own motion or on the motion of any interested party, may appoint a new temporary guardian without issuing additional citation if the court finds that the appointment is necessary to protect the proposed ward or the proposed ward's estate. A temporary guardian appointed under this subsection must qualify in the same form and manner required of a guardian under this code. The term of the temporary guardian expires at the conclusion of the hearing challenging or contesting the application or on the date a permanent guardian the court appoints for the proposed ward qualifies to serve as the ward's guardian.

Added by Acts 1993, 73rd Leg., ch. 957, § 1, eff. Sept. 1, 1993. Amended by Acts 1995, 74th Leg., ch. 76, § 8.074, eff. Sept. 1, 1995; Acts 1995, 74th Leg., ch. 1039, § 64, eff. Sept. 1, 1995; Acts 1999, 76th Leg., ch. 997, § 2, eff. Sept. 1, 1999.

For applicability provisions of the 1993 Act, see notes following V.A.T.S. Probate Code, § 601.

Section 3 of Acts 1999, 76th Leg., ch. 997 provides:

"(a) This Act takes effect September 1, 1999, and applies only to a proceeding for the appointment of a guardian instituted on or after the effective date of this Act.

"(b) A proceeding for the appointment of a guardian instituted before the effective date of this Act is governed by the law in effect on the date on which the proceeding was instituted, and the former law is continued in effect for that purpose."

§ 876. Authority of Temporary Guardian

When the temporary guardian files the oath and bond required under this chapter, the court order appointing the temporary guardian takes effect without the necessity for issuance of letters of guardianship. The clerk shall note compliance with oath and bond requirements by the appointed guardian on a certificate attached to the order. The order shall be evidence of the temporary guardian's authority to act within the scope of the powers and duties set forth in the order. The clerk may not issue certified copies of the order until the oath and bond requirements are satisfied.

Added by Acts 1993, 73rd Leg., ch. 957, § 1, eff. Sept. 1, 1993.

§ 877. Powers of Temporary Guardian

All the provisions of this chapter relating to the guardianship of persons and estates of incapacitated persons apply to a temporary guardianship of the persons and estates of incapacitated persons, insofar as the same may be made applicable.

Added by Acts 1993, 73rd Leg., ch. 957, § 1, eff. Sept. 1, 1993.

§ 878. Accounting

At the expiration of a temporary appointment, the appointee shall file with the clerk of the court a sworn list of all property of the estate that has come into the hands of the appointee, a return of all sales made by the appointee, and a full exhibit and account of all of the appointee's acts as temporary appointee.

Added by Acts 1993, 73rd Leg., ch. 957, § 1, eff. Sept. 1, 1993.

§ 879. Closing Temporary Guardianship

The court shall act on the list, return, exhibit, and account filed under Section 878 of this code. Whenever temporary letters expire or cease to be effective for any reason, the court shall immediately enter an order requiring the temporary appointee to deliver the estate remaining in the temporary appointee's possession to the person who is legally entitled to the possession of the estate. The temporary appointee shall be discharged and the sureties on the bond of the temporary appointee shall be released as to future liability on proof that the appointee delivered the property as required by this section.

Added by Acts 1993, 73rd Leg., ch. 957, § 1, eff. Sept. 1, 1993.

SUBPART B. GUARDIANSHIPS FOR NONRESIDENTS

§ 881. Nonresident Guardian

(a) A nonresident of this state may be appointed and qualified as guardian or coguardian of a nonresident ward's estate located in this state in the same manner provided by this code for the appointment and qualification of a resident as guardian of the estate of an incapacitated person if:

(1) a court of competent jurisdiction in the geographical jurisdiction in which the nonresident resides appointed the nonresident guardian;

(2) the nonresident is qualified as guardian or as a fiduciary legal representative by whatever name known in the foreign jurisdiction of the property or estate of the ward located in the jurisdiction of the foreign court; and

(3) with the written application for appointment in the county court of any county in this state in which all or part of the ward's estate is located, the nonresident files a complete transcript of the proceedings from the records of the court in which the nonresident applicant was appointed, showing the applicant's appointment and qualification as the guardian or fiduciary legal representative of the ward's property or estate.

(b) The transcript required by Subsection (a) of this section must be certified to and attested by the clerk of the foreign court or the officer of the court charged by law with custody of the court records, under the court seal, if any. The certificate of the judge, chief justice, or presiding magistrate, as applicable, of the foreign court must be attached to the transcript, certifying that the attestation of the transcript by the clerk or legal custodian of the court records is in correct form.

(c) If the nonresident applicant meets the requirements of this section, without the necessity of any notice or citation, the court shall enter an order appointing the nonresident. After the nonresident applicant qualifies in the manner required of resident guardians and files with the court a power of attorney appointing a resident agent to accept service of process in all actions or proceedings with respect to the estate, the clerk shall issue the letters of guardianship to the nonresident guardian.

(d) After qualification, the nonresident guardian shall file an inventory and appraisement of the estate of the ward in this state subject to the jurisdiction of the court, as in ordinary cases, and is subject to all applicable provisions of this code with respect to the handling and settlement of estates by resident guardians.

(e) A resident guardian who has any of the estate of a ward may be ordered by the court to deliver the estate to a duly qualified and acting guardian of the ward.

Added by Acts 1993, 73rd Leg., ch. 957, § 1, eff. Sept. 1, 1993. Amended by Acts 1995, 74th Leg., ch. 1039, § 65, eff. Sept. 1, 1995.

For applicability provisions of the 1993 Act, see notes following V.A.T.S. Probate Code, § 601.

§ 881A. Nonresident Guardian's Removal of Ward's Property From State

A nonresident guardian, regardless of whether the nonresident guardian is qualified under this code, may remove personal property of the ward out of the state if:

(1) the removal does not conflict with the tenure of the property or the terms and limitations of the guardianship under which the property is held; and

(2) all debts known to exist against the estate in this state are paid or secured by bond payable to and approved by the judge of the court in which guardianship proceedings are pending in this state.

Added by Acts 1995, 74th Leg., ch. 1039, § 66, eff. Sept. 1, 1995.

§ 882. Nonresident as Ward

Guardianship of the estate of a nonresident incapacitated person who owns property in this state may be granted, if necessary, in the same manner as for the property of a resident of this state. A court in the county in which the principal estate of the ward is located has jurisdiction to appoint a guardian. The court shall take all actions and make all necessary orders with respect to the estate of the ward for the maintenance, support, care, or education of the ward, out of the proceeds of the ward's estate, in the same manner as if the ward were a resident of this state and was sent abroad by the court for education or treatment. If a qualified nonresident guardian of the estate later qualifies in this state under Section 881 of this code, the court shall close the resident guardianship.

Added by Acts 1993, 73rd Leg., ch. 957, § 1, eff. Sept. 1, 1993.

SUBPART C. INCAPACITATED SPOUSE AND COMMUNITY PROPERTY

§ 883. Incapacitated Spouse

When a husband or wife is judicially declared to be incapacitated, the other spouse, in the capacity of surviving partner of the marital partnership, acquires full power to manage, control, and dispose of the entire community estate, including the part of the community estate that the incapacitated spouse legally has the power to manage in the absence of the incapacity, without an administration. If the court finds that it is in the best interest of the incapacitated spouse and that the other spouse would not be disqualified to serve as guardian under Section 681 of this code, guardianship of the estate of the incapacitated spouse may not be necessary when the other spouse is not incapacitated unless the incapacitated spouse owns separate property, and the guardianship will be of the separate property only. The qualification of a guardian of the estate of an incapacitated spouse does not deprive the competent spouse of the right to manage, control, and dispose of the entire community estate as provided in this chapter.

Added by Acts 1993, 73rd Leg., ch. 957, § 1, eff. Sept. 1, 1993.

For applicability provisions of the 1993 Act, see notes following V.A.T.S. Probate Code, § 601.

§ 883A. Recovery of Capacity

The special powers of management, control, and disposition vested in the same [1] spouse by this code shall terminate when the decree of a court of competent jurisdiction finds that the mental capacity of the other spouse has been recovered.

Added by Acts 1995, 74th Leg., ch. 1039, § 67, eff. Sept. 1, 1995.

[1] So in enrolled bill.

§ 884. Delivery to Spouse

A guardian of the estate of an incapacitated married person who, as guardian, is administering community property as part of the estate of the ward, shall deliver on demand the community property to the spouse who is not incapacitated.

Added by Acts 1993, 73rd Leg., ch. 957, § 1, eff. Sept. 1, 1993.

SUBPART D. RECEIVERSHIP FOR MINORS AND OTHER INCAPACITATED PERSONS

§ 885. Receivership

(a) When the estate of a minor or other incapacitated person or any portion of the estate of the minor or other incapacitated person appears in danger of injury, loss, or waste and in need of a guardianship or other representative and there is no guardian of the estate who is qualified in this state and a guardian is not needed, the county judge of the county in which the minor or other incapacitated person resides or in which the endangered estate is located shall enter an order, with or without application, appointing a suitable person as receiver to take charge of the estate. The court order shall require a receiver appointed under this section to give bond as in ordinary receiverships in an amount the judge deems necessary to protect the estate. The court order shall specify the duties and powers of the receiver as the judge deems necessary for the protection, conservation, and preservation of the estate. The clerk shall enter an order made under this section on the minutes of the court. The person who is appointed as receiver shall make and submit a bond for the judge's approval and shall file the bond, when approved, with the clerk. The person who is appointed receiver shall proceed to take charge of the endangered estate pursuant to the powers and duties vested in the person by the order of appointment and subsequent orders made by the judge.

(b) During the pendency of the receivership, when the needs of the minor or other incapacitated person require the use of the income or corpus of the estate for the education, clothing, or subsistence of the minor or other incapacitated person, the judge, with or without application, shall enter an order on the minutes of the court that appropriates an amount of income or corpus that is sufficient for that purpose. The receiver shall use the amount appropriated by the court to pay a claim for the education, clothing, or subsistence of the minor or other incapacitated person that is presented to the judge for approval and ordered by the judge to be paid.

(c) During the pendency of the receivership, when the receiver has on hand an amount of money that belongs to the minor or other incapacitated person that is in excess of the amount needed for current necessities and expenses, the receiver, under direction of the judge, may invest, lend, or contribute the excess money or any portion of the money in the manner, for the security, and on the terms and conditions provided by this chapter for investments, loans, or contributions by guardians. The receiver shall report to the judge all transactions made under this subsection in the same manner that a report is required of a guardian under this chapter.

(d) All necessary expenses incurred by the receiver in administering the estate may be rendered monthly to the judge in the form of a sworn statement of account that includes a report of the receiver's acts, the condition of the estate, the status of the threatened danger to the estate, and the progress made toward abatement of the danger. If the judge is satisfied that the statement is correct and reasonable in all respects, the judge shall promptly enter an order approving the expenses and authorizing the receiver to be reimbursed from the funds of the estate in the receiver's hands. A receiver shall be compensated for services rendered in the receiver's official capacity in the same manner and amount as provided by this chapter for similar services rendered by guardians of estates.

(e) When the threatened danger has abated and the estate is no longer liable to injury, loss, or waste because there is no guardian or other representative of the estate, the receiver shall report to the judge, file with the clerk a full and final sworn account of all property of the estate the receiver received, had on hand when the receivership was pending, all sums paid out, all acts performed by the receiver with respect to the estate, and all property of the estate that remains in the receiver's hands on the date of the report. On the filing of the report, the clerk shall issue and cause to be posted a notice to all persons interested in the welfare of the minor or other incapacitated person and shall give personal notice to the person who has custody of the minor or other incapacitated person to appear before the judge at a time and place specified in the notice and contest the report and account if the person desires.

(f) If on hearing the receiver's report and account the judge is satisfied that the danger of injury, loss, or waste to the estate has abated and that the report and account are correct, the judge shall enter an order finding that the danger of injury, loss, or waste to the estate has abated and shall direct the receiver to deliver the estate to the person from whom the receiver took possession as receiver, to the person who has custody of the minor or other incapacitated person, or to another person as the judge may find is entitled to possession of the estate. A person who receives the estate under this subsection shall execute and file with the clerk an appropriate receipt for the estate that is delivered to the person. The judge's order shall discharge the receivership and the sureties on the bond of the receiver. If the judge is not satisfied that the danger has abated, or if the judge is not satisfied with the receiver's report and account, the judge shall enter an order that continues the receivership in effect until the judge is satisfied that the danger has abated or is satisfied with the report and account.

(g) An order or a bond, report, account, or notice in a receivership proceeding must be recorded in the minutes of the court.

Added by Acts 1993, 73rd Leg., ch. 957, § 1, eff. Sept. 1, 1993.

For applicability provisions of the 1993 Act, see notes following V.A.T.S. Probate Code, § 601.

§§ 886 to 886F. Repealed by Acts 1999, 76th Leg., ch. 1081, § 7, eff. Sept. 1, 1999

SUBPART E. PAYMENT OF CLAIMS WITHOUT GUARDIANSHIP

§ 887. Payment of Claims Without Guardianship and Administration of Terminated Guardianship Assets

(a) When a resident person who is a minor or other incapacitated person, or the former ward of a guardianship terminated under Subpart C, Part 4,[1] of this code, who are referred to in this section as "creditor," are without a legal guardian of the person's estate, and the person is entitled to money in an amount that is $50,000 or less, the right to which is liquidated and is uncontested in any pending lawsuit, the debtor may pay the money to the county clerk of the county in which the creditor resides to the account of the creditor, giving the creditor's name, the creditor's social security identification number, the nature of the creditor's disability, and, if the creditor is a minor, the minor's age, and the creditor's post-office address. The receipt for the money signed by the clerk is binding on the creditor as of the date of receipt and to the extent of the payment. The clerk, by letter mailed to the address given by the debtor, shall apprise the creditor of the fact that the deposit was made. On receipt of the payment by the clerk,. the clerk shall call the receipt of the payment to the court's attention and shall invest the money as authorized under this chapter pursuant to court order in the name and for the account of the minor or other person entitled to the money. Any increase, dividend, or income from an investment made under this section shall be credited to the account of the minor or other person entitled to the investment. Any money that is deposited under the terms of this section that has not been paid out shall be subject to the provisions of this chapter not later than October 1, 1993.

(b) Not later than March 1 of each calendar year, the clerk of the court shall make a written report to the court of the status of an investment made by the clerk under this section. The report must contain:

(1) the amount of the original investment or the amount of the investment at the last annual report, whichever is later;

(2) any increase, dividend, or income from such investment since the last annual report;

(3) the total amount of the investment and all increases, dividends, or income at the date of the report; and

(4) the name of the depository or the type of investment.

(c) The father or mother, or unestranged spouse, of the creditor, with priority being given to the spouse who resides in this state or if there is no spouse and both father and mother are dead or are nonresidents of this state, then the person who resides in this state who has actual custody of the creditor, as custodian and on filing with the clerk written application and bond approved by the county judge of the county, may withdraw the money from the clerk for the use and benefit of the creditor, the bond to be in double the amount of the money and to be payable to the judge or the judge's successors in office and to be conditioned that the custodian will use the money for the creditor's benefit under directions of the court and that the custodian, when legally called on to do so, will faithfully account to the creditor and the creditor's heirs or legal representatives for the money and any increase to the money on the removal of the disability to which the creditor is subject, or on the creditor's death, or the appointment of a guardian for the creditor. A fee or commission may not be allowed to the custodian for taking care of, handling, or expending the money withdrawn by the custodian.

(d) When the custodian has expended the money in accordance with directions of the court or has otherwise complied with the terms of the custodian's bond by accounting for the money and any increase in the money, the custodian shall file with the county clerk of the county the custodian's sworn report of the custodian's accounting. The filing of the custodian's report, when approved by the court, operates as a discharge of the person as custodian and of the person's sureties from all further liability under the bond. The court shall satisfy itself that the report is true and correct and may require proof as in other cases.

(e) When a nonresident minor, a nonresident person who is adjudged by a court of competent jurisdiction to be incapacitated, or the former ward of a guardianship terminated under Subpart C, Part 4, of this code who has no legal guardian qualified in this state is entitled to money in an amount that is not more than $50,000 owing as a result of transactions within this state, the right to which is liquidated and is uncontested in any pending lawsuit in this state, the debtor in this state may pay the money to the guardian of the creditor who is duly qualified in the domiciliary jurisdiction or to the county clerk of any county in this state in which real property owned by the nonresident person is located. If the person is not known to own any real property in any county in this state the debtor has the right to pay the money to the county clerk of the county of this state in which the debtor resides. In either case, the debtor's payment to the clerk is for the use and benefit and for the account of the nonresident creditor. The receipt for the payment signed by the clerk that recites the name of the creditor and the post office address of the creditor, if known, is binding on the creditor as of the date and to the extent of the payment. The clerk shall handle the money paid to the clerk by the debtor in the same manner as provided for cases of payments to the accounts of residents of this state under Subsections (a)–(d) of this section. All applicable provisions of Subsections (a)–(d) of this section apply to the handling and disposition of money or any increase, dividend, or income paid to the clerk for the use, benefit, and account of the nonresident creditor.

(f) If a person who is authorized to withdraw the money does not withdraw the money from the clerk as provided for in this section, the creditor, after termination of the creditor's disability, or the subsequent personal representative of the creditor or the creditor's heirs may withdraw, at any time and without special bond for the purpose, the money on simply exhibiting to the clerk an order of the county or probate court of the county where the money is held by the clerk that directs the clerk to deliver the money to the creditor, to the creditor's personal representative, or to the creditor's heirs named in the order. Before the court issues an order under this subsection, the person's identity and the person's credentials must be proved to the court's satisfaction.

(g) When it is made to appear to the judge of a county court, district court, or other court of this state, by an affidavit executed by the superintendent, business manager, or field representative of any eleemosynary institution of this state, that a certain inmate in the institution is a person who has a mental disability, an incapacitated person, or a person whose mental illness or mental incapacity, or both, renders the person incapable of caring for himself and of managing the person's own property and financial affairs, there is no known legal guardian appointed for the estate of the inmate, and there is on deposit in the court registry a certain sum of money that belongs to the inmate that does not exceed $10,000, the court may order the disposition of the funds as provided by this subsection. The court, on satisfactory proof by affidavit or otherwise that the inmate is a person who has a mental disability, an incapacitated person, or a person whose mental illness or mental incapacity, or both, renders the inmate incapable of caring for the inmate's self and of managing the inmate's own property and financial affairs and is without a legally appointed guardian of the inmate's estate, may by order direct the clerk of the court to pay the money to the institution for the use and benefit of the inmate. The state institution to which the payment is made may not be required to give bond or security for receiving the fund from the court registry, and the receipt from the state institution for the payment, or the canceled check or warrant by which the payment was made, shall be sufficient evidence of the disposition of the payment. The clerk of the court is relieved of further responsibility for the disposition. On receipt of the money, the institution shall deposit all of the amount of money received to the trust account of the inmate. The money deposited by the institution in the trust account is to be used by or for the personal use of the owner of the trust account under the rules or custom of the institution in the expenditure of the funds by the inmate or for the use and benefit of the inmate by the responsible officer of the institution. This subsection is cumulative of all other laws affecting the rights of a person who has a mental disability, an incapacitated person, or a person who has a mental illness and affecting money that belongs to the person as an inmate of a state eleemosynary institution. If the inmate dies leaving a balance in the inmate's trust account, the balance may be applied to the burial expenses of the inmate or applied to the care, support, and treatment account of the inmate at the eleemosynary institution. After the expenditure of all funds in the trust account or after the death of the inmate, the responsible officer shall furnish a statement of expenditures of the funds to the nearest relative who is entitled to receive the statement. A copy of the statement shall be filed with the court that first granted the order to dispose of the funds in accordance with the provisions of this chapter.

Added by Acts 1993, 73rd Leg., ch. 957, § 1, eff. Sept. 1, 1993. Amended by Acts 1997, 75th Leg., ch. 295, § 1, eff. Sept. 1, 1997.

[1] V.A.T.S. Probate Code, § 745 et seq.

For applicability provisions of the 1993 Act, see notes following V.A.T.S. Probate Code, § 601.

SUBPART F. SALE OF PROPERTY OF MINORS AND CERTAIN WARDS

Acts 1997, 75th Leg., ch. 295, § 3 amended the Subpart heading

§ 889. Sale of Property of a Minor by a Parent Without Guardianship

(a) When the net value of the minor's interest in real or personal property in an estate does not exceed $50,000, a natural or adoptive parent, or the managing conservator, of a minor who is not a ward may apply to the court for an order to sell the real or personal property of a minor in an estate without being appointed guardian. A minor may not disaffirm a sale of property pursuant to a court order under this section.

(b) The parent shall apply to the court under oath for the sale of the property. Venue for the application under this section is the same as venue for an application for the appointment of a guardian for a minor. The application must contain:

(1) a legal description of the real property and a description that identifies the personal property;

(2) the name of the minor and the minor's interest in the property;

(3) the name of the purchaser;

(4) a statement that the sale of the minor's interest in the property is for cash; and

(5) a statement that all funds received by the parent shall be used for the use and benefit of the minor.

(c) On receipt of the application, the court shall set the application for hearing at a date not earlier than five days from the date of the filing of the application. If the court deems it necessary, the court may cause citation to be issued.

(d) At the time of the hearing of the application filed under this section, the court shall order the sale of the property if the court is satisfied from the evidence that the sale is in the best interests of the minor. The court may require an independent appraisal of the property to be sold to establish the minimum sale price.

(e) When the court enters the order of sale, the purchaser of the property shall pay the proceeds of the sale belonging to the minor into the court registry.

(f) Nothing in this section prevents the proceeds deposited in the registry from being withdrawn from the court registry under Section 887 of this code.

Added by Acts 1993, 73rd Leg., ch. 957, § 1, eff. Sept. 1, 1993. Amended by Acts 1995, 74th Leg., ch. 1039, §§ 68, 69, eff. Sept. 1, 1995; Acts 1997, 75th Leg., ch. 295, § 2, eff. Sept. 1, 1997.

For applicability provisions of the 1993 Act, see notes following V.A.T.S. Probate Code, § 601.

§ 890. Sale of Property of Ward Without Guardianship of the Estate

(a) This section applies only to a ward who has a guardian of the person but does not have a guardian of the estate.

(b) When a ward has an interest in real or personal property in an estate and the net value of the interest does not exceed $50,000, the guardian may apply under oath to the court for an order to sell the ward's interest in the property without being appointed guardian of the estate. A ward may not disaffirm a sale of property pursuant to a court order under this section.

(c) Venue for an application under this section is the same as venue for an application for the appointment of a guardian for the ward. The application must contain the same information required by Section 889(b) of this code.

(d) On receipt of the application, the court shall set the application for hearing at a date not earlier than five days from the date of the filing of the application. If the court considers it necessary, the court may cause citation to be issued.

(e) The procedures and evidentiary requirements for a hearing of an application filed under this section are the same as the procedures and evidentiary requirements for a hearing of an application filed under Section 889 of this code.

(f) When the court enters the order of sale, the purchaser of the property shall pay the proceeds of the sale belonging to the ward into the court registry.

(g) Nothing in this section prevents the proceeds deposited in the court registry from being withdrawn as prescribed by Section 887 of this code.

Added by Acts 1997, 75th Leg., ch. 295, § 4, eff. Sept. 1, 1997.

SUBPART G. NONRESIDENT GUARDIANS [REPEALED]

§§ 891, 892. Repealed by Acts 1995, 74th Leg., ch. 1039, § 73(2), eff. Sept. 1, 1995

HEALTH AND SAFETY CODE

TITLE 2. HEALTH

SUBTITLE H. PUBLIC HEALTH PROVISIONS

CHAPTER 166. ADVANCE DIRECTIVES

SUBCHAPTER A. GENERAL PROVISIONS

SUBCHAPTER B. DIRECTIVE TO PHYSICIANS

SUBCHAPTER C. OUT-OF-HOSPITAL DO-NOT-RESUSCITATE ORDERS

SUBCHAPTER D. MEDICAL POWER OF ATTORNEY

Acts 1999, 76th Leg., ch. 450, § 1.01 inserted the chapter heading.

SUBCHAPTER A. GENERAL PROVISIONS

§ 166.001. Short Title

This chapter may be cited as the Advance Directives Act.

Added by Acts 1999, 76th Leg., ch. 450, § 1.02, eff. Sept. 1, 1999.

Sections 3.02 and 3.03 of Acts 1999, 76th Leg., ch. 450 provide:

"Sec. 3.02. (a) The change in law made by this Act does not affect the validity of a document executed under Chapter 672 or 674, Health and Safety Code, or Chapter 135, Civil Practice and Remedies Code, before the effective date of this Act. A document executed before the effective date of this Act is governed by the law in effect on the date the document was executed, and that law continues in effect for that purpose.

"(b) A reference in a law to a durable power of attorney for health care means a medical power of attorney, as defined by Section 166.002, Health and Safety Code, as added by this Act.

"Sec. 3.03. (a) The change in law made by this Act applies only to the punishment for an offense committed on or after the effective date of this Act. For purposes of this section, an offense is committed before the effective date of this Act if any element of the offense occurs before the effective date.

"(b) An offense committed before the effective date of this Act is covered by the law in effect when the offense was committed, and the former law is continued in effect for that purpose."

§ 166.002. Definitions

In this chapter:

(1) "Advance directive" means:

(A) a directive, as that term is defined by Section 166.031;

(B) an out-of-hospital DNR order, as that term is defined by Section 166.081; or

(C) a medical power of attorney under Subchapter D.

(2) "Artificial nutrition and hydration" means the provision of nutrients or fluids by a tube inserted in a vein, under the skin in the subcutaneous tissues, or in the stomach (gastrointestinal tract).

(3) "Attending physician" means a physician selected by or assigned to a patient who has primary responsibility for a patient's treatment and care.

(4) "Competent" means possessing the ability, based on reasonable medical judgment, to understand and appreciate the nature and consequences of a treatment decision, including the significant benefits and harms of and reasonable alternatives to a proposed treatment decision.

(5) "Declarant" means a person who has executed or issued a directive under this chapter.

(6) "Ethics or medical committee" means a committee established under Sections 161.031–161.033.

(7) "Health care or treatment decision" means consent, refusal to consent, or withdrawal of consent to health care, treatment, service, or a procedure to maintain, diagnose, or treat an individual's physical or mental condition.

(8) "Incompetent" means lacking the ability, based on reasonable medical judgment, to understand and appreciate the nature and consequences of a treatment decision, including the significant benefits and harms of and reasonable alternatives to a proposed treatment decision.

(9) "Irreversible condition" means a condition, injury, or illness:

(A) that may be treated but is never cured or eliminated;

(B) that leaves a person unable to care for or make decisions for the person's own self; and

(C) that, without life-sustaining treatment provided in accordance with the prevailing standard of medical care, is fatal.

(10) "Life-sustaining treatment" means treatment that, based on reasonable medical judgment, sustains the life of a patient and without which the patient will die. The term includes both life-sustaining medications and artificial life support, such as mechanical breathing machines, kidney dialysis treatment, and artificial nutrition and hydration. The term does not include the administration of pain management medication or the performance of a medical procedure considered to be necessary to provide comfort care, or any other medical care provided to alleviate a patient's pain.

(11) "Medical power of attorney" means a document delegating to an agent authority to make health care decisions executed or issued under Subchapter D.

(12) "Physician" means:

(A) a physician licensed by the Texas State Board of Medical Examiners; or

(B) a properly credentialed physician who holds a commission in the uniformed services of the United States and who is serving on active duty in this state.

(13) "Terminal condition" means an incurable condition caused by injury, disease, or illness that according to reasonable medical judgment will produce death within six months, even with available life-sustaining treatment provided in accordance with the prevailing standard of medical care. A patient who has been admitted to a program under which the person receives hospice services provided by a home and community support services agency licensed under Chapter 142 is presumed to have a terminal condition for purposes of this chapter.

(14) "Witness" means a person who may serve as a witness under Section 166.003.

Added by Acts 1999, 76th Leg., ch. 450, § 1.02, eff. Sept. 1, 1999.

Section 3.02 of Acts 1999, 76th Leg., ch. 450 provides:

"Sec. 3.02. (a) The change in law made by this Act does not affect the validity of a document executed under Chapter 672 or 674, Health and Safety Code, or Chapter 135, Civil Practice and Remedies Code, before the effective date of this Act. A document executed before the effective date of this Act is governed by the law in effect on the date the document was executed, and that law continues in effect for that purpose.

"(b) A reference in a law to a durable power of attorney for health care means a medical power of attorney, as defined by Section 166.002, Health and Safety Code, as added by this Act."

§ 166.003. Witnesses

In any circumstance in which this chapter requires the execution of an advance directive or the issuance of a nonwritten advance directive to be witnessed:

(1) each witness must be a competent adult; and

(2) at least one of the witnesses must be a person who is not:

(A) a person designated by the declarant to make a treatment decision;

(B) a person related to the declarant by blood or marriage;

(C) a person entitled to any part of the declarant's estate after the declarant's death under a will or codicil executed by the declarant or by operation of law;

(D) the attending physician;

(E) an employee of the attending physician;

(F) an employee of a health care facility in which the declarant is a patient if the employee is providing direct patient care to the declarant or is an officer, director, partner, or business office employee of the health care facility or of any parent organization of the health care facility; or

(G) a person who, at the time the written advance directive is executed or, if the directive is a nonwritten directive issued under this chapter, at the time the nonwritten directive is issued, has a claim against any part of the declarant's estate after the declarant's death.

Added by Acts 1999, 76th Leg., ch. 450, § 1.02, eff. Sept. 1, 1999.

For application provisions of Acts 1999, 76th Leg., ch. 450, see notes following V.T.C.A., Health & Safety Code § 166.001.

§ 166.004. Statement Relating to Advance Directive

(a) In this section, "health care provider" means:

(1) a hospital;

(2) an institution licensed under Chapter 242, including a skilled nursing facility;

(3) a home and community support services agency;

(4) a personal care facility; and

(5) a special care facility.

(b) A health care provider shall maintain written policies regarding the implementation of advance directives. The policies must include a clear and precise statement of any procedure the health care provider is unwilling or unable to provide or withhold in accordance with an advance directive.

(c) Except as provided by Subsection (g), the health care provider shall provide written notice to an individual of the written policies described by Subsection (b). The notice must be provided at the earlier of:

(1) the time the individual is admitted to receive services from the health care provider; or

(2) the time the health care provider begins providing care to the individual.

(d) If, at the time notice is to be provided under Subsection (c), the individual is incompetent or otherwise incapacitated and unable to receive the notice required by this section, the provider shall provide the required written notice, in the following order of preference, to:

(1) the individual's legal guardian;

(2) a person responsible for the health care decisions of the individual;

(3) the individual's spouse;

(4) the individual's adult child;

(5) the individual's parent; or

(6) the person admitting the individual.

(e) If Subsection (d) applies and except as provided by Subsection (f), if a health care provider is unable, after diligent search, to locate an individual listed by Subsection (d), the health care provider is not required to provide the notice.

(f) If an individual who was incompetent or otherwise incapacitated and unable to receive the notice required by this section at the time notice was to be provided under Subsection (c) later becomes able to receive the notice, the health care provider shall provide the written notice at the time the individual becomes able to receive the notice.

(g) This section does not apply to outpatient hospital services, including emergency services.

Added by Acts 1999, 76th Leg., ch. 450, § 1.02, eff. Sept. 1, 1999.

For application provisions of Acts 1999, 76th Leg., ch. 450, see notes following V.T.C.A., Health & Safety Code § 166.001.

§ 166.005. Enforceability of Advance Directives Executed in Another Jurisdiction

An advance directive or similar instrument validly executed in another state or jurisdiction shall be given the same effect as an advance directive validly executed under the law of this state. This section does not authorize the administration, withholding, or withdrawal of health care otherwise prohibited by the laws of this state.

Added by Acts 1999, 76th Leg., ch. 450, § 1.02, eff. Sept. 1, 1999.

For application provisions of Acts 1999, 76th Leg., ch. 450, see notes following V.T.C.A., Health & Safety Code § 166.001.

§ 166.006. Effect of Advance Directive on Insurance Policy and Premiums

(a) The fact that a person has executed or issued an advance directive does not:

(1) restrict, inhibit, or impair in any manner the sale, procurement, or issuance of a life insurance policy to that person; or

(2) modify the terms of an existing life insurance policy.

(b) Notwithstanding the terms of any life insurance policy, the fact that life-sustaining treatment is withheld or withdrawn from an insured qualified patient under this chapter does not legally impair or invalidate that person's life insurance policy and may not be a factor for the purpose of determining, under the life insurance policy, whether benefits are payable or the cause of death.

(c) The fact that a person has executed or issued or failed to execute or issue an advance directive may not be considered in any way in establishing insurance premiums.

Added by Acts 1999, 76th Leg., ch. 450, § 1.02, eff. Sept. 1, 1999.

For application provisions of Acts 1999, 76th Leg., ch. 450, see notes following V.T.C.A., Health & Safety Code § 166.001.

§ 166.007. Execution of Advance Directive May Not be Required

A physician, health facility, health care provider, insurer, or health care service plan may not require a person to execute or issue an advance directive as a condition for obtaining insurance for health care services or receiving health care services.

Added by Acts 1999, 76th Leg., ch. 450, § 1.02, eff. Sept. 1, 1999.

For application provisions of Acts 1999, 76th Leg., ch. 450, see notes following V.T.C.A., Health & Safety Code § 166.001.

§ 166.008. Conflict Between Advance Directives

To the extent that a treatment decision or an advance directive validly executed or issued under this chapter conflicts with another treatment decision or an advance directive executed or issued under this chapter, the treatment decision made or instrument executed later in time controls.

Added by Acts 1999, 76th Leg., ch. 450, § 1.02, eff. Sept. 1, 1999.

For application provisions of Acts 1999, 76th Leg., ch. 450, see notes following V.T.C.A., Health & Safety Code § 166.001.

§ 166.009. Certain Life-Sustaining Treatment Not Required

This chapter may not be construed to require the provision of life-sustaining treatment that cannot be provided to a patient without denying the same treatment to another patient.

Added by Acts 1999, 76th Leg., ch. 450, § 1.02, eff. Sept. 1, 1999.

For application provisions of Acts 1999, 76th Leg., ch. 450, see notes following V.T.C.A., Health & Safety Code § 166.001.

SUBCHAPTER B. DIRECTIVE TO PHYSICIANS

Acts 1999, 76th Leg., ch. 450, § 1.03 redesignated Chapter 672, Health & Safety Code as this Subchapter B.

§ 166.031. Definitions

In this subchapter:

(1) "Directive" means an instruction made under Section 166.032, 166.034, or 166.035 to administer, withhold, or withdraw life-sustaining treatment in the event of a terminal or irreversible condition.

(2) "Qualified patient" means a patient with a terminal or irreversible condition that has been diagnosed and certified in writing by the attending physician.

Acts 1989, 71st Leg., ch. 678, § 1, eff. Sept. 1, 1989. Amended by Acts 1991, 72nd Leg., ch. 14, § 208, eff. Sept. 1, 1991; Acts 1993, 73rd Leg., ch. 107, § 5.04, eff. Aug. 30, 1993. Renumbered from § 672.002 and amended by Acts 1999, 76th Leg., ch. 450, § 1.03, eff. Sept. 1, 1999.

Sections 3.02 and 3.03 of Acts 1999, 76th Leg., ch. 450 provide:

"Sec. 3.02. (a) The change in law made by this Act does not affect the validity of a document executed under Chapter 672 or 674, Health and Safety Code, or Chapter 135, Civil Practice and Remedies Code, before the effective date of this Act. A document executed before the effective date of this Act is governed by the law in effect on the date the document was executed, and that law continues in effect for that purpose.

"(b) A reference in a law to a durable power of attorney for health care means a medical power of attorney, as defined by Section 166.002, Health and Safety Code, as added by this Act.

"Sec. 3.03. (a) The change in law made by this Act applies only to the punishment for an offense committed on or after the effective date of this Act. For purposes of this section, an offense is committed before the effective date of this Act if any element of the offense occurs before the effective date.

"(b) An offense committed before the effective date of this Act is covered by the law in effect when the offense was committed, and the former law is continued in effect for that purpose."

§ 166.032. Written Directive by Competent Adult; Notice to Physician

(a) A competent adult may at any time execute a written directive.

(b) The declarant must sign the directive in the presence of two witnesses who qualify under Section 166.003, at least one of whom must be a witness who qualifies under Section 166.003(2). The witnesses must sign the directive.

(c) A declarant may include in a directive directions other than those provided by Section 166.033 and may designate in a directive a person to make a treatment decision for the declarant in the event the declarant becomes incompetent or otherwise mentally or physically incapable of communication.

(d) A declarant shall notify the attending physician of the existence of a written directive. If the declarant is incompetent or otherwise mentally or physically incapable of communication, another person may notify the attending physician of the existence of the written directive. The attending physician shall make the directive a part of the declarant's medical record.

Acts 1989, 71st Leg., ch. 678, § 1, eff. Sept. 1, 1989. Amended by Acts 1991, 72nd Leg., ch. 14, § 209, eff. Sept. 1, 1991; Acts 1997, 75th Leg., ch. 291, § 1, eff. Jan. 1, 1998. Renumbered from § 672.005 and amended by Acts 1999, 76th Leg., ch. 450, § 1.03, eff. Sept. 1, 1999.

Section 4 of Acts 1997, 75th Leg., ch. 291 provides:

"This Act takes effect January 1, 1998, and applies to a directive executed on or after that date. A directive executed before January 1, 1998, is governed by the law in effect when the directive was executed, and the former law is continued in effect for that purpose."

For application provisions of Acts 1999, 76th Leg., ch. 450, see notes following V.T.C.A., Health & Safety Code § 166.031.

§ 166.033. Form of Written Directive

A written directive may be in the following form:

DIRECTIVE TO PHYSICIANS AND FAMILY OR SURROGATES

Instructions for completing this document:

This is an important legal document known as an Advance Directive. It is designed to help you communicate your wishes about medical treatment at some time in the future when you are unable to make your wishes known because of illness or injury. These wishes are usually based on personal values. In particular, you may want to consider what burdens or hardships of treatment you would be willing to accept for a particular amount of benefit obtained if you were seriously ill.

You are encouraged to discuss your values and wishes with your family or chosen spokesperson, as well as your physician. Your physician, other health care provider, or medical institution may provide you with various resources to assist you in completing your advance directive. Brief definitions are listed below and may aid you in your discussions and advance planning. Initial the treatment choices that best reflect your personal preferences. Provide a copy of your directive to your physician, usual hospital, and family or spokesperson. Consider a periodic review of this document. By periodic review, you can best assure that the directive reflects your preferences.

In addition to this advance directive, Texas law provides for two other types of directives that can be important during a serious illness. These are the Medical Power of Attorney and the Out-of-Hospital Do-Not-Resuscitate Order. You may wish to discuss these with your physician, family, hospital representative, or other advisers. You may also wish to complete a directive related to the donation of organs and tissues.

DIRECTIVE

I, ________, recognize that the best health care is based upon a partnership of trust and communication with my physician. My physician and I will make health care decisions together as long as I am of sound mind and able to make my wishes known. If there comes a time that I am unable to make medical decisions about myself because of illness or injury, I direct that the following treatment preferences be honored:

If, in the judgment of my physician, I am suffering with a terminal condition from which I am expected to die within six months, even with available life-sustaining treatment provided in accordance with prevailing standards of medical care:

________ I request that all treatments other than those needed to keep me comfortable be discontinued or withheld and my physician allow me to die as gently as possible; OR

________ I request that I be kept alive in this terminal condition using available life-sustaining treatment. (THIS SELECTION DOES NOT APPLY TO HOSPICE CARE.)

If, in the judgment of my physician, I am suffering with an irreversible condition so that I cannot care for myself or make decisions for myself and am expected to die without life-sustaining treatment provided in accordance with prevailing standards of care:

________ I request that all treatments other than those needed to keep me comfortable be discontinued or withheld and my physician allow me to die as gently as possible; OR

________ I request that I be kept alive in this irreversible condition using available life-sustaining treatment. (THIS SELECTION DOES NOT APPLY TO HOSPICE CARE.)

Additional requests: (After discussion with your physician, you may wish to consider listing particular treatments in this space that you do or do not want in specific circumstances, such as artificial nutrition and fluids, intravenous antibiotics, etc. Be sure to state whether you do or do not want the particular treatment.)

____

____

____

After signing this directive, if my representative or I elect hospice care, I understand and agree that only those treatments needed to keep me comfortable would be provided and I would not be given available life-sustaining treatments.

If I do not have a Medical Power of Attorney, and I am unable to make my wishes known, I designate the following person(s) to make treatment decisions with my physician compatible with my personal values:

1.________

2.________

(If a Medical Power of Attorney has been executed, then an agent already has been named and you should not list additional names in this document.)

If the above persons are not available, or if I have not designated a spokesperson, I understand that a spokesperson will be chosen for me following standards specified in the laws of Texas. If, in the judgment of my physician, my death is imminent within minutes to hours, even with the use of all available medical treatment provided within the prevailing standard of care, I acknowledge that all treatments may be withheld or removed except those needed to maintain my comfort. I understand that under Texas law this directive has no effect if I have been diagnosed as pregnant. This directive will remain in effect until I revoke it. No other person may do so.

Signed________ Date________ City, County, State of Residence ________

Two competent adult witnesses must sign below, acknowledging the signature of the declarant. The witness designated as Witness 1 may not be a person designated to make a treatment decision for the patient and may not be related to the patient by blood or marriage. This witness may not be entitled to any part of the estate and may not have a claim against the estate of the patient. This witness may not be the attending physician or an employee of the attending physician. If this witness is an employee of a health care facility in which the patient is being cared for, this witness may not be involved in providing direct patient care to the patient. This witness may not be an officer, director, partner, or business office employee of a health care facility in which the patient is being cared for or of any parent organization of the health care facility.

Witness 1 ________ Witness 2 ________

Definitions:

"Artificial nutrition and hydration" means the provision of nutrients or fluids by a tube inserted in a vein, under the skin in the subcutaneous tissues, or in the stomach (gastrointestinal tract).

"Irreversible condition" means a condition, injury, or illness:

(1) that may be treated, but is never cured or eliminated;

(2) that leaves a person unable to care for or make decisions for the person's own self; and

(3) that, without life-sustaining treatment provided in accordance with the prevailing standard of medical care, is fatal.

Explanation: Many serious illnesses such as cancer, failure of major organs (kidney, heart, liver, or lung), and serious brain disease such as Alzheimer's dementia may be considered irreversible early on. There is no cure, but the patient may be kept alive for prolonged periods of time if the patient receives life-sustaining treatments. Late in the course of the same illness, the disease may be considered terminal when, even with treatment, the patient is expected to die. You may wish to consider which burdens of treatment you would be willing to accept in an effort to achieve a particular outcome. This is a very personal decision that you may wish to discuss with your physician, family, or other important persons in your life.

"Life-sustaining treatment" means treatment that, based on reasonable medical judgment, sustains the life of a patient and without which the patient will die. The term includes both life-sustaining medications and artificial life support such as mechanical breathing machines, kidney dialysis treatment, and artificial hydration and nutrition. The term does not include the administration of pain management medication, the performance of a medical procedure necessary to provide comfort care, or any other medical care provided to alleviate a patient's pain.

"Terminal condition" means an incurable condition caused by injury, disease, or illness that according to reasonable medical judgment will produce death within six months, even with available life-sustaining treatment provided in accordance with the prevailing standard of medical care.

Explanation: Many serious illnesses may be considered irreversible early in the course of the illness, but they may not be considered terminal until the disease is fairly advanced. In thinking about terminal illness and its treatment, you again may wish to consider the relative benefits and burdens of treatment and discuss your wishes with your physician, family, or other important persons in your life.

Acts 1989, 71st Leg., ch. 678, § 1, eff. Sept. 1, 1989. Amended by Acts 1991, 72nd Leg., ch. 14, § 209, eff. Sept. 1, 1991; Acts 1997, 75th Leg., ch. 291, § 2, eff. Jan. 1, 1998. Renumbered from § 672.004 and amended by Acts 1999, 76th Leg., ch. 450, § 1.03, eff. Sept. 1, 1999.

For application provisions of Acts 1997, 75th Leg., ch. 291, see note following V.T.C.A., Health and Safety Code § 166.032.

For application provisions of Acts 1999, 76th Leg., ch. 450, see notes following V.T.C.A., Health & Safety Code § 166.031.

§ 166.034. Issuance of Nonwritten Directive by Competent Adult Qualified Patient

(a) A competent qualified patient who is an adult may issue a directive by a nonwritten means of communication.

(b) A declarant must issue the nonwritten directive in the presence of the attending physician and two witnesses who qualify under Section 166.003, at least one of whom must be a witness who qualifies under Section 166.003(2).

(c) The physician shall make the fact of the existence of the directive a part of the declarant's medical record, and the names of the witnesses shall be entered in the medical record.

Acts 1989, 71st Leg., ch. 678, § 1, eff. Sept. 1, 1989. Renumbered from § 672.005 and amended by Acts 1999, 76th Leg., ch. 450, § 1.03, eff. Sept. 1, 1999.

For application provisions of Acts 1999, 76th Leg., ch. 450, see notes following V.T.C.A., Health & Safety Code § 166.031.

§ 166.035. Execution of Directive on Behalf of Patient Younger Than 18 Years of Age

The following persons may execute a directive on behalf of a qualified patient who is younger than 18 years of age:

(1) the patient's spouse, if the spouse is an adult;

(2) the patient's parents; or

(3) the patient's legal guardian.

Acts 1989, 71st Leg., ch. 678, § 1, eff. Sept. 1, 1989. Renumbered from § 672.006 by Acts 1999, 76th Leg., ch. 450, § 1.03, eff. Sept. 1, 1999.

§ 166.036. Notarized Document Not Required; Requirement of Specific Form Prohibited

(a) A written directive executed under Section 166.033 or 166.035 is effective without regard to whether the document has been notarized.

(b) A physician, health care facility, or health care professional may not require that:

(1) a directive be notarized; or

(2) a person use a form provided by the physician, health care facility, or health care professional.

Added by Acts 1999, 76th Leg., ch. 450, § 1.03, eff. Sept. 1, 1999.

For application provisions of Acts 1999, 76th Leg., ch. 450, see notes following V.T.C.A., Health & Safety Code § 166.031.

§ 166.037. Patient Desire Supersedes Directive

The desire of a qualified patient, including a qualified patient younger than 18 years of age, supersedes the effect of a directive.

Acts 1989, 71st Leg., ch. 678, § 1, eff. Sept. 1, 1989. Renumbered from § 672.007 and amended by Acts 1999, 76th Leg., ch. 450, § 1.03, eff. Sept. 1, 1999.

For application provisions of Acts 1999, 76th Leg., ch. 450, see notes following V.T.C.A., Health & Safety Code § 166.031.

§ 166.038. Procedure When Declarant is Incompetent or Incapable of Communication

(a) This section applies when an adult qualified patient has executed or issued a directive and is incompetent or otherwise mentally or physically incapable of communication.

(b) If the adult qualified patient has designated a person to make a treatment decision as authorized by Section 166.032(c), the attending physician and the designated person may make a treatment decision in accordance with the declarant's directions.

(c) If the adult qualified patient has not designated a person to make a treatment decision, the attending physician shall comply with the directive unless the physician believes that the directive does not reflect the patient's present desire.

Acts 1989, 71st Leg., ch. 678, § 1, eff. Sept. 1, 1989. Renumbered from 672.008 and amended by Acts 1999, 76th Leg., ch. 450, § 1.03, eff. Sept. 1, 1999.

For application provisions of Acts 1999, 76th Leg., ch. 450, see notes following V.T.C.A., Health & Safety Code § 166.031.

§ 166.039. Procedure When Person Has Not Executed or Issued a Directive and is Incompetent or Incapable of Communication

(a) If an adult qualified patient has not executed or issued a directive and is incompetent or otherwise mentally or physically incapable of communication, the attending physician and the patient's legal guardian or an agent under a medical power of attorney may make a treatment decision that may include a decision to withhold or withdraw life-sustaining treatment from the patient.

(b) If the patient does not have a legal guardian or an agent under a medical power of attorney, the attending physician and one person, if available, from one of the following categories, in the following priority, may make a treatment decision that may include a decision to withhold or withdraw life-sustaining treatment:

(1) the patient's spouse;

(2) the patient's reasonably available adult children;

(3) the patient's parents; or

(4) the patient's nearest living relative.

(c) A treatment decision made under Subsection (a) or (b) must be based on knowledge of what the patient would desire, if known.

(d) A treatment decision made under Subsection (b) must be documented in the patient's medical record and signed by the attending physician.

(e) If the patient does not have a legal guardian and a person listed in Subsection (b) is not available, a treatment decision made under Subsection (b) must be concurred in by another physician who is not involved in the treatment of the patient or who is a representative of an ethics or medical committee of the health care facility in which the person is a patient.

(f) The fact that an adult qualified patient has not executed or issued a directive does not create a presumption that the patient does not want a treatment decision to be made to withhold or withdraw life-sustaining treatment.

(g) A person listed in Subsection (b) who wishes to challenge a treatment decision made under this section must apply for temporary guardianship under Section 875, Texas Probate Code. The court may waive applicable fees in that proceeding.

Acts 1989, 71st Leg., ch. 678, § 1, eff. Sept. 1, 1989. Amended by Acts 1997, 75th Leg., ch. 291, § 3, eff. Jan. 1, 1998. Renumbered from § 672.009 and amended by Acts 1999, 76th Leg., ch. 450, § 1.03, eff. Sept. 1, 1999.

For application provisions of Acts 1997, 75th Leg., ch. 291, see note following V.T.C.A., Health and Safety Code § 166.032.

For application provisions of Acts 1999, 76th Leg., ch. 450, see notes following V.T.C.A., Health & Safety Code § 166.031.

§ 166.040. Patient Certification and Prerequisites for Complying With Directive

(a) An attending physician who has been notified of the existence of a directive shall provide for the declarant's certification as a qualified patient on diagnosis of a terminal or irreversible condition.

(b) Before withholding or withdrawing life-sustaining treatment from a qualified patient under this subchapter, the attending physician must determine that the steps proposed to be taken are in accord with this subchapter and the patient's existing desires.

Acts 1989, 71st Leg., ch. 678, § 1, eff. Sept. 1, 1989. Amended by Acts 1991, 72nd Leg., 1st C.S., ch. 14, § 6.01, eff. Nov. 12, 1991. Renumbered from § 672.010 and amended by Acts 1999, 76th Leg., ch. 450, § 1.03, eff. Sept. 1, 1999.

For application provisions of Acts 1999, 76th Leg., ch. 450, see notes following V.T.C.A., Health & Safety Code § 166.031.

§ 166.041. Duration of Directive

A directive is effective until it is revoked as prescribed by Section 166.042.

Acts 1989, 71st Leg., ch. 678, § 1, eff. Sept. 1, 1989. Renumbered from § 672.011 and amended by Acts 1999, 76th Leg., ch. 450, § 1.03, eff. Sept. 1, 1999.

For application provisions of Acts 1999, 76th Leg., ch. 450, see notes following V.T.C.A., Health & Safety Code § 166.031.

§ 166.042. Revocation of Directive

(a) A declarant may revoke a directive at any time without regard to the declarant's mental state or competency. A directive may be revoked by:

(1) the declarant or someone in the declarant's presence and at the declarant's direction canceling, defacing, obliterating, burning, tearing, or otherwise destroying the directive;

(2) the declarant signing and dating a written revocation that expresses the declarant's intent to revoke the directive; or

(3) the declarant orally stating the declarant's intent to revoke the directive.

(b) A written revocation executed as prescribed by Subsection (a)(2) takes effect only when the declarant or a person acting on behalf of the declarant notifies the attending physician of its existence or mails the revocation to the attending physician. The attending physician or the physician's designee shall record in the patient's medical record the time and date when the physician received notice of the written revocation and shall enter the word "VOID" on each page of the copy of the directive in the patient's medical record.

(c) An oral revocation issued as prescribed by Subsection (a)(3) takes effect only when the declarant or a person acting on behalf of the declarant notifies the attending physician of the revocation. The attending physician or the physician's designee shall record in the patient's medical record the time, date, and place of the revocation, and, if different, the time, date, and place that the physician received notice of the revocation. The attending physician or the physician's designees shall also enter the word "VOID" on each page of the copy of the directive in the patient's medical record.

(d) Except as otherwise provided by this subchapter, a person is not civilly or criminally liable for failure to act on a revocation made under this section unless the person has actual knowledge of the revocation.

Acts 1989, 71st Leg., ch. 678, § 1, eff. Sept. 1, 1989. Renumbered from § 672.012 and amended by Acts 1999, 76th Leg., ch. 450, § 1.03, eff. Sept. 1, 1999.

For application provisions of Acts 1999, 76th Leg., ch. 450, see notes following V.T.C.A., Health & Safety Code § 166.031.

§ 166.043. Reexecution of Directive

A declarant may at any time reexecute a directive in accordance with the procedures prescribed by Section 166.032, including reexecution after the declarant is diagnosed as having a terminal or irreversible condition.

Acts 1989, 71st Leg., ch. 678, § 1, eff. Sept. 1, 1989. Renumbered from § 672.013 and amended by Acts 1999, 76th Leg., ch. 450, § 1.03, eff. Sept. 1, 1999.

For application provisions of Acts 1999, 76th Leg., ch. 450, see notes following V.T.C.A., Health & Safety Code § 166.031.

§ 166.044. Limitation of Liability for Withholding or Withdrawing Life-Sustaining Procedures

(a) A physician or health care facility that causes life-sustaining treatment to be withheld or withdrawn from a qualified patient in accordance with this subchapter is not civilly liable for that action unless the physician or health care facility fails to exercise reasonable care when applying the patient's advance directive.

(b) A health professional, acting under the direction of a physician, who participates in withholding or withdrawing life-sustaining treatment from a qualified patient in accordance with this subchapter is not civilly liable for that action unless the health professional fails to exercise reasonable care when applying the patient's advance directive.

(c) A physician, or a health professional acting under the direction of a physician, who participates in withholding or withdrawing life-sustaining treatment from a qualified patient in accordance with this subchapter is not criminally liable or guilty of unprofessional conduct as a result of that action unless the physician or health professional fails to exercise reasonable care when applying the patient's advance directive.

(d) The standard of care that a physician, health care facility, or health care professional shall exercise under this section is that degree of care that a physician, health care facility, or health care professional, as applicable, of ordinary prudence and skill would have exercised under the same or similar circumstances in the same or a similar community.

Acts 1989, 71st Leg., ch. 678, § 1, eff. Sept. 1, 1989. Renumbered from § 672.015 and amended by Acts 1999, 76th Leg., ch. 450, § 1.03, eff. Sept. 1, 1999.

For application provisions of Acts 1999, 76th Leg., ch. 450, see notes following V.T.C.A., Health & Safety Code § 166.031.

§ 166.045. Liability for Failure to Effectuate Directive

(a) A physician, health care facility, or health care professional who has no knowledge of a directive is not civilly or criminally liable for failing to act in accordance with the directive.

(b) A physician, or a health professional acting under the direction of a physician, is subject to review and disciplinary action by the appropriate licensing board for failing to effectuate a qualified patient's directive in violation of this subchapter or other laws of this state. This subsection does not limit remedies available under other laws of this state.

(c) If an attending physician refuses to comply with a directive or treatment decision and does not wish to follow the procedure established under Section 166.046, life-sustaining treatment shall be provided to the patient, but only until a reasonable opportunity has been afforded for the transfer of the patient to another physician or health care facility willing to comply with the directive or treatment decision.

(d) A physician, health professional acting under the direction of a physician, or health care facility is not civilly or criminally liable or subject to review or disciplinary action by the person's appropriate licensing board if the person has complied with the procedures outlined in Section 166.046.

Acts 1989, 71st Leg., ch. 678, § 1, eff. Sept. 1, 1989. Renumbered from § 672.016 and amended by Acts 1999, 76th Leg., ch. 450, § 1.03, eff. Sept. 1, 1999.

Section 3.04 of Acts 1999, 76th Leg., ch. 450 provides:

"The change in law made by this Act to Subsection (b), Section 166.045, and Subsection (b), Section 166.095, Health and Safety Code, as redesignated by this Act, applies only to conduct that occurs on or after January 1, 2000. Conduct that occurs before January 1, 2000, is governed by the law as it existed immediately before the effective date of this Act, and that law is continued in effect for that purpose."

§ 166.046. Procedure if Not Effectuating a Directive

(a) If an attending physician refuses to honor a patient's advance directive or a treatment decision under Section 166.039, the physician's refusal shall be reviewed by an ethics or medical committee. The attending physician may not be a member of that committee. The patient shall be given life-sustaining treatment during the review.

(b) The patient or the person responsible for the health care decisions of the individual who has made the decision regarding the directive or treatment decision:

(1) shall be informed of the committee review process not less than 48 hours before the meeting called to discuss the patient's directive, unless the time period is waived by mutual agreement; and

(2) is entitled to:

(A) attend the meeting; and

(B) receive a written explanation of the decision reached during the review process.

(c) The written explanation required by Subsection (b)(2)(B) must be included in the patient's medical record.

(d) If the attending physician, the patient, or the person responsible for the health care decisions of the individual does not agree with the decision reached during the review process under Subsection (b), the physician shall make a reasonable effort to transfer the patient to a physician who is willing to comply with the directive. If the patient is a patient in a health care facility, the facility's personnel shall assist the physician in arranging the patient's transfer to:

(1) another physician;

(2) an alternative care setting within that facility; or

(3) another facility.

(e) If the patient is requesting life-sustaining treatment that the attending physician and the review process have decided is inappropriate treatment, the patient shall be given available life-sustaining treatment pending transfer under Subsection (d). The patient is responsible for any costs incurred in transferring the patient to another facility. The physician and the health care facility are not obligated to provide life-sustaining treatment after the 10th day after the written decision required under Subsection (b) is provided to the patient or the person responsible for the health care decisions of the patient unless ordered to do so under Subsection (g).

(f) Life-sustaining treatment under this section may not be entered in the patient's medical record as medically unnecessary treatment until the time period provided under Subsection (e) has expired.

(g) At the request of the patient or the person responsible for the health care decisions of the patient, the appropriate district or county court shall extend the time period provided under Subsection (e) only if the court finds, by a preponderance of the evidence, that there is a reasonable expectation that a physician or health care facility that will honor the patient's directive will be found if the time extension is granted.

(h) This section may not be construed to impose an obligation on a facility or a home and community support services agency licensed under Chapter 142 or similar organization that is beyond the scope of the services or resources of the facility or agency. This section does not apply to hospice services provided by a home and community support services agency licensed under Chapter 142.

Added by Acts 1999, 76th Leg., ch. 450, § 1.03, eff. Sept. 1, 1999.

For application provisions of Acts 1999, 76th Leg., ch. 450, see notes following V.T.C.A., Health & Safety Code § 166.031.

§ 166.047. Honoring Directive Does Not Constitute Offense of Aiding Suicide

A person does not commit an offense under Section 22.08, Penal Code, by withholding or withdrawing life-sustaining treatment from a qualified patient in accordance with this subchapter.

Acts 1989, 71st Leg., ch. 678, § 1, eff. Sept. 1, 1989. Renumbered from § 672.017 and amended by Acts 1999, 76th Leg., ch. 450, § 1.03, eff. Sept. 1, 1999.

For application provisions of Acts 1999, 76th Leg., ch. 450, see notes following V.T.C.A., Health & Safety Code § 166.031.

§ 166.048. Criminal Penalty; Prosecution

(a) A person commits an offense if the person intentionally conceals, cancels, defaces, obliterates, or damages another person's directive without that person's consent. An offense under this subsection is a Class A misdemeanor.

(b) A person is subject to prosecution for criminal homicide under Chapter 19, Penal Code, if the person, with the intent to cause life-sustaining treatment to be withheld or withdrawn from another person contrary to the other person's desires, falsifies or forges a directive or intentionally conceals or withholds personal knowledge of a revocation and thereby directly causes life-sustaining treatment to be withheld or withdrawn from the other person with the result that the other person's death is hastened.

Acts 1989, 71st Leg., ch. 678, § 1, eff. Sept. 1, 1989. Renumbered from § 672.018 and amended by Acts 1999, 76th Leg., ch. 450, § 1.03, eff. Sept. 1, 1999.

For application provisions of Acts 1999, 76th Leg., ch. 450, see notes following V.T.C.A., Health & Safety Code § 166.031.

§ 166.049. Pregnant Patients

A person may not withdraw or withhold life-sustaining treatment under this subchapter from a pregnant patient.

Acts 1989, 71st Leg., ch. 678, § 1, eff. Sept. 1, 1989. Renumbered from § 672.019 and amended by Acts 1999, 76th Leg., ch. 450, § 1.03, eff. Sept. 1, 1999.

For application provisions of Acts 1999, 76th Leg., ch. 450, see notes following V.T.C.A., Health & Safety Code § 166.031.

§ 166.050. Mercy Killing Not Condoned

This subchapter does not condone, authorize, or approve mercy killing or permit an affirmative or deliberate act or omission to end life except to permit the natural process of dying as provided by this subchapter.

Acts 1989, 71st Leg., ch. 678, § 1, eff. Sept. 1, 1989. Renumbered from § 672.020 and amended by Acts 1999, 76th Leg., ch. 450, § 1.03, eff. Sept. 1, 1999.

For application provisions of Acts 1999, 76th Leg., ch. 450, see notes following V.T.C.A., Health & Safety Code § 166.031.

§ 166.051. Legal Right or Responsibility Not Affected

This subchapter does not impair or supersede any legal right or responsibility a person may have to effect the withholding or withdrawal of life-sustaining treatment in a lawful manner, provided that if an attending physician or health care facility is unwilling to honor a patient's advance directive or a treatment decision to provide life-sustaining treatment, life-sustaining treatment is required to be provided the patient, but only until a reasonable opportunity has been afforded for transfer of the patient to another physician or health care facility willing to comply with the advance directive or treatment decision.

Acts 1989, 71st Leg., ch. 678, § 1, eff. Sept. 1, 1989. Renumbered from § 672.021 and amended by Acts 1999, 76th Leg., ch. 450, § 1.03, eff. Sept. 1, 1999.

For application provisions of Acts 1999, 76th Leg., ch. 450, see notes following V.T.C.A., Health & Safety Code § 166.031.

SUBCHAPTER C. OUT-OF-HOSPITAL DO-NOT-RESUSCITATE ORDERS

Acts 1999, 76th Leg., ch. 450, § 1.04 redesignated Chapter 674, Health & Safety Code as this Subchapter C.

§ 166.081. Definitions

In this subchapter:

(1) "Cardiopulmonary resuscitation" means any medical intervention used to restore circulatory or respiratory function that has ceased.

(2) "DNR identification device" means an identification device specified by the board under Section 166.101 that is worn for the purpose of identifying a person who has executed or issued an out-of-hospital DNR order or on whose behalf an out-of-hospital DNR order has been executed or issued under this subchapter.

(3) "Emergency medical services" has the meaning assigned by Section 773.003.

(4) "Emergency medical services personnel" has the meaning assigned by Section 773.003.

(5) "Health care professionals" means physicians, physician assistants, nurses, and emergency medical services personnel and, unless the context requires otherwise, includes hospital emergency personnel.

(6) "Out-of-hospital DNR order":

(A) means a legally binding out-of-hospital do-not-resuscitate order, in the form specified by the board under Section 166.083, prepared and signed by the attending physician of a person, that documents the instructions of a person or the person's legally authorized representative and directs health care professionals acting in an out-of-hospital setting not to initiate or continue the following life-sustaining treatment:

(i) cardiopulmonary resuscitation;

(ii) advanced airway management;

(iii) artificial ventilation;

(iv) defibrillation;

(v) transcutaneous cardiac pacing; and

(vi) other life-sustaining treatment specified by the board under Section 166.101(a); and

(B) does not include authorization to withhold medical interventions or therapies considered necessary to provide comfort care or to alleviate pain or to provide water or nutrition.

(7) "Out-of-hospital setting" means a location in which health care professionals are called for assistance, including long-term care facilities, in-patient hospice facilities, private homes, hospital outpatient or emergency departments, physician's offices, and vehicles during transport.

(8) "Proxy" means a person designated and authorized by a directive executed or issued in accordance with Subchapter B to make a treatment decision for another person in the event the other person becomes incompetent or otherwise mentally or physically incapable of communication.

(9) "Qualified relatives" means those persons authorized to execute or issue an out-of-hospital DNR order on behalf of a person who is incompetent or otherwise mentally or physically incapable of communication under Section 166.088.

(10) "Statewide out-of-hospital DNR protocol" means a set of statewide standardized procedures adopted by the board under Section 166.101(a) for withholding cardiopulmonary resuscitation and certain other life-sustaining treatment by health care professionals acting in out-of-hospital settings.

Added by Acts 1995, 74th Leg., ch. 965, § 10, eff. June 16, 1995. Renumbered from § 674.001 and amended by Acts 1999, 76th Leg., ch. 450, § 1.04, eff. Sept. 1, 1999.

Sections 3.02 and 3.03 of Acts 1999, 76th Leg., ch. 450 provide:

"Sec. 3.02. (a) The change in law made by this Act does not affect the validity of a document executed under Chapter 672 or 674, Health and Safety Code, or Chapter 135, Civil Practice and Remedies Code, before the effective date of this Act. A document executed before the effective date of this Act is governed by the law in effect on the date the document was executed, and that law continues in effect for that purpose.

"(b) A reference in a law to a durable power of attorney for health care means a medical power of attorney, as defined by Section 166.002, Health and Safety Code, as added by this Act.

"Sec. 3.03. (a) The change in law made by this Act applies only to the punishment for an offense committed on or after the effective date of this Act. For purposes of this section, an offense is committed before the effective date of this Act if any element of the offense occurs before the effective date.

"(b) An offense committed before the effective date of this Act is covered by the law in effect when the offense was committed, and the former law is continued in effect for that purpose."

§ 166.082. Out-Of-Hospital DNR Order; Directive to Physicians

(a) A competent person may at any time execute a written out-of-hospital DNR order directing health care professionals acting in an out-of-hospital setting to withhold cardiopulmonary resuscitation and certain other life-sustaining treatment designated by the board.

(b) The declarant must sign the out-of-hospital DNR order in the presence of two witnesses who qualify under Section 166.003, at least one of whom must be a witness who qualifies under Section 166.003(2). The witnesses must sign the order. The attending physician of the declarant must sign the order and shall make the fact of the existence of the order and the reasons for execution of the order a part of the declarant's medical record.

(c) If the person is incompetent but previously executed or issued a directive to physicians in accordance with Subchapter B, the physician may rely on the directive as the person's instructions to issue an out-of-hospital DNR order and shall place a copy of the directive in the person's medical record. The physician shall sign the order in lieu of the person signing under Subsection (b).

(d) If the person is incompetent but previously executed or issued a directive to physicians in accordance with Subchapter B designating a proxy, the proxy may make any decisions required of the designating person as to an out-of-hospital DNR order and shall sign the order in lieu of the person signing under Subsection (b).

(e) If the person is now incompetent but previously executed or issued a medical power of attorney designating an agent, the agent may make any decisions required of the designating person as to an out-of-hospital DNR order and shall sign the order in lieu of the person signing under Subsection (b).

(f) The board, on the recommendation of the department, shall by rule adopt procedures for the disposition and maintenance of records of an original out-of-hospital DNR order and any copies of the order.

(g) An out-of-hospital DNR order is effective on its execution.

Added by Acts 1995, 74th Leg., ch. 965, § 10, eff. June 16, 1995. Renumbered from § 674.002 and amended by Acts 1999, 76th Leg., ch. 450, § 1.04, eff. Sept. 1, 1999.

For application provisions of Acts 1999, 76th Leg., ch. 450, see notes following V.T.C.A., Health & Safety Code § 166.081.

§ 166.083. Form of Out-Of-Hospital DNR Order

(a) A written out-of-hospital DNR order shall be in the standard form specified by board rule as recommended by the department.

(b) The standard form of an out-of-hospital DNR order specified by the board must, at a minimum, contain the following:

(1) a distinctive single-page format that readily identifies the document as an out-of-hospital DNR order;

(2) a title that readily identifies the document as an out-of-hospital DNR order;

(3) the printed or typed name of the person;

(4) a statement that the physician signing the document is the attending physician of the person and that the physician is directing health care professionals acting in out-of-hospital settings, including a hospital emergency department, not to initiate or continue certain life-sustaining treatment on behalf of the person, and a listing of those procedures not to be initiated or continued;

(5) a statement that the person understands that the person may revoke the out-of-hospital DNR order at any time by destroying the order and removing the DNR identification device, if any, or by communicating to health care professionals at the scene the person's desire to revoke the out-of-hospital DNR order;

(6) places for the printed names and signatures of the witnesses and attending physician of the person and the medical license number of the attending physician;

(7) a separate section for execution of the document by the legal guardian of the person, the person's proxy, an agent of the person having a medical power of attorney, or the attending physician attesting to the issuance of an out-of-hospital DNR order by nonwritten means of communication or acting in accordance with a previously executed or previously issued directive to physicians under Section 166.082(c) that includes the following:

(A) a statement that the legal guardian, the proxy, the agent, the person by nonwritten means of communication, or the physician directs that each listed life-sustaining treatment should not be initiated or continued in behalf of the person; and

(B) places for the printed names and signatures of the witnesses and, as applicable, the legal guardian, proxy, agent, or physician;

(8) a separate section for execution of the document by at least one qualified relative of the person when the person does not have a legal guardian, proxy, or agent having a medical power of attorney and is incompetent or otherwise mentally or physically incapable of communication, including:

(A) a statement that the relative of the person is qualified to make a treatment decision to withhold cardiopulmonary resuscitation and certain other designated life-sustaining treatment under Section 166.088 and, based on the known desires of the person or a determination of the best interest of the person, directs that each listed life-sustaining treatment should not be initiated or continued in behalf of the person; and

(B) places for the printed names and signatures of the witnesses and qualified relative of the person;

(9) a place for entry of the date of execution of the document;

(10) a statement that the document is in effect on the date of its execution and remains in effect until the death of the person or until the document is revoked;

(11) a statement that the document must accompany the person during transport;

(12) a statement regarding the proper disposition of the document or copies of the document, as the board determines appropriate; and

(13) a statement at the bottom of the document, with places for the signature of each person executing the document, that the document has been properly completed.

(c) The board may, by rule and as recommended by the department, modify the standard form of the out-of-hospital DNR order described by Subsection (b) in order to accomplish the purposes of this subchapter.

(d) A photocopy or other complete facsimile of the original written out-of-hospital DNR order executed under this subchapter may be used for any purpose for which the original written order may be used under this subchapter.

Added by Acts 1995, 74th Leg., ch. 965, § 10, eff. June 16, 1995. Renumbered from § 674.003 and amended by Acts 1999, 76th Leg., ch. 450, § 1.04, eff. Sept. 1, 1999.

For application provisions of Acts 1999, 76th Leg., ch. 450, see notes following V.T.C.A., Health & Safety Code § 166.081.

§ 166.084. Issuance of Out-Of-Hospital DNR Order by Nonwritten Communication

(a) A competent person who is an adult may issue an out-of-hospital DNR order by nonwritten communication.

(b) A declarant must issue the nonwritten out-of-hospital DNR order in the presence of the attending physician and two witnesses who qualify under Section 166.003, at least one of whom must be a witness who qualifies under Section 166.003(2).

(c) The attending physician and witnesses shall sign the out-of-hospital DNR order in the place of the document provided by Section 166.083(b)(7) and the attending physician shall sign the document in the place required by Section 166.083(b)(13). The physician shall make the fact of the existence of the out-of-hospital DNR order a part of the declarant's medical record and the names of the witnesses shall be entered in the medical record.

(d) An out-of-hospital DNR order issued in the manner provided by this section is valid and shall be honored by responding health care professionals as if executed in the manner provided by Section 166.082.

Added by Acts 1995, 74th Leg., ch. 965, § 10, eff. June 16, 1995. Renumbered from § 674.004 and amended by Acts 1999, 76th Leg., ch. 450, § 1.04, eff. Sept. 1, 1999.

For application provisions of Acts 1999, 76th Leg., ch. 450, see notes following V.T.C.A., Health & Safety Code § 166.081.

§ 166.085. Execution of Out-Of-Hospital DNR Order on Behalf of a Minor

The following persons may execute an out-of-hospital DNR order on behalf of a minor:

(1) the minor's parents;

(2) the minor's legal guardian; or

(3) the minor's managing conservator.

Added by Acts 1995, 74th Leg., ch. 965, § 10, eff. June 16, 1995. Renumbered from § 674.005 by Acts 1999, 76th Leg., ch. 450, § 1.04, eff. Sept. 1, 1999.

For application provisions of Acts 1999, 76th Leg., ch. 450, see notes following V.T.C.A., Health & Safety Code § 166.081.

§ 166.086. Desire of Person Supersedes Out-Of-Hospital DNR Order

The desire of a competent person, including a competent minor, supersedes the effect of an out-of-hospital DNR order executed or issued by or on behalf of the person when the desire is communicated to responding health care professionals as provided by this subchapter.

Added by Acts 1995, 74th Leg., ch. 965, § 10, eff. June 16, 1995. Renumbered from § 674.006 and amended by Acts 1999, 76th Leg., ch. 450, § 1.04, eff. Sept. 1, 1999.

For application provisions of Acts 1999, 76th Leg., ch. 450, see notes following V.T.C.A., Health & Safety Code § 166.081.

§ 166.087. Procedure When Declarant is Incompetent or Incapable of Communication

(a) This section applies when a person 18 years of age or older has executed or issued an out-of-hospital DNR order and subsequently becomes incompetent or otherwise mentally or physically incapable of communication.

(b) If the adult person has designated a person to make a treatment decision as authorized by Section 166.032(c), the attending physician and the designated person shall comply with the out-of-hospital DNR order.

(c) If the adult person has not designated a person to make a treatment decision as authorized by Section 166.032(c), the attending physician shall comply with the out-of-hospital DNR order unless the physician believes that the order does not reflect the person's present desire.

Added by Acts 1995, 74th Leg., ch. 965, § 10, eff. June 16, 1995. Renumbered from § 674.007 and amended by Acts 1999, 76th Leg., ch. 450, § 1.04, eff. Sept. 1, 1999.

For application provisions of Acts 1999, 76th Leg., ch. 450, see notes following V.T.C.A., Health & Safety Code § 166.081.

§ 166.088. Procedure When Person Has Not Executed or Issued Out-Of-Hospital DNR Order and is Incompetent or Incapable of Communication

(a) If an adult person has not executed or issued an out-of-hospital DNR order and is incompetent or otherwise mentally or physically incapable of communication, the attending physician and the person's legal guardian, proxy, or agent having a medical power of attorney may execute an out-of-hospital DNR order on behalf of the person.

(b) If the person does not have a legal guardian, proxy, or agent under a medical power of attorney, the attending physician and at least one qualified relative from a category listed by Section 166.039(b), subject to the priority established under that subsection, may execute an out-of-hospital DNR order in the same manner as a treatment decision made under Section 166.039(b).

(c) A decision to execute an out-of-hospital DNR order made under Subsection (a) or (b) must be based on knowledge of what the person would desire, if known.

(d) An out-of-hospital DNR order executed under Subsection (b) must be made in the presence of at least two witnesses who qualify under Section 166.003, at least one of whom must be a witness who qualifies under Section 166.003(2).

(e) The fact that an adult person has not executed or issued an out-of-hospital DNR order does not create a presumption that the person does not want a treatment decision made to withhold cardiopulmonary resuscitation and certain other designated life-sustaining treatment designated by the board.

(f) If there is not a qualified relative available to act for the person under Subsection (b), an out-of-hospital DNR order must be concurred in by another physician who is not involved in the treatment of the patient or who is a representative of the ethics or medical committee of the health care facility in which the person is a patient.

(g) A person listed in Section 166.039(b) who wishes to challenge a decision made under this section must apply for temporary guardianship under Section 875, Texas Probate Code. The court may waive applicable fees in that proceeding.

Added by Acts 1995, 74th Leg., ch. 965, § 10, eff. June 16, 1995. Renumbered from § 674.008 and amended by Acts 1999, 76th Leg., ch. 450, § 1.04, eff. Sept. 1, 1999.

For application provisions of Acts 1999, 76th Leg., ch. 450, see notes following V.T.C.A., Health & Safety Code § 166.081.

§ 166.089. Compliance With Out-Of-Hospital DNR Order

(a) When responding to a call for assistance, health care professionals shall honor an out-of-hospital DNR order in accordance with the statewide out-of-hospital DNR protocol and, where applicable, locally adopted out-of-hospital DNR protocols not in conflict with the statewide protocol if:

(1) the responding health care professionals discover an executed or issued out-of-hospital DNR order form on their arrival at the scene; and

(2) the responding health care professionals comply with this section.

(b) If the person is wearing a DNR identification device, the responding health care professionals must comply with Section 166.090.

(c) The responding health care professionals must establish the identity of the person as the person who executed or issued the out-of-hospital DNR order or for whom the out-of-hospital DNR order was executed or issued.

(d) The responding health care professionals must determine that the out-of-hospital DNR order form appears to be valid in that it includes:

(1) written responses in the places designated on the form for the names, signatures, and other information required of persons executing or issuing, or witnessing the execution or issuance of, the order;

(2) a date in the place designated on the form for the date the order was executed or issued; and

(3) the signature of the declarant or persons executing or issuing the order and the attending physician in the appropriate places designated on the form for indicating that the order form has been properly completed.

(e) If the conditions prescribed by Subsections (a) through (d) are not determined to apply by the responding health care professionals at the scene, the out-of-hospital DNR order may not be honored and life-sustaining procedures otherwise required by law or local emergency medical services protocols shall be initiated or continued. Health care professionals acting in out-of-hospital settings are not required to accept or interpret an out-of-hospital DNR order that does not meet the requirements of this subchapter.

(f) The out-of-hospital DNR order form or a copy of the form, when available, must accompany the person during transport.

(g) A record shall be made and maintained of the circumstances of each emergency medical services response in which an out-of-hospital DNR order or DNR identification device is encountered, in accordance with the statewide out-of-hospital DNR protocol and any applicable local out-of-hospital DNR protocol not in conflict with the statewide protocol.

(h) An out-of-hospital DNR order executed or issued and documented or evidenced in the manner prescribed by this subchapter is valid and shall be honored by responding health care professionals unless the person or persons found at the scene:

(1) identify themselves as the declarant or as the attending physician, legal guardian, qualified relative, or agent of the person having a medical power of attorney who executed or issued the out-of-hospital DNR order on behalf of the person; and

(2) request that cardiopulmonary resuscitation or certain other life-sustaining treatment designated by the board be initiated or continued.

(i) If the policies of a health care facility preclude compliance with the out-of-hospital DNR order of a person or an out-of-hospital DNR order issued by an attending physician on behalf of a person who is admitted to or a resident of the facility, or if the facility is unwilling to accept DNR identification devices as evidence of the existence of an out-of-hospital DNR order, that facility shall take all reasonable steps to notify the person or, if the person is incompetent, the person's guardian or the person or persons having authority to make health care treatment decisions on behalf of the person, of the facility's policy and shall take all reasonable steps to effect the transfer of the person to the person's home or to a facility where the provisions of this subchapter can be carried out.

Added by Acts 1995, 74th Leg., ch. 965, § 10, eff. June 16, 1995. Renumbered from § 674.009 and amended by Acts 1999, 76th Leg., ch. 450, § 1.04, eff. Sept. 1, 1999.

For application provisions of Acts 1999, 76th Leg., ch. 450, see notes following V.T.C.A., Health & Safety Code § 166.081.

§ 166.090. DNR Identification Device

(a) A person who has a valid out-of-hospital DNR order under this subchapter may wear a DNR identification device around the neck or on the wrist as prescribed by board rule adopted under Section 166.101.

(b) The presence of a DNR identification device on the body of a person is conclusive evidence that the person has executed or issued a valid out-of-hospital DNR order or has a valid out-of-hospital DNR order executed or issued on the person's behalf. Responding health care professionals shall honor the DNR identification device as if a valid out-of-hospital DNR order form executed or issued by the person were found in the possession of the person.

Added by Acts 1995, 74th Leg., ch. 965, § 10, eff. June 16, 1995. Renumbered from § 674.010 and amended by Acts 1999, 76th Leg., ch. 450, § 1.04, eff. Sept. 1, 1999.

For application provisions of Acts 1999, 76th Leg., ch. 450, see notes following V.T.C.A., Health & Safety Code § 166.081.

§ 166.091. Duration of Out-Of-Hospital DNR Order

An out-of-hospital DNR order is effective until it is revoked as prescribed by Section 166.092.

Added by Acts 1995, 74th Leg., ch. 965, § 10, eff. June 16, 1995. Renumbered from § 674.011 and amended by Acts 1999, 76th Leg., ch. 450, § 1.04, eff. Sept. 1, 1999.

For application provisions of Acts 1999, 76th Leg., ch. 450, see notes following V.T.C.A., Health & Safety Code § 166.081.

§ 166.092. Revocation of Out-Of-Hospital DNR Order

(a) A declarant may revoke an out-of-hospital DNR order at any time without regard to the declarant's mental state or competency. An order may be revoked by:

(1) the declarant or someone in the declarant's presence and at the declarant's direction destroying the order form and removing the DNR identification device, if any;

(2) a person who identifies himself or herself as the legal guardian, as a qualified relative, or as the agent of the declarant having a medical power of attorney who executed the out-of-hospital DNR order or another person in the person's presence and at the person's direction destroying the order form and removing the DNR identification device, if any;

(3) the declarant communicating the declarant's intent to revoke the order; or

(4) a person who identifies himself or herself as the legal guardian, a qualified relative, or the agent of the declarant having a medical power of attorney who executed the out-of-hospital DNR order orally stating the person's intent to revoke the order.

(b) An oral revocation under Subsection (a)(3) or (a)(4) takes effect only when the declarant or a person who identifies himself or herself as the legal guardian, a qualified relative, or the agent of the declarant having a medical power of attorney who executed the out-of-hospital DNR order communicates the intent to revoke the order to the responding health care professionals or the attending physician at the scene. The responding health care professionals shall record the time, date, and place of the revocation in accordance with the statewide out-of-hospital DNR protocol and rules adopted by the board and any applicable local out-of-hospital DNR protocol. The attending physician or the physician's designee shall record in the person's medical record the time, date, and place of the revocation and, if different, the time, date, and place that the physician received notice of the revocation. The attending physician or the physician's designee shall also enter the word "VOID" on each page of the copy of the order in the person's medical record.

(c) Except as otherwise provided by this subchapter, a person is not civilly or criminally liable for failure to act on a revocation made under this section unless the person has actual knowledge of the revocation.

Added by Acts 1995, 74th Leg., ch. 965, § 10, eff. June 16 1995. Renumbered from § 674.012 and amended by Acts 1999, 76th Leg., ch. 450, § 1.04, eff. Sept. 1, 1999.

For application provisions of Acts 1999, 76th Leg., ch. 450, see notes following V.T.C.A., Health & Safety Code § 166.081.

§ 166.093. Reexecution of Out-Of-Hospital DNR Order

A declarant may at any time reexecute or reissue an out-of-hospital DNR order in accordance with the procedures prescribed by Section 166.082, including reexecution or reissuance after the declarant is diagnosed as having a terminal or irreversible condition.

Added by Acts 1995, 74th Leg., ch. 965, § 10, eff. June 16, 1995. Renumbered from § 674.013 and amended by Acts 1999, 76th Leg., ch. 450, § 1.04, eff. Sept. 1, 1999.

For application provisions of Acts 1999, 76th Leg., ch. 450, see notes following V.T.C.A., Health & Safety Code § 166.081.

§ 166.094. Limitation on Liability for Withholding Cardiopulmonary Resuscitation and Certain Other Life-Sustaining Procedures

(a) A health care professional or health care facility or entity that in good faith causes cardiopulmonary resuscitation or certain other life-sustaining treatment designated by the board to be withheld from a person in accordance with this subchapter is not civilly liable for that action.

(b) A health care professional or health care facility or entity that in good faith participates in withholding cardiopulmonary resuscitation or certain other life-sustaining treatment designated by the board from a person in accordance with this subchapter is not civilly liable for that action.

(c) A health care professional or health care facility or entity that in good faith participates in withholding cardiopulmonary resuscitation or certain other life-sustaining treatment designated by the board from a person in accordance with this subchapter is not criminally liable or guilty of unprofessional conduct as a result of that action.

(d) A health care professional or health care facility or entity that in good faith causes or participates in withholding cardiopulmonary resuscitation or certain other life-sustaining treatment designated by the board from a person in accordance with this subchapter and rules adopted under this subchapter is not in violation of any other licensing or regulatory laws or rules of this state and is not subject to any disciplinary action or sanction by any licensing or regulatory agency of this state as a result of that action.

Added by Acts 1995, 74th Leg., ch. 965, § 10, eff. June 16, 1995. Renumbered from § 674.016 and amended by Acts 1999, 76th Leg., ch. 450, § 1.04, eff. Sept. 1, 1999.

For application provisions of Acts 1999, 76th Leg., ch. 450, see notes following V.T.C.A., Health & Safety Code § 166.081.

§ 166.095. Limitation on Liability for Failure to Effectuate Out-Of-Hospital DNR Order

(a) A health care professional or health care facility or entity that has no actual knowledge of an out-of-hospital DNR order is not civilly or criminally liable for failing to act in accordance with the order.

(b) A health care professional or health care facility or entity is subject to review and disciplinary action by the appropriate licensing board for failing to effectuate an out-of-hospital DNR order. This subsection does not limit remedies available under other laws of this state.

(c) If an attending physician refuses to execute or comply with an out-of-hospital DNR order, the physician shall inform the person, the legal guardian or qualified relatives of the person, or the agent of the person having a medical power of attorney and, if the person or another authorized to act on behalf of the person so directs, shall make a reasonable effort to transfer the person to another physician who is willing to execute or comply with an out-of-hospital DNR order.

Added by Acts 1995, 74th Leg., ch. 965, § 10, eff. June 16, 1995. Renumbered from § 674.017 and amended by Acts 1999, 76th Leg., ch. 450, § 1.04, eff. Sept. 1, 1999.

Section 3.04 of Acts 1999, 76th Leg., ch. 450 provides:

"The change in law made by this Act to Subsection (b), Section 166.045, and Subsection (b), Section 166.095, Health and Safety Code, as redesignated by this Act, applies only to conduct that occurs on or after January 1, 2000. Conduct that occurs before January 1, 2000, is governed by the law as it existed immediately before the effective date of this Act, and that law is continued in effect for that purpose."

For application provisions of Acts 1999, 76th Leg., ch. 450, see notes following V.T.C.A., Health & Safety Code § 166.081.

§ 166.096. Honoring Out-Of-Hospital DNR Order Does Not Constitute Offense of Aiding Suicide

A person does not commit an offense under Section 22.08, Penal Code, by withholding cardiopulmonary resuscitation or certain other life-sustaining treatment designated by the board from a person in accordance with this subchapter.

Added by Acts 1995, 74th Leg., ch. 965, § 10, eff. June 16, 1995. Renumbered from § 674.018 and amended by Acts 1999, 76th Leg., ch. 450, § 1.04, eff. Sept. 1, 1999.

For application provisions of Acts 1999, 76th Leg., ch. 450, see notes following V.T.C.A., Health & Safety Code § 166.081.

§ 166.097. Criminal Penalty; Prosecution

(a) A person commits an offense if the person intentionally conceals, cancels, defaces, obliterates, or damages another person's out-of-hospital DNR order or DNR identification device without that person's consent or the consent of the person or persons authorized to execute or issue an out-of-hospital DNR order on behalf of the person under this subchapter. An offense under this subsection is a Class A misdemeanor.

(b) A person is subject to prosecution for criminal homicide under Chapter 19, Penal Code, if the person, with the intent to cause cardiopulmonary resuscitation or certain other life-sustaining treatment designated by the board to be withheld from another person contrary to the other person's desires, falsifies or forges an out-of-hospital DNR order or intentionally conceals or withholds personal knowledge of a revocation and thereby directly causes cardiopulmonary resuscitation and certain other life-sustaining treatment designated by the board to be withheld from the other person with the result that the other person's death is hastened.

Added by Acts 1995, 74th Leg., ch. 965, § 10, eff. June 16, 1995. Renumbered from § 674.019 and amended by Acts 1999, 76th Leg., ch. 450, § 1.04, eff. Sept. 1, 1999.

For application provisions of Acts 1999, 76th Leg., ch. 450, see notes following V.T.C.A., Health & Safety Code § 166.081.

§ 166.098. Pregnant Persons

A person may not withhold cardiopulmonary resuscitation or certain other life-sustaining treatment designated by the board under this subchapter from a person known by the responding health care professionals to be pregnant.

Added by Acts 1995, 74th Leg., ch. 965, § 10, eff. June 16, 1995. Renumbered from § 674.020 and amended by Acts 1999, 76th Leg., ch. 450, § 1.04, eff. Sept. 1, 1999.

For application provisions of Acts 1999, 76th Leg., ch. 450, see notes following V.T.C.A., Health & Safety Code § 166.081.

§ 166.099. Mercy Killing Not Condoned

This subchapter does not condone, authorize, or approve mercy killing or permit an affirmative or deliberate act or omission to end life except to permit the natural process of dying as provided by this subchapter.

Added by Acts 1995, 74th Leg., ch. 965, § 10, eff. June 16, 1995. Renumbered from § 674.021 and amended by Acts 1999, 76th Leg., ch. 450, § 1.04, eff. Sept. 1, 1999.

For application provisions of Acts 1999, 76th Leg., ch. 450, see notes following V.T.C.A., Health & Safety Code § 166.081.

§ 166.100. Legal Right or Responsibility Not Affected

This subchapter does not impair or supersede any legal right or responsibility a person may have under a constitution, other statute, regulation, or court decision to effect the withholding of cardiopulmonary resuscitation or certain other life-sustaining treatment designated by the board.

Added by Acts 1995, 74th Leg., ch. 965, § 10, eff. June 16, 1995. Renumbered from § 674.022 and amended by Acts 1999, 76th Leg., ch. 450, § 1.04, eff. Sept. 1, 1999.

For application provisions of Acts 1999, 76th Leg., ch. 450, see notes following V.T.C.A., Health & Safety Code § 166.081.

§ 166.101. Duties of Department and Board

(a) The board shall, on the recommendation of the department, adopt all reasonable and necessary rules to carry out the purposes of this subchapter, including rules:

(1) adopting a statewide out-of-hospital DNR order protocol that sets out standard procedures for the withholding of cardiopulmonary resuscitation and certain other life-sustaining treatment by health care professionals acting in out-of-hospital settings;

(2) designating life-sustaining treatment that may be included in an out-of-hospital DNR order, including all procedures listed in Sections 166.081(6)(A)(i) through (v); and

(3) governing recordkeeping in circumstances in which an out-of-hospital DNR order or DNR identification device is encountered by responding health care professionals.

(b) The rules adopted by the board under Subsection (a) are not effective until approved by the Texas State Board of Medical Examiners.

(c) Local emergency medical services authorities may adopt local out-of-hospital DNR order protocols if the local protocols do not conflict with the statewide out-of-hospital DNR order protocol adopted by the board.

(d) The board by rule shall specify a distinctive standard design for a necklace and a bracelet DNR identification device that signifies, when worn by a person, that the possessor has executed or issued a valid out-of-hospital DNR order under this subchapter or is a person for whom a valid out-of-hospital DNR order has been executed or issued.

(e) The department shall report to the board from time to time regarding issues identified in emergency medical services responses in which an out-of-hospital DNR order or DNR identification device is encountered. The report may contain recommendations to the board for necessary modifications to the form of the standard out-of-hospital DNR order or the designated life-sustaining procedures listed in the standard out-of-hospital DNR order, the statewide out-of-hospital DNR order protocol, or the DNR identification devices.

Added by Acts 1995, 74th Leg., ch. 965, § 10, eff. June 16, 1995. Renumbered from § 674.023 and amended by Acts 1999, 76th Leg., ch. 450, § 1.04, eff. Sept. 1, 1999.

For application provisions of Acts 1999, 76th Leg., ch. 450, see notes following V.T.C.A., Health & Safety Code § 166.081.

SUBCHAPTER D. MEDICAL POWER OF ATTORNEY

§ 166.151. Definitions

In this subchapter:

(1) "Adult" means a person 18 years of age or older or a person under 18 years of age who has had the disabilities of minority removed.

(2) "Agent" means an adult to whom authority to make health care decisions is delegated under a medical power of attorney.

(3) "Health care provider" means an individual or facility licensed, certified, or otherwise authorized to administer health care, for profit or otherwise, in

the ordinary course of business or professional practice and includes a physician.

(4) "Principal" means an adult who has executed a medical power of attorney.

(5) "Residential care provider" means an individual or facility licensed, certified, or otherwise authorized to operate, for profit or otherwise, a residential care home.

Added by Acts 1991, 72nd Leg., ch. 16, § 3.02(a), eff. Aug. 26, 1991. Renumbered from V.T.C.A., Civil Practice & Remedies Code § 135.001 and amended by Acts 1999, 76th Leg., ch. 450, § 1.05, eff. Sept. 1, 1999.

Sections 3.02 and 3.03 of Acts 1999, 76th Leg., ch. 450 provide:

"Sec. 3.02. (a) The change in law made by this Act does not affect the validity of a document executed under Chapter 672 or 674, Health and Safety Code, or Chapter 135, Civil Practice and Remedies Code, before the effective date of this Act. A document executed before the effective date of this Act is governed by the law in effect on the date the document was executed, and that law continues in effect for that purpose.

"(b) A reference in a law to a durable power of attorney for health care means a medical power of attorney, as defined by Section 166.002, Health and Safety Code, as added by this Act.

"Sec. 3.03. (a) The change in law made by this Act applies only to the punishment for an offense committed on or after the effective date of this Act. For purposes of this section, an offense is committed before the effective date of this Act if any element of the offense occurs before the effective date.

"(b) An offense committed before the effective date of this Act is covered by the law in effect when the offense was committed, and the former law is continued in effect for that purpose."

§ 166.152. Scope and Duration of Authority

(a) Subject to this subchapter or any express limitation on the authority of the agent contained in the medical power of attorney, the agent may make any health care decision on the principal's behalf that the principal could make if the principal were competent.

(b) An agent may exercise authority only if the principal's attending physician certifies in writing and files the certification in the principal's medical record that, based on the attending physician's reasonable medical judgment, the principal is incompetent.

(c) Notwithstanding any other provisions of this subchapter, treatment may not be given to or withheld from the principal if the principal objects regardless of whether, at the time of the objection:

(1) a medical power of attorney is in effect; or

(2) the principal is competent.

(d) The principal's attending physician shall make reasonable efforts to inform the principal of any proposed treatment or of any proposal to withdraw or withhold treatment before implementing an agent's advance directive.

(e) After consultation with the attending physician and other health care providers, the agent shall make a health care decision:

(1) according to the agent's knowledge of the principal's wishes, including the principal's religious and moral beliefs; or

(2) if the agent does not know the principal's wishes, according to the agent's assessment of the principal's best interests.

(f) Notwithstanding any other provision of this subchapter, an agent may not consent to:

(1) voluntary inpatient mental health services;

(2) convulsive treatment;

(3) psychosurgery;

(4) abortion; or

(5) neglect of the principal through the omission of care primarily intended to provide for the comfort of the principal.

(g) The power of attorney is effective indefinitely on execution as provided by this subchapter and delivery of the document to the agent, unless it is revoked as provided by this subchapter or the principal becomes competent. If the medical power of attorney includes an expiration date and on that date the principal is incompetent, the power of attorney continues to be effective until the principal becomes competent unless it is revoked as provided by this subchapter.

Added by Acts 1991, 72nd Leg., ch. 16, § 3.02(a), eff. Aug. 26, 1991. Renumbered from V.T.C.A., Civil Practice & Remedies Code § 135.002 and amended by Acts 1999, 76th Leg., ch. 450, § 1.05, eff. Sept. 1, 1999.

For application provisions of Acts 1999, 76th Leg., ch. 450, see notes following V.T.C.A., Health & Safety Code § 166.151.

§ 166.153. Persons Who May Not Exercise Authority of Agent

A person may not exercise the authority of an agent while the person serves as:

(1) the principal's health care provider;

(2) an employee of the principal's health care provider unless the person is a relative of the principal;

(3) the principal's residential care provider; or

(4) an employee of the principal's residential care provider unless the person is a relative of the principal.

Added by Acts 1991, 72nd Leg., ch. 16, § 3.02(a), eff. Aug. 26, 1991. Renumbered from V.T.C.A., Civil Practice & Remedies Code § 135.003 by Acts 1999, 76th Leg., ch. 450, § 1.05, eff. Sept. 1, 1999.

For application provisions of Acts 1999, 76th Leg., ch. 450, see notes following V.T.C.A., Health & Safety Code § 166.151.

§ 166.154. Execution and Witnesses

(a) The medical power of attorney must be signed by the principal in the presence of two witnesses who qualify under Section 166.003, at least one of whom must be a witness who qualifies under Section 166.003(2). The witnesses must sign the document.

(b) If the principal is physically unable to sign, another person may sign the medical power of attorney with the principal's name in the principal's presence and at the principal's express direction.

Added by Acts 1991, 72nd Leg., ch. 16, § 3.02(a), eff. Aug. 26, 1991. Renumbered from V.T.C.A., Civil Practice & Remedies Code § 135.004 and amended by Acts 1999, 76th Leg., ch. 450, § 1.05, eff. Sept. 1, 1999.

For application provisions of Acts 1999, 76th Leg., ch. 450, see notes following V.T.C.A., Health & Safety Code § 166.151.

§ 166.155. Revocation

(a) A medical power of attorney is revoked by:

(1) oral or written notification at any time by the principal to the agent or a licensed or certified health or residential care provider or by any other act evidencing a specific intent to revoke the power, without regard to whether the principal is competent or the principal's mental state;

(2) execution by the principal of a subsequent medical power of attorney; or

(3) the divorce of the principal and spouse, if the spouse is the principal's agent, unless the medical power of attorney provides otherwise.

(b) A principal's licensed or certified health or residential care provider who is informed of or provided with a revocation of a medical power of attorney shall immediately record the revocation in the principal's medical record and give notice of the revocation to the agent and any known health and residential care providers currently responsible for the principal's care.

Added by Acts 1991, 72nd Leg., ch. 16, § 3.02(a), eff. Aug. 26, 1991. Renumbered from V.T.C.A., Civil Practice & Remedies Code § 135.005 and amended by Acts 1999, 76th Leg., ch. 450, § 1.05, eff. Sept. 1, 1999.

For application provisions of Acts 1999, 76th Leg., ch. 450, see notes following V.T.C.A., Health & Safety Code § 166.151.

§ 166.156. Appointment of Guardian

(a) On motion filed in connection with a petition for appointment of a guardian or, if a guardian has been appointed, on petition of the guardian, a probate court shall determine whether to suspend or revoke the authority of the agent.

(b) The court shall consider the preferences of the principal as expressed in the medical power of attorney.

(c) During the pendency of the court's determination under Subsection (a), the guardian has the sole authority to make any health care decisions unless the court orders otherwise. If a guardian has not been appointed, the agent has the authority to make any health care decisions unless the court orders otherwise.

(d) A person, including any attending physician or health or residential care provider, who does not have actual knowledge of the appointment of a guardian or an order of the court granting authority to someone other than the agent to make health care decisions is not subject to criminal or civil liability and has not engaged in unprofessional conduct for implementing an agent's health care decision.

Added by Acts 1991, 72nd Leg., ch. 16, § 3.02(a), eff. Aug. 26, 1991. Renumbered from V.T.C.A., Civil Practice & Remedies Code § 135.006 and amended by Acts 1999, 76th Leg., ch. 450, § 1.05, eff. Sept. 1, 1999.

For application provisions of Acts 1999, 76th Leg., ch. 450, see notes following V.T.C.A., Health & Safety Code § 166.151.

§ 166.157. Disclosure of Medical Information

Subject to any limitations in the medical power of attorney, an agent may, for the purpose of making a health care decision:

(1) request, review, and receive any information, oral or written, regarding the principal's physical or mental health, including medical and hospital records;

(2) execute a release or other document required to obtain the information; and

(3) consent to the disclosure of the information.

Added by Acts 1991, 72nd Leg., ch. 16, § 3.02(a), eff. Aug. 26, 1991. Renumbered from V.T.C.A., Civil Practice & Remedies Code § 135.007 and amended by Acts 1999, 76th Leg., ch. 450, § 1.05, eff. Sept. 1, 1999.

For application provisions of Acts 1999, 76th Leg., ch. 450, see notes following V.T.C.A., Health & Safety Code § 166.151.

§ 166.158. Duty of Health or Residential Care Provider

(a) A principal's health or residential care provider and an employee of the provider who knows of the existence of the principal's medical power of attorney shall follow a directive of the principal's agent to the extent it is consistent with the desires of the principal, this subchapter, and the medical power of attorney.

(b) The attending physician does not have a duty to verify that the agent's directive is consistent with the principal's wishes or religious or moral beliefs.

(c) A principal's health or residential care provider who finds it impossible to follow a directive by the agent because of a conflict with this subchapter or the medical power of attorney shall inform the agent as soon as is reasonably possible. The agent may select another attending physician. The procedures established under Sections 166.045 and 166.046 apply if the agent's directive concerns providing, withholding, or withdrawing life-sustaining treatment.

(d) This subchapter may not be construed to require a health or residential care provider who is not a physician to act in a manner contrary to a physician's order.

Added by Acts 1991, 72nd Leg., ch. 16, § 3.02(a), eff. Aug. 26, 1991. Renumbered from V.T.C.A., Civil Practice & Remedies Code § 135.008 and amended by Acts 1999, 76th Leg., ch. 450, § 1.05, eff. Sept. 1, 1999.

For application provisions of Acts 1999, 76th Leg., ch. 450, see notes following V.T.C.A., Health & Safety Code § 166.151.

§ 166.159. Discrimination Relating to Execution of Medical Power of Attorney

A health or residential care provider, health care service plan, insurer issuing disability insurance, self-insured employee benefit plan, or nonprofit hospital service plan may not:

(1) charge a person a different rate solely because the person has executed a medical power of attorney;

(2) require a person to execute a medical power of attorney before:

(A) admitting the person to a hospital, nursing home, or residential care home;

(B) insuring the person; or

(C) allowing the person to receive health or residential care; or

(3) refuse health or residential care to a person solely because the person has executed a medical power of attorney.

Added by Acts 1991, 72nd Leg., ch. 16, § 3.02(a), eff. Aug. 26, 1991. Renumbered from V.T.C.A., Civil Practice & Remedies Code § 135.009 and amended by Acts 1999, 76th Leg., ch. 450, § 1.05, eff. Sept. 1, 1999.

For application provisions of Acts 1999, 76th Leg., ch. 450, see notes following V.T.C.A., Health & Safety Code § 166.151.

§ 166.160. Limitation on Liability

(a) An agent is not subject to criminal or civil liability for a health care decision if the decision is made in good faith under the terms of the medical power of attorney and the provisions of this subchapter.

(b) An attending physician, health or residential care provider, or a person acting as an agent for or under the physician's or provider's control is not subject to criminal or civil liability and has not engaged in unprofessional conduct for an act or omission if the act or omission:

(1) is done in good faith under the terms of the medical power of attorney, the directives of the agent, and the provisions of this subchapter; and

(2) does not constitute a failure to exercise reasonable care in the provision of health care services.

(c) The standard of care that the attending physician, health or residential care provider, or person acting as an agent for or under the physician's or provider's control shall exercise under Subsection (b) is that degree of care that an attending physician, health or residential care provider, or person acting as an agent for or under the physician's or provider's control, as applicable, of ordinary prudence and skill would have exercised under the same or similar circumstances in the same or similar community.

(d) An attending physician, health or residential care provider, or person acting as an agent for or under the physician's or provider's control has not engaged in unprofessional conduct for:

(1) failure to act as required by the directive of an agent or a medical power of attorney if the physician, provider, or person was not provided with a copy of the medical power of attorney or had no knowledge of a directive; or

(2) acting as required by an agent's directive if the medical power of attorney has expired or been revoked but the physician, provider, or person does not have knowledge of the expiration or revocation.

Added by Acts 1991, 72nd Leg., ch. 16, § 3.02(a), eff. Aug. 26, 1991. Renumbered from V.T.C.A., Civil Practice & Remedies Code § 135.010 and amended by Acts 1999, 76th Leg., ch. 450, § 1.05, eff. Sept. 1, 1999.

For application provisions of Acts 1999, 76th Leg., ch. 450, see notes following V.T.C.A., Health & Safety Code § 166.151.

§ 166.161. Liability for Health Care Costs

Liability for the cost of health care provided as a result of the agent's decision is the same as if the health care were provided as a result of the principal's decision.

Added by Acts 1991, 72nd Leg., ch. 16, § 3.02(a), eff. Aug. 26, 1991. Renumbered from V.T.C.A., Civil Practice & Remedies Code § 135.011 by Acts 1999, 76th Leg., ch. 450, § 1.05, eff. Sept. 1, 1999.

For application provisions of Acts 1999, 76th Leg., ch. 450, see notes following V.T.C.A., Health & Safety Code § 166.151.

§ 166.162. Disclosure Statement

A medical power of attorney is not effective unless the principal, before executing the medical power of attorney, signs a statement that the principal has received a disclosure statement and has read and understood its contents.

Added by Acts 1991, 72nd Leg., ch. 16, § 3.02(a), eff. Aug. 26, 1991. Renumbered from V.T.C.A., Civil Practice & Remedies Code § 135.014 and amended by Acts 1999, 76th Leg., ch. 450, § 1.05, eff. Sept. 1, 1999.

For application provisions of Acts 1999, 76th Leg., ch. 450, see notes following V.T.C.A., Health & Safety Code § 166.151.

§ 166.163. Form of Disclosure Statement

The disclosure statement must be in substantially the following form:

INFORMATION CONCERNING THE MEDICAL POWER OF ATTORNEY

THIS IS AN IMPORTANT LEGAL DOCUMENT. BEFORE SIGNING THIS DOCUMENT, YOU SHOULD KNOW THESE IMPORTANT FACTS:

Except to the extent you state otherwise, this document gives the person you name as your agent the authority to make any and all health care decisions for you in accordance with your wishes, including your religious and moral beliefs, when you are no longer capable of making them yourself. Because "health care" means any treatment, service, or procedure to maintain, diagnose, or treat your physical or mental condition, your agent has the power to make a broad range of health care decisions for you. Your agent may consent, refuse to consent, or withdraw consent to medical treatment and may make decisions about withdrawing or withholding life-sustaining treatment. Your agent may not consent to voluntary inpatient mental health services, convulsive treatment, psychosurgery, or abortion. A physician must comply with your agent's instructions or allow you to be transferred to another physician.

Your agent's authority begins when your doctor certifies that you lack the competence to make health care decisions.

Your agent is obligated to follow your instructions when making decisions on your behalf. Unless you state otherwise, your agent has the same authority to make decisions about your health care as you would have had.

It is important that you discuss this document with your physician or other health care provider before you sign it to make sure that you understand the nature and range of decisions that may be made on your behalf. If you do not have a physician, you should talk with someone else who is knowledgeable about these issues and can answer your questions. You do not need a lawyer's assistance to complete this document, but if there is anything in this document that you do not understand, you should ask a lawyer to explain it to you.

The person you appoint as agent should be someone you know and trust. The person must be 18 years of age or older or a person under 18 years of age who has had the disabilities of minority removed. If you appoint your health or residential care provider (e.g., your physician or an employee of a home health agency, hospital, nursing home, or residential care home, other than a relative), that person has to choose between acting as your agent or as your health or residential care provider; the law does not permit a person to do both at the same time.

You should inform the person you appoint that you want the person to be your health care agent. You should discuss this document with your agent and your physician and give each a signed copy. You should indicate on the document itself the people and institutions who have signed copies. Your agent is not liable for health care decisions made in good faith on your behalf.

Even after you have signed this document, you have the right to make health care decisions for yourself as long as you are able to do so and treatment cannot be given to you or stopped over your objection. You have the right to revoke the authority granted to your agent by informing your agent or your health or residential care provider orally or in writing or by your execution of a subsequent medical power of attorney. Unless you state otherwise, your appointment of a spouse dissolves on divorce.

This document may not be changed or modified. If you want to make changes in the document, you must make an entirely new one.

You may wish to designate an alternate agent in the event that your agent is unwilling, unable, or ineligible to act as your agent. Any alternate agent you designate has the same authority to make health care decisions for you.

THIS POWER OF ATTORNEY IS NOT VALID UNLESS IT IS SIGNED IN THE PRESENCE OF TWO COMPETENT ADULT WITNESSES. THE FOLLOWING PERSONS MAY NOT ACT AS ONE OF THE WITNESSES:

(1) the person you have designated as your agent;

(2) a person related to you by blood or marriage;

(3) a person entitled to any part of your estate after your death under a will or codicil executed by you or by operation of law;

(4) your attending physician;

(5) an employee of your attending physician;

(6) an employee of a health care facility in which you are a patient if the employee is providing direct patient care to you or is an officer, director, partner, or business office employee of the health care facility or of any parent organization of the health care facility; or

(7) a person who, at the time this power of attorney is executed, has a claim against any part of your estate after your death.

Added by Acts 1991, 72nd Leg., ch. 16, § 3.02(a), eff. Aug. 26, 1991. Renumbered from V.T.C.A., Civil Practice & Remedies Code § 135.015 and amended by Acts 1999, 76th Leg., ch. 450, § 1.05, eff. Sept. 1, 1999.

For application provisions of Acts 1999, 76th Leg., ch. 450, see notes following V.T.C.A., Health & Safety Code § 166.151.

§ 166.164. Form of Medical Power of Attorney

The medical power of attorney must be in substantially the following form:

MEDICAL POWER OF ATTORNEY
DESIGNATION OF HEALTH
CARE AGENT.

I,__________(insert your name) appoint:

Name:______________________________

Address:______________________________

Phone______________________________

as my agent to make any and all health care decisions for me, except to the extent I state otherwise in this document. This medical power of attorney takes effect if I become unable to make my own health care decisions and this fact is certified in writing by my physician.

LIMITATIONS ON THE DECISION-MAKING AUTHORITY OF MY AGENT ARE AS FOLLOWS:

____

____

DESIGNATION OF ALTERNATE AGENT.

(You are not required to designate an alternate agent but you may do so. An alternate agent may make the same health care decisions as the designated agent if the designated agent is unable or unwilling to act as your agent. If the agent designated is your spouse, the designation is automatically revoked by law if your marriage is dissolved.)

If the person designated as my agent is unable or unwilling to make health care decisions for me, I designate the following persons to serve as my agent to make health care decisions for me as authorized by this document, who serve in the following order:

A. First Alternate Agent

Name:______________________________

Address:______________________________

Phone______________________________

B. Second Alternate Agent

Name:______________________________

Address:______________________________

Phone______________________________

The original of this document is kept at:

____

____

____

The following individuals or institutions have signed copies:

Name:______________________________

Address:______________________________

Name:______________________________

Address:______________________________

____

DURATION.

I understand that this power of attorney exists indefinitely from the date I execute this document unless I establish a shorter time or revoke the power of attorney. If I am unable to make health care decisions for myself when this power of attorney expires, the authority I have granted my agent continues to exist until the time I become able to make health care decisions for myself.

(IF APPLICABLE) This power of attorney ends on the following date: __________

PRIOR DESIGNATIONS REVOKED.

I revoke any prior medical power of attorney.

ACKNOWLEDGMENT OF DISCLOSURE STATEMENT.

I have been provided with a disclosure statement explaining the effect of this document. I have read and understand that information contained in the disclosure statement.

(YOU MUST DATE AND SIGN THIS POWER OF ATTORNEY.)

I sign my name to this medical power of attorney on ________ *day of* ________*(month, year) at*

____

(City and State)

____

(Signature)

____

(Print Name)

STATEMENT OF FIRST WITNESS.

I am not the person appointed as agent by this document. I am not related to the principal by blood or marriage. I would not be entitled to any portion of the principal's estate on the principal's death. I am not the attending physician of the principal or an employee of the attending physician. I have no claim against any portion of the principal's estate on the principal's death. Furthermore, if I am an employee of a health care facility in which the principal is a patient, I am not involved in providing direct patient care to the principal and am not an officer, director, partner, or business office employee of the health care facility or of any parent organization of the health care facility.

Signature:______________________________
Print Name: ________ Date: ____________
Address:______________________________

SIGNATURE OF SECOND WITNESS.

Signature:______________________________
Print Name: ________ Date: ____________
Address:______________________________

Added by Acts 1991, 72nd Leg., ch. 16, § 3.02(a), eff. Aug. 26, 1991. Renumbered from V.T.C.A., Civil Practice & Remedies Code § 135.016 and amended by Acts 1999, 76th Leg., ch. 450, § 1.05, eff. Sept. 1, 1999.

For application provisions of Acts 1999, 76th Leg., ch. 450, see notes following V.T.C.A., Health & Safety Code § 166.151.

§ 166.165. Civil Action

(a) A person who is a near relative of the principal or a responsible adult who is directly interested in the principal, including a guardian, social worker, physician, or clergyman, may bring an action in district court to request that the medical power of attorney be revoked because the principal, at the time the medical power of attorney was signed:

(1) was not competent; or

(2) was under duress, fraud, or undue influence.

(b) The action may be brought in the county of the principal's residence or the residence of the person bringing the action.

(c) During the pendency of the action, the authority of the agent to make health care decisions continues in effect unless the district court orders otherwise.

Added by Acts 1991, 72nd Leg., ch. 16, § 3.02(a), eff. Aug. 26, 1991. Renumbered from V.T.C.A., Civil Practice & Remedies Code § 135.017 and amended by Acts 1999, 76th Leg., ch. 450, § 1.05, eff. Sept. 1, 1999.

For application provisions of Acts 1999, 76th Leg., ch. 450, see notes following V.T.C.A., Health & Safety Code § 166.151.

§ 166.166. Other Rights or Responsibilities Not Affected

This subchapter does not limit or impair any legal right or responsibility that any person, including a physician or health or residential care provider, may have to make or implement health care decisions on behalf of a person, provided that if an attending physician or health care facility is unwilling to honor a patient's advance directive or a treatment decision to provide life-sustaining treatment, life-sustaining treatment is required to be provided the patient, but only until a reasonable opportunity has been afforded for transfer of the patient to another physician or health care facility willing to comply with the advance directive or treatment decision.

Added by Acts 1991, 72nd Leg., ch. 16, § 3.02(a), eff. Aug. 26, 1991. Renumbered from V.T.C.A., Civil Practice & Remedies Code § 135.018 and amended by Acts 1999, 76th Leg., ch. 450, § 1.05, eff. Sept. 1, 1999.

For application provisions of Acts 1999, 76th Leg., ch. 450, see notes following V.T.C.A., Health & Safety Code § 166.151.

INDEX

Abbreviations

H & S .... Health and Safety Code
Prob .... Probate Code

INDEX

INDEX

INDEX

INDEX

INDEX

INDEX

INDEX

INDEX

INDEX